SCOTTISH RECORD SOCIETY
NEW SERIES 1

Fasti
Ecclesiæ Scoticanæ
Medii Aevi

ad annum 1638

SECOND DRAFT
by
D. E. R. Watt

EDINBURGH
Printed for the Society by Smith and Ritchie Ltd.
1969

The Council of the Scottish Record Society wishes
to thank the Fasti Committee for making this
volume available to the Society as a joint publica-
ion.

PREFACE

Since the First Draft of the Fasti Ecclesiae Scoticanae Medii Aevi was circulated in duplicated typescript in 1959, it has been an essential working tool for scholars using the sources for the history of medieval Scotland. Many of them have assisted the editor in supplying corrections and additions, so that a Second Draft is now possible on a much bigger scale. Every section of the First Draft has been enlarged and extra categories of offices filled by secular clergy have been added. A Second Draft is therefore now in its turn offered for the use and criticism of interested scholars.

There is an important reason for emphasising that this publication is again a draft rather than a definitive work. Such collections can never be complete, for corrections and additions are constantly coming to hand. This edition suffers particularly from this defect, since the editor chose to close his collections for writing up into publishable form at a time when it was known that a large mass of new and relevant source material for Scottish history extracted from the Vatican Archives and elsewhere was being assembled at Glasgow University under the direction of the Ross Fund there. All this new evidence must some day be sifted for Fasti purposes, and it is clear from initial sampling that it contains a great deal of additional information for the fourteenth, fifteenth and sixteenth centuries. The materials which the Ross Fund in its early days collected from the Vatican Transcripts now in the Public Record Office in London have been used for this draft; but the much larger section of material microfilmed in the Vatican Archives itself remains to be examined. As this will take some years to accomplish, it seems best to make this Second Draft available now as it stands - not least to aid scholars who wish to make good use of the Ross Fund Collections.

Another warning needs to be emphasised. For a definitive work it would be necessary to check the many thousands of references to sources. These have been supplied by many different people, and when spot-checked some of them have proved to be misleading or erroneous. The editor has added his share of errors in the process of transcription, typing and proof-correction. Many references have in fact had to be checked for one reason or another; but it has seemed best not to delay publication by so much as the long time that would be needed for complete checking. *Thus this work stands declaredly as an unchecked draft, and users will be well advised to check the statements in it against the sources cited before accepting anything as accurate.*

As before, this draft is essentially a co-operative work. Apart from items individually attributed, generous contributions have been received over the last ten years from: Mr A.J. Aitken, Mrs M.O. Anderson, Mr A.E. Anton, Miss M. Ash, Messrs. G.W.S. Barrow, J.H. Baxter, A.L. Brown, C. Burns, J.H. Burns, R.G. Cant, D.S. Chambers, J.H. Cockburn, R.B. Dobson, G. Donaldson, A.A.M. Duncan, Mrs A.I. Dunlop, Messrs. J. Durkan, N. Macdougall, L.J. Macfarlane, Mr and Mrs R.W. Munro, Messrs. W.F.H. Nicolaisen, T.I. Rae, N.Shead, G.G. Simpson, R.N. Smart, D.B. Smith, J.A.F. Thomson, J.M. Todd, A.B. Webster and J.A. Wright. The editor is most grateful for all this help in the basic task of assembling a pool of information. He is grateful too for the research assistance of Mrs Teresa Vilardi McGinniss for a time, and to Columbia University, New York for making this assistance available. He hopes that all users of this draft will feel as free to offer further corrections and additions (however small); they should be sent to him at the Department of Mediaeval History, St Salvator's College, St Andrews.

In a different category are the thanks owed by the editor to his two fellow-members of the Fasti Committee - Dr I.B. Cowan of Glasgow University and Dr A.L. Murray of the Scottish Record Office, Edinburgh. The great bulk of the new information from unprinted sources which is now published has been supplied by these two friends, who have most generously made their findings available to this co-operative Fasti project. Over the years too they have cheerfully helped with chasing up innumerable elusive references, and they have patiently commented on the editor's little theories about this and that. Without their help this Second Draft could never have been the major advance on the First Draft that it is. In one way it would be only right that their names should appear on the title-page along with that of the editor; but that would not be fair to them, for they have no responsibility for the ways in which the single editor has used and abused their material and their advice. The merits of this work are largely due to them, while its short-comings are entirely the fault of the editor. He well knows and is properly grateful that these friends will remain his keenest critics.

CONTENTS

INTRODUCTION

The following lists are an attempt at increasing knowledge of the succession in the principal offices of the dioceses, cathedrals and collegiate foundations of the medieval Scottish church. They concentrate on the evidence for the dates of appointment and death or resignation, and when these are unknown references are provided for the earliest and latest dates of occurrences which connect a holder with an office.

The lists go back in time as far as datable evidence is available for the existence of each office. Sometimes a date of foundation can be cited; more often it is a question of pointing to the first known holder of the office. The lists of the bishops of the Isles, Orkney and St Andrews begin in the eleventh century. Elsewhere the starting dates fall in the twelfth century or later.

The year 1638 has been chosen as a more suitable finishing date for this draft than the year 1560 which was adopted for the First Draft. December 1638 saw the overthrow of episcopacy for the time being in Scotland, and this made an effective break in the episcopal succession such as had not occurred in 1560. At the same time the Glasgow Assembly excluded from the kirk the traditional titles of dignity associated with cathedral chapters (Peterkin, *Records,* 37, article 19); and though this was not to be the end of the story of the cathedral dignities of the medieval church, it is a convenient enough date to terminate these lists. The point to emphasise is that the medieval cathedral and collegiate dignities continued to be occupied by a succession of holders with little interruption until as late as 1638.

The post-1560 lists here presented are more uneven in quality than those for pre-1560, for there has been time so far to tackle only a portion of the possibly helpful sources that are available - another draft will be necessary to raise the coverage of the last period to parity with that of the earlier centuries. It should be noted that no attempt is made to establish when benefices (whether before or after 1560) were held by laymen rather than by clergy; and there is another obvious field of research open to those who wish to discover when and how far the dignities of the medieval church came to be held by ministers of the reformed church. The reader will find some suggestions towards this end (but also many puzzles) if he consults the latest edition of Hew Scott's *Fasti Ecclesiae Scoticanae* (Edinburgh, 1915 - 61) alongside the post-1560 lists here offered.

Though bishops and chapters, collegiate churches and university colleges survived the upheaval of 1560, the administrative and judicial offices of dean of christianity and official were presumably included in the so-called abolition of ecclesiastical jurisdictions of 17 August 1560 (*Acts Parl. Scot.*,ii,534). The existence of this act does not, however, necessarily mean that all these officers immediately ceased to perform their functions, though some probably did so and most others appear to have faded away soon after. The office of commissary too was perhaps covered by the same act of 1560. But then the commissary courts throughout the country were specifically and comprehensively reformed by council order on 28 December 1563 (*Reg.Privy Council,* i, 252), and the first four commissaries at Edinburgh under the new system were

appointed on 8 February 1564 (*The Practicks of Sir James Balfour,* ii (Stair Society, 1963), 670–3; cf. *Reg.Sec.Sig.,* v, no.1633). The lists here therefore for all these officers end for the most part by the 1560s, though one or two later occurrences of holders under the old titles have been noted.

DIOCESAN CLERGY

The bulk of the work is arranged under the headings of the thirteen dioceses of medieval Scotland (together with Edinburgh) arranged in alphabetical order. There are five sections under which the information for each diocese may be grouped:

1. BISHOPS. These lists offer an advance on the outline succession in each diocese established by J. Dowden in his *Bishops of Scotland* (Glasgow, 1912), in the second edition of C. Eubel's *Hierarchia Catholica Medii Aevi* (Munster, 1913-23), and by Olaf Kolsrud (for the sees of the Isles and Orkney) in *Diplomatarium Norvegicum,* xvii B (Christiania, 1913). Full advantage has been taken of the lists of bishops in the second edition of the *Handbook of British Chronology* (London, 1961), though the policy of that work in not offering references to authorities has meant that a number of dates suggested there could not be checked, and that some open questions remain unresolved. Wherever these new lists differ silently from earlier ones, it is to be assumed that the editor thinks that he is offering an advance in knowledge, even if there is not always room to argue negative points as well as to justify positive ones.

It is a general assumption that bishops demitted other benefices which they happened to hold when elevated to their sees at the date of their consecration, except when they had special authority to retain them. Scottish practice in this connection may in fact have been more variable than such a general assumption suggests, and more evidence on this subject would be welcome.

2. CHAPTERS. Some introductory remarks are offered as collections towards a study of the cathedral chapters of Scotland. More is said about some than others, but the editor hopes that everything is at least relevant if incomplete at this stage. The attempt is in some cases made to pinpoint the date when diocesan chapters of a synodal character came to be superseded in at least some functions by collegiate bodies of clergy attached to the cathedral church. One significant stage appears to come when the archdeacon ceases to take precedence over the dean and the latter comes to preside over meetings of the cathedral chapter, both for the conduct of episcopal elections and for the transaction of ordinary corporate business. A distinction is thus drawn in the lists between 'early deans' *in* the dioceses (who appear in witness-lists in a humbler position than that of archdeacons) and the deans *of* the cathedral chapters of the dioceses. This distinction may sometimes have an artificial look to it, but it does appear to be significant. After 1560 the chapters kept going as corporate owners of substantial property, while various efforts were made to revive the synodal type of diocesan chapter at least for episcopal elections.

The lists are concerned just with the secular clergy who were holders of cathedral dignities, only brief mention being made of the regular clergy who were priors at St Andrews and Whithorn in Galloway, or who had an *ex officio* position in the chapters of Argyll and Dunblane. As in the First Draft the lists are confined to the principal dignitaries in each cathedral, and nothing has been done for Scotland (as the various editions of Le Neve's *Fasti* have attempted for England) by way of lists of holders of simple canonries with prebend. It is not that they would not also be of interest; but the labour involved would be disproportionate to the utility of the work - the sources are few and scattered, and after all it is mainly the dignitaries whom scholars are likely to come across mentioned only by title in historical sources, and it is for such occasions that the Fasti is most needed as work of reference.

3. DEANS OF CHRISTIANITY. These lists are grouped under alternative titles which appear to have been used successively for officers having jurisdiction over the same geographical divisions of the diocese. In early practice this title could vary according to the parochial benefice held by the man appointed as dean; but gradually the office came to be associated with an area which is regularly given the same name under different holders. The lists of deans in each diocese where they have been found are generally arranged according to a geographical order, one deanery being as far as possible followed by another contiguous to it.

4. OFFICIALS. All the medieval dioceses came to employ at least one principal judicial officer under the name of the official, who presided over the bishop's court. In some dioceses (Argyll, Galloway, Glasgow, Isles, Orkney and St Andrews at any rate) lesser officials appear additionally from time to time with more limited jurisdiction, usually based on some centre away from the seat of the bishop himself. It is convenient to list under the same general heading the few officials of archdeacons who appear in Glasgow and St Andrews dioceses for a time in the thirteenth and fourteenth centuries.

5. COMMISSARIES. These were not listed in the First Draft, and it needs to be emphasised that very little is known about these officers in Scotland. The lists now offered omit persons who were clearly commiss-aries appointed temporarily for specific tasks, and are intended to establish the succession in what is presumed to be a more permanent kind of office; but it must be admitted that the distinction between the two classes of commissaries is not always clear. The significance of the variant titles - commissary-general, commissary, commissary (-general) of the bishop, commissary (-general) of the official, commissary depute and commissary substitute - is not at present obvious. In some cases the officer apparently has jurisdiction throughout a diocese, while in others his authority is confined to a section of the diocese or to a jurisdictional peculiar within it. The existence of some of these lesser jurisdictions before the re-organisation of 1563-4 can be suggested only by reading back from later evidence. For the present commissaries of different kinds can be grouped only loosely under apparently suitable headings (which may not be the right ones), and in each case an

abbreviated form of the officer's precise title as found in the source is provided. The lists are offered as a basis for further study.

THE CHAPEL ROYAL

The constitution of this collegiate body was from 1501 modelled largely on the existing cathedral chapters. Lists of the dignitaries and officials are therefore provided along similar lines. These are prefaced by some notes on the changing character of the chapels royal in Scotland before 1501, in an attempt to explain the possible significance of the title 'dean of the chapel royal' which can be traced from 1456 onwards.

HEADS OF COLLEGIATE CHURCHES

This draft offers something new here too. The persons who became heads of the many collegiate churches founded in Scotland in the later middle ages were often the same people who held cathedral dignities. It is therefore convenient to collect lists of such heads here. This has been done for all such churches where evidence has been found for the existence of a beneficed secular clerk (usually distinguished from parochial clergy by the title of provost or dean) as the head of a collegiate corporation of clergy. Vicars and presidents of the large burgh churches with communities of chaplains have not been included; and there are other variations also from the list of collegiate churches published by D.E. Easson in his *Medieval Religious Houses Scotland* (London, 1957) in the cases where no names of provosts or deans have so far been found to substantiate the other evidence of possible collegiality.

HEADS OF UNIVERSITY COLLEGES

These lists are included again for the sake of completeness, because the names of some of these academic heads are found also in other lists in the Fasti. Together they form a considerable addition to our knowledge of the succession of heads of the colleges that were either within or identical with the universities of medieval and early modern Scotland.

DATING

Wherever the date of the source cited contains at least the month as well as the year, it is expressed in modern form according to the calender which begins the year on 1 January. Thus most dates in Scottish sources from before 1600 which fall between 1 January and 24 March have been silently amended to conform with modern chronology, though a few have been left as they are found in the source because there is reason to believe that the clerk or chronicler followed a dating-system where the

year began at Christmas or 1 January. There remain difficult cases where it is not at present possible to interpret the dating evidence with certainty.

Where a date is expressed just as a year in the heading of an entry (e.g. '1199 - 1207' or '1329'), this is a shorthand way of indicating the period of time according to modern chronology during which the person was connected in some way with the office in question. But when such simple year-dates are mentioned in connection with a specific source, they should in most cases be understood to run from 25 March in the year stated to 24 March in the following year by modern reckoning. A main exception are the year-dates deriving from the Chronicle of Melrose, which usually approximate to the modern calendar year as they stand.

The sign 'x' is used to mean 'not earlier than the earliest point of time implied by' the *preceding* date and 'not the later than the point of time implied by' the *succeeding* date. It can be used in the forms '1228 x 1229', '12 May 1189 x 14 Sept. 1190', '27 Mar. x 23 July 1272', '1288 x' or 'x 1250'.

Many early occurrences of office-holders are based simply on appearances as witnesses in undated charters. Limits of date have in every case been suggested for such evidence, usually depending on the terms of office of other witnesses to the charter as well as on that of the man in question. As work on this draft of the Fasti has proceeded, it has been constantly possible to revise and narrow previously accepted datings - with the difficulty that entries in the Fasti have them themselves had to be revised. It has not been possible to find room for explanations of the many new datings of undated charters which differ from those suggested in the printed sources cited; but usually the reader will easily find the reasons for himself by checking the evidence here provided for revised ideas on the terms of office of the relevant witnesses.

FORMS OF NAMES

No wholly satisfactory system is possible where such a variety of sources is cited from so long a period. Christian names are usually standardised on a form in modern use. Some common surnames have been standardised on a single modern spelling e.g. Graham, Kennedy, Stewart. Others are standardised on the modern spelling of a well-known place-name e.g. Aberdeen, Dundee, Stirling. But when a name is based on a less familiar place-name whose identification may be debatable, the surname is left in form in which it is most commonly found in the sources cited. The particle 'de' is retained so long as it appears in contemporary sources, and becomes uncommon from the early fifteenth century onwards. Any name-forms that are at all unusual are given in the form in which they have been found, even where this is obviously corrupt. The editor has no knowledge of Gaelic, and so meanwhile names of Gaelic provenance are offered just in the forms in which they have been found. Some names found only in a Latin form have been retained in that form wherever there are no clear grounds for a translation e.g. de Cellario, de Prebenda, and genitives such as Donaldi, which can denote either the prefix

'Mac-' or the suffix '-son'. No doubt many further standardisations of
name-forms will be possible in a future edition, and it is most important
to try to spot single name-forms which at present appear in various
guises, so that further useful identifications of persons may be made.
But for the present the editor has prefered to remain cautious, though
he will probably be thought by some to have been too bold and foolish
as it is.

Where two christian names or surnames are given for the same
person and divided by an oblique stroke (e.g. Gamelial/Gamelin,
William Malveisin/Malvoisin), the implication is that both forms are
found in good contemporary sources, so that the editor has no clear
grounds for standardising on one form rather than the other. The
editor's preference is usually for the first form mentioned, however, and
for the purposes of the index the first form is used for the main entry to
which other entries refer.

Where a surname is placed within round brackets with a query, there
is doubt whether the surname is validly attachable to the christian name
in question.

Where a surname is followed by one or more spellings within round
brackets, the purpose is *either* to make clear some contemporary name-
forms from which the editor has been bold to standardise, *or* to give the
reader some examples of the more puzzling contemporary spellings and
forms of the well-authenticated name which may be encountered. All
these variants are indexed.

ABBREVIATIONS AND CROSS-REFERENCES

The various entries are compiled in as brief a space as possible to
establish the character of the known evidence for a man's succession to
an office and his demission of it. The reader will find the key to
reconstituting this pemmican in the list of abbreviated words on p. xiii
below.

The references to sources are also given in abbreviated forms. For
unprinted works the key is provided on p. xiv below; and for published
works consult p. xvi below. The usual convention is followed that unprinted sources are mentioned in roman type, while the titles of printed
works are cited in italic type. As a general rule roman numbers in
citations indicate volumes, while arabic numbers are used for pages
(though also for volumes when the number is very large). All the references are to a page of the source except where specific mention is made
of the foliation of a manuscript or the number of a printed document.

Cross-references are commonly made to other sections of the Fasti.
The convention is to mention another list in abbreviated form in italic
type e.g. 'cons. *G. abp.* 5 Feb. 1525', where the implication is that the
man ceased to hold his current office on 5 February 1525 when he was
consecrated archbishop of Glasgow. The reader should turn to the list of
archbishops of Glasgow to find the authority for this statement. Some
cross-references are based on editorial suggestion rather than on clear
contemporary evidence that two office-holders of the same name were
the same person (cf. introductory notes to the index, p. 386 below).

LISTS OF ABBREVIATIONS

1. WORDS

Ab.	Aberdeen
abp.	archbishop, archbishopric
adm.	admitted, admission
app.	appendix
Ar.	Argyll
archd.	archdeacon, archdeaconry
B.	Brechin
ben.	benefice
bp.	bishop, bishopric
C.	Caithness
(C)	commissary
c.	circa
can.	canon, canonry
(CB)	commissary of the bishop
cert.	certainly
(C depute)	commissary-depute
cf.	confer (i.e. compare)
(CG)	commissary - general
(CGB)	commissary - general of the bishop
(CGO)	commissary - general of the official
ch.	church
chanc.	chancellor, chancellorship
chr./chrs.	charter/charters
(CO)	commissary of the official
coadj.	coadjutor
coll.	collated, collation; college
comm.	commissary, commissaryship
com. priv.	*commissio privationis*
conf.	confirmed, confirmation
cons.	consecrated, consecration
(C substitute)	commissary-substitute
d.	died, death
Db.	Dunblane
dean.	deanery
dean. christ.	deanery of christianity
dem.	demitted, demission
depriv.	deprived, deprivation
dioc.	diocese
disp.	dispensed, dispensation
Dk.	Dunkeld
el.	elected, election
exch.	exchanged, exchange
exp.	expectation, expectative
fo./fos.	folio/folios
G.	Glasgow
Ga.	Galloway
I.	Isles

ibid.	ibidem
lic.	licensed, licence
lit.	litigating, litigated, litigation
M.	Moray
mand.	mandate
misc.	miscellaneous
nom.	nominated, nomination
O.	Orkney
occ.	occurs, occurred
O. Cist.	order of Cistercians
O. Clun.	order of Cluniacs
offic.	official, officialship
O.F.M.	order of Friars Minor (Franciscans)
O.P.	order of Preachers (Dominicans)
O. Prem.	order of Premonstratensians
ord.	ordinary
O.S.A.	order of St Augustine (canons)
O. Savigny	order of Savigny (later Cistercians)
O.S.B.	order of St Benedict
O. Tiron.	order of Tironensians
pl.	plate
poss.	possession
preb.	prebend
prec.	precentor, precentorship
pres.	presented, presentation
princ.	principal, principalship
prob.	probably
prov.	provided, provision; provost
R.	Ross
reg.	register
res.	resign, resigned, resignation
St A.	St Andrews
subch.	subchanter, subchantership
subd.	subdean, subdeanery
subpr.	subprincipal, subprincipalship
succ.	succeeded, succession; succentor, succentorship
surrog.	surrogated, surrogation
temps.	temporalities
trans.	translated, translation
treas.	treasurer, treasurership
uncons.	unconsecrated
v. inf.	vide infra
vic.	vicar, vicarage
v. sup.	vide supra

2. UNPRINTED SOURCES

a. MANUSCRIPT REPOSITORIES

Abdn. Univ. Archives	Aberdeen University Archives
BM	British Museum, London
Durham, D & C	Durham, Dean & Chapter Archives
Edin. Univ. Lib.	Edinburgh University Library
Glas. Univ. Lib.	Glasgow University Library
NLS	National Library of Scotland, Edinburgh
NRA	National Register of Archives (Scotland)
PRO	Public Record Office, London
St A. Univ. Mun.	St Andrews University Muniments
SRO	Scottish Record Office, Edinburgh
Vat. Arch.	Vatican Archives

b. COMMONLY CITED SOURCES

It is not practicable to list here the full titles of all the unprinted sources which are cited. Those which are cited only infrequently may be identified further by reference to the repository indicated. But there follows a select list of sources which are frequently cited.

Abbrev. Feu Chrs.	Abbreviates of Feu Charters of Kirklands (E. 14), in SRO.
Acts and Decreets	Register of Acts and Decreets, in SRO.
ADC	Acta Dominorum Concilii, in SRO.
ADC & S	Acta Dominorum Concilii et Sessionis, in SRO.
Bk. of Assumption of Benefices	Books of Assumption of the Thirds of Benefices (E. 48/1), in SRO.
Collect.	Collectorie, in Vat. Arch.
Comm. Edin. Decreets	Commissariat of Edinburgh Register of Decreets, in SRO.
Dunblane Tests.	Dunblane Testaments, in SRO.
Edin. Tests.	Edinburgh Testaments, in SRO.
GD.1	Call number for items in the section Miscellaneous Gifts and Deposits, in SRO.
Glas. Tests.	Glasgow Testaments, in SRO.
Hamilton & Campsie Tests.	Hamilton & Campsie Testaments, in SRO.
Ob. et Sol.	Obligationes et Solutiones, in Vat. Arch.
Orkney Tests.	Orkney Testaments, in SRO.
Part. Reg. Sasines Argyll (etc.)	Particular Register of Sasines for Argyll (etc.), in SRO.
PRO 31/9 (etc.)	Call number for items in the section Collections of Transcripts, in PRO.
Reg. Av.	Registra Avinionensia, in Vat. Arch.
Reg. Deeds	Register of Deeds (Books of Council and Session), in SRO.
Reg. Lat.	Registra Lateranensia, in Vat. Arch.
Reg. of Retours	Register of Retours (C.22), in SRO.
Reg. Pres.	Register of Presentations to Benefices (CH. 4/1), in SRO.
Reg. Supp.	Registra Supplicationum, in Vat. Arch.
Reg. Vat.	Registra Vaticana, in Vat. Arch.

*

RSS	Registrum Secreti Sigilli (Privy Seal Register, Old Series, PS.1), in SRO.
St A. Tests.	St Andrews Testaments, in SRO.
Secretary's Reg. Sasines Abdn. (etc.)	Secretary's Register of Sasines for Aberdeen (etc.), in SRO.
Sent. Offic. Laud.	Liber Sententiarum Officialis S. Andree infra Laudoniam (CH. 5/3/1), in SRO.
Sent. Offic. St A.	Liber Sententiarum Officialis S. Andree Principalis (CH. 5/2/1), in SRO.
Stirling Tests.	Stirling Testaments, in SRO.

3. PUBLISHED SOURCES

The abbreviations used here follow the standard *List of Abbreviated Titles of the Printed Sources of Scottish History to 1560* which was published as a supplement to the *Scottish Historical Review*, xlii (1963). The many titles listed there are not repeated here; but the following abbreviated titles are used in addition:

Abdn.Kirk.Recs.	*Selections from the Records of the Kirk Session, Presbytery, and Synod of Aberdeen* (Spalding Club, 1846).
Aberdeen Council Letters	*Aberdeen Council Letters*, ed. L.B. Taylor (London, 1942-61).
Acta Sanctorum	*Acta Sanctorum*, edd. the Bollandists (Antwerp/Brussels, 1643-, cited by month and volume).
Acts of Privy Council	*Acts of the Privy Council of England*, ed. J.R. Dasent (London, 1890-1907).
A.I. Dunlop, *Kennedy*	A.I. Dunlop, *The Life and Times of James Kennedy Bishop of St Andrews* (Edinburgh, 1950).
Arch. & Hist. Coll. Renfrew	*Archaeological and Historical Collections relating to the County of Renfrew* (Paisley, 1885).
Baillie, *Journals*	*The Letters and Journals of Robert Baillie* (Bannatyne Club, 1841-2).
BUK	*Acts and Proceedings of the General Assemblies of the Kirk of Scotland from the Year 1560: The Booke of the Universall Kirk of Scotland* (Bannatyne and Maitland Clubs, 1839-45).
Cal. Chancery Warrants	*Calendar of Chancery Warrants* (London, 1927).
Cal. Chr. Rolls	*Calendar of Charter Rolls* (London, 1903-27).
Calderwood, *History*	D. Calderwood, *The History of the Kirk of Scotland* (Wodrow Society, 1842-9).
Cart. Gyseburne	*Cartularium Prioratus de Gyseburne* (Surtees Society, 1889-94).

CCR	*Calendar of Close Rolls* (London, 1892-)
Chartularium Studii Bononiensis	*Chartularium Studii Bononiensis* (Bologna, 1909-40).
Chartularium Universitatis Parisiensis	*Chartularium Universitatis Parisiensis,* edd. H. Denifle and E. Chatelain (Paris, 1889-97).
Chron. Rishanger	*Willelmi Rishanger . . . Chronica et Annales,* ed. H.T. Riley (Rolls Series, 1865).
Clan Campbell	*The Clan Campbell,* ed. H. Paton (Edinburgh, 1913-22).
C. Lib. R.	*Calendar of Liberate Rolls* (London, 1917-64).
Complete Peerage	*The Complete Peerage,* new edn. edd. V. Gibbs and others (London, 1910-59).
Cotton, *Fasti Ecclesiae Hibernicae*	H. Cotton, *Fasti Ecclesiae Hibernicae* (Dublin, 1845-78).
Cowan, *Parishes*	I.B. Cowan, *The Parishes of Medieval Scotland* (SRS, 1967).
CPR	*Calendar of Patent Rolls* (London, 1893-).
Craven, *Church in Orkney*	J.B. Craven, *History of the Church in Orkney, 1558-1662* (Kirkwall, 1897).
CSP Foreign	*Calendar of State Papers, Foreign Series* (London, 1861-1950).
CSP Ireland	*Calendar of State Papers relating to Ireland* (London, 1860-1911).
Dict. Nat. Biog.	*Dictionary of National Biography* (London, 1885-1900, cited by article).
Die Register Innocenz III	*Die Register Innocenz III,* edd. O. Hageneder and A. Haidacher (Graz/Koln, 1964-).
Diplomatic Documents	*Diplomatic Documents* (London, 1964-).
Emden, *Biog. Reg. Univ. Cambridge*	A.B. Emden, *A Biographical Register of the University of Cambridge to 1500* (Cambridge, 1963).
Emden, *Biog. Reg. Univ. Oxford*	A.B. Emden, *A Biographical Register of the University of Oxford* (Oxford, 1957-9).
Eubel, *Hierarchia*	C. Eubel, *Hierarchia Catholica Medii Aevi,* 2nd edn. (Munster, 1913-23).
Fasti Mariscal.	*Fasti Academiae Mariscallanae Aberdonensis* (New Spalding Club, 1889-98).
Furness Coucher Bk.	*The Coucher Book of Furness Abbey,* vol. ii (Chetham Society, 1915-19).
Gunn, *Peebles Ch.*	C.B. Gunn, *The Book of Peebles Church* (Galashiels, 1908).
Haller, *Conc.Bas.*	*Concilium Basiliense,* edd. J. Haller and others (Basle, 1896-1936).
Herkless & Hannay, *Archbishops*	J. Herkless and R.K. Hannay, *The Archbishops of St Andrews* (Edinburgh, 1907-15).

Historians of York	*Historians of the Church of York,* ed. J. Raine (Rolls Series, 1879-94).
History of Clan Gregor	A.G.M. MacGregor, *History of the Clan Gregor* (Edinburgh, 1898-1901).
Hoberg, *Taxae*	H. Hoberg, *Taxae pro Communibus Servitiis* (Studi e Testi, Vatican, 1949).
Holm Cultram Reg.	*The Register and Records of Holm Cultram,* edd. F. Grainger and W.G. Collingwood (Cumberland and Westmorland Antiquarian and Archaeological Society, Record Series, 1929).
Hugh the Chantor, *History*	Hugh the Chantor, *History of the Church of York,* ed. C. Johnson (Edinburgh, 1961).
Innes, *Sketches*	C. Innes, *Sketches of Early Scotch History and Social Progress* (Edinburgh, 1861).
Innocentii III . . . Opera Omnia	*Innocentii III . . . Opera Omnia,* ed. J.P. Migne (Patrologiae Latinae Cursus Completus, Paris, 1858).
Invernessiana	*Invernessiana,* ed. C. Fraser-Mackintosh (Inverness, 1875).
Journ. Eccles. Hist.	*Journal of Ecclesiastical History* (London/ Cambridge, 1950-).
Le Neve, *Fasti Ecclesiae Anglicanae*	J. Le Neve, *Fasti Ecclesiae Anglicanae,* new edn., all citations from the volumes for *1300-1541* (London, 1962-7).
Leonis X Regesta	*Leonis X Pontificis Maximi Regesta,* ed. J. Hergenroether (Freiburg, 1884-91).
Liber Censuum	*Liber Censuum de l 'Eglise romaine,* edd. P. Fabre and L. Duchesne (Paris, 1905).
LP Henry VIII	*Letters and Papers, Foreign and Domestic, of the Reign of Henry VIII,* edd. J.S. Brewer and others (London, 1864-1932).
Macgill, *Old Ross-shire*	W. Macgill, *Old Ross-shire and Scotland* (Inverness, 1909-11).
Martine, *Reliquiae*	G. Martine, *Reliquiae Divi Andreae* (St Andrews, 1797).
Melville, *Diary*	*The Diary of Mr James Melvill* (Bannatyne Club, 1829); or *The Autobiography and Diary of Mr James Melvill* (Wodrow Society, 1842).
Mon. Conc. Bas.	*Monumenta Conciliorum Generalium Seculi XV: Concilium Basilense* (Vienna, 1857-86).
Mon. Ins. Man.	*Monumenta de Insula Manniae* (Manx Society, 1860-2).

Nicoll's Diary	*A Diary of Public Transactions and Other Occurrences,* by John Nicoll (Bannatyne Club, 1836).
Northern Registers	*Historical Papers and Letters from the Northern Registers,* ed. J. Raine (Rolls Series, 1873).
Obituaires de la province de Sens	*Obituaires de la province de Sens* (Receuils des historiens de la France, Obituaires, Paris, 1902-).
Original Letters	*Original Letters relating to the Ecclesiastical Affairs of Scotland* (Bannatyne Club, 1851).
Orkneyinga Saga	*Orkneyinga Saga,* ed. A.B. Taylor (Edinburgh, 1938).
Papal Negotiations with Queen Mary	*Papal Negotiations with Mary Queen of Scots during her Reign in Scotland* (SHS, 1901).
Peterkin, *Records*	*Records of the Kirk of Scotland . . . from the Year 1638,* ed. A. Peterkin (Edinburgh, 1838).
Peterkin, *Rentals of Orkney*	A Peterkin, *Rentals of the Ancient Earldom and Bishoprick of Orkney* (Edinburgh, 1820).
Provosts of Methven	T. Morris, *The Provosts of Methven* (Edinburgh, 1875).
Reg. Alexandre IV	*Les registres d'Alexandre IV,* edd. C. Bourel de la Roncière and others (Paris, 1931-).
Reg. Benoit XII	*Les registres de Benoît XII; lettres communes,* ed. J.-M. Vidal (Paris, 1903-11).
Reg. Boniface VIII	*Les registres de Boniface VIII,* edd. G. Digard and others (Paris, 1907-39).
Reg. Clement V	*Regestum Clementis Papae V . . . nunc primum editum,* cura et studio monachorum O.S.B. (Rome, 1885-92).
Reg. Cobham	*The Register of Thomas Cobham, Bishop of Worcester* (Worcestershire Historical Society, 1930).
Reg. Corbridge	*The Register of Thomas of Corbridge, Lord Archbishop of York* (Surtees Society, 1925-8).
Reg. Gray	*The Register or Rolls of Walter Gray, Lord Archbishop of York* (Surtees Society, 1872).
Reg. Grégoire IX	*Les registres de Grégoire IX,* edd. L. Auvray and others (Paris, 1896-).
Reg. Halton	*The Register of John de Halton, Bishop*

	in Scotland and England 1624-1645 (Spalding Club, 1850-1).
Spottiswoode, *History*	John Spottiswoode, *History of the Church of Scotland* (Spottiswoode Society, 1851).
Stirling's Register	*The Earl of Stirling's Register of Royal Letters,* ed. C. Rogers (Edinburgh, 1885).
State Papers Henry VIII	*State Papers during the Reign of Henry the Eighth* (Record Commission, 1830-52).
Thirds of Benefices	*Accounts of the Collectors of Thirds of Benefices 1561-1572* (SHS, 1949).
Trans. Royal Hist. Soc.	*Transactions of the Royal Historical Society,* 5th series (London, 1951-).
Vatikanische Quellen	*Vatikanische Quellen zur Geschichte der päpstlichen Hof- und Finanzverwaltung 1316-1378,* edd. E. Göller and others (Paderborn, 1910-).
VCH Lancashire	*The Victoria History of the County of Lancaster* (London, 1906-14).
Wedderburn Bk.	A. Wedderburn, *The Wedderburn Book* (privately printed, 1898).
Wodrow, *Collections*	R. Wodrow, *Collections upon the Lives of the Reformers* (Maitland Club, 1834-48).
Wodrow, *Selections*	*Selections from Wodrow's Biographical Collections: Divines of the North-East of Scotland* (New Spalding Club, 1890).

ABERDEEN DIOCESE

BISHOPS OF ABERDEEN

First known date: 1131 x 1132.

The names of three early bishops - Bean, Denortius and Cormac - were remembered in Aberdeen tradition as predecessors of Nechtan (*Abdn. Reg.*,ii,246-7; Boece, *Vitae*, 6-7); they were supposed to have been based at Mortlach in Banffshire rather than at Aberdeen (*Abdn. Reg.*,i,pp.xi-xix; *ES*,i,433,525; *MRHS*, 167); all the bishops from Nechtan onwards are associated with Aberdeen.

This see was directly subject to the pope until placed under the metropolitan authority of St Andrews 14 Aug. 1472 (*Vet.Mon.*,no. 852).

Nechtan 1131 x 1132.
    Occ. Apr. 1131 x Apr. 1132 (*ESC*,no.97).

Edward 1147 x 1151 - 1171.
    Occ. 1147 x 1151 (*Dunf.Reg.*, 8;cf. *Chron.Holyrood*,121-2); d. 1171 (*Chron.Melrose*, 39).

Matthew 1172 - 1199.
    El. when *St A.archd.* and cons. 2 Apr. 1172 (ibid.,40); d. 20 Aug. 1199 (ibid.,50).

John O.Tiron. 1199 - 1207.
    El. before 26 Dec. 1199 (*Moray Reg.*,13); cons. by 20 June 1200 (*Arb.Lib.*,i,35); d. 13 Oct. 1207 (*Chron.Melrose*,53 for year; *Abdn. Reg.*, ii,247 for month and day).

Adam de Kalder 1207 - 1228.
    El. Oct. x Dec. 1207 (*Chron.Melrose*,53); papal mand. for conf. 29 Jan. 1208 (*CPL*,i,30; cf. Dowden,*Bishops*,102,n.1); d. 1228 (*Chron. Bower*,ii,58).

Matthew Scot (?) 1228 x 1229.
Gilbert de Stirling 1228 - 1239.
    Scot perhaps el. on Kalder's death, but turned it down in favour of a right in *Dk.bp.* which became vacant in 1229 (ibid.; Boece, *Vitae*, 11); but is never in fact found even as 'elect' in numerous royal chrs. of 1228 and 1229, and so the tradition of his el. is suspect.
    Stirling el. 1228 (*Chron.Bower*,ii,58); cons. by 1230 (*SHS Misc.*,viii,6); d. 1239 (*Chron.Melrose*,86), before 17 June (v.inf.).

Ralph de Lamley O.Tiron. 1239 - 1247.
    Succ. Stirling 1239 when abbot of Arbroath (ibid.); had had el. when granted mand. for conf. and cons. 17 June 1239 (*Vet.Mon.*,no. 99); cons. before 20 Aug. 1240 (*Abdn.Reg.*,i,15); d. 1247 (*Chron. Melrose*,107), before 13 May (v.inf.).

Peter de Ramsay (Ramseya) 1247 - 1256.
    Succ. Lamley 1247 (ibid.); after el. gets mand. for cons. 13 May 1247 (*Vet.Mon.*,no.122); occ. 18 Apr. 1256 (*Abdn.Reg.*,ii,49); d.

later in 1256 (*Chron. Melrose*,113); but death was not yet known at
curia 9 Jan. 1257 (*Abdn.Reg.*, i,19); cf. Aberdeen tradition that he
died in 1257 (ibid.,ii,247; cf. *Chron.Bower*,ii,92).

Richard de Pottun   1256 - 1270 or 1272.
       Succ. Ramsay 1256 (*Chron.Melrose*,113); grant of temps. 10
May 1256 is spurious (*Abdn.Reg.*, i,18); occ. as 'elect' 4 Oct. 1257
(*Vet.Mon.*, 78); cons. before 25 Aug. 1258 (*Abdn.Reg.*,ii,50); d.
1270 (*Chron.Bower*,ii,113) or 26 Apr. 1272 (*Abdn.Reg.*,ii,247).

Hugh de Benham   1272 - 1281 x 1282.
       El. when *Ab.chanc*. and cons. at curia under Gregory X 27 Mar.
x 23 July 1272 (*Vet.Mon.*, 101-2); occ. 30 Apr. 1281 (*Arb.Lib.*, i,
164); d. 1282 (*Abdn.Reg.*,ii,247), before 17 June (v.inf.).

Henry de Chene   1282 - 1328.
       El. when *Ab.prec*. and then prov. with mand. for cons. 17 June
1282 (*CPL*, i,465,467); d. 1328 (*Abdn.Reg.*,ii,248) and certainly
before 11 June 1329 (*ER*, i,247).

Walter Herok   1329.
Alexander de Kininmund   1329 - 1343 x 1344.
       Herok el. when *M.dean* i.e. after 15 Mar. 1329 (when still in
poss. of deanery in papal eyes) and prov., but d. at curia without cons.
before 21 Aug. 1329 (v. inf.).
       Kininmund prov. when *St A.archd.Lothian* and employed at
curia 21 Aug. 1329, and cons. at same time (*Vet.Mon.*,no.482), occ.
1 May 1343 (Dowden, *Bishops*,lll,n.1); still thought to be alive by
curia 9 Jan. 1344 (*CPL*,iii,lll); d. before 13 Sept. 1344 (v.inf.).

William de Deyn   O.Tiron.   1344 - 1350.
       Had el. when abbot of Kilwinning and gets prov. 13 Sept. 1344
(*Vet.Mon.*,no.562); cons. by 27 Sept. 1344 (*CPL*,iii,170); for
surname see Boece, *Vitae*,20; cf. *Abdn.Reg.*,ii,148 for form 'de la
Deyne'; d. 20 Aug. 1350 (*Abdn.Reg.*,ii,148).

John de Rate   1350 - 1354 x 1355.
       El. when *Ab.archd*. and then prov. 19 Nov. 1350 (*Vet.Mon.*,
294); cons. 26 Jan. x 14 Mar. 1351 (Hoberg, *Taxae*, 3; *CPL*,iii,384);
occ. 22 Nov. 1354 (*Foedera* [O] ,v,812); perhaps d. before 6 June
1355 (Boece, *Vitae*,22).

Alexander de Kininmund   1355 - 1380.
       El. when *Ab.archd*. and then prov. 4 Dec. 1355 (*Vet.Mon.*,
309-10); cons. before 12 July 1356 (*Abdn.Reg.*, i,82-83); occ. 24
June 1380 (ibid., i,130-1); d. 29 July 1380 (ibid.,ii,248).

Adam de Tyninghame   1380 - 1389.
       Prov. when *Ab.dean* 15 Oct. 1380 (Eubel, *Hierarchia*, i,65);
said to have been cons. by 16 Nov. 1380 (Dowden,*Bishops*,116,no
source quoted); certainly cons. by 24 Oct. 1381 (*Abdn.Reg.*, i, 135);
d. 18 Sept. 1389 (ibid.,ii,248).

Gilbert de Greenlaw   1390 - 1421.

El. and then prov. 19 Jan. 1390 (Eubel, *Hierarchia*, i,65); prob. cons. before 19 Feb. 1390 (*Ob. et Sol.*,l,fo.126); granted temps. before 10 Aug. 1390 (*Abdn.Reg.*, i,201-2); certainly cons. before 18 Mar. 1391 (*APS*, i,579); still alive 24 July 1421 (*HBC*,175,no source quoted; see also *ER*,iv,337); d. before 1 Apr. 1422 (v. inf.); perhaps d. 1422 (*Abdn.Reg.*,ii,248), but more prob. d. 20 Sept. 1421, which was the date of his obit (ibid.,18-19,218).

Henry de Lichton   1422 - 1440.

Trans. from *M.bp.* on Greenlaw's death 1/3 Apr. 1422 (*CPL*, vii,248; cf. *ACSB*, 9); d. after Martinmas 1440 (*ER*,v,94-95) and before 11 Jan. 1441 (*Abdn.Reg.*,ii,68); prob. d. 12 or 14 Dec. 1440 (ibid.,24,205,221).

Ingram de Lindsay   1441 - 1458.
James Douglas   1441 - 1442.

Lindsay had el. and gets prov. by Eugenius IV 28 Apr. 1441 (*CPL*,ix,224); occ. 2 June 1458 (*Abdn.Reg.*, i,282); prob. d. 24 Aug. 1458 (ibid.,ii,203; cf. Dowden,*Bishops*,123-4).

Douglas prov. by Anti-Pope Felix V 30 May 1441 (*St A.Cop.*, 313-14); held temps. for a time c. May 1442 (ibid.,322).

Thomas Spens   1457 - 1480.
William Forbes   x 1459.

Spens trans. from *Ga.bp.* on false report of death of Lindsay 21 Nov. 1457 (*CPL*,xi,310; *ACSB*,46,48); trans. from *Ga.bp.* again 15 Dec. 1458 (*CPL*,xiii,15); trans. became effective 3 x 10 Mar. 1459 (*RMS*,ii,nos. 685-6); d. 15 Apr. 1480 (Boece, *Vitae*,54).

Forbes said to have been el. recently before 27 Feb. 1459 (*CPL*,xi,528); no. poss.

Robert Blackadder   1480 - 1483.

El. before 12 June 1480 (*ADC*, i,49); prov. 14 July 1480 (*ACSB*,76; Eubel, *Hierarchia*,ii,77); trans. to *G.bp.* when still not cons. 19 Mar. 1483 (Eubel, *Hierarchia*,ii,160; cf. *Vet.Mon.*, no. 894).

William Elphinstone junior   1483 - 1514.

Trans. from *R.bp.* when still not cons. 19 Mar. 1483 (Eubel, *Hierarchia*,ii,77; cf. *Vet.Mon.*, no.894); cons. 25 Apr. 1488 x 24 Apr. 1489 (*AUR*,xxiii, 135-6; cf. xxxvi,230); d. 25 Oct. 1514 (*Abdn.Reg.*, ii,249).

Alexander Gordon   x 1515 - 1518.
James Ogilvie   1514 x 1515.
Robert Forman   x 1515 - 1515 - 16.

Gordon nom. and el. before 20 Jan. 1515 (*ADCP*,49); prov. 6 June 1516 (Eubel, *Hierarchia*,iii,91); d. 30 June 1518 (*Abdn.Reg.*, ii,249; cf. Dowden, *Bishops*,136,n.6).

Ogilvie had nom. from duke of Albany, but res. his right on getting commend of abbey of Dryburgh (Boece, *Vitae*,113;cf.91); occ. as commendator 24 Sept. 1515 (*TA*, v,40).

Forman prov. by pope before 22 Mar. 1515 when he paid some

common services (Dowden, *Bishops*,136, quoting sources in Vatican
Archives); res. without poss. by 1515-16 (*James V Letters*,29, cf. *St
A.Form.*, i,46; Boece, *Vitae*,113).

Gavin Dunbar senior   1518 - 1532.
George Learmonth O.S.B.   1529 - 1531.
       Dunbar nom. as *St A.archd.* before 31 Oct. 1518 (Dowden,
Bishops,137); prov. 5 Nov. 1518 (ibid.); dem. *M.dean.* by 12 Dec.
1518; cons. 20 Feb. 1519 (ibid.,137-8); d. 10 Mar. 1532 (*Abdn.Reg.*,
ii,211-12).
       Learmonth as prior of Pluscarden prov. as coadj. and successor
to Dunbar 20 May 1529 (Dowden, *Bishops*,139); but d. before Dunbar
18 Mar. 1531 (Forbes, *Kalendars*, xxviii).

William Stewart   1532 - 1545.
       Crown nom. as Lincluden prov. 22 Mar. 1532 (*James V Letters*,
217); prov. 13 Nov. 1532 (PRO 31/10 - 14/96-97); cons. 22 Mar. x
10 Apr. 1533 (Dowden, *Bishops*,140,n.2); d. 10 Apr. 1545 (*Spalding
Misc.*,i,66; cf. Dowden, *Bishops*,140-1).

William Gordon   1545 - 1577.
       Crown nom. to pope for appointment as coadj. to Stewart
'about a month' before 28 Apr. 1545 (*ERS*,ii,250; cf. *Abdn. Reg.*,
i,lviii; cf. also *HBC*,283 for nom. as coadj. 21 Jan. and 15 Mar.
1545, no sources quoted), granted temps. 20 Aug. 1545 (*RSS*,iii,
no.1297); prov. 17 May 1546 (Brady, *Episcopal Succession*, i,133-4);
cons. 23 Dec. 1546 x 26 Jan. 1547 (*RSS*,iii,p.334n and no.2124);
d. 6 Aug. 1577 (*Spalding Misc.*,ii,46).

David Cunningham   1577 - 1600.
       Crown conf. after el. 5 Oct. or 5 Nov. 1577 (Reg.Pres., i,146v,
RSS,vii,no.1254); cons. 11 Nov. 1577 (*Spalding Misc.*,ii,46-47),
granted temps. 22 Feb. 1578 (*RSS*,vii,no.1476); d. 30 Aug. 1600
(Wodrow, *Selections*, p.1v, no source quoted).

Peter Blackburn   1600 - 1616.
       Crown prov. 2 Sept. 1600 (ibid.,p.lvi, no source quoted), cons.
just before 3 May 1611 (*Original Letters*, i,270); d. 14 June 1616
(*Abdn.Kirk Recs.*,84).

Alexander Forbes   1616 - 1617.
       Trans. from *C.bp.* 16/21 July 1616 (*Original Letters*,ii,485;
Reg.Pres.,iv,134v); d. 24 Nov. 1617 (Dowden, *Bishops*,396,n.1,
quoting Edin.Tests.).

Patrick Forbes   1618 - 1635.
       Crown nom. on or before 27 Jan. 1618 (*Original Letters*,
ii,542-3), el. 24 Mar. 1618 (*Funerals of ... Patrick Forbes*
[Spottiswoode Soc.] ,pp.lxiv,208); crown prov. 8 Apr. 1618 (ibid.,
214); cons. 17 May 1618 (ibid.,214-16); d. 28 Mar. 1635 (ibid.,
xciv).

Adam Bellenden   1635 - 1638.
       Trans. from *Db.bp.* 19 May 1635 (Baillie, *Journals*, i,436;

Wodrow, *Selections*,122); crown prov. 2 Aug. 1635 (RSS,cvi,fo.324);
depriv. by general assembly 13 Dec. 1638 (Peterkin, *Records*, i,27);
buried after death in England 4 Mar. 1648 (Dowden, *Bishops*,399).

CHAPTER OF ABERDEEN

Early see for this area before time of Bp. Nechtan was prob. at Mortlach
in Banffshire (v.sup.); the *monasterium* there (meaning perhaps a
minster rather than a monastery - suggestion of Dr I. B. Cowan) is listed
along with the *monasterium* of Clova in Aberdeenshire as having
become possession of ch. of Aberdeen by time of a papal bull of conf.
granted 10 Aug. 1157 (*Abdn. Reg.*, i,5-7; *AMW*,26-29; *SGS*,vi,58-88);
Aberdeen was clearly the see of the diocese at this date, but there was
apparently no community of clergy serving the cathedral, for Bp.
Edward received a papal faculty to introduce monks or canons there
at his choice (ibid.); perhaps he had a community of regular rather
than secular clergy in mind, following recent examples at St Andrews
and perhaps Whithorn in Galloway (cf. Glasgow and Dunkeld); but no
immediate advantage was taken of this faculty.

A cleric with designation 'canon' appears among witnesses to an
act of Bp. John 1199 - 1207 (*Kel.Lib.*,ii,no.444); under Bp. Kalder
1207 - 1228 such canons become numerous as members of assemblies
of a synodal character which are associated with episcopal acts, with
the archd. as the leading figure and a dean second to him (e.g. *St A.
Lib.*,299-301; see also *A. B.Ill.*,ii,17-18; cf. *Arb. Lib.*, i,no.199 prob.
from early in episcopate, where no canons yet appear); development
continues under Bp. Stirling 1228 - 1239, with this assembly now
being designated a 'chapter' and using a common seal (*Kel. Lib.*, ii,
no.435; cf. i,no.224; see also *St A.Lib.*,301-2; cf. *Arb. Lib.*, i,no.200);
one of the canons is sometimes now distinguished as the treas., but
the dean remains inferior to the archd. (a lonely exception is found
in a papal letter of 29 Jan. 1208 dealing with the election of Bp.
Kalder, when it is asserted that the election had been carried out by
the dean, archd. and chapter (*Innocentii III Opera*, ed. Migne,ii,
1303);though both men were present at the curia at the time, it is
likely that the clerks there were mistaken about their relative local
status); but when Bp. Lamley was elected early in 1239 it was in
an assembly apparently under the dean, comprising both the chapter
on the one hand as something separable and the clergy of the city
of Aberdeen on the other; and the two groups shared in the election
in the proportion of 4 : 3 (*Vet.Mon.*,no.99); this was the last time
that the non-capitular clergy shared in the bishop's election, for in
1247 it was the dean and canons alone who elected Bp. Ramsay
(ibid.,no.122).

Robert de Leicester was prob. elevated from his indeterminate
position in familia of Bp. Stirling to the dignity of dean by Bp.
Lamley; at first his status was inferior to that of the archd. as before
(*Arb. Lib.*, i,no.202, which prob. dates from June 1239 x Aug.
1240; and note that here a canon found under the previous bp. is

now distinguished as prec.); but the new bp. was active in building up common funds so as to maintain a resident chapter at the cathedral, and as early as 20 Aug. 1240 this community comprised four dignitaries apart from the archd. (for a chanc. now appears) and at least seven simple canons (*Abdn. Reg.*, i,15); the dean is now the leading member of this chapter and his precedence over the archd. is clear by time of a formal chapter act of 24 Apr. 1243 (*St A. Lib.*, 304-5); by this time the bp. and archd. had both become canons additional to those found in 1240; the chapter had now a sophisticated corporate character (presumably in consequence of episcopal constitutions now lost), and it had reached the same size of 13 members that was to be conf. in the cathedral statues of Bp. Ramsay 18 Apr. 1256 (*Abdn. Reg.*,ii,38-49); by then the process of allocating prebends to each canon, which had been supposedly started by Bp. Edward and continued by Bps. Stirling and Lamley (ibid.,38), was completed for the time being.

Additions were made to this chapter in succeeding centuries, with a temporary subd. in mid-14th century and a succ. in 16th century (*MRHS*,167;*RSCHS*,xiv,21,29,41-42).

EARLY DEANS IN ABERDEEN

Roger   1189 x 1196, 1175 x 1199.
      Occ. 1189 x 1196 (*Kel. Lib.*,ii,no.449) and 1175 x 1199 (*Arb. Lib.*, i,no.197).

Robert   1189 x 1199 - 1204 x 1211.
      Occ. 1189 x 1199 (*Kel. Lib.*,ii,no.450) and 11 June, 1204 x 1211 (*Arb. Lib.*, i,no.81 bis).

Alexander   1211 x 1214 - 1228 x 1239.
      Occ. 1211 x 1214 (ibid.,no.130) and 1228 x 1239 (ibid.,no. 200;*Kel. Lib.*,nos.224,435).

DEANS OF ABERDEEN

First known date: 1238 x 1240.
      Prebend: ch. of St Machar, Aberdeen in 1256 (*Abdn. Reg.*,ii, 39; Cowan, *Parishes*, 2).

Robert de Leicester   1238 x 1240 - 1277.
      Occ. 20 Aug. 1240 (*Abdn. Reg.*, i,15;*Inchcolm Chrs.*,no.19), having succ. since 31 Dec. 1238 (*Inchaff. Chrs.*,no.65); occ. 6 Feb. 1277 (*Abdn. Reg.*, i,34).

Matthew de Crambeth   1288.
      In poss. when conf. and cons. *Dk.bp.* 10 Apr. 1288.

Hervey de Crambeth   1291 - 1292 x 1296.
      Occ. (as 'Henry') 5 June 1291 (Palgrave, *Docs.Hist.Scot.*, illustrations, v); occ. 21 June 1292 (Glas. Univ. Lib., Cowie MS, no.21; cf. *Abdn. Reg.*,ii,pl.I); moved to *Dk.dean.* by 17 July 1296.

Walter Blackwater   1296 - 1297.
   Occ. 19 July 1296 (*CDS*,ii,195); occ. 27 Aug. 1297 (*Abdn. Reg.*, i,38).

Freskyn de Chene   1321.
   Occ. 15 Dec. 1321 (*Abdn. Reg.*, i,47).

Andrew Fleming   1321 x 1330.
   Held it at death before 20 Aug. 1330 (v. inf.).

Gilbert Fleming   1330 - 1347 x 1348.
   Prov. on Andrew's death 20 Aug. 1330 (*CPL*,ii,321); in poss. 10 Nov. 1347 (*CPL*,iii,256); d. before 18 July 1348 (Collect.,14,fo.161).

Walter de Coventre   1348 - 1361.
   Prov. on Gilbert's death 20 Dec. 1348 (*CPL*,iii,290); prov. *Db.bp.* 18 June 1361.

Michael de Monymusk 1361 - 1364 x 1365.
Adam de Tyninghame   1362 - 1380.
   Monymusk prov. 24 Aug. x 6 Nov. 1361 (*CPP*, i,325,375; Collect.,14,fo.167,190), occ. 10 Feb. 1363 (*Abdn. Reg.*, i,93), but lit. went against him Feb. 1364 x June 1365 (*CPP*, i,480,506), and he may have returned to *Db.dean.*
   Tyninghame prov. 20 Mar. 1362 and got poss. (Collect.,14,fo. 167v); turned out by Monymusk, but won lit. (v.sup.), occ. 20 Mar. 1366 (*Rot.Scot.*, i,901), prov. *Ab. bp.* 15 Oct. 1380.

Simon de Ketenis   1380 - 1386 x 1387.
   Prov. 16 Nov. 1380 (Reg.Supp.,61,fo.7); occ. 3 July 1386 (*Abdn.Reg.*, i,174-6); d. before 13 June 1387 (*CPP*, i,568).

William de Spynie   1388 - 1397.
   Occ. 18 July 1388 (*Moray Reg.*,350-1); prov. *M.bp.* 1 Sept. 1397.

Patrick de Spalding   1397 - 1422.
James de Lindsay   1419.
   Spalding prov. 23 Oct. 1397 (Reg. Vat.,322,fo.36-38); in poss. 22 May 1422 (*Sussidi ... dell' Archivio Vaticano*,ii,14); d. before 30 Aug. 1422 (*CPL*,vii,242).
   Lindsay prov. 17 July 1419 (*CSSR*, i,89).

Nicholas de Tunnok   1422 - 1428 x 1429.
Richard Militis   1423.
Edward de Lauder   1423.
Nicholas de Atholl   1424.
James Scrymgeour   1425, 1428 - 1429.
   Tunnok prov. on Spalding's death 30 Aug. 1422 (*CPL*,vii,243); in poss. 22 June 1428, but lit. with Scrymgeour (*CSSR*,ii,221-2); expelled before 2 Sept. 1429 (Reg.Supp.,246,fo.91); never regained poss. (ibid.,245,fo.177v).
   Militis prov. 24 May 1423 (*CSSR*,ii,26-27).
   Lauder prov. 12 Sept. 1423 (ibid.,ii,35).

Atholl prov. 28 Sept. 1424 (ibid.,ii,71-72).

Scrymgeour prov. 27 Mar./26 June 1425 unfruitfully (*CPL*,vii, 404; *CSSR*,ii,98-99); prov. 22 June 1428 (ibid.,ii,221-2); got poss. by 2 Sept. 1429 after lit. with Tunnok (v.sup.); prob. dead by 8 Nov. 1429 (v.inf.).

David Hamilton	1429 - 1446 x 1449.
John Wincester	1431.
Duncan de Lichton	1433(?), 1434 - 1435 x 1436.

Hamilton prov. 8 Nov. 1429 (Reg.Supp.,246,fo.15v), but letters not expedited; new prov. 11 Mar. 1431 (*CPL*,vii,412-13), but letters delayed until 1435 (Reg.Supp.,310,fo.3v; cf. *CPL*,viii,533); no poss. 12 Sept. 1433 (Reg.Supp.,289,fo.87v); cert. in poss. 1 June 1437 (*ACSB*,23); new prov. 11 June 1446 (*CPL*,ix,558), in poss. 21 Nov. 1446 (Reg.Supp.,414,fo.91); d. before 16 May 1449 (*CPL*, x,193).

Wincester prov. shortly before 21 Mar. 1431; no. poss. then (Reg.Supp.,267,fo.116).

Lichton perhaps had poss. by 12 Sept. 1433 (v.sup.); cert. poss. by 5 Mar. 1434 when he is incorporated at Basel (Haller, *Conc.Bas.*,iii,38; *Mon.Conc.Bas.*,ii,618); moved to *Ab.chanc.* 4 Feb. 1435 x 26 Nov. 1436; res. his right cert. before 30 May 1446 (Reg. Supp.,412,fo.24v).

Andrew de Durisdeer	1449 - 1455/1457.

Prov. on Hamilton's death 23 May 1449 (*CPL*, X,197); prov. *G.bp*. with disp. to retain *Ab.dean* for two years more 7 May 1455 (Reg.Supp.,479,fo.281).

Andrew Stewart	1455 - 1456.
Richard Forbes	1456 - 1483.

Stewart given dean. in commend when it becomes vacant 7 May 1455 (*CPL*,xi,2); said on 31 Jan. 1456 to have res. (v.inf.), but claimed poss. 23 June 1456 (Reg.Supp.,491,fo.274v).

Forbes prov. 31 Jan. 1456 (*CPL*,xi,33); occ. 12 June 1483 (*Abdn.Reg.*, i,315); perhaps d. 17 Aug. [1483] , this being his obit (ibid.,ii,205; cf. death-date of 30 Sept. 1480 given ibid.,ii,19,219).

James Chisholm	1483(?) - 1487.
James Brown	1483 - 1503 x 1505.
Gavin Vaiche	1485 - 1486.
David Abercrombie	1487 - 1488.

Chisholm prob. got poss. on death of Forbes and before prov. of Brown in 1483; in poss. when prov. *Db.bp*. 31 Jan. 1487; cf. *M.dean*.

Brown prov. on Forbes' death 1 Nov. 1483, but still no poss. 30 Mar. 1484 (*CPL*,xiii,914; *ACSB*, 211); prov. *si neutri*, prob. after lit. between Chisolm and Vaiche, 12 May 1485 (*ACSB*,211); in poss. in papal eyes 7 Apr. 1487 (*ACSB*, 213); occ. 9 June 1499 (*Abdn.Reg.*, i,346); occ. 29 Sept. 1503 (*Abdn.Fasti*,47).

Vaiche prov. on Forbes' death 5 Jan. 1485 (*ACSB*,213), but d. without poss. (ibid.) before 26 Dec. 1486 (see *M.dean*.).

Abercrombie was pres. by crown on promotion of Chisholm;

in poss. 11 Jan. 1488 when parliament supported his right against barrators (*APS*,ii,184).

Henry Babington   1505 - 1506 x 1507.
Pres. by crown on Brown's death 2 Dec. 1505 (*RSS*, i,no. 1172); conf. by pope 4 May 1506 (Reg.Supp.,1236,fo.12-13).

James Kincragy   1507 - 1539 x 1540.
Pres. by crown on Babington's death 24 May 1507 (*RSS*, i, no.1478); prov. 16 Aug. 1507 (PRO 31/9 - 31/121); occ. 25 Sept. 1538 (*ADCP*, 474) and 17 Sept. 1539 (*TA*,vii,231); said to have died 27 July 1539 (*Abdn.Reg.*,ii,15, 216).

Robert Erskine   1540 - 1563.
Pres. by crown for prov. on Kincragy's death 1 Aug. 1540 (*James V Letters*, 406-7); occ. 28 Apr. 1541 (*RMS*,iii,no.2347); made will 13 Feb. 1563 (SRO, Acts and Decreets,xxvii,fo.370), and d. before 31 July 1563 (ibid.).

Robert Maitland   1565 - 1578 x 1579.
Pres. by crown on Erskine's death 27 July 1565 (*RSS*, v,no. 2217); occ. 24 Dec. 1578 (*RMS*,iv,no.2834); res. before 8 Apr. 1579 when dean. annexed to college of Aberdeen (ibid.,no.2862; *Abdn.Fasti*,130-1).
Note: for details of the following subsequent deans see *Ab.King's coll.princ.*:

Walter Stewart	x 1585 - 1587 x
David Rait	x 1592 - 1629 x 1632.
William Leslie	1632 - 1639.

PRECENTORS/CHANTERS OF ABERDEEN

First known date: 1240.
Prebend: ch. of Auchterless in 1256 (*Abdn.Reg.*,ii,39; Cowan, *Parishes*,10).

Jordan   1240 - 1244.
Occ. 20 Aug. 1240 (*Abdn.Reg.*, i,15); occ. 24 Apr. 1243 (*St A.Lib.*,305); but styled simply as canon 1240 and 1244 (ibid., 303-4).

Roger de Derby   1259 x 1266 - 1268 x 1270.
Occ. 6 Feb. 1266 (*Pais.Reg.*, 422), having obtained it since 1 Aug. 1259 (*Abdn.Reg.*, i,27); occ. 16 Oct. 1268 (*A.B.Coll.*, 568); d. before 19 Nov. 1270 (*Rot. Gravesend*, 44; cf. 275).

Henry de Chene   1277 - 1282.
Occ. 22 Jan. 1277 (*Abdn.Reg.*,ii,278); prov. *Ab.bp*. 17 June 1282.

Thomas de Salcop   1312 x 1321.
Occ. 15 Dec. 1321 (*Abdn.Reg.*, i,47), having obtained it since 3 July 1312 (*Arb.Lib.*, i,287; cf. *Abdn.Reg.*, i,40); moved to *Ab. chanc.*

Gilbert Fleming   1330.
In poss. when prov. *Ab.dean*. 20 Aug. 1330 (*CPL*, ii,321).

George de Stirling   1331.
Prov. 12 Jan./27 Oct. 1331 (*CPL*,ii,339,360).

Reginald   1357.
Occ. 13 Sept. 1357 (*Foedera* [O] ,vi,40).

John de Cromdale   1362.
Occ. 12 Nov. 1362 (*CPP*, i,384).

John Penny   c.1364.
Robert Monypenny   1365.
Penny said in May 1366 to have held it for more than one month at some date more than two years earlier (*CPP*, i,527; Collect.,14,fo.172); cf. *G.subd*.
Monypenny prov. after coll. by ord. on Cromdale's death 14 Sept. 1365 (*CPP*, i,508).

William de Spynie   1371 - 1372 x 1373.
Occ. 1 Mar. 1371 (Reg.Av.,174,fo.101); res. on exch. after 1 May 1372 (see *M.prec*.).

William Boyl   1373.
Exch. conf. for Spynie 14 Sept. 1373 (*CPL*,iv,188).

Robert Boyl   1377 - 1392.
Occ. 3 Oct. 1377 (SRO, Transcripts from Vatican, i,no.42); occ. 24 Apr. 1392 (*Abdn.Reg*., i,185-6).

William de Lauder   1392 x 1408.
Alexander de Etal   1392 x 1407.
Lauder said in 1419 to have held it for several months by prov. (*CSSR*, i,41-42), must have been before prov. *G.bp*. 9 July 1408.
Etal said in 1419 to have held it at death at some much earlier date (*CSSR*, i,41-42), prob. after Lauder and before Simon de Etal.

Simon de Etal   1407 - 1416 x 1419.
Occ. 4 Apr. 1407 (*Abdn.Reg*.,i,211); occ. 27 May 1416 (*A.B.Ill*.,iii,26), d. before 3 May 1419 (*CSSR*, i,41).

William de Crawford   1419 - 1425.
Nicholas Tunnok   1419.
Crawford prov. after coll. by ord. having poss. 31 May 1419 (*CSSR*, i,61-62), occ. 2 June 1425 (*Abdn.Reg*., i,223); prob. res. on exch. with Barber (v.inf.).
Tunnok prov. unfruitfully 3/5 May 1419 (*CSSR*, i,41-42).

John Barber   1427 - 1438.
Occ. 20 Oct. 1427 (*Abdn.Reg*., i,227), prob. after exch. with Crawford; occ. 10 May 1438 (ibid., i,234-5).

David Ogilvie   1438.
Papal conf. after coll. by ord. on Barber's death having poss. 5

Dec. 1438 (Reg.Supp.,353,fo.194); prob. res. on exch. with Hervy for *M.archd*. which he held by 8 June 1440.

Henry Hervy   1440 - 1457.
       Had given up *M.archd*. by 8 June 1440; occ. 11 Jan. 1441 (*Abdn. Reg*.,ii,68); occ. 7 Apr. 1456 (*CPL*,xi,258); d. 26 Aug. 1457 (*Abdn. Reg*.,ii,17,217).

Henry Clerk   1457.
Robert de Forrest   1460.
William Lindsay   1460.
       Clerk prov. on Hervy's death 22 Oct. 1457 (*CPL*,xi,338); res. before 6 May 1460 (v.inf.).
       Forrest in poss. after res. of Clerk, gets prov. *si neutri* 6 May 1460 (Reg.Supp.,531,fo.118).
       Lindsay lit. 6 May 1460 (v.sup.); new prov. 10 June 1460 (Reg. Supp., 531,fo.134), res. on exch. with James Lindsay (v.inf.).

James Lindsay   1461 - 1465 x 1471.
       In poss. after exch. with William Lindsay though ord. 11 Apr. 1461 (*CPL*,xii,373n - 374n; *ACSB*,141); occ. 16 Jan. 1465 (*Spalding Misc*.,v,287); dem. before 6 Feb. 1471 (*CPL*,xii,373n - 374n).

Walter (sic) **Lindsay** (?)   x 1482.
       Res. on exch. through ord. before 15 Nov. 1485 (v.inf.), and so presumably before 15 Mar. 1482; perhaps error for James Lindsay.

Archibald Lindsay   1482 - 1516.
Henry Allan   1505.
       Lindsay occ. 15 Mar. 1482 (St A.Univ. Mun.,SM 110, B12. P2.7); got prov. following exch. with Walter Lindsay 15 Nov. 1485 (*CPL*,xiv,183-4); given royal permission to res. to pope, retaining fruits 12 Apr. 1516 (*RSS*, i,no.2745).
       Allan said to be in poss. 20 Dec. 1505 (*Prot.Bk.Foular*, i, no.211).

David Dischington   1516 - 1545.
       Pres. by crown on Archibald Lindsay's res. 12 Apr. 1516 (*RSS*, i,no.2745); occ. 14 Oct. 1543 (*HMC* 34, *14thR*.,iii,233); d. 26 Jan. 1545 (*Abdn.Reg*.,ii,210).

Archibald Betoun   1545 - 1582.
       Pres. by crown on Dischington's death 1 Nov. 1545 (*RSS*, iii,nos.1396-7); occ. 20 Jan. 1547 (*ADCP*,562); occ. as 'Al(exander)' 1 Nov. 1570 (*Abdn.Fasti*,128); d. in poss. 31 July 1582 (Edin.Tests.); cf. inf.

Gideon Murray   1582 - 1590.
       Pres. by crown on res. of Betoun 8 July 1582 (RSS,xlix,fo.19); occ. 10 Oct. 1590 (*RPC*,iv,538); was styled 'of Elibank' from 1595 (*SP*,iii,504).

William Meldrum   1593.
       Occ. abroad as *prefectus cantus* 6 Apr. 1593 (*Abdn.Fasti*,134).

Robert Maitland   1598 - 1614.
   Occ. 11 Feb. 1598 (SRO,Dalhousie,sec.16,no.2373); occ. 16
July 1607 (SRO,Secretary's Reg.Sasines Abdn.,vi,fo.207); occ. 10
Aug. 1614 (Stevenson & Wood, *Seals*,iii,490).

William Gray   1617 - 1626.
   Occ. 10 Sept. 1617 (SRO,Part.Reg.Sasines Abdn.,i,fo.66) and
29 Apr. 1626 (ibid.,v,fo.246).

John Forbes   1628 - 1636.
   Occ. 15 Nov. 1628 (SRO,Part.Reg.Sasines Banff,iii,fo.20); occ.
6 Apr. 1636 (ibid.,iv,fo.143).

CHANCELLORS OF ABERDEEN

First known date: 1240.
   Prebend: ch. of Birse in 1256 (*Abdn.Reg.*,ii,39; Cowan,*Parishes*,
18).

John   1240.
   Occ. 20 Aug. 1240 (*Abdn.Reg.*, i,15).

Hugh de Benham   1266 - 1272.
   Occ. 11 Nov. 1266 (*Abdn.Reg.*, i,29); cons. *Ab.bp*. 27 Mar. x
23 July 1272.

Thomas de Benham   1277.
   Occ. 22 Jan. 1277 (*Abdn.Reg.*,ii,278); occ. 1272 x 1281
(SRO,Benholm & Hedderwick, no.224x).

Walter de Blackwater   1282 x 1296, 1292 x 1296.
   Occ. 1282 x 1296 (*Abdn.Reg.*, i,37); moved to *Ab.dean* 21
June 1292 x 19 July 1296.

Henry Martini   1310.
   Occ. 29 Mar. 1310 (*Abdn.Reg.*, i,40).

Roger Paternoster   1321.
   Occ. 15 Dec. 1321 (*Abdn.Reg.*, i,47; another *Ab.chanc*. in same
document (Garioch) was prob. *Ab.treas.*).

Thomas de Salcop   1330 - 1335.
   Prob. in poss. before 20 Aug. 1330 (see *Ab.prec.*); prob. occ.
Mar. 1335, though text has 1305 (*Abdn.Reg.*, i,40); occ. 10 July
1335 (ibid.,i,62-64).

Andrew de Bosco   1350 - 1353.
   Occ. 10 Feb. 1350 (*Family of Rose*,119); occ. 2 July 1353
(*CPP*, i,250).

Malcolm de Drumbreck   1362 - 1369.
   Occ. 27 Nov. 1362 (*CPP*, i,389); prov. *C.bp*. 21 Feb. 1369.

John de Drumbeck   1369 - 1407.
   Prov. 24 Apr. 1369 (Collect.,14,fo.174v); occ. 4 Apr. 1407
(*Abdn.Reg.*, i,210-11).

Duncan Petit   1414 x 1418 - 1435.
      Occ. 10 Oct. 1418 (*Abdn.Recs.*, i,4-5), having prob. got it since
18 May 1414 (see *M.chanc.*); occ. 4 Feb. 1435 (*Abdn.Reg.*,i,223-4).

Duncan de Lichton   1436 - 1475.
David Reid   1438.
      Lichton occ. 26 Nov. 1436 (*A.B.Ill.*,iii,317); occ. 6 May 1475
(*Abdn.Reg.*,i,299).
      Reid gets *com.priv.* against Lichton 7 Nov. 1438 (Reg.Supp.,
351,fo.253v); unsuccessful.

Alexander Inglis   1476 - 1480.
      Occ. 27 Feb. 1476 (St A.Univ.Mun.,SM110.B12.P2.9); still in
poss. 14 July 1480 (*RMS*,ii,no.1446); prob. res. on getting *St A.
archd.*; he is wrongly called *Ab.archd.* in document of 12 July 1480
(ibid.,no.1445).

John Nisbet   1480 x 1481.
      Held it at death before Aug. 1481 (v.inf.).

Giles Boyce   1480 x 1481.
      Prov. on Nisbet's death, but d. without poss. Aug. 1480 x Aug.
1481 (*CPL*,xiii,816,904, where christian name is given as 'Files').

Andrew Young   1482.
      Prov. on Boyce's death 30 May 1482 (*CPL*,xiii,816); res. at curia
without having had poss. 20 June 1482 (ibid.).

George Brown   1482 - 1483.
      Prov. on Boyce's death and res. of Young 20 June 1482 (*CPL*,
xiii,816; *ACSB*, 206); prov. *Dk.bp.* 22 Oct. 1483.

John Flestone   1485.
Nicholas Greenlaw   1485 - 1494.
John Fletcher   1492 - 1523.
      Flestone in poss. 24 Nov. 1485 (*ACSB*,221); prob. same as John
Fletcher (v.inf.).
      Greenlaw gets *com.priv.* against Flestone 24 Nov. 1485 (*ACSB*,
221); promised annates 31 Aug. 1487 (ibid.); prov. and promises
annates again 24 Aug. 1494 (PRO 31/9 - 30/378).
      Fletcher is to be prov. and admitted 26 Aug. 1492 (Reg.Lat.,
952,fos.32-35; Reg.Vat.,777,fo.137-9); occ. 7 Sept. 1493 (*Abdn.Reg.*,
i,333); occ. 11 July 1516 (*Abdn.Chrs.*,399); given coadj. 1521
(v.inf.); d. 9 Feb. 1523 (*Abdn.Reg.*,ii,4,211; but obit is dated 9 Feb.
1521 by Abdn. Franciscans, see *Spalding Misc.*, i,63).

Patrick Dunbar   1521 - 1525.
John Dingwall   1525 - 1532.
      Dunbar promises annates as coadj., with consent of Fletcher,
20 Feb. 1521 (PRO 31/9 - 31/361, 369, name being 'Dumbach'); prob.
in poss. by 20 July 1524 (see *C.chanc.*) and may have retained a right
until after 23 Aug. 1525 (see. *M.succ.*).
      Dingwall occ. 21 July 1525 (Fraser, *Eglinton*,ii,101), and prob.
made exch. with Dunbar for *M.succ.* after 23 Aug. 1525; occ. 10 Apr.

1532 (SRO, Swinton,no.107); d. 6 Sept. 1532 x 7 Jan. 1533
(see *Edin.Trin.prov*.).

William Symple	1533 - 1534.
David Douglas	1532 x 1533 - 1534.
John Reid	1534 - 1540 x 1541.

Symple pres. by crown on Dingwall's death 8 Jan. 1533 (*RSS*,ii,
no.1474; cf. no.1471); res. in favour of Reid on or about 13 Oct.
1534 (*James V Letters*,276-7).

Douglas had papal prov. Mar. 1532 x Mar. 1533, and has poss.
13 Oct. 1534 (*James V Letters*,277).

Reid gets pres. by crown to curia against Douglas 13 Oct. 1534
(*James V Letters*, 276-7); occ. Aug. 1536 x Sept. 1537 (*ER*,xvii,
56); occ. 18 Dec. 1540 (SRO, Erroll,no.379); d. before July 1541
(v.inf.).

George Marschell	1540 x 1541 - 1546 x 1547.
William Meldrum	1540 x 1541 - 1542.
James Salmond	1542.

Marschell coll. by ord. on Reid's death, and on 14 Feb. 1542
pres. by crown to curia for prov. (*James V Letters*,436); has been
seeking prov. for more than a year, and lit. in curia when on 8 July
1542 king writes again on his behalf (ibid.,440-1); occ. 16 Aug.
1542 (*TA*,viii,l); occ. 14 Oct. 1543 (*HMC*,34,*14thR*.,iii,233); d.
16 Dec. 1546 x 16 Sept. 1547 (see *Lincluden prov*.).

Meldrum had prov. more than a year before 8 July 1542, when
king proposed he res. his right to Marschell for a pension (*James V
Letters*,440-1); still claiming this pension 7 Sept. 1551 (*Prot.Bk.
Cristisone*,no.459).

Salmond promised annates 17 July 1542, though prov. on
Reid's death was not effective since Marschell was in poss. (PRO
31/9 - 33/140).

| **Alexander Seton** | 1547 - 1600 x 1601. |

Occ. 17 Dec. 1547 (SRO,Dunecht,no.38); occ. wrongly as
'William' 1 Nov. 1570 (*Abdn.Fasti*,128); occ. 2 Aug. 1581 (SRO,
Erroll,no.957); occ. 26 Mar. 1600 (SRO,Reg.Ho.Chr.no.2375); d.
by 16 Nov. 1601 (v.inf.).

| **George Seton of Barra** | 1591 - 1626. |
| **Alexander Irving** | 1601. |

Seton occ. already with title of chancellor during Alexander
Seton's lifetime 8 Feb. 1591 (*RPC*,iv,581) and 17 Sept. 1597
(*Laing Chrs*.,no.1337); occ. thereafter 16 July 1607 (SRO,
Secretary's Reg.Sasines Abdn.,vi,fo.207) and 29 Apr. 1626 (SRO,
Part.Reg.Sasines Abdn.,v,fo.246); d. in office Aug. 1626 (SRO,
Reg. of Retours,ix,fo.230).

Irving gets crown pres. on Alexander Seton's death 16 Nov.
1601 (RSS,lxxii,fo.171); but never occ. as chanc.

| **John Ross/Rose** | 1628 - 1636. |

Occ. 15 Nov. 1628 (SRO, Part.Reg. Sasines Banff,iii,fo.20)

and 6 Apr. 1636 (ibid.,iv,fo.143).

TREASURERS OF ABERDEEN

First known date: 1228 x 1239.
    Prebend: ch. of Daviot in 1256 (*Abdn.Reg.*,ii,39; Cowan, *Parishes*, 45).

William   1228 x 1239 - 1243.
    Occ. 1228 x 1239 (*Arb.Lib.*, i,no.200); occ. 24 Apr. 1243 (*St A.Lib.*,305).

Robert   1277.
    Occ. 22 Jan. 1277 (*Abdn.Reg.*,ii,278); occ. 1272 x 1281 (SRO, Benholm & Hedderwick,no.224x).

William de Moffat   1291.
    Occ. 30 Apr. 1291 (*Melr.Lib.*,no.353).

Andrew de Garioch   1297 - 1321.
    Occ. 27 Aug. 1297 (*Abdn.Reg.*,i,38); prob. occ. 15 Dec. 1321, though printed text calls him *Ab.chanc.* (ibid., i,47).

John de Kininmund   1321 x 1361.
    Held it at death before 9 Nov. 1361 (Collect.,14,fo.167v.)

William de Rotha   1361.
William de Ormskirk   1361 x 1363 - 1392.
    Rotha prov. on Kininmund's death 9 Nov. 1361 (*CPP*, i,379).
    Ormskirk coll. by ord. on Kininmund's death and gets prov. 3 Mar. 1363 (Collect.,14,fo.168v); had occ. 10 Feb. 1363 (*Abdn.Reg.*, i,93); occ. 24 Apr. 1392 (ibid.,i,186).

James de Lindsay   1407 - 1412.
Alexander Barber   1410.
    Lindsay occ. 4 Apr. 1407 (*CPP*, i,594; *Abdn.Reg.*, i,210-11); in poss. when given disp. to exch. his benefices 20 Dec. 1412 (*CPP*, i, 599); in fact res. in curia in favour of Alexander de Lindsay on or before 26 Nov. 1412 (v.inf.).
    Barber prov. 18 May 1410 (*CPP*, i,596) unfruitfully.

Alexander de Lindsay   1412 - 1436.
    Prov. on res. of James de Lindsay 26 Nov. 1412, expedited 20 Dec. 1412 (Reg.Av.,340,fos.503-4); in poss. 27 Oct. 1413 (*CPP*,i, 601, where date is wrong) and 29 Mar. 1436 (Reg.Supp.,324,fo. 235v).

Henry Rynd   1436 - 1461.
    Coll. by ord. on Alexander Lindsay's death, then prov. 27 Apr. 1436 (Reg.Supp.,322,fo.285v); occ. 22 Oct. 1456 (*HMC* 34, *14thR*.,iii,27); date of death given as 10 Mar. 1471 (*Abdn.Reg.*, ii,6,211), but this is prob. error for 1461.

Andrew Lyell   1461 - 1503.
David Meldrum   1461 x 1462.

Alexander Preston   1464.
Thomas Myrton   1499 - 1508 x 1510/1512.
  Lyell prov. on Rynd's death 19 Mar. 1461, following exp. grace
(*ACSB*,140; cf.Reg.Supp.,542,fo.51); no poss. 9 July 1461 (ibid.); lit.
and promises annates 9 Dec. 1461 (*ACSB*,140); in poss. 19 Mar. 1462
(*Abdn.Reg*.,ii,91); surrog. to Meldrum's right 30 Mar. 1462 (Reg.
Supp.,549,fo.141); new prov. after lit. with Preston 12 Mar. 1464 (ibid.,
572,fo.243); occ. 28 Oct. 1501 (*Abdn.Fasti*,39); still alive 4 Sept.
1503 (see *Ab.offic*.); d. 13 Dec. 1503 (*Abdn.Reg*.,ii,24,221).
  Meldrum lit.with Lyell and res. right to him prob. by 30 Mar.
1462 (v.sup.) and cert. by 18 May 1462 (Reg.Supp.,551.fo.107).
  Preston lit. with Lyell 12 Mar. 1464 (Reg.Supp.,572,fo.243);
res. right to Lyell 11 Apr. 1464 (ibid.,573,fo.6v).
  Myrton occ. 31 May 1499 (*RSS*, i,no.396). though perhaps then
a coadj.; occ. 13 Jan. 1504 (*Abdn.Fasti*,44); occ. 9 Aug. 1508 (*RSS*,
i,no.1713); prob. made exch. with Elphinstone for *Ab.archd*. x 8
May 1512 or x 15 July 1510 (see *R.archd*.).

Robert Elphinstone   1512 - 1535.
  Occ. 30 July 1512 (*Abdn.Fasti*,72); occ. 23 Jan. 1535 (*Prot.
Bk.Cristisone*,no.143).

George Marschell   1535 - 1541.
  Occ. 30 July 1535 (*TA*,vi,239; SRO,Exchequer Roll no.403A);
occ. 16 Feb. 1538 (*AbdnReg*.,ii,112); coll. to *Ab.chanc*. c. July 1541.

John Stewart   1542 - 1551.
  Occ. 25 Sept. 1542 (*RMS*,iii,no.2789); occ. 13 Aug. 1549
(SRO,Sent.Offic.Laud.,fo.340); moved to *Ab.archd*. presumably on
exch. with Myrton 6 July x 13 Aug. 1551.

Patrick Myrton senior   1551 - 1571 x 1573.
  Occ. 9 Dec. 1551 (St A.Univ.Mun.,UY305/2,p.42); occ. 18
Aug. 1571 (*A.B.Ill*.,iii,255); depriv. by 10 June 1573 (v.inf.).

Patrick Myrton junior   1573.
George Paterson   1573 - 1608.
  Myrton junior gets crown pres. on depriv. of Myrton senior
10 June 1573 (*RSS*,vi,no.1983); not fruitful.
  Paterson gets crown pres. for same reason 13 July 1573
(ibid.,no.2034); occ. 18 Apr. 1608 (SRO, Secretary's Reg.Sasines
Abdn.,vii,fo.354).

William Strachan   1617 - 1636.
  Occ. 10 Sept. 1617 (SRO, Part.Reg.Sasines Abdn.,i,fo.66)
and 6 Apr. 1636 (SRO, Part. Reg. Sasines Banff,iv,fo.143).

SUBDEAN OF ABERDEEN

Only known date: 1363.
  Prebend: none known.

Richard de Moray 1363.
Occ. 10 Feb. 1363 (*Abdn.Reg.*, i,93).

SUCCENTORS/SUBCHANTERS OF ABERDEEN

First known date: 1526 x 1534.
Ben. was not yet established 1526 (*Abdn.Reg.*,ii,254-5).
Prebend: ch. of Spittal at Reformation (SRO, Bk. of Assumption of Benefices, fo.379v); this ch. had been erected 1427 (*Abdn.Reg.*, i,226-7; Cowan, *Parishes*,2).

Note: **John Chalmer** is said in his obit to have been *Ab.succ.* x 1477 ? (*Abdn.Reg.*,ii,215); but see *M.succ.*; see also *Abdn.Reg.*, ad indicem, where a John Chalmer is active in Aberdeen in 1540s and 1550s.

Alexander Kyd 1533 x 1534 - 1563.
Occ. Aug. 1533 x Sept. 1534 (*ER*,xvi,370); occ. 9 July 1547 under wrong name 'Rynd' (*Abdn.Reg.*,ii,319; cf. *Spalding Misc.*,iv, 57-9 for spelling 'Bryd'), occ. 29 Nov. 1563 (SRO, Gordon Castle, 5.8.3); obit came to be celebrated 22 Sept. (*Abdn.Reg.*,ii,19,218-19).

John Collisoun 1565 - 1584.
Alexander Hervy 1566.
Arthur Jaffrey 1568.
Collisoun occ. 20 Oct. 1565 (SRO, Abbrev.Feu.Chrs.,ii,fo.102), had had coll. by ord. on Kyd's death, and got crown conf. 19 May 1566 (*RSS*,v,no.2836); at horn 18 May 1579 (*RSS*,vii,no.1896); occ. 2 Aug. 1581 (SRO, Erroll, no.957); d. in poss. 25 July 1584 (*Spalding Misc.*,ii,56); but note that this benefice had been annexed to New College i.e. King's College of Aberdeen 10 Sept. 1574 (*RSS*, vi,no.2680; *RMS*,iv,no.2304; *Abdn.Fasti*,129-30).
Hervy pres. by crown on Kyd's death 25 May 1566 (*RSS*,v, no.2851).
Jaffrey pres. by crown on Kyd's death 1 Sept. 1568 (*RSS*, vi,no.467).

Note: by royal ordinance 28 June 1617 (but not apparently earlier as in the case of the principalship and the deanery) the subprincipal of King's College, Aberdeen was henceforth to be the subchanter in the chapter of Aberdeen diocese (*Abdn.Fasti*, 140-2). The following succession ensues:

Patrick Guthrie 1619.
Apparently in office as subpr. 1610-1619 (*Abdn.Grads.*,40); occ. as subch. 21 Jan. 1619 (SRO,Part.Reg.Sasines Abdn., i,fo.381); still subpr. 14/16 Sept. 1619 (*Abdn.Fasti.*,275).

William Forbes 1620 - 1623.
Apparently subpr. 1619 - 1623 (*Abdn.Grads.*,40); occ. as subch. 10 Oct. 1620 and 2 May 1623 (SRO, Part.Reg.Sasines Abdn., iii,fo.53; iv,fo.243).

B

William Leslie   1627 - 1632.
　　/ Apparently subpr. 1623 - 1632 (*Abdn.Grads*.,40); occ. as
subch. 19 Apr. 1627 and 18 Apr. 1632 (SRO, Part.Reg.Sasines Abdn.,
v,fo.491;viii,fo.154); moved to *Ab.King's coll.princ*. and *Ab.dean*. by
31 Aug. 1632.

David Leche (Leech)   1632 - 1638.
　　Pres. and adm. to subpr. 6 Nov. 1632 (*Abdn. Fasti*,289); occ.
as subch. 25 Mar. 1633 (SRO, Part.Reg.Sasines Abdn.,viii,fo.198)
and 6 Apr. 1636 (SRO, Part.Reg.Sasines Banff,iv,fo.143): dem. subpr.
30 Apr. 1638 (*Abdn. Fasti*,409).

Robert Ogilvie   1638 - 1640 x 1641.
　　El. and adm. as subpr. 30 Apr. 1638 (ibid.,409-10); dem. 16
Nov. 1640 x 14 June 1641, apparently on or before 10 Mar. 1641
(ibid.,418,420; cf. *Abdn.Grads*.,41).

ARCHDEACONS OF ABERDEEN

First known date: 1172 x 1179.
　　Prebend: ch. of Rayne in 1256 (*Abdn.Reg*.,ii,40; Cowan,
Parishes,169).

Malcolm   1172 x 1179, 1175 x 1178.
　　Occ. 1172 x 1179 (*St A.Lib*.,298-9); occ. 1175 x 1178 ·
(*Abdn.Reg*., i,10).

Simon   1189 x 96 - 1202 x 1203.
　　Occ. 1189 x 1196 (*Kel.Lib*.,no.449); occ. 1175 x 1199
(*Arb.Lib*., i,no.197); occ. 1202 x 1203 (*Lind.Cart*.,8).

Omer   x 1207 - 1208 x .
　　Occ. x 1207 (*Kel.Lib*.,ii,340); occ. 1204 x 1211 (*Arb.Lib*., i,
54-5); occ. 1208 x 1228 (*St A.Lib*.,300-1).

Malcolm   1224 x 1226 - 1250.
　　Occ. 19 Apr. 1224 x 18 Sept. 1226 (*Moray Reg*.,no.73);
occ. 4 May 1250 (*Abdn.Reg*.,ii,275).

Geoffrey   1259 - 1281.
　　Occ. 1 Aug. 1259 (*Abdn.Reg*., i,27); occ. 20 June 1281
(*Reg.Sutton*, i,14).

Alan de Moray   1335 - 1341.
　　Prob. occ. Mar. 1335 (*Abdn.Reg*., i,40, but printed text has
1305); prov. *C.bp*. 16 Jan. 1341.

John de Rate   1342 - 1350.
　　Prov. 22 May 1342 (*CPL*,iii,75); prov. *Ab.bp*. 19 Nov. 1350.

Alexander de Kininmund   1352 - 1355.
　　Occ. 8 Mar. 1352 (Collect.,14,fo.163v.); prov. *Ab.bp*. 4 Dec.
1355.

John Barber   1357 - 1395.

Occ. 13 Aug. 1357 (*Rot.Scot.*, i,808-9); occ. 22 Apr. 1392 (*Abdn.Reg.*, i,190); d. in poss. 13 Mar. 1395 (ibid.,ii,212).

Henry de Lichton	1395 - 1396.
Thomas Trail	1395.
John de Lichton	1395 x 1402.

Henry de Lichton had coll. by ord. (presumably on Barber's death), and lit. in curia by 9 Jan. 1396 (Reg.Av.,300,fo.216v).

Trail got prov. on Barber's death 16 Apr. 1395 (*CPP*, i,583).

John de Lichton held it at death, apparently as predecessor of Falconer (*CPL*,vii,234); d. sometime before 15 Sept. 1402 (*CPP*, i,618).

David Falconer	1407 - 1411.

Occ. 4 Apr. 1407 (*Abdn.Reg.*, i,210-11); res. on exch. with Tyninghame c. June 1411 (*CPP*, i,597; Reg.Supp.,265,fo.214v).

Thomas de Tyninghame	1411 - 1439.
Simon Bowmaker	1431.

Tyninghame in poss. 19 Aug. 1413, having got it on exch. some two years before (*CPP*, i,600); new prov. 22 Apr. 1422 (*CPL*,vii,234); occ. 24 July 1439 (*Abdn.Reg.*, i,237).

Bowmaker prov. 24 Jan. 1431 (Reg.Supp.,265,fo.214v) unfruitfully.

Walter Stewart	1440.

Prov. on Tyninghame's death 8 Jan. 1440 (*CPL*,ix,75); res. on exch. with Piot at curia without poss. 20 Feb. 1440 (*CPL*,viii,276,295).

Laurence Piot	1440 - 1453 x 1454, 1455 - 1465 x 1468.
Robert de Crannach	1442.
James Lindsay	1454 - 1456.

Piot prov. on exch. 20 Feb. 1440 (*CPL*,viii,276,295); in poss. 3 Nov. 1440 (Reg.Supp.,369,fo.4v); occ. 24 Oct. 1453 (*Abdn.Reg.*, i, 274); res. to ord. sometime before 20 Dec. 1454 (v.inf.), but by 16 Jan. 1455 had reasserted his right (Reg.Supp.,478,fo.271); occ. 2 Jan. 1465 (*Abdn.Reg.*, i,295); d. before 29 May 1468 (v. inf.; cf. *Abdn.Reg.*, i,301).

Crannach gets *com.priv.* against Piot 13 Jan. 1442 (Reg.Supp., 379,fo.125) unfruitfully.

Lindsay occ. 20 Dec. 1454 (*Abdn.Reg.*, i,268); had been coll. by ord. on res. of Piot and got poss., now gets prov. 16 Jan. 1455 (Reg.Supp.,478,fo.271); res. his right in exch. for *M.prec.* from Piot 12 June 1456 (ibid.,491,fo.242).

Alexander Rate	1468 - 1475 x 1479.
James Inglis	1468.
Robert Stewart	1472 - 1474.

Rate gets papal conf. after getting it by exp. grace on Piot's death 29 May 1468 (Reg.Supp.,624,fo.196v); lit. 1 Oct. 1471 (ibid., 672,fo.190v); new prov. against Stewart 30 Mar. 1472 (*CPL*,xiii,16-17); new prov. after deaths of Inglis and Stewart 7 Jan. 1474 (Reg.Supp., 700,fo.193); but still lit. 30 Apr. 1474 (ibid.,704,fo.289v); apparently in poss. 8 June 1475 (ibid.,721,fo.202v); d. 2 Oct. 1475 x 5 Apr. 1479

(v.inf.; cf. *Dk.dean*.).

Inglis prov. 2 June 1468 (Reg.Supp.,630,fo.412); d. before 7 Jan. 1474 (v.sup.).

Stewart lit. against Rate, perhaps by 1 Oct. 1471 (v.sup.), cert. by 30 Mar. 1472 (*CPL*,xiii,16-17); occ. in poss. 26 Sept. 1472 (SRO, Forglen, box 1, bundle 1); d. before 7 Jan. 1474 (v.sup.).

Andrew Young	1479.
George Brown	1479.
Robert Blackadder	1475 x 1479 - 1480/1483.
James Lindsay	1479 - 1490/1495.
John Fraser	1480 - 1488.
Gavin Vaiche	1485 x 1486.
Gavin Dunbar	1487.

Young prov. on Rate's death 5 Apr. 1479 (Reg.Supp.,779,fos. 275v -6).

Brown prov. on Rate's death 16 Apr. 1479 (Reg.Supp.,780, fo.178).

Blackadder got poss. without fruits by right of an exp. grace on Rate's death, and gets papal prov. 11 Aug. 1479 (*CPL*,xiii,664-5); prov. *Ab.bp*. 14 July 1480, but not cons. until Apr. 1483.

Lindsay prov. on Rate's death 24 Aug. 1479 (*ACSB*, 199-200); promised annates 4 Sept. 1480 (ibid.); occ. 17 June 1490 (*CPL*,xiv, 267); obit dated 1495 (Bryce, *Grey Friars*,ii,334).

Fraser prov. on Blackadder's promotion 14 July 1480 (*CPL*, xiii,83-84); still without poss. 5 May 1488 since he did not have the king's assent (*ACSB*,199).

Vaiche had some right at his death (v.inf.) 5 Jan. 1485 x 26 Dec. 1486 (see *Ab.dean* and *M.dean*).

Dunbar promised annates and got prov. on Vaiche's death 4 Apr. 1487 (PRO 31/9 - 30/69); cf. *M.dean*.

Adam Elphinstone	1490/1495 x 1499.

Held it at death before 29 Apr. 1499 (v.inf.).

Robert Elphinstone	1499 - 1508 x 1510/1512.
William Dowy	1499 - 1500.
Thomas Halkerston	c. 1508.

Elphinstone occ. 7 Dec. 1499 (*Abdn.Fasti*,29); had had coll. by ord., and still has poss. 6 Jan. 1500 (*RSS*, i,no.441); prob. made exch. with Myrton for *Ab.treas*. 9 Aug. 1508 x 8 May 1512 or x 15 July 1510 (cf. *R.archd*.).

Dowy prov. conditionally 29 Apr. 1499 (Reg.Lat.,1051,fos. 159-160); condemned by king for barratry over this ben. 6 Jan. 1500 (*RSS*, i,no.441); promised annates 21 Feb. 1500 (PRO 31/9 - 31/5-6).

Halkerston pres. by crown before 26 Mar. 1508, but may not have had coll. (*James IV Letters*, 102-3); his right challenged by Ab.bp. before 22 Oct. [? 1508] (Lyon, *St Andrews*,ii,351).

Thomas Myrton	1512 - 1540.
Patrick Myrton　senior	1530 - 1551.

Thomas Myrton occ. 8 May 1512 (*Abdn.Fasti*,70); res. but promised annates on keeping fruits 18 Oct. 1530 (PRO 31/9 - 32/186-7; cf. *St A.Form.*, i,189-90); occ. 16 Dec. 1536 (*Laing.Chrs.*,109); d. 30 July 1540 (*Abdn.Reg.*,ii,15,216; cf. Bryce, *Grey Friars*,ii,324, where obit is dated 1515).

Patrick Myrton promised annates and got prov. but no fruits 18 Oct. 1530 (PRO 31/9 - 32/187); occ. 16 Feb. 1538 (*Abdn.Reg.*,ii,112); occ. 6 July 1551 (St A.Univ.Mun.,UY305/2,p.42); moved to *Ab.treas.*, prob. on exch. with Stewart.

John Stewart   1551 - 1563.
Occ. 13 Aug. 1551 (*Abdn.Reg.*, i,455); occ. 24 June 1563 (*RSS*, v,no.1403

James Erskine   1565 - 1579.
Crown pres. on Stewart's death 15 Apr. 1565 (*RSS*,v,no.2025); occ. 27 Jan. 1579 (*A.B.Ill.*,iii,400).

Robert Murray   1584 - 1585.
Crown pres. on death of Erskine 23 Oct. 1584 and 26 Mar. 1585 (Reg.Pres.,ii,114,128).

Walter Abercrombie   1586 - 1620.
Walter Richardson   1586.
Abercrombie gets crown pres. on res. of Murray 31 Jan. 1586 (Reg.Pres.,ii,141); despite reputed res. later in 1586 (v.inf.), he retained poss. until occ. 12 Oct. 1620 (SRO, Part.Reg.Sasines Abdn., iii,fo.116).
Richardson gets crown pres. by reason of res. of Abercrombie 16 Apr. 1586 (Reg.Pres.,ii,144) abortively.

Andrew Logie   1624 - 1636.
Occ. 21 Oct. 1626 (SRO, Part.Reg.Sasines Abdn.,iv,fo.583) and 6 Apr. 1636 (SRO, Part.Reg.Sasines Banff,iv,fo.143); cf. *Powis Papers* [3rd Spalding Club] ,203, where this name is misread as 'William Brown' 6 Jan. 1634 (see original SRO, Burnett of Powis, no.297).

DEANS OF CHRISTIANITY

DEANS OF ABERDEEN

First known date: 1274 (*SHS Misc.*,vi,42).

N (?) 1282.
Occ. 25 Jan. 1282 (*Lind.Cart.*,159).

Gilbert Chalmer   1502 x 1503 - 1503 x 1504.
Occ. 29 July 1502 x 12 July 1503 (*ER*,xii,173); occ. 12 July 1503 x 26 June 1504 (ibid.,272).

John Strathauchin   1541 x 1542.

Occ. Aug. 1541 x July 1542 (*ER*,xvii,470).

DEANS OF MAR: STRATHDON: STRATHDON WITH STRATHDEE

First known dates: Mar: 1274 (*SHS Misc.*,vi,41).
  Strathdon: 1524.
  Strathdon with Strathdee: 1537 (SRO, Erroll,no.370).

Thomas Scherar (Strathdon) 1524.
  Occ. 8 Apr. 1524 (*Prot.Bk.Cristisone*,no.29).

DEANS OF GARIOCH

First known date: 1274 (*SHS Misc.*,vi,40).

John de Moray   1445.
  Occ. 5 Nov. 1445 (*HMC* 60, *Mar and Kellie*,ii,18).

Andrew Scherar   1532.
  Occ. 4 Apr. 1532 (*Prot.Bk.Cristisone*,no.90).

Duncan Udny   1535 - 1537.
  Occ. 23 Jan. 1535 (ibid.,no.142); occ. 8 Jan. 1537 (ibid.,no. 229).

Robert Allardice   1550.
  Occ. 18 Jan. 1550 (ibid.,no.417).

DEANS OF FORMARTINE

Known dates: 1537 (SRO, Erroll,no.370).
  1547 (*A.B.Coll.*,309).

No names known.

DEANS OF BUCHAN

First known date: 1199 x 1207.

John   1199 x 1207 - 1228 x 1239.
  Occ. 1199 x 1207 (*Kel.Lib.*,ii,340); occ. 1211 x 1233 (*Abdn. Reg.*,i,15); occ. 1228 x 1239 (*Arb.Lib.*,i,no.200).

William Feryare   1456.
  Occ. 13 Dec. 1456 (*Abdn.Reg.*,i,282).

DEANS OF BOYNE

First known date: 1274 (*SHS Misc.*,vi,43).

Robert de Forglen   1375 - 1376.
    Occ. 27 Aug. 1375 (*C.A.Chrs.*, i,203); occ. 5 May 1376 (ibid., i, 251).

OFFICIALS

OFFICIALS OF ABERDEEN

First known date: 1172 x 1199.

Matthew   1172 x 1199.
    Occ. 1172 x 1199 (*Abdn.Reg.*,ii,316).

Walter   1202 x 1203.
    Occ. 1202 x 1203 (*Lind.Cart.*,p.8,no.3).

Richard   1239 x 1240 - 1245.
    Occ. 1239 x 1240 (*A.B.Coll.*,293); occ. 24 June 1240 (ibid.,293-4;*Kel.Lib.*, i,187); occ. 26 Apr. 1245 (*St A.Lib.*,307-8).

W.   1247 x 1250.
    Occ. 1247 x May 1250 (*Abdn.Reg.*, i,17; cf.ii,273-5).

Roger de Scartheburg   1261 - 1263.
    Occ. 23 Sept. 1261 (ibid.,ii,277); occ. 23 Jan. 1263 (*Arb.Lib.*, i,193).

John de Derby   1268.
    Occ. 16 Oct. 1268 (*A.B.Coll.*,568).

W.   1293.
    Occ. 21 July/15 Sept. 1293 (Druham,D&C Misc.Chrs.,no.4454; *Durham Seals*,no.3596).

Waldeve Story   1325.
    Occ. 26 Aug. 1325 (*Arb.Lib.*, i,no.353;*A.B.Coll.*,196).

Thomas de Salcop   1335.
    Occ. Mar. 1335 (*Abdn.Reg.*, i,40, where printed text has 1305); occ. 10 July 1335 (ibid., i,64).

Reginald (de Ogston?)   1357.
    Occ. 13 Sept. 1357 (*Foedera* [O] ,vi,40).

John Forrester   1389 - 1406 x 1414.
    Occ. 18 Dec. 1389 (*CPP*, i,574); prob. moved to *G.offic*. Mar. 1406 x Feb. 1414.

Henry Hervy   1421 - 1428.
    Occ. 25 Mar. 1421 (*CPL*,vii,189); occ. 5 May 1428 (*ER*,iv,459).

Walter Idill 1446 (?) - 1468.
Occ. 11 Nov. ?1446 (*Abdn.Reg.*, i,210); occ. 9 June 1452 (ibid., i,270); occ. 4 Apr. 1468 (ibid., i,300); d. 3 July 1468 (*Logan's Collections* [3rd Spalding Club] , 171).

Alexander Vaus 1469 - 1479.
Occ. 1469 (*Arb.Lib.*,ii,160,no.180); occ. 1 Apr. 1470 (*Abdn. Reg.*, i,307-8); occ. 2 Feb. 1479 (ibid., i,321).

Richard Forbes 1482 - 1483.
Occ. 26 Nov. 1482 (Fraser, *Douglas*,iii,426); d. 12 June x 1 Nov. 1483 (see. *Ab.dean*.).

Andrew Lyell 1490 - 1503.
Occ. 18 Sept. 1490 (NRA, Pitcaple, chr.no.3); occ. 4 Sept. 1503 (SRO, Erroll,no.184); d. 13 Dec. 1503 (see *Ab.treas*.).

Alexander Galloway 1516.
Occ. 1516 (*Abdn.Grads.*,7).

John Leslie 1553.
Occ. 3 Dec. 1553 (SRO, Comm.Edin.Decreets, i,fo.160; but this date [though checked with MS] may be an error).

John Wawane 1553.
Occ. 22 Dec. 1553 (SRO, Erroll,no.528).

John Leslie 1557 - 1564.
Occ. 11 Apr. 1557 (NLS,Adv.MS34.4.4,fo.79); said to have been appointed 18 Apr. 1558 (Keith, *Bishops*,199); occ. 12 Apr. 1560 (*RMS*,iv,no.1725); perhaps still in office 28 Jan. 1564 (*RSS*,v,no. 1549); moved to *R.bp*. from 20 Apr. 1566.

COMMISSARIES

COMMISSARIES OF ABERDEEN

First known date: 1446.

Henry Hervy 1446 - 1453.
Occ. (CB) 22 Sept. 1446 (*A.B.Ill.*,iii,318); see *Ab.offic*.; occ. (C) 21 Apr. 1453 (*Frasers of Philorth*,ii,197).

Laurence Duncan 1456.
Occ. (C depute) 9 Nov. 1456 (*SHR*,xxiv,284).

Robert Elphinstone 1508.
Occ. (C) 15 Jan. 1508 (SRO, Erroll,no.226).

Alexander Hay 1527 - 1528.
Occ. (CG) 6 June 1527 (*A.B.Ill.*,iii,66); occ. (CG) 10 Oct. 1528 (SRO, Forbes,no.422).

Arthur Boyce 1529 - 1533.
Occ. (CG) 1 Apr. 1529 (Fraser, *Sutherland*,iii,87); occ. (C) 19

Sept. 1533 (*Prot.Bk.Cristisone*,no.104); occ. (CG) 14 Nov. 1533
(*RMS*,iii,no.1323).

John Galloway   1534.
    Occ. (C) 13 Apr. 1534 (*Prot.Bk.Cristisone*,no.122).

John Reid   1539.
    Occ. (CG) 17 Jan. 1539 (*Abdn.Counc*.,i,151); d. Dec. 1540 x
July 1541 (see *Ab.chanc*.).

Alexander Kyd   1542 - 1551.
John Spittal   x1546.
John Watson   1547.
    Kyd occ. (C) 1 Feb. 1542 (SRO, ADC&S,xvii,fo.144); occ. (C)
20 and 24 May 1550 (SRO, Dunecht,no.41; *Prot.Bk.Cristisone*,no.
440); occ. (CG) 12 Oct. 1551 (SRO, Sent.Offic.St A.,fo.248).
    Spittal held office (CG) before 7 Sept. 1548 (SRO, Sent.
Offic. St A.,fo.171); date was presumably before his move to *St A.
offic*. Sept. x Nov. 1546.
    Watson occ. (C for confirmation of greater testaments) 13 Dec.
1547 (SRO, Prot.Bk. Robert Lumsden,fo.6).

Nichol Hay   c. 1551 - c.1591.
David Seton   1553.
John Leslie   1556.
William Leslie   1557.
Thomas Burnett   1564 - 1583.
    Hay held office for about 40 years before dem.prob. shortly
before 20 Nov. 1591 (RSS,lxiii,fo.17); occ. with David Seton (CO)
3 Dec. 1553 (SRO, Comm.Edin.Decreets, i,fo.160 - but date must
be erroneous, see *Ab.offic*.); occ. (C) 22 Dec. 1553 (SRO, Erroll,
no.531); occ. (C) 15 July 1559 and 28 July 1564 (ibid.,no.605;
RSS,v,no.1549).
    Seton occ. with Hay (CO) 3 Dec. 1553 (v.sup.).
    John Leslie occ. (C) 21 Aug. 1556 (Fraser, *Grant*,iii,119).
    William Leslie occ. (CB) 2 Jan. 1557 (SRO, Reg.Ho.Chr. no.
1692).
    Burnett occ. (C) 9 Aug. 1564 and 8 Feb. 1566 (Stevenson &
Wood, *Seals*, i,126; *Family of Burnett*, 26); d. in office 24 Feb.
1583 (*Spalding Misc*.,ii,55).

ARGYLL DIOCESE

BISHOPS OF ARGYLL : LISMORE

First known date: 1183 x 1189 (*Liber Censuum*,i,text,pp.230-2; *Chron.Bower*,i, 356-7).

Bishops are sometimes designated 'of Lismore' after the site of their cathedral.

This see was directly subject to the pope until placed under metropolitan authority of St Andrews 14 Aug. 1472 (*Vet.Mon.*, no.852), and then transferred to that of Glasgow 9 Jan. 1492 (ibid., no.889).

Harald x 1189 (?) - 1228 x 1232.
Cons. on erection of see (*Chron.Bower*, i,357); occ. 17 Aug. 1228 (*Moray Reg.*,25); d. before 10 June 1232 (*Pais.Reg.*,342, where name is wrongly extended as 'Hugh').

Note: see in charge of *I.bp*. 1228 x 1236 (*Vet.Mon.*,33); Bp. Simon occ. as 'ecclesie Lesmorensis per dominum papam cure gestor' 1230 x 1236 (*Pais.Reg.*,135, where name is wrongly extended as 'Stephen').

William 1238 x 1239 - 1241.
M.bp. ordered to arrange an election 7 July 1236 (*Vet.Mon.*,33); el. as *M.chanc.* after May 1238 (*Moray Reg.*,275) and before 16 Feb. 1239 when mand. issued for cons. (*CPL*, i,178); cons. before 20 May 1240 (*PSAS*,xc,219); d. 1241 (*Chron.Melrose*,89).

Note: see vacant for at least seven years before 23 Dec. 1248, when mand. went to bps. of Glasgow and Dunblane to arrange an election (*Vet.Mon.*,no.139); during at least part of this time see was in charge of *Db.bp.*; Bp. Clement occ. in this capacity c. 1247 (*Inchaff.Chrs.*, 65; cf. Dowden,*Bishops*,378-9).

Alan 1248 x 1250 - 1262.
Occ. as elect 27 Sept. 1250 (*Pais.Reg.*,134); cons. before 27 Sept. 1253 (ibid.,129); d. 1262 (*Chron.Melrose*,118).

Laurence de Argyll (Ergadia) O.P. 1264 - 1299.
El. in succession to Alan (*Chron.Melrose*,118; cf.p.lxiii), mand. for conf. and cons. 31 Mar. 1264 (*CPL*, i,411; cf. *Reg.Urbain IV*,iii,214); occ. 20 June 1268 (*Dryb.Lib.*,7); occ. 29 Oct. 1299 (*Pais.Reg.*,131).

Andrew O.P. 1300 - 1327 x.
El. on death of Laurence, and gets prov. and cons. 18 Dec. 1300 (*Vet.Mon.*,no.368; cf. Eubel, *Hierarchia*, i,241); occ. 18 Nov. 1327 *(Pais.Reg.*,137; *Vet.Mon.*,258).

Martin de Argyll (Ergaill) O.P. 1342 - 1362.
Angus de Argyll (Ergardia) / Cowall (?) (Congallis) 1342 - 1343 x 1344.
Martin el. by chapter before 16 Mar. 1342 (*Rot.Scot.*, i,623); lit. with Angus followed at curia; then after death of Angus, Martin res. his right and obtained prov. and cons. 20 Dec. 1344 (*Vet.Mon.*,no. 564); occ. 9 June 1362 (*Pais.Reg.*,145).

Angus el. by clergy of city and diocese, and went to curia to lit. with Martin before death of Benedict XII i.e. before 25 Apr. 1342 (*Vet.Mon.*,no.564); still lit. 15 Jan. 1343 (*CPL*,iii,82); d. at curia while lit. still in progress before 20 Dec. 1344 (v.sup.).

John Dugaldi 1387 - 1390.
El. when *Ar.archd.* and then prov. 26 Apr. 1387 (Eubel, *Hierarchia*, i,241); prob. cons. by 8 June 1387 (Ob. et Sol.,45A, fo. 134v), and perhaps as early as 30 May 1387 (*CPP*, i,568); in poss. 8 July 1390 (Ob. et Sol.,50,fo.161).

Bean Johannis/ Johannis Andree/ Macgillandris 1397 - 1411.
El. when *Ar.dean* and then prov. 17 Sept. 1397 (Eubel, *Hierarchia*, i,241); occ. 8 July 1411 (*Highland Papers*,iv,162-5).

Finlay de Albany (Albania) O.P. 1420 - 1426.
El. and then prov. 31 Jan. 1420 (Eubel, *Hierarchia*, i,241); prob. cons. by 11 Mar. 1420 when he paid common services (*ACSB*,2,225); occ. 3 May 1425 in Scotland, but fled to Ireland thereafter (*Chron. Bower*,ii,483); still thought at curia to be alive 13 May 1426 (*Brech. Reg.*, i,100-2), but said to be dead before prov. of Lauder (v.inf.).

George Lauder 1427 - 1461.
Prov. 26 May 1427 (Brady, *Episcopal Succession*, i,159); mand. for cons. 20 Dec. 1427 (*CPL*,viii,17); cons. by 21 Apr. 1428 (Brady, op.cit.,i,160); occ. 7 Mar. 1461 (*APS*,xii,28); d. soon after (Dowden, *Bishops*,386).

Robert Colquhoun 1475 - 1493 x 1496.
Prov. 24 Apr. 1475 (Eubel, *Hierarchia*,ii,179); occ. 20 Nov. 1475 (*APS*,ii,108); cons. 3 Dec. 1475 x 2 Dec. 1476 (*Glas. Reg.*,ii, 439); occ. 20 June 1493 (*ADA*,179); d. before 13 Feb. 1496 (Dowden, *Bishops*,387).

David Hamilton 1497 - 1522 x 1523.
Prov. 3 Apr. 1497 (Eubel, *Hierarchia*,ii,179); still elect 3 Jan. 1498 (Brady, *Episcopal Succession*, i,160); occ. 13 Mar. 1504 (*APS*, ii,273); occ. 28 Mar. 1522 (*Laing Chrs.*,no.333); d. before 13 Dec. 1523 (*James V Letters*,95).

Robert Montgomery 1525 - 1533 x 1538.
Prov. 28 July 1525 (Eubel, *Hierarchia*,iii,226); not yet cons. 26 May 1533 (PRO 31/9 - 32/241); was cons. sometime (*St A.Form.*, ii,25); d. before 29 Aug. 1538 (SRO,Acts and Decreets, l,387).

William Cunningham 1539 - 1553.
Crown nom. to pope when *Edin.Trinity prov.* 1 Feb. 1539 (*Vet.Mon.*,no.1047); prov. 7 May 1539 (Eubel, *Hierarchia*,iii,226); never cons. and still called 'elect' when res. on exch. with Hamilton for *B.dean.* on or before 14 July 1553 (Brady, *Episcopal Succession*, i,161).

James Hamilton 1553 - 1580.
Prov. when *G.subd.* on exch. with Cunningham for *B.dean.* 14

July 1553 (ibid.; *SHR*,xxii,38); cons. not recorded (Dowden, *Bishops*,391); d. 6 Jan. 1580 (Edin.Tests.,18 Jan. 1591).

Neil Campbell 1580 - 1608.
> Licence to elect issued to chapter with no name given 12 Jan. 1580 (*RSS*,vii,no.2190); said to have been el. and got crown prov. 1580 (*HBC*,284, no sources quoted); occ. 4 Jan. 1608 (*The Genealogist*,xxxviii,143); res. 1608 (RSS,lxxvii,fo.28), before 1 June (v.inf.); d. c. Jan. 1613, i.e. about 14 years 6 months before 21 July 1627 (SRO, Reg. of Retours,ix,fo.295).

John Campbell 1608 - 1613.
> Crown prov. 1 June 1608 (Reg.Pres.,iv,16); prob. cons. 23 Jan./ 24 Feb. 1611 (Calderwood, *History*,vii,154); d. Jan. 1613 (ibid.,176).

Andrew Boyd 1613 - 1636.
> Crown prov. 4 Mar. 1613 (Reg.Pres.,iv,91v); d. 22 Dec. 1636 (Keith, *Bishops*,291, no source quoted).

James Fairlie 1637 - 1638.
> El. 21 June 1637 (RSS,cviii,fo.71); crown prov. 10 July 1637 (ibid.); cons. 8 Aug. 1637 (Row, *Historie*, 410); depriv. 13 Dec. 1638 (Peterkin, *Records*, i,27-28); d. Feb. 1658 (Edin.Tests., 9 Apr. 1658 i.e. vol.69,fo.105).

CHAPTER OF ARGYLL

See was sited on island of Lismore in Loch Linnhe apparently from 1225 and prob. from time of erection of the diocese (cf. *PSAS*,xc,209; *TSES*,xv,pt.1, 41-50); at the end of the long episcopal vacancy after 1241, when the bishops of Glasgow and Dunblane had been ordered 23 Dec. 1248 to arrange for election of a new bishop, they were also ordered by the pope 2 Jan. 1249 to move the see to a more suitable place (*Vet.Mon.*,no.140); the king was then said to be willing to endow a new cathedral church in a more convenient place, and Alexander II's gift of ch. of Kilbride (near modern Oban) on his deathbed within the bounds of that parish 8 July 1249 may be a pointer to where it was intended to place the see (*PSAS*,xc,218; cf.210); but the king's death in fact prevented any move from Lismore.
> The dean found in 1240 is apparently of the early type who were of lesser status than the archdeacon; but there soon came a change, prob. in connection with the arrangements which the experienced bishops of Glasgow and Dunblane must have made for the episcopal election of 1248 x 1250, and by the time of the next election 1262 x 1264 the dean presided over the chapter and acted as its proctor to the curia (*Reg.Urbain IV*,iii,no.1496); it is note-worthy that though this election was managed *concorditer*, things were arranged too *singulariter* and not sufficiently *communiter* to satisfy the demands of canon law (ibid.); though at least one canon appears by 27 Sept. 1250 (*Pais.Reg.*,134), there is no sign as yet of a collegiate community; the electoral chapter appears to have

remained of a synodal character until the mid-14th century, when as late as 26 Sept. 1357 the bishop could not (as other Scottish bishops did) bring a common chapter seal with him to commit his capitular clergy to the arrangements for the ransom of King David II 'quia totus clerus eligit' (*APS*, i,294; *CDS*,iii no.1650); yet some kind of lesser chapter of a collegiate character was emerging within the synodal framework before then - the seal of some kind of chapter was attached to an episcopal act done at the cathedral 18 Nov. 1327 (*Pais.Reg.*, 137), and matters no doubt had to be clarified after the double episcopal election of 1342, when the 'chapter' (presumably those clergy associated with the cathedral) acted separately from the 'clergy of the city and diocese' (v.sup.); it was prob. thereafter during the time of Bp. Martin de Argyll (and presumably after 1357 - v.sup.) that the kind of chapter by then usual in the other mainland dioceses with secular cathedrals was organised, with three dignities in addition to the deanery and the old office of archdeacon appearing by the early 15th century, together with a number of simple prebends (*RSCHS*,xiv, 37-38, 47); perhaps c.1371 was the critical date, when the precentorship was made a secular benefice after being held for some time by the prior of Ardchattan.

Once the property of the old Cistercian abbey of Saddell in Kintyre had been united to the bishopric 1507-8 (*MRHS*, 66; cf. *James V Letters*,364), the king proposed to pope that the cathedral be moved from Lismore to Saddell 22 Apr. 1512 (*James IV Letters*, no.446); the cathedral on the island was then said to be ruinous and deserted, having neither bishop nor chapter (though this can only mean no resident chapter, as the succession of dignitaries does not appear to have been significantly interrupted at this period); but nothing came of this proposal to rebuild the cathedral and re-endow the chapter.

EARLY DEANS IN ARGYLL

Gillemoluag 1240.
> Occ. 22 May 1240 (*PSAS*,xc,219).

DEANS OF ARGYLL

First known date: 1262 x 1264.
> Prebend: a ben. with cure was associated with this dignity by 1350 (v.inf.); vic. of Lismore in 1497 (*OPS*,II,ii,159; cf. Cowan, *Parishes*,134).

Note: an unnamed dean presided over an episcopal election of 1262 x 1264 (*Reg.Urbain IV*,iii,no.1496).

Lachlan / Roland son of Lochlan 1350 or earlier.
> Prob. still in poss. 13 June 1350 when a ben. which he had long

held in plurality with the deanery without disp. was granted to another (Collect.,14,fo.163, where name is Lachlan; cf. *CPP*,i,201, where name is Roland son of Lochlan); as Lachlan he was dead and the ben. thereafter had long been vacant before 13 Nov. 1388 and 19 Jan. 1389 (*CPP*, i,573; cf. 576).

James Johannis de 'Tinetur' 1388.
  In poss. 13 Nov. 1388 (ibid.,573).

Bean Johannis/ Johannis Andree/ Macgillandris 1388 - 1397.
Celestine Johannis   1391.
  Bean prov. 13 Nov. 1388 and 19 Jan. 1389 (*CPP*, i,573); had held it for over a year and was still in poss. 26 Aug. 1391 (ibid.,576); prov. *Ar.bp*. 17 Sept. 1397.
  Celestine prov. 26 Aug. 1391 (*CPP*, i,576) unfruitfully.

Bean Johannis/ Bean Mauritii/ John Campbell c.1398 - 1420 x 1433.
Cristin Davidson   x1432.
John Foster   1432.
  Bean/John coll. by ord. of same name who had just been cons. c.1398 (*CSSR*, i,179-80); new prov. 21 Feb. 1420 (ibid.); in poss. 19 Mar. 1420 (ibid.,184); occ. under name of Campbell 1392 x 1425 (*Lenn.Cart.*,66), a successor (v. inf.) claimed to follow in 1433 on death of John Campbell (Reg.Supp.,313,fo.90v), or alternatively of Bean Mauritii (*CPL*,xii,743) - for identification of these two see *M.subd*.
  Davidson said to have been in poss. at death before 3 Oct. 1432 (Reg.Supp.,280,fo.176v).
  Foster prov. on Davidson's death 3 Oct. 1432 (ibid.).

Malcolm Johannis/ de Dunblane/ Mathan de Lovri 1432 x 1433 - 1462.
  Coll. by ord. after 15 June 1432 when still *Db.offic*., following death of John Campbell/ Bean Mauritii; conf. 30 Sept. 1435 after more than two years' poss. (Reg.Supp.,313, fo.90v.; *CPL*,xii,743); prob. prov. 2 Mar. 1437 (*ACSB*,116); occ. 26 Jan. 1462 (*Inchaff.Chrs*.,150); res. to ord. prob. by June 1462 (Reg.Supp.,596,fo.93, where name is Mathan de Lovri; *CPL*,xii,743, where name is Malcolm de Dunblane).

Robert Muir   c.1462 - 1473.
Kenneth Beani   1466.
Malcolm son of Saloman David   1470.
  Muir coll. by ord. on res. of Lovri some 4-5 years before 3 June 1466, when in poss. (Reg.Supp.,596,fo.93; cf. *CPL*,xii,743, where coll. is dated 8 or 10 years before 23 July 1470); occ. 4 Jan. 1473 (*Scot. Antiq*., x,118).
  Beani gets *com.priv*. against Muir 3 June 1466 (Reg.Supp.,596 fo. 93).
  Malcolm gets *com.priv*. against Muir 23 July 1470 (*CPL*,xii, 743), prov. being based on death of Bean Mauritii (PRO 31/9 - 29/184); in poss. in papal eyes 19 Nov./31 Dec. 1470 (Reg.Supp.,661, fo. 50; PRO 31/9 - 29/185).

Malcolm Makylker 1494.
    Occ. 28 June 1494 (*RMS*,ii,no.2221).

Malcolm Salmond 1497.
    Occ. 1497 (*OPS*,II, i,161); res. to earl of Argyll 19 June 1497
(NLS, Hutton [Shires] ,xiii,17; Inverary, Argyll Inventory of 1680,
i,394).

Alexander Macleod 1510.
    Occ. 18 May 1510 (*RSS*, i,no.2069).

James Macgregor   1514 - 1551.
Nicholas Campbell   1542 - 1566.
    Macgregor occ. 10 Mar. 1514 (*History of Clan Gregor*,323); d.
apparently in poss. 12 Dec. 1551 (*Taymouth Bk.*,123).
    Campbell occ. 28 Mar. 1542 (*Laing Chrs.*,122); occ. 1 July 1566
(*Prot.Bk.Grote*, no.276); d. by 22 Mar. 1588 (v.inf.).

Donald Campbell 1588 - 1622.
    Crown pres. 22 Mar. 1588 on death of Nicholas Campbell (RSS,
lvii, fo.72); occ. 15 May 1622 (SRO, Part.Reg.Sasines Argyll, i, fo. 227).

PRECENTORS/CHANTERS OF ARGYLL

This dignity was for some time held by the prior of Ardchattan; but he
res. his right in exch. for ch. of St Bean in Lower Lorne c.1371; a later
prior obtained papal approval for the annulment of this exch. 27 Aug.
1425, but this does not appear to have been effective (*CPP*, i,584;
CSSR,ii,112).

First secular holder: c.1371.
    Prebend: one-quarter teinds of Lismore parsonage in 16th
century (Cowan, *Parishes*,134).

Cristin McGillemichel c.1371.
    Got poss. on exch. with prior of Ardchattan some 24 years before
1 July 1395 (*CPP*, 1,584).

Celestine   x1424.
Congham MacPaden 1423 - 1425.
Bean David   1424 - 1425.
    Celestine held it at death before 2 Nov. 1424 (*ACSB*,91).
    MacPaden in poss. 27 Aug. 1425 (*CSSR*,ii,112); had prob.
obtained it by 6 Mar. 1423 (see *Ar.archd.*).
    David prov. on Celestine's death 2 Nov. 1424 (*ACSB*,91);
promised annates 27 Aug. 1425 (*ibid.*), but has doubts whether he will
obtain poss. 31 Aug. 1425 (*CSSR*,ii,113).

Robert Dalustone 1451.
    Had poss. on David's death, and gets papal conf. 14 Jan. 1451
(Reg.Supp.,447,fo.273).

Bean David 1470.
    Said to occ. 1470 (*OPS*,II, i,161).

Donald Macfadzen 1507 - 1511.
    Occ. 12 Apr. 1507 (*RMS*,ii,no.3133); occ. 11 Sept. 1511 (*The Genealogist*,xxxviii,183).

Dugall McOnill 1556.
    Occ. 1556 (*OPS*,II, i,161).

John Campbell 1569.
    Occ. 12 Aug. 1569 (*Taymouth Bk.*,215).

Neil Campbell 1574 - 1580 (?).
    Occ. 1574 (*OPS*,II, i,166): occ. 28 Dec. 1574 (Stevenson & Wood, *Seals*,ii,274); prob. in poss. 9 Nov. 1575 (*RSS*,vii,no.340); perhaps same as prov. *Ar.bp.* 1580.

Gavin Hamilton 1584.
    Occ. 22 Oct. 1584 (*The Genealogist*,xxxviii,185); cf. *Ar.chanc*.

Colin Campbell 1622.
    Occ. 1622 while also parson of Craiginch (*OPS*,II, i,96,161).

J. Campbell 1629.
    Occ. 1629 (ibid.,161).

CHANCELLORS OF ARGYLL

First known date: 1424.
    Prebend: one-quarter teinds of Lismore parsonage in 16th century (Cowan, *Parishes*,134).

Gilbert McLochlan/Torleti 1424 - 1425.
    Had coll. by ord. more than a year before 21 May 1425 when in poss. (*CSSR*,ii,89).

Gilbert Barrouch 1491.
    Occ. 18 Apr. 1491 (*Prot.Bk.Young*,ii,no.428).

Archibald Leche 1511.
    Occ. 24 Jan. 1511 (Fraser, *Lennox*,ii,190); occ. 11 Sept. 1511 (*The Genealogist*,xxxviii, 183).

Neil McGillespy 1556.
    Occ. 1556 (*OPS*,II, i,161).

Nigel McVellen 1558.
    D. in poss. 27 Mar. 1558 (*Taymouth Bk.*,127).

Dougall McGregor 1574 - 1575.
    Occ. 28 Dec. 1574 (*History of Clan Gregor*,176); occ. 21 May 1575 (SRO, Macgregor Transcripts,box 26,s.a); prob. in poss. 9 Nov. 1575 (*RSS*,vii,no.340).

Gavin Hamilton 1578.
>Occ. 1578 (*OPS*,II, i,161-2); cf. *Ar.prec*.

Neil Campbell 1623.
>Occ. 1623 (*OPS*,II, i,162).

TREASURERS OF ARGYLL

First known date: 1390.
>Prebend: one-quarter teinds of Lismore parsonage in 16th century (Cowan, *Parishes*,134).

Congham MacPaden 1390 - 1391.
>In poss. 23 Dec. 1390 when prov. *Ar.archd*. (*CPP*, i,575); new prov. on exch. for same archd. with Leche 6 Dec. 1391.

John Leche 1391.
>Prov. prob. on exch. c. 6 Dec. 1391 when MacPaden prov. *Ar.archd*. (Reg.Vat.,302,fo.148v; 321,fos. 83-85).

Donald Colini x1451.
>Held it at death before 13 Feb. 1451 (v.inf.).

Maurice Macfadzen 1451 - 1467.
Duncan Nigelli Nenaici 1451.
>**Macfadzen** in poss. 13 Feb. 1451 (Reg.Supp.,448,fo.206v); occ. 6 May 1467 (NLS, Adv.MS 19.2.20, fo.76).
>**Duncan** prov. 13 Feb. 1451 (Reg.Supp.,448,fo.206v).

Patrick Clarkson 1486.
>Occ. 22 June 1486 (Fraser, *Lennox*,ii,128).

John Fisher 1517.
>Occ. 30 Aug. 1517 (*Taymouth Bk*.,180).

Neil Fisher 1528.
>Occ. 7 Oct. 1528 (Nisbet, *Heraldry*, i,33).

Archibald McNoril (McNerl ?) 1546.
>Occ. 16 Sept. 1546 (*Highland Papers*,iv,31).

John Carswell 1551 - 1552.
>Occ. 14 Oct. 1551 (*RMS*,iv,no.641); occ. 14 Feb. 1552 (SRO, Breadalbane, Comm. of Justiciary, etc.).

John Campbell 1556 - 1573.
>Occ. 1556 (*OPS*,II, i,161); occ. 1573 (ibid.,161,165); d. 18 Sept. 1573 (Edin.Tests.).

Ewen Cameron 1574.
>Occ. 1574 (*OPS*,II, i,161).

John Cameron 1604 - 1622.
>Occ. 11 June 1604 (*HMC* 3, *4th R*.,481,no.141); occ. 15 May 1622 (SRO, Part.Reg.Sasines Argyll, i,fo.227).

C

Ewen Cameron 1626.

Said to have been pres. by Lord Lorne 30 Oct. 1626 (Scott, *Fasti*, iv,23 no source cited).

ARCHDEACONS OF ARGYLL

First known date: 1230 x 1236.

Prebend: one-quarter teinds of Elanmunde in 16th century (*OPS*,II, i,170; Cowan, *Parishes*, 61).

Cristin 1230 x 1236 - 1240.

Occ. 1230 x 1236 (*Pais.Reg.*, 135 - 6); occ. 22 May 1240 (*PSAS*, xc,219).

Gilbert 1262 - 1270.

Occ. 1 Jan. 1262 (*Pais.Reg.*,122-3); occ. 9 July 1270 (ibid., 138).

Maurice 1304.

Occ. 10 Sept. 1304 (*RMS*,ii,no.3136).

Laurence c.1353.

Occ. c. 1353 (*Lamont Papers*,10); occ. 1352 x 1357 (Maidment, *Analecta*,ii, 16 - but possibly this man is *Db.archd*.).

John Dugaldi 1361 - 1387.

Occ. 16 Aug. 1361 (SRO, Transcripts Misc.Chrs. s.d.); occ. 2 Nov. 1364 (*Scrymgeour Inventory*,20); prov. *Ar.bp*. 26 Apr. 1387.

Walter de Wardlaw 1387.

Prov. as cardinal 30 May 1387 (*CPP*, i,568); d. before 5 Oct. 1387 (*CPL*,iv,255).

Alexander de Wardlaw 1387 x 1389.

Prov. on Walter's death, but d. without poss. (*CPP*, i,568,572; Reg. Vat.,302,fo.148v).

David Macmurchard/Marcard 1389 - 1390.
John Leche   1387 x 1391.
Congham MacPaden   1390 - 1397.

Macmurchard prov. on Alexander de Wardlaw's death 19 Jan. 1389 (*CPP*, i,573); in poss. following coll. by ord. 23 Dec. 1390 (*CPP*, i,575).

Leche had prov. on Alexander de Wardlaw's death, but res. without poss. on exch. with MacPaden for *Ar.treas*. on or before 6 Dec. 1391 (v.inf.).

MacPaden prov. 23 Dec. 1390 (*CPP*, i,575); prov. again on exch. with Leche 6 Dec. 1391 (Reg.Vat.,302,fo.148v; 321,fos. 83-85); prob. in poss. 11 Nov. 1395 and 19 Oct. 1397 when he was to be summoned before abbot of Saddell on charge of simony (v.inf.).

Nigel Colini Campbell 1395 - 1433 x 1437.
 Prov. on simony of MacPaden 11 Nov. 1395 (Reg.Vat.,321,fos. 83-85), and again 19 Oct. 1397 (Reg.Av.,304,fos.520v-521v); occ. 6 Mar. 1423 (*Highland Papers*,iv,176-8); occ. 17 Feb. 1433 (*Lamont Papers*,13); d. before or during visit of legate to Scotland 1436-7 (v.inf.).

Dougal Campbell de Lochawe   1437 - 1453.
Peter de Dalkeith   1441.
 Campbell coll. by legate 1436-7 and had new prov. 29 July 1441 (Reg.Supp.,375,fo.75v); occ. 11 May 1453 (NLS,Adv.MS 19.2.20, p.45).
 Dalkeith had coll. by ord. but is not in poss. 29 July 1441 (Reg. Supp.,375,fo.75v), nor 23 Sept. 1441 (ibid.,376,fo.172).

John de Lauder 1467.
 Occ. 6 May 1467 (NLS, Adv.MS 19.2.20,p.76); retained it until death (v.inf.).

Peter de Sandilands 1473 - 1475.
Robert de Houston 1475.
John Whitelaw   1475.
 Sandilands in poss. 13 Apr. 1475 (Reg.Supp.,718,fo.46v), and by 31 May 1475 had held it more than two years following Lauder's death (ibid.,721,fo.146v.).
 Houston prov. on plea that Sandilands is not in orders 13 April 1475 (Reg.Supp.,718,fo.46v.).
 Whitelaw prov. on same plea 31 May 1475 (ibid.,721,fo.146v.).

William Elphinstone junior   1478 - 1480 x 1481 (?).
John de Bickertone   1479.
 Elphinstone occ. 4 Dec. 1478 (*RMS*,ii,no.1408); is to res. on exch. with Bickertone 2 Dec. 1479 (v.inf.); occ. 12 June 1480 (*ER*,ix,i); perhaps dem. before 25 June 1481 (ibid.,ix,92); prov. *R.bp.* 3 Aug. 1481.
 Bickertone is to get it on exch. 2 Dec. 1479 (*Glas.Reg*.,ii,439); but this was prob. not effective.

John Brown (Browain) x1483.
 Browain held it at death before John Campbell had poss. (v.inf.); prob. not same man as Bickertone (v.sup.), but identifiable with John Brown, and so may have succ. Elphinstone here in return for giving up his right to *G.archd. Teviotdale*; d. 3 July x 3 Nov. 1483 (see *G.coll. princ.*).

John Campbell 1486 - 1487.
 Occ. 2 Aug. 1486 (*RMS*,ii,no.1662); had had prov. on Browain's death (*CPL*,xiv,54), prov. *I.bp.* 19 Jan. 1487.

Robert Campbell   1487 - 1490.
David Cunningham   1489 - 1509.
 Campbell prov. 19 Jan. 1487 (*CPL*,xiv,54); promises annates 14 June 1490 (PRO 31/9 - 30, Ob. et Sol. 1489-92,fo.53).

Cunningham occ. 2 May 1489 (*RMS*,ii,no.1848); occ. 3 Oct. 1500 (*Glas.Reg.*,ii,501-2); d. 18 Apr. 1509 (see *G.offic.*).

Robert Barry 1509 - 1526.
    Occ. 18 May 1509 (*Prot.Bk. Simon*,ii,284); occ. 10 Dec. 1526 (SRO,Reg.Ho.Chr.no.997).

John Makaw 1531 - 1554.
    Pres. by crown on Barry's death 11 July 1531 (*RSS*,ii,no.959); occ. 8 Feb. 1554 (SRO,Prot.Bk.John Robeson,fo.56).

Robert Montgomery 1554 - 1574 x 1601.
    Pres. by crown on Makaw's death 26 Feb. 1554 (*RSS*,iv,no. 2429); occ. 1574 (*OPS*,II, i,162); res. before 10 Nov. 1601 (v.inf.).

Duncan Campbell 1601.
    Pres. by crown on res. of Montgomery 10 Nov. 1601 (RSS, lxxii,fo.173).

James Kirk 1604 - 1622 x 1623.
    Pres. by crown on death of Campbell 7 Feb. 1604 (RSS,lxxiv, fo.130); occ. 15 May 1622 (SRO,Part.Reg.Sasines Argyll; i,fo.227); d. by 27 June 1623 (v.inf.).

Adam Boyd 1623 - 1629.
    Occ. 28 May 1623 (*HMC* 3, *4th R.*,481,no.134; cf. *OPS*,II,i, 170); crown pres. on death of Kirk 27 June (*sic*) 1623 (Reg.Pres.,v, 81); occ. 1629 (*OPS*,II,i,162).

DEANS OF CHRISTIANITY

DEANS OF KINTYRE: KINTYRE AND KNAPDALE

First known dates: Kintyre: 1222(?)
                      Kintyre and Knapdale: 1520.

Gillifelan (Kintyre) x 1222(?)
    Occ. c.1220 x 1240, prob. before 1222 (*RMS*,ii,no.3136; cf. *PSAS*,xc,219).

Gillecund (Kintyre) 1240.
    Occ. 22 May 1240 (*PSAS*,xc,219).

Malcolm Macdowell (Kintyre) 1406.
    Occ. 27/28 Jan. 1406(*RMS*,ii,nos.403,379).

Cornelius (Kintyre and Knapdale) 1520.
    Occ. 1520 (SRO,Prot.Bk.Matthew Forsyth,fo.33v).

DEANS OF GLASSARY: COWAL

First known dates: Glassary: 1240
Cowal: 1364

Maluin (Glassary) 1240.
Occ. 22 May 1240 (*PSAS*,xc,219).

Odo (Glassary) 1284 - 1285.
Occ. 2 Sept. 1284 and 21 Aug. 1285 (*Pais.Reg.*,124).

Adam (Cowal) 1364.
Occ. 2 Nov. 1364 (SRO, Dalhousie,sec.27,no.9).

DEANS OF LORNE: LOCH AWE: KILMARTIN

First known dates: Lorne: 1240.
Loch Awe: 1434 (*HMC 3,4th R.*,479; cf. *OPS*,
II, i,121n).
Kilmartin: 1541

John (Lorne) 1240.
Occ. 22 May 1240 (*PSAS*,xc,219).

Neil Campbell (Loch Awe/Kilmartin) 1533 - 1544.
Occ. as vic. of Kilmartin and dean of Loch Awe 10 Dec. 1533
(*The Genealogist*,xxxviii,138); occ. as dean of Kilmartin 26 Mar. 1541
(*Lamont Papers*,no.158); occ. as vic. of Kilmartin and dean of Loch
Awe 20 Apr. 1541 (SRO,Prot.Bk.John Graham,fo.24); occ. as dean of
Loch Awe 6 Oct. 1544 (Inverary, Glenample Writs); styled rector of
Kilmartin 20 Oct. 1547 (*The Genealogist*,xxxviii,139).

DEANS OF KNOYDART: MORVEN

First known dates: Knoydart: 1506 x 1510.
Morven: 1545.

John Macvurich (Knoydart) 1506 x 1510.
Has been identified as dean while holding ch. of Knoydart 1506
x 1510 (*TGSI*,xliii,287-8).

Roderick/ Rore Macallister (Morven) 1545.
In office when found as *I.bp.-elect* 28 July 1545 (*State Papers
Henry VIII*,v,477; cf. iii,531,533,549,553,567-8; v,508).

Note: the deaneries of Argyll are in 1539-41 mentioned as Argyll, Lorne
and Bute (*MW*, i,291).

OFFICIALS

OFFICIALS WITH GENERAL AUTHORITY

OFFICIALS OF ARGYLL

First known date: 1240.

Daniel 1240.
  Occ. 22 May 1240 (*PSAS*,xc,219).

Maurice 1250
  Occ. 27 Sept. 1250 (*Pais.Reg.*,134).

OFFICIALS WITH LIMITED AUTHORITY

OFFICIALS OF LOCH AWE AND COWAL

First known date: 1410.

John Campbell 1410.
  Occ. 29 Nov. 1410 (*Highland Papers*,iv,236); cf. *Ar.dean*.

COMMISSARIES

None known.

BRECHIN DIOCESE

BISHOPS OF BRECHIN

First known date: c.1150.

    This see was directly subject to the pope until placed under metropolitan authority of St Andrews 14 Aug. 1472 (*Vet.Mon.*, no.852).

Samson c.1150 - 1165 x 1169.

    Occ. c.1150 and certainly before 24 May 1153 (*ESC*,180); occ. 1165 x 1169 (*St A.Lib.*,133).

Turpin 1178 - 1189 x 1198.

    El. by 1178 (*Arb.Lib.*, i,9); still just elect 1178 x 1184 (*St A. Lib.*,147); cons. by 1178 x 1188 (*Arb.Lib.*, i,134); prob. one of the two unnamed Scottish bps. cons. at 3rd Lateran Council Mar. 1179 (*ES*,ii,300); occ. 1189 x·1198 (ibid.,123-5).

Radulf 1198 x 1199 - 1212.

    El. by Aug. 1198 x Mar. 1199 (ibid.,103); cons. 1202 (*Chron. Melrose*, 51), before July (*C.A.Chrs.*, i,19); occ. 31 May 1212 (*Dunf.Reg.*,124).

Hugh 1214 x 1215 - 1218.

    Occ. 1214 x 1215 (*Arb.Lib.*, i,129-30) and 17 Feb. 1215 (ibid.,74); d. 1218 (*Chron.Melrose*,70).

Gregory 1218 - 1242.

    Succ. when *B.archd.* 1218 (ibid.); after el. gets mand. for conf. and cons. 15 Dec. 1218 (*Vet.Mon.*,no.19); occ. 1242 (*Arb.Lib.*, i, 206).

Albin 1246 - 1269.

    El. when *B.prec.* before 19 July 1246, when mand. was issued for conf. of his postulation and cons. (*Vet.Mon.*,no.116); cons. by 13 May 1247 (*CPL*, i,232); d. 1269 (*Chron.Melrose*,144).

William 1269 x 1275.

    El. when *B.dean*, but d. prob. without cons. before 24 May 1275 (*Vet.Mon.*,no.262), perhaps at general council of Lyons May-July 1274 (*Chron.Extracta*,112; cf. ibid.,108; see also *Chron.Bower*,ii, 106,116).

William Comyn/ de Kilconquhar (Kilconcath) O.P. 1275 - 1291 x 1296 or 1297.

    As Kilconcath succ. Albin (*Chron.Melrose*,144); as Comyn had el. after death of Bp.-elect William and then got mand. for conf. and cons. 24 May 1275 (*Vet.Mon.*,no.262); cons. before 29 Apr. 1276 (*St A.Lib.*,111); occ. June 1291 (*SHR*, xxxvi,119); d. before Jan. 1296 or Jan. 1297 (v.inf.).

Nicholas 1296 or 1297 x 1298.

    Prov. when *B.subd.* and cons. 21 Jan. 1297 (*Reg. Boniface VIII*,·

i,no.1518); but note that same letter is dated 26 Jan. 1296 by other editors (*Vet.Mon.*,no.350, *CPL*, i,567; cf. *B.dean*.), d. before 1 June 1298 (v.inf.).

John de Kininmund 1298 - 1323 x 1327.
El. when *B.archd.* on death of Nicholas and got conf. and cons. 1 June 1298 (*Vet.Mon.*,no.361), occ. Oct. 1323 x Sept. 1327 (*Arb. Lib.*, i,339).

Adam de Moray 1328 - 1349.
El. before 15 Oct. 1328 (*Vet.Mon.*,no.474), prov. and cons. 31 Oct. 1328 (ibid.,no.475), occ. 30 Apr. 1349 (*Rot.Scot.*, i,727).

Philip Wilde/ de Brechin 1350 - 1351.
El. when *B.dean* and then gets prov. 17 Feb. 1350 (*Vet.Mon.*, no.585, cf. *Brech.Reg.*,ii,393), perhaps cons. by 2 June 1350 (*CPL*, iii,413), and certainly by 16 Mar. 1351 (*Brech.Reg.*,ii,7); occ. 3 May 1351 (*Spalding Misc.*,v,249); d. before 17 Nov. 1351 (v.inf.).

Patrick de Leuchars (Locrys) O.S.A. 1351 - 1373 x 1383.
El. when canon of St Andrews and then gets prov. 17 Nov. 1351 (*Vet.Mon.*,no.600); cons. by 11 Dec. 1351 (*CPL*,iii,431); occ. 3 Apr. 1373 (*APS*, i,562); res. in curia on account of old age presumably on or before 12 June 1383 (v.inf.), and granted pension on revenues of the see 20 June 1383 (Reg.Av.,234,fo.596).

Stephen de Cellario 1383 - 1404 x 1405.
El. when *B.archd.* on res. of Leuchars and gets prov. 12 June 1383 (Reg.Av.,232,fos.119,596v,598; Eubel, *Hierarchia*, i,145), cons. by 23 Feb. 1385 (*Brech.Reg.*, i,21); d. 11 Nov. 1404 x 7 June 1405 (*ER*,iii,638).

Walter Forrester/ Jordani 1407 - 1425 x 1426.
El. as Jordani before 11 Apr. 1407 when pope was considering his suitability (Reg.Av.,332,fo.7), described as *B.subd.* when prov. as Forrester 26 Nov. 1407 (Eubel, *Hierarchia*, i,145); described as bp. in royal records 28 Oct. 1408 (*RMS*, i,386; cf. *ER*,iv,72), but not cons. until 11 May 1410 x 10 May 1411 (*Brech.Reg.*,ii,273); occ. 7 May 1425 (*ER*,iv,379), prob. d. before 15 Apr. 1426 (ibid,400).

John de Crannach 1426 - 1453.
Trans. from *C.bp.* 7 June 1426 (PRO 31/10 - 14/36; Eubel, *Hierarchia*, i,145); not cons. until after 5 Oct. 1426 (*Brech.Reg.*, i, 155); occ. 17 Nov. 1453 (ibid.,ii,96-97).

George Schoriswood 1454 - 1462.
Prov. when *Dk.chanc.* 8 Mar. 1454 (Eubel, *Hierarchia*,ii,110); cons. before 1 July 1454 (*ER*,v,609); still in poss. 11 Nov. 1462 (*ER*,vii,223-4).

Patrick Graham 1463 - 1465.
Described as elect and had papal promotion 28/29 Mar. 1463 (*ACSB*,54; *Vet.Mon.*,no.828); temps. still in royal hands 29 May 1463 (*ER*,vii,223-4); cons. 3 Nov. x 29 Dec. 1464 (*Spalding Misc.*,iv,6-7;

Arb.Lib.,ii,154), though had been active as bp. as early as Jan. 1464
(Herkless & Hannay, *Archbishops*, i,23-24); trans. to *St. A.bp.* 4 Nov.
1465.

John Balfour 1465 - 1488.

Prov. 29 Nov. 1465 (Brady, *Episcopal Succession*, i,138; *ACSB*,
56-57); cons. 8 Dec. 1465 (Dowden, *Bishops*, 187); still in poss. 4
June 1488 when expected to res. in favour of Meldrum (*Brech.Reg.*,
ii,124).

William Meldrum 1488 - 1514 x 1516.

Prov. when B.canon 4 July 1488 (Eubel, *Hierarchia*,ii,110); cons.
30 Jan. x 7 July 1489 (*ADC*, i,103,121); still in poss. 8 Dec. 1514
(Eubel, *Hierarchia*,iii,139n); d. before 19 Mar. 1516 (*RSS*, i, no.2727).

John Hepburn 1516 - 1557.

Prov. 29 Oct. 1516 (Dowden, *Bishops*, 189); cons. June 1522 x
23 Feb. 1523 (*Brech.Reg.*,ii,194,310; cf. Dowden, *Bishops*, 189 and
n; cf. also *St A.Form.*,i,183, which appears to imply that he had been
cons. before 21 Sept. 1516); d. 27 Mar. x 22 May 1557 (*RMS*,v,no.
1294; *RSS*,v,no.134).

Donald Campbell 1557 - 1559.

Said to have had crown nom. Dec. 1557 (*HBC*,285, no source
cited); certainly nom. before July 1558 when papal approval was being
sought (*Correspondence of Sir Patrick Waus*, ed. R Vans Agnew, 10);
pope still making difficulties because of his desire to retain abbacy of
Coupar Angus 11 May 1559 (Maidment, *Analecta*, ii,381-2); was
reported 19 May 1559 to have put on the 'secular weed' (*CSP Scot.*,
i,212,no.455); still called abbot of Coupar Aug. 1560 (*APS*,ii,525);
prob. never obtained this see (cf. Lesley, *De Origine*,539); d. 16 Dec.
1562 x 20 Jan. 1563 (*RMS*,iv,no.1436; *RSS*,v,no.1199).

John Sinclair 1565 - 1566.

Prov. by pope after crown nom. when *Restalrig dean* 7 Sept.
1565, following vacancy said to have lasted seven years (Eubel,
Hierarchia,iii,139; Brady, *Episcopal Succession*, i,138); cons. doubtful
(Dowden, *Bishops*,192), d. 9 Apr. 1566 (*Diurnal of Occurrents*, 98).

Alexander Campbell 1566 - 1607.

Crown prov. while a minor 6 May 1566 (*RSS*,v,no.2806); crown
nom. to pope 21 July 1566 (*Papal Negotiations with Queen Mary*,
262); cons. uncertain; res. on or before 22 Apr. 1607 (v.inf.); d.
Feb. 1608 (Edin.Tests.,24 June 1608).

Andrew Lamb 1607 - 1619.

Crown prov. 22 Apr. 1607 (Reg.Pres.,iv,4v); cons. 21 Oct. 1610
(Spottiswoode, *History*,iii,209); trans. to *Ga.bp*. 4 Aug. 1619.

David Lindsay 1619 - 1634.

El. 10 Apr. 1619 (*RMS*,vii,no.2128); cons. 23 Nov. 1619
(Calderwood, *History*,vii,396); trans. to *E.bp*. 16 Sept. 1634.

Thomas Sydserf 1634 - 1635.
Cons. 29 July 1634 when *E.dean* (Row, *Historie*,375); crown prov. 16 Sept. 1634 (*RMS*,ix,no.218); trans. to *Ga.bp*. 30 Aug. 1635.

Walter Whiteford 1635 - 1638.
Crown prov. 15 Sept. 1635 (*RMS*,ix,no.403); cons. 7 Dec. 1635 (*HBC*,285, no source cited); depriv. 13 Dec. 1638 (Peterkin, *Records*, i, 26-27); buried at Westminster 16 June 1647 (*Dict.Nat.Biog.*, lxi,128).

CHAPTER OF BRECHIN

This chapter in early 12th century comprised the prior and culdees of Brechin together with certain other clerks unspecified e.g. 1212 x 1218 (*Arb.Lib.*, i,no.188) and presumably at episcopal election of 1218 (*Vet. Mon.*,no.19); by time of next episcopal election in early 1246 a college of canons had emerged (ibid.,no.116), apparently by means of an act of Bp. Gregory now lost whereby the culdees were converted into secular canons (cf. *Lind.Cart.*,no.99 of 18 Feb. 1250); prob. at least four of the dignities in addition to the older office of archdeacon were founded at this time, and there were at least six prebends by 1274 and eleven by 1372 (*MRHS*,190,167; *RSCHS*,xiv,29-30,42).

EARLY DEANS IN BRECHIN

Matussali 1178 x 1188.
Occ. 1178 x 1188 (*Arb.Lib.*,i,134).

Matthew 1189 x 1198 - 1212 x 1218.
Occ. 1189 x 1198 (*Arb.Lib.*,i,124); occ. 1212 x 1218 (ibid.,131).

DEANS OF BRECHIN

First known date: 1248.
Prebend: ch. of Farnell at Reformation and prob. by 1274 (Reg. Pres.,ii,62v; Cowan, *Parishes*,64).

William (de Crachin ?) 1248 - 1269 x 1275.
Occ. 22 Sept. 1248 (*Arb.Lib.*,i,175,cf. NLS,Adv.MS 34.6.24); occ. 1256 x 1261 *or* Mar. x July 1267 (*Brech.Reg.*,i,no.3); el. *B.bp*. 1269 x, but d. uncons. x 24 May 1275, by which date *another* dean had been in poss. (*Vet.Mon.*,106).

Thomas de Dundee (Dono Dei) 1295.
In poss. when prov. *R.bp*. 18 Nov. 1295.

Imbert Aurei 1296.
Prov. on promotion of Dundee 27 Jan. 1296 (*CPL*, i,566).

Fulco 1323 x 1327 - 1339.

Occ. Oct. 1323 x Sept. 1327 (*Arb.Lib.*,i,339); occ. 7 Mar. 1339 (*Abdn.Reg.*,i,65).

Thomas de Fingask 1342.
In poss. when prov. *C.bp*. 29 Nov. 1342; cons. by 1 Dec. 1342.

Philip Wilde/ de Brechin 1343 - 1350.
Prov. 8 Mar. 1343 (Reg.Av.,182,fo.119; *CPL*,iii,54); prov. *B.bp*. 17 Feb. 1350.

Alexander de Kininmund 1350.
Prov. 28 May 1350 (*CPL*,iii,413); had poss. and res. before 8 Mar. 1352 (v.inf.).

John de Crail 1352 - 1393.
Conf. after el. 8 Mar. 1352 (Collect.,14,fo.163v); res. on exch. at curia 25 May 1393 (v.inf.).

Andrew de Kyle   1393 - 1397 x 1399.
John de Hawick   x1394.
Patrick de Spalding 1394 - 1397.
Kyle prov. on exch. with Crail 25 May 1393 (Reg.Vat.,306,fos. 246,267); papal mand. to St A.bp. 12 Oct. 1394 (expedited 26 Jan./ 3 Feb. 1395) to summon him on 8 June 1395 and deprive him if found to have perpetrated fraud (Reg.Av.,280,fos.196v-197); prob. still in poss. 23 Oct. 1397 (v.inf.); d. before 24 June 1399 (v.inf.).
Hawick had prov. before 16 Oct. 1394 (Reg.Av.,292,fos.153v-154), but prob. never had poss.
Spalding prov. on depriv. of Kyle or death of Crail 12 Oct. 1394 (expedited 26 Jan./3 Feb. 1395) to take effect 10 July 1395 (Reg.Av., 278,fos.224v-226); lit. in curia 28 Aug. 1395 (ibid.,281,fos.216v-217) and 23 Oct. 1397 (Reg.Vat.,322,fos.36-38); on this latter date his ambitions prob. switched to *Ab.dean*.; prov. to another B.preb. 15 Sept. 1402 (*CPP*, i,618) which he retained until death in 1422 (*CPL*, vii,242), and it was prob. this preb. for which he got conf. and new prov. 14 Feb. 1415 (*CPP*, i,602, where preb. is said to be the deanery).

Cuthbert de Brechin/ Henrici/ Alanson 1399 - 1437.
Prov. on death of Kyle 24 June 1399, expedited 29 Mar. 1404 (Reg.Av.,304,fos.40-40v); occ. 9 Nov. 1409 (*Brech.Reg.*, i,34); d. in poss. 28 Apr. 1437 (*CPL*,ix,23).

Duncan de Lichton 1437 - 1439 x 1440.
David de Crannach 1437 - 1440.
John de Lichton   1438 - 1451.
Robert de Tulloch x1441.
Richard Cady   1450.
Duncan de Lichton prov. on Alanson's death 7 May 1437 (*CPL*, viii,651); claimed to have won lit. with Crannach 2 June 1439 (*CPL*, ix,51-52); claimed poss. 11 July 1439 (Reg.Supp.,359,fo.233v); res. on exch. with John de Lichton before 21 July 1440 (ibid.,366,fo.21).
Crannach occ., being newly el., 31 May 1437 (*St A.Acta*,44); prov. after coll. by ord. on Alanson's death and lit. with Duncan de

Lichton 16 Apr. 1438 (*CPL*,ix,23); claims poss. 26 Apr. 1438 (Reg.
Supp.,345,fo.256v); res. right to John de Lichton, who has poss. 23
Sept. 1440 (ibid.,367,fo.290v); cf. *Dk.subd*.

John de Lichton claimed poss. 31 Dec. 1438 (Reg.Supp.,353,
fo.147); obtained Duncan de Lichton's right by exch. before 21 July
1440 (v.sup.; cf. *CPL*,ix,83); surrog. to Crannach's right 23 Sept. 1440
(*ACSB*,127); still in poss. 1 July 1451 (BM,Add.MS 33245,fo.169).

Tulloch prov. unsuccessfully before 17 June 1441 (Reg.Supp.,
377,fo.179v).

Cady prov. on death or res. of John de Lichton 17 Oct. 1450
(Reg.Supp.,446,fo.193).

David de Crannach 1452 - 1453.

Prov. on John de Lichton's death 3 May 1452 (*CPL*, x, 588);
occ. 17 Nov. 1453 (*Brech.Reg.*,ii,97).

Walter Stewart 1454.

Prov. on Crannach's death 19 Apr. 1454 (*CPL*,x,256); paid
annates 22 May 1454 (*ACSB*, 273).

William Forbes 1454 - 1455.

Prov. on Stewart's death 8 Oct. 1454 (*CPL*,x,260); in poss.
7 June 1455 (*CPL*,xi,12); res. in favour of Spalding (v.inf.).

John Spalding 1456 - 1487.
John Barry   1477 - 1487.
Hugh Douglas 1487 - 1512.

Spalding occ. 8 May 1456 (*Brech.Reg.*,i,182), having got it on
res. of Forbes, conf. 5 Oct. 1458 (Reg.Supp.,512,fo.173); res. on
exch. with Douglas for *B.prec.*, after holding it for more than thirty
years by right of papal prov. on or before 17 Feb. 1487 (v.inf.).

Barry got *com.priv.* against Spalding 14 May 1477 (*CPL*,xiii,
864); promised annates 2 Jan. 1487 (*ACSB*,217); still lit. 17 Feb.
1487 (*CPL*,xiv,141,162); withdrew claim in return for pension 19
May 1487 (*ACSB*,220).

Douglas prov. on exch. with Spalding 17 Feb. 1487 (*CPL*,
xiv,141,162); occ. 2 July 1512 (*Brech.Reg.*,ii,166).

Alexander Stewart 1523 - 1534.

Occ. 1523 and 1524-5 (SRO,Dalhousie,section 13,no.309);
in poss. when prov. *M.bp*. with disp. to retain dean. 13 Sept. 1529
(Dowden, *Bishops*,170); res. commend in favor of White 1 July
1534 (PRO 31/9 - 32/286-7).

Henry White   1534 - 1541 x 1542.
Patrick Stewart 1536 - 1545.
John Erskine   1542.

White wrongly said to occ. 9 Feb. 1532 (Fraser, *Menteith*,ii,400 -
there is no such designation in original text i.e. SRO, ADC,xliii.fo.
148); prov. and promises annates 17 Aug. 1534 (PRO 31/9 - 32/284);
in poss. and proposes to res. 22 Feb. 1536 (*James V Letters*,313);
occ. June 1541 (*Brech.Reg.*,ii,192-4); d. by 31 May 1542 (St A.Univ.

Mun.,SCB,fo.109v).

Stewart gets crown nom. for papal prov. 22 Feb. 1536 (*James V Letters*,313); promised annates as coadj. to White 11 Nov. 1536 (PRO 31/9 - 33/46); in poss. and is to res. 20 Nov. 1542 (*James V Letters*, 445); but occ. 19 Jan. 1545 (SRO, Airlie, sec.42,no.10).

Erskine gets crown nom. for papal prov. 20 Nov. 1542 (*James V Letters*,445).

James Nasmyth 1545.
Res. to Cardinal Betoun as legate 5 Oct. 1545 (*SHR*,xxii,37).

James Hamilton 1545 (?) - 1554.
Prov. by legate 5 Oct. 1545? (*SHR*,xxii,37); occ. 16 Nov. 1549 (*RSS*,iv,no.498); prov. *Ar.bp.* 14 July 1553 (*SHR*,xxii,38); occ. 10 Mar. 1554 (*RSS*,iv,no.2523).

William Cunningham 1555 - 1558 x 1560.
Occ. 1555 (SRO, Acts and Decreets,xii,30), having got it on exch. for his right in see of Argyll (*SHR*,xxii,37); occ. 27 Mar. 1556 (*Laing Chrs.*,169); occ. 4 Dec. 1558 (*Brech.Reg.*,ii,280); d. by 19 Feb. 1560 (*Laing Chrs.*,184).

James Thornton 1563 - 1577.
Crown pres. on Cunningham's death 3 July 1563 (*RSS*,v,no. 1416); escheated 8 Oct. 1577 (*RSS*,vii,no.1208).

James Nicolson 1577 - 1580.
Crown pres. on death (*sic*) of Thornton 24 Nov. 1577 (*RSS*, vii,no.1282); occ. 26 Aug. 1578 (*RMS*,iv,no.2795); occ. 20 Apr. 1580 (SRO, Bks. of Sederunt,iii,fo.119).

Dougal Campbell 1581 - 1619.
Crown pres. on death of Nicolson 30 Nov. 1581 (Reg.Pres.,ii, 62); occ. 20 Sept. 1619 (SRO, Dalhousie, section 13, no.328).

David Carnegie 1633 - 1668.
Crown pres. on death of Campbell 8 July 1633 (RSS,civ,fo.466); occ. as dean again after Restoration 9 Mar. 1668 (SRO, Part.Reg. Sasines Forfar,v,fo.240).

PRECENTORS/CHANTERS OF BRECHIN

First known date: 1246.
Prebend: ch. of Stracathro in 1274 (*SHS Misc.*,vi,52; Cowan, *Parishes*,189).

Albin 1246.
In poss. when conf. *B.bp.* after el. 19 July 1246.

Thomas de Perth/ Bell 1259 - 1275.
Occ. 22 Aug. 1259 (*Reg.Alexandre IV*,iii,59); occ. Dec. 1275 (*SHS Misc.*,vi,69; cf.52); see *Scone Liber*, 124-5 for surname as 'Perth dictus Bell'.

William de Cluny 1296 - 1298.
 Occ. 28 Aug. 1296 (*CDS*,ii,208); occ. 1 June 1298 (*Vet.Mon.*, 164-5).

Fergus de Tulloch 1372.
 Occ. 24 May 1372 (*Brech.Reg.*,i,19-20).

Salomon Rae 1380.
 In poss. 16 Nov. 1380 (*CPP*, i,556, where text says *B.succ.*); known to have held *B.prec.* before death 29 Nov. 1385 x 4 Sept. 1389 (*CPP*, i,574; Reg.Vat.,305,fos.191-2; cf. *Dk.dean*.).

Alexander Doig (Dog) x1393.
 Held it at death before 3 May 1393 (v.inf.).

Cuthbert de Brechin 1393 - 1399.
 Prov. after coll. by ord. on Doig's death 3 May 1393 (Reg.Vat., 305,fos.191-2); prov. *B.dean* 24 June 1399.

Gilbert Brown 1399 - 1439.
 Prov. 24 June 1399 (Reg.Av.,305,fos.7-8v); occ. 9 Nov. 1409 (*Brech.Reg.*,i,34); occ. 13 June 1439 (ibid.,87).

Robert de Crannach 1440 - 1453.
Andrew Fife   1440 - 1442.
 Crannach had coll. by ord. on Brown's death and gets papal conf. 1 Sept. 1440 (*CPL*,ix,101-2); new prov. after lit. with Fife 12 Sept. 1442 (Reg.Supp.,385,fo.210); occ. 17 Nov. 1453 (*Brech.Reg.*,ii,97).
 Fife had prov. before 1 Sept. 1440, when pope decided against his prior right (*CPL*,ix,101-2); no poss. 12 Sept. 1442 (Reg.Supp., 381, fo.278).

George Seres 1457 - 1480.
James Lindsay 1459.
 Seres occ. 10 Sept. 1457 (*Brech.Reg.*,ii,274); occ. 13 June 1480 (*RMS*,ii,no.1441).
 Lindsay gets disp. to hold some right in it with other benefices 8 Mar. 1459 (Reg.Supp.,517,fo.216).

Hugh Douglas 1485 - 1487.
 Occ. 9 June 1485 (SRO, Cupar Burgh Chrs.,no.8); res. at curia on exch. with Spalding for *B.dean*. 17 Feb. 1487 (v.inf.).

John Spalding 1487.
 Prov. on exch. with Douglas, being aged 69, 17 Feb. 1487 (*CPL*, xiv,162; *ACSB*,218).

Henry Meldrum 1489 - 1496.
 Occ. 13 July 1489 (*ER*, x,148), having prob. got poss. since William Meldrum became *B.bp*. 1488-9; occ. 21 Mar. 1496 (*Brech.Reg.*, ii,135).

William Meldrum 1500 - 1517 x 1518.
 Occ. 6 May 1500 (*Brech.Reg.*,i,217); occ. 2 Jan. 1515 (*Laing Chrs.*,78); prob. res on exch. with Ferne 20 June 1517 x 12 Jan. 1518

(see *Dk.archd.*).

George Ferne   1518 - 1527.
James Scrymgeour   1521 - 1541.
     Ferne prob. had poss. by 12 Jan. 1518 (v.sup.); occ. 28 Feb.
1520 (St A.Univ.Mun.,Acta Rectorum,i,72); res. but promises annates
on retaining fruits 24 Apr. 1521 (PRO 31/9 - 31/365-6); occ. 9 July
1527 (SRO, ADC,xxxvii,fo.150).
     Scrymgeour promises annates and gets prov. 24 Apr. 1521 (PRO
31/9 - 31/365-6), occ. 3 Mar. 1528 (Glamis, Strathmore Writs, box 2,
no.31), occ. 6 June 1541 (*Brech.Reg.*,i,228).

Thomas Scrymgeour 1543 - 1562.
     Occ. 24 May 1543 (Stevenson & Wood, *Seals*,iii,581), occ.
wrongly called *B.succ*. 20/31 Mar. 1553 (*Scrymgeour Inventory*,32,
37), occ. 27 June 1556 (*Brech.Reg.*,ii,204), d. Mar. 1562 (*Thirds of
Benefices*,10n).

Robert Fraser 1564.
     Pres. by crown on death of Thomas Scrymgeour 10 Oct. 1564
(*RSS*,v,no.1785).

Robert Fraser 1565.
     Pres. by crown on his father's sickness 2 Apr. 1565 (ibid.,no.
2007); res. by July 1566 (v.inf.).

Paul Fraser 1566 - 1609.
     Pres. by crown on res. of both Frasers 18 July 1566 (ibid.,no.
2978), occ. 15 May 1608 (*Brech.Reg.*,ii,296); d. in poss. 22 Aug.
1609 (Brech.Tests., under 14 Sept. 1609).

Robert Norie 1611 - 1623.
     Occ. 13 Feb. 1611 (*RMS*,vii,no.579) and 1 Oct. 1623 (SRO,
Airlie, sec.48,no.82).

CHANCELLORS OF BRECHIN

First known date: 1274 (*SHS Misc.*,vi,52).
     Prebend: ch. of Navar at Reformation and prob. by 1274
(RSS,lxix,95;cf.*SHS Misc.*,vi,52; Cowan, *Parishes*,154).

Philip Wilde/ de Brechin 1342 - 1343.
     In poss. 28 July 1342 (*CPP*, i,3); moved to *B.dean*. by prov. 8
Mar. 1343.

Hugh 1348.
     Occ. 21 Aug. 1348 (*Brech.Reg.*,i,11).

Richard de Mowat 1372.
     Occ. 24 May 1372 (ibid.,19-20).

Geoffrey de Arbroath 1410 - 1439.
     Occ. 9 Apr. 1410 (ibid.,131), occ. 13 June 1439 (ibid.,85-87).

Richard Wylie   1444 - 1446 x 1448.
Richard Dot (Doid) 1444.
David de Crannach   1444 - 1452.
William Gylespy   1444.
Patrick Reid   1445.
Laurence Wylie   1448.

    Richard Wylie had poss. on Arbroath's death on strength of exp.
prov., and gets new prov. 8 July 1444 (Reg.Supp.,398,fo.69); lit. with
Crannach 19 Sept. 1444 (ibid.,fo.79); new prov. after lit. with Dot 3
Sept. 1446 (ibid.,413,fo.49v), lost poss. by 3 Nov. 1446 (v.inf.) and
res. right by 14 Feb. 1448 (Reg.Supp.,423,fo.105v).

    Dot was nom. by bp. and had prov.; by 30 July 1444 lit. with
Richard Wylie and Crannach (*CPL*,ix,415); res. without poss. before
19 Sept. 1444 (Reg.Supp.,398,fo.79).

    Crannach lit. with Richard Wylie and Dot 30 July 1444 (*CPL*,
ix,415), no poss. 11 Mar. 1445 (Reg.Supp.,404,fo.44); prov. after lit.
with Reid 28 Apr. 1445 (*CPL*,ix,490); occ. apparently in poss. 3
Nov. 1446 (*St A.Acta*, 67), prov. after res. of Richard Wylie 14 Feb.
1448 (Reg.Supp.,423,fo.105v), prov. *B.dean*. 3 May 1452.

    Gylespy had coll. by ord. on Arbroath's death and gets prov.
19 Sept. 1444 (Reg.Supp.,398,fo.79).

    Reid had right which he res. in curia in return for pension 28
Apr. 1445 (*CPL*,ix,490).

    Laurence Wylie prov. on res. of Richard Wylie 5 Sept. 1448
(Reg.Supp.,430,fo.132) unfruitfully.

Walter Stewart   1452 - 1454.
David Ogilvie   1453 - 1457 x 1458.

    Stewart prov. 3 May 1452 (*CPL*,x,588); in poss. 11 Aug. 1453
(Reg.Supp.,471,fo.188v); prov. *B.dean*. 19 Apr. 1454.

    Ogilvie gets *com.priv*. against Stewart 11 Aug. 1453 (ibid.); in
poss. 12 Feb. 1456 (*CPL*,xi,34); prob. res. on exch. with William
Ogilvie for *R.dean*. after 31 May 1457 and before death x 21 Oct.
1458.

William Ogilvie 1457 x 1458 - 1481.

    Prob. obtained it by exch. 31 May 1457 x 21 Oct. 1458 (v.sup.);
in poss. 12 Jan. 1459 (Reg.Supp.,510,fo.150), occ. 27 Apr. 1461
(*Brech.Reg*.,ii,275), occ. 27 May 1476 (ibid.,277); d. 2 Mar. 1481
(*Spalding Misc*.,i,64).

James Balfour 1483 - 1490 x 1492.

    Occ. 13 Mar. 1483 (*ADC*,ii,cix); occ. 6 Oct. 1490 (*Brech.Reg*.,
ii,135); d. by 10 Mar. 1492 (SRO, ADC,i,228).

Walter Fenton 1500.

    Occ. 6 May and 24 Oct. 1500 (*Brech.Reg*.,i,217; ii,277).

William Cadzow 1506.

    Pres. by crown on Fenton's death 9 Feb. 1506 (*RSS*,i,no.1221).

Thomas Meldrum 1509 x 1510 - 1524.

    Moved from *B.subd*. 26 Apr. 1509 x 20 Jan. 1510; occ. 26 Aug.

1510 (*Brech.Reg.*,ii,278); occ. 3 July 1524 (SRO, Douglas Collection, vol.xvi,no.51).

John Colden 1532 - 1538 x 1540.
 Occ. 22 Sept. 1532 (SRO, Shairp of Houston,no.5); occ. 28 Feb. 1538 (*RSS*,ii,no.2457); prob. res. on exch. with Turing for *Methven prov.*.

Alexander Turing 1540 - 1548.
William Cuni   1541.
 Turing occ. 6 Mar. 1540 (SRO, ADC & S,xii,fo.77v); revoked earlier intention to res. in favour of Cuni 28 May 1541 (PRO 31/9 - 33/115); occ. 31 Aug. 1548 (SRO, Sent.Offic.St A.,fo.170).
 Cuni had some expectations x 28 May 1541 (v.sup.).

George Hepburn 1548 - 1580.
 Pres. by crown on death of Turing 11 Oct. 1548 (*RSS*,iii,no. 2990); bp. refused coll. 16 Oct. 1548 (*Brech.Reg.*,ii,196; *HMC* 57, *Home*,264), but he must have got poss. after that; occ. 7 June 1580 (*Brech.Reg.*,ii,215).

Edward Hepburn 1585 - 1596 x 1597.
 Pres. by crown on res. of George Hepburn 21 Oct. 1585 (Reg. Pres.,ii,138); occ. 20 July 1596 (SRO, Dalhousie, sec.16,no.971); res. by 14 May 1597 (v.inf.).

David Lindsay 1597.
James Shewan 1597 - 1613.
 Lindsay pres. by crown on res. of Edward Hepburn 14 May 1597 (Reg.Pres.,iii,6); perhaps same as prov. *R.bp.* 5 Nov. 1600.
 Shewan pres. by crown on res. of Edward Hepburn 23 May 1597 (Reg.Pres.,iii,5); occ. 20 June 1599 and 10 Oct. 1613 (SRO, Dalhousie, sec.16,nos.979,982).

Laurence Skinner 1623.
 Occ. 1 Oct. 1623 (SRO, Airlie, sec.48,no.82).

TREASURERS OF BRECHIN

First known date: 1219 x 1246.
 Prebend: ch. of Glenbervie by 1274 (*SHS Misc.*,vi,52); but this ch. became separate preb. in 1422 (*CSSR*, i,305; SRO, Transcripts from Vatican, Petitions, no.24; Cowan, *Parishes*, 74).

Henry (?) 1219 x 1236.
 Holds ch. of Glenbervie 1219 x 1236 (*Arb.Lib.*,i,179; cf. *Brech. Reg.*,ii,3).

A. 1219 x 1246.
 Occ. 1219 x 1246 (*Arb.Lib.*,i,185).

David de Inverbervie c.1256 - 1274-6.
 Holds ch. of Glenbervie c. 1256 (Fraser, *Grant*,iii,5); in poss.

1274-6 (*SHS Misc.*,vi,52,60).

John de Stowe (?) 1296.
Holds ch. of 'Glenkerny' i.e. Glenbervie 28 Aug. 1296 (*CDS*, ii,203).

Robert de Dundee 1298.
Occ. 1 June 1298 (*CPL*, i,575).

Radulf de Kininmund c.1329 x 1339.
Occ. c.1329 x 1339 (*Abdn.Reg.*,i,65).

Matthew de Arbroath 1372.
Occ. 24 May 1372 (*Brech.Reg.*,i,20).

John Lyell 1409 - 1436.
Occ. 9 Nov. 1409 (*Brech.Reg.*,i,34); occ. 1 Feb. 1436 (ibid.,73).

Patrick Reid 1438.
Got poss. on Lyell's death and gets papal conf. 5 Dec. 1438 (Reg.Supp.,353,fo.183v).

Thomas Archer 1439 - 1442.
David Reid 1440 - 1441 x 1442.
Archer occ. 13 June 1439 (*Brech.Reg.*,i,87); in poss. 19 Dec. 1442 (*CPL*,ix,263).
Reid lit. without poss. 23 Sept. 1440 (Reg.Supp.,367,fo. 290v); no poss. 11 Jan. 1441 (ibid.,370,fo.272v); res. right on exch. before 28 Apr. 1442 (ibid.,381,fo.290v).

Stephen Johannis/ de Mayr (cf. **Angus**) 1444.
Donald Machmahary 1444.
Johannis/ de Mayr held it before 24 Apr. 1444, by which date he was said to have adhered to Council of Basel (Reg.Supp.,396,fos.68, 268v).
Machmahary prov. on Archer's death or Johannis' depriv. 24 Apr. 1444 (Reg.Supp.,396,fo.68), unfruitfully.

Stephen de Angus (cf. **Johannis**) 1444 - 1477.
David Seton 1471.
Thomas de Camera 1476 - 1477.
Angus had prov. before 20 Nov. 1444 (Reg.Supp.,401,fo.55v); new prov. 20 Nov. 1445 (ibid.,408,fo.236v); occ. 19 Aug. 1448 (*Brech.Reg.*,i,124); occ. 27 May 1476 (ibid.,ii,277); still in poss. 5 Mar. 1477 (Reg.Supp.,748,fo.62).
Seton prov. on supposed death of Angus 18 Sept. 1471 (Reg. Supp.,671,fo.277v).
Camera had *com.priv.* against Angus 1 Aug. 1476 (Reg.Supp., 740,fos.168v-9), and again 5 Mar. 1477 (ibid.,748,fo.62).

Patrick Boyce 1493 - 1526.
Occ. 8 June 1493 (*Brech.Reg.*,ii,138); occ. 16 June 1526 (ibid., ii,181).

Arthur Boyce 1527 - 1532.

Occ. 21 Jan. 1527 (*Abdn.Fasti*,77-78); res. on exch. with right of return 26 Aug. 1532 (PRO 31/9 - 2/sub 8 Apr. 1533).

Charles Fotheringain 1532 - 1536.

Promises annates on exch. and gets prov. 26 Aug. 1532 (PRO 31/9 - 32/259-60); bp. has refused to obey prov., and is made to do so 8 Apr. 1533 (PRO 31/9 - 2/s.d.); res. promising annates to retain fruits 20 Oct. 1536 (PRO 31/9 - 33/45-46).

Robert Monypenny 1536 - 1537.

Promises annates and gets prov. without fruits 20 Oct. 1536 (PRO 31/9 - 33/46); occ. 24 Aug. 1537 (*RMS*,iii, no.1710).

Henry Sinclair 1538.

Occ. 15 July 1538 (*ER*,xvii,70); occ. 24 Sept. 1538 (*TA*,vi,367).

Thomas de Huchesoun/ Hugonis 1539.
David Methven 1539.

Hucheson had a right on papal authority and res. in Methven's favor 25 Aug. 1539 (PRO 31/9 - 33/88).

Methven prov. 25 Aug. 1539 after supp. granted 14 Aug. 1539 (ibid.).

James Arott 1541.

Occ. June 1541 (*Brech.Reg.*,ii,194).

James Wawane 1543.
James Ard 1543 - 1547.
Henry Sinclair 1543.

Wawane occ. 31 Jan. 1543 (SRO, Prot.Bk.Edward Diksoun, pp. 169-73); grants procuratory for res. 5 Feb. 1543 (ibid.).

Ard is to be coll. 31 Jan. 1543 (ibid.); occ. 19 Aug. 1547 (*Brech.Reg.*,ii.279).

Sinclair coll. by bishop's authority 6 June 1543 (SRO, Prot.Bk. Edward Diksoun, pp.169-73).

John Hepburn 1552 - 1596 x 1598.

Occ. 12 Nov. 1552 (SRO, Dalhousie, no.16/2215); occ. 20 July 1596 (ibid.,16/971); d. before 2 Jan. 1598 (v.inf.).

Henry Stirling 1598 - 1599.

Pres. by crown on Hepburn's death 2 Jan. 1598 (Reg.Pres.,iii, 35); occ. 20 June 1599 (SRO, Dalhousie, sec.16,no.979); cf. *Db.dean*.

John Norie 1613 - 1623 x 1625.

Occ. 10 Oct. 1613 (SRO, Dalhousie, sec. 16,no.982) and 1 Oct. 1623 (SRO, Airlie, sec. 48,no.82); d. before 15 Nov. 1625 (v.inf.).

Patrick Lindsay 1625.

Pres. by crown on Norie's death 15 Nov. 1625 (RSS,lxxxviii, fo.333).

William Ogilvie 1633.

Pres. by crown on Lindsay's death 19 Apr. 1633 (RSS,civ, fo.464).

SUBDEANS OF BRECHIN

First known date: 1296.
Prebend: called just subdeanery in 1372 (*Brech.Reg*.,i,19); ch. of Cookston at Reformation (*RMS*,vi,no.1730; Cowan, *Parishes*,35).

Nicholas 1296.
Prov. *B.bp*. when in poss. 26 Jan. 1296.

William de Fores 1355 - 1358 x 1371.
In poss. 11 Oct. 1355 after coll. by ord. and papal conf. (*CPP*, i,289; cf. Collect.,14,fos.180,189); still in poss. 11 Feb. 1358 (*CPP*, i,326); prob. d. 6 Mar. 1370 x 30 Mar. 1371 (see *M.archd*.).

Radulf Wild 1372.
Occ. 24 May 1372 (*Brech.Reg*.,i,19-20).

Walter Forrester 1386 x 1390 - 1407.
Prob. obtained poss. June 1386 x Nov. 1390 (see *St A.archd. Lothian*); occ. 20 May 1400 (*ER*,iii,508); prov. *B.bp*. 26 Nov. 1407.

Walter de Lichton 1410 - 1415.
Occ. 9 Apr. 1410 (*Brech.Reg*.,i,130-1) and in poss. 23 May 1415 (Reg.Av.,345,fo.595).

Hugh Henrici/ de Brechin 1430 - 1435.
In poss. 8 Dec. 1430 (*CPL*,viii,199); occ. 24 May 1435 (*Brech. Reg*.,i,132).

Henry Rynd 1448 - 1461.
Occ. 20 Aug. 1448 (*Brech.Reg*.,ii,72); prob. died 10 Mar. 1461 (see *Ab.treas*.).

William Rynd (Lion) 1461 - 1464.
Prov. on Henry Rynd's death under name 'Lion' 9 Apr. 1461 (Reg.Supp.,533,fo.78v); occ. 27 Apr. 1461 and 14 May 1464 under name 'Rynd' (*Brech.Reg*.,ii,275,103).

William Meldrum 1474.
Occ. 13 Sept. 1474 (*Brech.Reg*.,i,198).

James Balfour 1478 - 1481 x 1483.
Occ. 27 Mar. 1478 (*RMS*,ii,no.1377); occ. 13 June 1480 (ibid., ii,no.1441); prob. moved to *B.chanc*. 2 Mar. 1481 x 13 Mar. 1483.

James Meldrum 1490 - 1496.
Occ. 6 Oct. 1490 (*Brech.Reg*.,ii,135); occ. 21 Mar. 1496 (ibid.).

Thomas Meldrum 1504 - 1509.
Occ. 28 Dec. 1504 (*RMS*,ii,no.2842); occ. 26 Apr. 1509 (*Brech. Reg*.,ii,304); moved to *B.chanc*.

Andrew Keith 1510.
Pres. by crown on res. of Thomas Meldrum 20 Jan. 1510 (*RSS*,

i,no.1989).

Henry Fenton 1510.
> Occ. 26 Aug. 1510 (*Brech.Reg.*,ii,278).

Adam Simpson x1525.
> Held it at death before 26 Oct. 1525 (v.inf.).

Alexander Kerss 1525.
> Promises annates and gets prov. on Simpson's death 26 Oct. 1525 (PRO 31/9 - 32/76).

Thomas Nudry 1526 x 1527.
> Held it at death (v.inf.) i.e. July 1526 x Dec. 1527 (see *M.archd.*).

Sixtus Zucchellus 1529.
> Prov. by a cardinal with rights on death of Nudry 3 Sept. 1529 (PRO 31/9 - 32/135-6).

Robert Steill   1536 - 1546.
Patrick Forhous   1538 - 1539.
> **Steill** occ. 28 Apr. 1536 (*RMS*,ii,no.2411); occ. 19 Aug. 1547 (*Brech.Reg.*,ii,279).
> **Forhous** lit. against Steill and is challenged in king's council 13 Aug. 1538 (*ADCP*,472); res. claim to Steill without having had poss. 11 Jan. 1539 (SRO, Prot.Bk.Edward Diksoun, fo.41).

Robert Carnegie   1556 - 1596 x 1597.
William Carnegie 1559.
> **Robert** occ. 27 Mar. 1556 (*Laing Chrs.*,169); is to res. 8 Aug. 1559 (*RSS*,v,no.639); still in poss. 31 July 1576 (*Brech.Reg.*,ii,286); occ. 20 July 1596 (SRO, Dalhousie, sec.16,no.971); d. by 19 Apr. 1597 (v.inf.).
> **William** gets crown pres. 8 Aug. 1559 (*RSS*,v,no.639).

John Wemyss   1597 - 1623.
John Marschell   1602.
> **Wemyss** gets crown pres. on death of Robert Carnegie 19 Apr. 1597 (Reg.Pres.,iii,4); occ. 15 May 1608 (*Brech.Reg.*,ii,296) and 1 Oct. 1623 (SRO, Airlie,sec.48,no.82).
> **Marschell** gets crown pres. on death of Robert Carnegie 13 Jan. 1602 (RSS,lxxii, fo.220).

ARCHDEACONS OF BRECHIN

First known date: 1189 x 1198.
> Prebend: ch. of Strachan in 1274 (*SHS Misc.*,vi,52; Cowan, *Parishes*,189).

Gregory 1189 x 1198 - 1218.
> Occ. 1189 x 1198 (*Arb.Lib.*,i,124,nos.177-8); prov. *B.bp.* 15 Dec. 1218.

Adam 1242 - c.1245, perhaps 1254.

Occ. as 'A.' 1242 (*Arb.Lib.*,i,206); occ. as 'Adam' c. 1245 (BM, MS Add. 33245, fo.149); perhaps same as 'A.' who occ. 22 June 1254 (*Arb.Lib.*,i,324).

Adam Perhaps 1254, 1264.

Perhaps the 'A.' who occ. 22 June 1254 (v.sup.); was coll. after 1246, being *nepos* of Bp. Albin, and mand. issued for his depriv. 23 Jan. 1264 (*Reg.Urbain IV*,iii,160).

John Scot (?) 1275.

Perhaps had some right in this ben. Dec. 1275 (*SHS Misc.*,vi,70; cf. 52).

William Cresswell 1284 - 1285 x 1294.

Occ. 23 Nov. 1284 (BM, MS Julius D. IV,fo.167v); occ. 10 Jan. 1285 (R.J. Brentano, *York Metropolitan Jurisdiction*,233); prob. moved to *M.chanc.* by 26 Oct. 1294.

John de Kininmund 1295 - 1298.

Occ. 13 Feb. 1295 (NLS, Adv. MS 15.1.18,no.8); conf. *B.bp.* 1 June 1298.

Hugh de Selkirk 1308 (?), 1309.

Seal of an unnamed *B.archd.* was used 29 Sept. 1308 (SRO, Transcripts of Misc.Chrs., s.d.); occ. 23 Sept. 1309 (C.M. Fraser, *Records of Anthony Bek*, 155); occ. 1307 x 1320 (*C.A. Chrs.*,i,195).

Laurence de Haddington 1323 x 1327.

Occ. Oct. 1323 x Sept. 1327 (*Arb.Lib.*,i,339).

David de Mar 1343 - 1344.

In poss. 8 Mar. 1343 (*CPP*, i,15); later res. on exch. with Donald de Mar for *M.treas.*.

Donald de Mar 1344 - 1349.

Prov. on exch. with David de Mar. 28 Oct. 1344 (Collect.,14,fo. 158v; M. Fournier, *Les Statuts ... universités françaises*, iii,452-3); occ. 2 Mar. 1349 (*Brech.Reg.*,ii,394-5).

Laurence de Erroll   1352.
William de Greenlaw   1352 - 1353.

Erroll has poss. following earlier coll. by ord. 27 Feb. 1352 (*Brech.Reg.*,ii,394-5).

Greenlaw prov. 27 Feb. 1352 (ibid.); conf. of prov. 20 May 1353 (ibid.), but failed to get poss. (*Vet.Mon.*,311); see *St A.archd.*

Laurence de Spens x1366, x1370.

A 'Laurence' occ. before 11 Feb. 1366 (*RMS*, i,82; cf. Collect., 14,fo.180); 'Laurence de Spens' held it at death before 26 Nov. 1370. (v.inf.).

Stephen de Cellario 1370 - 1383.

Prov. after coll. by ord. on death of Spens 26 Nov. 1370 (Reg.Av., 172,fo.349v; *CPL*,iv,82); prov. *B.bp.* 12 June 1383.

Cuthbert de Brechin/ Henrici 1383.

Prov. 25 June 1383 (Reg.Av.,232,fo.145); if he had poss. he presumably res. on getting *B.prec*.

Thomas Stewart x1393.

Had some right which he res. in curia before 15 Apr. 1393 (v.inf.).

William de Ramsay 1393 - 1395.

Prov. on Stewart's res. 15 Apr. 1393 (Reg.Vat.,305,fo.197-8); in poss. 20 Oct. 1394 (Reg.Supp.,87,fo.134); in poss. still when related bull was expedited 15/19 Jan. 1395 (Reg.Av.,279,fos.492v-494).

John de Innes (?) 1397.

In poss. 24 Sept. 1397 (Reg.Av.,301,fos.382-382v); but prob. error for *C.archd*.

David de Idvy 1404 - 1420 x 1425.

In poss. 21 Mar. 1404 (*CPP*, i,625); occ. 10 May 1420 (*Brech. Reg*.,ii,273); held it at death before 4 May 1425 (*CSSR*,ii,81).

Richard de Crag	1426 - 1428.
Gilbert Forrester	1428 - 1459 x 1462.
William Fechet	1438.
David Hedewe	x1448.
David Stewart	1448.

Crag had poss. for two years before losing lit. with Forrester 10 Feb. 1428 (v.inf.).

Forrester had prov. but no poss. on Idvy's death, and wins lit. with Crag in curia 10 Feb. 1428 (*CPL*,viii,45); occ. 29 Oct. 1429 (*Brech.Reg*.,ii,70); still in poss. 28 June 1459 (*CPL*,xi,384); retained it until death (v.inf.).

Fechet gets *com.priv*. against Forrester 19 May 1438 (Reg.Supp., 347,fo,116), unfruitfully.

Hedewe had some right at death before 18 June 1448 (v.inf.).

Stewart prov. on Hedewe's death 18 June 1448 (*CPL*, x,380).

Richard Wylie	1458 - 1467.
George Liddell (Lydel)	1462.
John Graham	x1467.
Alexander Meldrum	1467.

Wylie had *com.priv*. against Forrester 16 May 1458 (Reg.Supp., 509,fo.277v); prov. on Forrester's death 31 July 1462 (*CPL*,xi,455-6); still in poss. 13 Nov. 1467 when appointed abbot of Kelso (ibid.,xii, 640).

Liddell prov. on Forrester's death 10 Aug. 1462 (*CPL*,xi,456-7); no poss. 31 Aug. 1462 (*CPL*,xii,150).

Graham said to have held it at death sometime before 27 Apr. 1467 (v.inf.).

Meldrum prov. on Graham's death 27 Apr. 1467 (Reg.Supp., 609, fo.43); d. before 20 Sept. 1468 (see *M.archd*.).

William Lowry/ Laurencii 1467 - 1490.

Prov. at king's request on Wylie's res. 19 Nov. 1467 (*CPL*,xii, 282); occ. in error as B. 'succentor' 9 Nov. 1470 (*A.B.Ill.*,iii,273); occ. 3 Nov. 1490 (*St A.Acta*,236).

David Pitcairn   1500 - 1552 x 1555.
James Pitcairn   1526, 1556 - 1564 x 1565.
Arthur Erskine   1563.

David Pitcairn occ. 15 Mar. 1500 (*Laing Chrs.*,61); occ. 12 Nov. 1552 (SRO, Dalhousie, no.16/2215); d. by 8 Jan. 1555 (NLS, MS Chr. 5875).

James Pitcairn apparently prov. on res. of David 8 Oct. 1526 (*Brech.Reg.*,ii,416; SRO, GD1/176/2/3); occ. 27 June 1556 (*Brech. Reg.*,ii,204); occ. 27 Oct. 1564 (SRO, Comm.Edin.Decreets, i,fo.199); d. before 15 Jan. 1565 (v.inf.).

Erskine occ. 1563 (*Thirds of Benefices*,230); res. right before 15 Jan. 1565 (v.inf.).

David Erskine   1565 - 1578.

Crown pres. on James Pitcairn's death and res. of Arthur Erskine 15 Jan. 1565 (*RSS*,v,no.1894); occ. 29 Nov. 1566 (*Brech. Reg.*,ii,284); occ. 3 Jan. 1578 (ibid.,ii,214).

Thomas Burnett   1608 - 1626.

Occ. 15 May 1608 (ibid.,ii,296); crown pres. on David Erskine's death 6 Dec. 1611 (RSS, lxxx, fo.195); occ. 16 Dec. 1626 (SRO, Part.Reg.Sasines Abdn.,v,fo.401).

OFFICIALS

OFFICIALS OF BRECHIN

First known date: 1202 x 1214.

William   1202 x 1214.
     Occ. 1202 x 1214 (*Arb.Lib.*,i,51,129).

Henry de Norham   1218 x 1222.
     Occ. 1218 x 1222 (ibid.,i,52).

John de Drum   1366.
     Occ. 14 Mar. 1366 (*CPP*, i,519).

Thomas Bell   1410 - 1433.
     Occ. 2 July 1410 (*Brech.Reg.*,i,26-27); occ. 10 Mar. 1433 (ibid., ii,37-39).

John Willelmi   1434 - 1470.
     Occ. 14 Apr. 1434 (ibid.,i,60); occ. 13 Oct. 1470 (St A.Univ. Mun.,SCB,fo.40v).

John Athilmar/ Aylmer/ Eldmer   1474 - 1480.
     Occ. 13 Sept. 1474 and 27 May 1476 (*Brech.Reg.*,i,198; ii,277); occ. 13 June 1480 (*RMS*,ii,no.1441).

David Garden (?) 1507.

As *B.comm.-general* uses seal of officialate 24 June 1507 (*Brech. Reg.*,ii,156-8).

Thomas Meldrum 1514 - 1519.

Occ. 1514 (Laing, *Seals*, i,no.986); occ. 2 Mar. 1519 (SRO, Dalhousie, section 17, no.6).

COMMISSARIES

COMMISSARIES OF BRECHIN

First known date: 1493.

But note that a 'sigillum commissariatus Brec.' from 12 Jan. 1411 is described from a March charter in Stevenson & Wood, *Seals*, i,133.

John Thomas 1493.

Occ. (C) 8 June 1493 (*Brech.Reg.*,ii,138).

David Garden 1507 - 1512.

Occ. (CG) 1500 x 1507 (SRO, Dalhousie, no.13/188); occ. (CG) 24 June 1507 (*Brech.Reg.*,ii,156); occ. (C) 10 Oct. 1507 and 8 Apr. 1512 (ibid.,ii,158; Stevenson & Wood, *Seals*, i,133).

James Robertson/ Robesoun 1545 - 1555 x 1562.

Occ. (CG) 12 Nov. 1545 (*RMS*,iii,no.3184) and 18 June 1550 (SRO, Dalhousie, no.18/631); occ. (C) 12 June 1555 (SRO, Acts and Decreets,xxi,fo.382); d. by 20 Mar. 1562 (ibid.,xxvi,fo.329).

Thomas Ramsay 1572.

Occ. (C) 30 Sept. 1572 (*RMS*,iv,no.2097).

CAITHNESS DIOCESE

BISHOPS OF CAITHNESS

First known date: 1147 x 1151.
　　This see was directly subject to the pope until placed under metropolitan authority of St Andrews 14 Aug. 1472 (*Vet.Mon*.,no. 852).

Angerius Brito (?) x1151.
　　May possibly have held this see before Andrew (cf. *Traditio*, xvii,475-7).

Andrew O.S.B. 1147 x 1151 - 1184.
　　Occ. 1147 x 1151 (*ESC*,no.189; *Dunf.Reg*.,8; cf. *Chron.Holyrood*, 121-2); had been a monk of Dunfermline (*Chron. Picts-Scots*,136); d. 29/30 Dec. 1184 (*Chron.Melrose*,45; *Chron.Bower*,ii,484; cf. Dowden, *Bishops*,232,n.1).

John 1187 (?), 1189 x 1199 - 1202.
　　Said to occ. 1187 (*HBC*,286, no source cited); occ. 1189 x 1199 (*Arb.Lib*.,i,17,99-100); in poss. 27 May 1198 (*Die Register Innocenz III*,i,no.218); prob. still in poss. after mutilation Aug./Sept. 1202 (*Innocentii III ... Opera Omnia*, ed.Migne, i,1062; cf. Dowden, *Bishops*, 233).

Adam O.Cist. 1213 - 1222.
　　El. when abbot of Melrose 5 Aug. 1213 (*Chron.Melrose*,57); cons. 11 May 1214 (ibid.,58); murdered 11 Sept. 1222 (ibid.,75-76).

Gilbert de Moravia 1222 or 1223 - 1245.
　　El. when *M.archd*. late 1222 or late 1223 (*Chron.Fordun*, i,289 ; *Chron.Wyntoun*,v,86-87; *Chron.Extracta*,93; *Chron.Bower*,ii,47-48); in poss. by 10 Apr. 1224 (*Vet.Mon*.,no.52); d. 1 Apr.,prob. 1245 (Sir R. Gordon, *Sutherland*, 32; cf. *CPL*,i,207; but see *ES*,ii,535, where 1243 is suggested).

William 1246 x 1247 - 1255.
　　Cons. 17 Sept. 1246 x 16 Sept. 1247 (*Rites of Durham*,152); occ. 16 Sept. 1255 (ibid.).

Walter de Baltroddie (Baltrodin) 1263 - 1270.
　　El. when C.canon and got mand. for conf. and cons. 13 June 1263 (*Vet.Mon*.,no.229); d. 1270 (*Chron.Bower*,ii,112).

Nicholas O.S.A. 1272 x 1273.
　　El. when abbot of Scone and C.canon and sought conf. from Gregory X i.e. after 27 Mar. 1272; but he was refused conf., and lic. issued for new el. 4 June 1273 (*CPL*, i,446).

Archibald Herok 1274 - 1275 x 1278.
　　El. when *M.archd*. in terms of mand. of 4 June 1273 (v.sup.), and got mand. for conf. and cons. 1 Nov. 1274 (*Vet.Mon*.,no.259); cons. 10 Jan. x 22 Sept. 1275 (*Beauly Chrs*.,57; *Bannatyne Misc*.,iii,21-24);

presumably d. before '9 Dec. 1278 (v.inf.).

Richard 1278 - 1279.
El. when *C.dean* before 9 Dec. 1278, but was refused conf. and mand. issued to persuade him to res. his right 9 Mar. 1279 (*Vet.Mon.*, no.270).

Harvey de Dundee (Donodei) O.S.A. 1279 x 1282.
El. as St A.canon after res. of Richard, but d. at curia while seeking conf.,prob. not long before 13 Apr. 1282 (*CPL*, i,464-5).

Alan de St Edmund 1282 - 1291.
Prov. and cons. at curia 13 Apr. 1282 (ibid.; cf. Dowden, *Bishops*, 238,n.3); d. 5 Nov. x 12 Dec. 1291 (*CDS*,ii,no.540; *Rot.Scot.*, i,6).

John 1291 x 1296.
El. when *C.archd.*, but this el.quashed by pope 29 Apr. 1296 (*CPL*, i,564).

Adam de Darlington 1296.
Prov. when *R.prec.* and cons. at curia 29 Apr. 1296 (*Vet.Mon.*, no.353); d. at Siena before 17 Dec. 1296 (v.inf.).

Andrew (de Buchan ?) O.Cist. 1296 - 1297 x 1304.
Prov. when abbot of Coupar Angus 17 Dec. 1296 (*Vet.Mon.*, no.359; cf. *C.A.Chrs.*,ii,269-70 for surname, for which the authority is not clear); see considered vacant still 29 July 1297 (*CDS*,ii,no.927); mand. for cons. 1 Aug. 1297 (*Vet.Mon.*,no.360); held it until his death sometime before 16 June 1304 (v.inf.).

Fercard Belegaumbe 1304 - 1321 x 1327.
El. when *C.dean* before 16 June 1304, when going to curia to get conf. (*CDS*,ii,no.1574); conf. with mand. for cons. at curia 22 Jan. 1306 (*CPL*,ii,8); temps. granted by Edward I 4 Apr. 1306 (*CDS*,ii,no.1752); occ. 10 July 1321 (*RMS*, i,no.84); see vacant by 11 Nov. 1327 (*ER*, i, 114).

David 1328 - 1329 x 1341.
Promised his common services on getting papal appointment 26 Jan. 1328 (Eubel, *Hierarchia*, i,176); prob. made fine for entry into his temps. 28 Aug. x 12 Nov. 1329 (*ER*, i,237; cf. 207; cf. Dowden, *Bishops*, 241, n.2); d. before 16 Jan. 1341 (v.inf.).

Alan de Moray 1341 - 1342.
El. when *Ab.archd.* and got conf. and cons. at curia 16 Jan. 1341 (*Vet.Mon.*,no.548); in poss. 22 May 1342 (*CPP*, i,l); d. in Scotland before 29 Nov. 1342 (v.inf.).

Thomas de Fingask 1342 - 1365 x 1369.
El. when *B.dean* and C.canon and got prov. 29 Nov. 1342 (*Vet. Mon.*,no.551); cons. by 1 Dec. 1342 (*CPL*,iii,68); occ. 13 Sept. 1360 (Fraser, *Sutherland*,iii,19); prob. still in poss. 21 Jan. 1365 (*CPL*,iv, 49); d. before 11 Jan. 1369 (v.inf.).

Malcolm de Drumbreck 1369 - 1379 x 1380.

El. when *Ab.chanc*. and C.canon before 11 Jan. 1369 (*ER*,ii, 300); prov. 21 Feb. 1369 (*Vet.Mon*.,no.681), cons. 24 Apr. 1369 x 16 Jan. 1370 (Collect.,14,fo.175v; *ER*,ii,328); occ. 3 Apr. 1373 (*APS*, i,562); prob. still in poss. Mar. 1379 x Feb. 1380 (*ER*,iii,25).

Alexander Man 1381 - 1412.

El. when *R.archd*. before 24 Sept. 1381 (*CPP*, i,556); prov. 21 Oct. 1381 (Eubel, *Hierarchia*, i,176), cons. before 10 Dec. 1381 (*CPP*, i,565); prob. still in poss. May 1412 (*ER*,iv,184).

Alexander Vaus 1414 - 1422.

Trans. from *O.bp*. without having yet had cons. 4 May 1414 (Eubel, *Hierarchia*, i,176), papal faculty for local cons. 22 Jan. 1415 (Reg.Av.,347,fo.403), cons. by 16 Jan. 1419 (*Melr.Lib*.,ii,499); trans. *Ga.bp*. 4 Dec. 1422.

John de Crannach 1422 - 1426.

Prov. 4 Dec. 1422 (Vat.Arch., Armaria, XII, 121,p.155,fo.79); new prov. 11 Dec. 1424 (*CPL*,vii,407); still not cons., though his agents have been drawing revenues from the see 9/14 May 1425 (*CSSR*,ii,85, 88-89); trans. to *B.bp*. still not cons. 7 June 1426.

Robert de Strathbrock (Strabrok) 1427 - 1445 x 1446.

El. and then prov. 4 June 1427 (*CPL*,viii,31; Eubel, *Hierarchia*, i,176); prob. cons. by 23 Jan. 1428 (*ACSB*,8), and certainly by 1 Apr. 1428 (*HMC* 26, *12th R*.,viii,123); occ. 10 Oct. 1444 (*RMS*,ii,no.281); prob. d. after 24 July 1445 (*ER*, v,235) and before 7 Apr. 1446 (v.inf.).

John de Innes 1446 - 1447 x 1448.

Prov. when *R.subd*. and *C.prec*. 7/8 Apr. 1446 (*ACSB*,35; *CPL*, ix,581; cf. x,290); still elect certainly 26 Feb. 1447 and prob. 5 June 1447 (Brady, *Episcopal Succession*, i,148); d. before 6 Jan. 1448 (v.inf.) after having had poss., but prob. no cons. (*CPL*, x,402).

Andrew Tulloch 1447 x 1448.
William Mudy   1448 - 1477.

Tulloch el. but not conf. (*CPL*, x,244), and d. before 23 Sept. 1448 (ibid.,45-46, 195).

Mudy prov. when *C.prec*. 6 Jan. 1448 (*ACSB*, 41; but see *CPL*, x,301); cons. 15 Mar. x 19 Apr. 1448 (*ACSB*, 41); occ. 30 June 1477 (*Brech.Reg*.,i,200).

Prosper Camogli de' Medici (de Camulio de Janua) 1478 - 1484.

Prov. 25 May 1478 (Eubel, *Hierarchia*, ii,122; cf. *ACSB*,xlvii - xlviii); granted temps. 12 Sept. 1481 (*RMS*,ii,no.1489); res. on or before 26 May 1484 (Dowden, *Bishops*,246).

John Sinclair 1484.

Prov. when *O.archd. Shetland* 26 May 1484 (Eubel, *Hierarchia*, ii,122); prob. never cons. as see is still considered vacant June 1494 and Aug. 1497 (*ADC*,i,334,341; *RSS*,i,nos. 119-20; cf. Dowden, *Bishops*,

247); d. before 21 Jan. 1501 (*RSS*, i,no.617).

Andrew Stewart senior 1501 - 1517.
    Prov. 26 Nov. 1501 (Eubel, *Hierarchia*,ii,122); prob. cons. by 26 Mar. 1502 when his common services were promised (Brady, *Episcopal Succession*,i,149), and certainly by 13 Mar. 1504 (*APS*,ii,273); d. June 1517, prob. 17 June 1517 (*Vet.Mon.*,no.927; cf. Dowden, *Bishops*, 248).

Andrew Stewart junior 1517 - 1540 x 1541.
    Crown nom. to pope 24 July 1517 (*Vet.Mon.*,no.919); prov. 14 Dec. 1517 (Eubel, *Hierarchia*,iii,159); occ. 10 Dec. 1540 (*RMS*,iii, no. 2232); d. shortly before 9 Aug. 1541 (*RSS*,ii,no.4157).

Robert Stewart   1541 - 1586.
Alexander Gordon   1544 - 1548.
    Stewart got crown nom. when *Dumbarton prov*. 8 Sept. 1541 (*James V Letters*,433; cf. *St A.Form.*,ii,143); papal grant of administration of see, being still under age, 27 Jan. 1542 (Eubel, *Hierarchia*,iii,159; Brady, *Episcopal Succession*, i,149); sequestered for treason 1545 (*St A.Form.*,ii,318-21); never cons., but retained title and some functions even after becoming earl of Lennox 1578 and then earl of March 1580 (Dowden, *Bishops*,249-50; *SP*,v,355); d. 29 Aug. 1586 (*SP*,ix,126).
    Gordon had crown nom. to replace Stewart 12 Dec. 1544 (*ERS*, ii,222-3), and again three more times 1545-6 (*HBC*,286, no sources cited); not known to have obtained prov. (Dowden, *Bishops*,249-50), and res. claim in Stewart's favour 6 Aug. 1548 (SRO, ADC & S,xxv, fo.32); retained pension on fruits at least until 1551 (Brady, *Episcopal Succession*,i,155-6).

Robert Pont 1586 - 1587.
    Crown prov. on death of Stewart, following crown nom. and el. by general assembly, dated '1586' but recorded after 20 June 1587 (Reg.Pres.,ii,176, where entry is cancelled); question was considered further by assembly, who notified king of their objection to episcopacy and of Pont's unwillingness to serve, 28 June 1587 (*BUK*, ii,688,696).

George Gledstanes 1600 - 1604.
    Crown prov. 5 Nov. 1600 (*RMS*,vi,no.1089); trans to *St A.bp*. 12 Oct. 1604.

Alexander Forbes 1604 - 1616.
    Crown prov. 12 Nov. 1604 (*RMS*,vi,no.1547); cons. just before 3 May 1611 (*Original Letters*, i,270); trans. to *Ab.bp*. 16/21 July 1616.

John Abernethy 1616 - 1638.
    Crown prov. 7 Dec. 1616 (Reg.Pres.,iv,139v); said to have res. on or before 5 Dec. 1638 (v.inf.); depriv. 13 Dec. 1638 (Peterkin, *Records*, i,28); d. before 27 Apr. 1639 (*RMS*,ix,no.1436).

Robert Hamilton 1638.

Crown nom. before 5 Dec. 1638 on renunciation of Abernethy, but this did not take effect (Baillie, *Journals*, i,152-3; cf. Peterkin, *Records*, i,181).

CHAPTER OF CAITHNESS

There were monks at Dornoch with some connection with Dunfermline abbey c.1139 x 1151 (*Dunf.Reg.*,no.23; *ESC*,no.132; cf. *RRS*, i,44); no doubt they had been brought there by their fellow-monk Bp. Andrew (cf. *Trans. Royal-Hist.Soc.*, 5th series,iii,98); this place was then under the influence of the earl of Orkney and may well have been ecclesiastically under the bishops of Orkney; about the same time (but it cannot be said whether before or after) the diocese of Caithness was separated from Orkney by David I as part of a deliberate move to detach the whole area north of the river Oykell from its Norse loyalties (cf. *PSAS*,lxxvii,115-16); possibly these monks at Dornoch were meant to serve the cathedral church of the new see; but nothing more is known of them, and in fact there is no evidence of the whereabouts of the cathedral under the first bishops, whose activities prob. centred on the episcopal manor of Halkirk on the Thurso river in the far north; it was there that Bp. Adam was murdered in 1222.

Under his successor Bp. Gilbert de Moravia (and with a new line of Scottish rather than Norse earls of Caithness after 1231) the centre of activity in the diocese moved to near its southern boundary with Ross, where the bishop and others of his family held lands around Dornoch (cf. *OPS*,II,ii,626-9; *Moray Reg.*, preface, nos. I - IV); he chose to develop the church at Dornoch as his cathedral, both by a building programme and by establishing a chapter of a collegiate character in place of the one priest who had previously served it; a draft survives of his constitution and statutes for a community of ten canons headed by himself and including five dignitaries (*Bannatyne Misc.*,iii,17-21 with facsimile; Fraser, *Sutherland*,iii,3-6); this document is incomplete and undated, but the details in it lie behind the papal bull of conf. issued 21 Mar. 1238 x 20 Mar. 1239 (*Reg. Gregoire IX*, no. 4423); this constitution affected the revenues of every parish in the diocese, and so it was probably some time before it was fully effective; but it was certainly working by the 1270s (*SHS Misc.*,vi,51-52, 68-69; Fraser, *Sutherland*,iii,8-9; cf. *MRHS*,167; *RCSHS*,xiv,35-37, 42-43).

DEANS OF CAITHNESS

First known date: 1238-9 (v.sup.).

Prebend: ch. of Clyne, etc. in 1238-9 (*Bannatyne Misc.*,iii,18: Cowan, *Parishes*,32).

Richard 1274 - 1282.

Occ. 1 Nov. 1274 (*Vet.Mon.*,104); has been el. *C.bp.*, but is told

to res. 9 Mar. 1279; prob. still in poss. 13 Apr. 1282 (*CPL*, i,464).

Fercard Belegaumbe 1304 - 1306.
Occ. 16 June 1304, when already *C.bp.-elect (CPR 1301-7*,232); conf. *C.bp.* 22 Jan. 1306.

Adam Herok 1341 x 1358.
Held it sometime before 11 Feb. 1358 (v.inf.), presumably after 16 Jan. 1341 when found as *C.chanc.*.

William de Fores 1358 - 1362 x.
Prov. after coll. by ord. 11 Feb. 1358 (*CPL*,iii,594-5); prob. retained it until he became *M.archd.* sometime after 23 Dec. 1362.

Malcolm de Alves 1363.
Occ. 12 Nov. 1363 (*Moray Reg.*,313).

Alexander de Sutherland c.1420/1426 - 1435.
Robert Scrymgeour 1432 - 1436.
Sutherland has poss. 18 Feb. 1432, when said to have held it for c. 6 years (Reg.Supp.,275,fo.230v); said 3 Aug. 1434 to have held it for c. 14 years (*CPL*,viii,496), loses lit. against Scrymgeour 17 Jan. 1435 (ibid.,viii,489).

Scrymgeour gets *com.priv.* against Sutherland 18 Feb. 1432 (Reg.Supp.,275,fo.230v) and again 3 Aug. 1434 (*CPL*,viii,496); wins lit. 17 Jan. 1435 (v.sup.); no peaceable poss. 17 June 1435 (Reg.Supp., 320,fo.92); claims poss. 17 Sept. 1435 (ibid.,312,fo.77), though was being molested 23 May 1436 (ibid.,325,fo.221v), d. by 5 Nov. 1436 (*CPL*,viii,604,606).

Patrick Fraser 1436 - 1455.
Andrew de Tulloch 1445.
Fraser prov. on Scrymgeour's death 8 Nov. 1436 (*CPL*,viii,606); occ. 18 Sept. 1455 (*RMS*,ii,no.1404).

Tulloch gets *com.priv.* against Fraser 10 July 1445 (Reg.Supp., 407,fo.22v; *Caithness Recs.*,i,241) unfruitfully.

James Kennedy 1462.
Andrew Symon 1462.
John de Ferne 1462.
Martin Vaus 1461 x 1462 - 1466 x 1468.
Alexander Lumsden 1466.
Kennedy prov. on Fraser's death 27 Aug. 1462 (*CPL*,xi,458).
Symon prov. 18 Sept. 1462 (Reg.Supp.,555,fo.75v).
Ferne prov. on Fraser's death 2 Oct. 1462 (*CPL*,xi,460).
Vaus prov. Sept. 1461 x Sept. 1462 (*CPL*,xii,p.xxvi; cf. *ACSB*, 278); lit. about his claim 19 Sept. 1462 (Reg.Supp.,555,fo.204); in poss. 19 Sept. 1466 (*CPL*,xii,552); prob. moved to *R.dean*. 27 Sept. 1466 x 14 May 1468.
Lumsden prov. on Kennedy's death 15 June 1466 (Reg.Supp., 596,fo.274v).

Donald Ross 1481 - 1487.

In poss. 27 Aug. 1481 (*ACSB*,203); occ. 12 Sept. 1487 (*RMS*, ii,no.1694).

Adam Gordon   1492 - 1514/1529.
Nicholas Grulatris   1507.
     Gordon occ. 4 Feb. 1492 (Fraser, *Grant*,iii,41); occ. 22 Sept. 1514 (*Laing Chrs.*,77); said to have died 5 June 1529 (Walcott, *Ancient Church in Scotland*,129); but obit held on 28 May (*PSAS*, ii,258).
     Grulatris had prov. but res. in favour of Gordon 24 Mar. 1507 (PRO 31/9 - 31/185).

Alexander Sutherland   1529 - 1552.
     Occ. 12 June 1529 (*Moray Reg.*,416,no.435); occ. 23 Oct. 1550 (SRO, Sent.Offic.St A.,fo.222); still alive 15 Jan. 1552 (see *M.offic.*); obit came to be held on 7 Apr. (*PSAS*,ii,257).

William Hepburn   1552 - 1563 x 1565.
     Occ. 13 May 1552 (SRO, Dalhousie, sec.17,no.646); occ. 14 June 1563 (SRO, Mackintosh Mun.,no.76); d. by 4 Jan. 1565 (*Thirds of Benefices*,169; cf. 120 for date).

Gavin Borthwick   1565 - 1606 x 1608.
Adam Hepburn   1565.
     Borthwick pres. by crown on William Hepburn's death 30 Nov. 1565 (*RSS*,v,no.2466); coll. by bp. 19 July 1566 (Sutherland Mun., xiii,l,4); occ. 16 Oct. 1606 (SRO, Secretary's Reg.Sasines Inverness, fo.163); dem. by 15 Jan. 1608 (v.inf.).
     Hepburn pres. by crown on William Hepburn's death 20 Dec. 1565 (*RSS*,v,no.2505); occ. 25 Dec. 1565 (SRO, Reg.Deeds,viii,fo. 200).

John Gray   1608 - 1638.
     Crown pres. on dem. of Borthwick 15 Jan. 1608 (RSS,lxxvi,fo. 208); d. in poss. Jan. 1638 (SRO, Reg. of Retours,xxiv,fo.30).

PRECENTORS/CHANTERS OF CAITHNESS

First known date: 1238-9 (v.sup.).
     Prebend: ch. of Creich, etc. in 1238-9 (*Bannatyne Misc.*,iii,18; Cowan, *Parishes*, 38-39).

Note: there was an unnamed incumbent Dec. 1274 - June 1275 (*SHS Misc.*,vi,51,69) and 22 Sept. 1275 (Fraser, *Sutherland*,iii,8).

Thomas de Urquhart   1350.
     Prob. in poss. 3 Nov. 1350 when described as prec. 'Chatenensis' in Ross dioc. (*Vet.Mon.*,294).

John Derling   1358 - 1368.
     Occ. 12 Nov. 1358 (Fraser, *Grant*,iii,10) and 1368 (*OPS*,II,ii,617).

Alexander Vaus 1398.

Apparently in poss. when prov. *C archd*. 25 July 1398.

Alexander de Sutherland x1420.

Held it for more than a year sometime before 16 Jan. 1428 (*CPL*, viii,44), prob. before 1420 (see *C.dean.*).

John Lichton 1422 x 1426.

Res. on exch. with Tulloch for a parochial ben. 1422 x 1426 (*CPL*,viii,44).

Robert de Tulloch 1422 x 1426 - 1437 x 1438.

Got poss. on exch. through ord. and then had papal prov. 16 Jan. 1428 (*CPL*,viii,44); still in poss. 3 Nov. 1437 (Reg.Supp.,344,fo.40v); res. by 24 July 1438 (v.inf.).

John de Innes   1438 - 1446.
John Kennochson   1444.

Innes had coll. by ord. on res. of Tulloch (cf. *M.succ.*) some six years before 24 July 1444, when still in poss. (Reg.Supp.,398,fo.174); in poss. when prov. *C.bp*. 7/8 Apr. 1446; d. prob. uncons. June 1447 x Jan. 1448.

Kennochson prov. 24 July 1444 (Reg.Supp.,398,fo.174); promised annates 26 Aug. 1444 (PRO 31/9 - 28/140-1); prob. no poss. (cf. Reg.Supp.,399,fo.48).

William Mudy   1446 - 1448.
William Wincester 1447.

Mudy prov. on Innes's promotion 29 Apr. 1446 (Reg.Supp.,411, fo.154); in poss. when prov. *C.bp*. 6 Jan. 1448.

Wincester had coll. by ord. and lit. with Mudy without poss. July/Oct. 1447 (*CPL*,x,312,346-7); lit. without poss. 21 Oct. 1447 (Reg.Supp.,420,fo.55v); res. right after prov. *M.treas*. 27 Oct. 1447 (ibid.,436,fo.166v).

Robert Stewart   1448 - 1450.
Gilbert Forrester x1449.
John Wylie   1449 - 1454.

Stewart prov. on Mudy's elevation 8 Mar. 1448 (*CPL*,x,370-1); lit. with Wylie 12 Mar. 1450 (Reg.Supp.,441,fo.168v).

Forrester res. some right before 29 Apr. 1449 (v.inf.).

Wylie had poss. after prov. by ord. in virtue of a papal indult, and got conf. after res. of Forrester and assecution of Wincester 29 Apr. 1449 (Reg.Supp.,436,fo.166v); new prov. while lit. with Stewart 12 Mar. 1450 (ibid.,441,fo.168v); still in poss. 7 Nov. 1454 (*CPL*,x, 687), but was depriv. by ord. (ibid.,xi,320).

John Kennochson/ Kenniti 1455 - 1457.

Occ. 18 Sept. 1455 (*RMS*,ii,1404); had been coll. by ord. on Wylie's depriv., and got papal prov. 7 May 1457 (*CPL*,xi,320).

Alexander Stewart 1478.

After prov. and poss. gets new prov. 1 Apr. 1478 (Reg.Supp., 767,fo.35).

James Auchinleck/ Achlek   c.1479 - 1496 x 1497.
David Maistertoun   1496.
    Auchinleck pres. by crown c.1479 (*ADC*,ii,37); occ. under name Achlek 28 Feb. 1484 (Fraser, *Cromartie*,ii,337); in poss. 19 July 1496 (*ADC*,ii,36); res. or d. before Sept. 1497 (v.inf.).
    Maistertoun has raised lit. in curia against Auchinleck, but withdraws in king's council 19 July 1496 (*ADC*,ii,36-37).

Nicholas Paterson   1497.
James Betoun   1497 - 1498 x 1499.
John Poilson   1497 - 1512.
    Paterson gets crown pres. on Kennochson's death 10 Aug. 1497 (*RSS*, i,no.119).
    Betoun gets crown pres. on Auchinleck's death 17 Sept./11 Oct. 1497 (ibid.,i,nos.136,145); gets condemnation of Poilson in king's council for barratry 3 Feb. 1498 (*ADC*,ii,98); res. before 3 Nov. 1499 (v.inf.).
    Poilson gets crown pres. on res. of Auchinleck 20 Sept. 1497 and again on res. of Betoun 3 Nov. 1499 (*RSS*, i,nos.138,426); occ.1512 (*TA*,iv,365).

Thomas Murray   1515 or 1516 - 1546.
Alexander Gray   1543.
    Murray occ. 9 Mar. 1515 or 1516 (*OPS*,II,ii,618); occ. 6 July 1522 (Fraser, *Sutherland*,iii,72); occ. 23 Apr. 1545 (Innes, *Sketches*, 85n); occ. 1546 (*OPS*,II,ii,618).
    Gray occ. 2 Mar. 1543 (Dunrobin, Sutherland Chrs.,v,26,200).

Angus Murray 1549 - 1550.
    Occ. 6 Aug. 1549 (SRO, Mey,no.50) and 6 Sept. 1550 (*RSS*,iv, no.883).

Robert Stewart 1557 - 1563.
    Occ. 26 Mar. 1557 (Fraser, *Sutherland*,iii,124) and 12 June 1563 (*RSS*, v,no.1340).

Gilbert Gray 1577 - 1583.
    Occ. 1 June 1577 (Sutherland Mun.,xiii,3,20); res. on or before 4 June 1583 (v.inf.).

Donald Logan 1583 - 1584.
    Crown pres. on res. of Gray 4 June 1583 (Reg.Pres.,ii,90); adm. and coll. by bp. 31 Dec. 1584 (Sutherland Mun.,xiii,1,10).

William Pape 1599 - 1607.
    Crown pres. on death of Logan 22 Nov. 1599 (Reg.Pres.,iii,31); occ. 29 Oct. 1607 (SRO, Secretary's Reg.Sasines Inverness,fo.347).

Alexander Duff 1625.
    Occ. 26 May 1625 (SRO, Part. Reg.Sasines Inverness,iii,fo.119).

John Hossack 1631.
    Occ. 8 June 1631 (ibid.,iv,fo.325).

CHANCELLORS OF CAITHNESS

First known date: 1238-9 (v.sup.).
      Prebend: ch. of Rogart, etc. in 1238-9 (*Bannatyne Misc*,iii,18-19; Cowan, *Parishes*, 172).

Note: there was an unnamed incumbent Dec. 1274 - June 1275 (*SHS Misc.*,51,69) and 22 Sept. 1275 (Fraser, *Sutherland*,iii,8-9).

Adam Herok 1330 x 1338 - 1341 x 1358.
      In poss. 16 Jan. 1341 (*Vet.Mon.*,276; *CPL*,ii,552), having prob. obtained it Dec. 1330 x Jan. 1338 (see *M.treas*.); prob. res. on getting *C.dean*. at some date before 1358.

John Wasil 1366 - 1371.
      In poss. 9 June 1366 (*CPP*,i,528) and 9 Aug. 1371 (Reg.Av., 177,fo.381v).

Thomas Wys 1381.
      In poss. 12 Dec. 1381 (*CPP*, i,561).

John de Aberchirder (Abyrkerdor) 1390.
      Held it and res. on exch. with Longforgan on or before 19 May 1390 (*Moray Reg.*,203).

William de Longforgan (Lonkfordyn, Loneford) 1390 x 1392.
      Aberchirder gets coll. by ord. on exch. to benefices which Longforgan has res. 19 May 1390 (ibid.); he had coll. by ord. on exch. too, and d. before 28 May 1392 (Reg.Av.,281,fos.129-129v).

Gilbert Vaus 1429.
      In poss. 8 Apr. 1429 (*CPL*,viii,85).

Walter Idill 1435 - 1439.
      Occ. 4 Nov. 1435 (*Mon.Conc.Bas.*,ii,832); occ. 24 July 1439 (*Abdn.Reg.*,i,237).

David de Dischington   1441 x 1442 - 1445.
Alexander de Rattray   1443 - 1445.
      Dischington had coll. by ord. on death of Vaus, and by 2 Nov. 1443 has been in poss. more than one year but less than two (*CPL*, ix,348); new prov. while lit. with Rattray 21 July 1445 (Reg.Supp., 407,fo.101v); still lit. 12 Aug. 1445 (*CPL*,ix,532).
      Rattray prov. 2 Nov. 1443 (*CPL*,ix,348); prob. no poss. 12 Aug. 1445 (v.sup.).

Thomas White 1455 - 1466.
      Occ. 18 Sept. 1455 (*RMS*,ii,no.1404); occ. 27 Oct. 1466 (Fraser, *Cromartie*,ii,334).

William Tarall 1497.
      Has poss. and is to res. 13 Aug. 1497 (v.inf.).

Patrick Dunbar 1497 - 1512, 1521/1523.

Crown pres. on res. of Tarall 13 Aug. 1497 (*RSS*, i,no.120);
occ. 1512 (*TA*,iv,364); prob. moved to *Ab.chanc*. 1521/1523.

William Fudes 1520(?) 1524 - 1527 x 1529.
Said to occ. 1520 (*TGSI*,xxviii,269, no source given); occ. 20
July 1524 (*Munro Writs*, no.45); occ. 18 Nov. 1527 (*RMS*,iii,no.527);
d. by 6 Mar. 1529 (*RSS*, i,no.4105).

John Matheson 1532 - 1554.
Occ. 4 Dec. 1532 (SRO, Reg.Ho.Chr.no.1082B) and 28 Feb.
1554 (*RSS*,iv,no.2441).

John Jackson/Jersone 1557 - 1567 x 1572.
Occ. under name Jersone 26 Mar. 1557 (Fraser, *Sutherland*,iii,
124); occ. as Jackson 20 Feb. 1558 (*RMS*,iv,no.1260) and 19 July
1567 (SRO,Mey,no.115); res. before 17 Apr. 1572 (v.inf.).

George Sinclair 1572 - 1593.
Crown pres. on Jackson's res. 17 Apr. 1572 (*RSS*,vi,no.1562);
occ. 28 Oct. 1574 (*RMS*,iv,no.2315) and 24 Jan. 1593 (SRO, Mey,
no. 2426); res. before 15 Feb. 1593 (v.inf.).

Thomas Pape 1593 - 1610.
Crown pres. on Sinclair's res. 15 Feb. 1593 (RSS,lxv,fo.19); occ.
1610 (*OPS*,II,ii,619).

John Sutherland 1617 - 1631.
Occ. 4 Apr. 1617 (Sutherland Mun.,xiii,8,62) and 8 June 1631
(SRO, Part.Reg.Sasines Inverness,iv,fo.325).

TREASURERS OF CAITHNESS

First known date: 1238-9 (v.sup.).
Prebend: ch. of Lairg, etc. in 1238-9 (*Bannatyne Misc*.,iii,18-19;
Cowan,*Parishes*, 126); ch. of Spittal in 1579 (*RSS*,vii,no.1939; cf.
Cowan,*Parishes*, 186).

Patrick 1274.
In poss. 1 Nov. 1274 (*CPL*, i,448).

Gilbert de Rosemarkie 1329 - 1341.
In poss. 24 Nov. 1329 (*CPL*,ii,301); still in poss. 16 Jan. 1341
(*Vet.Mon*.,276; *CPL*,ii,552).

Thomas Murchie   x1431.
Thomas Wiseman   x1431.
Murchie held it sometime before 12 May 1431 (Reg.Supp.,269,
fo.231).
Wiseman held it prob. after Murchie and res. before 12 May 1431
(ibid.).

Patrick de Wardlaw 1431 - 1445 x 1447.
William Leuchars   1445.

Wardlaw had coll. by ord. and has poss. when gets new prov. 12 May 1431 (Reg.Supp.,269,fo.231); conf. after two years of poss. without disp. 5 Aug. 1433 (ibid.,287,fo.276v); still in poss. 19 June 1445 (ibid.,406,fo.169v); res. before 20 Dec. 1447 (v.inf.).

Leuchars gets *com.priv.* against Wardlaw 3 Apr. 1445 (ibid.,404, fo.242) unfruitfully.

David Stewart 1447 - 1448.

Got it on res. of Wardlaw, and gets new prov. 20 Dec. 1447 (Reg. Supp.,421,fo.235v); res. to ord. before 18 June 1448 (v.inf.; cf. *CPL*, x,378).

Thomas de Dingwall 1448 - 1454.

After coll. by ord. on res. of Stewart, gets prov. 18 June 1448 (Reg.Supp.,427,fo.196; *CPL*,x,378); occ. 4 Oct. 1451 and 21 Apr. 1454 (Fraser, *Cromartie*,ii,325,327).

Thomas Tulloch 1455.

Res. some right to ord. certainly before 8 Jan. 1456 and prob. just before William Tulloch got coll. (*CPL*,xi,246-7).

William Tulloch 1455 - 1456 x 1461.

Occ. 18 Sept. 1455 (*RMS*,ii,no.1404); had had coll. by ord. less than one year before 8 Jan. 1456, when he got papal prov. (*CPL*,xi, 246-7); res. to ord. some time before prov. *O.bp.* 11 Dec. 1461 (*CPL*, xii,134,170,194).

Andrew Wishart 1461 - 1481.

Had coll. by ord. on res. of William Tulloch before 11 Dec. 1461 (v.sup.); papal prov. 18 May 1463 (*CPL*,xii,170, 194-5); occ. 24 Oct. 1481 (*Orkney Recs.*,194).

Thomas Myrton 1494.
Thomas Hay 1494.

Both claim it and agree to accept arbitration 23/27 June 1494 (*ADC*, i,334-5, 341-2).

Walter Mersare 1515.

Occ. 31 [May] 1515 (*RSS*, i,no.2570).

Thomas Stewart 1528 - 1546.

Occ. 16 Jan. 1528 (NRA, Balledmund Chrs.,11); occ. 23 Apr. 1545 (Innes, *Sketches*, 85n); occ. 1546 (*OPS*,II,ii,620; see also Stevenson & Wood, *Seals*,iii,617, where he is wrongly called *R.treas.* at this date).

William Gordon 1547 - 1566 x 1571.
David Carnegie 1547?, 1548.
John Gordon 1560 - 1575.

William Gordon gets crown pres. on death or res. of Stewart 27 Mar. 1547 (*RSS*,iii,no.2228); occ. 18 May 1561 (*RMS*.iv,no.2995); is to res. or had res. 20 May 1566 (*RSS*,v,no.2838); d. by 23 Apr. 1571 (*RSS*,vi,no.1150; cf. no. 1207).

Carnegie said to occ. 1547 (*TGSI*,xxviii,269, no source quoted); pres. by crown on Stewart's death 15 Apr. 1548 (*RSS*,iii,no.2717).

John Gordon occ. 25 May 1560 (SRO, Reg.Deeds,v,fo.115), gets royal conf. of rights obtained from pope 20 May 1566 (*RSS*,v,no. 2838); occ. 20 July 1575 (SRO, Comm. Edin.Decreets,vii,s.d.).

William Gray 1577 - 1607.
Alexander Barclay 1579.

Gray occ. 1577 (*OPS*,II,ii,620); gets crown pres. on death of John Gordon 29 July 1580 (*RSS*,vii,no.2437); dem. before 16 June 1606 in favour of his son James (v.inf.), but occ. still in poss. 29 Oct. 1607 (SRO, Secretary's Reg. Sasines Inverness,fo.347).

Barclay gets crown pres. on death of John Gordon 18 June 1579 (Reg.Pres.,ii,20; *RSS*,vii,no.1939).

James Gray 1606 - 1638.

Crown pres. on dem. of William Gray 16 June 1606 (RSS,lxxv, fo.114); occ. 7 June 1638 (SRO, Reg.Deeds, vol. 527, fo.310); the 'Alexander' Gray said to occ. 1610 (*OPS*,II,ii,620) is presumably an error.

ARCHDEACONS OF CAITHNESS

First known date: 1238-9 (v.sup.).

Prebend: chs. of Bower and Watten, etc. in 1238-9 (*Bannatyne Misc.*,iii,18-19; Cowan, *Parishes*,22,207).

Note: this ben. is not mentioned in accounts of papal collector for period Dec. 1274-June 1276 (*SHS Misc.*,vi,51-52,68-69); but an unnamed incumbent occ. 22 Sept. 1275 (Fraser, *Sutherland*,iii,8).

John 1296.

In poss. 29 Apr. 1296 after el. as *C.bp*. had been cancelled by pope (*CPL*, i,564).

Fercard Belegaumbe 1297.

Pres. by Edward I 29 July 1297 (CDS,ii,no.927); became *C.dean* before 16 June 1304.

Andrew de Hirdmaniston 1328 - 1329.

Occ. 8 May 1328 (*Moray Reg.*,152); prov. *M.dean*. and is to res. 19 Sept. 1329 (*CPL*,ii,298).

John Todd 1329.

Prov. 24 Nov. 1329 (*CPL*,ii,302).

William de Fores 1355.
John de Lancford 1358.

Fores prov. on Todd's death 11 Oct. 1355 (*CPL*,iii,543; *CPP*,i, 289), but did not get poss. (Collect.,14,fo.165).

Lancford had coll. by ord. on Todd's death and got prov. 12 Feb. 1358 (*CPL*,iii,594).

John de Moray 1365.

Occ. 1365 (*OPS*,II,ii,620-1).

William de Forrester 1382.
    In poss. 25 Jan. 1382 (*CPP*, i,563).

John de Innes 1396 - 1398.
    Occ. 1396 (*Moray Reg.*,206); still in poss. 25 July 1398 when depriv. (v.inf.).

Alexander Vaus 1398.
    Prov. 25 July 1398 on depriv. of Innes (Reg.Av.,322,fos.368v-369v); in poss. when prov. *O.bp*. at some date before 7 Nov. 1407 (v.inf.).

Alexander Barber	1407 - 1419 x 1421.
Thomas de Greenlaw	1414 - 1419 x 1428.
Nicholas Tunnok	1421 - 1422.
Thomas Duncan	1426.
Thomas de Tulloch	1428 - 1437.

    Barber prov. 7/20 Nov. 1407 (Reg.Supp.,102,fo.257v; Reg. Av., 329,fos.203v-204v); occ. 25 Oct. 1408 (Fraser, *Douglas*,iii,367-8); lit. with Greenlaw by 9 June 1414 (v.inf.); claims poss. 3 Jan. 1416 (*CPP*, i,605); new prov. 10 June 1419 (*CSSR*, i,71-72); d. before 7 Apr. 1421 while still lit. (*CPL*,vii,185).
    Greenlaw had coll. by ord. and is said to have poss. while lit. with Barber 9 June 1414 (*CPP*, i,602; *CSSR*, i,62-63); new prov. 1 June 1419 (*CSSR*, i,62-63), but lit. continued; res. on local exch. with Tulloch before 12 Mar. 1428 (*ACSB*,96).
    Tunnok gets surrog. to Barber's right 7 Apr. 1421 (*CPL*,vii,185); new prov. 20 Apr. 1422 (*CSSR*, i,302) but perhaps no poss.
    Duncan prov. in succession to Tunnok 4 Aug. 1426 (*ACSB*,93).
    Tulloch had local exch. with Greenlaw and then gets prov. 12 Mar. 1428 (*ACSB*,96); still in poss. 6 July 1437 (Reg.Supp.,337,fo. 127v); is to res. on prov. to parochial ben. 15 July 1437 (*CPL*,viii, 583).

James Bruce	1437.
Laurence Piot	1437 - 1440.
Alexander de Rattray	1438 - 1440 x 1443.
Alexander de Lichton	1440.
David Reid	1440.
David Stewart	1440.
James de Innes	1440 - 1442.
Richard Dor	1441.
William de Sutherland	1443 - 1443 x 1445.

    Bruce prov. on res. of Tulloch 15 July 1437 (*CPL*,viii,583); is to dem. in favour of Piot if he gets another ben. 12 Sept. 1437 (Reg. Supp.,341,fo.107v).
    Piot had expectations 12 Sept. 1437 (v.sup.); claimed a right Oct. 1438 (Reg.Supp.,368,fo.196v), but had no poss. before this right was extinguished on prov. as *Ab.archd*. 20 Feb. 1440 (*CPL*,viii,295; cf. ix, 107; *ACSB*,130).
    Rattray had coll. by ord. on supposed death of Piot and by 26 Oct. 1440 had had poss. for two years (Reg.Supp.,368, fo.196v); lost

poss. before 18 May 1443 (v.inf.).

Lichton prov. 27 July 1440 (Reg.Supp.,366,fo.14v); had no poss. by 23 Sept. 1440 when prov. *Db.chanc*. and instructed to resign right here (Reg.Supp.,367,fo.290v; *CPL*,ix,131).

Reid prov. 23 Sept. 1440 (Reg.Supp.,367,fo.290v); res. right without poss. 26 Oct. 1440 (ibid.,368,fos.196v,104v).

Stewart lit. 19 Oct. 1440 (ibid.,368,fo.107) - perhaps error for Reid.

Innes prov. on Reid's res. 26 Oct. 1440 (Reg.Supp.,368,fo. 196v); new prov. 4 Aug. 1442 (ibid.,383,fo.213); new prov. in succ. to right of Piot and Reid 20 Aug. 1442 (*ACSB*,130-1); d. May x Oct. 1447 prob. without poss. (see *M.dean/treas*.).

Dor prov. 27 Jan. 1442 (Reg.Supp.,379,fo.251).

Sutherland got. poss. in succ. to right of Lichton, and then got prov. 18 May 1443 (Reg.Supp.,390,fo.50v); res. on exch. through ord. with Holland before 3 Feb. 1445 (*CPL*,ix,465).

Richard de Holland   1443 x 1445 - 1448.
Alexander de Sutherland 1445 - 1477.
Hector de Tulloch   1445.

Holland got poss. on exch. through ord. before 3 Feb. 1445 (v.sup.); lost poss. but won sentence in lit. with Alexander de Sutherland 17 June 1446 (*CPL*,ix,543-4); still lit. 18 July 1448 (v.inf.).

Sutherland got *com.priv*. against Holland 3 Feb. 1445 (*CPL*, ix,465); had poss. by 17 June 1446 when Holland was winning lit. (ibid.,543-4); continuing lit. against Holland 18 July 1448 (Reg. Supp.,428,fo.135v); presumably successful as still in poss. 12 Feb. 1477 (ibid.,748,fo.184v).

Tulloch got prov. against rights of both Holland and Sutherland 18 May 1445 (Reg.Supp.,405,fo.262).

James Forrester 1497 - 1498.
    Occ. 2 Nov. 1497 and 17 July 1498 (*ADC*,ii,83,281).

George Stewart 1512.
    Occ. 26 Feb. 1512 (*RSS*, i,no.2377).

John Dingwall   1516 - 1532 x 1533.
James Brady   1525 - 1556.
William Gordon 1529.

Dingwall occ. 13 Oct. 1516 (*TA*,v,57); agrees to pension on fruits for John Thornton 8 Sept. 1522 (*St A.Form*.,ii,79); occ. 21 July 1525 (Fraser, *Eglinton*, ii,101); res. but promises annates for keeping fruits 26 Oct. 1525 (PRO 31/9 - 32/77-78; cf. *Edin. Trin.prov*.); prob. still in poss. 15 June 1531, though source describes him as *C.chanc*. (*RMS*,iii,no.1065); d. 6 Sept. 1532 x 7 Jan. 1533 (see *Edin. Trin.prov*.).

Brady prov. without fruits 26 Oct. 1525 (PRO 31/9 - 32/78); occ. 1 Mar. 1533 (St A.Univ.Mun.,UY305/1,91); had Sinclair as coadj. by 1550 or 1551 (v.inf.); occ. 12 Sept. 1556 (*RMS*, v,no. 1077).

Gordon occ. 1529 (*OPS*,II,ii,621).

John Sinclair 1550 or 1551 - 1574 x 1575, 1577 or 1578(?).
Occ. as coadj. and successor to Brady 1550 or 1551 (*OPS*,II,ii, 621); occ. in similar capacity 12 Sept. 1556 (*RMS*,v,no.1077); occ. as archd. 9 June 1560 (SRO, Abbrev. Feu Chrs.,i,fo.295); said 28 Feb. 1562 to have been long in office (SRO, Acts and Decreets,xxiii,fo. 170v); occ. 17 May 1574 (*RMS*,iv,no.2267); prob. d. before 21 May 1575 (see *Innerpeffray prov*.); but said to occ. 4 Jan. 1577 or 1578 (*OPS*,II,ii,621).

Robert Innes 1577 - 1581.
Occ. 1 June 1577 (*OPS*,II,ii,621); gets crown pres. on Sinclair's death 4 May 1580 (Reg.Pres.,ii,35; *RSS*,vii,no.2340); occ. 1581 (*OPS*,II,ii,621).

Zachary Pont 1608.
Crown pres. on death of Innes 2 Sept. 1608 (Reg.Pres.,iv.23).

Richard Merchiston 1619 - 1626 x 1633.
Crown pres. on death of Pont 29 Jan. 1619 (Reg.Pres.,v,22); occ. 30 Aug. 1626 (SRO, Part.Reg. Sasines Inverness,iii,fo.286); said to have been murdered before 26 Mar. 1633 (Scott, *Fasti*,vii,114).

OFFICIALS

OFFICIALS OF CAITHNESS

First known date: 1443 x 1445.

John de Strathbrock 1443 x 1445.
Occ. 1443 x 1445 (*CPL*,ix,348,532).

David Tulloch (Tulch) 1445 x 1446.
Occ. Feb. 1445 x June 1446 (Reg.Supp.,428,fo.135v; cf. *CPL*, ix,465,543-4).

COMMISSARIES

COMMISSARIES OF CAITHNESS

First known date: 1522.

Robert McRaith 1522.
Occ. (C substitute) 6 July 1522 (Fraser, *Sutherland*,iii,71).

Alexander Gray 1538 - 1539.
Occ. (C) 20 Dec. 1538 and 6 June 1539 (Pitcairn, *Trials*, i,222x).

William Sinclair   1539 - 1557.
Alexander Thomson   1552.
Malcolm Reid   1557 - 1558.
Sinclair occ. (C) 1539 (*OPS*,II, ii,623); occ. (C) 16 Feb. 1540

(SRO, Reg.Ho.Chr.no.1218); occ. (CG) 22 Apr. 1557 (SRO, Mey, no.66).

     Thomson occ. (C) 19 July 1552 (SRO, Sent. Offic. St A.,fo.263).

     Reid occ. (C Substitute) 22 Apr. 1557 (SRO,Mey,no.66); occ. (C) 22 June 1558 (ibid.,no.108).

Thomas Brady 1579.

     Occ. (C) 13 Oct. 1579 (*RMS*,iv,no.2931).

DUNBLANE DIOCESE

BISHOPS OF DUNBLANE: STRATHEARN

First known date: 1155.

At least Bp. Osbert sometimes used the title 'of Strathearn' in place of that of Dunblane.

This see was directly subject to the pope until placed under the metropolitan authority of St Andrews 14 Aug. 1472 (*Vet.Mon.*, no. 852); it was transferred to province of Glasgow 9 Jan. 1492 (ibid., no.889), and then back to province of St Andrews 28 Jan. 1500 (Dowden, *Bishops*,333).

Laurence 1155 - 1165 x 1171.

Occ. 27 Feb. 1155 under initial which has been transcribed as 'M.' or as 'La.' (Haddan & Stubbs, *Councils*,ii,231; see also *AMW*, 18-19, where several of the initials used for names of bishops on this occasion are shown to be wrong; cf. Dowden, *Bishops*, 193); occ. as Laurence 1161 (*RRS*, i,223) and 28 Mar. 1165 x 1171 (*Camb.Reg.*, 313-14).

Simon (Simeon) 1179 - 1191 x 1194.

Prob. one of the two unnamed Scottish bps. cons. at 3rd Lateran Council Mar. 1179 (*ES*,ii,300); occ. 14 Oct. 1178 x 17 Sept. 1184 (*St A.Lib.*,147) and 1191 x 1194 (*Arb.Lib.*, i,no.211); occ. once under wrong initial 'W.' 1191 x 1198 (*Camb.Reg.*,no.122; but see ibid.,no. 221 and *N.B.Chrs.*, no.5 for acts certainly of Bp. Simon with similar witnesses; cf. Dowden. *Bishops*,195n).

Jonathan 1195 x 1198 - 1210.

Occ. 1195 x 1198 (*Arb.Lib.*,i,no.212). having prob. previously held *Db.archd.*; d. 1210 (*Chron.Bower*, i,529).

Abraham 1210 x 1214 - 1220.

Occ. as elect 1210 x 1214 (*Inchaff.Chrs.*,no.28; cf. no.29); cons. before 4 Dec. 1214 (*Arb.Lib.*,i,147); in poss. 7 Feb. 1220 (*Dunf. Reg.*, 66).

Radulf 1223 x 1225 - 1226.

Occ. as elect 1223 x 1225 (*Arb.Lib.*,i,59); but res. his right prob. without cons. on or before 12 Jan. 1226, when mand. was issued for a new election (Dowden, *Bishops*,195; see also Eubel, *Hierarchia*, i,229).

Osbert 1226 x 1227 - 1231.

Unnamed bp. occ. 11 Apr. 1227 (*Dunf.Reg.*,125-6), having been el. since 12 Jan. 1226 (v.sup.); occ. as Osbert 1227 x 1231 (*Camb.Reg.*, no.124), and as 'O.' 1230 (*SHS Misc.*,viii,6); d. as professed canon of Holyrood abbey 1231 (*Chron.Bower*,ii,59).

Clement O.P. 1233 - 1258.

Cons. 4 Sept. 1233 after selection under papal mand. by bps. of St Andrews, Brechin and Dunkeld (*Chron.Melrose*,82; see also *Vet. Mon.*,no.91); occ. July x Oct. 1257 (*Chron.Melrose*,114; *ES*,ii,589);

thought at curia to be alive 14 Feb. 1258 (NLS, Adv.MS 15.1.19,no.13);
d. in spring of 1258 (*Chron.Melrose*,115), prob. on date of later obit 19
Mar. (Forbes, *Kalendars*,301).

Robert de Prebenda 1259 - 1284.

El. by 2 Jan. 1259 when *Db.dean* (*Glas.Reg.*,i,166); cons. 22 Aug.
1259 x 1 Sept. 1260 (*CPL*, i,367; *CDS*, i,no.2216); occ. 11 Sept. 1283
(*CDS*,ii,no.245); prob. still alive 5 Feb. 1284 (*APS*, i,424).

William O.Tiron. 1284 - 1291.

El. when abbot of Arbroath and Db. canon, and gets conf. and
cons. 18 Dec. 1284 (*Vet.Mon.*,no.284); in poss. 31 July 1291 (ibid.,
no.343).

Alpin de Strathearn 1295 x 1296 -

El. when Db. canon at some date after 4 May 1295 (*Reg.Halton*,
i,21); got conf. and cons. 16 Oct. 1296 (*Vet.Mon.*,no.355; Stevenson,
Documents,ii,115-18); promised common services 6 Nov. 1296 (*SNQ*,
3rd series,viii,201).

Nicholas O.Tiron. 1301 - 1306 x 1307.

El. when abbot of Arbroath and Db.canon on death of Strathearn; went to curia and got prov. and cons. 13 Nov. 1301 (*Vet.Mon.*,
no.369), having previously promised common services 15 Oct. 1301
(*Reg. Clement V*, app.,271,n.4, where wrong surname is attributed
to him); paid some services 26 Jan. 1306 (ibid.,no.269); d. before 11
Dec. 1307 (v.inf.).

Nicholas de Balmyle 1307 - 1319 x 1320.

El. on death of Nicholas when Db.canon, and got conf. and cons.
11 Dec. 1307 (*Vet.Mon.*,no.386); occ. 8 Feb. 1319 (*C.A.Chrs.*,i,216);
prob. d. before 30 Jan. 1320 when see was said to be vacant (*Cal.
Chancery Warrants 1244-1326*, p.504; *CDS*,iii,no.689).

Richard de Pontefract O.P. 1320.
Maurice O.S.A. 1319 x 1322 - 1347.
Roger de Ballinbreich 1319 x 1322.

Pontefract nom. by Edward II to pope for prov. 30 Jan./ 25 June
1320 (ibid.; *Foedera*,II,i,428).

Maurice occ. as bishop 5 Dec. 1318 (*Abdn.Reg.*,i,45, where text
must be faulty); el. when abbot of Inchaffray and *Db.prec*. on death of
Balmyle; lit. at curia with Ballinbreich; res. right and got prov. 5 Mar.
1322 (*Vet.Mon.*,no.441); cons. before 23 Mar. 1322 (ibid.,no.443); d.
before 23 Oct. 1347 (v.inf.), prob. not long before (cf. *CPP*, i,124
where a pet. which he had supported was granted by pope in Nov.
1347).

Ballinbreich also el. on death of Balmyle, and lit. with Maurice
in curia, and res. his right before 5 Mar. 1322 (*Vet.Mon.*,no.441).

William 1347 - 1358 x 1361.

El. on death of Maurice when Db.canon, and got prov. and cons.
23 Oct. 1347 (*Vet.Mon.*,no.576); occ. 11 Apr. 1358 (*Inchaff.Chrs.*,
no.132); d. before 18 June 1361 (v.inf.).

Walter de Coventre 1359 x 1361 - 1371.

El. after 4 Sept. 1359 (*HMC* 60, *Mar and Kellie*,ii,6) when *Ab.dean* and following death of William; prov. 18 June 1361 (*Vet.Mon.*,no.644); promised common services 20 Sept. 1361 (Hoberg, *Taxae*,47); cons. before 30 June 1362 (*Glas.Reg.*,i,265-8); occ. 27 Mar. 1371 (*APS*,i, 545).

Andrew (Magnus ?) 1372 - 1373.

El. when *Db.archd.*, and then got prov. 27 Apr. 1372 (Eubel, *Hierarchia*, i,230); cons. by 4 Apr. 1373 (*APS*,i,549).

Dougal (de Lorne/ de Argyll/ Petri ?) 1380 - 1396.

El. when Db.canon, and then prov. 20 Sept. 1380 (Eubel, *Hierarchia*,i,230); for suggested identification with alternative sur-names, see Dowden, *Bishops*,205 and *Highland Papers*,ii,147-8 and iv, 137-8; cons. by 13 Feb. 1381 (Dowden, *Bishops*,205); in poss. 1 Aug. 1396 (Reg.Supp.,91,fo.234v; cf. *CPP*,i,591-2).

Finlay Colini 1403 - 1419.

El. when *Db.archd.* and then prov. 10 Sept. 1403 (Eubel, *Hierarchia*,i,230); cons. before 28 Apr. 1404 (*SHR*,xxxv,134); d. 1419 (*Chron.Bower*,ii,459).

William Stephenson 1419 - 1428 x 1429.

Trans. from *O.bp.* 30 Oct. 1419 (*CPL*,vii,133); occ. 17 July 1428 (L.Barbé, *Margaret of Scotland and the Dauphin Louis*, 22); d. by 25 Feb. 1429 (Reg.Supp.,232,fo.244).

Michael de Ochiltree 1429 - 1446.

Prov. when *Db.dean* 22 June 1429 (Eubel, *Hierarchia*, i,230); cons. 4 July 1430 x 12 Apr. 1431 (*CPL*,vii,176,368-9); occ. 23 Sept. 1446 (*HMC* 6, *7th R.*,707b).

Walter Stewart   1446 x 1447.
Robert Lauder   1447 - 1466.

Stewart el. when *Db.archd.* before 27 Oct. 1447 (v.inf.), but not conf. (Reg.Supp.,421,fo.158, as quoted in A.I. Dunlop, *James Kennedy*, 97,n.3).

Lauder prov. 27 Oct. 1447 (Eubel, *Hierarchia*,ii,147); cons. by 13 Nov. 1447 (*ACSB*,40); res. 12 Sept. 1466 (*CPL*,xii,454).

John 'Herspolz' / Hepburn (?)   1466 - 1485 x 1487.
John Spalding   x1467.

'Herspolz' prov. 12 Sept. 1466 on res. of Lauder (ibid.,458; see *ACSB*, 58 for surname); cons. 22 June x 28 Sept. 1467 (Dowden, *Bishops*,206; *ACSB*,61); occ. 3 Feb. 1485 (*ADC*,i,106^X,107^X); d. before 31 Jan. 1487 (v.inf.).

Spalding had crown nom. to pope for this see sometime before 19 Nov. 1467 when *B.dean* (*CPL*,xii,278-9).

James Chisholm 1487 - 1534 x 1546.

Prov. when *Ab.dean* and with some right to *M.dean*. 31 Jan. 1487 on death of 'Herspolz' (*ACSB*,84); not yet cons. 11 July 1487 (*Camb. Reg.*,no.92); cons. by 11/29 Jan. 1488 (*APS*,ii,184); res. in favour of

William Chisholm senior, but retaining fruits and right of return 6 June
1526 (Brady, *Episcopal Succession*,i,140); still administrator of the
fruits 26 Mar. 1534 (*Camb.Reg.*,no.183); d. before 20 Jan. 1546 (*RSS*,
iii,no.1499).

William Chisholm senior 1526 - 1564.

Prov. when Db.canon without fruits on res. of James Chisholm his
brother 6 June 1526 (v.sup.; Eubel, *Hierarchia*,iii,188); said to have been
cons. 14 Apr. 1527 (Dowden, *Bishops*,207); active as bp. by 28 May
1527 (*Arb.Lib.*,ii,no.643); accepted his nephew as coadj. 2 June 1561
(v.inf.); at point of death 14/15 Dec. 1564 (*CSP Scot.*,ii,p.100).

William Chisholm junior 1561 - 1569.

Prov. when Db.canon after crown nom. as coadj. to his uncle 2
June 1561 (Brady, *Episcopal Succession*, i,140-1); occ. in Scotland
as bp. in his own right 30 Mar. 1565 (*CSP Scot.*,ii,no.161) and 23
May 1567 (*RMS*,iv,no.1999); depriv. on or before 25 Aug. 1569 (*RSS*,
vi,no.729); as an exile from Scotland given administration of see of
Vaison in France until he might return to Dunblane 8 Nov. 1570
(Eubel, *Hierarchia*,iii,327; Brady, *Episcopal Succession*, i,142-3); res.
Db.bp. 10 Mar. 1580 (J.H. Cockburn, *The Medieval Bishops of
Dunblane*,229); res. Vaison bp. to join O.Carthus. 4 Nov. 1585
(Eubel, *Hierarchia*,iii,327); rehabilitated as *Db.bp.* in Scotland 28
Mar./29 July 1587 (*RMS*,v,no.1173; *APS*,ii,469); this rehabilitation
annulled 27 May 1589 (*RPC*,iv,388-9); d. 26 Sept. 1593 (Cockburn,
loc.cit.).

Andrew Graham 1573 x 1575 - 1603.

Licence for el. on depriv. of Chisholm junior issued 3 July 1573
(*RSS*,vi,no.2024); crown conf. of Graham with mand. for cons. 17
May 1575 (ibid.,vii,no.186); granted temps. 28 July 1575 (ibid., no.
260); res. in or before Feb. 1603 (v.inf.).

George Graham 1603 - 1615.

Crown prov. Feb. 1603 on res. of Andrew Graham (Reg.Pres.,
iii,63); cons. certainly 21 Oct. 1610 x 3 May 1611 (Spottiswoode,
History,iii,209; *Original Letters*,i,270) and prob. 23 Jan./24 Feb.
1611 (Calderwood, *History*,vii,154); trans. to *O.bp.* 26 Aug. 1615.

Adam Bellenden 1615 - 1635.

Crown prov. 24 Sept. 1615 (Reg.Pres.,iv,123; RSS,lxxxiv,fo.
115); cons. by 3 Apr. 1616 (*HBC*,287, no source cited); trans to
Ab.bp. 19 May 1635.

James Wedderburn 1636 - 1638.

Crown prov. 11 Feb. 1636 (*RMS*,ix,no.480); depriv. 13 Dec.
1638 (Peterkin, *Records*, i,27); d. 23 Sept. 1639 (*Wedderburn Bk.*,
i,31, quoting memorial inscription in Canterbury Cathedral).

CHAPTER OF DUNBLANE

Bp. Osbert appears to have given weight to the Strathearn section of

his diocese rather than to the Menteith section in which Dunblane itself lay (v.sup.); this is not surprising when it is known that Bp. Clement his successor in 1233 found the cathedral church at Dunblane roofless and served, not by any college of clergy, but just by 'quidam capellanus ruralis' (cf. *Db.early deans* and *Db.dean.christ. Menteith*); he obtained a papal mand. 11 June 1237 to bps. of Glasgow and Dunkeld to help him either to establish a chapter with dean and canons at Dunblane, or to move the cathedral to the Augustinian abbey of Inchaffray in Strathearn (*Vet.Mon.*,no.91); in fact the first course of action was chosen; no single comprehensive act of constitution survives, but a series of agreements made with interested monasteries 1238-1240 illustrates part of the process whereby some of the prebends of Dunblane were established (*RSCHS*,xiv,34-35, 43; cf. *MRHS*,168); two of the new dignitaries along with the older-established archdeacon are found acting as the chapter of Dunblane and using a capitular seal 29 Jan. 1240 (*Inchaff. Chrs.*,no.67); the two other dignities first found 1274 and 1296 may in fact have been founded about the same time, but it is apparent that the build-up of the cathedral chapter to its maximum size by the early 16th century was a gradual process.

As late as 1234 it was said that the right to elect the bishop belonged to the whole clergy of the diocese (*Inchaff.Chrs.*,no.60); the papal mand. of 11 June 1237 is not wholly clear on this matter - it states that the power of electing the bishop is henceforth to be restricted to a group of canons, and the construction seems to require the interpretation that this restriction is to apply only if the alternative of moving the cathedral to Inchaffray is chosen; but this alternative was not chosen, and it is not clear whether the new chapter at Dunblane was similarly to have exclusive rights in episcopal elections; as established 1238-1240 it came to comprise both secular and regular clergy, and perhaps it is significant of the usual exclusive trend found in other dioceses that when the next election came in 1258 it was the current dean of Dunblane who was chosen; but, though the subsequent elections happen to be comparatively well documented, it is hard to be sure just when the cathedral chapter managed to exclude other diocesan clergy from their share in elections; certainly it was for long the custom to elect a member of the chapter.

EARLY DEANS IN DUNBLANE

John de Dunblane (?) c. 1170.
    Perhaps may have been dean c.1170 (*Camb.Reg.*,no.218).

Gillemure c. 1190.
    Occ. c.1190 (*Inchaff.Chrs.*,no.1).

Thomas 1178 x 1197, 1194 x 1210.
    Occ. 1178 x 1197 (*N.B.Chrs.*,no.5) and 1194 x 1210 (*Inchaff. Chrs.*,nos.3,13).

Brice 1210 x 1225.

Occ. 1210 x 1225 (*Camb.Reg.*,no.123).

Matthew 1210 x 1225 - 1227 x 1231.
Occ. 1210 x 1225 (*Arb.Lib.*,i,no.213) and 1227 x 1231 (*Camb. Reg.*,no.124); perhaps identifiable with the 'capellanus ruralis' whom Bp. Clement found officiating in the unroofed Dunblane Cathedral in 1233 (*Vet.Mon.*,35); but see *Db.dean.christ.Menteith*.

DEANS OF DUNBLANE

First known date: is to be established 1237 (*Vet.Mon.*,35).
Prebend: vic. of Dunblane and one-quarter fruits of Tullibole at Reformation and prob. much earlier (Assumptions, fos.299,321v; Cowan, *Parishes*, 51, 201).

W. 1239 - 1240.
Occ. 7 Apr. 1239 (*Lind.Cart.*,no.54), occ. 29 Jan. 1240 (*Inchaff.Chrs.*,no.67).

Luke de Muthill 1240 x 1255.
Occ. twice 1240 x 1255 (ibid.,no.75; *Lind.Cart.*,no.28); for surname see *Inchaff.Chrs.*,53.

Robert de Prebenda 1255 - 1258 x 1260.
In poss. 23 June 1255 (*CPL*,i,319), having prob. succ. since Mar. 1255 (*Reg.Gray*,121); still in poss. 30 Sept. 1257 (*CPL*,i,350); el. *Db.bp.* 19 Mar. 1258 x 2 Jan. 1259 and cons. 22 Aug. 1259 x 1 Sept. 1260.

Henry 1266.
Occ. 16 May 1266 (*Inchaff.Chrs.*,157).

Thomas 1273 - 1285 x 1296.
Occ. 12 Feb. 1273 (*Camb.Reg.*,no.14); occ. 1285 x 1296 (*Moray Reg.*,469-70).

John 1296 - 1302.
In poss. 16 Oct. 1296 (*CPL*,i,567); occ. 24 Aug. 1302 (*Lind. Cart.*,no.136).

William de Yetholm (Yetham) 1309 - 1309 x 1313.
Occ. 23 Sept. 1309 (C.M. Fraser, *Records of Anthony Bek*, 155); moved to *Db.archd.* by 9 Dec. 1313.

Donald 1322 x 1328 - 1333 x 1334.
Occ. 1322 x June 1328 (*C.A.Chrs.*,nos.103-4); occ. July 1333 x July 1334 (SRO, Transcripts Royal Chrs.,s.d.).

Michael de Monymusk   1352 x 1357 - 1362 x 1363, 1365 x 1366 - 1366 x 1368.
Adam de Tyninghame   1361 - 1365 x 1366.
Monymusk occ. 1352 x 1357 (Maidment, *Analecta*,ii,16); in poss. 23 Aug. 1361 (*CPP*,i,375); moved to *Ab.dean.* by 10 Feb.

1363; lit. with Tyninghame which may have resulted in his return to this ben. 28 Nov. 1365 x 20 Mar. 1366 (v.inf.; cf. *Ab.dean.*); moved to *G.dean.* 21 June 1366 x 21 Jan. 1368.

Tyninghame prov. 9 Nov. 1361 (*CPP*,i,379); occ. 28 Nov. 1365 (*Inchaff.Chrs.*,129); prob. res. on getting re-possession of *Ab.dean.* by 20 Mar. 1366.

Adam de Carnbo 1375.

In poss. 24 Oct. 1375 (Reg.Av.,198,fo.135v).

Henry de Dunblane x1381.

Held it at death before 20 May 1381 (v.inf.).

David de Stirling 1381.

Prov. on Dunblane's death 20 May 1381 (*CPP*,i,556).

Gilbert de Ochtertyre/ Johannis 1381 x 1394.

Occ. 1371 x 1398, possibly 1371 x 1390, presumably 1381 x 1390 (Fraser, *Southesk*,ii,508-10); occ. 1380 x 1398, presumably 1380 x 1394 (*RMS*,ii,42); called Ochtertyre on both these occasions; but it was a Gilbert Johannis who held it at death sometime before 27 Oct. 1394 (v.inf.).

Donald de Bute 1394 - 1408.

Had coll. by ord. on death of Gilbert Johannis, and then got prov. 27 Oct. 1394 (Reg.Av.,282,fos.517v-518v); occ. 27 Mar. 1408 (*ER*,iv, 64).

Michael de Ochiltree 1419 x 1420 - 1429.
John Stewart 1421.
John de Keremor 1422.

Ochiltree had coll. by ord. on Bute's death some time after Oct. 1419, and got prov. 25 Nov. 1420 (*CSSR*,i,235); lit. with Stewart by 11 Mar. 1421 (ibid.,245-6); occ. 25 Jan. 1423 (*HMC* 55, *Var.Coll.*,v, 10); prov. *Db.bp.* 22 June 1429.

Stewart lit. 11 Mar. 1421 (v.sup.); had had prov., but as late as 22 Sept. 1421 had still not expedited letters and still lit. without poss. (*CSSR*,i,260).

Keremor prov. while at curia 20/27 Apr. 1422 (*CSSR*,i,298-9, 302-3) unfruitfully.

Robert de Crannach 1430 - 1439 x 1440.
William Spalding x1431.

Crannach prov. on Ochiltree's elevation 4 July 1430 (*CPL*,viii, 176); prov. on Spalding's death 25 Oct. 1431, having poss. and getting conf. as Ochiltree may have dem. on getting a parish ben. before his elevation (Reg.Supp.,271,fo.204v); in poss. 11 Mar. 1439 (ibid.,356, fo.109v); res. on exch. with Murray for *Db.chanc.* before Mar. 1440 (v.inf.).

Spalding had some right at death before 25 Oct. 1431 (v.sup.).

Henry Murray 1440 - 1455.
Patrick de Birnie (Brineth) 1448.

Murray in poss. by Mar. 1440 (v.inf.) having got it on exch. with

F

Crannach (Reg.Supp.,423,fo.195; cf. *CPL*,ix,131); new prov. 2 Mar. 1448 after more than eight years' poss. (Reg.Supp.,423,fo.195; 425, fo.11); res. on exch. with Scott 4 Dec. 1455 (*CPL*,xi,249,279).

Birnie gets *com.priv.* against Murray 2 Mar. 1448 (Reg.Supp., 423,fo.247v) unfruitfully.

William Scott 1455.
Prov. on exch. with Murray 4 Dec. 1455 (*CPL*,xi,279).

John Donaldson (Donaldi) 1456.
Andrew Moschet 1456.
Donaldson prov. on Scott's death 16 Sept. 1456 (Reg.Supp., 493,fo.74).
Moschet prov. on Scott's death 6 Nov. 1456 (ibid.,494,fo.188).

John Drummond 1462-3 - 1495.
Occ. 1462-3 (*St A.Acta*,150); occ. 20 Jan. 1495 (*RMS*,ii,no. 2230); res. before 11 Dec. 1495.

Walter Drummond 1495 - 1513.
Occ. 11 Dec. 1495 (*RMS*,ii,no.2292); prov. after res. of John Drummond 30 Dec. 1495 (PRO 31/9 - 30/285); occ. 26 Nov. 1513 (*APS*,ii,281).

John Chisholm c. 1513 - 1515.
Gilbert Strathauchin 1515.
Chisholm gets crown pres. to pope for prov. on Walter Drummond's death c.1513 (*James V Letters*, 3); in poss. and lit. 12/13 Dec. 1515 (*ADCP*, 62).
Strathauchin lit. on basis of same papal right 12/13 Dec. 1515 (ibid.).

William Drummond 1522 - 1533 (?).
Occ. 29 Apr. 1522 (*Fife Ct.Bk.*,250); occ. 26 Mar. 1533? (*Camb. Reg.*,267).

Malcolm Fleming 1536 - 1539.
Crown pres. on Drummond's death 20 Nov. 1536 (*RSS*,ii,no. 2191); crown pres. to pope for prov. to priory of Whithorn 2 Jan. 1539 (*James V Letters*, 362-3); occ. 9 Feb. 1539 (SRO,Prot.Bk. Edward Diksoun, p.72).

William Gordon 1539 - 1551.
Crown pres. to pope for prov. on Fleming's elevation 17 Jan. 1539 (*Vet.Mon.*,608); occ. 26 Feb. 1551 (*Wigt.Chrs.*,no.322).

Roger Gordon 1554 - 1577 x 1587.
Occ. 13 Apr. 1554 (SRO, Drummond Castle, box 28, 'Ledmachany', 1/1); occ. 12 July 1577 (SRO, Burnett-Stuart, no.25); d. before 12 May 1587 (*RMS*,v,no.1234); cf. *Ga.bp*.

John Johun 1588.
Crown pres. on dem. of Roger Gordon 21 Feb. 1588 (RSS, lvii,fo.29).

John Graham 1597.
>Crown pres. on Johun's death 23 May 1597 (Reg.Pres.,iii,5).

Henry Stirling 1602.
>Crown pres. on Graham's death 18 Nov. 1602 (RSS,lxxii,fo.103);
cf. *B.treas*.

James Stirling 1603 - 1617 x 1618.
>Crown pres. on deaths of Johun, Graham and Stirling 19 Dec. 1603
(RSS,lxxiv,fo.105); granted lic. to go abroad 11 May 1617 (*RPC*,xi,62);
depriv. by 10 Mar. 1618 (v.inf.).

William Fogo 1618 - 1622.
>Crown pres. on James Stirling's dem.,non-residence or depriv. 10
Mar. 1618 (Reg.Pres.,v,6); occ. 1 July 1622 (SRO, Reg.Ho.Chr.,s.d.).

James Pearson 1624 - 1651.
>Crown pres. on dem. of Fogo 3 Mar. 1624 (Reg.Pres.,v,89); occ.
23 June/ 27 Oct. 1630 (Stevenson & Wood, *Seals*,iii,542); conf. 24
July 1651 (RSS,cxvi,fo.195).

PRECENTORS/CHANTERS OF DUNBLANE

This dignity was held by successive abbots of Inchaffray probably from
1240 (*Inchaff.Chrs*.,xxxviii). For lists see ibid.,249-57, and *Bibliotheck*,
ii,15-16.

CHANCELLORS OF DUNBLANE

First known date: 1296.
>Prebend: vic. of Kilmadock in 1429 (*ACSB*, 97-98; Cowan,
Parishes, 102-3).

Peter 1296.
>In poss. 16 Oct. 1296 (*CPL*, i,567).

Thomas de Row 1372.
>In poss. 10 Sept. 1372 (Reg.Av.,186,fo.380v).

Adam de Port	x1423.
John Willelmi (William Clerk)	1423 - 1429 x 1431.
John Gilston (Gylyston)	x1425.
John Bowmaker	1425.
Nicholas de Atholl	1425.
Gilbert de Bannay/Bannori	1429.
William Stephenson	1429.
Andrew Young	1429 - 1431.

>**Port** held it at death before June 1423 (v.inf.).
>**Willelmi/Clerk** coll. by ord. on Port's death more than two years
before 26 June 1425 when, after lit. with Bowmaker, he got new prov.
(*CSSR*,ii,86-87, 99); in poss. and has held it for some five years 28 July

1429 (Reg.Supp.,244,fo.36); res. on exch. with Moray some time before 29 Sept. 1431 (v.inf.).

Gilston held it at death sometime before May 1425 (v.inf.).

Bowmaker had prov. on Gilston's death, and, while lit. with Willelmi (who has poss.), res. in favour of Atholl 13 May 1425 (*CSSR*,ii,86-87).

Atholl gets surrog. to Bowmaker's right 13 May 1425 (ibid.); still no poss. 14 Aug. 1425 (ibid.,111).

Bannay/Bannori prov. on Port's death 11 May 1429 (*ACSB*, 97-98); died at curia before 28 July 1429 (v.inf.).

Stephenson prov. 28 July 1429 (Reg.Supp.,244,fo.36) prob. unfruitfully.

Young prov. on Port's death 5 Dec. 1429 (*ACSB*,102); claims right but has no poss. 29 Sept. 1431 (Reg.Supp.,269,fo.292v).

John de Moray   1431 - 1431 x 1433.
Laurence Piot   1431.
Moray got it on exch. with Clerk and then had prov. 29 Sept. 1431 (Reg.Supp.,269,fo.292v); d. in poss. more than two years before 17 Sept. 1435 (ibid.,312,fo.77v).

Piot had prov. sometime before 8 May 1431 but no poss. then (*CPL*,viii,335).

William Clerk   1431 x 1435.
John Cristisoun   1433 - 1435.
Clerk sought to regain poss. on Moray's death, but d. without success before 17 Sept. 1435 (Reg.Supp.,312,fo.77v).

Cristisoun got poss. more than two years before 17 Sept. 1435, when still in poss. (ibid.).

Henry Murray 1439 x 1440.
Held it but res. on exch. with Crannach for *Db.dean*. after 11 Mar. 1439 and before Mar. 1440 (v.inf.).

Robert de Crannach 1439 x 1440.
Obtained it on exch. with Murray 11 Mar. 1439 x Mar. 1440 and res. before 23 Sept. 1440 (Reg.Supp.,423,fo.195; cf. *CPL*,ix,131).

Alexander de Lichton   1440 - 1446.
David Reid   1441 - 1442.
Lichton prov. on res. of Crannach 23 Sept. 1440 (*CPL*,ix,131); lit. with Reid 16 Dec. 1441 (Reg.Supp.,378,fo.221v); in poss. 12 Mar. 1446 (ibid.,410,fo.191v).

Reid prov. 11 Jan. 1441 on suggestion that Lichton's prov. be set aside (Reg.Supp.,370,fo.272v); lit. with Lichton 16 Dec. 1441 (ibid.,381,fo.221v); letters still not expedited 27 Mar. 1442 (ibid.,381, fo.118).

John Cristisoun 1448 - 1462.
Occ. 5 Sept. 1448 (Fraser, *Keir*,224); occ. 26 Jan. 1462 (*Inchaff.Chrs*.,148-50).

Henry Boyce 1466 - 1474.

Thomas de Carribus 1466.
David Nobil 1466.

Boyce got poss. by virtue of an exp. grace on Cristisoun's death, and got prov. 5 Jan. 1466 (Reg.Supp.,589,fo.212); no poss. yet 21 Jan. 1466 (ibid.,590,fo.242v); new prov. after winning lit. with Carribus and Nobil 27 Jan. 1466 (ibid.,590,fo.225v); occ. 1 Feb. 1473 (*CDS*,iv,no. 1403); in poss. when prov. (prob. ineffectively) *Dk.dean*. 20 May 1474 (Reg.Supp.,705,fo.193).

Carribus and Nobil known only as having lost lit. with Boyce by 27 Jan. 1466 (v.sup.).

Andrew Makbrek (Aiton) 1490 - 1528.

Occ. 25 June 1490 (Floors Castle, Roxburghe Mun., tin box no. 4, bundle 20, no.1); occ. 1 Aug. 1526 (*RMS*,iii,no.384); under name 'Aiton' res. in favour of Kaill 11 Oct. 1528, in terms of supp. granted 19 June 1528 (PRO 31/9 - 32/129); as 'Aiton' said to have died 12 Oct. 1528 (*Notes and Queries*, III,viii,246); certainly as 'Makbrek' d. by 8 Dec. 1529 (v.inf.).

Thomas Kaill 1528.

Prov. on res. of Makbrek 11 Oct. 1528 (PRO 31/9 - 32/129).

Patrick Forhous 1529, 1538 - 1545.
John Chisholm 1531 - 1542.
John Thornton 1531.

Forhous promised annates and had prov. on Makbrek's death 8 Dec. 1529 (PRO 31/9 - 32/160); lit. with Chisholm 13 Aug. 1538 (*ADCP*,472); Chisholm res. in his favour 19 Apr. 1542 (v.inf.); occ. 21 May 1545 (*N.B.Chrs.*,61); made will 28 Sept. 1545 (Dunblane Tests., i,124).

Chisholm in poss. when made coadj. *Db.archd*. 24 Jan. 1531 (PRO 31/9 - 32/190-1); retained it when had succ. as archd.; occ. 26 Mar. 1533? (*Camb.Reg.*,267), 6 July 1535 (*RMS*,iii,no.1487) and 1538 x 1539 (*MW*,i,239); res. in favour of Forhous 19 Apr. 1542 (SRO, Prot.Bk. Edward Dikson, fo.70v).

Thornton granted reversionary right if a pension not paid 26 Jan. 1531 (PRO 31/9 - 32/190-1).

James Kennedy 1546 - 1571.

Occ. 3 July 1546 (NLS, MS Chr. no. 2241); occ. 1 Apr. 1571 (SRO, Reg.Deeds. xi,fo.365).

Alexander Forgy 1576 - 1581.

Occ. 19 Jan. 1576 (SRO, Drummond Castle, box 37, 'Corskaiple', 2/8) and 24 June 1581 (ibid.,box 6,10/9).

William Edmonston 1626 - 1635.

Occ. 12 June 1626 (SRO, Burnett-Stuart,no.27) and 8 Jan. 1635 (SRO, Drummond Castle, box 6,10/9).

TREASURERS OF DUNBLANE

First known date: 1274 (*SHS Misc.*,vi,54).
Prebend: vic. of Strogeith at Reformation (NLS,Adv.MS 34.4.8;
cf. Cowan, *Parishes*, 192 and *RSCHS*,xiv,43).

Geoffrey 1292 - 1296.
Occ. 6 June 1292 (*Rot.Scot.*,i,7); in poss. 16 Oct. 1296 (*CPL*,i,
567).

Michael Manyson x1379.
Held it sometime before Oct. 1379 (*CPP*,i,541).

Eugene de Dumbarton 1401.
Has had coll. by ord. before 28 Jan. 1401 (*CPP*,i,615-16).

Laurence de Prendergast x1417.
Held it and dem. before 6 Feb. 1417 (v.inf.).

William de Athray 1417 - 1423.
Had coll. by ord. on dem. of Prendergast and gets prov. from
Pope Benedict XIII 6 Feb. 1417 (Reg.Av.,349,fos.230-1); occ. 13
Mar. 1423 (Fraser, *Grandtully*,i,154x).

John de Athray 1453 - 1466.
Occ. 11 May 1453 (NLS, Adv.MS 19.2.20, p.45); wrongly
described as *Dk.treas.* 12 Mar. 1459 (*HMC* 4, *5th R.*, 630; see MS
in SRO, GD 49/5); occ. 21 Mar. 1466 (SRO, Reg.Ho.Chr. no.396).

David Kay (Ray)   1470.
John Lockhart   1470 - 1470 x 1476.
Kay occ. 8 June 1470 (Fraser, *Wemyss*,ii,96-97); lit. with
Lockhart 6 July 1470 (*CPL*,xii,742-3).
Lockhart gets new prov. 6 July 1470, after getting it on John de
Athray's death by right of exp. grace. (*CPL*,xii,742-3); res. to ord. before
10 Aug. 1476 (v.inf.).

William Elphinstone junior 1476 - 1481x.
Had coll. by ord. on res. of Lockhart before 10 Aug. 1476 (*CPL*,
xiii,506; cf. 558); prov. *R.bp.* 3 Aug. 1481, though not cons. until Apr.
1488 x Apr. 1489.

Patrick Murray   1507 - 1550 or 1551.
William Murray   1534 - 1563 x 1567.
Alexander Murray   1550 or 1551 - 1564.
Patrick occ. 20 June 1507 (Fraser, *Lennox*,ii,183-4); res. in favour
of William promising annates to keep fruits 14 Aug. 1534 (PRO 31/9 -
32/280); occ. 10 Feb. 1535 (SRO, Reg.Ho.Chr. no.1105); res. in favour
of Alexander (retaining fruits as pension in terms of supp. granted 23
June 1547) 29 Sept. 1550 or 1551 (PRO 31/9 - 33/261-2, text is
contradictory).
William promises annates and gets prov. without fruits 14 Aug.
1534 (v.sup.); occ. 25 Feb. 1547 (SRO, Reg.Ho.Chr. no. 1399B); occ.

1 Nov. 1563 (*RMS*,iv,no.2153); res. to ord. before 19 Apr. 1567 (v.inf.).

Alexander obtained right without fruits on res. of Patrick 29 Sept. 1550 or 1551 (v.sup.); claimed poss. 15 May/ 5 June 1564, when lit. over title to this ben. since Patrick's death (SRO, Comm.Edin.Decreets, i,fos.21,44).

William Murray 1567 - 1581.
Crown conf. of coll. by ord. on res. of namesake 19 Apr. 1567 (*RSS*,v,no.3433); occ. 24 June 1581 (SRO, Drummond Castle, box 6, 10/9).

Mungo Murray 1618 - 1622.
Occ. 5 May 1618 (ibid.) and 1 July 1622 (SRO, Reg.Ho.Chrs., s.d.).

James Govane 1626 - 1635.
Occ. 12 June 1626 (SRO, Burnett-Stuart,no.27) and 8 Jan. 1635 (SRO, Drummond Castle, box 6, 10/9).

SUBDEANS OF DUNBLANE

First known date: 1468.
Prebend: vic. of Muthill in 1468 (Reg.Supp.,626,fo.144; Cowan, *Parishes*,154).

Patrick Reid x1468.
Held it and res. before 1 June 1468 (v.inf.).

George Brown 1468.
Had been pres. by king *sede vacante*, i.e. 12 Sept. 1466 x, and got papal conf. 1 June 1468 (Reg.Supp.,626,fo.144).

William Glendinning (Glendinwyn) 1475.
Occ. 25 Oct. 1475 (*Glas.Mun.*,ii,85).

James Belses (Belches) 1497 - 1498.
Occ. 15 Dec. 1497 (*HMC* 10, *10th R.*,i,67); occ. 20 June 1498 (*RMS*,ii,no.2474).

Thomas Leiss 1506 - 1530.
Occ. 30 Sept. 1506 (*Prot.Bk.Simon*,ii,147,no.192); occ. 8 Mar. 1530 (*Glas.Mun.*,i,49-50).

Malcolm Chisholm 1533.
Occ. 18 Jan. 1533 (*RMS*,iii,no.1257).

James Blackwood 1546 - 1550.
Occ. 3 July 1546 (NLS, MS Chr. no.2241); wrongly called *Dk. subd.* 31 Dec. 1549 (*RSS*,iv,no.529; see RSS,xxiii,fo.56); occ. 23 Mar. 1550 (Fraser, *Keir,* 402).

Edmund Chisholm 1557 - 1581 x 1590.
Occ. 12 May 1557 (Fraser, *Keir*,411); occ. 24 June 1581 (SRO, Drummond Castle, box 6, 10/9); d. by 6 June 1590 (RSS,lx,fo.137).

James Burdon 1606 - 1626.
Occ. 18 June 1606 (SRO, Drummond Castle, box 4,6) and 12 June 1626 (SRO, Burnett-Stuart, no.27).

ARCHDEACONS OF MUTHILL/DUNBLANE/STRATHEARN

First known date: 1165 x 1171.
Andrew used title 'Muthill'; Jonathan, Gilbert and Luke used 'Dunblane'; John and Duncan used 'Strathearn'; and from Augustine de Nottingham onwards 'Dunblane' was the standard title.
Prebend: various garbal teinds by agreement with Inchaffray abbey confirmed 29 Jan. 1240 (*Inchaff.Chrs.*,59-60); then vic. of Findogask by 1358 (ibid.,no.132; cf. *Thirds of Benefices*,15; Cowan, *Parishes*,66).

Andrew 1165 x 1171.
Occ. 1165 x 1171 (*Camb.Reg.*,no.219, where title is 'Modhel' but source is a late transcript).

Jonathan 1178 x 1197, 1191 x 1194, 1198.
Occ. 1178 x 1197 (*N.B.Chrs.*,no.5); occ. 1191 x 1194 (*Arb.Lib.*, i,no.211); occ. 1179 x 20 Mar. 1198 (*Lind.Cart.*,165); prob. became *Db.bp.* 1198.

John 1194 x 1199 - 1203 x 1210.
Occ. 1194 x 1199, prob. 1198 x 1199 (*Inchaff.Chrs.*,no.3); occ. 1203 x 1210 (ibid.,no.25).

Gilbert x1210 - 1235.
Occ. as 'G' 1171 x 1210 (*Inchaff.Chrs.*,no.27); occ. in error as 'Galfridus' 1210 x 1216 (*Pais.Reg.*,229, a late text); occ. as 'Gilbert' 1211 x 1214 (*Lind.Cart.*,no.42); occ. as 'Gilbert' 7 May 1235 (ibid., no.51).

Luke de Muthill 1239 - 1240.
Occ. 7 Apr. 1239 (ibid.,no.54; cf. no.53, prob. of same date); occ. 29 Jan. 1240 (*Inchaff.Chrs.*,no.67); moved to *Db.dean.*; for surname see *Inchaff.Chrs.*,no.61.

Duncan 1240 x 1255.
Occ. 1240 x 1255 (*Lind.Cart.*, no.28).

Augustine de Nottingham 1268 - 1283.
Occ. 23 Jan. 1268 (*Chartularium Studii Bononiensis*,vii,224; cf. viii,251); occ. 25 Mar. 1283 (*Inchaff.Chrs.*,no.113).

Walter de Montrose (Monros) 1287 - 1296.
Occ. 28 Sept. 1287 (*Inchaff.Chrs.*,no.118); in poss. 16 Oct. 1296 (*CPL*,i,567).

William de Yetholm (Iheteme) 1309 x 1313 - 1320 x 1321.
Occ. 9 Dec. 1313 (*PSAS*,xc,80) after moving from *Db.dean.* since 23 Sept. 1309; occ. 13 Mar. 1320 (*Dunf.Reg.*,239); prob. moved to *G.archd. Teviotdale* by 11 July 1321; mentioned in 1345

under name 'Iheteme' (*CPL*,iii,198).

Thomas 1322 x 1328.
Occ. Mar. 1322 x July 1328 (*Dunf.Reg*.,242).

Walter de Coventre 1345.
Prov. 7 Dec. 1345 (*CPL*,iii,198), perhaps unfruitfully.

Laurence (?) 1352 x 1357.
Occ. as an archd. 1352 x 1357 (Maidment, *Analecta*,ii,16), but is prob. *Ar.archd*.

Nicholas de Kinbuck 1358 - 1360.
Occ. 11 Apr. 1358 (*Inchaff.Chrs*.,124-5); occ. 4 May 1360 (*ER*,ii,43).

Andrew (Magnus?) 1365 - 1372.
Occ. 28 Nov. 1365 (*Inchaff.Chrs*.,128-9); see Collect., 14, fo. 174 for surname; prov. *Db.bp*. 27 Apr. 1372.

David Bell O.S.A.   1375 - 1377.
Maurice de Strathearn 1377 - ⁻1391.
Bell occ. 5 Feb. 1375 (*ER*,ii,469), after coll. by ord. (Reg.Av., 202,fo.124v); occ. 28 Jan. 1377 (*ER*,ii,569).
Strathearn prov. on Bp. Andrew's promotion 29 May 1377 (Reg.Av., 202, fo.124v); occ. 7 Dec. 1391 (*Inchaff.Lib*.,1).

Finlay Colini 1394 - 1403.
In poss. 13 Oct. 1394 (Reg.Av.,306,fos.32-32v); prov. *Db.bp*. 10 Sept. 1403.

Thomas Graham 1410 or 1411 - 1414 x 1419.
Occ. 31 Mar. 1410, though perhaps 1411 is meant (*HMC* 34, *14th R*.,iii,25-26); proposed to res. on exch. with Erskine sometime 1414 x 1419, but this was abortive (*CSSR*,i,181-2;ii,38-40).

John de Erskine 1414 x 1419.
Planned to obtain it by exch. 1414 x 1419, but failed (ibid.).

Walter Stewart 1433 - 1456.
In poss. 12 Feb. 1433 (Reg.Supp.,283,fo.21); occ. 3 Nov. 1456 (*St A. Acta*, 116); cf. *St A.archd*.

Andrew Purves x1474(?). 1478 - 1479 x 1480.
Alexander Rate   1474 - 1475 x 1479.
William Scheves 1474.
John Cant   1479 - 1479 x 1480.
Purves coll. by ord. on Stewart's death; had poss.; lit. with Rate (*CPL*,xiii,103-4); his coll. prob. before prov. of Rate and Scheves in 1474 (v.inf.); in poss. 23 Feb. 1478 (Reg.Supp.,765,fo.155); new prov. 12 Aug. 1479 (ibid.,785,fos.32v-33); res. on exch. with Bully on ord. auth. before 15 Aug. 1480 (v.inf.).
Rate prov. on Stewart's death 30 Apr. 1474 (*CPL*,xiii,33); still claimed right, but no poss. 20 June 1475 (ibid.,43,103-4); d. after 2 Oct. 1475 (see *Dk.dean*.) and before 5 Apr. 1479 (Reg.Supp.,779,

fos.275v-6).

Scheves prov. on res. of Stewart 2 May 1474 (Reg.Supp.,704, fo.53v) unfruitfully; cf. *Dk.dean*.

Cant surrog. to Rate's right 9 July 1479 (Reg.Supp.,784,fo.85); res. without poss. before 15 Aug. 1480 (*CPL*,xiii,103-4).

Duncan Bully (Bulle) 1480 - 1490.
　　Prov. after coll. on exch. 15 Aug. 1480 (*CPL*,xiii,103-4); occ. 29 Dec. 1490 (SRO, Airlie, 46/4).

Henry Allan (Alane, Alani) 1492 - 1504.
　　Occ. 1492 (*TA*,i,206); occ. 13 July 1504 (*ER*,xii,629).

John Doby 1506 - 1513.
　　Occ. 1 May 1506 (*RMS*,ii,no.2971); occ. 1513 (*Prot.Bk.Foular*, no. 913).

Patrick Blackadder (?) c.1519.
　　Said to have been in poss. when murdered c.1519 (Fraser, *Douglas*,ii,171, but no source quoted).

George Newton 1521 - 1531 x 1533.
John Chisholm 1531 - 1542.
　　Newton occ. 11 July 1521 (*Camb.Reg.*,122); accepts coadj. 24 Jan. 1531 (v.inf.); d. by 18 Jan. 1533 (*RMS*,iii,no.1257), though occ. as apparently alive 26 Mar. 1533? (*Camb.Reg.*,267).
　　Chisholm promises annates as coadj., with agreement of Newton 24 Jan. 1531 (PRO 31/9 - 32/190); occ. 18 Jan. 1533 (*RMS*,iii,no. 1257); in poss. when res. *Db.chanc.* 19 Apr. 1542; d. in poss. Nov. 1542 (*Vet.Mon.*,614).

John Danielston 1542 - 1545.
William Gordon 1545.
James Thornton 1545.
　　Danielston gets crown pres. to pope for prov. 21 Nov. 1542 (*James V Letters*,445-6; *Vet.Mon.*,614); occ. 21 May 1545 (*N.B.Chrs.*, 61); prov. 1 June 1545 having poss. (PRO 31/9 - 33/179).
　　Gordon lit. with Danielston and res. in his favour 9 Mar. 1545 (PRO 31/9 - 33/177-8).
　　Thornton had prov. on Chisholm's death, but res. without poss. in Danielston's favour 1 June 1545 (PRO 31/9 - 33/179).

George Wawane 1550 - 1558 x 1564.
　　Occ. 23 Mar. 1550 (Fraser, *Keir*,402); occ. 19 Feb. 1558 (ibid., 412-13); d. by 5 June 1564 (SRO, Comm.Edin.Decreets,i,fo.44).

James Chisholm 1566 - 1595.
　　Occ. 1566 (*Thirds of Benefices*,255); cf. *Edin. St Giles prov.*; occ. 6 May 1595 (*RMS*,vii,no.960).

Patrick Stirling 1606 - 1607.
　　Occ. before crown pres. 18 June 1606 (SRO, Drummond Castle, box 4,6); crown pres. on Chisholm's death 19 June 1607 (RSS, lxxvi,fo.106).

Alexander Gaw 1610 - 1615.
Occ. 1 Aug. 1610 (SRO, Drummond Castle, box 39,2/11) and 8 Feb. 1615 (ibid.,box 6,10/9).

John Fife 1616 - 1633.
Occ. from 19 June 1616 (ibid.,box 6,10/4), but did not get crown pres. on Gaw's death until 28 Mar. 1633 (Reg.Pres.,vii,18).

William Bannatyne 1635.
Crown pres. on dem. of Fife 1 Jan. 1635 (RSS,cvi,fo.333).

DEANS OF CHRISTIANITY

DEANS OF MENTEITH : DUNBLANE

First known dates: Menteith : 1235.
                     Dunblane : 1512.

Martin (Menteith) 1235.
Occ. 7 May 1235 (*Lind.Cart.*,55); perhaps identifiable with the 'capellanus ruralis' whom Bp. Clement found officiating in the unroofed Dunblane Cathedral in 1233 (*Vet.Mon.*,35); but see *Db.early deans*.

James Belses (Dunblane) 1512.
Occ. 23 June 1512 (NRA, Napier Papers, 18).

James Blackwood (Dunblane) 1550.
Occ. 31 Jan. 1550 (Fraser, *Keir*, 397).

DEANS OF MUTHILL : STRATHEARN

First known date: Muthill (?) : 1266 x 1287.
                    Strathearn : 1271.

Donald (?) (Muthill) 1266 x 1287.
Occ. 1266 x 1287, prob. early in period (*Inchaff.Chrs.*,no.102); but a Donald was *prior* of Muthill 1284 x 1296 (*Moray Reg.*,469).

John (Strathearn) 1271.
Occ. when rector of Glendevon 23 Nov. 1271 (*Inchaff.Chrs.*,nos. 98, 100).

Clement (Strathearn) 1284 x 1296.
Occ. 1284 x 1296 (*Moray Reg.*,469; *Inchaff.Lib.*,xxxvii).

OFFICIALS

OFFICIALS OF DUNBLANE

First known date: 1266.

Richard de Stirling 1266.
Occ. 16 May 1266 (*Inchaff.Chrs.*,157).

B. 1269.
Occ. 21 Feb. 1269 (ibid.,159).

William de Eckford 1322 x 1328.
Occ. 1322 x 1328 (*C.A. Chrs.*,i,223).

Malcolm Johannis 1425 - 1432 x 1433.
Occ. 10 May 1430 (Fraser, *Grandtully*,i,159 x); occ. 15 June 1432, having been seven years in office (*CPL*,viii,437); prob. dem. on becoming *Ar.dean.* by 30 Sept. 1433.

John Cristisoun (Cristini) x 1445 - 1464 x 1466.
Occ. 17 Feb. 1445, having been in office for 'several years' (Reg. Supp.,403,fo.161); occ. 23 June 1464 (St A.Univ.Mun.,REP, fo.68); prob. d. by 5 Jan. 1466 (see *Dk.chanc.*).

Henry Boyce 1470.
Occ. 17 July 1470 (St A.Univ.Mun., REP,fo.72).

John de Ockerburn x1471.
Said to have held office before 23 Jan. 1471 (*CPL*,xii,788); but see John de Otterburn who was *St A.offic.Lothian* at this time.

Luke Arnot 1472.
Occ. 6 Nov. 1472 (*Scot.Antiq.*,x,117); perhaps dem. on becoming *Db.comm.* 18 May 1474 x 11 Dec. 1476.

John Fraser 1476.
Occ. 26 Aug. 1476 (*Stirling Recs.*,260).

John Moffat 1480.
Occ. 26 May 1480 (*Scot.Antiq.*,x,166).

William Forbes 1495 - 1498 x 1503.
Occ. 20 Jan. 1495 (*RMS*,ii,no.2230); occ. as 'Walter' 19 Jan. 1498 (*ADC*,ii,218); prob. d. before 11 Mar. 1503 (see *Edin.St Giles prov.*).

Henry White 1506 - 1534.
Occ. 4 June 1506 (*RMS*,ii,no.2969) and 26 Mar. 1533? (*Camb. Reg.*,267); prov. *B.dean* 17 Aug. 1534.

COMMISSARIES

COMMISSARIES OF DUNBLANE

First known date: 1474.

John Moffat 1474.
Occ. (C) 18 May 1474 (*ADA*,34); cf. *Db.offic*.

Luke Arnot 1476.
Occ. (CB) 11 Dec. 1476 (Fraser, *Lennox*,ii,lll); had been *Db.offic.*,
but successor found there by 26 Aug. 1476.

David Guthynd (Gwynde) x1548.
Occ. (CG) before 7 Sept. 1548 (SRO, Sent.Offic. St A.,fo.172).

James Wilson 1551.
Occ. (C) 2 Jan. 1551 (SRO, Comm. Db. Act Bk.,s.d.).

John Sinclair 1552.
Occ. (C) 7 Jan. 1552 (ibid.).

John Sinclair 1553.
John Wright 1553.
Sinclair occ. (CG) 17 June 1553 (SRO, Sent. Offic. St A.,fo.278).
Wright occ. (CG) 17 June 1553 (ibid.).

John Wright 1553.
Occ. (C) 23 Oct. 1553 (SRO, Comm. Db.Act Bk.,s.d.).

William Custny 1553.
Occ. (C) 27 Oct. 1553 (ibid.).

Archibald Gaw 1556.
Occ. (C) 29 June 1556 (*Prot.Bk.Gaw*,no.166).

Malcolm Chisholm x1562.
An action before him (C) had by 12 Mar. 1562 been stopped by
reason of the cessation of consistorial laws (SRO, Acts and Decreets,
xxiii,fo.252v).

DUNKELD DIOCESE

BISHOPS OF DUNKELD

First known date: c. 1114 or c. 1120.

For death of a Celtic predecessor in 865, see *ES*,i,296 and *PSAS*, lxxxvii,109-10.

See of Argyll was detached from this diocese 1183 x 1189 (cf. Myln, *Vitae*, 8).

This see was directly subject to the pope until placed under the metropolitan authority of St Andrews 14 Aug. 1472 (*Vet.Mon.*,no. 852); it was transferred to province of Glasgow 9 Jan. 1492 (ibid.,no. 889), and then restored to St Andrews on or before 25 May 1515 (Dowden, *Bishops*, 333-4).

Cormac c. 1114 or c. 1120, 1127 x 1131? - 1131 x 1132.

Occ. just as 'bishop' c.1114 if charter evidence is genuine (*Scone Liber*, no.1; cf. *ESC*,280-3; cf. also *Trans.Royal Hist.Soc.*, 5th series,iii,83, where date c.1120 is suggested); occ. with style 'bishop of Dunkeld' 1127 x 1131? (*Dunf.Reg.*,4; cf. *ES*,ii,149) and Apr. 1131 x Apr. 1132 (*Deer Bk.*,93).

John (?) 1138 - 1139.

Occ. on mission to Orkney as Bp. John from Atholl in Scotland Dec. 1138 - Jan. 1139 (*Orkneyinga Saga*, ed. A.B. Taylor, 261-2).

Gregory x1147 - 1169.

Occ. c.1136 x 1147, perhaps 1141 x 1147 (*RRS*,i,no.29); cf. Gregory *M.bp.*; d. 1169 (*Chron.Bower*,i,460; cf. 443).

Richard 1170 - 1178.

Cons. 9 Aug. 1170 (*Chron.Melrose*,38); d. 1178, prob. Feb. x Apr. (ibid.,42; cf. *Chron.Holyrood*,164,n.1).

Walter de Bidun 1178.

D. as elect of Dunkeld 1178 (*Chron.Melrose*,42).

John Scot 1183 - 1203.

Granted this see by the pope on resigning his right to *St A.bp.* 1183, before July (*SAEC*,285-6; cf. *Chron.Holyrood*,168n for dating); received final royal recognition in this see 1188 (*SAEC*,298); d. 1203 (*Chron.Melrose*,51).

Richard de Prebenda 1203 - 1210.

Succ. John 1203 (ibid.); d. Apr./May 1210 (ibid.,54; *Chron. Bower*,i,528,531).

John de Leicester 1211 - 1214.

El. when *St A.archd.Lothian* 22 July 1211 (*Chron.Melrose*,55); papal mand. issued for his cons. 13 June 1212 (*Innocentii III ... Opera Omnia*, ed. Migne,iii,634-5; *AMW*,373-4); d. 7 Oct. 1214 (*Chron.Melrose* 58).

Hugh de Sigillo 1214 - 1229 or 1230.

Succ. Leicester 1214 (ibid.); cons. by 29 Sept. 1216 (ibid.,63); d.
1229 (*Chron.Bower*,ii,58), or perhaps 6 Jan. 1229/30 (Dowden, *Bishops*,
53).

Matthew Scot (?)   1229 or 1230.
Gilbert   1229 or 1230 - 1236.

Scot said to have dem. a right in *Ab.bp.* when el. to this see on
death of Sigillo, but to have d. 1229 without cons. (*Chron.Bower*,ii,
58); this date of death is inaccurate, for he remained in office as king's
chancellor until some date 30 Apr. 1230 x 30 Mar. 1231 (*HBC*,174);
and even as late as his last known appearance as chancellor on 30 Apr.
1230 (*Camb.Reg.*,297) he is never found as 'elect' in royal charters;
but may have d. as elect of Dunkeld later in 1230,

Gilbert (who had been a chaplain of Bp. Hugh) said to have been
el. on Scot's death 1229 (*Chron. Bower*,ii,58); perhaps 1230 is correct
date (v.sup.), possibly after Dundee council of that year (*SHS Misc.*,
viii,5-6) when no Dk.bp. was present; buried 6 Apr. 1236 (*Chron.
Melrose*,85; Myln, *Vitae*,9).

Geoffrey de Liberatione 1236 - 1249.

El. when Dk.canon in succ. to Gilbert 1236 (*Chron.Melrose*,85);
got papal mand. for conf. and cons. 6 Sept. 1236 (*Vet.Mon.*,no.85);
cons. 3 x 31 Dec. 1236 (Dowden, *Bishops*,55-56); d. 22 Nov. 1249
(*Chron.Bower*,ii,78; Myln, *Vitae*,11).

Richard de Inverkeithing 1250 - 1272.

El. 1250 (*Chron.Bower*,ii,83), prob. before 3 Dec. (*RMS*.ii,no.
804; cf. Dowden, *Bishops*,56-57); cons. 3 Aug. x 20 Oct. 1251 (*Inchaff.
Chrs.*,79-80; *Moncreiffs*,ii,636-7); d. 16 Apr. 1272 (*Chron.Bower*,ii,115).

Robert de Stuteville 1273 - 1277, 1282 (?).

El. when *Dk.dean* and got mand. for conf. and cons. 7 May 1273
(*Vet.Mon.*,no.255); cons. by 9 Nov. 1273 (*Inchcolm Chrs.*,28-29); occ.
29 Sept. 1277 (Durham, Dean & Chapter MSS, Misc.Chr.no.1047);
see prob. not yet vacant when a *Dk.offic.* is found in office 9 Oct.
1282 (*Fraser Papers*,218).

Hugh de Stirling (Strivelin) 1282 x 1283.

El. when Dk.canon, but d. at papal court without cons. before 13
Dec. 1283 (*CPL*,i,469).

William 1283 - 1285 x 1288.

El. when *Dk.dean* after death of Stirling, and got conf. and cons.
13 Dec. 1283 (ibid.); occ. 18 May 1285 (*Rites of Durham*,155); d.
before 10 Apr. 1288 (v.inf.).

Matthew de Crambeth 1288 - 1309.

El. when *Ab.dean* and Dk.canon on death of William, and got
conf. and cons. 10 Apr. 1288 (*Vet.Mon.*,no.306; cf. *CPL*,i,491 for
date); occ. 15 Sept. 1305 (*APS*,i,119); prob. still in poss. 16/17 Mar.
1309 (BM, MS Harleian 4694, fo.6; cf. G.W.S. Barrow, *Robert Bruce*,
264,n.2, 374,n.1); d. before 28 Aug. 1309 (*CDS*,iii,19; cf.21).

John de Leek/ Leche   1309 - 1311.
William Sinclair   1309 - 1337.

    Leek el. when Dk.canon by some of the chapter with support of Edward II before 28 Aug. 1309 when that king commended him to the pope (*Foedera*,II,i,86); lit. followed at curia with Sinclair which was still unresolved when Leek was appointed to Dublin abp. 18 May 1311 (*Vet.Mon.*,no.398; Eubel, *Hierarchia*,i,229).

    Sinclair el. when Dk.canon by some of the chapter, prob. a little before Leek's el. by others of the chapter (cf. Dowden, *Bishops*, 61-62); went to curia for conf.; lit. there with Leek until May 1311 (v.sup.), but did not obtain conf. and cons. until 8 May 1312 (*Vet. Mon.*,no.398); d. 27 June 1337 (Myln, *Vitae*, 15).

Richard de Pilmuir   1337 x 1338 - 1345 x 1347.
Malcolm de Innerpeffray 1337 x 1338 - 1338 x 1342.
Duncan de Strathearn   1337 x 1342 - 1344.

    Pilmuir el. when Dk.canon on death of Sinclair and presumably before 3 Jan. 1338 (see Innerpeffray below); lit. at curia with Innerpeffray and Strathearn; prov. 5 July 1344 (*Vet.Mon.*,no.559); cons. 14 July x 27 Sept. 1344 (ibid.,no.560; *CPL*,iii,170); occ. 20 Oct. 1345 (*Moray Reg.*,156); d. before 15 Oct. 1347 (v.inf.), prob. not long before (cf. *CPP*,i,124 where a pet. which he had supported was granted by pope in Nov. 1347).

    Innerpeffray el. when Dk.canon on death of Sinclair, prob. about same time as Pilmuir (v.sup.) and certainly before 3 Jan. 1338 when granted a safe-conduct to go to the curia for conf. (*CDS*,iii,no.1254); lit. with Pilmuir and Strathearn, but d. in curia without any result before death of Pope Benedict XII i.e. before 25 Apr. 1342 (*Vet.Mon.*, no.559).

    Strathearn challenged rights of both Pilmuir and Innerpeffray (being himself *Dk.prec.*) before death of Pope Benedict i.e. before 25 Apr. 1342 (ibid.); granted stipend at curia while called elect of Dunkeld 13 Mar. 1344 (*Vatikanische Quellen*,iii,699); lost lit. with Pilmuir by 5 July 1344 (v.sup.; cf. *M.prec.*).

Robert de Den   1347 x 1348.
Duncan de Strathearn 1347 - 1354.

    Den el. when *Dk.archd.* presumably on death of Pilmuir, but had apparently res. right having failed to get conf. before 28 Jan. 1348 (*CPL*,iii,245); d. before 30 Sept. 1349 (*CPP*,i,176).

    Strathearn prov. when *M.prec.* and *Dk.prec.* 15 Oct. 1347 on death of Pilmuir (*Vet.Mon.*,no.575); cons. by 9 Nov. 1347 (*CPL*,iii, 264); occ. 1 Apr. 1354 (*Kel.Lib.*,ii,385,389; *APS*,xii,9-11); prob. still in poss. 14 Dec. 1354 (*CPL*,iii,520).

John Luce 1355 - 1369.

    El. when *Dk.prec.* on death of Strathearn, and gets prov. 18 May 1355 (*Vet.Mon.*,no.621); surname is taken from that of his father James Luce (Ob.et Sol.,32,fo.59v); cons. by 29 June 1355 (*Vet.Mon.*, no.623); occ. 20 July 1369 (*Rot.Scot.*,i,939).

John de Carrick   1370 x 1371.
Michael de Monymusk   1370 - 1377.

    Carrick el. when royal chancellor (*HBC*,174) and given a grant from royal funds by David II to go to curia in pursuit of his right Jan. 1370 x Jan. 1371 (*ER*,ii,356); not successful.

    Monymusk el. when *G.dean* and got prov. 13 Nov. 1370 (Reg. Av.,172,fo.498; Dowden, *Bishops*,67); cons. 5 x 8 Jan. 1371 (Reg.Av., 176,fo.171v); d. 1 Mar. 1377 (Myln, *Vitae*,15).

Andrew Umfray 1377 x 1378.

    El. when *Dk.dean* and got prov. 17 June 1377 (Reg.Av.,202,fo. 47; Eubel, *Hierarchia*,i,232); promised common services 1 July 1377 (Hoberg, *Taxae*,48); d. at curia without cons. (*CPP*,i,555), before death of Pope Gregory XI i.e. before 27 Mar. 1378 (see Peebles below).

John de Peebles (Peblis) 1378 - 1390.

    El. when *St A.archd.* and royal chancellor and got prov. from Gregory XI i.e. before 27 Mar. 1378 (SRO, Transcripts from Vatican, i,no.34; *CPP*,i,538); cons. by authority of Urban VI c. June 1378 i.e. before doubts had been raised over legitimacy of this pope (SRO, Transcripts from Vatican,i,no.34; cf. *Dundee Chrs.*,12-13 and *RMS*, i,289-90); accepted regularly as bishop in royal records from Oct. 1378 (e.g. *Oliphants in Scotland*, 8, no.10, where editorial dating is wrong; *Family of Burnett*,157-8; *ER*,ii,588); got mand. from Clement VII for his cons. 21/22 Feb. 1379 (Reg.Av.,215,fo.70v-71); cons. by July 1379 in eyes of this pope (ibid.,215,fos.121v-122v; Vatican Archives, Introitus et Exitus,350,fo.27v); occ. 15 Aug. 1390 (*Chron. Wyntoun*,vi,367).

Note: For notes on English suffragans who bore the Dunkeld title during Great Schism and later, see Dowden, *Bishops,* 94-95 and *C.A. Rent.,*i,66-71.

Robert de Sinclair 1391 - 1395 x 1398.

    Trans. from *O.bp*. when also *M.dean* 1 Feb. 1391 (Eubel, *Hierarchia*,i,232; cf. *CPP*,i,575); occ. 11 Feb. 1395 (*Camb.Reg.*,317); d. before 27 Nov. 1398 (*Dipl.Norv*.,xvii B,300).

Robert de Cardeny   1398 - 1437.
William (?)   1430.

    Cardeny prov. when *Dk.dean* 27 Nov. 1398 (Eubel, *Hierarchia*, i,232); cons. by 20 Nov. 1399 (*APS*,i,574); d. 16/17 Jan. 1437 (Myln, *Vitae*,17; *Chron. Bower*,ii,502).

    William is said to pay part of his services for this see 4 July 1430 (PRO 31/9 - 27/216-7); prob. an error.

Donald de Macnachtan 1437.
James Kennedy   1437 - 1440.

    Macnachtan perhaps el. when *Dk.dean* Jan. x Feb. 1437 (Myln, *Vitae*,17-18; cf. Kennedy below); but there is no evidence that he sought papal conf. as Myln says, and he certainly was still alive as *Dk.dean* until July x Sept. 1440.

Kennedy el. when Dk.canon under royal pressure before 16 Feb. 1437 (*ACSB*,23; Myln, *Vitae*,18); prov. 1 July 1437 (*CPL*,viii,653); cons 16 May x 7 July 1438 (Dowden, *Bishops*,72); trans. to *St A.bp*. 22 April/ 1 June 1440.

Alexander de Lauder 1440.
El. May 1440 (*Chron.Extracta*,239); prov. when *Dk.archd*. 6 June 1440 (*CPL*,viii,265; *ACSB*,25); d. without cons. 11 Oct. 1440 (*Chron. Bower*,ii,502; Myln, *Vitae*,19).

Thomas Livingstone   1440 - 1460.
James Bruce (Brois)   1441 - 1447.
Livingstone prov. as abbot of Dundrennan by Pope Felix V 29 Nov. 1440 (*St A.Cop*.,305-7); cons., but never had poss.; d. 9 Apr. x 10 July 1460 (Dowden, *Bishops*,95-96; *RSCHS*,xii,120-55).
Bruce el. when *Dk.archd*. and got prov. 6 Feb. 1441 (*CPL*,ix, 129-30); cons. 4 Feb. 1442 (*HBC*,289, no source cited); trans. *G.bp*. 3 Feb. 1447.

William Turnbull 1447.
Prov. when G.canon 10 Feb. 1447 (*ACSB*,37); trans *G.bp*. when not yet cons. 27 Oct. 1447.

John de Ralston 1447 - 1451 x 1452.
Prov. as *Dk.dean* on trans. of Turnbull 27 Oct. 1447 (*ACSB*,39); cons. perhaps by 4 Apr. 1448, and certainly by 20 Apr. 1448 (Dowden, *Bishops*, 74-75); occ. 5 July 1451 (*Foedera* (O),xi,286); d. before 28 Apr. 1452 (v.inf.).

Thomas Lauder   1452 - 1475.
Thomas   1464.
Lauder prov. when *St A.chanc*. on death of Ralston 28 Apr. 1452 (*CPL*,x,599; *ACSB*,44); prob. still not yet cons. when granted temps. 22 June 1452 (*RMS*,ii,no.578); res. on pension 2 Oct. 1475 (*ACSB*, 179); d. 4 Nov. 1481 (Myln, *Vitae*,25).
Thomas paid common services as elect of Dunkeld 31 Jan. and 3 Feb. 1464, but money was repaid as the see was not then vacant (*ACSB*,280,54; there is no evidence for the identification with Thomas Spens suggested ibid.,54n).

James Livingstone 1475 - 1483.
Prov. when *Dk.dean* 2 Oct. 1475 (*ACSB*,71); cons. 30 June 1476 (Myln, *Vitae*,26); d. 28 Aug. 1483 (ibid.).

Alexander Inglis   1483 - 1485.
George Brown   1483 - 1515.
James Betoun   1507 - 1508.
Inglis el. when *Dk.dean* and *St A.archd*. on king's nom. before 17 Sept. 1483 (*Laing Chrs*.,no.191; cf. Myln, *Vitae*,27); still recognised as elect by king 26 May 1485 (*APS*,ii,171); but Brown won royal recognition by 16 Aug. 1485, and Inglis remained in his previous benefices without cons.
Brown prov. when *Ab.chanc*. 22 Oct. 1483 (*ACSB*,82; Myln,

Vitae,27); cons. 13 June 1484 at Rome (Brady, *Episcopal Succession*, i,p.xxii; PRO 31/9 - 29/493); prob. accepted as bp. by James III by 16 Aug. 1485 when witness of crown chrs. (*RMS*,ii,nos.1623-4; cf. no. 1581 which is misdated), and certainly by 22 Sept. 1485 (*Rot.Scot.*, ii,469; cf. Myln, *Vitae*,28-29); d. 15 Jan. 1515 (ibid.,54; cf. Dowden, *Bishops*,81).

Betoun when abbot/commendator of Dunfermline appointed vicar-general of Dunkeld to take charge because of senility of Brown; but pope at same time refused royal request that see should be reserved for him as Brown's successor 20 Dec. 1507 (PRO 31/9 - 1/85-86); nom. by king to *Ga.bp.* 1 Mar. 1508.

Andrew Stewart   1515 - 1516.
Gavin Douglas   1515 - 1522.
  Stewart el. under pressure from his brother the earl of Atholl soon after death of Brown; gained crown consent from duke of Albany in or soon after May 1515 when Albany came to Scotland, and forced chapter to hand over temps. of the see; gave these over to Douglas 16 x 28 Sept. 1516 after failing to obtain conf. (Myln, *Vitae*, 70-75; *James V Letters*,32).
  Douglas got crown nom. with support of his Aunt (Queen) Margaret when *Edin.St Giles prov.* and on giving up his right to *St A. abp.* 17 Jan. 1515 (*LP Henry VIII*,ii,no.31; *James V Letters*,17-18; cf. *ADCP*,49); prov. 25 May 1515 (Eubel, *Hierarchia*,iii,189; cf. *James V Letters*,23-24); imprisoned for more than a year on orders of Albany 16 July 1515 (*LP Henry VIII*,ii,no.779; Myln, *Vitae*,72); granted temps. by Albany after compromise with Stewart 16 Sept. 1516 (*RSS*,i,no.2807); cons. 21 Sept. 1516 (Dowden, *Bishops*,430; cf. *St A. Form.*,i,183-4); forfeited for treason 12 Dec. 1521 and fruits of see sequestered after his flight to England 21 Feb. 1522 (*LP Henry VIII*, iii,nos.1857,2063); d. in London 10 x 19 Sept. 1522 (Dowden, *Bishops*, 85).

Robert Cockburn   1524 - 1526.
  Trans. from *R.bp.* 27 Apr. 1524 (Eubel, *Hierarchia*,iii,189); active in Scotland as bp. by 6 May 1524 (*RMS*,iii,no.262); granted temps. 14 Sept. 1524 (*RSS*,i,no.3286); d. 12 Apr. 1526 (*Arch.Scotica*,iii,327).

George Crichton O.S.A. 1526 - 1544.
  Crown nom. when abbot of Holyrood 21 June 1526 (*APS*,ii,305); prov. by pope 25 June 1526 (Brady, *Episcopal Succession*,i,130; Eubel, *Hierarchia*,iii,189); still elect 17 July 1526 (PRO 31/9 - 32/110); d. Jan. 1544, before 20 Jan. (*ERS*,ii,183-5; cf. inf.).

Robert Crichton   1543 - 1571.
John Hamilton   O.Clun. 1544 - 1549.
Donald Campbell O.Cist. 1549 - 1553 x 1554.
  Crichton said to have had crown nom. when *Edin.St Giles prov.* as coadj. and successor to George Crichton (*HBC*,289, no source cited); not in fact likely to have had such support from the governor (the earl of Arran), who protested to pope 14 May 1543 that a res. and prov. had taken place regarding this see in the curia since death of James V (14

Dec. 1542) without any consultation with him (*LP Henry VIII*,xviii,pt.1, nos. 542-3; cf. no. 801 and pt. 2, nos. 477-8); appointment of Robert as coadj. and successor to George, with pension to George, must surely therefore be datable 17 Mar. 1543 (PRO 31/10 - 14/114; Eubel, *Hierarchia*,iii,189, where in both cases the date is given as 17 Mar. 1544, by which time George was certainly dead); lit. with Hamilton followed latter's prov. 17 Dec. 1544, and was in progress at curia 8 Jan. 1546 (Brady, *Episcopal Succession*, i,131-2) and 22 Dec. 1547, when Robert still based his claim on having acted as coadj. to George for a time (PRO 31/9 - 33/221-5); after trans.of Hamilton to *St A.abp*. lit. with Campbell by 22 Apr. 1550 (*RPC*,i,91); still lit. without poss. 18 Sept. 1553 (*RSS*,iv,nos. 2142-3); first occ. in poss. at parliament which effected change of governorship from Chatelherault (i.e. Arran) to Queen Mary of Guise 12 Apr. 1554 (*APS*,ii,603), and he res. his *Edin. St Giles prov*. on or before 1 May 1554; retained sec thereafter until forfeited 30 Aug. 1571 (*HBC*,289, no source cited).

   Hamilton granted temps. when abbot of Paisley on death of George Crichton 20 Jan. 1544 (*RSS*,iii,no.601); crown nom. to pope by Governor Arran 24 Jan. 1544 (*ERS*,ii,183-4,187; *LP Henry VIII*, xix,pt.1,nos.56-57); prov. 17 Dec. 1544 (Brady, *Episcopal Succession*, i,130-1); granted faculty to change his religious habit for dress of secular bishops 15 Mar. 1546 (Eubel, *Hierarchia*,iii,189); cons. 22 Aug. 1546 (SRO, Accts. of Master of Household (E.31/13), fo.219v); trans. to *St A.abp*. 28 Nov. 1547, but this was not effective until June 1549.

   Campbell when abbot of Coupar Angus granted temps. on trans. of Hamilton 23 June 1549 (*RSS*,iv,no.310); had got crown nom. to pope from Governor Chatelherault before 22 Apr. 1550, by which date he lit. in curia with Robert Crichton (*RPC*,i,91); still lit. with Crichton 18 Sept. 1553, being still the official crown nominee, prob. in poss. of fruits, but not papally conf. (*RSS*,iv,nos.2142-3); lost to Crichton prob. soon before 12 Apr. 1554 (v.sup.).

James Paton   1571 - 1596.
Robert Crichton 1584 - 1585.
Peter Rollock   1585 - 1607.

   Paton got crown nom. 8 Sept. 1571 following forfeiture of Crichton (*RSS*,vi,no.2812); lic. to elect issued to chapter 16 Feb. 1572 (ibid.,no.1486); crown conf. and mand. for cons. 20 July 1572 (ibid.,no.1672; Reg.Pres.,i,78); granted temps. 27 Apr. 1573 (*RSS*,vi,no.1943); not known how he stood in relation to the restored Crichton and Rollock; d. 20 July 1596 (inscription on headstone in parish of Muckhart, quoted Keith, *Bishops*, 97).

   Crichton progressively restored to see 1583 - 1584, getting conf. of full restoration 22 Aug. 1584 (*APS*,iii,373; Reg.Pres.,ii,114); acted as bp. 21 Jan. 1585 (*Laing Chrs*.,no.1092); d. soon before 26 Mar. 1585, when permission was given for his burial (*Edin.Recs*.,iv,405).

   Rollock gets crown prov. on death of Crichton 26 Mar./2 Apr. 1585 (Reg.Pres.,ii,132v; RSS,lii,fo.66); occ. in parliament as bp. 31 July 1585 (*APS*,iii,38lb); occ. 23 Dec. 1606 (*APS*,v,493); res. on or before 23 Apr. 1607 (RSS,lxxvi,fo.215); d. 31 Mar. 1631 x 30 June

1632 (*SP*,vii,191).

James Nicolson 1607.

    Crown prov. on res. of Rollock 23 Apr. 1607 (Reg.Pres.,iv,8v); d. 7 x 27 Aug. 1607 (Edin.Tests.,xliv,fo.8 of 4 June 1608; Calderwood, *History*,vi,671,677).

Alexander Lindsay 1607 - 1638.

    Crown prov. 28 Dec. 1607 (Reg.Pres.,iv,12v); cons. certainly 21 Oct. 1610 x 3 May 1611 (Spottiswoode, *History*,iii,209; *Original Letters* i,270), and prob. 23 Jan./ 24 Feb. 1611 (Calderwood, *History*,vii,154); depriv. 13 Dec. 1638 (Peterkin, *Records*,i,28); d. Oct. 1639 (*Dict.Nat. Biog.*,xxxiii,282, no clear source cited).

CHAPTER OF DUNKELD

There was prob. a community of culdees still at Dunkeld in early 12th century (see evidence cited *MRHS*,192; *RRS*,i,98,166-7,183), but there is no evidence that they ever formed a chapter for the see. The Dunkeld tradition of the 16th century was that a new college of secular canons was established in the time of David I along with the restored bishopric (Myln, *Vitae*, 4-5). In fact such a collegiate body does not appear until the early 13th century.

    Pope Alexander III confirmed the right to elect the bp. to the 'canons of Dunkeld' 'by common consent' 7 June 1163 (Fraser, *Wemyss*,ii,1-3; cf. Myln, *Vitae*,5); the language of this papal letter seems to be based in part on a request from Bp. Gregory, but the meaning of 'canons' at this date is obscure, for clerks with this designation are not found among the witnesses of surviving 12th century documents concerning this see (cf. Glasgow and Aberdeen). At the first documented episcopal election thereafter - that of 1211 - the archd. appears to have presided over a gathering of a synodal character which included both the 'chapter' and 'all the clergy' of the diocese (*AMW*, 373); clearly more than just some distinguishable group of 'canons' were involved, though the 'chapter' may have comprised an inner group of more important clergy. This chapter was still itself of a synodal character with a wide membership, as is clear from an act of the chapter (still under the archd.), authenticated by the chapter seal, which dates from 1214 x 1223, probably early in the period, and so early in the time of Bp. Hugh de Sigillo (*Lind.Cart.*,35-36).

    Very soon afterwards a varying proportion of the clergy who customarily witnessed acts of Bp. Hugh came for the first time to be distinguished from the others as 'canons', and among them one canon was sometimes identified as the precentor, e.g. 1214 x 1221 (*Inchaff. Chrs.*, 30-31, 43-44), 1214 x 1225 (*Holy.Lib.*,53), 1220 x 1225 (*Inchaff.Chrs.*, 42-43), 1221 x 1229 (*C.A.Chrs.*,i,63-66) and 1225 x 1229 (*St A.Lib.*,295-6); the archd. is still the leading figure of this group; this was still the position at first under Bp. Gilbert (1229/1230 - 1236), who had long been at Dunkeld as canon and bishop's chaplain

before his own election to the see, e.g. 1229 x 1236 (*Inchcolm Chrs.*, 12-13); but it appears to have been this bp. and not Bp. Geoffrey de Liberatione his successor (cf. Myln, *Vitae*, 10) who took the most important step in converting this synodal diocesan chapter into a collegiate body at the cathedral; no act of constitution survives, but a dean (who had previously been one of the canons) is found presiding over the 'chapter of Dunkeld' in place of the archd. 1231 x 1236 (*Dunf.Reg.*,77-78), and it is the dean and chapter who elected Bp. Geoffrey in 1236 (*Vet.Mon.*,no.85); the dean had certainly become superior in status to the archd by 21 Dec. 1238 (*Inchaff.Chrs.*,56-57), by which date all the eventual total of six cathedral dignities in addition to the older archd. had been established, with the doubtful exception of the chancellorship whose existence is not proved until towards the end of the century; Bp. Geoffrey had been Dk.canon under his predecessor, and 16th century tradition may well be right in reporting him as taking things further by introducing chapter statutes on the model of Salisbury and by providing endowments of such a character as to encourage the devlopment of a larger resident community of clergy at the cathedral (Myln, *Vitae*, 9-10); additions were still being made, however, to this cathedral chapter as late as the 15th century (cf. *MRHS*,169; cf. *RSCHS*, xiv, 30-32, 43-44).

EARLY DEANS IN DUNKELD

Elwyn 1178 x 1188.
    Occ. 1178 x 1188 (*Camb.Reg.*,no.191).

Matthew 1214 x 1221 - 1229 x 1236.
    Occ. 1214 x 1221 (*Inchaff.Chrs.*,no.36), 1214 x 1229 (*Arb.Lib.*, i,150, no.218; *Lind.Cart.*,36), 6 Dec. 1228 (*Holy.Lib.*,218), and 1229 x 1236 (*Inchaff.Chrs.*,no.59); possibly same as contemporary Matthew *Dk.dean.christ.Rattray*.

Denis (Dionisius) 1221 x 1229.
    Occ. 1221 x 25 May 1229 (*Laing Chrs.*,2).

DEANS OF DUNKELD

First known date: 1231 x 1236.
    Prebend: chs. of Inchaiden and Clunie by 1236 x 1249 (Myln, *Vitae*,10; Cowan, *Parishes*, 32, 84-85).

Adam de Prebenda 1231 x 1236 - 1245.
    Occ. 1229 x 1236 (*Dunf.Reg.*,nos. 131-3). having become dean since 1231 (*Balm.Lib.*,22); occ. 26 Apr. 1245 (*St A.Lib.*,307).

Robert de Stuteville 1245 x 1250 - 1273.
    Occ. 1245 x July 1250 (*St A.Lib.*,284); conf. after el. *Dk.bp.* 7 May 1273; cons. by 9 Nov. 1273.

William 1283.
    As dean conf. after el. *Dk.bp*. 13 Dec. 1283.

Simon (de Kinross?) 1288.
    Occ. 10 Apr. 1288 (*CPL*,i,491).

Hervey de Crambeth 1292 x 1296 - 1303.
    Occ. 17 July 1296 (*CDS*,ii,195), having got poss. since 21 June
1292 (see *Ab.dean*.); occ. 9 Feb. 1303 (*C.A. Chrs*.,i,168).

Matthew de Kinross 1304 - 1312 x 1321.
    Occ. 13 Aug. 1304 (*CDS*,ii,no.1573); occ. 1312 x 1321 (*RMS*,i,
464).

Nicholas de Hay 1324.
    Occ. 6 May 1324 (*Perth Blackfriars*, no.13).

William Bell 1329 - 1342 x 1343.
    Occ. 11 Nov. 1329 (*CPL*,ii,301); occ. 20 Feb. 1342 (*CPL*,ii,557);
d. 7 Feb. 1343 as canon (O.S.A.) of St. Andrews (*Chron.Bower*,i,363).

Robert Kinnaird/ Kennande/ Keneth(Kenes) 1351 - 1374 x 1376.
    As Kinnaird/Kennande got papal conf. 12 May 1351 (Collect.,14
fos. 162v, 182, 191v); occ. as Kenes 1347 x 1355 and 25 July 1362
(*Inchcolm Chrs*.,32,36); res. on exch. with Umfray for *Dk.prec*. 23
Oct. 1374 x 5 Feb. 1376 (v.inf.).

Andrew Umfray 1374 x 1376 - 1377.
    Conf. of coll. by ord. on exch. with Kinnaird 5 Feb. 1376 (*CPL*,
iv,222), which had taken place since 23 Oct. 1374 (*Scone Liber*,145-6);
prov. after el. *Dk.bp*. 17 June 1377, but died uncons. before 27 Mar.
1378.

Walter Trail 1380 - 1385.
    Prov. 18 Nov. 1380 (*CPP*,i,555); not known whether he ever had
poss.; prov. *St A.bp*. 29 Nov. 1385.

Salomon Rae x1389.
    Held it at death before 4 Sept. 1389 (v.inf.).

Thomas Stewart 1389.
    Prov. on Rae's death 4 Sept. 1389 (*CPP*,i,574). prob. unfruitfully.

William de Spynie (?) 1397.
    Said to be in poss. shortly before 24 Sept. 1397 (Reg.Av.,301,fos.
382-382v); but see *Ab.dean*. and *M.bp*.

Robert de Cardeny 1398.
    In poss. when prov. *Dk.bp*. 27 Nov. 1398.

Thomas de Machran (?) x1404.
    Perhaps held it and res. on exch. with Ramsay before Aug. 1404
(v.inf.).

William Ramsay 1404, 1407 - 1419 x 1420.
    In poss. 30 Aug. 1407, having obtained a 'ben. in Dk. dioc.' more
than three years before on exch. with Machran (*CPP*,i,635,632); occ.

13 May 1416 (*St A.Cop.*,65); prob. res. on exch. with Macnachtan for *Dk.treas.* 28 Aug. 1419 x 25 Mar. 1420 (v.inf.).

Adam de Gordon   1420.
Donald de Macnachtan 1419 x 1420 - 1440.
    Gordon prov. on Ramsay's death 25 Mar. 1420 (*CSSR*,i,185) unfruitfully.
    Macnachtan in poss. 3 June 1420 (*CSSR*,i,204), prob. after coll. by ord. on exch. for *Dk.treas.* 28 Aug. 1419 x 25 Mar. 1420; in poss. 9 July 1440 (*CPL*,ix,110).

John Painter   1440.
Robert de Tulloch   1440 - 1443.
Alexander de Lichton 1440.
Fergus Macaloven   x1442.
Andrew de Fife   1442.
David Ogilvie   1443.
    Painter claimed poss. 9 Sept. 1440 (*St A.Cop.*,493).
    Tulloch prov. on Macnachtan's death 29 Sept. 1440 (*CPL*,ix,130); is to res. right on exch. with Lichton without poss. 29 Oct. 1440 (ibid., 147); obtained poss. on Macaloven's death by 24 Apr. 1442 (Reg.Supp., 381,fo.278); is to res. on exch. with Ogilvie for *M.archd.* 30 Jan. 1443 (ibid.,388,fo.89v); but died before 10 July 1443 (v.inf.).
    Lichton prov. on exch. with Tulloch 29 Oct. 1440 (*CPL*,ix,147), prob. unfruitfully.
    Macaloven held it at his death before 24 Apr. 1442 (Reg.Supp., 381,fo.278).
    Fife got *com.priv.* against Tulloch 24 Apr. 1442 (Reg.Supp.,381, fo.278) unfruitfully.
    Ogilvie prov. on exch. with Tulloch 30 Jan. 1443 (ibid.,388,fo. 89v); but unfruitfully because of Tulloch's death.

John Stewart 1443.
Simon Reid   1444.
    Stewart prov. after el. on Tulloch's death 10 July 1443 (Reg. Supp.,388,fo.89v); new prov. 19/21 Dec. 1443 (ibid.,393,fo.237; *CPL*,ix,390); d. before 14 July 1445 (v.inf.), but annates paid to curia as late as 19 Jan. 1446 (*ACSB*,269).
    Reid had an earlier grace of prov. cancelled 8 Jan. 1444 (Reg. Supp.,394,fo.35v).

Robert Lauder   1445.
Richard (John) Clepham 1445.
John de Ralston   1445 - 1447.
    Lauder prov. on Stewart's death 14 July 1445 (Reg.Supp.,406, fo.300v *or* 310v).
    Clepham prov. under name 'John' 12 Nov. 1445 (ibid.,408,fo. 152), but res. before letters were expedited (ibid.; see *CPL*,ix,528,530 for name 'Richard').
    Ralston prov. on Stewart's death 26 Nov. 1445 (*CPL*,ix,529-30); prov. *Dk.bp.* 27 Oct. 1447.

Patrick Young 1447 - 1471 x 1474.

Prov. 6 Nov. 1447 (*CPL*,x,183); occ. 19 May 1468 (SRO, Airlie, 5/2); d. after 27 Nov. 1471 (see *Ga.archd*) and before 20 May 1474 (v.inf.); possibly res. on exch. with Livingstone for *Dk.prec*. 5 July 1473 x 18 May 1474 i.e. just before death.

Duncan Bunch   1471 x 1475.
James Livingstone 1473 x 1474 - 1475.
Henry Boyce   1474.
Alexander Rate   1475.
William Scheves   1475 - 1478.

Bunch prov. prob. on Young's death, but died without poss. after 3 Nov. 1473 and before 19 Dec. 1474 (see *G.coll.princ.*; *CPL*,xiii,42, 40).

Livingstone occ. 18 July 1474 (*C.A.Chrs.*,ii,67); prob. had moved from *Dk.prec.* by ord. coll. on Young's res. or death after 5 July 1473 (and before 18 May 1474); occ. 8 Nov. 1474 (SRO, Supp.Reg.Ho.Chrs., s.d.); prov. *Dk.bp.* 2 Oct. 1475, cons. 30 June 1476.

Boyce prov. on Young's death 20 May 1474 (Reg.Supp.,705,fo. 193).

Rate prov. on deaths of Young and Bunch 7 Jan. 1475 (*CPL*, xiii,40); after lit. with Livingstone gets new prov.on his elevation 2 Oct. 1475 (ibid.,47); d. before 5 Apr. 1479 (see *Ab.archd.*) prob. without poss.

Scheves prov. on Livingstone's elevation 2 Oct. 1475 (*CPL*,xiii, 42); prov. *St A.abp.-coadj.* 13 Sept. 1476; said to have poss. when prov. *St A.abp.* 11 Feb. 1478.

Alexander Inglis 1477 - 1496.

Prov. on elevation of Scheves 26 Nov. 1477/ 13 Feb. 1478 (Reg. Supp.,761,fo.23; *ACSB*,191), occ. 29 Apr. 1495 (*St A.Acta*,247); d. 25 Feb. 1496 (ibid.,263).

Gavin Douglas   1497 - 1498.
George Hepburn   1497 - 1527.

Douglas occ. 28 Jan. 1497 (Fraser, *Douglas*,iii,164); gets royal judgment in his favour against Hepburn 28 Oct. 1497 (*ADC*,ii,81-82); still lit. before king's council June/July 1498 (ibid.,241,284).

Hepburn had papal prov. and is condemned for this by king's council 28 Oct. 1497 (*ADC*,ii,81-82); still lit. June/July 1498 (v.sup.); occ. 4 Nov. 1504 (*St A.Acta*,276); occ. 28 Feb. 1527 (St A.Univ.Mun., AR,i,83); cf. *M.treas.*

James Hepburn 1526 - 1566.

Promised annates when appointed coadj. and successor to George Hepburn 29 Jan. 1526 (PRO 31/9 - 32/92-93); occ. 2 Mar. 1530 (*HMC* 3, *4th R.*,537); escheated before 29 Aug. 1552 (*RSS*,iv,no.1679); occ. 12 Oct. 1566 (*RMS*,iv,no.1805); d. before 30 Dec. 1566 (v.inf.); erroneously appears to occ. 5 Jan. 1568 (*RSS*,vi,no.90; cf. *Crichton prov.*).

John Barton (Bertoun) 1566 - 1586 x 1589.

Crown pres. on James Hepburn's death 30 Dec. 1566 (*RSS*,v,no. 3156); occ. 20 Feb. 1567 (*RSS*,vi,no.2306); appointed coadj. to *Dk.bp*. 7 Oct. 1584 (Reg.Pres.,ii,40), but did not succeed to see; occ. as dean 10 Feb. 1586 (SRO, Airlie, sec.48,no.38); d. by 20 Jan. 1589 (v.inf.).

Henry Lindsay 1589.
George Graham 1589 - 1603, 1617 (?).
    Lindsay gets crown pres. on Barton's death 20 Jan. 1589 (RSS, lviii,fo.15).
    Graham gets crown pres. on Barton's death 24 May 1589 (ibid., fo.154); occ. 15 June 1595 (SRO, Reg.Ho.Chr.no.3335) and 29 Sept. 1602 (*RMS*,vi,no.1539); appointed to *Db.bp*. Feb. 1603 and trans. to *O.bp*. 26 Aug. 1615; but occ. still as dean 10 Oct. 1611 (SRO, Airlie, sec.48,no.56) and 8 Mar. 1617 (*RMS*,vii,no.1602).

William Young 1610 - 1637 x 1641.
    Occ. 1 Sept. 1610 (SRO, Airlie,sec.5,no.50) and 12 June 1637 (SRO,Part.Reg.Sasines Edin.,xxvi,fo.281); d. by 30 June 1641 (Reg. Pres.,vii,97).

PRECENTORS/CHANTERS OF DUNKELD

First known date: 1214 x 1225.
    Prebend: ch. of Kinclaven in 1260 (*Camb.Reg*.,no.184; Cowan, *Parishes*,111).

Robert de Raperlaw 1214 x 1225, 1221 x 1229.
    Occ. 1214 x 1225 (*Holy.Lib*.,53); occ. 1221 x 1229 (*C.A.Chrs*., no.29); but note that both he and Carstairs appear in chr. of 1229 x 1236 simply as canons (*Inchcolm Chrs*.,no.14).

Peter de Carstairs 1238 - 1239.
    Occ. 31 Dec. 1238 (*Inchaff.Chrs*.,no.65) and Oct./Nov. 1239 (*Inchcolm Chrs*.,no.18).

Malcolm 1246 - 1258 x 1261.
    Occ. 26 May 1246 (BM, Add.Chrs.,nos.66, 569); occ. 1258 x 1261 (*St A.Lib*.,309).

William de Tylloel 1291.
    In poss. 19 Jan. 1291 (*CPL*, i,524).

Walter Bacon (Bakon) 1298.
    Pres. by Edward I 10 Aug. 1298 (*CDS*,ii,no.1003).

Duncan de Strathearn 1307 - 1347.
    Occ. 19 May 1315 when had had poss. for eight years (*Camb. Reg*.,270); prov. to *M.prec*. 8 July 1344, but seems to have retained poss. until prov. *Dk.bp*. 15 Oct. 1347 (*Vet.Mon*.,288-9; cf. *CPL*, iii,154,200).

John Luce 1355.

In poss. when prov. *Dk.bp*. after el. 18 May 1355.

John Barber x1356.
Held it sometime before 12 July 1356 (v.inf.).

Andrew Umfray 1356 - 1374 x 1376.
Prov. after coll. by ord. 12 July 1356 (Collect.,14,fos.165v, 182v); occ. 23 Oct. 1374 (*Scone Liber*, 145-6); res. on exch. with Robert Keneth/Kinnaird (v.inf.).

Robert Keneth/Kinnaird 1374 x 1376 - .
In poss. 5 Feb. 1376 after coll. by ord. on exch. with Umfray (*CPL*,iv,222).

Fergus de Tulloch x1411.
Held it, and either res. on exch. (presumably with Spalding or Masson), or retained it until death, before 7 Apr. 1411 (*CPP*,i, 597).

Patrick de Spalding 1402.
In poss. 15 Sept. 1402 (ibid.,618); res. before 7 Apr. 1411 (ibid.,597).

John Masson 1409.
In poss. 5 May 1409 when is to res. to ord. in favour of Atholl (Reg.Av.,332,fos.390v-392).

Nicholas de Atholl	1409 - 1447.
Thomas de Kinghorn	1411.
David Ogilvie	1435.
Richard Clepham	1446 - 1447.

Atholl gets papal mand. for coll. by ord. on res. of Masson 5 May 1409 (ibid.); this took effect, but lit. with Kinghorn followed in curia; got. prov. *Si neutri* 7 Apr. 1411 (*CPP*, i,597); claimed peaceable poss. from before July 1411 (*CSSR*,i,95); in poss. 18 Aug. 1435 (*CPL*,ix, 42); in poss. 13 May 1447 (Reg.Supp.,417,fo.187); res. on exch. with John de Atholl before 2 Sept. 1447 (ibid.,419,fo.269) and prob. before 26 Aug. 1447 (ibid.,419,fo.66).
Kinghorn lit. with Atholl 7 Apr. 1411 (*CPP*,i,597).
Ogilvie prov. on reported death of Atholl 17 June 1435 (Reg. Supp.,320,fo.192) unfruitfully.
Clepham prov. on reported death of Atholl 11 May 1446 (ibid., 411,fo.156); absolved for irregularity in this prov., Nicholas de Atholl being still alive, 13 May 1447 (ibid.,417,fo.187).

John de Atholl	1447 - 1458 x 1460.
Thomas Penven (?)	1447.
Henry Logan	1447.
Richard Clepham	1447 - 1449.
Alan Clepham	1449.

Atholl coll. by ord. on exch. with Nicholas de Atholl for *Dk.chanc*. 13 May x 26 Aug. 1447 (v.sup.), and got new prov. 2 Sept. 1447 (Reg. Supp.,419,fo.269); had had poss. for over a year by 28 Jan. 1449 (*CPL*, x,382); res. on exch. with Livingstone for *Dk.treas*. 16 Feb. 1458 x 10

June 1460 (Reg.Supp.,532,fo.29v; cf. *CPL*,xi,180).

Penven said to have been prov. on death or res. of Nicholas de Atholl 26 Aug. 1447 (Reg.Supp.,419,fo.66); but this may be an error for *Dk.chanc.*

Logan was pres. by dean and chapter *sede vacante* on reputed death of Nicholas de Atholl and got poss.; new prov. 2 Sept. 1447 (Reg. Supp.,419,fo.270v); prob. dispossessed by John de Atholl.

Richard Clepham prov. anew on basis that exch. by Nicholas de Atholl was invalid 12 Sept. 1447 (Reg.Supp.,420,fo.35); new prov. after coll. 23 Nov. 1447 (ibid.,421,fo.116v); claims poss. after new prov. 28 Feb. 1448 (ibid.,423,fo.220v); prov. on death of Nicholas de Atholl 28 Jan. 1449 (*CPL*,x,382); no poss. 2 May 1449 (Reg.Supp.,436,fo.97v); res. right in favour of Alan Clepham before 24 May 1449 (v.inf.).

Alan Clepham prov. on dem. of Richard Clepham 24 May 1449 (Reg.Supp.,436,fo.200) unfruitfully.

James Livingstone	1458 x 1460 - 1473 x 1474.
Nicholas Monypenny	1466.
James Inglis	1472.
Patrick Young (?)	1473 x 1474.

Livingstone in poss. 10 June 1460 (Reg.Supp.,531,fo.129) after exch. with John de Atholl for *Dk.treas.* since 16 Feb. 1458; still in poss. 5 July 1473 (*CPL*,xiii,554); moved to *Dk.dean.* certainly by 18 July 1474 and presumably before 18 May 1474 (v.inf.) perhaps on exch. with Young.

Monypenny gets *com.priv.* against Livingstone 19 Nov. 1466 (*CPL*,xii,554) unfruitfully.

Inglis prov. on reported dem. of Livingstone 13 Nov. 1472 (Reg. Supp.,684,fo.83v); d. by 7 Jan. 1474 (see *Ab.archd.*).

Young said to have held it at death before 18 May 1474 (v.inf.) and so may have been coll. on exch. with Livingstone for *Dk.dean.* just before his death.

Robert Blackadder	1474 - 1474 x 1476.
Patrick Young	1474 - 1480 x 1490.

Blackadder prov. on death of first Patrick Young 18 May 1474 (*CPL*,xiii,33); no poss., and by 2 Mar. 1474 was content with pension on fruits (*ACSB*,182); cons. *G.bp.* Apr. 1483.

Young (second of name) occ. 8 Nov. 1474 (SRO, Reg.Ho.Supp. Chrs.,s.d.); had presumably succ. to right of first Patrick Young; occ. 27 Oct. 1480 (*SHS Misc.*,viii,15); d. by 5 Oct. 1490 (v.inf.).

William Lindsay 1490.

Prov. on Young's death 5 Oct. 1490 (*CPL*,xiv,280).

Walter Brown 1491 - 1493.

Occ. 10 Jan. 1491 (SRO, Airlie,44/3); occ. 28 Feb. 1493 (*Arb. Lib.*,ii,273).

Robert Boswell 1500.

Res. on exch. at curia with Wood for *Restalrig dean.* 10 Jan. 1500 (PRO 31/9 - 31/3).

Henry Wood 1500 - 1501.
Prov. on exch. with Boswell 10 Jan. 1500 (ibid.); res. on exch. with Fenton for *Dk.treas*. 20 Feb. x 7 Dec. 1501 (v.inf.).

James Fenton 1501 - 1524.
Occ. 7 Dec. 1501 (SRO, Dalguise, no.8), having prob. obtained it on exch. since 20 Feb. 1501 (see *Dk.treas*.); consents to have Hay as coadj. 6 Dec. 1521 (PRO 31/9 - 31/371-2); occ. 12 Jan. 1524 (SRO, King James VI Hospital, sec.4,no.24).

Alexander Hay 1521 - 1527 x 1530.
Is to be coadj. to Fenton 6 Dec. 1521 (v.sup.); occ. 13 July 1527 (*RMS*,iii,no.479); dem. by Mar. 1530 (v.inf.).

Robert Crichton	1530 - 1534.
John Douglas	1530 - 1534 x 1537.
David Douglas	1533.
Robert Montgomery	1533.

Crichton lit. 26 May 1533 (PRO 31/9 - 32/241); stated 22 Mar. 1534 to have had coll. by ord. and papal prov. more than four years before, and to have poss. (*James V Letters*,260).

John Douglas lit. 26 May 1533 (PRO 31/9 - 32/241); by 22 Mar. 1534 had lit. for over four years and had lost (*James V Letters*,260); d. before 8 Jan. 1537 (v.inf.).

David Douglas had prov. and lit. with Crichton and John Douglas; res. right in favour of Montgomery 26 May 1533 (PRO 31/9 - 32/241).

Montgomery surrog. to right of David Douglas 26 May 1533 (ibid.).

David Bonar	1537.
James Salmond	1537 - 1538.
Mark Ker	1538 - 1547.

Bonar had prov. on death of John Douglas, and res. right in favour of Salmond 26 Jan.1537 (PRO 31/9 - 33/35-36; cf. 33/53).

Salmond prov. on death of John Douglas 8 Jan. 1537 (PRO 31/9 - 33/53); lit. with Ker, and res. right in his favour in return for pension 27 Sept. 1538 (ibid.,33/90 - 91; cf. *St A.Form*.,ii,56-57).

Ker had ord.coll. and poss. (ibid.); won lit. with Salmond 27 Sept. 1538, in terms of supplication granted 28 Apr. 1538 (PRO 31/9 - 33/90-91); occ. 25 July 1540 (Fraser, *Grandtully*, i,83); occ. 3 June 1547 (SRO, Acts and Decreets, viii,fo.567).

William Adamson 1558 - 1563 x 1565.
Occ. 2 Dec. 1558 (SRO, Airlie, sec.28,no.10); occ. 8 Sept. 1563 (*RSS*,v,no.1450); d. before 10 June 1565 (v.inf.).

William Curll 1565 - 1566 x 1571.
Crown pres. on Adamson's death 10 June 1565 (*RSS*,v,no.2113); occ. 2 Feb. 1566 (ibid.,no.2602); escheated before 6 Nov. 1571 (ibid., vi,no.1346).

George Ruthven x1571.
Held it at death before 13 Sept. 1571 (v.inf.).

James Ruthven   1571 - 1595.
John Crichton   1584.

     Ruthven pres. by crown on George Ruthven's death 13 Sept. 1571 (*RSS*,vi,no.1281); occ. 22 July 1572 (ibid.,no.1674); occ. 16 Jan. 1585 (Fraser, *Grandtully*, i,105); crown pres. confirmed on Curll's death 9 Mar. 1585 (Reg.Pres.,ii,125); occ. 20 Dec. 1595 (*HMC* 72, *Laing*, i,83).

     Crichton pres. by crown on Curll's death 10 Dec. 1584 (Reg.Pres., ii,119).

Alexander Ireland   1602 - 1637.

     Crown pres. on Curll's death 10 July 1602 (RSS,lxxiii,fo.40); occ. 12 June 1637 (SRO, Part.Reg. Sasines Edin.,xxvi,fo.281).

CHANCELLORS OF DUNKELD

First known date: 1274 (*SHS Misc*.,vi,48).

     Prebend: ch. of Lethendy at Reformation and prob. by 1274 (*Dunk.Rent*.,347; cf. Cowan, *Parishes*,131).

Note: the 'Thomas the chancellor' found 6 Oct. 1226 (*Dunf.Reg*.,no. 218) was presumably Thomas de Stirling the king's chancellor (*HBC*, 174), or just possibly the bishop's chancellor.

Thomas de Preston (?)   1274-5 *or* 1287.

     Perhaps (by inference only) in poss. 1274-5 or 1287 (*SHS Misc*., vi,48, 30).

Robert   1283.

     In poss. 13 Dec. 1283 (*CPL*,i,469-70).

William Sibbald   x1371.

     Held it at death before 13 Sept. 1371 (v.inf.).

Alexander Man   1371 - 1376.

     Prov. on Sibbald's death 13 Sept. 1371 (Reg.Av.,176,fo.291); in poss. 4 Oct. 1374 (ibid.,193,fo.506v); prob. res. on getting *R.archd*. in terms of prov. of 19 Aug. 1376.

John de Glasgow   1378 - 1387.

     Occ. 24 Jan. 1378 (*Glas.Reg*.,i,289-92); res. on exch. with Lang for *Dk.subd*. some 26 years before Aug. 1413, i.e. 1387 (v.inf.).

John Lang   1387 - 1419.
John de Rattray (Retro)   1405.

     Lang coll. by ord. on exch. for *Dk.subd*. c.Aug. 1387 (*CPP*, i, 600); in poss. 24 May 1405 (*CPP*,i,601); is to res.in favour of Child 23 Aug. 1419 (*CPL*,vii,114).

     Rattray prov. 24 May 1405 (*CPP*,i,631) unfruitfully.

Nicholas Child   1418 - 1419.

     Prov. by Benedict XIII on res. of Lang 15 June 1418 (Reg.Vat., 329,fos.51-52v); prov. again by Martin V 23 Aug. 1419 (*CPL*,vii,114).

John Wincester 1426 - 1426 x 1431.

    Occ. 15 Mar. 1426 (*RMS*,ii,15-16), after coll. by ord. (*CSSR*,ii, 144); dem. before 17 Dec. 1431 (Reg.Supp.,272,fo.244).

John Gyl 1439.

    Occ. 18 Mar. 1439 (R.K. Hannay, *Statutes of the Faculty of Arts*, 112; cf. *IR*,xiii,104-7).

John de Atholl 1445 - 1447.

    Occ. 13 Mar. 1445 (Fraser, *Wemyss*,ii,69); res. on exch. with Nicholas de Atholl for *Dk.prec*. 13 May x 26 Aug. 1447.

Nicholas de Atholl 1447.

    Coll. by ord. on exch. after 13 May 1447 (Reg.Supp.,419,fo.269), but died before 26 Aug. 1447 (v.inf.).

Thomas Penven	1447 - 1461.
Richard Clepham	1447 - 1448 x 1452.
George Schoriswood	1451 x 1452 - 1454.
John Donaldson (Donaldi)	1452 - 1480.

    Penven prov. on death of Nicholas de Atholl 26 Aug. 1447 (*CPL*, x,366); cf. *Dk.prec*. for prov. on same date to that dignity (Reg.Supp., 419,fo.66); in poss. 9 May 1450 (ibid.,445,fo.22v) and 3 Nov. 1450 (*CPL*,x,473); prob. lost poss. to Schoriswood 1451-1452, and perhaps earlier to Clepham (v.inf.); lit. with Donaldson and Schoriswood 12 Jan. 1454 (Reg.Supp.,470,fo.249); no poss. 16 Nov. 1458 (*CPL*,xii, 29); res. right to Donaldson for pension on fruits 5 Mar. 1561 (Reg. Supp.,536,fo.245).

    Clepham claims poss. 27 Oct. 1447 (*CPL*,x,291); perhaps this is an error for *Dk.prec*.; prov. on death of Nicholas de Atholl or res. of John de Atholl only on 12 Aug. 1448 (Reg.Supp.,430,fo.2); perhaps obtained poss. c.1451 (see Penven); still had some right at death before 21 Jan. 1452 (v.inf.).

    Schoriswood had crown pres. *sede vacante* i.e. 5 July 1451 x 22 June 1452 (Reg.Supp.,471,fo.38v), perhaps on Clepham's death; occ. 20 Nov. 1452 (*ER*,v,491); lit. with Penven and Donaldson 12 Jan. 1454 (Reg.Supp.,470,fo.249); had poss. when prov. *B.bp*. 8 Mar. 1454 (*CPL*,x,625-6) and when granted prov. to this dignity at king's request 20 Mar. 1454 (Reg.Supp.,471,fo.38v); cons. by 1 July 1454.

    Donaldson prov. on Clepham's death 21 Jan. 1452 (*CPL*,x,232); claims poss. 13 Oct. 1453 (*CPL*,x,163); lit. with Penven and Schoriswood 12 Jan. 1454 (Reg.Supp.,470,fo.249); surrog. to Schoriswood's right 12 Mar. 1454 (*CPL*,x,728-9); in poss. 15 Jan. 1456 (ibid.,xi,33); new prov. on res. of Penven 5 Mar. 1461 (Reg.Supp.,536,fo.245; cf. *CPL*,xii,125); occ. 17 Feb. 1467 (*Brech.Reg*.,i,193); in poss. 18 Dec. 1480 (v.inf.).

Walter Drummond 1480 - 1496.

    Gets *com.priv*. against Donaldson 18 Dec. 1480 (*CPL*,xiii,722-3); occ. 3 Aug. 1489 (Fraser, *Wemyss*,ii,112); occ. 21 Mar. 1496 (*Brech.Reg*.,ii,134).

George Brown 1500 - 1504.
Occ. 20 June 1500 (SRO, Airlie, sec. 12,no.209) and 7 Feb. 1504 (*Arb.Lib.*,ii,350,no.438); d. before 25 Oct. 1507 (*Dunk.Rent.*,165; cf.307).

Walter Small 1505.
Occ. 3 Nov. 1505 (*St A.Acta*, 279); moved to *Dk.treas*.

Robert Cockburn 1507.
In poss. when prov. *R.bp* 9 July 1507.

Gilbert Strathauchin 1507 - 1510.
Patrick Painter 1509 - c.1517.
Strathauchin promises annates and gets prov. on cons. of Cockburn 23 Dec. 1507 (PRO 31/9 - 31/179); mand. for poss. 1 Jan. 1508 (ibid., 1/89-90); still no poss. 24 Apr. 1510 (ibid.,31/179).
Painter occ. 18 May 1509 (*Glas.Reg.*,ii,520); occ. c.1517 (*Dunk. Rent.*,338).

James Laycock (?) x c.1517.
Said to have held it before 1517 (Myln, *Vitae*,63); but prob. error for *Dk.subd*.

William Douglas 1534 - 1540.
George Newton x1536.
James Strathauchin 1536.
Douglas occ. 3 Apr. 1534 (*TA*,vi,207); occ. 25 July 1540 (Fraser, *Grandtully*,i,83).
Newton had some right at death before 27 June 1536 (v.inf.).
Strathauchin promises annates and gets prov. on Newton's death 27 June 1536 (PRO 31/9 - 33/43) unfruitfully.

George Ogilvie 1542 - 1543.
Occ. 19 June 1542 and 3 May 1543 (*RMS*,iii,nos.2887, 2929).

Alexander Ogilvie 1550 - 1553.
Occ. 30 July 1550 (*RMS*,iv,no.496); is to res. on exch. with Gordon 18 June 1553 (v.inf.).

William Gordon 1553 - 1568 x 1571.
Crown pres. on exch. with Ogilvie 18 June 1553 (*RSS*,iv,no. 1997); occ. 22 Nov. 1568 (SRO, Reg.Deeds,xi,fo.155); d. before 23 Apr. 1571 (v.inf.).

William Edmonston (Edmeston) 1571 - 1596.
Crown pres. on Gordon's death 23 Apr. 1571 (*RSS*,vi,no.1150); pres. again 18 Jan. 1576 (*RSS*,vii,no.403); occ. 21 Aug. 1596 (SRO, Erroll Chrs.,no.1409).

George Pitullo 1605.
Crown pres. on Edmonston's death 25 Nov. 1605 (RSS,lxxiv, fo.407).

William Banewis 1619 - 1622.
Occ. 14 Apr. 1619 and 18 Jan. 1622 (SRO, Part.Reg.Sasines

Edin.,xx,fo.328 and xvi,fo.87).

James Drummond 1623 - 1633.
Occ. 12 Aug. 1623 (SRO, Airlie, sec.48,no.80) and 30 Oct. 1633 (SRO, Drummond Castle, box 6,10/5).

John Strachan 1634 - 1637.
Occ. 28 June 1634 (ibid.,box 23, 3/9) and 12 June 1637 (SRO, Part.Reg.Sasines Edin.,xxvi,fo.281).

TREASURERS OF DUNKELD

First known date: 1238.
An apparent treasurer appears x 1178 (*C.A.Rent.*,i,334-5,nos. 39-41); but this source is suspect.
Prebend: a preb. was in existence by 1274 (*SHS Misc.*,vi,48, 73); by Reformation this preb. comprised vic. fruits of Little Dunkeld, Caputh and Dowally (Reg.Pres.,i,100v); Caputh and Dowally formed part of Little Dunkeld until 1484 x 1506 (Myln, *Vitae*, 42-43; cf. Cowan, *Parishes*, 26-27, 47, 134).

Robert 1238 - 1271.
Occ. 31 Dec. 1238 (*Inchaff.Chrs.*,no.65); occ. 5 Mar. 1271 (*C.A.Chrs.*,i,17).

John Painter (Payntour, Pictoris) 1328 - 1329.
In poss. 13 Oct. 1328 and 27 Jan. 1329 (*CPL*,ii,284,286); perhaps moved to *M.dean*.

John de Kinnaird 1345.
Occ. 20 Oct. 1345 (*Moray Reg.*,156-7).

Donald de Macnachtan 1417 - 1418 x 1420.
In poss. in eyes of Benedict XIII 1 Mar. 1417 (Reg.Av.,349,fos. 92-92v); in poss. in eyes of Martin V 29 Jan. 1418 (*CPL*,vii,102-3); occ. 28 Aug. 1419 (Fraser, *Grant*,iii,15-16); prob. res. on exch. with Ramsay for *Dk.dean*.

William de Ramsay x1420.
Prob. obtained it on exch. with Macnachtan; held it at death before 25 Mar. 1420 (*CSSR*,i,185,234).

Richard de Creich 1420.
Prov. on Ramsay's death 25 Nov. 1420 (*CSSR*,i,234).

Walter Stewart 1428 - 1428 x 1429.
In poss. 11 Aug. 1428 (*CSSR*,ii,235); res. in favour of Archer in return for his right in *M.dean*.before May 1429 (*CPL*,viii, 411-12).

Thomas Archer 1429 - 1432.
Presumably had coll. by ord. by May 1429 (v.sup.); but new prov. to a different preb. in Dunkeld 27 Apr. 1432 (*ACSB*,108).

Ninian Spot 1454.
   Occ. 24 Sept. 1454 (SRO, Bargany Papers, no.1).

Maurice Macnab (Makab) x1456.
   Held it at death before 10 Jan. 1456 (Reg.Supp.,486,fo.190;
cf. 532, fo.29v.).

James Livingstone   1456 - 1458 x 1460.
Nicholas Monypenny   1456.
Walter Stewart   1456.
   Livingstone obtained it on Macnab's death and had poss. 10 Jan.
1456 (Reg.Supp.,486,fo.190); in poss. 16 Feb. 145ε (*CPL*,xi,180); res.
on exch. with Atholl for *Dk.prec.* before 10 June 1460 (v.inf.).
   Monypenny had prov. on Macnab's death, and obtained new prov.
10 Jan. 1456 (Reg.Supp.,486,fo.190).
   Stewart said to have some right 10 Jan. 1456 (ibid.).

John de Atholl 1458 x 1460 - 1460.
   Got it on exch. with Livingstone by 10 June 1460 (Reg.Supp.,531,
fo.129); new prov. 3 July 1460 (ibid.,532,fo.29v).

David Hay 1470.
   Occ. 8 June 1470 (Fraser, *Wemyss*, ii,96).

William Livingstone   1474 - 1494.
Alexander Tours/Toure/Towris 1479 - 1479 x 1492.
   Livingstone occ. 8 Nov. 1474 (SRO, Reg.Ho.Supp.Chrs.,s.d.); occ.
31 Jan. 1494 (*RMS*,ii,no.2354).
   Tours claimed poss. 14 Apr. 1479 (Reg.Supp.,780,fo.89; *CPL*,
xiii,627); had had coll. by ord. and poss., then prov. 22 Apr. 1479 (Reg.
Supp.,780,fo.211); moved to *Dk.archd.* 6 Nov. 1479 x 8 Mar. 1492.

James Fenton 1499 - 1501.
   Occ. 15 Feb. 1499 (SRO, Reg.Ho.Supp.Chrs.,s.d.); occ. 20 Feb.
1501 (*RMS*,ii,no.2568); prob. res. on exch. with Wood for *Dk.prec.*
before 7 Dec. 1501.

Henry Wood 1501 - 1502.
   Occ. 7 Dec. 1501 (SRO, Dalguise, no.8), having prob. obtained it
on exch; occ. 30 May 1502 (*RMS*,ii,no.2655).

Walter Small 1505 x 1507 - 1532.
   Prob. moved from *Dk.chanc.* 3 Nov. 1505 x 9 July 1507; occ. 19
Feb. 1508 and c.1517 (*Dunk.Rent.*,245,338); accepted Tailliefeir as
coadj. 7 Nov. 1532, with both agreeing to a pension for George Small
in terms of supplication granted 14 Sept. 1532 (PRO 31/9 - 32/211-12).

Laurence Tailliefeir 1532 - 1543 x 1545.
   Promised annates as coadj. 19 Nov. 1532 (ibid.,32/262-3); occ.
Aug. 1534 x Aug. 1535 (*ER*,xvi,375); George Small res. pension in
Tailliefeir's favour 21 Sept. 1540 (PRO 31/9 - 33/105-6); occ. 6 June
1543 (SRO, Prot.Bk. Edward Dickson, fo.85); d. before 9 Dec. 1545,
and prob. before 30 July 1545 (v.inf.).

David Hamilton 1545 - 1548.

Occ. 30 July 1545 (*TA*,viii,387); crown pres. on Tailliefeir's death 9 Dec. 1545 (*RSS*,iii,no.1421), occ. 2 May 1548 (*RSS*,iii,no.2755); res. but promises annates for right of return 13 July 1548 (v.inf.).

John Hamilton 1548 - 1549.

Promises annates and gets prov. 13 July 1548 (PRO 31/9 - 33/239-40; but note that source transfers names of John and David); in poss. and is to res. 6 Oct. 1549 (*RSS*,iv,no.445).

John Moncreiff	1549 - 1561.
Stephen Culross/ Wilson	1554 - 1561.
Robert Abercrombie	c.1561 - 1561 x 1573.

Moncreiff gets crown pres. 6 Oct. 1549 (ibid.); occ. 26 Nov. 1549 (*RMS*,iv,no.765) and 1561 (*Thirds of Benefices*,92).

Culross occ. 30 Aug. 1554 (SRO, Prot.Bk. James Harlaw,fo.90v); lit. with Abercrombie under name 'Wilson' c.1561 (*Dunk.Rent.*,347-8); perhaps d. before 12 Apr. 1561 (see *O.treas.*).

Abercrombie lit. with Culross/Wilson c.1561 (v.sup.); became Jesuit overseas before 19 Dec. 1573 (v.inf.).

Duncan McNair 1573 - 1577.

Crown pres. on depriv. of Abercrombie 19 Dec. 1573 (*RSS*,vi,no. 2241); occ. 16 Apr. 1574 (*Laing Chrs.*,224) and 22 Mar. 1577 (SRO, Airlie,sec.5,no.34).

Walter Stewart	1582.
William Glass senior	1583 - 1623.

Stewart gets crown pres. on McNair's death 17 Feb. 1582 (Reg. Pres.,ii,69).

Glass gets crown pres. on McNair's death 1 Aug. 1583 (ibid.,ii, 92); occ. 16 Jan. 1585 (Fraser, *Grandtully*,i,105); occ. 12 Aug. 1623 (SRO, Airlie, sec.48,no.80).

Note: this ben. was granted as part of stipend of minister of Little Dunkeld 14 Feb. 1588 (RSS,lvii,fo.20).

William Glass junior 1633 - 1637.

Occ. 30 Oct. 1633 (SRO, Drummond Castle, box 6,10/5); said to be son of William Glass senior (Scott, *Fasti*,iv,158); occ. 12 June 1637 (SRO, Part.Reg.Sasines Edin.,xxvi,fo.281).

Alexander Rollo 1637 x 1638 - 1641.

Had pres. from bp. (and so presumably June 1637 x Dec. 1638), and then gets crown conf. to ben. 8 Nov. 1641 (*RMS*,ix,no.1013).

SUBDEANS OF DUNKELD

First known date: 1238.

Prebend: ch. of Obney in 1419 (*CSSR*,i,81); this ch. had been a simple preb. in 1274 (*SHS Misc.*,vi,49) and its holder is not customarily identified as the subdean until the time of William Croyser

from 1419 onwards (cf. Cowan, *Parishes*,158).

William 1238.
    Occ. as subdean 31 Dec. 1238 (*Inchaff.Chrs*.,no.65).

William de Yetholm (Iheteme) 1309 x 1321.
    Held it as subdean before 7 Dec. 1345 (*CPL*,iii,198), prob.
in period 1309 x 1321 (see *Db.archd*.).

John Lang 1387.
    Res. 'vic. of Obney' on exch. with Glasgow for *Dk.chanc.*
some 26 years before Aug. 1413 i.e. 1387 (*CPP*,i,600).

John de Glasgow   1387 - 1403.
Richard de Creich   1403 - 1415.
    Glasgow coll. by ord. to 'vic. of Obney' on exch. for *Dk.chanc.*
c. Aug. 1387 (v.sup.); lit. with Creich over Obney preb. in curia 21
Oct. 1403 (Reg.Supp.,98,fo.283v); lost poss. eventually (*CSSR*,i,
38-39).
    Creich lit. with Glasgow 21 Oct. 1403 (v.sup.); in poss. of
Obney preb. 10 Oct. 1404 (*CPP*,i,620) and 6 Jan. 1413 (ibid.,599);
is to res. on prov. to another ben. 20 June 1415 (v.inf.).

William Croyser   1415 - 1430.
Michael de Ochiltree 1419.
Robert de Crannach   1424.
John Malcolmi   1425.
    Croyser prov. to Creich's preb. 20 June 1415 (*CPP*,i,603); in
poss. 2 May 1419 (*CSSR*,i,39); restored after erroneous prov. to
Robert de Crannach 31 July 1426 (*CPL*,vii,464-5); agrees to res. subd.
in favour of David de Crannach 31 Oct. 1430 (Reg.Supp.,263,fo.179).
    Ochiltree prov. to Obney preb. i.e. subdean, 2 May/26 June 1419
(*CSSR*,i,39,81) unfruitfully.
    Crannach prov. to subd. 8 Dec. 1424 on (mistaken) res. or depriv.
of Croyser (*CSSR*,ii,77).
    Malcolmi prov. to subd. 4 Sept. 1425 (ibid.,ii,115).

David de Crannach   1430 - 1440.
Thomas Bell (Bele)   1431.
Alexander de Lichton 1440.
    Crannach prov. to subd. on dem. of Croyser 31 Oct. 1430 (v.sup.)
prov. as part of a deal with him (see *St A.archd.Lothian*) 11 Mar. 1431
(*ACSB*,108); res. in curia on exch. with Tulloch 23 Sept. 1440 (*CPL*,
ix,105-6; cf. *B.dean*.).
    Bell prov. 21 Mar. 1431 (Reg.Supp.,267,fo.117) unfruitfully.
    Lichton gets *com.priv*. against Crannach for adherence to Council
of Basel 5 July 1440 (*CPL*,ix,103).

Thomas de Tulloch 1440.
    Prov. on exch. with Crannach in curia 23 Sept. 1440 (*CPL*,ix,105-
6); res. on same day in favour of Ker (Reg.Supp.,367,fo.290v); prov.
R.bp. 26 Sept. 1440.

Stephen Ker 1440 - 1449 x 1454.
Alexander Piot 1445.
Ker prov. on Tulloch's res. 23 Sept./3 Oct. 1440 (Reg. Supp.,367, fo.290v; *CPL*,ix,143-4); d. Feb. 1449 x May 1454 (see *Bothans prov.*).
Piot said 28 July 1445 to have had recent prov. to Obney (Olmer) preb., but no poss. (*CPL*,ix,508).

Alexander Inglis 1469 - 1477-8.
In poss. 8 Aug. 1469 (*CPL*,xii,683); prov. *Dk.dean.* 26 Nov. 1477/ 13 Feb. 1478.

James Laycock x1490.
Held it prob. at death some time before 30 Mar. 1490 (*RMS*,ii,no. 1942).

David Abercrombie 1494 - c.1517 x 1531.
Occ. 31 Jan. 1494 (*RMS*,ii,no.2354); occ. c.1517 (*Dunk.Rent.*, 338); d. by 29 Nov. 1531 (v.inf.).

Alexander Erskine 1531 - 1550 x 1553.
Crown pres. on Abercrombie's death 29 Nov. 1531 (*RSS*,ii,no. 1065); occ. 27 Nov. 1549 (Patrick, *Statutes*,88); prob. still in poss. 10 June 1550 (Stevenson & Wood, *Seals*,ii,349, where he is called 'subdeacon'); d. by 5 Sept. 1553 (v.inf.).

Robert Hamilton 1553.
Crown pres. on Erskine's death 5 Sept. 1553 (*RSS*,iv,no.2128, where printed text wrongly refers to *Dk.dean.*).

Richard Haldane 1558 - 1606.
Occ. 2 Dec. 1558 (SRO, Airlie, sec.28,no.10); occ. 15 June 1595 (SRO, Reg.Ho.Chr.no.3335); d. Nov. 1606, when described as constable of Stirling Castle, but still in fact retaining this ben. (Stirling Tests., 9 Apr. 1614; J.A.L. Haldane, *The Haldanes of Gleneagles*, 39-40).

Thomas Glass 1633 - 1636.
Occ. 30 Oct. 1633 (SRO, Drummond Castle, box 6,10/5) and 12 Feb. 1636 (J. Hunter, *Diocese and Presbytery of Dunkeld*,ii,307, quoting Perth sasines).

SUCCENTORS/SUBCHANTERS OF DUNKELD

First known date: 1238.
But this dignity is not again mentioned by its title until 1475 and thenceforward.
Prebend: ch. of Rattray said to have been granted to this dignity 1147 x 1169 (Myln, *Vitae*, 5); but it is found just as a simple preb. 1274 (*SHS Misc.*,vi,48) and as late as 1420 (*CSSR*,i,215); this ch. certainly attached to this dignity by Reformation (Reg.Pres.,i,106v; Cowan, *Parishes*,169).

Malcolm 1238.
    Occ. as succentor 31 Dec. 1238 (*Inchaff.Chrs.*,no.65).

Stephen de Segrave 1309 - 1323 x 1324.
    In poss. of Rattray preb. 27 Dec. 1309 (*CPL*,ii,68; cf. Emden, *Biog.Reg.Univ.Cambridge*, 516-17); prov. Armagh abp. 16 Mar. 1323 and cons. Apr. 1324 (*HBC*,308).

Robert de Fuxo 1325.
    Prov. to Rattray preb. on Segrave's promotion 7 June 1325 (*CPL*,ii,244).

William de Angus 1345.
    Held Rattray preb. some time before 25 Jan. 1345, when prob. still in poss. (v.inf.).

Thomas de Pilmuir 1345.
    Prov. to Rattray preb. 25 Jan. 1345 (*CPL*,iii,149).

Alexander Trail x1417.
    Held Rattray preb. at death some time before 4 Nov. 1417 (v.inf.).

Richard de Creich 1417.
    Prov. to Rattray preb. on Trail's death 4 Nov. 1417 (*CPP*,i,607).

Robert Stewart 1419 - 1420 x 1431.
    In poss. of Rattray preb. 5 Sept. 1419 and 10 July 1420 (*CSSR*, i,117,215); d. before 20 Mar. 1431 (see *M.prec.*).

David Colden 1475 - 1493.
    Occ. as succentor 2 Oct. 1475 (Myln, *Vitae*,25; Dowden, *Bishops*, 77); occ. as succentor 28 Feb. 1493 (*Arb.Lib.*,ii,274,no.338).

David Balbirnie 1507.
    Occ. Jan. 1507 x June 1508 (*Dunk.Rent.*,19; cf. 324).

Robert Shaw 1507 - c.1517 x 1542.
    Occ. 27 July 1507 (*Prot.Bk.Simon*,ii,204; year is calculated from given weekday); occ. c.1517 (*Dunk.Rent.*,338); dem. before 14 Feb. 1542 (*RMS*,iii,no.2597).

Simon Shaw 1544.
    Occ. 9 Dec. 1544 (SRO, Airlie, no.12/211).

William Crichton 1558 - 1562 x 1565.
    Occ. 22 May 1558 (SRO, Reg.Deeds,iii,fo.409); occ. 10 July 1562 (SRO, Airlie, sec.5,no.15); d. by 30 Apr. 1565 (v.inf.).

Andrew Abercrombie 1565 - 1591.
    Crown pres. on Crichton's death 30 Apr. 1565 (*RSS*,v,no.2039); occ. 16 Jan. 1585 (Fraser, *Grandtully*,i,105) and 10 Feb. 1586 (SRO, Airlie, sec.48,no.38); cf. Silvester Rattray below; occ. 18 Jan. 1591 (Stevenson & Wood, *Seals*,ii,223).

Silvester Rattray 1585, 1592 - 1623.
    Occ. 7 Jan. 1585 (SRO, Airlie, sec.48,no.36); but cf. Aber-

crombie above; occ. 13 June 1592 (SRO, Reg.Ho.Chr.no.3170); occ. 18 Jan. 1622 (SRO, Part.Reg.Sasines Edin.,xvi,fo.87); d. 30 Jan. 1623 (Scott, *Fasti*,iv,170, quoting tombstone).

John Rattray 1624 - 1634.
Occ. 7 Apr. 1624 (SRO, Part.Reg.Sasines Edin.,ix,fo.58) and 28 June 1634 (SRO, Drummond Castle, box 23,3/9).

Thomas Lundie 1637.
Had crown pres. on 'transportation' of John Rattray sometime before 9 May 1637, when found in poss. (J. Hunter, *Diocese and Presbytery of Dunkeld*,ii,349-50); occ. 12 June 1637 (SRO, Part.Reg. Sasines Edin.,xxvi,fo.281).

ARCHDEACONS OF DUNKELD

First known date: 1177.
Prebend: ch. of Lagganallachie annexed 1312 x 1319 (Myln, *Vitae*,13; *Chron.Extracta*, 147); ch. of Tealing annexed in addition 1274 x 1442 (*SHS Misc.*,vi,48; Reg.Supp.,386,fo.40; cf. Cowan, *Parishes*, 126,196).

Jocelin 1177 - 1194.
Occ. 1177 (*Kel.Lib.*,ii,no.448); occ. 1189 x 1198 (*Moray Reg.*, 11); occ. 2 Feb. 1194 (*ND*, no.462).

Henry 1200 x 1209 - 1220 x 1225.
Occ. 1203 x 1210 (*C.A.Chrs.*,i,35) and 1208 x 1209 (*Melr.Lib.*, i,no.133, (having got it since 1200 x 1203 (*Camb.Reg.*,313); occ. 1220 x 1225 (*Inchaff.Chrs.*,43).

William de Ednam 1221 x 1225 - 1245.
Occ. 19 Apr. 1225 (SRO, Maitland Thomson Transcripts, file 3, but with '?'); occ. 4 July 1225 (*Scone Liber*,no.83), having got poss. since 1221 x 1225 (*Dunf.Reg.*,no.216); occ. 26 Apr. 1245 (*St A.Lib.*, 308).

John de Everley 1251 x 1257 - c.1263 x 1272.
Occ. 5 Apr. 1257 (*C.A.Chrs.*,i,129), having got it since 7 Apr. 1251 (*Inchaff.Chrs.*,154-5); occ. c.1263 (*Inchcolm Chrs.*,24-25); d. before 1265 x 1272 (ibid.,25-26).

W. 1282.
Occ. 9 Oct. 1282 (*Fraser Papers*,218).

Matthew de Kinross 1304.
Occ. 19 Mar. 1304 (*CDS*,ii,no.1473); moved to *Dk.dean.* by 13 Aug. 1304.

William de Pilmuir 1329 - 1330 x .
In poss. 28 Nov. 1329 (*CPL*,ii,303); moved to *St A.archd.* after 4 June 1330.

Robert de Den/ Valle 1340 - 1347 x 1349.
Occ. as Valle 28 Feb. 1340 (*Vatikanische Quellen*,iv,81); occ. as Den 9 Nov. 1347 (ibid.,v,51); d. before 30 Sept. 1349 (*CPP*,i,176).

Walter de Wardlaw 1349.
Prov. 23 Oct. 1349 (*CPL*,iii,315) prob. unfruitfully.

Adam Pullur 1351 - 1351 x 1352.
Had coll. by ord. and gets papal conf. 26 Apr. 1351 (Collect., 14,fo.161v,182); d. before 13 July 1352 (v.inf.).

John de Ethie 1352.
Prov. on Pullur's death 13 July 1352 (Collect.,14,fo.163v; cf. *CPP*,i,230) unfruitfully.

Ingram de Ketenis   1359 - 1398 x 1407.
Walter Trail   1379.
Ketenis occ. 13 Aug. 1359 (*Moray Reg*.,367-8); occ. 1398 x (SRO, Transcripts of Misc.Chrs.); res. on exch. with Cornell before 25 Feb. 1407 (*CPP*,i,638; v.inf.).
Trail prov. 26 Feb. 1379 (*CPP*,i,540) unfruitfully; cf. *Dk.dean*.

Richard de Cornell 1398 x 1407 - 1408.
Occ. 25 Feb. 1407 (*RMS*,i,382-3) after exch. with Ketenis (v. sup.); prov. to *St A.archd.Lothian* 14 July 1408; still in poss. of this archd. 3 Aug. 1408 (SRO, Transcripts from Vatican,ii,no.33) and 5 Oct. 1408, when he is to dem. on getting his new archd. (Reg.Av., 330,fos. 547 - 547v).

Alexander de Lilliesleaf   1408 - 1415.
Richard Hunter   x1408.
Lilliesleaf prov. in succession to Cornell 14 July 1408 (*CPP*,i, 638-9); cf. *St A.archd.Lothian*; said to have poss. when given papal conf. 5 Oct. 1408 (Reg.Av.,330,fos.548v-549); cf.sup.; d. in or soon before Jan. 1415 (v.inf.).
Hunter had a right based on prov. at death before 5 Oct. 1408 (Reg.Av.,330,fos.548v-549); cf. *R.prec*.

Alexander de Lauder   1415 - 1440.
John Stewart   1418.
Ingram de Lindsay   1421.
Lauder had coll. by ord. on death of Lilliesleaf some three months before 5 Apr. 1415 when he got prov. (Reg.Av.,345,fos.387v-388v); in poss. 3 Jan. 1416 (*CPP*,i,604); prov. *Dk.bp*. 6 June 1440, but d. uncons. 11 Oct. 1440 (*Chron.Bower*,ii,502).
Stewart prov. 11 Dec. 1418 by Pope Benedict XIII (*CPP*,i,610) unfruitfully.
Lindsay prov. 11 Jan. 1421 by Pope Martin V (*CSSR*,i,243) unfruitfully.

James Bruce   1440 - 1441.
Adam de Montgomery 1440 - 1455.
Bruce pres. by king and in poss. by 2 Nov. 1440 (Reg.Supp.,369,

fo.162); in poss. when prov. *Dk.bp.* 6 Feb. 1441; prob. had been recently at Council of Basel (Haller, *Conc.Bas.*,vii,347); cons. 4 Feb. 1442.

Montgomery prov. in exp. of Lauder's elevation 8 June 1440 (*ACSB*,128); in poss. 23 June 1446 (*CPL*,viii,245); res. in curia on or before 22 Nov. 1455 (v.inf.).

John Carrick	1455 - 1468.
James Lindsay	1465.
Nicholas Graham	1467.
William Livingstone (Lynolisan)	1468.

Carrick prov. on res. of Montgomery 22 Nov. 1455 (*CPL*,xi,25); in poss. 22 Nov. 1468 (Reg.Supp.,634,fo.4v).

Lindsay gets *com.priv.* against Carrick 12 Sept. 1465 (*CPL*,xii, 241).

Graham gets *com.priv.* against Carrick 3 Apr. 1467 (Reg.Supp., 609,fo.62).

Livingstone (spelled Lynolisan) gets *com.priv.* against Carrick 22 Nov. 1468 (ibid.,634,fo.4v).

David Luthirdale	1475 - 1479.
William Elphinstone junior	x1476.

Luthirdale in poss. 26 Oct. 1475 (Reg.Supp.,729,fo.23v), having prob. moved from *G.archd.Teviotdale* since 5 June 1475; occ. 6 Nov. 1479 (*HMC* 34, *14th R.*,iii,17).

Elphinstone lit. with Luthirdale, but desisted before 10 Aug. 1476 (*CPL*,xiii,506).

Alexander Tours 1492 - 1507.
        Occ. 8 Mar. 1492 (*Prot.Bk.Young*,ii,nos.502,507-8); occ. 14 Jan. 1507 (SRO, ADC,xviii,pt.2,fo.86).

George Ferne	1508 - 1517 x 1518.
John Carnavel/Carwenall	1512.

Ferne occ. 19 Feb. 1508 (*Dunk.Rent.*,245; cf. 324); lit. in curia with Carnavel and by 18 July 1512 had had sentence in his favour (*James IV Letters*,256-7); occ. 20 June 1517 (*Crail Register*,no.103); prob. res. on exch. with William Meldrum for *B.prec.* before 12 Jan. 1518.

Carnavel was an Englishman (*Dunk.Rent.*,324, where the 'Carwenall' spelling is found); had crown pres. on papal authority, but by 18 July 1512 (despite royal support) had lost lit. in curia with Ferne (ibid.; *James IV Letters*,256-7).

William Meldrum 1517 x 1518 - 1527.
        Prob. coll. on exch. with Ferne; occ. 12 Jan. 1518 (*Fife Ct.Bk.*, 92); occ. 9 July 1527 (SRO, ADC,xxxvii,fo.150).

David Meldrum 1532 - 1550.
        Occ. 25 Jan. 1532 (*Brech.Reg.*,ii,184); res. on or before 23 Dec. 1547 (PRO 31/9 - 33/235); but found still in poss. 31 Aug. 1548 (SRO, Sent.Offic.St A.,fo.170) and 4 Sept. 1550 (*RMS*,iv,no.514).

David Spens 1547 - 1586.

Alexander Crichton 1558 - 1559.
James Spens   1581.

David Spens promises annates and gets prov. 23 Dec. 1547 (PRO
31/9 - 33/235); cf. David Meldrum above; occ. 22 Oct. 1554 (*Laing
Chrs*.,163); after lit. with Crichton (and dispossession for a time,v.inf.)
gets papal sentence in his favour 16 June 1559 (*Dunk.Rent*.,348);
occ. 18/21 Jan. 1585 (SRO, GD 1/446/27) and 10 Feb. 1586 (SRO,
Airlie, sec.48,no.38).

Crichton occ. 22 May 1558 (SRO, Reg.Deeds,iii,fo.409); lost
lit. with David Spens in curia 16 June 1559 (*Dunk.Rent*.,348).

James Spens got crown pres. on supposed death of David Spens
14 Mar. 1581 (Reg.Pres.,ii,52); effect unknown.

John Ramsay 1591 x 1610 - 1618.

Given crown pres. to parsonage of Tealing, which was thereupon
disjoined from Dk.archd. 30 Apr. 1591 (RSS,lxii,fo.42); but later occ.
as archd. 1 Sept. 1610 (SRO, Airlie, sec.5,no.50); still in poss. at death
10 May 1618 (*PSAS*,x,292).

Alexander Bruce 1619 - 1633.

Occ. 14 Apr. 1619 (SRO, Part.Reg.Sasines Edin.,xx,fo.328) and
30 Oct. 1633 (SRO, Drummond Castle, box 6,10/5).

DEANS OF CHRISTIANITY

DEANS OF ATHOLL : ATHOLL AND DRUMALBAN

First known dates: Atholl : 1203 x 1210.
                              Atholl and Drumalban : 1508 x 1509.

Duncan (Atholl) 1203 x 1210 - 1212 x 1214.

Occ. 1203 x 1210 (*C.A.Chrs*.,i,35-36) and 1212 x 1214 (*Inchaff.
Chrs*.,27-28); perhaps one of series of *Dk.early deans*.

W. (Atholl) 1294.

Occ. 31 Mar. 1294 (*C.A.Chrs*.,i,139).

Thomas Greig (Atholl/Atholl and Drumalban) 1505 - c.1517.

Appointed dean of Atholl 22 Apr. 1505 (*Dunk.Rent*.,12); occ.
23 June 1508 under this title, which had been changed to dean of
Atholl and Drumalban by 5 July 1509 (ibid.,13,14); occ. still as dean
of Atholl and Drumalban 20 Apr. 1515 and c.1517 (ibid.,16,328).

David Cunningham (Atholl and Drumalban) 1542.

Occ. 11 Aug. 1542 (*RSS*,ii,no.4829).

DEANS OF RATTRAY : ANGUS

First known dates :   Rattray : 1183 x 1203.
                              Angus : 1479 (cf. *Dunk.Rent*.,304).

Matthew (Rattray) 1183 x 1203 - 1225 x 1229.
   Occ. 1183 x 1203 and 1221 x 1229 (*C.A.Chrs*.,i,12-16,63); occ.
as 'M.' 4 July 1225 (*Scone Liber*,53); possibly same as contemporary
early dean in Dunkeld of same name.

Thomas of Durham (Angus) 1479.
   Occ. 2 Oct. 1479 (*C.A.Rent*.,i,216).

Alexander Myln (Angus) 1505 - 1514.
   Appointed 22 Apr. 1505 (*Dunk.Rent*.,17); occ. 6 Nov. 1514
(ibid.,24).

John Thomson (Angus) 1515 x 1516.
   Occ. 1515 x 1516 (ibid.,148).

James Lauder (Angus) 1516 x 1517 - 1538-9.
   Occ. 1516 x 1517 (ibid.,297); occ. 1538-9 (*MW*,i,199).

DEANS OF FIFE AND STRATHEARN : FIFE :
FIFE, FOTHRIFF AND STRATHEARN

First known dates: Fife and Strathearn: 1501.
                     Fife: 1505.
                     Fife, Fothriff and Strathearn: c.1505 (*Dunk.
                        Rent*.,304).

John Marschell (Fife and Strathearn) 1501.
   Occ. 24 Apr. 1501 (SRO, Breadalbane GD.112/26/1,s.d.).

Alexander Wilson (Fife, Fife and Strathearn) 1505 - 1509.
   Appointed to Fife 22 Apr. 1505 (*Dunk.Rent*.,9); responsible
for Fife and Strathearn from 24 Nov. 1506 (ibid.,10); occ. 30 June
1509 (ibid.).

DEANS FOR WHOLE DIOCESE

First known date: 1484 x 1505 (cf. *Dk.early deans*).

David Abercrombie 1484 x.
   As *Dk.subd*. made *Dk.comm*. and rural dean for whole dioc. 1484
x (*Dunk.Rent*.,304).

Walter Brown x1505.
   As *Dk.offic*. made rural dean for whole dioc. in succ. to Abercrombie and before re-organisation into four deaneries arranged apparently in April 1505 (ibid.; see other deaneries for dating); d. 5 Sept.
1505 (*Taymouth Bk*.,114).

DEANS SOUTH OF FORTH

First known date: 1505.

Thomas Greenlaw 1505.
Appointed prob. 22 Apr. 1505 (*Dunk.Rent.*,304; cf. other deaneries for dating).

Matthew Ker 1505 x 1511.
Succ. Greenlaw (ibid.), must have dem. before 11 June 1511 when Lyne is found as *Dk.dean christ. Strathearn, Fife and Lothian* - the last area designating the South of Forth parishes.

DEANS OF STRATHEARN, FIFE AND LOTHIAN

First known date: 1511.

James Lyne x1511 - 1514.
Held office 11 June 1511 - 7 May 1514 (*Dunk.Rent.*,11); had apparently held same office (which was regarded as a single-deanery) for an earlier term which had ended 11 June 1511 (ibid.); in office just as dean of Lothian 18 May 1510 x 17 Nov. 1513 (ibid.,280); had moved to Dk. dioc. from *St A.ped.princ.* 5 Oct. 1509 x (cf. *Dunk.Rent.*, 304-5).

OFFICIALS

OFFICIALS OF DUNKELD

First known date: 1203 x 1210.

Matthew 1203 x 1210.
Occ. 1203 x 1210 (*C.A.Chrs.*,i,35-36); *not* same as Matthew *Dk. dean christ. Rattray*.

Thomas de Perth 1263.
Occ. 2 Aug. 1263 (*Inchaff.Chrs.*,80).

H. 1282.
Occ. 9 Oct. 1282 (*Fraser Papers*,218).

Nicholas de Atholl 1414 - 1418.
Prob. still in office 28 Jan. 1418 after holding it for four years (*CPL*,vii,102).

Donald de Macnachtan 1433.
Occ. 16 May 1433 (*Brech.Reg.*,i,56-59).

William Ramsay 1432 x 1437.
Occ. May 1432 x Aug. 1437 (*CPL*,viii,426,620).

Robert de Tullous 1445.
    Occ. 13 Mar. 1445 (Fraser, *Wemyss*,ii,69).

Robert Todd 1449,
    Occ. 19 May 1449 (*HMC* 8, *9th R*.,ii,187).

David Meldrum 1467 - 1478 x 1479.
    Occ. 17 Feb. 1467 (*Brech.Reg*.,i,193); occ. 12 Aug. 1478 (*HMC* 6, *7th R*.,709); moved to *St A.offic*. 18 Nov. 1478 x 3 Nov. 1479.

Walter Brown 1493 x 1498 - 1505.
    Appointed 1484 x 1505 (*Dunk.Rent*.,304,326), prob. after 28 Feb. 1493 (see *Dk.comm*.); occ. 3 Aug. 1498 (SRO, Erroll,no.152); d. 5 Sept. 1505 (*Taymouth Bk*.,114).

Alexander Myln 1513 - 1518 x 1519.
    Occ. 31 May 1513 (*Dunk.Rent*.,42); occ. 19 Jan. 1518 (*Arb.Lib*., ii,424,no.545) and 1518 (*IR*,ix,132); prov. abbot of Cambuskenneth 8 Aug. 1519 (SRO, GD 1/194/2).

Simon Young 1543 x 1545 - 1547.
    Occ. 4 Mar. 1545 (*Dunf.Reg*.,394); had prob. been recently appointed (ibid.) and had moved to Dk. dioc. since 1543 (cf. *St.A.dean. christ. Gowrie*); occ. 4 July 1547 (SRO, Sent.Offic.St A.,fo.156).

Alexander Erskine 1549 - 1549 x 1553.
    Occ. 27 Nov. 1549 (Patrick, *Statutes*,88); d. before 5 Sept. 1553 (see *Dk.subd*.).

COMMISSARIES

COMMISSARIES WITH GENERAL AUTHORITY

COMMISSARIES OF DUNKELD

First known date: 1467.

John de Myrton 1467.
    Occ. (CB) 2 Jan. 1467 (Fraser, *Haddington*,ii,236).

David Abercrombie 1484 x 1505.
    Appointed (C and CG) prob. for whole dioc. 1484 x 1505, holding office apparently early in the period and before Brown (*Dunk.Rent*., 304,324).

Walter Brown 1491 - 1493.
    Occ. (CG) and vicar of bp. in spirituals 10 Jan. 1491 (SRO, Airlie, sec.44,no.3); occ. (C) 28 Feb. 1493 (*Arb.Lib*.,ii,273); found as *Dk.offic*. by 3 Aug. 1498.

Walter Leslie   c.1517.

William Ireland c.1517.
> **Leslie** occ. (CG) with Ireland c.1517 (*Dunk.Rent.*,326-7).
> **Ireland** occ. (CG) with Leslie c. 1517 (ibid.).

James Crombie 1534.
> Occ. (CG) 15 Apr. 1534 (SRO, Maitland Thomson Notebook 24, p.10 [back] , from Kinnoull Chrs., box 10).

John Etal (Ettell) 1541.
> Occ. (CG) 11 Aug. 1541 (SRO, Airlie, sec.44,no.5).

John Barton 1566.
> Occ. (C) 30 Dec. 1566 (*RSS*,v,no.3156); given crown appointment to Dunkeld North of Forth 5 Feb. 1567 (ibid.,no.3209).

COMMISSARIES WITH LIMITED AUTHORITY

COMMISSARIES OF TULLILUM

First known date: 1513.

Note: Document of 1530 describes this man as 'commissarius Dunkeldensis in causis apud Tulilum tractandis' and it is sealed with his seal of office. He may in fact have been the commissary of Dunkeld acting at Tullilum, an administrative centre of the diocese near Perth (cf. *Dunk.Rent.*,passim).

Andrew Elder 1513.
> Occ. (C) 3 Mar. 1513 (SRO, ADC,xxiv,fo.161).

Simon Young 1530.
> Occ. (C) 29 May 1530 (SRO, Forglen, box 2, bundle 3).

COMMISSARIES SOUTH OF FORTH

First known date: 1505 x 1511.

Thomas Greenlaw　　1505 x 1511.
Matthew Ker　　　　1505 x 1511.
> In office successively while *Dk.dean.christ. South of Forth* 1505 x 1511 (*Dunk.Rent.*,304).

John Letham 1530 - 1541.
> Occ. 8 Jan. 1530 (PRO 31/9 - 32/215-22); cf. *Chapel Royal comm.*; occ. 26 Oct. 1541 (SRO, Sent.offic. St A.,fo.6).

EDINBURGH DIOCESE

BISHOPS OF EDINBURGH

First known date: see erected out of St A.dioc. 29 Sept. 1633 under metropolitan authority of St Andrews (*RMS*,viii,no.2225; Keith, *Bishops*, 44-60).

William Forbes 1634.
Appointment expected 11 Dec. 1633 (*Fasti Mariscal.*,i,230); crown prov. 26 Jan. 1634 (*RMS*,ix,no.21); d. 12 Apr. 1634 (Spalding, *History*,i,24; cf. *Stirling's Register*,ii,743 for an order for his cons. dated 13 May 1634).

David Lindsay 1634 - 1638.
Trans. from *B.bp.* 16 Sept. 1634 (*RMS*,ix,no.219); depriv. 13 Dec. 1638 (Peterkin, *Records*, i,26-27); d. Dec. 1641 (Edin.Tests.,under 25 Mar. 1642).

CHAPTER OF EDINBURGH

DEANS OF EDINBURGH

First known date: erected with the see 29 Sept. 1633, with arrangement that the principal minister of St Giles is to be the first dean (*RMS*, viii,no.2225; Keith, *Bishops*,49); no other dignities were erected among the other twelve prebendaries.

William Struthers 1633.
Presumably became dean 29 Sept. 1633 (v.sup.); d. 9 Nov. 1633 (Edin.Tests., under 8 Aug. 1635).

Thomas Sydserf 1634.
Crown pres. on death of Struthers to deanery and to first minister's place 18 Jan. 1634 (Reg.Pres.,vii,fo.19; *Stirling's Register*,ii,711-12,714); el. by burgh council as minister of N.W. parish in succ. to Struthers 12 Feb. 1634 (*Edin.Recs. 1626-41*, 139); said to have been adm. 19 Feb. 1634 (Scott, *Fasti*, i,56, no clear source cited); cons. *B.bp.* 29 July 1634.

James Hannay 1634 - 1639.
Crown pres. (in Latin) in anticipation of coming promotion of Sydserf 13 May 1634 (Reg.Pres.,vii,fo.29; *Stirling's Register*,ii,749); in poss. in crown eyes when given pres. again (in Scots), though there are delays over the formalities of the appointment 19/20 Oct. 1634 (RSS, cv,fo.421; *Stirling's Register*,ii,791,801-2); appointed by burgh council as minister of N.W. parish in succ. to Sydserf 30 Mar. 1635 (*Edin.Recs. 1626-41*,157); said to have been adm. soon after (Scott, *Fasti*,i,56, no clear sources cited); depriv. 1 Jan. 1639 (*Edin.Recs.1626-41*, 212; cf. 321, 322, 324).

GALLOWAY DIOCESE

BISHOPS OF GALLOWAY: WHITHORN: CANDIDA CASA

First known date: 1128.

For a succession of bishops of Whithorn in eighth century, see *SAEC*, 53, 55, 58-59, *ES*,i,246,248,254 and *SHR*,xxxii (1953), 144-6. For use of alternative titles by the bishops from 1128 onwards, see *TDGAS*, 3rd series,xxvii (1950), 127-8.

These bishops recognised the metropolitan authority of archbishops of York from 1128 until 1355; but no bishop thereafter is known to have offered formal obedience to York (ibid.,129-34); the see was in practice subject to direct papal authority until placed under metropolitan authority of St Andrews 14 Aug. 1472 (*Vet.Mon.*,no. 852), and then transferred to province of Glasgow 9 Jan. 1492 (ibid., no.889).

These bishops were associated with *Chapel Royal dean./bp.* from 1504 onwards.

Gilla-Aldan 1128.

El. sometime before 9 Dec. 1128, when given papal mand. to go to York abp. for cons.; his profession of obedience 1128 x 1140 survives (Haddan & Stubbs, *Councils,* II,i,24-25; *Historians of York,* iii,48-49, 60; cf.ii,385; for year-date see W. Holtzman, *Papsturkunden in England*,ii,105; cf.147).

Christian 1154 - 1186.

Cons. 19 Dec. 1154 (*Chron.Holyrood*,127); d. 7 Oct. 1186 (*Chron.Melrose*,45).

John 1189 - 1209.

El. before 3 Sept. 1189, and then cons. 17 Sept. 1189 (*SAEC*, 306); said to have become a monk of Holyrood abbey 1206 (*Chron. Bower*,i,520); d. 1209 (*Chron.Melrose*,54).

Walter 1209 - 1235.

Succ. 1209 when chamberlain of Alan son of Roland lord of Galloway (ibid.); cons. by 2 Nov. 1214 (*Rot.Litt.Claus.* (Record Comm.),i,173); d. 1235, presumably Jan./Feb. (*Chron.Melrose*, 83; cf. inf.).

Gilbert   O.Cist.   1235 - 1253.
Odo Ydonc O.Prem.   1235 - 1241.

Gilbert, when monk of Melrose, el. by clergy and people (including *Ga.archd.*) with the exception of the prior and convent of Whithorn 25 Feb. 1235 (ibid.); assent of King Alexander given 23 Apr. 1235, and lit. at York with Ydonc followed mand. of abp. 4 June 1235 (*Reg.Gray*,170-3); cons. at York 2 Sept. 1235 (*Chron.Melrose*,83); d. 1253 (ibid.,111).

Ydonc, when canon of Whithorn, el. by prior and convent as the chapter 11 Mar. 1235 (*Chron.Melrose*, 83; see *Reg.Gray*,170-3 for surname); King Alexander wrote to York abp. against him 19 May

1235, and by 2 Sept. 1235 he had lost lit. there with Gilbert (ibid.; *Historians of York*,iii,144-9; *SAEC*,347-8); got papal mand. for further enquiries into his right 19 June 1241 (*Reg.Gregoire IX*,iii,532-5,no. 6077; cf. *CPL*, i,198 and *TDGAS*, 3rd series, xxxvii (1960), 62-69); but failed to obtain poss.

Henry O.S.A. 1253 - 1293.

El. when abbot of Holyrood with support of the Comyn councillors of the young King Alexander III, but with opposition from John de Balliol in the name of the rights of the lordship of Galloway, apparently in 1253 (*Chron.Melrose* 111; *Chron.Lanercost*,59); but perhaps election was in fact delayed until after Oct. 1254, for Henry occ. simply as abbot then, and not as bp.-elect (*Dunf.Reg.*,no.309); the interested parties were summoned to the usual examination of the election at York 11 Feb. 1255 and this led to conf. by York abp. 24 Feb. 1255 (*Reg.Gray,* 120-2); it is reported that despite this conf. there was a delay before cons. (*Chron.Lanercost*,59), and this is perhaps not surprising in view of the fact that Balliol was one of the Comyn faction and events led in Sept. 1255 to the loss of political control in Scotland by the Comyns in favour of the Durwards (*CDS*,i,no.2013); Henry occ. still as bp.-elect in company of Gamelin *St A.bp.elect* 22 Dec. 1255 (*Dunf.Reg.*,no.206), who was also of the Comyn faction; the Melrose chronicler reports his cons. after that of Bp.Gamelin which took place 26 Dec. 1255 (*Chron.Melrose*,113), and this is the likely time for it; but the chronicler also states that this cons. was by Walter abp. of York who d. 1 May 1255, and the Lanercost chronicler is puzzlingly specific in stating that this cons. was by the bp. of Durham near Richmond on 7 Feb. preceding cons. of Gamelin i.e. 7 Feb. 1255 (*Chron.Lanercost*, 52); the same source states a bp. of Carlisle was cons. on same occasion, and this does seem go have been the probable date for cons. of Bp. Thomas Vipont of that see (cf. *HBC*,213); but it is not a possible date for Henry's cons. in view of the other evidence already quoted; it seems likely that the true date of cons. was early 1256, while there was still no consecrated abp. at York following Abp. Walter's death and at a time when things were difficult for Comyn supporters in Scotland; this is to suggest that both chroniclers are mistaken in some particulars and to prefer the facts in the record evidence instead (*Chron. Lanercost*, 62 is certainly confused, for it has two entries about the death of the York abp.; cf. a differing conjectural account of the order of these events in *TDGAS*, 3rd series, xxvii,137, which appears to be based on the partial summation of the evidence in Haddan & Stubbs, *Councils*, II,i,58-60 and Dowden, *Bishops,* 357-8); d. 1 Nov. 1293 (*Chron. Lanercost,* 154-5).

Thomas de Dalton/ Kirkcudbright/ Galloway 1294 - 1324 x 1326.

El. by chapter when chaplain of Robert Bruce (and with his support) before 13 Jan. 1294, when King John opposed his conf. *Northern Registers,* 104-5; *Reg.Romeyn*,ii,115-16); obtained King John's approval 19 May 1294 (ibid.,129-30); professed obedience to York and received spiritualities 30 May 1294 (ibid.,127-8, 130);

cons. 10 Oct. 1294 (ibid.,131; cf. *Chron.Lanercost*,155; see discussion in *IR*,iv,71-83); loyalty to York began to come into question by 28 May 1319 (*Northern Registers*, 287-9; but note that in the source, i.e. York, MS Reg.Melton,fo. 504v, this letter is attributed to the bp. of Galloway only in a fifteenth-century, partially-legible rubric - it may well not refer to Dalton at all); but Edward II still counted on his loyalty 19 July 1319 (*Foedera*,II,i,401; *CPR 1317-21*, 381); see still occupied in York eyes 5 Mar. 1324 (*Northern Registers*, 346-7,n.1), and Bp. 'T.' was summoned to a York council in the belief that he had never adhered to King Robert I 4 Apr. 1324 (York, MS Reg. Melton, fo. 516v); Dalton held this see until his death before 23 Sept. 1326 (v.inf.).

Note: date of a cartulary copy of a chr. by Simon bp. of Galloway given as 8 July 1321 (BM, MS Harley 3960, fo.109, printed in *Melr.Lib*.,ii, 390) is prob. erroneous; abp. of York appears to have been wrongly informed in Apr. 1323 that see of Galloway was then vacant (cf.sup.), so that he then appointed a *Ga.offic.* for the vacancy; this was connected with rumours which he was hearing that an unnamed bp.-elect of Galloway was seeking conf. and cons. at the curia; he protested to pope and cardinals 10/18 Apr. 1323 that this man should be sent back to York for cons. there in the customary way (York, MS Reg.Melton,fos. 463-4; cf. Haddan & Stubbs, *Councils*, II,i,62; *Wigt.Chrs*.,p.1x); if this bp.-elect ever existed, he cannot now be identified.

Simon de Wedale O.S.A. 1326 - 1355.

Occ. simply as abbot of Holyrood 10 June 1326 (*Midl.Chrs*.,46; cf. 42); el. as abbot to this see following recent death of Dalton 23 Sept. 1326 (*Northern Registers*,335); abp. ordered examination of this election 16 Oct. 1326 (York, MS Reg.Melton,fo.467v); conf. at York 16 Dec. 1326 and cons. at Westminster 1 Feb. 1327, with profession of obedience to York made at Tottenham near London 8 Feb. 1327 (*Northern Registers*,336-9; *CDS*,iii,no.902); d. 11 Mar. 1355 (Haddan & Stubbs, *Councils*, II ,i,63).

Michael de Malconhalgh/ Mackenlagh O.Prem. 1355 - 1358 x 1359.

El. when prior of Whithorn before 4 June 1355 (*CDS*,iii,no. 1584); conf. by York 26 June 1355 and cons. by commission of York abp. 12 July 1355 (Haddan & Stubbs, *Councils*,II,i,63); occ. 17 Jan. 1358 (*Foedera*,iii,387); d. before 31 Dec. 1359 (v.inf.).

Thomas MacDowell 1358 x 1360.
Thomas 1359 - 1362.

Thomas MacDowell claimed unanimous el. on death of Malconhalgh, but failed to get conf. and had given up his right by 4 Feb. 1360 (*CPP*,i,351).

Thomas gets prov. and cons. at Avignon on death of Malconhalgh 31 Dec. 1359 (*Vet.Mon*.,no.638); occ. 2 Sept. 1362 (*Glas.Reg*.,i,271).

Adam de Lanark O.P. 1363 - 1378.

El. and then got prov. 17 Nov. 1363 (Reg.Av.,157,fo.136v); cons by 2 Jan. 1364 (*CPP*,i,476); in poss. 16 Dec. 1370 (Ob. et Sol.,38,fo. 49v); d. during a vacancy in the papal see i.e. possibly 19 Dec. 1370 x

5 Jan. 1371, but more prob. 27 Mar. x 31 Oct. 1378 (*Reg.Av.*,217,fo. 524).

Oswald O.Cist.   1378 x 1379 - 1417.
Ingram de Ketenis   1378 x 1379.
Thomas de Rossy O.F.M. 1379 - 1393 x 1406.

 Oswald el. when prior of Glenluce, got prov. from Urban VI i.e. after 18 Apr. 1378, and prob. cons. before 26 Mar. 1379 when he was intending to visit Scotland (*Rot.Scot.*,ii,14; cf. *Reg.Av.*,226,fo.287); prov. cancelled by Clement VII prob. before 26 Feb. 1379 in favour of Ketenis (v.inf.), and certainly by 15 July 1379 (*Reg.Av.*,217,fo.524); prob. had poss. for a short time, but was ousted by Rossy, and then lost lit. with him in curia of Clement VII by 29 Oct. 1381 (v.inf.); active in England until Sept. x Dec. 1417 (*Reg.Langley*,v,90-91, 108).

 Ketenis , when *Dk.archd.*, prov. by Clement VII 31 Oct. 1378 x 26 Feb. 1379 (*CPP*,i,540); by 15 July 1379 he had raised objections against his elevation, and papal mand. was then issued to investigate the facts and prov. Rossy instead if Ketenis sustained his objections (*Reg.Av.*,217,fo.524).

 Rossy prov. conditionally (provided Ketenis wished in fact to res. his right), and given mand for cons. from Clement VII 15 July 1379 (ibid.); cons. by 16 July 1380 (Fraser, *Carlaverock*,ii,426-8); conf. from Clement VII after winning lit. with Oswald 29 Oct. 1381 (*Reg.Av.*, 226,fo.287); still in poss. 14 June 1393 (*CPP*,i,577); d. before 28 May 1406 (v.inf.).

Elisaeus Adougan 1406 - 1412? x 1415.
 El. when *Lincluden prov.* and got prov. from Benedict XIII 28 May 1406 (Eubel, *Hierarchia*,i,162); occ. 1412 (Keith, *Bishops*,274 - source now lost); d. before 14 June 1415 (v.inf.).

Gilbert Cavan   1412(?) x 1415.
Thomas de Buittle (Butil) 1415 - 1420 x 1422.
 Cavan el. by chapter on death of Adougan, but failed by 20 June 1415 to get papal conf. (*CSSR*,i,220; *CPP*,i,603).

 Buittle prov. when *Ga.archd.* 14 June 1415 (*Reg.Av.*,345,fo.245 v; cf. Eubel, *Hierarchia*,i,162); cons. by 5 Sept. 1415 (*Reg.Av.*,347,fo. 581); occ. 16 July 1420 (*SES*,ii,77-78); d. before 4 Dec. 1422 (v.inf.).

Alexander Vaus 1422 - 1450.
 Trans. from *C.bp.* on death of Buittle 4 Dec. 1422 (*CPL*,vii,287); res. in favour of Spens 8 Jan. 1450 (*ACSB*, 42).

Thomas Spens   1450 - 1458.
Thomas Vaus   1457.
 Spens prov. when said to have some right in *Ga.archd.* 8 Jan. 1450 (ibid.); cons. 27 May 1450 x 1 Apr. 1451 (Brady, *Episcopal Succession*,i,158; *Abdn.Reg.*,i,308; cf. Dowden, *Bishops*, 368, 127 and n.1); trans. to *Ab.bp.* 21 Nov. 1457, but this was subsequently cancelled; trans. to *Ab.bp.* again 15 Dec. 1458.

 Vaus prov. when *G.dean* on trans. of Spens 21 Nov. 1457; but this was not effective as Spens was not in fact trans. then, and moneys

paid for services on behalf of Vaus were repaid (*ACSB*,46).

Ninian Spot 1458 - 1480 x 1482.
     Prov. 15 Dec. 1458 (*CPL*,xii,11); cons. 12 Mar. x 16 Apr. 1459 (*HMC* 4, *5th R*.,629; *Holy.Lib*.,148); granted temps. 27 Apr. 1459 (*RMS*,ii,no.698); occ. 12 June 1480 (*ER*,ix,1); d. before 9 Dec. 1482 (v.inf.).

George Vaus 1482 - 1508.
     Prov. on death of Spot 9 Dec. 1482 (Eubel, *Hierarchia*,ii,116; *ACSB*, 78-79); cons. by 9 Oct. 1483 (*ADA*,116ˣ); occ. 25 Oct. 1507 (*RSS*,i,no.1564); d. by 30 Jan. 1508 when mass said for his soul, and so he had prob. died just before (*TA*,iv,37-38).

James Betoun 1508 - 1509.
     Crown nom. when abbot (i.e. commendator) of Dunfermline 1 Mar. 1508 (*James IV Letters*, 98-99; cf. 137); postulated by chapter at some stage (Dowden, *Bishops*,338); prov. by pope 12 May 1508 (Eubel, *Hierarchia*,iii,150); granted temps. 17 July 1508 (*RSS*,i,no. 1707); el. to *G.abp*. 9 Nov. 1508 and trans. 19 Jan. 1509 without yet having had cons.

David Arnot O.S.A. 1508 - 1526.
     Crown nom. when abbot of Cambuskenneth [8] Nov. 1508 (*James IV Letters*, 123); prov. 29 Jan. 1509 (Eubel, *Hierarchia*,iii,150); granted temps. 27 May 1509 (*RSS*,i,no.1889); res. on pension in favour of Wemyss retaining right of return 23/24 Jan. 1526 (v.inf.); bull for pension of half the fruits released 2 Mar.1526 (PRO 31/9 - 32/110); d. 10 July 1536 x 25 Aug. 1537 (SRO, Reg.Ho.Chrs.nos. 1132,1154).

Henry Wemyss 1526 - 1541.
     Prov. when *Ga.archd*. on res. of Arnot 23/24 Jan. 1526 (Eubel, *Hierarchia*,iii,150; Brady, *Episcopal Succession*,i,158; cf. *St A.Form*., ii,1-2); still elect 1 Mar. 1526 (PRO 31/9 - 32/97); d. 14 Mar. x 21 May 1541 (*RMS*,iii,no.2303; *RSS*,ii,no.4024).

Andrew Dury O.Cist. 1541 - 1558.
     Crown nom. when abbot of Melrose 3 July 1541 (*James V Letters*,425); papal prov. 22 Aug. 1541 on death of Wemyss (Eubel, *Hierarchia*,iii,150; Brady, *Episcopal Succession*,i,159); still elect 3 Apr. 1542 (PRO 31/9 - 33/147); occ. 14 Dec. 1557 (*APS*,ii,514); prob. d. Sept. 1558 (Dowden, *Bishops*, 374).

Alexander Gordon   1559 - 1575.
Archibald Crauford 1564.
John Gordon   1568.
     Alexander Gordon was trans. from *I.bp*. following crown nom. 24 Mar. x 10 Apr. 1559 (Lesley, *History*, 267; *SES*,ii,145, 154; cf. *Diplom.Norv*.,xvii B,348); still elect 5 Mar. 1564 (*RMS*,iv,no.1846); perhaps had papal prov. 1564 (*RMS*,iv,nos. 1719, 1743); res. in favour of his son John 4 Jan. 1568 (v.inf.), but this did not take effect; d. in poss. 11 Nov. 1575 (Edin.Tests.).

Crauford had some right on papal authority which he res. in Alexander Gordon's favour before 13 June 1564 (*Papal Negotiations with Queen Mary*, 184-5 and n.).

John Gordon got crown prov. on res. of his father Alexander 4 Jan. 1568 (*RMS*,iv,no.1804); but this was not effective before his father's death (v.inf.).

John Gordon 1575 - 1586.
Roger Gordon 1578 - 1579 x 1587.

 John Gordon made good his claim after his father's death (v.sup.), and then res. in favour of his brother George 8 July 1586 (v.inf.; see *TDGAS*, 3rd series,xxvii,143).

 Roger Gordon el. on death of Alexander Gordon, and got crown conf. with mand. for cons. 17 Sept. 1578 (*RSS*,vii,no.1646); called 'pretended bishop' 27 June 1579 (SRO, Acts and Decreets,lxxvi,fo. 202), and may never have had effective poss.; d. before 12 May 1587 (see *Db.dean.*; cf. *TDGAS*, 3rd series,xxvii, 143,n.22a, where death 1590 x 1598 is suggested).

George Gordon 1586 - 1588.

 Crown prov. on res. of his brother John 8 July 1586, and then d. prob. never cons. 1 Apr. x 5 Nov. 1588 (*TDGAS*, 3rd series,xxvii, 143).

Note: see appears to have been vacant 1588 - 1605.

Gavin Hamilton 1605 - 1612.
John Gordon 1610.

 Hamilton got crown prov. at Whitehall 6 Feb. 1605 and then at Edinburgh 3 Mar. 1605 (RSS,lxxiv,fo.359); cons. 21 Oct. 1610 (Spottiswoode, *History*,iii,209); d. Feb. 1612 (Hamilton and Campsie Tests, ii,pt.1,fo.243).

 Gordon renewed his claim 1610 (*RPC*,ix,569); had been dean of Salisbury since 1603, and d. 3 Sept. 1619 (*SP*,ix,110).

William Couper 1612 - 1619.

 Crown prov. 31 July 1612 (Reg.Pres.,iv,74); cons. 4 Oct. 1612 (*Chron.Perth*,6); d. 15 Feb. 1619 (*Theater of Mortality* (1704), 15-16).

Andrew Lamb 1619 - 1634.

 Trans. from *B.bp*. 4 Aug. 1619 (*RMS*,vii,no.2070); d. 1634 (Keith, *Bishops*, 281, no source cited).

Thomas Sydserf 1635 - 1638.

 Trans. from *B.bp*. 30 Aug. 1635 (*RMS*,ix,no.399); depriv. 13 Dec. 1638 (Peterkin, *Records*,i,26-27); trans. to *O.bp*. 14 Nov. 1661 (*RMS*, xi,no.126) and d. 29 Sept. 1663 (*Nicoll's Diary*,400).

CHAPTER OF GALLOWAY

Status of ch. at Whithorn from which Bp. Gilla-Aldan took his title in 1128 is obscure; but once the Premonstratensian canons had been

brought to Scotland starting first at Dryburgh in 1150 (*Chron.Melrose*,
35; *MRHS*,86), a community of this order came to be established at
Whithorn; since the recognised founders were Bp. Christian and Fergus
lord of Galloway, the probable date is 1154 x 1161 (*TDGAS*, 3rd series,
xxvii,103); but there is late evidence which asserts that the Premon-
stratensians were introduced only in 1177 by Bp. Christian to replace
canonicos iam regulares who were already there (ibid.,104), and it has
been concluded that the cathedral community was an Augustinian one
for some time before it was converted to Premonstratensian (*IR*,iv,38-
39); Fergus was certainly interested in the Augustinians among whom
he died as a canon of Holyrood (*Chron.Holyrood*,137-9), and the models
of cathedral convents of this order at Carlisle 1133-6 and St Andrews
1144 must have been in people's minds; but there is no firm evidence
regarding the existence of this short-lived Augustinian community; yet
a major rebuilding of the ch. at Whithorn has been dated c.1150
(*TDGAS*, 3rd series,xxvii,102, 125-6; cf. xxxiv,183-5); and two priors
can be traced before the first known Premonstratensian one - an Adam
who was in some sense the 'first prior and prelate' at Whithorn 1154 x
1161 (*IR*,iv,38), and a William prior of Galloway who occ. in a St
Andrews/Augustinian context 2 Apr. 1172 x 13 May 1178 (*St A.Lib.*,
135; cf. *TDGAS*, 3rd series, xxvii,145,n.30); then the Michael remembered as the first Premonstratensian abbot in Galloway (*IR*,iv,38) may
well be the same as the Michael prior of Whithorn who certainly occ.
along with his chapter when witness of an act of Bp. John 19 Dec.
1200 x 1209 (*Holy.Lib.*,no.49); the rebuilding of the cathedral again
was undertaken from c.1200 onwards (*TDGAS*, 3rd series, xxvii,105;
xxxiv,185-9).

This regular community at the cathedral prob. from the first
shared the duty of electing the bp. with some or all of the secular clergy
of the diocese (cf. ibid.,134-6); such a background made possible the
rival claims made at the double election of 1235; the candidate who
ultimately obtained poss. then was an outsider elected with the en-
couragement of King Alexander II, who was actively interested in
spreading royal influence in Galloway after the death in 1234 of Alan
lord of Galloway; this Bp. Gilbert's right was based on election by an
assembly representative of the clergy and people (led by the archd. and
including both rectors from the parishes and two abbots and a prior
from outside the diocese - *Reg.Gregoire IX*,iii,no.6077; *Reg.Gray*,
170-3), which acted specifically without the participation of the prior
and convent of Whithorn (*Chron.Melrose*,83); the latter responded by
electing a local candidate of their own, claiming that an election by
themselves alone was valid; they lost their case prob. because of the
political pressures of the time, but also because they could not establish
at York or Rome the validity of their claim to be the proper electing
body (cf. *TDGAS*, 3rd series,xxxvii,67-68; cf. also xxvii,136-7). It is not
known how the election was conducted at the next vacancy 1253-5;
there was controversy between the crown and the traditional Galloway
interests over the person elected, when it was objected that the election
was irregular (*irrite factam* - see *Chron.Lanercost*, 59), though in fact
it was prob. more the matter of patronage that was mainly at stake

(ibid.,59, 62); but no legal difficulties appear to have been raised at York over the method of election this time (*Reg.Gray*, 120-2); the archd. was active at Whithorn as the abp.'s official in the vacancy (see *Ga.offic.*), and he certainly co-operated in the process which led to the conf. of the bp.-elect; the candidate was apparently acceptable also to the prior and convent, and it is reasonable to assume that he was again the joint-choice of both the cathedral chapter and at least some representatives of the secular clergy of the diocese.

This was certainly the case at the next election 1293-4, when the prior and convent acted along with 'others from the clergy of the see and diocese' (*Northern Registers*, 104-5; *Reg.Romeyn*,ii,no.1388); alternatively it was then stated to be the custom in Galloway for election to be in the hands of the prior and chapter of Whithorn together with (all) the clergy of the diocese (ibid.,nos.1389, 1403); and the archd. and convent are found in co-operation over how the diocese should be administered during the vacancy so that the election might not be impeded (ibid.). The same joint electoral chapter acted in 1326 (*Northern Registers*,335). From later evidence it appears that the right of election came to be exercised by a body loosely described just as 'the chapter' (e.g. Cavan in 1415 or Betoun in 1508), but it is not clear that in this context it was just the prior and convent of Whithorn alone that was meant.

At convention of Leith 16 Jan. 1572 it was noted that measures would have to be taken to establish a new chapter for episcopal elections and spiritual affairs, while the temporality of the cathedral priory would remain for life in the hands of the prior and canons (*BUK*,i,223); detail⸋ were then worked out for the parallel and immediately urgent case of St Andrews (ibid.,222-3), but not for Galloway; some kind of new chapter of reformed parish clergy may be assumed to have carried through the election of Bp. Roger Gordon 1575 x 1578; the priory was annexed to the bishopric of Galloway 29 Sept. 1605 (RSS, lxxiv,fo. 405) and confirmed to subsequent bps. 1612, 1619 and 1633 (*APS*, iv, 522; *RMS*,vii,no.2070; *APS*,v,72; see *TDGAS*, 3rd series,xxvii, 129, 148); but there remained a 'chapter of Whithorn' which succeeded to some of the interests and duties of the old cathedral priory, and it is found by 25 Jan. 1614 to comprise the archd. and a number of paro-chial clergy (SRO, Reg.Ho.Chrs.,s.d.; cf. *RMS*,vii,no.123).

The erection of an office of Dean of Galloway appears to have been contemplated in 1637, when the bp. granted chrs. with consent of the 'dean and chapter'; but no appointments appear to have been made, as the archd. is found signing *vicem decani supplens* (*RMS*, ix,no.833; SRO, Part.Reg.Sasines Dumfries,iv,fo.328).

PRIORS OF WHITHORN : CANDIDA CASA

For lists of known holders of this office see *TDGAS*, 3rd series, xxvii (1950), 145-8, and *The Bibliotheck*,ii,27 (to c.1300).

ARCHDEACONS OF GALLOWAY

First known date: 1154 x 1174.
      Prebend: ch. of Kells c. 1320 (*RMS*,i,app.1,no.22); but this
appropriation was ineffective; half of fruits of ch. of Penninghame
1410, and then of whole ch. c.1425 (SRO, Transcripts from Vatican,
ii,no.50; *CPL*,vii,297; *CSSR*,ii,68,159,218,224-5,231-2; Cowan,
Parishes, 92,163).

Robert 1161 x 1174, 1164 x 1174, 1154 x 1186.
      Occ. 1161 x 1174 (*TDGAS*, 3rd series,v,250); occ. 1164 x 1174
(*Holy.Lib.*,42); occ. 1154 x 1186 (*Cal.Chr.Rolls*, iii ,91).

John 1154 x 1186, 1200 x 1209 - 1222.
      Occ. 1154 x 1186 (*Holy.Lib.*,20); occ. 19 Dec. 1200 x 1209
(ibid.,40); occ. 1209 x 1222 (*CDS*,ii,422, no.1606; *Cal.Chr.Rolls*,iii,
92); occ. 1222 (*Holm Cultram Reg.*,53).

Michael 1235, 1235 x 1253.
      Occ. as 'M.' 1235 (*Reg.Gregoire IX*,iii,533); occ. as Michael 1235
x 1253 (*Holm Cultram Reg.*,47).

Geoffrey   1254 - 1294.
John Nepos   1293 - 1294.
      Geoffrey presumably in poss. by 7 May 1254 (*Reg.Gray*, 272);
occ. 15 Oct. 1254 (ibid.,273; cf. *IR*,iv,80); old and blind when Nepos
made his curator x 1 Nov. 1293 and 7 May 1294 (v.inf.).
      Nepos appointed curator before death of Bp. Henry i.e. x 1 Nov.
1293; conf. in this office by abp. of York during vacancy of see of
Galloway 7 May 1294 (*Reg.Romeyn*,ii,127).

Gilbert de Galloway (Galwidia) c.1320 - 1321.
      Occ. c.1320 (*RMS*,i,app.1,no.22); occ. 11 July 1321 (*Glas.Reg.*,
i,228).

Patrick Macdowell 1331 - 1360.
      Occ. 21 Sept. 1331 (Fraser, *Carlaverock*,ii,408); in poss. 4 Feb.
1360 (SRO, Maitland Thomson Notebook 42, from Reg.Av.,144,fo.
433).

Stephen de Makerstoun (Malcarston)   x1367.
Duncan Petit   1363 x 1369 - 1383.
      Makerstoun held it (prob. by papal prov.) and res. before 24
Jan. 1367 (*CPL*,iv,61-62).
      Petit had coll. by Bp. Lanark (i.e. Nov. 1363 x) on Macdowell's
death, and got papal conf. 26 Nov. 1369 (*CPL*,iv,82); in poss. 13 June
1383 (ibid.,248).

Richard Smerles x1391.
      Held it sometime before 2 Mar. 1391 (v.inf.).

Thomas de Buittle (Butil) 1391 - 1415.

Prov. 2 Mar. 1391 (*CPP*,i,575); lit. 9 Aug. 1393 (Reg.Supp.,81,fo. 210); in poss. 21 Oct. 1394 (ibid.,82,fo.28v); prov. *Ga.bp.* 14 June 1415.

Gilbert Cavan 1415 - 1415 x 1417.

Prov. 20 June 1415 (*CPP*,i,603); res. on exch. through ord. with Gray before 20 May 1417 (v.inf.).

John Gray	1415 x 1417 - 1425.
Patrick Young (Juvenis)	1423 - 1471.
David de Hamilton	1425.
John Betoun	1427 - 1428.
John Benyng	1430.
Thomas Spens (?)	x1450.

Gray gets conf. after exch. through ord. 20 May 1417 (*CPP*,i, 606); prov. to a parish ben. and is to res. 29 May 1425 (*CPL*,vii,399; cf. *G.chanc*); in poss. when given rehabilitation 19 Sept. 1425 (PRO 31/9 - 27/159).

Young prov. in exp. 10 Jan. 1423 (*ACSB*,90); promised annates 27 Mar. 1425 (ibid.); obtained poss. Apr. 1426 x Feb. 1427 (*CSSR*, ii,159,209); new prov. after lit. with Betoun 11 July 1428 (ibid., 225); in poss. 27 Nov. 1471 when granted faculty to res. on exch. with Otterburn for *Methven prov.* (*ACSB*,170; Reg.Supp.,673,fo. 245v).

Hamilton prov. 30 May 1425, but failed to expedite his papal letters (*CSSR*,ii,68).

Betoun prov. 25 July 1427 and 22 June 1428 (*CSSR*,ii,159, 220), but lost lit. with Young by 11 July 1428 (v.sup.).

Benyng prov. 25 Oct. 1430 (Reg.Supp.,263,fo.112) unfruitfully.

Spens said to have held it on crown pres. before prov. as *Ga.bp.* 8 Jan. 1450 (Boece, *Vitae*,37).

John Otterburn 1471 - 1478.
George Brown 1477 - 1478.

Otterburn obtained poss. on exch. with Young on or shortly after 27 Nov. 1471 (Reg.Supp.,673,fo.245v); occ. 20 Sept. 1473 (*RMS*,ii,no.1320); new prov. on res. of Brown 25 Feb. 1478 (Reg. Supp.,765,fo.139); occ. 4 June 1478 (*St Giles Reg.*,128-30).

Brown prov. on claim that Otterburn's appointment was null 1 Mar. 1477 (Reg.Supp.,747,fo.200); res. in Otterburn's favour without having had poss. 25 Feb. 1478 (ibid.,765,fo.139).

Andrew Stewart 1502 - 1507.

Occ. 23 July 1502 and 17 Nov. 1507 (*Prot.Bk.Simon*,ii,58, 225-6); d. by 7 Dec. 1507 (v.inf.).

Walter Betoun 1507.
Thomas Nudry 1509 - 1510 x 1512.

Betoun got crown pres. on Stewart's death 7 Dec. 1507 (*RSS*,i, no.1575).

Nudry promises annates and gets prov. on Stewart's death 15 Nov. 1509 (PRO 31/9 - 31/196); in poss. 6 Apr. 1510 (*James IV Letters*, 169); prob. res. on getting *M.archd.* July 1510 x Feb. 1512.

Alexander Shaw 1512 - 1513.
    Occ. 12 July 1512 (SRO, Supp.Reg.Ho.Chrs.,s.d.); occ. 9 Nov.
1513 (SRO, Reg.Ho.Chr.no.810).

Henry Wemyss   1522 - 1531.
Patrick Arnot   1529 - 1543.
Thomas Hay   1531.
    Wemyss occ. 9 Dec. 1522 (SRO, Ailsa, sec.1,no.263); prov. *Ga.bp*.
23/24 Jan. 1526; promised annates to retain it with see 1 Mar. 1526
(PRO 31/9 - 32/97); res. in favour of Arnot 11 Feb. 1531 (PRO 31/9 -
32/206).
    Arnot occ. 4 Jan. 1529 (*TDGAS*, 3rd series,xxxvi,23); promised
annates and got prov. 22 Apr. 1531 (PRO 31/9 - 32/198); occ. 16 Apr.
1540 (SRO, Lochnaw Chrs.; cf. *Wigt.Chrs.*,no.273); res. 14 Oct. 1543,
but promised annates to retain fruits (PRO 31/9 - 33/145-6).
    Hay res. some right in curia in favour of Arnot in return for
pension 28 Feb. 1531 (PRO 31/9 - 32/207-8; cf. 32/198).

Andrew Arnot   1543 - 1575.
William Blair   1550 - 1559.
    Arnot promises annates without fruits 14 Oct. 1543 (PRO 31/9 -
33/146); occ. 24 Nov. 1546 (*RSS*,iii,no.2012); res. 19 Jan. 1550, but
retained whole fruits less pension to Blair (*Wigt.Chrs.*,no.316); res.
annexed ch. 22 Apr. 1566, but retained life-rent until death Oct. 1575
(*TDGAS*, 3rd series, xxx,52).
    Blair prov. 19 Jan. 1550 (*Wigt.Chrs.*,no.316); occ. 1 June 1557
(ibid.,no.347); occ. 24 Mar. 1559 (Patrick, *Statutes*,155).

Lyon Brown 1576 - 1577.
    Crown pres. on Andrew Arnot's death 24 May 1576 (Reg.Pres.,
i,128; *RSS*,vii,no.617); occ. 20 Mar. 1577 (SRO, Galloway Chrs.,no.
142).

James Adamson 1614 - 1637.
    Occ. 25 Jan. 1614 (SRO, Reg.Ho.Chr.,s.d.) and 27 May 1637
(Part.Reg.Sasines Dumfries,iv,fo.328).

DEANS OF CHRISTIANITY

EARLY DEANS IN GALLOWAY

Macbeth/ Malbec 1165 x 1174.
    Occ. 1165 x 1174, though diocese is not certain (*Holy Lib.*,42,
no.52; *AHCAG*,iv,55; cf. *HMC* 3, *4th R.*,535).

James 1185 x 1197.
    Occ. 1 Jan. 1185 x 24 Mar. 1197 (*St Bees Reg.*,no.62).

DEANS OF DESNES : KIRKCUDBRIGHT

First known dates: Desnes: 1200 x 1209.
                     Kirkcudbright: 1529.

Note: Part of this deanery is found as separate deanery of Glenken in 1275 (*SHS Misc.*,vi,74).

Matthew (Desnes) 1200 x 1209 - 1209 x 1222.
      Occ. 19 Dec. 1200 x 1209 (*Holy.Lib.*,40); occ. undated (ibid., 60); occ. 1209 x 1222 (*Cal.Chr.Rolls*,iii,92).

Thomas (Desnes) 1250.
      Occ. 1250 (*Melr.Lib.*,no.317).

John Wallace (Walays) (Desnes) 1331.
      Occ. 21 Sept. 1331 (Fraser, *Carlaverock*,ii,408).

Herbert Dunn (Kirkcudbright) 1529.
      Occ. 4 Jan. 1529 (*TDGAS*, 3rd series, xxxvi,23).

DEANS OF FARINES : WIGTOWN

First known dates: Farines: 1200 x 1209.
                     Wigtown: 1254.

William (Farines) 1200 x 1209.
      Occ. 19 Dec. 1200 x 1209 (*Holy.Lib.*,40).

S. (Wigtown) 1254 - 1257.
      In office 3 Apr. 1257, having held it for at least three years (*CPL*,i,344).

DEANS OF RHINNS

First known date: 1200 x 1209.

Gilbert 1200 x 1209.
      Occ. 19 Dec. 1200 x 1209 (*Holy.Lib.*,40).

DEANS OF FARINES AND RHINNS

First known date: 1538.

John McCracken 1538 - 1552.
      Occ. 20 Sept. 1538 (*Wigt.Chrs.*,no.268); occ. 9 Mar. 1552 (ibid.,no.327).

Michael Hawthorn 1559.
      Occ. 24 Mar. 1559 (Patrick, *Statutes*, 154).

OFFICIALS

OFFICIALS WITH GENERAL AUTHORITY

OFFICIALS OF GALLOWAY

First known date: 1209 x 1222.

Durand 1209 x 1222.
> Occ. 1209 x 1222 (*Cal.Chr.Rolls*,iii,92).

Geoffrey 1254 - 1255.
> As *Ga.archd.* is appointed official by York abp. *sede vacante* 7 May 1254 (*Reg.Gray*, 272; cf. 273); ordered to hand over spiritualities to new bp. 24 Feb. 1255 (ibid.,121).

Ralph de Ponthieu (Ponthou)   1293.
Robert le Vavasour   1294.
Walter   1293 x 1294.
> **Ponthieu** appointed by York abp. *sede vacante* 1 Dec. 1293 (*Reg. Romeyn*,ii,114); but ineffective.
> **Vavasour** in office 23 Jan. 1294 (ibid.,116,118).
> **Walter** as vic. of Twynholm appointed *sede vacante* by prior and convent of Whithorn and archd. of Galloway Dec. 1293 x Jan. 1294 (ibid.,116-17, 121-3; cf. R.J. Brentano, *York Metropolitan Jurisdiction*, ch.6).

Robert de Sauthorp 1294.
> Appointed by York abp. in place of Vavasour 12 Feb. 1294 (*Reg. Romeyn*,ii,119); ordered to hand over to new bp. and return to York 30 May 1294 (ibid.,129).

Robert de Ouston 1323.
> Appointed by York abp. who believed see to be vacant 17 Apr. 1323 (York, MS Reg.Melton,fo.463); prob. ineffective as see was not in fact vacant.

John de Blekeburne 1331.
> Occ. 21 Sept. 1331 (Fraser, *Carlaverock*,ii,408).

Stephen (de Makerstoun ?) 1381.
> Stephen prior of St Mary's Isle occ. 16 July 1381 (ibid.,427).

Fergus Macdowell 1491 - 1504.
> Occ. 7 Nov. 1491 (SRO, Broughton and Cally,no.620); occ. 4 Jan. 1504 (*Hist.Chapel Royal*, 39).

David Abercrombie 1512.
> Occ. 5 Mar. 1512 (ibid.,90).

Henry Wemyss 1517 - 1522.
> Occ. 18 Feb. 1517 (*RMS*,iii,no.145); occ. 16 Jan. 1522 (*Chronicles of Lincluden*,77); prov. *Ga.bp.* 23/24 Jan. 1526.

Andrew Arnot 1535 - 1536.
    Occ. 1 June 1535 (SRO, Reg.Ho.Chrs.,no.1108); occ. 10 July 1536 (SRO, Calendar of Chrs.,no.1136).

David Abercrombie 1540 - 1541.
    Occ. 1 Nov. 1540 (*Wigt.Chrs.*,no.274); occ. 9 May 1541 (ibid., no.276).

OFFICIALS WITH LIMITED AUTHORITY

OFFICIALS OF FARINES AND RHINNS

First known date: 1552.

John McCracken 1552.
    Occ. 9 Mar. 1552 (*Wigt.Chrs.*,no.327); cf. *Ga.dean.christ.Farines and Rhinns* and *Ga.comm.Farines and Rhinns*.

COMMISSARIES

COMMISSARIES WITH GENERAL AUTHORITY

COMMISSARIES OF GALLOWAY

First known date: 1506.

John Oliver 1506.
    Occ. (CB) 3 Sept. 1506 (Fraser, *Maxwell Inventories*,145).

COMMISSARIES WITH LIMITED AUTHORITY

COMMISSARIES OF DESNES AND GLENKEN : KIRKCUDBRIGHT

First known dates: Desnes and Glenken: 1467.
                       Kirkcudbright: 1529.

Note: This jurisdiction is once found under name 'Galloway under Cree' 1537-8 (*MW*,i,200).

Hugh Witherspune (Desnes and Glenken) 1467.
    Occ. (C) 13 Feb. 1467 (Robison, *Kirkcudbright,* 156; cf. *HMC* 3, *4th R.*,539).

Herbert Dunn (Kirkcudbright) 1529 - 1550.
    Occ. (C) 4 Jan. 1529 (*TDGAS*, 3rd series, xxxvi,23) and 4 Nov. 1537 (*RMS*,iii,no.1737); occ. (C) with jurisdiction named 'Kirkcudbright, Desnes, and Glenken' 19 July 1550 (SRO, Reg.Ho.Chr. no. 1492A).

Thomas Anderson (Kirkcudbright) 1578.
 Occ. (C) 5 Oct. 1578 (*RMS*,iv,no.2830).

COMMISSARIES OF FARINES : WIGTOWN : FARINES AND RHINNS

First known dates: Farines: 1501.
                    Wigtown: 1525.
                    Farines and Rhinns: 1540.

William McGirve/Makgarwy (Farines) 1501 - 1507.
 Occ. (C) with jurisdiction named 'Farines in Rhinns' 1 June 1501 (*Wigt.Chrs*.,185); occ. (C) with jurisdiction named 'Farines' 8 Mar. 1507 (ibid.,188).

John McCracken (Wigtown) 1525 - 1536.
 Occ. (C) 11 June 1525, when an appeal is made from commissary of Wigtown to bp. of Galloway and his official (SRO, Broughton and Cally, no.554); occ. (C) 7 July 1536 (*Wigt.Chrs*.,30).

Thomas Foulis (Wigtown: Farines and Rhinns) 1537 - 1540.
 Occ. (C) with jurisdiction named 'Wigtown' 24 Apr. 1537 (ibid., 215); occ. (C) with name 'Farines and Rhinns' 16 Apr. 1540 (ibid., 219).

John McCracken (Farines and Rhinns: Wigtown) 1545 - 1549.
 Occ. (C) with name 'Farines and Rhinns' 7 Jan. 1545 (ibid.,227); occ. (C) with name 'Wigtown' 3 Apr. 1549 (SRO, Ailsa, 1/520).

Herbert Anderson (Wigtown) 1557.
 Occ. (C) 13 Mar. 1557 (*Wigt.Chrs*.,246).

Michael Hawthorn (Farines and Rhinns: Wigtown) 1559 - 1560.
 Occ. (C) with name 'Farines and Rhinns' 24 Mar. 1559 (Patrick. *Statutes*,154); occ. (C) with name 'Wigtown' 23 Mar. 1560 (*RSS*,v,no. 781).

William Macgowan (Makgowne) (Wigtown) 1572.
 Occ. (C) 6 Feb. 1572 (*RMS*,iv,no.2098).

GLASGOW DIOCESE

BISHOPS/ARCHBISHOPS OF GLASGOW

First known date: (1055 x 1060), c.1114 x 1118.

The first three bishops listed below may in practice have acted mainly (or even only) as suffragan - bishops of abp. of York within his diocese, though given the ancient Glasgow title associated with St Kentigern (suggestion of Mr N.F. Shead in an unpublished Glasgow university thesis); they may never have had anything to do with Glasgow itself, though by the time Hugh the Chantor was recording York tradition about them (i.e. x 1127), at least plans were afoot for re-storing the church of Glasgow as a diocesan centre (see below, and Bp. John, and notes on *Chapter of Glasgow*); it is noteworthy that Bp. Michael, besides being active for at least some of his time within York diocese, is reported to have died within bounds of 'English Cumbria' i.e. the area south of the Solway under the political control of the English king in the early 12th century; York was prob. wishing to extend its ecclesiastical influence into that area, and so may well have appointed a bishop to serve it and given him an old title that had some time before been borne by bishops serving the whole ancient province of Cumbria both north and south of the Solway (cf. G.W.S. Barrow, *The Border* [University of Durham, 1962], 3-4); Mr Shead considers that, despite his title, Bp. Michael is more properly regarded as a forerunner of the bishops of Carlisle than of Glasgow.

With Bp. John comes a conscious effort to resist York metro-politan authority (v.inf.); one result of his attitude was that he was deprived of any claims which he might have had to jurisdiction over 'English Cumbria' when the diocese of Carlisle was erected 1133 (D.Nicholl, *Thurstan Archbishop of York* (York,1964). 140-50; cf. 15th century tradition about this in *Chron.Bower*,i,449); but this may have meant little to him in practice or even in theory, and it is noteworthy that when 'English Cumbria' came to be ruled by the king of Scots 1136 - 1157, no attempt appears to have been made to dispossess the new bishop there (Barrow, *The Border*, 7-8; this Bp. Athelulf was in any case a close friend of Robert *St A.bp. - see Trans. Royal Hist.Soc.*, 5th series, iii,82-84); the reason for this attitude is probably connected with the fact that when c.1122 efforts were being made by Earl David to restore the ancient possessions of the church of Glasgow for Bp. John's benefit, no claims were made to any lands south of the Solway (*ESC*,no.50; cf. Barrow, *The Border*, 7-8); some of these traditional lands of this church, on the other hand, lay in Teviotdale, and it is significant of Bp. John's outlook also that nothing more is heard under him of a claim raised by York as recently as 1109 x 1114 that Teviotdale lay in the diocese of Durham (*SAEC*,133,n.3; cf. 97,n.5 and 129,n.1, where it is perhaps too easily assumed that Teviotdale had in fact formed part of Durham diocese until 1101); Bp. John, then, was unlike his predecessor in exercising authority over an area that was wholly Scottish in its political allegiance; from such a secure base his successors continued the anti-York tradition until the

status of direct subjection to Rome as a *filia specialis* was won for the
see of Glasgow in 1175 and confirmed in 1176 and 1192 (*AMW*, 198-
200, 206-17, 275-6; *Chron.Holyrood*, 159-61).

This see was placed under the metropolitan authority of St
Andrews 14 Aug. 1472 (*Vet.Mon.*,no.852); then Glasgow itself was
erected into a metropolitan see with the sees of Dunkeld, Dunblane,
Galloway and Argyll transferred from St Andrews to this new
ecclesiastical province 9 Jan. 1492 (ibid.,no.889; *Glas.Reg.*,470-3);
Dunblane was transferred back to province of St Andrews 28 Jan.
1500, and Dunkeld was similarly restored to St Andrews on or before
25 May 1515 (Dowden, *Bishops*, 333-4); by 1617 the see of the Isles
had come to be transferred from St Andrews to Glasgow (*APS*,iv,530).

Magsuen/ Magnus (?)/ MacSuein (?)   1055 x 1060.
Said in York tradition (recorded x 1127) to have been cons. by
Abp. Cynsige as a predecessor of the Michael mentioned below
(Hugh the Chantor, *History*, 32, where form 'Magnus' is suggested;
cf. *SAEC*, 134 for suggestion of 'MacSuein'; an older reading of the
name in same source was 'Magsuea' - see *Historians of York*,ii,127);
date is prob. 1055 x 1060, since this abp. did not get his pallium
until 1055 (*The Anglo-Saxon Chronicle*, ed.D.Whitelock,p.130; cf.
p.128,n.5; cf. *HBC*,264).

John   1055 x 1060 - 1066 (?).
Similarly said to have been cons. by same York abp. 1055 x
1060 (Hugh the Chantor, *History*,32; cf.sup.); see also John *O.bp.*
1043 x 1072; possibly same as the John from 'Scotland' appointed
by abp. of Bremen as bp. of Mecklenburg and d. there 10 Nov.
1066 (Adam of Bremen, *History of the Archbishops of Hamburg-
Bremen*, ed. F.J.Tschan,pp.131,157; *ES*,ii,9).

Michael   1109 x 1114 (?).
Said in same York tradition to have been appointed to see of
Glasgow by Earl David and cons. by Thomas abp. of York after
profession of abedience (Hugh the Chantor, *History*,32); cons. must
therefore have been June 1109 x Feb. 1114, and 25 Dec. 1113 x
Feb. 1114 if David is understood literally to have been styled earl
at the time; but this title was prob. irrelevant to the authority which
he exercised in southern Scotland from 1107 onwards (*ES*,ii,147,n.2;
cf. *Trans.Royal Hist.Soc.*, 5th series,iii,85), and in any case Hugh the
Chantor may be mistaken in saying that Earl David appointed this
man - there may be a confusion with the next Bp. John; apparently
same man as the 'certain Briton' described in a Canterbury source of
1119 as having been cons. by York to the 'British' ch. of Glasgow
after a long vacancy there (*Historians of York*,ii,246-7; *SAEC*,133);
performed episcopal acts in York diocese at least for a time after his
cons. there, and was buried at Morland in Westmorland (Hugh the
Chantor, *History*, 32); perhaps these latter facts are indicative of his
outlook and sphere of activity (see introductory notes above).

John   O.Tiron. (?)   c.1114 x 1118 - 1147.

Possibly of French origin (R.L.G.Ritchie, *The Normans in Scotland*, 153); appointed when a monk (perhaps with Tiron connections) by Earl David, whose tutor he had been, after c.1114 (*Trans.Royal Hist.Soc.*, 5th series, iii,99; cf.86,88), and cons. by Pope Paschal II i.e. x 21 Jan. 1118, at a time when York had no consecrated abp. (*ESC*, p.45; *Glas.Reg.*,i,4); occ. x 1 May 1118 (*ESC*,no.30); directed by Pope Calixtus II to obey abp. of York as metropolitan 20 Nov. 1119 (Hugh the Chantor, *History*,76), and was believed at curia of same pope 15 Jan. 1122 to have been elected in chapter of York and given papal cons. at request of ch. of York (*ESC*,no.44; cf. Hugh, the Chantor, *History*,126); but he resisted all efforts of York to obtain his submission to York metropolitan authority (for discussions of this dispute see e.g. *ESC*,pp.267-8, and more recently Nicholl, *Thurstan Archbishop of York*, ad indicem sub John); occ. at Coldingham 3 May 1147 (*ND*,no.21); d. later in 1147 before 24 Aug. (v.inf.) and was buried at Jedburgh (*Chron.Melrose*,34; *SAEC*,221).

Herbert O.Tiron. 1147 - 1164.

Cons. when abbot of Kelso by Pope Eugenius III at Auxerre in France 24 Aug. 1147 (*Chron.Melrose*,34; *SAEC*,221); d. 1164, before 20 Sept. (*Chron.Melrose*, 37; cf.inf.).

Ingram 1164 - 1174.

El. when *G.archd*. and royal chanc. 13/20 Sept. 1164 (*Chron. Bower*,i,461-2; cf. *ES*,ii,253,n.1); cons. by Pope Alexander III at Sens in France 28 Oct. 1164 (*Chron.Melrose*,37; cf. *Glas.Reg.*,i,no.19); d. 2 Feb. 1174 (*Chron.Melrose*,41).

Jocelin O.Cist. 1174 - 1199.

El. when abbot of Melrose at Perth 23 May 1174 (ibid.); papal conf. with mand. for cons. 16 Dec. 1174 (*Glas.Reg.*,i,no.35); cons. in 1175 at Clairvaux by abp. of Lund (*Chron.Melrose*,41), date being prob. x 10 Apr. 1175 (*Glas.Reg.*,i,no.36; cf. no.37) and certainly before 14/23 May 1175 (*Chron.Melrose*,41); d. at Melrose 17 Mar. 1199 and buried there (ibid.,50; *SAEC*, 319-20).

Hugh (de Roxburgh ?) 1199.

Succ. when *St A.archd*. (and so prob. x 6 June 1199) and royal chanc., but d. when still bp.-elect 10 July 1199, and buried at Jedburgh (*SAEC*,321; *Chron.Bower*,i,514; cf. *Chron.Melrose*,50).

William Malveisin/ Malvoisin (Malevicinus) 1199 - 1202.

El. when *St A.archd.Lothian* and royal chanc. Oct. 1199 (*SAEC*, 321); cons. under papal mand. by abp. of Lyons at Lyons 24 Sept. 1200 (ibid.,323); postulated for trans. to *St A.bp*. 18/20 Sept. 1202.

Florence 1202 - 1207.

El. prob. in 1202 (*Chron.Melrose*,51; *Chron.Bower*,i,516); but perhaps it was not until after 4 Nov. 1203, when styled royal chanc. only (*Holy.Lib.*,36); res. right while still bp.-elect 1207, before 15 May (*Chron.Melrose*,53; *Pais.Reg.*,428).

Walter 1207 - 1232.

El. when royal chaplain 9 Dec. 1207 (*Chron.Melrose*,53); cons. under papal mand. at Glasgow 2 Nov. 1208 (ibid.,54); occ. 19 May 1232 (*Kel.Lib.*,nos.279,433; *Dryb.Lib.*,no.51); d. later in 1232, before 2 Nov. (*Chron.Melrose*,81).

William de Bondington 1233 - 1258.
    Perhaps *St A.archd.Lothian* when el. to this see; date is uncertain - el. when royal chanc. perhaps 1232 (ibid.) or more probably in period 11 Apr. x 7 June 1233 (*Balm.Lib.*,31; *Kel.Lib.*,i,309); cons. at Glasgow 11 Sept. 1233 (*Chron.Melrose*,82); d. 10 Nov. 1258 and buried at Melrose (ibid.,116).

Nicholas de Moffat 1259.
John de Cheam 1259 - 1268.
    Moffat el. by chapter when *G.archd.Teviotdale* 2 Jan. x 2 Feb. 1259 (*Glas.Reg.*,i,166-7; *Chron.Melrose*,116); obtained royal conf. and went to curia seeking papal conf; but his right was quashed on or before 13 June 1259 (ibid.;cf.inf.).
    Cheam, when archd. of Bath and at curia, got papal appointment on quashing of Moffat's right on or before 13 June 1259 (*CDS*,i,no. 2158); cons. presumably at curia by 28 Oct. 1259 (*Glas.Reg.*,i,nos. 210,212); pope rejected royal request for cancellation of this prov., and asked king to grant the temps. 21 May 1260 (*Vet.Mon.*,no.225; *CDS*,i,nos.2182,2194); accepted by King Alexander III and enthroned at Glasgow later in 1260 (*Chron.Melrose*,117); occ. at Tournai 11 June 1268 (*Glas.Reg.*,i,no.218); d. at Meaux in France 1268 (*Chron.Melrose*, 141), prob. before 13 Oct. (*Glas.Reg.*,i,no.213).

Nicholas de Moffat 1268 - 1270.
    El again when still *G.archd.Teviotdale* after pre-election compact of 13 Oct. 1268 (ibid.); but d. without cons. 1270 (*Chron.Lanercost*, 53; *Chron.Bower*,ii,109,112).

William Wishart 1270 - 1271.
    El. when *St A.archd.* and royal chanc. at instance of king on Moffat's death (ibid.,112; cf. *Chron.Melrose*,141); still not cons. when el. to *St A.bp.* 3 June 1271; cons. to St A. 15 Oct. 1273.

Robert Wishart 1271 - 1316.
    El. when *St A.archd.Lothian* on el. of his uncle William Wishart to St A. (*Chron.Melrose*,141); this was at instance of king, and he went to curia to seek conf. for both his uncle and himself (*Chron.Bower*, ii,114); cons. at Aberdeen 29 Jan. 1273 (ibid.,116); occ. 15 Apr. 1273 (*Midl.Chrs.*,no.44); occ. 25 June 1316 (*Melr.Lib.*,ii,364); perhaps d. 26 Nov. 1316 (Dowden, *Bishops*, 308).

Stephen de Dunnideer (Donydoir/ Dundore) 1316 x 1317.
    El. when *M.archd.* sometime after 18 Oct. 1316 and before 13 June 1317 when he was at the curia and pope delayed conf. and cons. for a year (*Reg.Jean XXII*,i,374; cf. *CPL*,ii,151); still thought by King Edward II to be alive 13 July 1317 (*Foedera*,ii,337); but d. without cons. at Paris on his way home from the curia before 18 Aug. 1317,

when pope reserved to himself prov. to this see (*CPL*,ii,132; *Vet.Mon.*, 202).

John de Lindsay   1317 x 1318 - 1334 x 1336.
John de Eglescliffe O.P. 1318 - 1323.

Lindsay el. when canon of Glasgow on death of Dunnideer, and went to curia for conf.; but el. was quashed there on or before 17 July 1318 (*Vet.Mon.*,202); an unnamed G.bp. is said to have sealed an act of parliament 3 Dec. 1318 (*APS*,i,465-6; cf.290, but source is suspect); but see is found in Scottish sources as vacant between 3 Feb. 1319 *(Pais.Reg.,* 238) and 31 Dec. 1321 (*Dunf.Reg.*,245); prov. by pope on trans. of Eglescliffe 15 Mar. 1323 (*Vet.Mon.*,226); still bp-elect 2 July 1323 (*Vatikanische Quellen*,i,662); cons. at curia before 10 Oct. 1323 when given papal mand. to go to his see (*Vet.Mon.*,227); for proof of surname see *Kel.Lib.*,ii,no.501; occ. 10/12 Feb. 1334 (*APS*,i,542); d. before 8 Feb. 1336 (*Glas.Reg.*,i,no.286).

Eglescliffe prov. when a papal penitentiary on quashing of Lindsay's election, with papal letters addressed to King Edward II following cons. at curia 17 July 1318 (*Vet.Mon.*,202); an Englishman who was not acceptable in Scotland Aug. 1320 (ibid.,nos.431,434; cf. *Foedera,* II,i,432); occ. in Worcestershire, England 27 June 1322 (*Reg.Cobham*,129); trans to see of Connor on or just before 15 Mar. 1323, when he had not been receiving any fruits from Glasgow (*Vet. Mon.*, 226; cf. *CDS*,iii,808); papal trans. again to see of Llandaff 20 June 1323 (Le Neve, *Fasti Ecclesiae Anglicanae,* xi,21); d. as Llandaff bp. 2 Jan. 1347 (ibid.).

John Wishart 1336 - 1337.

El. when *G.archd.* on death of Bp. Lindsay prob. after 8 Feb.1336 (*Glas.Reg.*,i,no.286), and had conf. and cons. at curia on or just before 17 Feb. 1337 (*Vet.Mon.*,no.540; cf. *Reg.Benoit XII*,i,377, for date); promised services 29 Apr. 1337 (ibid.,ii,428); captured by English at sea when returning from France with arms, money and agreements c. 15 Aug. 1337 (*Chron.Lanercost*,291; Walsingham, *Historia Anglicana* (Rolls Series),i,198) and d. in consequence before 20 Aug. 1337 prob. near Great Yarmouth (*CCR 1337-9,* 172; cf. Dowden, *Bishops,* 312 for mis-dating).

William Rae 1339 - 1367.

El. when *G.prec.* on Bp. Wishart's death, and got conf. and cons. at curia on or just before 22 Feb. 1339 (*Vet.Mon.*,no.543); d. 27 Jan. 1367 (*Glas.Reg.*,ii,615).

Walter de Wardlaw 1367 - 1387.

El. when *St A.archd.Lothian* on death of Rae, and prob. went to curia for prov. 14 Apr. 1367 (*Vet.Mon.*,331); prob. cons. at curia soon afterwards, and certainly before 1 July 1367 when on his way home to Scotland through England (*Rot.Scot.*,i,912); created cardinal without title by Pope Clement VII, retaining administration of see of Glasgow 23 Dec. 1383 (Ob.et Sol.,43,fo.93; Reg.Av., 235,fo.63; cf. *CPL*,iv,250); occ. at Edinburgh 22 May 1387 (SRO, Transcripts of Royal Chrs.,s.d.); d. before 5 Oct. 1387 (*CPL*,iv,255).

Matthew de Glendinning (Glendonwyn)   1387 - 1408.
John Framysden O.F.M.   1391 - 1418.

   Glendinning promised his services at curia of Clement VII 18 Dec. 1387 (Ob. et Sol.,43,fo.117), presumably following prov.; prob. cons. by time pope accepted a roll of petitions from him as from 21 Dec. 1387 (*CPP*,i,569) and certainly by 24 Feb. 1388 (*Melr.Lib.*,ii,511); d. at his manor of Lochwood near Glasgow 10 May 1408 (*Glas.Reg.*,ii, 615; cf. *Pais.Reg.*,337-8).

   Framysden was prov. by Pope Boniface IX 1 Mar. 1391 (*CPL*, iv,383); active as suffragan in London and Salisbury dioceses 1392 - 1396 (*HBC*,271 and Eubel, *Hierarchia*,i,551, no sources cited); a John bp. of Glasgow was active at curia of Martin V 27 July 1418 (PRO 31/9 - 52B/75); not known to have ever been recognised in Scotland (cf. *Proceedings of the Privy Council* (Record Comm.),i,95-96).

William de Lauder   1408 - 1425 x 1426.

   Prov. by Pope Benedict XIII when *St A.archd.Lothian* 9 July 1408 (Eubel,*Hierarchia*,i,265); granted faculty to be ordained by any catholic bp. 11 July 1408 (Reg.Av.,330,fo.613); not then in person at curia at Perpignan (cf. Dowden, *Bishops*,318), but had been cons. by time of a safe-conduct to travel from France to Scotland via England 24 Oct.1408 (*Rot.Scot.*,ii,189); this points to cons. somewhere in France; granted temps. with effect from half-way through the term Nov.1408 - May 1409 (*ER*,iv,99; cf. Dowden,*Bishops*,318); occ. 7 Aug. 1425 (SRO, Cal.Chrs.,ii,no.268); prob. still in poss. 14 Dec. 1425 (*RMS*,ii,5-6); had been succ. in office of royal chanc. by a keeper of the great seal by 25 Feb.1426 (*HBC*,175), and so prob. had d. by then; certainly d. by 14 Apr. 1426 (*Glas.Reg.*,ii,318-19; cf.616 for obit date 14 June 1425).

John Cameron   1426 - 1446.

   El. when *Lincluden prov.* on death of Lauder and gets prov. 22 Apr. 1426 (*CPL*,vii,478); mand. for cons. 16 July 1426 (ibid.,465); cons. 12 Jan. 1427 (*SHR*,xxiii,190-6); d. 24 Dec. 1446 at or near Glasgow (*Glas.Reg.*,ii,616; cf. Dowden, *Bishops*,321).

James Bruce (Brois)   1447.

   Trans. from *Dk.bp.* on Cameron's death 3 Feb. 1447 (Eubel, *Hierarchia*,ii,160;*ACSB*,37); occ. 19 June 1447 (*ER*,v,258); d. before 4 Oct. 1447 (*Glas.Reg.*,ii,no.350).

William Turnbull   1447 - 1454.

   Trans. from being bp.-elect of Dunkeld on Bruce's death 27 Oct. 1447 (*CPL*,x,229); cons. 1 Dec. 1447 x 7 May 1448 (*Glas.Reg.*,ii,no. 375; *RMS*,ii,No.1791); occ. 17 July 1454 (*APS*,xii,23); d. 3 Sept. 1454 (*Glas.Reg.*,ii,616; see discussion in J.Durkan, *William Turnbull*, 51-52).

Andrew de Durisdeer/Muirhead   1455 - 1473.

   Prov. when *Ab.dean* and *G.subdean* under name Durisdeer on Turnbull's death 7 May 1455 (*Vet.Mon.*,no.772; *ACSB*,45); cons. 6 Mar. x 3 May 1456 (Dowden, *Bishops*, 326); occ. 6 Aug. 1473 (*ADA*, 28); d. 20 Nov. 1473 (*Glas.Reg.*,ii,616, where name is Muirhead; cf. Dowden *Bishops*.328).

John Laing 1474 - 1483.
　　　Prov. on Durisdeer's death 28 Jan. 1474 (*Glas.Reg.*,ii,no.402; *ACSB*,68); cons. 9 May x 2 Dec. 1474 (*APS*,ii,106; *Glas.Reg.*,ii, no.406); occ. 25 Dec. 1482 (*RMS*,ii,no.1533); d. 11 Jan.1483 (*Glas.Reg.*,ii,615).

George Carmichael 1483.
Robert Blackadder 1483 - 1508.
　　　Carmichael occ. as bp-elect 18 Feb. 1483 (*RMS*,ii,no.1560); had been el. by chapter when *G. treas.*, but this el. was annulled by pope in favour of Blackadder 13 Apr. 1483 (*Vet.Mon.*,no.873); still recognised as bp.-elect in Scottish royal administration prob. as late as 28 Feb. 1484 (*ADA*,137*; see Dowden, *Bishops*, 330); d. as *G.treas.* 12 July x 10 Sept. 1485.
　　　Blackadder was trans. from being bp.-elect of Aberdeen 19 Mar. 1483 (Eubel, *Hierarchia*,ii,160; *ACSB*,79). and conf. 13 Apr. 1483 (*Vet.Mon.*,no.873); cons. at curia 13 x 30 Apr. 1483 (ibid.; *Glas.Mun*,i, 40); occ. as witness to royal act at Edinburgh 20 Nov. 1483 (*Brech.Reg.*, i,208); appointed abp. on raising of this see to metropolitan status 9 Jan. 1492 (*Vet.Mon.*,no.889; *Glas.Reg.*,ii,470-3); d. 28 July 1508 while on pilgrimage to Palestine (*Glas.Reg.*,ii,616; Dowden, *Bishops*, 334-5).

James Betoun 1508 - 1523.
　　　El. by chapter when *Ga.bp.(-elect)* following crown nom. on death of Blackadder 9 Nov. 1508 (*Prot.Bk.Simon*,232; cf. *St A.Form.*, i, 331-4); trans. from *Ga.bp.* 19 Jan. 1509 (Eubel, *Hierarchia*,iii,203); cons. at Stirling 15 Apr. 1509 (*Prot.Bk.Simon*, 337,507); trans. to *St A.abp.* 10 Oct. 1522; but still called G.abp. as late as 2 May 1523 (*RMS*,iii,no.233) and trans. did not become effective until 5 June 1523 (*Prot.Bk.Simon*,337; cf. Dowden, *Bishops*,340).

Gavin Dunbar junior 1523 - 1547.
　　　El. when *M.dean* by 15 Aug. 1523 (*Letters and Papers Henry VIII*, III,ii,no.3241; see also Pinkerton, *History*,ii,222,n.5); nom. by Governor Albany to pope (*St A.Form.*,i,43-44); prov. 8 July 1524, with pallium granted 29 July 1524 (Eubel, *Hierarchia*,iii,203; Brady, *Episcopal Succession*,i,155); temps. granted 27 Sept. 1524 (*RSS*,i,no.3298); bulls published in Scotland 21 Dec. 1524 (*ADCP*, 217); cons. at Edinburgh 5 Feb. 1525 (*Prot.Bk.Simon*,337); d. 30 Apr. 1547 (Dowden,*Bishops*, 345).

James Hamilton　　　　1547 - 1548.
Donald Campbell　O.Cist. 1548.
James Betoun　　　　　1550 - 1570.
Alexander Gordon　　　1550 - 1551.
　　　Hamilton got crown nom. on Dunbar's death 31 July 1547 (*Vet. Mon.*,no.1074); but this nom. was rejected in summer of 1548, ostensibly because of his illegitimacy (*SHR*,xxii,33-34; cf. *B.dean*.).
　　　Campbell when abbot of Coupar Angus got crown nom. to a papal nuncio in Scotland in place of Hamilton, but negotiations were broken off when this nuncio died 9 Aug. 1548 (*SHR*,xxii,34).

Betoun (who was son of a nephew of previous Abp. James Betoun - see Dowden, *Bishops*,337) was granted temps. until an abp. should be appointed 6 Jan. 1550 (*RSS*,iv,no.533); crown nom. and then postulated (being under age) by chapter on Dunbar's death both on 27 Feb. 1550 (*Glas.Reg.*,ii,no.509); prov. on res. of Gordon, with disp. for age, 4 Sept. 1551 (ibid.,nos.511-19); granted pallium 24 Aug. 1552 (Brady, *Episcopal Succession*,i,157); cons. at Rome 28 Aug. 1552 (*Glas.Reg.*, ii,no.521); left for France 17/18 July 1560 (*CSP Scot.*,i,455); forfeited 18/19 Sept. 1570 (*Diurnal of Occurrents*, 188; *RSS*,vi,no. 2142; cf. no. 1472), though he administered temps. in fact until as late as 20 Jan. 1571 (*Glas.Rent.*,29).

Gordon was prov. on Dunbar's death 5 Mar. 1550 and granted pallium as abp.-elect 10 Mar. 1550 (Brady, *Episcopal Succession*,i,155-6) commended as abp.-elect to king of France for help to get poss. of his see 25 Apr. 1550 (Eubel, *Hierarchia*,iii,203n; see also *Mary of Lorraine Corresp.*,323-4;cf.349,352); prob. cons. thereafter at Rome (Lesley, *History*,242; cf. *IR*,xiv,32); his position was under enquiry at curia at request of Scottish crown 9 May 1551 (*SHR*,xxii,33-35); res. on or before 4 Sept. 1551, when trans. to abp. of Athens *in partibus infidelium* (*Glas .Reg.*,ii,no.513-15; Brady, *Episcopal Succession*,i,156).

Note: John Willock was reported 28 Aug. 1560 as having been made 'bishop of Glasgow' in some sense in place of Betoun (Keith, *History*, iii,10); his position was regularised as that of superintendent, 14 Sept. 1561 (ibid.,ii,87; *CSP Scot.*,i,555).

John Porterfield 1571 - 1572 (?).

A crown prov. to this see on forfeiture of Betoun was anticipated 26 Jan. 1571 (*RSS*,vi,no.1107); an unnamed G.abp. occ. in parliament 7 Sept. 1571 (*APS*,iii,69-70); this was Porterfield who had had crown nom. and prov.; but on 8 Sept.1571 a commission was appointed to examine his fitness for his see and that of John Douglas for see of St. Andrews (*RSS*,vi,nos.2810-11); prob. granted temps. before 20 Oct. 1571, when occ. as abp. (*RMS*,iv, no. 2068); perhaps lic. to elect on forfeiture of Betoun which was issued with no name mentioned 8 Feb. 1572 (*RSS*,vi,no.1472) was intended to secure his election; this lic. was presumably directed to the *ad hoc* electoral chapter named in the convention of Leith 16 Jan. 1572 (*BUK*,i,224-6); but while Abp. Douglas got el. and cons. 6/10 Feb. 1572, Porterfield is not found again as G.abp.

James Boyd of Trochrague 1573 - 1581.

Lic. to elect on forfeiture of Betoun issued again with no name mentioned 30 Sept. 1573 (*RSS*,vi,no.2142); crown conf. of el. 3 Nov. 1573 (ibid.,no.2175;see Wodrow,*Collections*,II,i,app., p.iv for his estate and family); cons. before 9 Nov.1573 (*RPC*, ii,301) when temps. were granted (*RSS*, vi,no,2192); occ. 5 June 1581 (*Glas.Reg.*,ii,no. 530) seal used 8 June 1581 (Stevenson & Wood, *Seals*,i,114-15); d. 21 June 1581 (Edin. Tests.,8 Mar.1582).

Robert Montgomery 1581 - 1585.

Lic. to elect on death of Boyd issued with no name mentioned 1 Aug. 1581 (RSS,xlviii,fo.32); granted crown prov. on or before 3 Oct. 1581, when expected to be el. and adm. soon (*Glas.Burgh Recs.*,i,89); not known to have had cons.; crown conf. in parliament against excommunication by kirk 22 May 1584 (*APS*,iii,311-12); occ. as G. abp. in parliament 31 July 1585 (ibid., 423-4); but king's support apparently withdrawn by 7 Dec. 1585 (Calderwood, *History*,iv,461-2), and he was depriv. on or before 21 Dec. 1585 (v.inf.).

William Erskine 1585 - 1587, 1594 (?).

Crown pres. on depriv. of Montgomery 21 Dec. 1585 (Reg.Pres., ii,139); not known to have been cons.; his seal as abp. used 17 Apr. 1587 (Stevenson & Wood, *Seals*,i,115; cf. *Scot. Antiq.*,xii,62-63); had been accepted by local presbytery on basis that he held only the temporality, leaving matters of ecclesiastical jurisdiction in hands of the kirk; but general assembly of June 1587 condemned this and ordered annulment of the arrangement by the next September (*BUK*,ii,690, 693); said to occ. as abp. still 8 June 1594 (Scott, *Fasti*,vii,321, no source cited).

Note: After crown annexation of temporalities of benefices 29 July 1587 (*APS*,iii,431 ff.), temps. of this see were dispersed by grants to more than one layman 9 Aug./1 Nov.1587 (*RMS*,v,nos.1346,1404, 1406; cf. no.1932; *Glas.Chrs.*,I,ii,no.lxxvii); some are said to have been res. back to crown before 2 Jan. 1596 (*HBC*,293, no source cited).

James Betoun 1598 - 1603.

Restored to see 29 June 1598 (*APS*,iv,169-70); d. at Paris 24 Apr. 1603 (Dowden, *Bishops*,350, quoting tomb inscription).

John Spottiswood 1603 - 1615.

Crown prov. 20 July 1603, 2 Nov. 1604 and 24 May 1608 (Reg. Pres., iii,68v,93v;iv,19v); cons. 21 Oct. 1610 (Spottiswoode, *History*, iii,209); trans. to *St A.abp.* 30/31 May 1615.

James Law 1615 - 1632.

Trans. from *O.bp.* 20 July 1615 (Reg.Pres.,iv,120v); d. 13 Oct. 1362 (J.McUre, *View of City of Glasgow* (1736),35, quoting tomb inscription - but note that tomb now appears to read 10 Oct. 1632).

Patrick Lindsay 1633 - 1638.

Trans. from *R.bp.* 16 Apr. 1633 (*RMS*, viii,no.2161); depriv. 13 Dec. 1638 (Peterkin, *Records*,i,26-27); buried 2 July 1644 (Baillie, *Journals*, ii,213 and n.).

CHAPTER OF GLASGOW

A new ch. at Glasgow was cons. 7 July 1136 (*Chron.Holyrood*,119; cf. *ESC*, 269 for movements of Bp. John at this time); presumably in this connection, Bp. John established a group of secular canons there, at first supported by a common fund, but later by individual prebends

created by successive bishops (*Glas. Reg.*,i,nos.28,32,51; the details have been worked out by Mr. N.F. Shead in an unpublished Glasgow university thesis); Bp. John himself started this process of erecting separate prebends before his death in 1147, and by death of Bp. Herbert in 1164 there were seven of them (*RSCHS*,xiv,26-27); prob. the single archd. of this period was at the head of this community at first, but a dean appears 1159 x 1164; this dean was regarded as the head of the community of canons by time that Archd. Ingram (who had presumably been an absentee as royal chancellor) was el. *G.bp.* Sept. 1164 (*Glas. Reg.*,i,no.19); the dean and canons confirmed their right to elect the bishop at the next vacancy 1174 (ibid., no.35), and by Feb. 1201 x Sept.1202 they were taking an exclusive attitude about their capitular rights against the claims of lesser clergy at Glasgow (ibid.,no.97); at the same time they were acknowledging the bishop's rights of patronage over vacant prebends (ibid.,no.95); a chapter act survives from Sept. 1195 x Feb.1196 (*Melr.Lib.*,i,no.122;cf.no.121).

No formal act of constitution for this chapter survives: but additional dignities emerge in late 12th and mid-13th centuries, and even as late as 1455 x 1471 for the succentorship; some features of the Salisbury constitution were adopted in 1258 (*MRHS*, 170;*RSCHS*, xiv, 27-29, 45-46).

By the convention of Leith 16 Jan. 1572 the old chapter was conf in its control of its temporalities; at the same time it was noted that only six of the dignities and canonries were then held by reformed ministers, and so a separate electoral chapter was erected comprising these six together with a further fifteen parish ministers; it was intended that the dignities of *G.dean*, *G.archd.*, *G.archd.Teviotdale* and *G.chanc.* should be added to this electoral chapter once their incumbents accepted the Reformation (*BUK*,i,224-6; cf. Calderwood, *History*,iii, 188-90); it was presumably a body such as this which conducted the elections of 1572 (when Porterfield was rejected), 1573 and 1581.

The ordinary chapter was restored to its property and conf. in its normal rights June 1617, when it was decided that for episcopal elections they should meet along with the three suffragan bps. of the province, with *Ga.bp.* as convening authority (*APS*,iv,529-30).

DEANS OF GLASGOW

First known date: 1159 x 1164.
Prebend: ch. of Cadzow/Hamilton had prob. been erected as a preb. by 1164 (*Glas.Reg.*,i,26); not known when it came to be attached to this dignity (cf. Cowan. *Parishes*, 80).

Salomon 1159 x 1164 - 1175.
Not yet dean Mar. x May 1159 (*RRS*,i,194); occ. 6 Jan. 1161 x 20 Sept. 1164 (*TDGAS*, 3rd series,xxvi, 153-4); occ. 1 Nov.1164 (*Glas. Reg.*,i,no.19); occ. 7 Mar. 1175 (ibid.,i,21).

Herbert 1179 x 1189 - 1204 x 1207.

Not yet dean 1179 x 1196 (*Melr.Lib.*,i,no.43); occ. 1188 x 1189 (ibid.,nos.94, 108); occ. 1179 x 1221 (*Newb.Reg.*,no.3); occ. 1204 x 1207 (*Melr.Lib.*,i,no.126).

Hugh de Mortimer 1221 - 1235.
Occ. 28 Dec.1221 (*Glas.Reg.*,i,100), having prob. become dean since 24 Apr. 1221 (*CDS*,i,142); occ. 16 Apr. 1235 (*Lind.Cart.*,52).

William de Lindsay 1235 x 1236 - 1247.
Occ. 21 Feb. 1236 (*Melr.Lib.*,ii,667), having succ. since 4 May 1235 (ibid.,no.418); c¬c. 14 Jan. 1247 (*Pais.Reg.*,87,113).

Walter de Mortimer 1250 - 1270.
Occ. on or before 14 Sept. 1250 (*Glas.Reg.*,i,160); occ. 23 May 1270 (ibid.,i,181).

William Fraser 1273 - 1280.
*Occ. 29 Jan. x 11 July 1273 (*Pais.Reg.*, 192-5; cf.197); cons. *St A.bp.* 19 May 1280.

Thomas Wishart c. 1286 - 1292.
Occ. c. 1286 (*Vet.Mon.*,256); occ. 1292 (Sarti & Fattorini, *De claris...Bononiensis professoribus,* ii,331).

Alexander Bruce 1304 x 1307 - 1307.
Occ. 10 Feb. 1307 (*SHR*,viii,169), having succ. since 25 Feb. 1304 (*Reg. Corbridge*,ii,155-6); executed 17 Feb.1307 (*SHR*,loc.cit.).

Stephen de Segrave 1307 - 1309.
In poss. 3 Aug. 1307 (*CPL*,ii,28; see also Emden, *Biog.Reg.Univ. Cambridge,* 516-17); occ. 10 Jan.1309 (*Foedera*,ii,66); in poss. 27 Dec. 1309 (*CPL*,ii,68).

Raymond de Monteboerii 1313 - 1313 x 1318.
In poss. 21 May 1313 (*Vet.Mon.*,256); res. before 27 Mar. 1318 (v.inf.).

Robert de Bardis/Barducii/de Florentia 1318 - 1335 x 1336.
Robert de Coucy 1319.
Bardis prov. 27 Mar.1318 (*CPL*,ii,170); in poss. 12 Sept. 1323 (*Reg.Jean XXII*,v,4); occ. 18 May 1325 (*Glas.Reg.*,i,233;cf. 234-5) and prob. 20 May 1330 (*Cart. Gyseburne*,ii,348-52); is to res. 6 Sept.1335 when not receiving fruits (*Reg.Benoit XII*,i,30-31); promoted to another ben. before 18 July 1336 (v.inf.).
Coucy pres. by Edward II 6 Aug.1319 (*CPR 1317-21*,381), prob. unfruitfully.

William Rae 1336.
Richard Small/Sivale/de Ratho x 1338 - 1342.
Rae prov. 18 July 1336 (Vatican Archives, Instr. Misc. 5195); but still holding *G.prec.* when conf. *G.bp.* 22 Feb. 1339.
'Ratheu' (i.e. Small rector of Ratho: e.g. *Mort.Reg.*,ii,33) prob. in poss. 6 July 1338, when Edward III considered him to have incurred forfeiture (*CDS*,iii,no.1278); occ. as Small c. 1340 and 23 July 1342

*(Glas.Reg.,*i,254,231); prob. still in poss. (as Sivale) 20 Oct. 1342 (*CPL,* iii,67).

Peter de Didonia 1343 - 1349.
> Prov. on promotion of Bardis 11 Nov. 1343 (*CPL,*iii,125); is to res. 8 Dec.1349 (v.inf.).

William de Greenlaw	1349 - 1366 x 1368.
Thomas de Harcars	1364.
Michael de Monymusk	1365 - 1370.
John de Peebles (Peblis)	1365.

> **Greenlaw** prov. on Didonia's promotion 8 Dec. 1349 (*CPL,*iii,341); in poss. 30 Dec. 1352 (ibid.,611); prov. to another Glasgow preb. Aug. 1366 (Collect.,14,fo.170v); still in poss. along with other preb. 21 June 1366 (*CPP,*i,528); res. before 21 Jan. 1368 (*CPL,*iv.73).
> **Harcars** prov. 31 Oct. 1364 (Collect.,14,fo.170v) unfruitfully.
> **Monymusk** prov. 26 June 1365 (*CPP,*i,506), but no poss.; new prov. 21 June 1366 (ibid.,528) with poss. by 21 Jan. 1368 (v.sup.); cons. *Dk.bp.* 5 x 8 Jan. 1371.
> **Peebles** prov. 27 June 1365 (*CPP,*i,506) unfruitfully.

Nicholas de Greenlaw 1371 - 1415.
> Prov. 14 May 1371 (Reg.Av.,176,fo.199); d. in poss. 25 Sept. 1415 (*Glas.Reg.,*ii,616).

George de Hawden 1415 - 1415 x 1418.
> Prov. on Greenlaw's death 8 Dec. 1415 (*CPP,*i,604); d. before 11 Dec. 1418 (v.inf.).

Walter Stewart	1418 - 1421.
Thomas de Myrton/Merton	1419 - 1452 x 1456.
David de Hamilton	1420 - 1433.
Alexander de Lauder	1421.
Patrick Leche (Leth)	x 1444.
Adam de Montgomery	1444.

> **Stewart** prov. by Benedict XIII on Hawden's death 11 Dec. 1418 (*CPP,*i,610); lit. followed with Myrton and Lauder; surrog. to Myrton's right 25 Feb. 1421 (*CSSR,*i,244-5).
> **Myrton** had prov. from Martin V on Hawden's death, but still no poss. 29 May 1419 (*CSSR,*i,56-57,244); in poss. when lit. with Stewart, Lauder and Hamilton 25 Feb. 1421 (ibid.); new prov. with poss. 15 Oct. 1421 (ibid.,262-3); prob. still in poss. 16 Dec. 1423 (*CSSR,*ii,42); lost poss. to Hamilton for a year, but regained poss. by 6 May 1425 (ibid., 84-85); prob. remained in poss. thereafter; occ. 16 Sept. 1452 (*Glas. Reg.,*ii,394-6); d. before 12 Feb. 1456 (v. inf.).
> **Hamilton** had prov. from Martin V on Hawden's death 2 Aug. 1420 (*ASCB,*86); lit. with Myrton and had poss. for one year in the period Dec. 1423 x May 1425 (v.sup.); res. right in Myrton's favour 8 Nov. 1429 (Reg.Supp.,246,fo.15v); prov. again 12 Sept. 1433 (ibid., 289,fo,87v) unfruitfully.
> **Lauder** lit. with Stewart and Myrton 25 Feb. 1421 (*CSSR,*i, 244-5); no poss.
> **Leche** had some right before 21 Apr. 1444 when found as *G.chanc.*

(v.inf.).

Montgomery prov. on res. of Leche 21 Apr.1444 (Reg.Supp., 396, fo.69).

James Inglis 1456.

Prov. on Myrton's death 12 Feb. 1456, but d. without poss. (*CPL*, xi,34,64,271).

Thomas Vaus 1456 - 1468.
James Lindsay 1463 - 1487 x 1488.
Richard Cady 1466.

Vaus prov. on death of Inglis 8 May 1456 (*CPL*,xi,271); in poss. and gets licence to res. on exch. 13 Mar.1464 (Reg.Supp., 572,fo.215); new prov. following molestation 27 Dec.1465 (ibid., 589, fo.234); still in poss. 31 Oct.1466 (ibid.,602,fo.254v); res. on exch. with Lindsay for *M.prec.*, effective apparently 11 Apr. x 7 Oct. 1468.

Lindsay gets *com.priv.* against Vaus 23 Dec. 1463 and again 3 Jan. 1464 (Reg.Supp.,570,fo.220v; 571,fo.87); said to be in poss. 29 Nov. 1466 (*Rot.Scot.*,ii,421); settlement with Vaus by exch. for *M.prec.* arranged after 11 Apr. and before 7 Oct. 1468 (*CPL*,xii,298-9); said to have d. in poss. 17 May 1487 (*Glas. Reg.*,ii,615); but occ. later, 19 Sept. and 26 Nov. 1487 (ibid.,ii,455-6, 456-7; cf. list of contents); certainly d. by 29 Feb. 1488 (v. inf.).

Cady gets *com.priv.* against Vaus 31 Oct. 1466 (Reg.Supp., 602, fo.254v).

Thomas Montgomery 1488.
Richard Muirhead 1488 - 1503 x 1504.

Montgomery prov. on Lindsay's death 29 Feb. 1488 (*ACSB*, 222) unfruitfully.

Muirhead occ. 22 Apr. 1488 (ibid.); promised annates and was prov. on Lindsay's death 30 Jan. 1489 (PRO 31/9 - 30/143 - 4); occ. 21 Sept. 1503 (*RMS*,ii,no.2755); prob. d. before 4 June 1504 (*Stirling Chrs.*,xxxv).

Robert Forman 1505 - 1530.

Occ. 3 Dec. 1505 (SRO, ADC,xvii,fo.66), having moved from *G. prec.* since 1 Mar. 1505; d. in poss. 29 Nov. 1530 (*James V Letters*, 184).

William Stewart 1530 - 1533.
James Lamb 1531.

Stewart given crown pres. to pope 25 Dec. 1530 (*ibid.*,185): el. 21 Jan. 1531 (*St A.Form.*,i,340); in poss. when nom. *Ab.bp.* 22 Mar.1532; cons. 22 Mar. x 10 Apr. 1533.

Lamb had papal prov. at Albany's request, and gets papal conf. despite crown nom. of Stewart 17 July 1531 (PRO 31/9 - 2/s.d.).

James Scrymgeour 1532 - 1532 x 1533.

Gets crown pres. to pope for prov 22 Mar.1532 (*James V Letters*, 218); occ. in a royal letter 25 Nov. 1532 (ibid.,232); installed by deputy after prov. (*St A.Form.*,ii,75-78); d. by Oct. 1533 (v.inf.).

George Lockhart 1533 - 1547.

John Lauder   1534.

Lockhart el. 11 Oct. 1533 (NLS, Riddell MS no.9, fo.9v); crown pres. to pope for prov. on Scrymgeour's death 13 Oct.1533 *(James V Letters,* 249); promises annates and gets prov. 17 Mar. 1534 (PRO 31/9 - 32/272-3); d. 22 June 1547 *(Glas.Reg.,*ii,614).

Lauder res. some right on or before 17 Mar. 1534 (v.sup.), prob. in exch. for right in *G.archd. Teviotdale.*

Alexander Hamilton   x 1548.

Had some right at death before 16 July 1548 (v.inf.).

Gavin Hamilton   1548 - 1551.
Henry Sinclair   1550 - 1561.

Hamilton promises annates and gets prov. 16 July 1548 (PRO 31/9 - 33/240); occ. 30 Apr. 1549 (RSS,iv.no.225) and 16 Jan. 1551 *(Prot.Bk.Glasgow,*i,24).

Sinclair granted crown permission to obtain it on exch. with Hamilton 10 Apr.1550 *(RSS,*iv,no.644); prov. *R.bp.* 2 June 1561; occ. 13 Nov. 1561 *(RPC,*i,187).

James Balfour 1561 - 1589.

Had prob. moved from *G.treas.* by 12 Dec. 1561; occ. 12 May 1562 (SRO, Dalhousie, 16/690); occ. 2 Oct. 1589 (SRO,Reg.Ho.Chrs., no.3027).

John Muirhead (Murehead) 1602 - 1603.

Crown pres. 26 Dec. 1602 (RSS,1xxiii,fo.165); d. 10 Oct. 1603 (Edin Tests., 28 Feb.1605).

James Hamilton 1610 - 1636.

Crown pres. on deaths of Balfour and Muirhead 4 Dec.1610 (RSS,1xxix,fo.213); occ. 30 Mar. 1636 (Edin.Univ.Lib., MS Laing Chr. no. 2660; *Laing Chrs.,*no. 2187).

PRECENTORS/CHANTERS OF GLASGOW

First known date: 1179 x 1221.

Prebend: ch. of Carstairs was held by Hertford in 1227 *(Glas.Reg.,*i 130); ch. of Kilbride perhaps in 1266, certainly by 1417 (Cowan *Parishes,* 96).

Simon 1179 x 1221.

Occ. 1179 x 28 Dec. 1221 *(Newb.Reg.,*no.3).

Robert Hertford 1223 x 1225 - 1228.

Occ. x 1 Aug. 1225 (Pais.Reg., 211-12), having obtained poss. since 30 Aug. 1223 *(Cart. Gyseburne,*ii,347; cf. *Glas.Reg.,*i,106); occ. as 'R.' 1 Mar. 1228 *(Glas.Reg.,*i,120).

W.   1229.

Occ. 28 Jan. 1229 (ibid.,i,123).

Geoffrey de Liberatione 1236.
Occ. 21 Feb. 1236 (*Melr.Lib.*,ii,667); cons. *Dk.bp.* 3 x 31 Dec. 1236.

David de Bernham 1238 x 1239 - 1240.
Occ. 1238 x 3 June 1239 (*Glas.Reg.*,i,141); cons. *St A.bp.* 22 Jan. 1240.

Simon de Biggar (Bygres) 1259 - 1266.
Occ. 2 Jan. 1259 and 19 Apr. 1266 (*Glas.Reg.*,i,166-7,174).

John 1269.
Occ. 19 Dec. 1269 (*Kel.Lib.*, no.179).

Robert c. 1290.
Occ. c. 1290 (*Glas.Reg.*,i,200).

William de Clyff 1319.
Pres. by Edward II 19 July 1319 (*CPR 1317-21*,380), prob. unfruitfully.

Walter de Rule 1321 - 1330.
Occ. 11 July 1321 (*Glas.Reg.*,i,228); still in poss. 24 Apr. 1330 (*Vet.Mon.*,254).

William Rae 1339.
Conf. *G.bp.* as prec. 22 Feb. 1339 (ibid.,274).

Gilbert de Cunningham 1341 x 1346 *or* 1356 x 1371.
Occ. 1341 x 1346 or 1356 x 1371, prob. earlier dating (*HMC 21, Hamilton*, 21).

Laurence de Kinghorn 1362 - 1362 x 1371.
Occ. 1 July 1362 (*Glas.Reg.*,i,268); d. by 7 Sept.1371 (v.inf.).

John Fabri 1371 - 1372.
Prov. as cardinal on Kinghorn's death 7 Sept. 1371 (Reg.Av.,176, fo.348); d. 6 Mar. 1372 (Eubel, *Hierarchia*,i,42).

Stephen de Poissy 1372 - 1373.
Prov. as cardinal on Fabri's death 25 May 1372 (Reg.Av.,183,fo. 212); d. 17 Oct. 1373 (Eubel, *Hierarchia*,i,40).

William de Wardlaw 1378.
In poss. 20 Nov. 1378 (*CPP*, i,550).

Walter de Wardlaw 1387.
In poss. as cardinal and bp. of Glasgow at death May x Oct.1387 (PRO 31/9 - 59/572).

Walter Bricii 1387 - 1388.
Henry de Wardlaw 1387 - 1403.
Bricii has some right and prob. poss. 5 Oct.1387 (*CPP*,i,568); prob. still in poss. 1 Feb. 1388 (v. inf.).
Wardlaw had crown pres. on Cardinal Wardlaw's death and had papal conf. 2 Dec. 1387 (PRO 31/9 - 59/572); no poss 1 Feb. 1388

(*CPP*,,i,570); occ. 12 Sept. 1388 (*Pais.Reg.*,332-4); prov. *G.archd.*
20 May 1398, but still in poss. when prov. *St A.bp.* 10 Sept. 1403.

John de Hawick   1398 - 1432.
William de Lauder   1403 - 1406.
   Hawick prov. on Henry de Wardlaw's prov. to *G.archd.* 20 May
1398 (*CPP*,i,596); later claimed to have had poss. by Feb. 1402 (ibid),
but it is doubtful that his prov. was effective until after promotion of
Wardlaw to his see; said to be in poss. 22 July 1404 (Reg.Av.,326,fo.
6v); dispossessed for a time by Lauder (v.inf.), but won lit. in curia
against him and got new prov. 20 Dec. 1404 (*CPP*,i,633) and 5 Apr.
1405, expedited 27 Jan. 1406 (Reg. Av., 318,fos.594v-595v); occ.
14 Jan. 1428 (*Glas.Reg.*,ii,319-21); d. 17 Mar. 1432 (ibid.,615).
   Lauder prov. on Wardlaw's elevation to his see 21 Sept. 1403
(Reg.Av.,307,fos.369v-370v); occ. 26 Nov. 1404 (*Melr.Lib.*,ii,480-7);
but lost lit. in curia with Hawick by 20 Dec. 1404/5 Apr. 1405/ 27
Jan. 1406 (v.sup.).

David de Cadzow   1432 x 1433 - 1456 x 1458.
Nicholas de Otterburn   1432 - 1432 x 1433.
Laurence Piot   1433 - 1436.
Robert Lauder   1440.
Patrick de Sinclair   1443.
   Cadzow coll. by ord. on Hawick's death (*CPL*,viii,607-8);
occ. 24 Mar. 1433 (*Glas.Reg.*,ii,329); papal conf. of poss. 23 July 1434
(Reg.Supp.,297,fo.37v) and 5 June 1436 (*CPL*,viii,607-8); occ. 19 Apr.
1456 (*Glas.Reg.*,ii,406); res. in favour of Dalgless before 8 May 1456
(v.inf.); had pension on fruits, conf. by pope 15 Nov. 1458 (*CPL*,xii,
49); still sometimes called prec. e.g. 29 July 1460 (*Glas.Mun.*,ii,67);
alternative dates of death are found - x 4 May 1460 (*Glas.Reg.*,ii,414),
19 Aug. 1467 (ibid.,616) and 7 Jan. 1468 (*Glas.Mun.*,i,20).
   Otterburn Prov. on Hawick's death 12 May 1432 (*CPL*,viii,453);
res. right on getting another preb. 29 June 1432 x 29 Aug. 1433 (Reg.
Supp.,278,fo.64v; 288,fo.72v.
   Piot prov. 29 Aug. 1433 (ibid.,288,fo.72v); lit. without poss. 9
Aug. 1434 (ibid.,296,fo.15v) and 26 July 1436 (*CPL*,viii,579).
   Lauder gets *com.priv.* against Cadzow 1 Sept. 1440 (Reg. Supp.,
369,fo.227v) unfruitfully.
   Sinclair gets *com.priv.* against Cadzow 21 Dec. 1443 (ibid., 394,
fo.8v) unfruitfully.

Simon de Dalgless   1456 - 1471 x 1476.
John de Montgomery   1459.
   Dalgless occ. 8 May 1456 (*SHS Misc.*,v,40), having got it from
ord. on Cadzow's res. (*CPL*,xii,49); occ. 6 Apr. 1471 (*HMC* 46, *Hope-
Johnstone*,12); d. 5 Jan. 1476 apparently in poss. (*Glas.Reg.*,ii,614).
   Montgomery got *com.priv.* against Dalgless 31 July 1459 (Reg.
Supp.,520,fo.230) unfruitfully.

John Crichton/Crechtone/Crethon 1474 - 1497.
   Occ. 29 Mar. 1474 (Fraser, *Lennox*, ii,22); occ. 13 May 1497

(*Glas.Reg.*,ii,496).

John Goldsmith 1498.
Charged with barratry after obtaining exp. grace from pope 10 May 1498 (*ADC*,ii,202).

Robert Forman 1500 - 1505.
'Helpit and supliit' to prec. before 11 Feb. 1500 (*ADC*,ii,387); lit. at curia while prob. in poss. 31 May 1500 (*Camb.Reg.*, 177-8); in poss. 24 Aug. 1501 (PRO 31/9 - 31/22); occ. 1 Mar. 1505 (*RMS*,ii,no.3007); moved to *G.dean.* by 3 Dec. 1505.

John Forman	1509 - 1543.
Andrew Cunningham	1512 - 1516.
Thomas Nudry	1513.
John Duncanson	1521 - 1544.
Alexander Hervy	1524.
Archibald Dunbar	1537 - 1538 x 1539.
John Bellenden/Ballantyne	1537 - 1547.
Patrick Bellenden	1543.

Forman occ. 31 May 1509 (*Prot.Bk.Simon*,285); is expected to res. on promotion to abbey of Kilwinning 1512 and 1513 (v.inf.), and lost poss. after 7 Apr. 1513 (ibid.,485) and before 16 May 1516 (v.inf.); claimed poss. and royal letters of support when lit. in curia with Duncanson 31 Jan. 1524 (*James V Letters*, 97-98); still drawing pension on fruits 1 Mar. 1543 (PRO 31/9 - 33/143).

Cunningham gets crown pres. to pope for prov. 1512 (*James IV Letters*,280); apparently in poss. July 1513 x July 1514 (*ER*,xiv,47); in poss. *de facto* when Forman's right was asserted 16 May 1516 (*ADCP*, 67).

Nudry promises annates and gets prov. on expected promotion of Forman 20 Apr. 1513 (PRO 31/9 - 31/272); no poss. 10 Oct. 1513 (ibid.,273).

Duncanson occ. 8 Oct. 1521 (*Melr.Lib.*,ii,632); lit. at curia with Forman 31 Jan. 1524 (*James V Letters*, 97-98); agrees to res. in favour of Hervy 19 Mar. 1524 (PRO 31/9 - 32/16), but does not; occ. 4 Jan. 1525 (SRO,Reg.Ho.Chr. no.966, quoted Bellenden, *Chronicles*,ii,429) and 23 Oct. 1526 (*Arb.Lib.*,ii,458); depriv. by abp. 9 Jan.1537 (Bellenden, *Chronicles*,ii,430) and escheated by crown 9 Sept. 1537 (*RSS*,ii,no.2368); but claimed at Rome to be still in poss. 12 Jan. 1538 (PRO 31/9 - 33/75); res. in curia in favour of Fogo 3 Sept. 1544 (ibid., 171); d. before 30 Mar. 1545 (ibid.,166-7).

Hervy prov. on Duncanson's res. 2 Mar. 1524 (PRO 31/9-32/16).

Dunbar in poss. Jan. 1537 (Bellenden, *Chronicles*,ii,428); occ. 5 Aug. 1537 (*Glas.Mun.*,i,494); prob. res. right on exch. with John Bellenden for *M.archd.* Dec. 1538 x Mar. 1539.

John Bellenden gets crown pres. on Duncanson's escheat 9 Sept. 1537 (*RSS*,ii,no.2368); prob. got poss. on exch. with Dunbar Dec. 1538 x Mar. 1539 (v. sup.); promises annates and gets prov. without fruits (cf. Forman above and Patrick Bellenden below) 1 Mar. 1543 (PRO 31/9 - 33/144); in poss. 30 Mar. 1545 (ibid., 166-7); occ. 5 Apr.

1547 (*RSS*,iii,no.2238).

Patrick Bellenden had some right which he res. 1 Mar. 1543 promising annates to retain fruits (PRO 31/9 - 33/143).

William Fogo   1544.
John Stevenson/Stevinstoun 1544 - 1563 x 1564.

Fogo prob. got prov. 3 Sept. 1544 (see Duncanson above); but res. without poss. in favour of Stevenson 17 Nov. 1544 (PRO 31/9 - 33/176; cf.ibid.,66/291).

Stevenson acquired some right from Fogo 17 Nov. 1544 (v.sup.); promised annates and got prov. on Duncanson's death 30 Mar.1545. though Bellenden then in poss. (PRO 31/9 - 33/166-7); occ. 12 Aug. 1549 (Macphail, *Pluscardyn,*242); occ. 11 Dec. 1563 (*Yester Writs,* no. 710); d. by 1 Feb. 1564 (v. inf.).

George Bellenden 1564 - 1568 x 1569.

Crown pres. on Stevenson's death 1 Feb. 1564 (*RSS*,v,no.1551); occ. 2 Aug. 1568 (*Orkney Recs.,*287); d. by 21 Mar. 1569 (*RSS,* vi,no.561).

John Colville   1569 - 1586.
William Fleming   1584 - 1585.

Colville gets crown pres. on Bellenden's death 20 Apr. 1569 (Reg.Pres.,i,19; *RSS*,vi,no.580); occ. 5 June 1581 (*Glas.Reg.*,ii,588); occ. 1586 (Stevenson & Wood, *Seals,*ii,292).

Fleming gets crown pres. on 'inhabilitie' of Colville 28 May 1584 (Reg.Pres.,ii.103), and again on Colville's forfeiture 10 Feb. 1585 (ibid.,122).

Robert Darroch 1586 - 1607.

Crown pres. on Colville's res. 22 July 1585 (Reg.Pres.,ii,154); d. Jan. 1607 (Hamilton Tests., 29 Oct. 1622).

David Sharp (Scharpe) 1608 - 1635.

Crown pres. on Darroch's death 14 Jan. 1608 (Reg.Pres.,iv.10); occ. as chanter 15 Nov.1632 (ibid.,vi,151) and as parson of Kilbride 22 Feb. 1635 (SRO, Part.Reg.Sasines Lanark,ivA,279).

CHANCELLORS OF GLASGOW

First known date: 1258.

By inference this dignity was not yet in existence as late as 20 Apr. 1249 (*CPL*,i,257).

Prebend: ch. of Campsie in 1266 (*Kel.Lib.*,i,187); Cowan, *Parishes,* 26).

Richard 1249 x 1258 - 1270.

Occ. 1247 x 1258, 11 Aug. 1258 and 23 May 1270 (*Glas.Reg.*,i, 142, 166, 181).

William de Lamberton 1293 - 1298.

Occ. 18 Feb. 1293 (ibid.,201); cons. *St A.bp.* 1 June 1298.

William Comyn 1298 - 1336 x 1337.
   Prov. 12 July 1298 (*CPL*,i,578); still in poss. 11 Nov. 1329 (ibid., ii,310); prob. d. 1336 x Feb. 1337 (see *St A.archd. Lothian*).

Gilbert de Southwick   1337 - 1343.
Reginald de Ogston   1343 - 1350.
   Southwick in poss. 17 Feb. 1337 (*CPL*, ii,540); had got it without papal prov., but still in poss. 5 Mar. 1343 (*CPP*,i,15).
   Ogston prov. on Comyn's death 5 Mar. 1343 (ibid.,14-15); occ. 20 Oct. 1345 (*Moray Reg.*, 156-7); still in poss. 13 June 1350 (*CPP*, i,201).

John de Carrick 1362 - 1362 x 1363.
   Occ. 30 June and 2 Sept. 1362 (*Glas.Reg.*,i,265,271); prob. res. before 14 Mar. 1363 (*Rot.Scot.*,i,872).

John de Erskine 1400 - c. 1414.
   Occ. 18 June 1400 (Fraser, *Wemyss*, ii,41); res. to ord. on exch. with Busby before 21 Mar. 1414 (v. inf.); said to be still retaining fruits 25 Oct. 1419 (*CSSR*,i,133-4; cf. ibid.,ii,39-40).

John Busby   c. 1414 - 1423.
John Weir (Wer)   1419 - 1422.
Thomas de Greenlaw 1419.
Robert Stewart   1423.
Edward de Lauder   1423.
John Gray   1425 x 1428.
   Busby got it on exch. with Erskine and then got prov. 21 Mar.1414 (Reg.Av.,343,fos. 261-262v;cf. *CSSR*,i,133-4; ii,38-40); occ. 12 June 1415 (SRO, J.M. Thomson Transcripts, sub 15 June 1415); involved in lit. (v.inf.); res. in curia retaining pension 4 Mar. x 27 May 1423 (*CSSR*, ii,5,24); still in poss. of pension when given habilitation for simony 1 Oct. 1423 (ibid.,38-40).
   Weir prov. 13 Sept. 1419 (*CPL*,vii,114-15); lit. in curia; new prov. 6 Dec. 1422 (*ACSB*,87); lit. had gone against him by 4 Mar. 1423 (*CSSR*, ii,5); prob. never had poss.
   Greenlaw prov. 25 Oct. 1419 (ibid.,i,133-4) unfruitfully.
   Stewart surrog.to Busby's right 27 Mar. 1423 (*CPL*,vii, 294-5); d. without poss. (v.inf.).
   Lauder prov. on Stewart's death 22 May 1423 (*CSSR*,ii,24) unfruitfully.
   Gray held it for a time by right of a papal exp. grace for a G.can. dated 25 Apr. 1424, but res. to ord. at king's request before 3 Mar. 1428, prob. in favour of Brown (*CPL*,viii,381-3; *CSSR*,ii,193-4); his poss. was prob. after 29 May 1425 when he held can. and unidentified preb. in Glasgow, which he was then to res. (*CPL*,vii,399).

David Brown 1428 - 1435.
   Prob. in poss. by 3 Mar. 1428 (v.sup.); occ. 12 Sept. 1428 (SRO, Cal.St A.Chrs.,no.18); new prov. 17 May 1430 (*ACSB*,114); occ. 28 Nov. 1435 (*St Giles Reg.*, 57-58).

L

Thomas Rule (Roulle) 1438.
   Occ. 8 July 1438 (*ER*,v,55); had had coll by ord. before 3 Nov. 1438 (*CPL*,ix,24).

Patrick Leche (Leth)   1444 - 1459 x 1464.
John Ochiltree (Uchtre)   1447.
   Leche obtained it shortly before 21 Apr. 1444 (Reg.Supp., 396. fo.69); occ. 18 June 1446 (*Glas.Reg.*,ii,365); occ. 12 May 1459 (ibid., 410); d. before 18 Feb. 1464 (*Glas. Mun.*,ii,199).
   Ochiltree gets *com.priv.* against Leche 4 May 1447 (Reg.Supp., 417,fo.91) unfruitfully.

David Livingstone   x 1465, 1466 (?).
Robert Hamilton   1465 - 1468.
   Livingstone held it sometime before 28 Dec. 1465, when no longer in poss.(Reg.Supp.,595, fo.283); said to be in poss. 6 Apr. 1466 (*CPL*, xii,535).
   Hamilton occ. 1 Apr. 1465 (*Melr.Lib.*,ii,593), following coll. by ord. (*CPL*,xii, 402-3); occ. 22 July 1468 (*Lag Chrs.*,no.12).

Martin Wan/Wane 1468 - 1478 x 1480.
Richard Cady   1472 - 1473.
   Wan occ. 28 July 1468 (Stevenson & Wood, *Seals*,iii,640); occ. 19 June 1470 (*Glas.Mun.*,ii,76); occ. 3 Nov. 1478 (*Yester Writs*,78); apparently ousted by Leche for a period by 1480 (v.inf.).
   Cady res. to ord. in terms of papal mand. of 31 July 1472, obtaining pension on fruits for which he promised annates 7 May 1473 (*ACSB*,173).

Patrick Leche 1480 - 1480 x 1481.
   Occ. 5 June and 7 Oct./3 Nov. 1480 (*Glas.Reg.*,ii,444;*Glas. Mun.*,ii,232); found holding another preb. in Glasgow by 25 Oct. 1481 (ibid.,ii,90).

Martin Wan 1480 x 1482 - 1505.
   Occ. again 25 Oct. 1482 (*Glas.Mun.*,ii,91); consents to Reid as coadj; 26 Nov. 1502 (PRO 31/9 - 31/44); occ. 15 Jan. 1504 (*Prot. Bk.Simon*,60); d. shortly before 12 June 1505 (v.inf.).

Martin Reid 1502 - 1516.
   Accepted as coadj. to Wan 26 Nov. 1502 (v.sup.); occ. as coadj. 15 Jan 1504 (*Prot.Bk.Simon*,59-60.no.78); instituted on Wan's death 12 June 1505 (ibid.,120); occ. 23 Aug. 1516 (*Prot.Bk.Ros*,no.147); d. before 1 May 1523 (ibid.,no.654).

David Betoun 1519 - 1523.
   Occ. 16 Oct. 1519 (*SHS Misc.*,ii,85); occ. 31 Dec. 1523 (*James V Letters*,96).

David 'Rinzeane' 1524.
   Said to have res. in favour of Lamb before Nov. 1524 (v.inf.); surname is prob. error for Betoun.

John Lecheman/Lescheman/Lichman   1524 - 1535.
James Lamb   1524 - 1527.
Thomas Erskine   1532 - 1535.

Lecheman pres. by Albany c. Nov. 1524 (*ADCP*, 270); in poss. 10 June 1532 when is to res. in Erskine's favour (*James V Letters*, 224); retained pension on fruits, which he res. 30 May 1535 on getting another ben. (PRO 31/9 - 33/21-22).

Lamb prov. by pope on res. of 'Rinzeane' in his favour while see was vacant Nov. 1524 (*ADCP*, 270); condemned for barratry 5 Nov. 1527 (ibid.).

Erskine gets crown pres. to pope for prov. on Lecheman's res. 10 June 1532 (*James V Letters*, 224); res. in curia on or before 20 Aug. 1535 (v. inf.).

Walter Maxwell 1535 - 1536.

Promises annates and gets prov. on Erskine's res. 20 Aug. 1535 (PRO 31/9 - 33/9-10); occ. 5 Aug. 1537 (*Glas.Mun.*, i, 494).

Thomas Erskine 1539 - 1548.

Occ. 7 Nov. 1539 (*James V Letters*, 380); res. 20 July 1548 (*RSS*, iii, no.2869).

John Erskine 1548 - 1552.

Crown pres. on res. of Thomas Erskine 20 July 1548 (ibid.); res. 10 Dec. 1552 (*RSS*, iv, no.1814).

David Erskine 1552 - 1554.

Crown pres. on John Erskine's res. 10 Dec. 1552 (ibid); occ. 2 Feb. 1554 (*SHR*, xxii, 29).

Adam Erskine 1560 - 1562.

Occ. 29 June 1560 (*Dryb.Lib.*, 325); crown pres. to abbey of Cambuskenneth 30 June 1562 (*RSS*, v, no.1066).

William Erskine   1563 - 1589.
John Stoddart (Stodhard) 1584.

Erskine occ. 8 June 1563 (SRO, Boyd, no. 172); crown pres. 26 Sept. 1563 (*RSS*, v, no, 1469); occ. 5 June 1581 (*Glas.Reg.*, ii, 588) and 2 Oct. 1589 (SRO, Reg. Ho.Chr. no. 3027).

Stoddart got crown pres. on Erskine's forfeiture 24 Aug. 1584 (RSS, li, fo.37).

James Stewart 1614 - 1619.

Occ. as prebendary of Campsie 7 Dec. 1614 (*Glas.Chrs.*, ii, 294), and as chanc. 6 Dec. 1619 (Edin.Univ.Lib., MS Laing Chr. no.2284; cf. *Laing Chrs.*, no.1596, where date is wrong).

William Crichton 1626 - 1629.

Occ. 31 Oct. 1626 (SRO, Moir Bryce Chr.no.188) and 5 Aug. 1629 (SRO, Part.Reg.Sasines Lanark, iiiB, 100).

Alexander Forbes 1636.

Occ. 30 Mar. 1636 (Edin.Univ.Lib., MS Laing Chr.no.2660; *Laing Chrs.*, no. 2187).

TREASURERS OF GLASGOW

First known date: 1195 x 1196.
    Prebend: ch. of Carnwath in 1438 and prob. earlier (Cowan,
*Parishes,*28).

John de Roxburgh 1195 x 1196 - 1196.
    Occ. Sept. 1195 x Feb. 1196 (*Melr.Lib.,*i,78); d. in poss. 2 Feb.
1196 (*Chron.Melrose,*49).

Robert de Tyndale 1223 - 1235.
    Occ. 14 Oct. 1223 (*CPL,*i,337), 30 Aug. 1223 x 1 Aug. 1225
(*Pais Reg.,* 211-12; see *G.prec.* for dating), 1225 (ibid.,373); occ. as
'R.' 28 Jan. 1229 (*Glas.Reg.,*i,123) and as 'Robert' 7 May 1235
(*Lind.Cart.,*no.51).

Robert 1251 x 1253 - 1299.
    Occ. 12 Mar. 1241 x 24 May 1253 (*Glas.Reg.,*i,145), 1273 (*Pais.
Reg.,*195), 1279 (Sarti and Fattorini, *De claris... Bononiensis
professoribus,*ii,318), c. 1285 (*HMC* 1,*2nd R.*,166), 23 Apr. 1293
(*Glas.Reg.,*i,208), and 29 Oct. 1299 (Pais.Reg.,131); there is no
evidence to show how many people are involved in this series of
references.

William de Herlaston 1319.
    Pres. by Edward II 19 July 1319 (*CPR 1317 - 21,*380), prob.
unfruitfully.
Robert Cameron (Cambrun) 1325.
    Occ. 17 May 1325 (*Glas.Reg.,*i,234).
Robert de Strathearn 1330 - 1339.
    In poss. 24 Apr. 1330 (*Vet.Mon.,*254) and 22 Feb. 1339
(*CPL,*ii,545).

John de Ketenis 1352.
    In poss. 3 May 1352 (*CPP,*i,226-7).

John de Peebles (Peblis) 1362 - 1368 x 1369.
    Occ. 22 July 1362 (*Rot.Scot.,*i,864); still in poss. 20 Jan.1368
(*CPL,*iv,74); apparently res. before 15 Jan. 1369 (*Pais Reg.,* 328-30)

Henry de Mangavilla x 1371.
    Held it at death before 23 Sept. 1371 (v. inf.).

William de Etal 1371.
    Had coll. by ord. on Mangavilla's death, and gets papal conf. 23
Sept. 1371 (*CPL,*iv,167).

Walter Trail 1378 - 1385.
    Had. prov. before 24 Nov. 1378, but no poss. then (*CPP,*i,540);
in poss. 27 June 1381 (ibid.,559); prov. *St A.bp.* 29 Nov. 1385.

David Falconer 1386 - 1403.
    Prov. 27 Jan. 1386 (Reg.Av.,243,fo.118); still in poss. 20 Oct.

1403 (*CPP*,i,625).

Thomas Trail 1424 - 1430.

     Occ. 26 Sept. 1434 (*St Mary Lib.*,242); is to res. in favour of
Moffat by papal authority 1 Feb. 1430 (*CPL*,viii,168).

Robert de Moffat   1430 - 1437 x 1438.
John de Wincester   1431.
Gilbert Herring (Heryng)   1431.

     Moffat prov. on exch. with Trail 1 Feb. 1430 (ibid.); still in poss.
7 Dec. 1437 (Reg. Supp.,342,fo.35v); d. by 13 Nov.1438 (v.inf.).

     Wincester prov. 11 Mar. x 19 Sept. 1431 (Reg.Supp.,270, fo.145);
still had a claim 23 Oct.1431 (ibid.,271,fo,190v).

     Herring prov. on (false) report of Moffat's death 22 Sept. 1431
(ibid.,271,fo.232).

Hugh Kennedy   1438 - 1451 x 1452.
James Inglis   1438 x 1439 - 1439 x 1440.

     Kennedy prov. on Moffat's death 13 Nov. 1438 (*CPL*,ix,1-2); won
lit. against Inglis by 17 Sept. 1439 (v.inf.); but still lit. 10 Oct. 1439
(Reg.Supp.,304,fo.178); perhaps retained this ben. until he moved to
St A.archd.,i.e. 3 Mar. 1451 x 4 Mar. 1454: Clepham's prov. (v.inf.)
was prob. subsequent to this move, which would then be datable 3 Mar.
1451 x 21 Jan. 1452.

     Inglis had coll. by ord. on Moffat's death (*CPL*,ix,123-4); claims
poss. at Basel 24 Apr. 1439 (Haller, *Conc.Bas.*,vi,372-3; *Mon.Conc.Bas.*,
iii,255); papal conf. 12 May 1439 (Reg. Supp.,361,fo.206); lost lit. in
curia against Kennedy by 17 Sept. 1439 (*CPL*,ix,48-49); res.right and
reverted to another G. preb. before 11 July 1440 (ibid.,123-4).

Richard Clepham x 1452.

     Had prov. sometime before death i.e. x 21 Jan 1452 (Reg.Supp.,
459,fo.440; see *Dk.chanc.* for death date).

Thomas Lauder   1452.
John Balfour   1452.
Walter Stewart   1452 - 1456 x 1457.

     Lauder had some right in this ben. and lit. with Stewart when prov.
Dk.bp. 28 Apr. 1452 (*CPL*,x,576).

     Balfour had surrog. to Lauder's right and continued lit. with
Stewart 29 Apr/20 May 1452 (Reg.Supp.,459,fo.440; *CPL*,x, 576).

     Stewart is found as lit. with Lauder and then Balfour Apr. - May
1452 (v.sup.); appears to have been successful; res. on exch. with
Douglas for *St A.archd.* certainly after 7 June 1455 (*CPL*,xi,12) and
prob. Nov. 1456 x Oct. 1457.

Hugh Douglas 1456 x 1457 - 1460.

     Got poss. on exch. with Stewart prob.Nov.1456 x Oct.1457 (v.
sup.); occ. 8 Apr. 1460 (*St A.Acta*, 135). still in poss. 21 Oct. 1460
(*CPL*,xi,422).

George Carmichael 1474 - 1485.

     Occ. 25 Apr. 1474 (*RMS*,ii,no.1169); still in poss. 12 July 1485

(*CPL*,xiv,56); d. by 10 Sept. 1485 (v. inf.).

Alexander Inglis   1485 - 1513.
John Stewart   1488.

Inglis prov. on Carmichael's death 10 Sept. 1485 (Reg. Supp., 850,fo.51-51v); still in poss. 9 Apr. 1513, when he agreed that abp. sho seek papal faculty to dispose of his benefices (*Prot. Bk.Simon*,486); d. by 2 July 1513 (ibid.,495).

Stewart said to be in poss. 14 July 1488 (NLS'Adv.MS 19.2.20,p

John Campbell   1513.
Thomas Nudry   1514.

Campbell gets crown pres. to pope for prov. on death of Inglis 13 Feb./10 July 1513 (*James IV Letters*, 292,309); prob. not the man for whom a proctor acted in claiming the treasurer's stall at Glasgow 2/4 July 1513 (*Prot.Bk.Simon*,'495); perhaps same as nom. *I.bp. 9* Sept. 1513 x 18 Sept. 1514.

Nudry perhaps had had new prov. before 2/4 July 1513 in terms of which a proctor acted for an anonymous new G. treas (v.sup.); in poss. 10 June 1514 (*James V Letters*,9).

Andrew Sibbald   1518.

Occ. 19 Jan. and 26 Aug. 1518 (*Arb.Lib.*,ii,424-5).

Peter Balfour   1526 - 1548.

Occ. 8 Sept. 1526 (SRO,ADC, xxxvi, fo.96); gets crown lic. to res. in papal court in favour of James Balfour 3 Jan. 1548 (*RSS*,iii, no. 2582); still in poss. 10 Nov. 1548 (*RSS*,iii,no.3016).

James Balfour   1548 - 1561.

Expects appointment 3 Jan. 1548 (v.sup.); occ. 27 Feb.1550 *(Glas.Reg.*,ii,562); occ. 25 Oct. 1558 (*Glas.Mun.*, ii,177); moved to *G. dean.* 13 Nov. 1561 x.

Thomas Livingstone   1561 - 1594.

Occ. 12 Dec. 1561 (SRO, Reg.Deeds,iv.fo.436); occ. 2 Oct. 1589 (SRO, Reg. Ho.Chr. no. 3027) occ. as parson of Carnwath 9 Aug. 1594 (SRO, Reg. Deeds xlviii,274).

Robert Bannatyne   1614 - 1628.

Occ. as prebendary of Carnwath 7 Dec. 1614 (*Glas.Chrs.*,ii,294); occ. with same style 14 Dec. 1626 (SRO, Part.Reg. Sasines Ayr, iv,113) d. May 1628 (Scott,*Fasti*,iii,289, quoting tombstone).

Alexander Anderson   1628 - 1635.

Occ. as prebendary of Carnwath and treas. 30 Oct. 1628 (*Glas. Chrs.*,ii,324) and 28 Oct. 1635 (*PSAS*,xli,368).

SUBDEANS OF GLASGOW

First known date: 1266.

By inference this dignity was not yet in existence as late as 2 Jan. 1259 (*Glas.Reg.*,i,166).

Prebend: ch. of Cadder in 1350 and prob. earlier (Cowan, *Parishes*, 24).

Robert de Lanark 1266-1273 x.

Occ. 19 Apr. 1266 and 23 May 1270 (*Glas.Reg.*,i,174,181); occ. 29 Jan. 1273 x (*Kel.Lib.*,ii,273).

Thomas Nicolson (Nicholay) 1283 x 1295.

Occ. 1283 x 1295 (*Pais. Reg.*, 127); perhaps same as Thomas de Dundee (v. inf.).

Thomas de Dundee (Dono Dei) 1293 - 1295 x 1296.

Occ. 18 Feb. and 24 Apr. 1293 (*Glas.Reg.*, i, 201, 205-7); prov. *R.bp.* 18 Nov. 1295.

John Penny 1344 - 1364.

In poss. 25 June 1344 (*CPL*,iii,156); occ. 2 Sept. 1362 (*Glas.Reg.*, i,271-2); prob. res. on moving to *Ab.prec.* early in 1364.

Hugh Rae 1364 - 1389.

Had coll. by ord. more than two years before 29 May 1366, when he got papal conf. (*CPP*,i,527); still in poss. 10 Apr. 1389 (ibid.,573); d. by 9 Mar. 1405 (v. inf.).

John Stewart 1405 - 1438 (?).
William de Glendinning 1413 - 1414.

Stewart got poss. on Rae's death, and gets conf. 9 Mar. 1405 (*CPP*,i,626); res. on exch. with Glendinning for a right in *G.archd.* 14 Jan. 1413 (v. inf.); but this exch. was abortive, and he got new prov. to this ben. again 25 Sept. 1414 (Reg.Av., 343, fos. 405v-407); said to have d. in poss. 19 Feb. 1428 (*Glas.Reg.*,ii,615); but see Kennedy below.

Glendinning prov. on exch. with Stewart 14 Jan. 1413 (Reg.Av., 340, fos. 487v-489); res. right without having had poss. 25 Sept. 1414 (ibid.,343,fos. 405v-407).

John Scrymgeour 1428 - 1433.
James Kennedy x 1428 - 1434 x 1437.

Scrymgeour claims right following exp. grace (*CSSR*,ii,222); still no poss. 28 Feb. 1433 (Reg. Supp.,283,fo.29v).

Kennedy gets papal conf. after 'several years' of poss. following Stewart's death 5 Dec. 1429 (ibid.,249,fo.199v); new prov. 28 Feb. 1433 (*ACSB*,112); prob. still in poss. 12 Feb. 1434 (ibid.); res. on exch. with Graham before 14 Mar. 1437 (v. inf.), and prob. before el. as *Dk.bp.* 16 Feb. 1437.

Henry Graham (Gharme) 1437.

Obtained it on exch. with Kennedy, and in poss. when prov. 14 Mar. 1437 (Reg. Supp.,333,fo.7).

David de Hamilton 1437 - 1446 x 1449.

Prov. 4 July 1437 (*ACSB*,119); still in poss. 21 Nov. 1446 (Reg. Supp.,414, fo. 91); d. in poss. before 16 May 1449 (v. inf.).

Christopher Gynnis 1449.

Prov. on Hamilton's death 16 May 1449 (*CPL*,x,195); res. his right before 17 June 1449 (ibid.,194); in fact d. without poss. before 18 June 1449 (Reg.Supp.,437,fo.90).

Andrew de Durisdeer 1449 - 1455.

Prov. on Hamilton's death or res. of Gynnis 17 June 1449 (*CPL*, x,194); in poss. 27 Mar. 1450 (ibid.,211); prov. *G.bp.* 7 May 1455, with lic. to retain this ben. until he got his temporalities (Reg. Supp.,479,fo.281).

Andrew Stewart 1455 - 1482.

Prov. on promotion of Durisdeer 7 May 1455 (*CPL*,xi,1-2); prov. *M.bp.* 12 Aug. 1482.

Archibald Whitelaw   1482 - 1498.
Alexander Gifford (Gisford) 1494 - 1500.

Whitelaw prov. on promotion of Stewart 12 Aug. 1482 (*CPL*, xiii,817); given Gifford as coadj. 26 Nov. 1494 (v. inf.); occ. 13 May 1497 (*Glas.Reg.*,ii, 496); d. 23 Oct. 1498 (ibid.,616).

Gifford promised annates and got prov. as Whitelaw's coadj. and successor 26 Nov. 1494 (PRO 31/9 - 30/380-1); paid some of these annates 9 June 1497 (ibid.,381); but did not in fact succeed Whitelaw in 1498, being found with just a pension on fruits 9 Sept. 1500 (ibid.,31/17).

Roland Blackadder 1498 x 1503 - 1541.
James Houston   1526 - 1550.

Blackadder prob. had local coll. on Whitelaw's death in 1498, the abp. being Robert Blackadder; occ. 27 May 1503 (*RMS*,ii,no.2723); res. 2 July 1526, but promising annates to retain fruits (PRO 31/9 - 32/114-15); still usufructuary 4 Aug. 1537 (SRO, Prot. Bk. Andrew Brounhill i, fo.30v); said to have d. 9 Mar. 1541 (*Glas.Reg.*,ii,615); but occ. 12 June 1541 (*Prot. Bk.Glasgow*,ii,113).

Houston promised annates and got prov. without fruits 2 July 1526 (PRO 31/9 - 32/115); occ. 2 May 1527 (*St Mary Lib.*, 85); occ. 8 Oct. 1550 (ibid.,1xxi-1xxiii); d. before 10 Oct. 1550 (v.inf.).

James Hamilton 1550 - 1580.

Crown pres. on Houston's death 10 Oct. 1550 (*RSS*,iv.no,931); prov. *Ar.bp.* 14 July 1553, but with disp. to retain this ben for life (*SHR*,xxii,38); d. 6 Jan. 1580 (Edin.Tests.,18 Jan 1591), having made some gesture of res. the year before (v. inf.).

Andrew Polwart 1579 - 1587.
John Graham   1586.

Polwart had crown pres. on res. of Hamilton 17 Mar. 1579 and again on his death 13 Feb. 1580 (Reg.Pres.,ii,15,32; *RSS*,vii, nos. 1848, 2229); d. in poss. 20 May 1587 (Edin.Tests.).

Graham had crown pres. on forfeiture of Pblwart for barratry, and then got pension on Polwart's restitution 24 Mar. 1586 (Reg.Pres., ii,151).

Patrick Walkinshaw 1588 - 1624.

Crown pres. on Polwart's death 16 Mar. 1588 (RSS,lvii,fo.53); occ. erroneously 23 Mar. 1562 (Stevenson & Wood, *Seals*,iii,639); d. Aug. 1624 (Hamilton Tests., 18 Jan. 1625).

James Fullarton 1627.

Had crown pres. before 18 Sept. 1627 on vacancy caused by dispute over patronage of ch. of Monkland, but this dispute prevented his adm. (*RPC,* 2nd series, ii,119-21).

Walter Whiteford   1628 - 1636.
John Galbraith   1629.

Whiteford gets crown pres. on Walkinshaw's death 9 Dec. 1628 (RSS,ci,fo.136); allowed to retain this ben. along with *B.bp.* 15 Sept. 1635 (*RMS*,ix,no.403).

Galbraith gets crown pres. on death of unnamed predecessor 5 Mar. 1629 (RSS, ci, fo.192) apparently without effect.

SUCCENTORS/SUBCHANTERS OF GLASGOW

First known date: 1455 x 1471.

Dignity was erected by Bp. Andrew de Durisdeer 1455 x *(CPL,* xii, xxiii; cf. *Glas.Reg.,* ii,346).

Prebend: ch. of Durisdeer annexed 1455 x 1471 (Cowan, *Parishes,* 56).

David Purdy/Prade 1471 - 1497.

In poss. 15 Jan. 1471 (*CPL*,xii, 800); occ. 6 June 1491 (*Glas.Reg.,* ii,478); promised annates on getting faculty to res. on exch. 8 Aug. 1494 (PRO 31/9 - 30/372-3); d. 20 Mar. 1497 (*Glas.Reg.,*ii,615).

James Silver 1497 - 1505.

Occ. 13 May 1497 (*Glas.Reg.,*ii,496); res. 13 Dec. 1505 (v.inf.).

John Rankine 1505.

Coll. by abp. on res. of Silver and installed 13 Dec. 1505 (*Prot. Bk.Simon,* 108); res. immediately (v.inf.).

William Silver 1505 - 1507.

Coll. by abp. on res. of Rankine and installed 14 Dec. 1505 (ibid.,109); occ. 22 May 1507 (ibid.,190).

Robert Clerk 1510 - 1539.

Occ. 28 June 1510 (ibid .,364); d. 10 Oct. 1539 (*Glas.Reg.,*ii, 615).

John Douglas x 1544.

Held it and res. on exch. with Dunbar (for parsonage of Kirkbride) x 1544 (SRO, Acts and Decreets, xx, fo.144).

Archibald Dunbar 1544 - 1548 x 1551.

Occ. 25 June 1544 (*Glas.Mun.,*ii,295-6), having got it on exch. (v.sup.); occ. 31 May 1548 (Glas.Tests.,i,fo.25); prob. res. before 6

July 1551 (v.inf.).

John Hamilton 1551 - 1570.
    Crown pres. on Dunbar's dem. 6 July 1551 (*RSS*,iv,no,1288); occ. 26 Oct. 1551 (*Glas.Mun.*,ii,172); occ. 6 May 1570 (ibid.,i, 82); prob.d. before 5 Aug. 1570 (v.inf.), but said erroneously to occ. 1 June 1580 (SRO, Abbrev. Feu Chrs.,ii,fo.196).

Peter Young 1570 - 1573.
    Crown pres. on Hamilton's death 5 Aug. 1570 (*RSS,* vi,no.879); said to be unable to hold it as he cannot reside 4 Nov. 1573(ibid., vi, no. 2818); but perhaps did not res. effectively (v. inf.).

Lyon Brown	1575.
James Lindsay	1575.
Alexander Bryson	1578.
James Bryson	1579.

    Brown gets crown pres. on res. of Young 25 Jan. 1575 (RSS,vii, no.17).
    Lindsay gets crown pres. on res of Young 18 Dec. 1575 (ibid., no. 369).
    Alexander Bryson gets crown pres. on res. of Young 15 Jan. 1578 (ibid.,no.1398).
    James Bryson gets crown pres. on res. of Young 14/26 Nov. 1579 (ibid.,no.2083; Reg.Pres.,ii,23).

George Cleland 1626 - 1637.
    Occ. 14 Dec. 1626 (SRO, Part. Reg. Sasines Ayr,iv,113) and 21 Aug. 1637 (SRO, Part. Reg. Sasines Dumfries, iv,301).

ARCHDEACONS OF GLASGOW

First known date: 1126 x 1127.
    Some early holders of this office in G.dioc. are styled archdeacons of Teviotdale e.g. 1172 x 1195, 1164 x 1174, 1177 (*Kel.Lib.*,nos. 268, 286, 448) and 1202 x 1204 (*Pais.Reg.*,13).
    Prebend: this was a matter of dispute 1227-9 (*Glas.Reg.*,i,125-6); none yet erected 31 Jan. 1231 when holder had pension until ch. of Peebles should become available (ibid.,i,130-1); ch. of Peebles and chapel of Manor erected as preb. 1233 x 1257 (ibid.,i,164; cf. Cowan, *Parishes,* 142-3, 162).

Ascelin 1126 x 1127 - 1153 x 1159.
    Occ. 23 Apr. 1126 x 24 Mar. 1127 (*ND*,nos. 15-16; *ESC*,no.65); occ. 1153 x 1159 (*Kel.Lib.*,ii,nos. 415, 436).

Ingram 1161 x 1162 - 1164.
    Occ. 6 Jan. 1161 x 24 Jan. 1162 (*RRS*,i,no,195); cons. *G.bp.* 28 Oct. 1164.

Simon 1166 x 1174 - 1195 x 1196.

Nepos of Robert Avenel (Fraser,*Buccleuch*,ii,410; *Fraser Facsimiles*, no. 18); occ. 1166 x 1174 (*Kel.Lib.*,i,no.286); occ. 10 Sept. 1195 x 2 Feb. 1196 (*Melr.Lib.*,i,no.122).

Robert 1195 x 1196 - 1222.

Occ. 10 Sept. 1195 x 2 Feb. 1196 (*Melr.Lib.*i,no.90); still in poss. 22 Mar. 1222 (*CPL*,i,87); d. 1222 (*Chron. Melrose*,76); the 'L.' found as archd. 7 Aug. 1205 x 16 July 1216 (*Dunf.Reg.*,68) is prob. an error

Thomas 1222.

As parson of Lilliesleaf succ. 1222 and d. in same year (*Chron. Melrose*, 76).

Thomas de Stirling/Contravel 1222 - 1227.

Succ. 1222 (ibid.); occ. as Stirling 22 June 1224 (*SHS Misc.*,iv, 313); occ. as Contravel Sept. 1224 (*HMC* 29, *Portland*,ii,1); occ. as Stirling 12 Oct. 1225 (*Balm.Lib.*,nos. 4-5); d. 1227 (*Chron.Melrose*, 79), after 26 Feb. 1227 (*RMS*,ii,no.2387) and before 16 May 1227 (*Glas.Reg.*, i,129); erroneously occ. 23 Sept. 1228 (*Midl.Chrs.*,24).

Hugh de Potton 1227 - 1238.

Anticipates coll. by ord. 16 May 1227 (*Glas.Reg.*,i,129-30); occ. 9 Nov. 1227 (ibid.,i,121); d. 1238, the archd. being divided into two on his death (*Chron.Melrose*,86); from dates of his successor in *G.archd. Teviotdale* his death must have been 1 Jan. x 24 Mar. 1238.

Matthew de Aberdeen 1238 x 1244.

Occ. 1 July 1238 (Fraser, *Menteith*, ii,329; *Inchaff. Lib.*,no.11); occ. 30 Aug. 1244 (*Glas.Reg.*,i,152).

Reginald de Irvine 1245 - 1266 x 1268.

Succ. 1245 (*Chron. Lanercost*,53); occ. 19 Apr. 1266 (*Glas.Reg.*, i,174); d. before 11 June 1268 (ibid.,i,178).

William de Lindsay 1275.

Occ. 5 Apr. and 26 July 1275 (*Glas.Reg.*,i,189,191).

James de Dalileye 1306 - 1308 x 1311.

Occ. 26 Sept. 1307 (*Reg.Woodlock*,i,208); had got poss. c. Aug. 1306, and still in poss. 5 Feb. 1308 (*CPL*,ii,37); d. before 22 Apr. 1311 (*CDS*,iii,no.206).

John Wishart x 1310 - 1337.

Described as 'formerly G.archd.' by Edward II 16 apr. 1310 when he was that king's prisoner (*CDS*,iii,no.143); prob. had been coll. by Bp. Robert Wishart, and may well have had poss. before Dalileye; occ. c.1320 (*HMC* 55, *Var.Coll.*,v,8); occ. 11 July 1321 (*Glas.Reg.*,i,228); cons. *G.bp.* on or before 16 Feb. 1337.

Guido Kieretti/Quiret 1342 - 1374.

In poss. 3 Dec. 1342 (*CPL*,iii,64); occ. 17 Aug. 1361 (*Foedera*, III, ii,625).

Gregory de Maybole (?) 1367 - 1387.

Said on poor authority to have held it in time of Bp. Wardlaw

1367 - 1387 (Dempster, *Historia*,ii,491).

Thomas Mercer 1374 x 1377 - 1379 x 1388.

    Had exp. grace which took effect after 4 Dec. 1374 when he was still holding another G.preb.; conf. 23 Apr. 1377 (Reg.Av.,193,fo.497; 201,fo.500); occ. 18 Oct. 1379 (*Rot.Scot*,ii,18); d. by c. 1388 (Reg. Vat.,321,fo.184v).

Duncan Petit	1388 - 1397.
John de Grangia	x 1394.
Henry de Wardlaw	x 1394 - 1403.
William Macmorrin	x 1403.
Simon de Mandeville	1403 - 1409.
William de Camera	1403.
John Forrester	1403.

    Petit occ. 10 Dec. 1388 (SRO, Crawford Priory Inventory, no. 372); occ. 14 Jan. 1397 (SRO, Reg.Ho.Chr.no.205); d. prob. by June 1397 (see *St Mary, St A.prov.*).

    Grangia held it as cardinal and res. before 16 Sept. 1394 (v.inf.).

    Wardlaw had prov. on res. of Grangia from Pope Clement VII i.e. before 16 Sept. 1394; granted new prov. on additional grounds of death of Petit, who was said to have held this ben. and *St Mary, St A.prov.*together without disp. 20 May 1398 (Reg.Vat.,322,fos. 271-2; cf. Reg.Av.,304,fos.176v-177v); prob. never obtained poss. (see *G.prec.*); lit. with Mandeville, Camera and Forrester when prov. *St A.bp.* 10 Sept. 1403 (Reg.Av.,320,fos.625-6).

    Macmorrin had poss. (presumably after death of Petit), and res. to ord. on exch. with Mandeville before 10 Aug.1403 (v.inf.).

    Mandeville had ord. coll. on exch. with Macmorrin some time before 10 Aug. 1403 when he had poss. (Reg.Vat.,323,fos.349v-350); lit. with Wardlaw, Camera and Forrester when Wardlaw prov. to his see 10 Sept. 1403 (Reg.Av.,320,fos.625-6); in poss. 18 Oct. 1403 (Reg.Supp.,98,fo.261); still in poss. 26 Oct. 1409 (Reg.Av.,335, fos. 163-4); d. before 6 Nov. 1409 (ibid.,334,fos.167-8).

    Camera had some right and lit. with Warlaw, Mandeville and Forrester 10 Sept. 1403 (Reg.Av.,320,fos.625-6).

    Forrester had some right and lit. with Wardlaw, Mandeville and Camera 10 Sept. 1403 (ibid.).

John Forrester	1409 - 1414.
William de Glendinning	1409 - 1413.
John Stewart	1413 - 1414.

    Forrester had ord. coll. on death of Mandeville (Reg. Av., 344, fos.790-1); in poss. 14 Jan. 1413 (ibid.,340,fos.487v-489) when Stewart got prov.; expected to res. his 'claim' on exch. 25 Sept. 1414 (ibid.,343,fos.405v-407); cf. *G.archd.Teviotdale.*

    Glendinning gor prov. on Mandeville's death 11 Nov. 1409 (*CPP*,i,595); obtained diffinitive sentence after lit. against Forrester, but res. without poss. on exch. with Stewart for *G.subd.* 14 Jan. 1413 (Reg.Av.,340,fos.487-489; cf. *CPP*,i,608); though this exch. was not in the end effective (v.inf.), he is not known to have resumed his

right to this ben.

Stewart got prov. on exch. with Glendinning 14 Jan. 1413 (Reg.Av., 340,fos.489-490); new prov. 21 Nov. 1413 following refusal of *G.bp.* to adm. him to archd. (Reg.Av.,344,fos.790-1); res. right when given new prov. to *G.subd.* again 25 Sept. 1414 (Reg.Av.,343,fos.405v-407); never had poss.

George de Borthwick 1414 - 1446.

Prov. on res. of Stewart 25 Sept. 1414 (ibid.); in poss. 1 Mar. 1418 (Reg.Vat.,329,fo.80); new prov. 31 Jan. 1420 (*CSSR*,i,160); occ. 17 July 1446 (*RMS,* ii,no.1607); held it until death (v.inf.).

John Arous	1447 x 1448 - 1468.
Andrew de Durisdeer	1449.
Richard Guthrie	x 1451.

Arous occ. 30 Aug. 1448 (*Glas.Reg.*,ii,369); had had crown pres. after 27 Oct. 1447 on Borthwick's death, and gets papal conf. despite Durisdeer's claim 30 Dec. 1449 (Reg.Supp.438,fo.256; *CPL*,x 203); occ. 16 May 1467 (*Glas.Reg.*,ii,414-16); d. 15 Feb. 1468 (ibid.,ii,615).

Durisdeer had some right which he res. after prov. to *G.subd.* 17 June 1449 (Reg.Supp.,438,fo.256).

Guthrie had some right sometime before 2 Mar. 1451 (ibid., 454, fo.61; cf. 449,fo.57v).

Archibald Whitelaw	1468.
Hugh 'Danslas'	1468.
Gilbert Rerik	1468 - 1495.

Whitelaw had prov. and claims poss. before 5 May 1468 when he got papal conf. (Reg.Supp.,626,fo.55v).

'Danslas' (perhaps an error for Douglas) got it by virtue of an exp. grace on death of Arous, and claims poss. when given papal conf. 17 May 1458 (ibid.,625,fo.161).

Rerik occ. 19 July 1468 (Fraser, *Pollok,* i,182); occ. 12 Feb. 1472 (*Glas.Mun.*,ii,79); the 'Duncan' mentioned in poss. 12 June 1474 (*ACSB*,247) is prob. an error for David Luthirdale *G.archd. Teviotdale*; occ. 30 May 1487 (*HMC* 10,*10th R.*,i,66); said to be dead by 6 June 1488 (*Glas.Reg.*,ii,457); but occ. 21 Feb.1495 (ibid.,ii,462).

John Gibson 1495.

Occ. 31 Aug. 1495 (Fraser, *Lennox,*ii,158).

Patrick Blackadder 1502(?), 1505 - 1521 x 1524.

Perhaps the unnamed 'iuvenis' in poss. at time of visitation of chapter 17 Feb. 1502 (*Glas.Reg.*,ii,611); occ. 25 Oct.1505 (*Glas.Mun.*, ii,120); occ. 19/24 Dec. 1521 (*RMS*,iii,no.212); dem. before 26 Feb. 1524 (SRO, Sent.Offic.Laud.,fo.119).

Alexander Dick 1523 (?),1538 - 1559 x 1560.

Perhaps took poss. by proctor 5 June 1523, but entry in MS is cancelled (NLS, Riddell MS no.9,fo.3v); occ. 25 Nov. 1538 (*RSS*,ii, no.2776); occ. 24 Mar. 1559 (Gunn, *Peebles Ch. 1195 - 1560*,156); said to have died before 28 Oct. 1560 (v.inf.), but appears at Roman

Court 7 Jan. 1562 when he agreed to Abercrombie as coadj. in return
for pension for himself on fruits (PRO 31/9 - 33/360; cf. 364); d. by
6 Sept. 1563 (v. inf.).

John Abercrombie   1562.
Andrew Betoun   1560 - 1563 x 1573.
    Abercrombie appointed coadj. and successor to Dick at curia
7 Jan. 1562 (PRO 31/9 - 33/360).
    Betoun coll. on supposed death of Dick 28 Oct. 1560 and
installed 20 Dec. 1560 (*Prot.Bk. Glasgow*,v,no.1398); occ. 8 June 1563
(SRO, Boyd, no. 172); crown pres. on Dick's death 6 Sept. 1563 (*RSS*,
v,no,1445); depriv. before 8 June 1573 (v.inf.).

Archibald Douglas 1573 - 1610.
    Crown pres. on Betoun's depriv. 8 June 1573 (*RSS*,vi,no.1981);
occ. 10 Mar. 1575 (ibid.,vii,no.83); pres. confirmed 25 Dec. 1577 (ibid.,
no.1352); held it until d. Mar. 1610 (SRO, Reg. of Retours, iv.431).

Theodore Hay 1610 - 1638.
    Crown pres. on death of Douglas 22 Dec. 1610 (RSS, 1xxix,fo
211); occ. 31 May 1638 (SRO, Hay of Haystoun, no. 411).

ARCHDEACONS OF TEVIOTDALE

First established: 1238.
    Some earlier holders of office of archdeacon of Glasgow are
sometimes called archdeacons of Teviotdale (v.sup.); but single archd.
was not in fact divided into two until Jan. x Mar. 1237/8 on death of
Hugh de Potton (*Chron.Melrose*, 86).
    Prebend: ch. of Morebattle by early 15th century (*Glas.Reg.*,
ii,416; see Cowan, *Parishes*, 152).

Peter de Alinton 1238 - 1242.
    Occ. 1237 (*Melr.Lib.*,i,no.273); as archd. was founded only in
1238 as computed in chronicle of Melrose (v.sup.), this reference must
be datable Jan. x Mar. 1238; d. 1242 (*Chron. Melrose*, 89).

Reginald de Irvine 1242 - 1245.
    Succ. 1242 (ibid.); occ. 30 Oct. 1244 (*Glas.Reg.*,i,152); moved
to *G. archd.* 1245.

Nicholas de Moffat 1245 - 1270.
    Succ. 1245 (*Chron. Lanercost*, 53); occ. 1250 (*Kel.Lib.*,i,no.
149); occ. 13 Oct. 1268 (*Glas.Reg.*,i,174-5); el. *G.bp.* later in 1268,
but d. uncons. 1270.

Note: an unnamed archd. Teviotdale is mentioned 18 Dec. 1273
(*Kel.Lib.*, i, 140-1).

William Wishart 1288 - 1297 x 1308.
    In poss. 10 Apr. 1288 (*CPL*,i,491); occ. 18 Feb. 1297 (*Glas.Reg.*,
i,213-14); imprisoned by English, prob. after Mar. 1306, certainly by

10 July 1307 (*CDS*,iii,no,288); by Mar. 1308 (and prob. earlier) the English considered him depriv. (ibid.,iii,no.37).

Roger de Welleton 1307 - 1310.
Pres. by Edward II 25 Dec. 1307 (*CPR 1307 - 13*,33); occ. 11 Apr. 1310 (*Rot. Scot.*,i,81).

William de Hillum 1312.
Pres. by Edward II to vacant archd. 3 Apr. 1312 (*CDS*,iii,no.261).

William de Yetholm 1320 x 1321 - 1329.
Occ. 11 July 1321 (*Glas.Reg.*,i,228), having prob. moved from *Db.archd.* since 13 Mar. 1320; occ. 5 May 1329 (*Kel.Lib.*,ii,376).

John de Berwick x 1354.
Held it at death before 27 Mar. 1354 (v. inf.).

John de Boulton 1354.
Pres. by Edward III 2 Jan. 1354. (*Rot.Scot.*,i,762).

Henry de Smalham 1354 - 1358 x 1364.
Prov. on Berwick's death 27 Mar. 1354 (*CPL*,iii,516); occ. 30 Sept. 1358 (*Kel.Lib.*,ii,398); d. by 5 Apr. 1364 (v. inf.).

John de Ancrum 1364 - 1393.
Prov. on Smalham's death 5 Apr. 1364 (Collect., 14, fo.170); occ. 19 Mar. 1393 (SRO, Brodie Writs, no. 3).

Thomas de 'Mathane' 1394.
In poss. 26 May 1394 (*CPP*,i,578).

John de Merton 1394 - 1400 x 1404.
In poss. 27 Feb. 1395, after prov. before 16 Sept. 1394 (*CPP*,i, 583);occ. 2/22 July 1400 (*CDS*,iv,115; *Foedera* (0),viii,149); res. on exch. with Mouswald for another G. preb. before 24 Aug. 1404 (Reg. Av.,330,fos.48v-50; *CDS*,iv,139).

Gilbert Mouswald	1400 x 1404 - 1408.
William Macmorrin/McMoyn	x 1408.
James Watson (Walteri)	1408 - 1418.

Mouswald had coll. by ord. on exch. with Merton before 24 Aug. 1404 (v.sup.); in poss. 31 Mar. 1408 (Reg.Av., 329 fos. 414-415; in this source the date 21 May 1408 found in *CPP*,i,636 has been deleted and this earlier date substituted)

Macmorrin held it at death sometime before 31 Mar. 1408 (ibid.); see *CPP*,i,579, 585, 586, 636 for different forms of this surname; cf. *G.archd.*

Watson gets prov. on Macmorrin's death 31 Mar. 1408 (v.sup.); in poss. 14 Oct. 1408 (Reg.Av.,333,fos.673v-674); occ. 10 July 1411 (*RMS*,i,404-5); d. in poss. 30 Mar. 1418 (*CSSR*,i,14-15,97).

John Forrester	1418.
William Croyser	1418 - 1440 x 1443; 1446 x 1451 - 1460 x 1461.
John de Scheves	1418 - 1419.
John Lyon	1418 - 1418 x 1423.

Edward de Lauder	x 1419.
Alexander de Foulertoun	1422 x 1424.
John Bowmaker	x 1424 - 1428.
Andrew de Hawick	1424 - 1425.
John Benyng	1426.
James Croyser	1440.
Walter Blair	1441 - 1447.
Patrick Hume	1443 - 1446 x 1451; 1453 x 1455 - 1472.
Alexander Inglis	1471.

Forrester obtained poss. (prob. by ord. coll) before 15 Apr. 1418, and was still in poss. 15 June 1418 (*CPP*,i,609); cf. *G.archd.*

Croyser prov. by Martin V on Watson's death 4 June 1418 (*CPL*, vii,93,66-67); new prov. 2 Apr. 1419 (ibid.,139-40), but did not have poss. until after res. of Scheves on 7 Sept. 1419 (v.inf.; Reg. Supp., 235, fo.133v), although by 8 Feb. 1424 was said to have had poss. for more than five years i.e. since before 8 Feb. 1419 (*CSSR*,ii,49); restored after mistaken res. or depriv. 31 July 1425 (*CPL*,vii,464-5; cf. Hawick below); new prov. after lit. 7 Feb. 1429 (Reg. Supp., 235, fo.133v); proposed to res. in favour of James Croyser 4 Aug. 1440 (ibid.,366,fo.92v); instead was depriv. by Eugenius IV for adherence to council of Basel on or before 12 Aug. 1441 (see Blair below); this was effective in Scotland before 3 June 1443 (see Hume below); restored 28 June 1446 x 22 June 1451 (*CPL*,x,529; cf. Hume below); occ. 6 Dec. 1453 (*Rot.Scot.*,ii 372), but had lost local poss. by 3 Mar. 1455 (see Hume below); abroad by this time and remained there until death, getting new prov. 1 July 1455 (Reg.Supp.,482,fo.182) and being recognised as archd. Teviotdale in papal sources dated 14 Mar., 1 Apr. and 19 July 1460 (ibid.,527,fo.283; 528,fo.71; 532,fo. 296; cf. *CPL*,xi,6,405); d. before 3 Sept. 1461 (Reg. Supp.,554,fo. 2), and prob. before 6 Aug. 1461 (see Hume below).

Scheves prov. by Benedict XIII 15 June 1418 (Reg.Vat.,329, fo.49v); had poss., but res. right in Croyser's favour 7 Sept. 1419 (*CSSR*,i,124,126-7).

Lyon pres. on Watson's death by James I (in captivity) to Pope Martin V and got prov. 16 Aug. 1418 (ibid.,14-15); retained some right until death before 12 Sept. 1423 (ibid.,ii,36,45).

Lauder had some right which he res. in Croyser's favour 2 Apr. 1419 (*CPL*,vii,139-40); see also *St A.archd. Lothian.*

Foulertoun had some right at death in curia 22 Apr. 1422 x 4 Jan. 1424 (*CSSR*,ii,45;cf.i.300-1); had been servant of the captive James I (ibid.), and so his right was prob. in succession to Lyon.

Bowmaker had prov. and raised lit. against Croyser the possessor sometime before 4 Jan. 1424, when he had prov. again *Si neutri* (*CSSR*,ii,45); prov. again 8 Feb. 1424 (ibid.,49-50); surrog. to Croyser's right on his (mistaken) res. 12 May 1425 (ibid., 85-86); promised annates 23 May 1427 (*ACSB*,94); lit. finally went against him in Croyser's favour 16 Nov. 1428 (*CPL*,viii,72); prob. never had poss.

Hawick prov. on (mistaken) res. or depriv. of Croyser 8 Dec. 1424 (*CSSR*,ii,77); d. at curia shortly before 22 May 1425 (ibid.,86).

Benyng prov. 15 July 1426 (ibid.,142) unfruitfully.

James Croyser prov. in event of res. of William Croyser 4 Aug.1440 (Reg.Supp.,366,fo.92v) unfruitfully.

Blair prov. on depriv. of William Croyser 12/26 Aug. 1441 (Reg. Supp.,375.fo.136v; *CPL*,ix,174); never had poss. (ibid.,ix,443), for he was involved in lit. with Hume; offered to res. in Hume's favour 8 Apr. 1446 (Reg.Supp.,410,fo.235v); still lit. 12 Sept. 1447 (ibid.,420,fo.214).

Hume had coll. by ord. (presumably after c.Aug. 1441 on depriv. of William Croyser) and is first found in poss. 3 June 1443 (*CPL*,viii, 306-8); prov. after winning lit. with Blair 28 June 1446 (*ACSB*,135); lost poss. to William Croyser by 22 June 1451 (v. sup.); won back local poss. again after 6 Dec. 1453 (v.sup.) and before 3 Mar. 1455 (*Melr. Lib.*,ii,578); by 6 Aug. 1461 had won recognition in papal sources (*CPL*, xi,425), presumably on death abroad of Croyser; res. on pension in favour of Lichton 18 Sept./29 Oct. 1472 (Reg.Supp.,683, fos. 1, 237v-8); still called archd. when abroad 5 Oct. 1474 (*CPL*,xiii,45); d. at Sutri, Italy shortly before 17 Oct. 1478 (v.inf.).

Inglis prov. on res. of Patrick Hume (Howat) 3 July 1471 (Reg. Supp.,668,fo.248), prob. unfruitfully.

John Lichton	1472.
David Luthirdale	1474 - 1475.
John Whitelaw	1475.

Lichton prov. on res. of Hume on pension 18 Sept. 1472 (Reg. Supp.,683,fo.1).

Luthirdale prob. same as 'Duncan archd. of Glasgow' found 12 June 1474 (*ACSB*,247; cf. *G.archd.*); occ. 5 June 1475 (*ER*,viii,266); prob. moved to *Dk.archd.* by 26 Oct. 1475.

Whitelaw prov. on assecution or res. of Hume 5 June 1475 (Reg. Supp.,721,fo.135v).

Nicholas Forman	1478 x 1479.
James Doles	1478.
John Brown	1479.
William Elphinstone junior	1479 - 1481.

Forman prov. on Hume's death 17 Oct. 1478 (ibid.,744,fo. 131v); but d. 24 Oct. 1478 x 10 Feb. 1479 before letters had been made out (ibid.,774,fo.126v; 778,fos. 9,10).

Doles prov. on Hume's death 20 Oct. 1478 (ibid.,774,fo.35v).

Brown prov. in place of Forman on Hume's death 10 Feb./8 Mar. 1479 (ibid.,778,fos.9-10; *ACSB*, 195-6); cf. *Ar.archd.*; cf.inf.

Elphinstone occ. 17 Mar. 1479 (*ADC*,i,23); may have obtained some right by ord. coll. on giving up his claim to *Dk.archd.* in Luthirdale's favour c. 1475-6; but it is as *Ar.archd.* that he is more usually designated in royal records x 4 Dec. 1478 - 12 June 1480 x; a plan to res. *Ar.archd.* in exch. for another G. preb. (namely Erskine) was under way 2 Dec. 1479 (*Glas.Reg.*,ii,439); but this exch. was prob. abortive, so that he is to be identified with the unnamed absentee holder of this dignity for whom William Elphinstone senior stood

proxy in the Glasgow chapter 5 June 1480 (ibid.,ii,444); may have satisfied claim of John Brown by ceding *Ar.archd.* to him after 12 June 1480; and prob. retained his right in this dignity until prov. *R.bp.* 3 Aug. 1481.

William Elphinstone senior 1481 x 1482 - 1486.

Certainly not in poss. 17 Mar. 1479 (v.sup.). for he occ. still just as G.canon and holder of Ancrum preb. 25 June 1479 (*Glas.Mun.*, ii,229); still holder of such an ordinary preb. 7 Oct.1480, 23 and 25 June 1481 (ibid.,ii,232;i,32;ii,233); prob. succ. to his son's right in this archd. after 3 Aug.1481 (v.sup.); occ. in poss. 25 Oct. 1482 and 9 Jan. 1483 (*Glas.Mun.*,ii,91,94; cf.ibid.,ii,238,96, where he occ. later just as G. canon 25 June and 25 Oct. 1483); said to have d. in poss. 30 June 1486 (*Glas.Reg.*,ii,616).

John Martini	1486 x 1491 (?), x 1510.
William Ker	1491, 1510 - 1511.
George 'Herher'	1509.

Martini res. some right before 27 Apr. 1510 (PRO 31/9 - 31/214 and 206); his tenure may have been in the period 30 June 1486 x 6 June 1491 before Ker is first found in poss. (v.inf.).

Ker occ. 6 June 1491 (*Glas.Reg.*,ii,478); at time of visitation of chapter 17 Feb. 1502 nothing was known about holder of this ben. (ibid.,ii,611); prov. on res. of Martini 27 Apr./7 May 1510 (PRO 31/9 - 33/214 and 206), and promised annates 18 Aug. 1511 (ibid., 233); but these efforts to obtain a papal title were prob. unfruitful.

'Herher' in poss. 8 Jan. 1509 when granted lic. to visit by deputy (PRO 31/9 - 1/131-2); name is prob. mistranscription of Lockhart (v.inf.).

George Lockhart   1509 (?) - 1533.

Prob. same as 'Herher' found in poss. 8 Jan. 1509 (v.sup.); and may well have remained in poss. until el as archd. to *G.dean.* 11 Oct. 1533 (NLS, Riddell MS no. 9, fo.9v).

Thomas Ker x 1534.

Held it at death before 17 Mar. 1534 (v.inf.); perhaps an error for William Ker (v.sup.).

John Lauder 1534 - 1551.

Promises annates and gets prov. on Thomas Ker's death 17 Mar. 1534 (PRO 31/9 - 32/275); another person is said then to be in poss., and this was prob. Lockhart with whom he came to terms over *G.dean.* on that day; occ. 4 Mar.1535 (*ADCP*,445); res. in favour of Hepburn, but promised annates to retain fruits 21 Jan.1544 (PRO 31/9 - 33/162); occ. 1551 (*THAS*,1907,p.46, no source quoted); d. before 12 Dec. 1551 (*RSS*,iv,no.1438).

John Hepburn	1544 - 1564 x 1565.
Robert Richardson	1552 - 1565.

Hepburn promised annates and got prov., but without fruits 21 Jan. 1544 (PRO 31/9 - 33/163); occ. 23 July 1556 (SRO, Reg.

Deeds,i,fo.426) and 28 July 1564 (SRO, Abbrev. Feu Chrs.,ii,fo.241); d. before 30 Jan. 1565 (SRO, Acts and Decreets,xxxi,fo.274).

Richardson prov. with no description of circumstances 8 Oct. 1552 (*Glas.Reg.*,ii,613-14); cf. *G.dean. christ. Teviotdale*; occ. 12 May. 1565 (*RMS*,iv,no.1938); res. before 22 June 1565 (v. inf.).

Thomas Ker 1565 - 1569, 1572 (?)
Crown pres. on Richardson's res. 22 June 1565 (*RSS*,v,no.2121); occ. 1569 (*Thirds of Benefices*, 286); bn. apparently occupied by an unnamed incumbent hostile to the Reformation 16 Jan. 1572 (*BUK*,i, 226).

DEANS OF CHRISTIANITY

ARCHDEACONRY OF GLASGOW

DEANS OF LENNOX : LUSS

First known dates: Lennox: 1178 x 1199.
                                   Luss   : x 1227.

Maldoven (Lennox/Luss) 1178 x 1199 - 1208 x 1214.
Occ. as dean of Lennox 1178 x 1199 (*Pais.Reg.*,157; *Lenn. Cart.*, 12); prob. still in office 2 Nov. 1208 x 4 Dec. 1214 when his son was known as 'filius Decani de Levenax' (*Glas.Reg.*,i,87-88); later remembered as dean of Luss when had dem. but was still alive and holding lands of Luss c. 1250? (Fraser, *Lennox*,ii,404; *Lenn.Cart.*, 96-98; cf. Fraser, *Colquhoun*,i, 13n).

Michael (Lennox) 1227 - 1232 x 1234.
Occ. 8 Jan. 1227 (*Glas.Reg.*,i,120); occ. 8 June 1232 x 30 Sept. 1234 (*Pais.Reg.*,173-4; cf.174-5).

Luke (Lennox) 1247 x 1270, 1248.
Occ. 1247 x 1270 (*Glas.Reg.*,i,146) and 1 Aug. 1248 (Fraser, *Lennox*,ii,11).

Laurence (Lennox) 1274.
Occ. c. 17 Nov. 1274 (*Lenn.Cart.*,85; cf. 85-86); see also *Pais. Reg.*,176 for another reference from the same period.

Maurice (Lennox) 1333 x 1364, 1349.
As vic. of Kilmarnock occ. 1333 x 1364 (*Lenn. Cart.*,53) and 30 July 1349 (*Highland Papers*, iv,12).

John Fleming (Lennox) 1459.
Occ. as vic. of Houston 15 Feb. 1459 (NLS,Adv.MS 19.2.20, p.49); Houston lay in Rutherglen deanery.

John Aikenhead (Lennox) 1473.
Occ. 21 July and 12 Oct. 1473 (Fraser, *Lennox*,ii,44,102).

Archibald Laing (Lennox) 1511 - 1512.
Occ. as vic. of Eastwood 9 Aug. 1511 (*Prot.Bk.Simon*, 419); occ.
24 Dec. 1512 (NRA, Napier Papers, 18); perhaps dem. when or before
succ. to *Semple prov.* 25 Oct. 1516 x 6 Mar.1518; see also *G. dean.
christ. Rutherglen;* Eastwood lay in Rutherglen deanery.

Andrew Smith (Lennox) 1527 - 1531.
Occ. 8 June 1527 (*Camb.Reg.*,213) and 18 Sept. 1531 (SRO,
Fraser Inventory, no. 97).

William Hamilton (Lennox) 1539 x 1541.
Occ. 1539 x 1541 (*MW*,i,268); see also *G. dean. christ. Rutherglen.*

DEANS OF RENFREW (?) : KILBRIDE : RUTHERGLEN

First known dates: Renfrew (?)   : 1204 x .
                       Kilbride   : 1211.
                       Rutherglen   : 1342 (*Glas.Reg.*,i,252).

Roger (?) (Renfrew) 1204 x .
Perhaps occ. 1204 x , but printed text ambiguously calls him just
'diaconus de Renfrw' (*Pais.Reg.*,379; cf. Chalmers, *Caledonia,* vi,829n).

J. (Kilbride) 1211.
Occ. 25 Feb. 1211 (*Melr.Lib.*,i,no.186); perhaps same as John
parson of Kilbride found 1175 x 1196 (*Pais.Reg.*,99); see also *G. dean.
christ.Clydesdale.*

David Cunningham (Rutherglen) 1490.
Occ. 31 Jan. 1490 (*Pais.Reg.*,352); became *G.offic.* 8 Mar. 1493
x 27 Feb. 1496.

Archibald Laing (Rutherglen) 1509 - 1511.
Occ. 1 May 1509 (*Prot.Bk.Simon*,280); had become vic. of
Eastwood 29 Aug. 1506 x 8 June 1507 (ibid.,144,193); as this vic.occ.
9 and 21 Aug. 1511 (ibid.,419, 422); perhaps dem. when or before
succ. to *Semple prov.* 25 Oct. 1516 x 6 Mar. 1518; see also *G.dean.
christ.Lennox.*

William Hamilton (Rutherglen) 1531 - 1541.
Occ. 25 Oct. 1531 (*Glas.Mun.*,ii,157); occ. as vic. of Inverkip
25 Oct. 1541 (ibid.,166); see also *G. dean.christ.Lennox* and *G.offic.*

DEANS OF CLYDESDALE : LANARK

First known dates: Clydesdale: 1175 x 1180.
                     Lanark   : 1262 x 1267.

Peter (Clydesdale) 1175 x 1180 - 1195 x 1196.
Occ. 1175 x 1180 (*Glas.Reg.*,i,41) and 10 Sept. 1195 x 2 Feb.

1196 (*Melr.Lib.*,i,no.122); see also *G.dean.christ.Stobo.*

John de Kilbride (Clydesdale) 1218 x 1220 - 1223 x 1225.
Occ. 1218 x 1220 (*Pais.Reg.*,1) and 1214 x 1225, prob. 1223 x 1225 (*Glas.Reg.*,i,103); see also *G.dean.christ.Kilbride.*

John de Kilbarchan (Kilberhan) (Clydesdale) 1225 - c.1227-8.
Occ. 1225 (*Pais.Reg.*,373), 1226 (*Glas.Reg.*,i,119) and c.1227-8 (ibid.,96).

Benedict (Lanark) 1249 - 1262 x 1267.
'Benedict the dean' occ. in connection with lands in Lanarkshire 18 June 1249 (*Midl.Chrs.*,30); 'B.dean of Lanark' occ. 5 June 1262 x 1267 (*CDS*,i,no.2676).

Yvan (Lanark) 1275.
Occ. 26 July and 15 Sept. 1275 (*Glas.Reg.*,i,190,187); see also *G. dean. christ.Peebles.*

Robert Hamilton (Lanark) 1515 - 1517.
Occ.27 Feb. 1515 and 9 Mar. 1517 (*Prot.Bk.Simon*,nos.106, 168); see also *G. comm. Hamilton, Douglas* and *Lesmahagow.*

John Weir (Lanark) 1574 - 1583.
Occ. 9 July 1574 (*RSS*,vi,no.2579); occ. as vic. of Lanark 20 Mar. 1583 (*Lanark Recs.*,363); see also *G.comm. Carnwath* and *Lesmahagow.*

DEANS OF STOBO : PEEBLES : TWEEDDALE

First known dates: Stobo   : 1164 x 1174 (*Glas.Reg.*,i,73).
                     Peebles : 1275.
                     Tweeddale : 1457.

Peter (Stobo) 1175 x 1178, 1175 x 1195.
Occ. 1175 x 1178 (*Holy.Lib.*,42) and 1175 x 1195 (*Kel.Lib.*,ii, 270); see also *G. dean.christ.Clydesdale.*

Yvan (Peebles) 1275.
Occ. 26 July and 15 Sept. 1275 (*Glas.Reg.*,i,190,187); found earlier just as vic. of Stobo 11 June 1268 (ibid.,179); see also *G.dean. christ. Lanark.*

William Adamson/Adam (Peebles) 1419 - 1421.
Occ. as Adamson 26 Jan 1419 and as Adam 12 Apr. 1421 (*Yester Writs*, nos. 51, 54).

John of Cockburn (Peebles) 1448.
Occ. 26 Nov. 1448 (ibid.,no.89).

Richard Purdy (Tweeddale/Peebles) 1459 - 1470.
Occ. as dean of Tweeddale 16 Sept. 1457 (SRO, ADC & S,vi,fo. 93); occ. as dean of Peebles 12 July 1459 (*Peebles Recs.*,133) and when

vic. of Pettinain 26 Dec. 1470 (ibid.,164); Pettinain lay in Lanark deanery.

William Tweedy (Peebles) 1473 - 1480.
　　　　Occ. 29 Jan. 1473 (*Peebles Recs.*,170); occ. as parson of Glenholm 23 July 1480 (ibid.,186).

James Stanhouse/Stannos (Peebles) 1511 - 1519.
　　　　Occ. as Stannos 20 Dec. 1511 and 28 Mar. 1519 (*Yester Writs,* nos. 325, 384); occ. as Stanhouse 26 Apr. 1515 (*HMC* 55, *Var.Coll.,* v,21);

John Colquhoun (Peebles) 1529 x 1564.
　　　　Occ. 29 Jan. 1529 (*Glas.Rent,*63); occ. as vic. of Govan 13 Nov. 1546 (*Yester Writs,* no. 623); occ. 4 Mar. 1564 (SRO, Peebles Burgh Prot.Bk.1549-65,fo.271); Govan lay in Rutherglen deanery.

DEANS OF CUNNINGHAM

First known date: 1175 x 1178.

Herbert 1175 x 1178.
　　　　Occ. 1175 x 1178 (*Glas.Reg.,*i,40-41);

William 1202 x 1207 - 1211.
　　　　Occ. 1202 x 15 May 1207 (*Glas.Reg.,*i,84); occ. 25 Feb. 1211 (*Melr.Lib.,*i.no.186); d. 1211 (*Chron. Melrose,* 55).

Humphrey 1211 x 1214 - 1214 x 1225.
　　　　Occ. 25 Feb. 1211 x 4 Dec. 1214 (*Melr. Lib.,*i,64[X]); had ceased to hold office before 21 July 1225 (*Glas.Reg.,*i,117).

Richard 1233 x 1234.
　　　　Occ. 12 Nov. 1233 x 18 May 1234 (*Pais.Reg.,*168).

William de Stewarton 1461 - 1462.
　　　　Occ. 2 May 1461 and 18 Feb. 1462 (SRO, Reg.Ho.Chrs.nos. 362,365).

Martin Reid 1508 - 1509 x 1510.
　　　　Occ. 5 Mar. 1508 (*Prot.Bk.Simon,*241); moved to *G.offic.*
18 Apr. 1509 x 3 Apr. 1510; see also *G.chanc.* and *G. dean.christ.Kyle.*

James Neilson 1510 - 1538-9.
　　　　Occ. 31 July 1510 (*Prot.Bk.Simon,* 371); occ. as vic. of Colmonell 25 Oct. 1514 and 25 Oct. 1517 (*Glas.Mun.*ii,128,131), occ. 1538-9 (*MW,*i,238); Colmonell lay in Carrick deanery; see also *G.dean. christ. Kyle.*

Lambert Blair 1547 x 1548 - 1548 x .
　　　　Occ. 31 May 1548 (*Cross.Chrs.,*i,109), having moved from *G.dean. christ.Carrick* since 2 July 1547.

DEANS OF AYR : KYLE

First known dates: Ayr : 1269.
                       Kyle : c. 1272.

Ralph de Par' (Ayr/Kyle) 1269 - c. 1272.
     Occ. as dean of Ayr 23 Oct. 1269 (*Pais.Reg.*,137); occ. as Ralph
vic. of Ayr and dean of Kyle c. Oct. 1272 (ibid.,233; cf. 232-3 for dating);
occ. as Ralph dean of Ayr in document of about same period, say 1260s
(*Melr.Lib.*,i,201).

Richard (Kyle) 1276.
     Occ. as vic. of Kilmaurs 4/17 May 1276 (*Pais.Reg.*,234-5); Kilmaurs
lay in Cunningham deanery.

Note: unnamed dean of Kyle is in office 25 June 1316 (*Melr.Lib.*,ii,
364);

Roger de Lauder (Kyle) 1416.
     Occ. as vic. of Ayr 24 Feb. 1416 (*Ayr Burgh Chrs.*,9).

Martin Reid (Kyle) 1508.
     Occ. 5 Mar. 1508 (*Prot.Bk.Simon*,241); moved to *G.offic.* 18 Apr.
1509 x 3 Apr. 1510; see also *G.chanc.* and *G. dean.christ.Cunningham.*

James Neilson (Kyle) 1514 - 1538-9.
     Occ. as vic. of Colmonell 25 Oct. 1514 and 25 Oct. 1517 (*Glas.
Mun.*,ii,128,131); occ. 1538-9 (*MW*,i,238); Colmonell lay in Carrick
deanery: see also *G.dean.christ. Cunningham.*

John Laing (Kyle) 1548.
     Occ. 31 May 1548 (*Cross.Chrs.*,i,109).

DEANS OF CARRICK

First known date: 1194 x 1196.

Christian 1194 x 1196.
     Occ. 1194 x 1196 (*N.B.Chrs.*,no.2).

'Macraht' 1202 x 1207.
     Occ. 1202 x 15 May 1207 (*Pais.Reg.*,110).

Alan 1189 x 1250.
     Occ. just as 'Alan the dean' in chr. of earl of Carrick concerned
with lands in Carrick 1189 x 1250 (*N.B.Chrs.*,no. 1).

John 1189 x 1250.
     Occ. just as 'John the dean' in chr. of earl of Carrick concerned
with ch. of Maybole 1189 x 1250 (ibid.,nos.13-14); John prob.
followed Alan (v.sup.) who may be the 'Master Alan' now a fellow-
witness with John.

T. 1225.
　　　Occ. 21 July 1225 (*Glas.Reg.*,i,117).

Laurence 1233 x 1234.
　　　Occ. 12 Nov. 1233 x 18 May 1234 (*Pais.Reg.*,168).

John 1406.
　　　Occ. 27/28 Jan. 1406 (*RMS*,ii,nos.379,403).

Robert Campbell 1478.
　　　Occ. 24 Feb. 1478 (Glasgow, Mitchell Library, MS Cartularium
Glasguense,ii,1061).

Robert Muir 1483.
　　　Occ. 9 Jan. 1483 (*Glas.Mun.*,ii,94).

John Kennedy 1505.
　　　Occ. 7 July 1505 (SRO,Ailsa,1/192).

David Kennedy 1531 - 1536.
　　　Occ. Feb. 1531 (*Prot.Bk.Ros*,no.115;cf.1205); occ. 27 Feb.
1536 (*RMS*,iii,no.1606).

Lambert Blair 1547.
　　　Occ. 2 July 1547 (SRO,Ailsa,1/496); see also *G.dean.christ.
Cunningham.*

John Campbell 1548.
　　　Occ. 31 May 1548 (*Cross. Chrs.*,i,109).

ARCHDEACONRY OF TEVIOTDALE

DEANS OF ROXBURGH : HASSENDEAN : TEVIOTDALE : ANCRUM

First known dates:	Roxburgh	: 1161 x 1162.
	Hassendean	: 1175 x 1195.
	Teviotdale	: 1175 x 1180.
	Ancrum	: 1214 x 1221.

Aldred (Roxburgh) 1124 x 1131 - 1161 x 1162.
　　　Occ. as 'Aldred the dean' 1124 x 1131 (*Glas.Reg.*i,10: *ESC*,no.83);
occ. as dean of Roxburgh 6 Jan 1161 x 13 Sept. 1162 (*ND*,no.451).

Richard de Hassendean (Hassendean/Teviotdale) 1175 x 1195.
　　　Occ. as Richard dean of Hassendean 1175 x 1195 (*Kel.Lib.*,ii,270);
prob. same person as the Richard de Hassendean found 1164 x 1174 (ibi
i,233), taking his name from his church.; occ. as dean of Teviotdale
1175 x 1180 (*Glas.Reg.*,i,41), 1175 x 1 Aug. 1189 (*Melr. Lib.*,i,153) and
1180 x 1185 (*Glas.Reg.*,i,46); see also *G.offic.*

John (Teviotdale/Roxburgh) 1195 x 1196 - 1204 x 1207.
　　　Occ. as dean of Teviotdale 10 Sept. 1195 x 2 Feb. 1196 (*Melr.
Lib.*,i, no.122; cf. no. 121); occ. as dean of Roxburgh 13 June 1204

(*Dryb.Lib.*,162-3); occ. as dean of Teviotdale 1204 x 1207 (*Melr.Lib.*,i, 118); *not* same person as John de Huntingdon *G.offic.*(ibid.).

Richard de Ancrum (Ancrum/Teviotdale) 1214 x 1221 - 1227.
   Occ as 'R. dean of Ancrum' Oct.1214 x Oct.1221 (*Melr.Lib.*,i, 229); occ. as Richard parson of Ancrum and dean of Teviotdale 1208 x 1225, prob. c.1223 (*Glas.Reg.*,i,100); occ. as dean of Teviotdale 13 Dec. 1225 (*Dryb.Lib.*,137) and 1227 (*Melr.Lib.*,i,249); ch. of Ancrum was in other hands by 31 Jan. 1231 (*Glas.Reg.*,i,131); see *G.offic.* for use of name of his church as his surname.

Walter (Teviotdale) 1227 x 1238.
   Occ. 1227 x 1238 (*Melr.Lib.*,i,258).

Geoffrey (Teviotdale) 1238 x 1234 - 1251.
   Occ. 1238 x 1245 (SRO, Reg.Ho.Chr.no.34) and 21 Nov. 1251 (*Kel.Lib.*,i,134).

William (Teviotdale) 1251 x 1274.
   Occ. 1251 x 1274 (*Midl.Chrs.*,10).

James Newton (Teviotdale) 1489.
   Occ. 3 Jan. 1489 (*Melr.Lib.*,ii,618); see also *G.comm.Teviotdale.*

Nicholas Rutherford (Teviotdale) 1548.
   Occ. 31 May 1548 (*Cross. Chrs.*,i,109).

Robert Richardson (Teviotdale) 1552.
   Occ. 1 Oct. 1552 (*Holy.Lib.*,288); see also *G.dean.christ. Annandale* and *G.archd.Teviotdale.*

DEANS OF ESKDALE : ESK : LIDDESDALE

First known dates: Eskdale   :   1195 x 1196.
                     Esk   :   1274 (*SHS Misc.*,v,93-95).
                     Liddesdale :   1539-41 (*MW*,i,291).

Richard (Eskdale) 1195 x 1196.
   Occ. 10 Sept. 1195 x 2 Feb. 1196 (*Melr.Lib.*,i, no.122; cf.no. 121).

Note: No other deans known by name; but an unnamed dean of Eskdale occ. 16 Sept. 1321 (*Melr.Lib.*,ii,353).

DEANS OF ANNANDALE : ANNAN

First known dates: Annandale :   1175 x 1189.
                     Annan   :   1274.

William (Annandale) 1175 x 1189.
   Occ. 1175 x 1189 (*CDS*,i,no.197;   *Glas.Reg.*,i,64; see *TDGAS*,

3rd series, xxxii,147 for suggested dating c.1187 x 1189).

Thomas (Annandale) 1195 x 1196.
    Occ. 10 Sept. 1195 x 2 Feb. 1196 (*Melr.Lib.*,i,no.122; cf. no. 121).

Robert (Annandale) c. 1258.
    Occ. just as 'Robert the dean' in an undated chr. relating to Annandale c. 1258 (*St Bees Reg.*,354; cf. *Glas.Reg.*,i,no.205, where one possible common witness is sole authority for date here suggested).

Note: an unnamed dean of Annandale occ. 28 Nov. 1273 (*Glas.Reg.*, i,186), and deanery of Annan existed 1274 (*SHS Misc.*,v,95-99).

Thomas Tynding (Annandale) 1443 - 1471.
    Occ. perhaps as rector of Annan 2 Aug. 1443 (*HMC* 44, *Drumlanrig*, i,45); occ. 7 Oct. 1471 (ibid.,64); see also *G.comm. Annandale*.

Note: deanery of Annandale existed 1538-9 (*MW*,i,239).

Robert Richardson (Annandale) 1548.
    Occ. 31 May 1548 (*Cross. Chrs.*,i,109); see also *G.dean.christ. Teviotdale*.

DEANS OF DUMFRIES : STRATHNITH : NITH : NITHSDALE

First known dates: Dumfries   :   1175 x 1178.
                    Strathnith   :   1195 x 1196.
                    Nith   :   1274.
                    Nithsdale   :   1540.

Waltheof (Dumfries) 1175 x 1178, 1175 x 1189.
    Occ. 1175 x 1178 (*Holy.Lib.*,no.53) and 1175 x 1189 (*CDS*,i, no.197; *Glas.Reg.*,i,64; see *TDGAS*, 3rd series, xxxii, 147 for suggested dating c. 1187 x 1189).

Radulf (Strathnith/Dumfries) 1195 x 1196 - 1198 x 1202.
    Occ. as dean of Strathnith 10 Sept. 1195 x 2 Feb.1196 (*Melr. Lib.*,i,no.122; cf. no.121); occ. as dean of Dumfries 15 Feb. 1198 x 7 July 1202 (*Kel.Lib.*,ii,260); see also *Holy.Lib.*,44 for late 12c. reference to a 'John son of Radulf dean of Dumfries'.

Note: deanery of Nith existed 1274 (*SHS Misc.*,v, 100-3).

John Walker (Nith) 1511.
    Occ. as rector of Luce 9 Apr. 1511 (*RMS*,ii,no.3564); Luce lay in Annandale deanery.

Note: deanery of Nithsdale existed 1540 (*MW*,i,290-1).

Archibald Menzies (Nith) 1542 - 1551.
    Occ. 19 Oct. 1542 (SRO, Prot.Bk.Herbert Anderson 1541-50, fo.9) and 11 Feb. 1551 (*Prot.Bk.Carruthers*,no.151); see also *G.offic. Nith* and *G. comm.Dumfries*

DEANS OF DESNES

First known date: 1195 x 1196.

Perhaps this deanery comprised churches transferred to Glasgow diocese from Desnes deanery in Galloway diocese c.1186 x 1189 (*TDGAS*, 3rd series, xxxiv, 109).

James 1195 x 1196.
Occ. 10 Sept. 1195 x 2 Feb. 1196 (*Melr.Lib.*,no.122; cf.no.121).

Thomas 1250.
Occ. 1250 (ibid.,i,279).

Note: This deanery still existed 1274 (*SHS Misc.*,v,104-6); but it appears to have been later incorporated within Dumfries deanery (*TDGAS*, 3rd series, xxxiv,106).

OFFICIALS

OFFICIALS WITH GENERAL AUTHORITY

OFFICIALS OF GLASGOW

First known date: 1175 x 1189.

Richard de Hassendean 1175 x 1189.
Occ. 1175 x 1 Aug. 1189 (*Melr.Lib.*,i,153); see *G.dean.christ. Teviotdale*.

John de Huntingdon 1201 x 1202 - 1204 x 1207.
Occ. Feb. 1201 x Sept. 1202 (*Glas.Reg.*,i,83); occ. thrice Sept. 1202 x 15 May 1207 (ibid.,i,84; *Pais.Reg.*,110; *Melr.Lib.*,i,37); occ. 1204 x 15 May 1207 (*Melr.Lib.*,i,118).

Richard de Ancrum 1221 - 1226.
Occ. 28 Dec. 1221 as '(Robert) Richard' or as 'Robert' (*Glas. Reg.*,i,101; *Kel.Lib.*,i,189; but note that witness lists in both versions of this text are imperfect); perhaps an otherwise unknown Robert; more likely same person as Richard de Ancrum found as official 1226 (*Glas.Reg.*,i,119); see also *G.dean.christ.Teviotdale*

Adam de Dertford 1260 x 1267, 1262 x 1267.
Occ. twice 1260 x 1267 (*Glas.Reg.*,i,177,183); occ. 5 June 1262 x 1267 (*CDS*,i,no.2676);

John de Lenne 1267 - 1268.
Appointed when Bp.Cheam went abroad 1267 (*Chron.Bower*, ii,108); bp. died 11 June x 13 Oct. 1268.

Thomas de Aberdeen 1273.
Occ. c.11 July 1273 (*Pais.Reg.*, 183, 189, 191, 201, 202, 203; cf. 195, 197) and 29 Jan. 1273 x (*Kel.Lib.*,ii,272).

Alexander de Kennedy 1295.
Occ. 23 Dec. 1295 (*Vet.Mon.*,no.349; cf. *CPL*,i,562 where name is given wrongly as Andrew).

John Fleming 1317 - 1325.
Occ. 2 Mar. 1317 (*Kel.Lib.*,i,252) and 18 May 1325 (*Glas.Reg.*, i,233).

William de Eckford 1328 x 1330.
Occ. 1328 x 1330 (*Chron.Bower*, ii,300; *Chron.Extracta*,159).

Walter de Fothes 1328 x 1335.
Occ. 1328 x 1335 (*Pais.Reg.*,239).

William de Corry 1342.
Occ. 3 Aug. 1232 (*Glas.Reg.*,i,253).

John de Peebles 1360-1363.
In office 29 Apr. 1363 and had been for three years (*CPP*,i,417).

Walter Trail 1379.
In office 26 Feb. 1379 (*CPP*,i,540).

Nicholas de Irvine 1381.
Occ. 15 Oct. 1381 (*Ayr Friars*, 23).

John de Merton 1386 - 1387 x 1395.
In office June 1386 (SRO, Transcrips from Vatican, i, 58); still in office 15 June 1387 (*CPP*,i,567-8); prob. res. 1394 x 1395 on becoming *G.arch.Teviotdale.*

Gilbert de Mouswald 1396 - 1406 x 1408.
In office 1 Feb. 1396 (Reg.Supp.,90,fo.36); occ. 26 Mar. 1406 (*HMC* 34, *14th R.*,iii,38, where name is given 'William'); prob. res. before 21 May 1408 on becoming *G.archd.Teviotdale.*

John Forrester 1414 - 1422.
Occ. 6 Feb. 1414 (*Pais.Reg.*,387-8); still in office 1 Mar. 1422 (*ACSB*,311-13).

David de Cadzow   1432 - 1454.
Stephen Ker   1438 - 1438 x 1440.
Simon de Dalgless   1452 - 1470.
Cadzow occ. 31 Mar. 1432 (*Pais.Reg.*,370), 16 Feb. 1441 (*Glas. Reg.*,ii,359) and 21 Oct. 1454 (SRO, Broughton & Cally Inventory, no. 14); perhaps not in office continuously in this period.
Ker occ. 3 Mar. 1438 (*Pais.Reg.*,289); prob. res. 1438 x 6 Aug. 1440 on becoming *Bothans prov.*
Dalgless occ. 14 Jan. 1452 (*Glas.Reg.*,ii,391), 25 Oct. 1457 (*Glas.Mun.*,ii,65) and 28 June 1470 (*Pais.Reg.*,344-7).

William Elphinstone junior 1471 - 1478.
Occ. 6 Apr. 1471 (*HMC* 46, *Hope-Johnstone*, 11) and 13 Mar. 1478 (*HMC* 8, *9th R.*,ii,233); cf. *St A. offic. Lothian.*

John Otterburn 1478.

Occ. 4 June 1478, having succ. to office since 4 May 1478 (*St Giles Reg.*, 128-30; cf. *RMS*,ii,no. 1382 when his titles at this date are given wrongly).

Patrick Leche 1483 - 1493 x 1494.

Occ. 19 Apr. 1483 (*Glas.Reg.*,ii,418); occ. 8 Mar. 1493 (Blair (Dalry) Papers, per Mr A.B. Webster); d. before 16 May 1494 (Fraser, *Douglas*,iii,208-10).

David Cunningham 1496 - 1509.

Occ. 27 Feb. 1496 (*Glas.Reg.*,ii,491); occ. 10 Oct. 1508 (*Glas. Chrs.*,ii,479-80); d. 18 Apr. 1509, having prob. retained office until then (*Glas.Reg.*,ii,615; see also *Prot. Bk.Simon,* 285).

Martin Reid 1510 - 1512.

Occ. 3 Apr. 1510 and 21 Apr. 1512 (*Prot.Bk.Simon,*327,438).

Andrew Sibbald 1516 - 1519.

Occ. 25 Aug. 1516 and 8 June 1519 (*Prot.Bk.Ros,*nos,145,331).

Thomas Coutts 1520 - 1524.

Occ. 18 May 1520 and 12 June 1523 (ibid.nos. 410,660); moved to *St A.offic.Lothian* Aug. x Dec. 1524.

Adam Colquhoun 1524 - 1541.

Occ. 25 Oct. 1524 (*Glas.Mun.*,ii,149); occ. 31 Oct. 1541 (Fraser, *Pollok*,i,284).

Alexander Dunbar 1544 - 1546.

Occ. 11 May 1544 (ibid.,i,285); occ. 22 May 1546 (SRO, ADC & S,xx, fo.131); moved to *M.succ.* later in 1546.

William Hamilton 1548 - 1552.

In office 13 Nov. 1548 (PRO 31/9 - 66/190); occ. 25 Oct. 1552 (*Glas.Mun.*,ii,172).

Archibald Menzies (?) 1557.

Occ. 13 Apr. 1557 (*Laing Chrs.*,no.669); but prob. this is an error for *G.offic.Nith*, the place-date being Dumfries.

Archibald Betoun 1557 - 1562.

Occ. 1 Oct. 1557 (Fraser, *Colquhoun Cartulary*, 401); occ. 19 Mar. 1562 (Fraser, *Eglinton*,ii,172).

OFFICIALS WITH LIMITED AUTHORITY

OFFICIALS OF DUMFRIES : NITH, DESNES AND ANNANDALE : NITH

First known dates: Dumfries : 17 June 1494 (*ADC*,i,327).
                Nith, Desnes and Annandale : 1535.
                Nith   :   1546.

Note: abp. had an 'officialis foraneus' 1525 (*St A.Form.*,i,264).

John Turner (Nith, Desnes and Annandale/Dumfries/Nith) 1535 - 1546.
Occ. as rector of Annan and offic. Nith,Desnes and
Annandale 22 Nov. 1535 (*Glas.Reg.*,ii,550); occ. as rector of
Annan and offic. Dumfries 20 July 1541 (*Wigt.Chrs.*,no.278);
occ. as rector of Annan and offic. Nith 8 Feb. 1546 (*Prot.Bk.
Carruthers*, no.107); see also *G.comm.Nith,Desnes and
Annandale*.

Archibald Menzies (Nith) 1557 (?) - 1560.
Prob. in office when described as *G.offic.* 13 Apr. 1557 (v.sup.);
occ. 10 Apr. and 31 Aug. 1560 (*Wigt.Chrs.*,nos. 355,355a); see also
G.dean christ. Nith and *G.comm.Dumfries*.

OFFICIALS OF STOBO

First known date: 15th century.
A seal-matrix survives with legend 'S.officii de Stobo' and has
been attributed to 15th century (Stevenson & Wood, *Seals*,i,116);
perhaps used by commissaries of Stobo (v.inf.).

No names known.

OFFICIALS OF ARCHDEACON OF GLASGOW

First known date: 1275.

William Salsarius 1275.
Occ. Apr./July 1275 (*Glas.Reg.*, i,189-91).

William de Eckford 1316.
Occ. 25 June 1316 (*Melr.Lib.*,ii,364).

OFFICIALS OF ARCHDEACON OF TEVIOTDALE

First known date: 1241 x 1274.

John de Musselburgh 1241 x 1274, 1251 x 1274.
Occ. 1241 x 1274 (*Cold.Cart.*,18); occ. as 'offic.Teviotdale'
1251 x 1274 (*Midl.Chrs.*,9, where text is prob. faulty); moved to
St A.offic. 15 Oct. 1273 x 18 July 1274.

Walter Cammoys c. 1297.
Occ. c. July 1297 (Stevenson, *Documents*, ii,200).

Hugh de Chirnside 1306.

Occ. 24 Mar./4 Apr. 1306 (*Melr.Lib.*,i,315).

COMMISSARIES

COMMISSARIES WITH GENERAL AUTHORITY
COMMISSARIES OF GLASGOW

First known date: 1486.

John Restoun 1486.
　　Occ. (C) 25 Feb. 1486 (*RMS*,ii,no.1644).

John Spreule 1505.
　　Occ. (CO) 25 Jan. 1505 (*Prot.Bk.Simon*, 84).

James Neilson 1506 - 1507.
　　Occ. (CO) 27 July 1506 and 27 Apr. 1507 (ibid.,143, 178).

John Spreule 1510 - 1511.
　　Occ. (CGO) 12 Aug. 1510 (ibid.,374); occ. (CO) 13 Aug. 1511
(*HMC* 4, *5th R.*, 614-15).

Thomas Coutts 1514 - 1517.
　　Occ. (CO) 14 June 1514 (SRO, Reg.Ho.Chr.no.818) and 20 Feb.
1517 (*Prot.Bk.Ros*,no.162A); became *G.offic.* himself 8 June 1519 x
18 May 1520.

John Spreule 1526.
　　Occ. (CO) 13 Oct. 1526 (SRO,Reg.Ho.Supp.Chr.,s.d.).

John Gledstanes 1537.
　　Occ. (C) 4 Feb. 1537 (SRO, Acts and Decreets,i,fo.341).

John Spreule 1539.
　　Occ. (CO) 14 Apr. 1539 (Fraser,*Keir*,361).

John Stewart 1551 - 1552.
　　Occ. (C) 10 Apr. and 31 Oct. 1551 (SRO, Reg.Ho.Chrs.nos.1398,
1536A) and (CG) 6 Sept. 1551 and 8 Feb. 1552 (*Prot.Bk.Carruthers*,
no.145; Fraser, *Colquhoun Cartulary*, 423).

John Hamilton 1552.
　　Occ. (CG) 4 July 1552 (Fraser, *Buccleuch*,ii,no.186).

John Spreule 1554.
　　Occ. (CG) 7 Mar. 1554 (SRO, Reg.Ho.Chr.no.1607).

Robert Herbisoune 1557 - 1562.
　　Occ. (C) 10 Feb. 1557 (*Prot.Bk.Glasgow*,ii,no.341); occ. (CG) 19
Mar.1562 (Fraser, *Eglinton*,ii,172).

Archibald Betoun 1564 - 1581 x 1582.

Occ. (C) under new organisation 14 June 1564 (SRO, Comm. Edin.Decreets,i,fo.59); occ. 6 Feb. 1572 (*RMS*,iv,no.2098); occ. 1581 (*Introduction to Scottish Legal History* [Stair Soc.] ,369, no source cited); d. 31 July 1582 (see *Ab.prec.*).

COMMISSARIES WITH LIMITED AUTHORITY

COMMISSARIES OF TEVIOTDALE

First known date: 1492.

James Newton 1492.
Occ. (C) as rector of Bedrule 15 Sept. 1492 (*RMS*,ii,no.2122A); see also *G.dean.christ. Teviotdale.*

Stephen Douglas 1513.
Occ (C) 6 Apr. 1513 (*Prot.Bk.Simon*,483; see also 445);

Archibald Rutherford 1542.
Occ. (C) 21 Mar. 1542 (SRO, Biel, no.605).

COMMISSARIES OF NITH : ANNANDALE : NITH, DESNES AND ANNANDALE : DUMFRIES

First known date: [   ] : 1459 (?)
Nith   : 9 Aug.1465 (SRO,Reg.Ho.Chr.no.384
Annandale : 1471.
Nith, Desnes and Annandale : 1506.
Dumfries   : 1543 (?), 1565.

William Heris   1459.
Thomas Tynding   1459.
Thomas Gilhagy   1459.
Gilhagy occ. as C depute for **Heris** (CB) and **Tynding** (CB) 4 May 1459 (SRO, Reg.Ho.Chr.no.354); as proceedings were at Dumfries, their area of jurisdiction was prob. Nith.

Thomas Tynding (Annandale) 1471.
Occ. (C) 7 Oct. 1471 (*HMC* 44, *Drumlanrig*,i,64); see also *G.dean. christ.Annandale.*

Roger de Carruthers (Nith) 1476.
Occ. (C) 5 Jan. 1476 (*TGDAS*,3rd series,xxxvii,54).

Herbert Gledstanes (Nith, Desnes and Annandale) 1496 - 1506.
Occ. (C in unspecified jurisdiction) 20 Apr. 1496 (Fraser, *Maxwell Inventories*,13); occ. (C) 2 Nov. 1506 (Fraser,*Carlaverock*,ii, 415).

Hugh Greenlaw (Nith,Desnes and Annandale) 1506 (?) - 1509.

Occ. (C) 18 Apr. 1509, having perhaps been in office as early as 1506 (*Prot.Bk.Simon*, 280).

John Oliver   (Nith)   1529.
John McKynnell   (Nith)   1529 - 1532.

Oliver occ. (C) jointly with McKynnell 5 Aug. 1529 (*TGDAS*, 3rd series, xxxvii, 54).

McKynnell occ. (C) jointly with Oliver 5 Aug. 1529 (ibid); occ. (C) alone 23 Oct. 1532 (*Prot.Bk.Carruthers*, no.14).

John Turner (Nith, Desnes and Annandale) 1539.

Occ. (CG) as rector of Annan 27 Nov. 1539 (*Glas.Reg.*, ii, 553); see also *G.offic. Nith, Desnes and Annandale*.

Archibald Menzies (Dumfries) c.1543 - 1579.

Appointed (C with unspecified jurisdiction) c. 1543 and held office for 36 years until depriv. on or before 20 Jan. 1579 (*RPC*, iii, 71); occ. (C) 22 Dec. 1565 (*RSS*, v, no.2506); occ. (C) 30 Oct. 1575 (ibid., vii, no.315); d. before 1 July 1579 (ibid., no.1964); see also *G.offic. Nith* and *G.dean christ.Nith.*

COMMISSARIES OF PECULIAR JURISDICTIONS OF CATHEDRAL PREBENDS

COMMISSARIES OF HAMILTON (Dean)

First known date: 1514.

Robert Hamilton 1514.

Occ. (C) 19 Mar. 1514 (*Prot.Bk.Ros*, nos.63-64), when reference is made to unnamed predecessors; occ. (C) as rector of Covington 8 June 1515 (ibid., no.111); see also *G.comm.Douglas* and *Lesmahagow* and *G.dean.christ.Lanark*.

John Hamilton 1558.

Occ. (C) 13 July 1558 (SRO, Reg.Ho.Chr.no.1307): see also *G.comm. Kilbride* and *Monkland and Cadder*.

COMMISSARIES OF KILBRIDE (Precentor)

First known date: 1513.

Matthew Stewart 1513.

Has been exercising this jurisdiction as vic. of Maybole though Kilbride prebend is vacant; is ordered not to act any more pending lit. 19 Dec. 1513 (*Prot.Bk.Simon*, 452).

James Lindsay 1521.

Occ. (C) 14 Oct. 1521 (*Prot.Bk.Ros*, no.528).

Alexander Hamilton 1534 - 1543 x 1548.

      Occ. (C) 29 May 1534 (SRO,Boyd,no. 83) and 10 Aug. 1543 (SRO,Comm. Hamilton and Campsie Decreets,i,fo.20v); prob. d. before 16 July 1548 (see *G.dean)*.

John Hamilton 1558.

      Occ. (C) 18 Apr. 1558 (SRO, Comm.Hamilton and Campsie Decreets, i,fo.9v); see also *G.comm. Hamilton* and *Monkland and Cadder.*

COMMISSARIES OF CAMPSIE (Chancellor)

First known date: 1506.

George Symontoun   1506.
Cuthbert Simonis   1506.

      Symontoun occ. (C) 26 June and 3 July 1506 when Simonis acts as his *locum tenens* (*Prot.Bk.Simon*,139-40); had been vic. of Mearns since 6 Jan. 1506 (ibid.,106) and d. 6 x 12 July 1507 (ibid., 200-1).

      Simonis acts for Symontoun 26 June and 3 July 1506 (v.sup.).

Adam Colquhoun 1508.

      Occ. (C *in hac parte*) as can. of Glasgow 19 Aug. 1508 (*Prot.Bk. Simon*,236-8).

Cuthbert Simonis 1508 - 1512.

      Occ. (C) 23 Dec. 1508 and 23 Mar. 1512 (ibid.,254-5, 436).

James Blair 1549.

      Occ. (C) 1 June 1549 (SRO, Comm.Hamilton and Campsie Decreets,i,fo.48v).

COMMISSARIES OF CARNWATH (Treasurer)

First known date: 1574.

John Weir 1574.

      In office 9 July 1574 when appointed first comm. Lanark under re-organisation (*RSS*.vi.no.2579). see also *G.comm. Lesmahagow* and *G.dean.christ. Lanark.*

Note: this jurisdiction was absorbed in new comm. Lanark at this date.

COMMISSARIES OF MONKLAND AND CADDER (Subdean)

First known date: 1555.

John Hamilton 1555.

Occ. (C) 28 Aug. 1555 (SRO, Prot.Bk.Thomas Stevin, fo.107v);
see also *G.comm.Kilbride* and *Hamilton.*

COMMISSARIES OF MANOR (Archdeacon of Glasgow)

First known date: 1511.

Patrick Tweedy 1511.
Occ. (C) 24 Apr. 1511 (*Yester Writs,*no. 322).

COMMISSARIES OF CARDROSS (Canon)

First known date: 21 Apr. 1512 (*Prot.Bk.Simon,*437-8).

No names known.

COMMISSARIES OF CARSTAIRS (Canon)

First known date: 1566.

John Young 1566.
Appointed 12 Jan. 1566 (*RSS,*v,no.2537).

Note: this jurisdiction was absorbed in new comm. Lanark erected 9
July 1574 (ibid.,vi,no.1579).

COMMISSARIES OF DOUGLAS (Canon)

First known date: 1516.

Robert Hamilton 1516.
Occ. (C) as rector of Covington 12 Jan. and 27 June 1516 (*Prot.
Bk. Ros,*nos.130,143); see also *G.comm. Hamilton* and *Lesmahagow*
and *G.dean.christ. Lanark.*

Note: this jurisdiction is mentioned without name of comm. Aug.1541
(SRO, ADC and S, xvii, fo.83).

COMMISSARIES OF STOBO (Canon)

First known date: 1504.
See *G.offic.Stobo* for a seal-matrix perhaps used by this
commissary in 15th century.

Andrew Young 1504.

Occ. (C) 20 Mar. 1504 (*Yester Writs*,no.272).

William Thomson 1540.
Occ. (C) 10 Nov. 1540 (*HMC* 55, *Var.Coll.*,v,14).

John Colquhoun 1552.
Occ. (C) 16 Dec. 1552 when also *G.dean.christ.Peebles* (SRO, Elibank, 5/4).

COMMISSARIES OF OTHER PECULIAR JURISDICTIONS

COMMISSARIES OF LESMAHAGOW (Kelso Abbey)

First known date: 1513.

Robert Hamilton 1513 - 1517.
Occ. (C) as rector of Covington Feb.1513 and Mar. 1516 (*Prot. Bk. Ros*,nos. 33-34, 169); see also *G.comm. Hamilton* and *Douglas* and *G.dean.christ.Lanark.*

John Davidson 1534.
Occ. (C) 9 Aug. 1534 (*RMS*,iii,no.2008).

John Weir 1574.
In office 9 July 1574 when appointed first comm. Lanark under re-organisation (*RSS*,vi,no.2579), see also *G.comm. Carnwath* and *G.dean.christ.Lanark.*

Note: this jurisdiction was absorbed in new comm. Lanark at this date.

ISLES DIOCESE

BISHOPS OF SKYE : MAN : THE ISLES : SUDREYS : SODOR

First known date: before 1079.

For names of some Celtic bishops in Man and the Western Isles of Scotland, see work of O.Kolsrud in *Diplom.Norv.*,xvii B, 311-18; cf. *HBC*,293,295; *PSAS*,1xxxvii,107,n.6, 111,n.1.

For use of alternative titles by these bishops from 1154 onwards, see *Diplom.Norv.*, xvii B,308.

These bishops appear to have recognised York metropolitan authority until 1153, when they were placed under Nidaros/Trondheim (see A.O. Johnsen, *Studier vedrorende Nicolaus Brekespears Legasjon til Norden* (Oslo, 1945),96-97 for date); some bishops, however, continued to seek conf. from York or (exceptionally) Dublin until as late as the early 13th century; patronage of this see was transferred by king of Norway to King Alexander III of Scotland by treaty of Perth 2 July 1266 (*APS*,i,420); Bp. Russell obtained a papal grace excusing him from a personal visit to Trondheim to profess obedience to his metropolitan 14 June 1349 (*Diplom.Norv.*, vii,no.222b; *CPP*,i,168); this marks the reduction of the rights of Trondheim over this see to a nominal level (cf. *Diplom.Norv.*,xvii B,308).

Two separate lines of bishops, now based on Man and the Isles respectively, emerge from the Great Schism from 1387 onwards (ibid., 308-9; see *HBC*, 254-5 for list of bishops of Sodor and Man recognised in England).

The Scottish see of Sodor or the Isles was placed under the metropolitan authority of St Andrews 17 Aug. 1472 (*Vet.Mon.*, no. 852); by 1617 this see had been transferred from province of St Andrews to that of Glasgow (*APS*,iv,530).

Roolwer x 1079.

D. as bp. and was buried on Isle of Man; held office before 1079 (*Chron.Man*,112-114); possibly associated with contemporary first Norse bp. of Dublin c.1030 - 1074 (A. Ashley, *The Church in the Isle of Man*, 11; cf. *HBC*,336).

William

Succ. Roolwer as bp. (*Chron.Man*,114).

Hamond 'filius Iole'/Wimund 1079 x 1095.

Succ. William as bp. under name 'Hamond filius Iole', a Manxman (*Chron.Man*,114); Dr D.P. Kirby suggests that he is identical with the 'Wimund' who obtained cons. as bp. of Skye from Thomas abp. of York 1070 - 1100 (*Historians of York*,ii,372, where the name 'Wimund' is to be taken as a misreading of 'Hamond' induced by knowledge of the later Wimund (v.inf.), and where a confusion is to be assumed between two abps. of York called Thomas, and where the entry is to be thought

to have been inserted alongside the profession of the wrong Radulf
O.bp.(cf.p.363); but note that A.O. Anderson considered and rejected
this identification of Hamond and Wimund-see *ES*,ii,96-97).

Note: Olaf I king of the Isles may possibly have presented an unnamed
bp. ('episcopus noster') to 'G' abp. of York for cons. 1103 x 1108
(*Monumenta de Insula Manniae* ii,7; but this text may be just a variant
of the similar letter to Abp. Thurstan mentioned below). Then, rather
than have his kingdom divided under the episcopal care of mercenary
strangers (which points to a period when this had been the case), King
Olaf decreed 1134 that there should be one bp. for his whole kingdom
of Man and the Isles, and that the duty of election should perpetually
lie with the monks of Furness abbey in Lancashire (*Furness Coucher
Bk.*,ii,pt.3, 708-9;*Mon.Ins.Man.*,ii,1-3;cf.*Chron.Man,* 62 for date); at
the same time he authorised the monks for this occasion to elect one
of their own number as bp., and he wrote to Thurstan abp. of York
to ask him to give conf. and cons. to whomsoever should be elected
(*Furness Coucher Bk.*,ii,709;*Mon.Ins.Man.*,ii,4-6; *Chron.Man,* app. no.3,
pp.269-71, Haddan & Stubbs, *Councils*,II,i,218-19; *Historians of York,*
iii,58-59).

Wimund O.Savigny 1134 x 1140 - 1143 x 1148.
       An Englishman who became a monk of Furness 1127 or later,
and then moved to the Isle of Man, presumably to the daughter-house
of Rushen after its foundation 1134; became bp., being called in one
chronicle the 'first bishop' of the Isle of Man (*SAEC,*223-4), though
he was not remembered in Man tradition (cf. *Chron.Man,*114); presumably the first to be el. by the monks of his mother-house of
Furness in terms of the grant by King Olaf of 1134 - to which he may
possibly have been witness as 'W.monachus' (cf.*Furness Coucher Bk.*,
ii,709,n.2) - and so prob. cons. by Thurstan abp. of York (cf. *SHR,*
iii,398); developed political ambitions as pretender to Scottish throne
against David I prob. after 1138, and on defeat retired to Byland
Abbey, Yorkshire i.e. 1143 (its date of foundation) or later (*SAEC,*
225-6,230; cf. 192-5; *ES*,ii,97-98; *SHR*,vii,29-36; *VCH Lancashire,*
ii,116-17); prob. res. or depriv. before 1148 (v.inf).

Nicholas   c. 1148.
John   O.S.B. (?) 1151 or 1152.
       Nicholas went to York as bp.-elect of King Olaf ('electus noster'),
who corresponded with dean and chapter of York about a delay in
his cons; Olaf wanted him cons. without delay by the abp.; the monks
of Furness were objecting, and Olaf threatened that in consequence they
might lose what they seemed to possess in his dominions (*Furness
Coucher Bk.*,ii,710;*Mon.Ins.Man.*,ii,49-52; *Chron.Man,*app.no.4,pp.
272-3; Haddan & Stubbs, *Councils*,II,i,219-20;*Historians of York*,iii,
59-60; see *Diplom.Norv.*,xvii B,320 for argument that this letter must
belong to Olaf I and not a later King Olaf); dating is partly controlled by
name of dean of York, 'R' for Robert (*Furness Coucher Bk.*,ii,710; cf.
*Chron.Man,*272n), which suggests 1143 x (C.T.Clay, *York Minster Fasti,*

i,1); but there was no York abp. with full metropolitan power or resident at York thereafter until after cons. at the curia of Abp. Henry Murdac 7 Dec. 1147 (D.Knowles, 'The case of St William of York', *Historian and Character and other Essays*, 76-97); most probable date for Nicholas being elect and at York is therefore early 1148, when the dean and chapter's jurisdiction in the vacancy would have lapsed and they were awaiting the arrival of the new abp.; his el. had prob. followed res. or depriv. of Wimund (v.sup.), and Olaf was apparently not willing to allow Furness freedom to exercise their privilege of election again after his unfortunate experience with their choice of Bp.Wimund; Nicholas prob. never had conf. or cons. since the abp. preferred John (cf. *Diplom.Norv.*,xvii B,320-1; *Chron.Man*,169n,236n; *ES*,ii,381-2).

John, when a monk of Seez in Normandy, was cons. by Henry abp. of York as 'second bishop' of Isle of Man 1151 or 1152 (*SAEC*, 224; *Historians of York*,ii,462); but he was not remembered in Man tradition (*Chron.Man*,114) and so was prob. not acceptable to King Olaf.

Note: right of monks of Furness to elect bp. of the Isles conf. by King Godred c.1154 (*Furness Coucher Bk.*,ii,710).

Gamaliel/Gamelin 1154 x .

An Englishman, 'Gamaliel' is first to be remembered in Man tradition since Hamond (*Chron.Man*,114); prob. had been el. by monks of Furness and was same as the 'Gamelin' who received cons. from Roger abp. of York 1154 x 1181 (*Historians of York*,ii,462); buried at Peterborough, England (*Chron.Man*,114).

Reginald/Nemar - c.1170.

A Norwegian, 'Reginald' succ. Gamaliel (ibid); is first bp. of Sudreys to be mentioned in Icelandic annals, and so was prob. first to have recognised metropolitan authority of Trondheim rather than York (cf.ibid.,238-9); as 'Nemar' d. some forty years before 1210 (*ES*, ii,381-2), and implication is that no bp. was recognised by Trondheim after him in the period c.1170 - 1210.

Cristin 1170 x .

An Argyll man (and so possibly el. by monks of Furness under pressure of sons of Somerled of Argyll, who were calling themselves kings of the Isles 1156 - c. 1192 - see *PSAS*,xc,197-8), succ. Reginald (*Chron.Man*,114); prob. cons by York; buried at Bangor (ibid.).

Michael O.Cist. - 1203.

A Manxman and a monk (prob. O.Cist.since he was to be buried at Fountains Abbey, Yorkshire), succ. Cristin as bp. of the Isles and d. 1203 (*Chron.Man*,114,80; cf.240); perhaps had been monk of Rushen, and prob. had been el. by monks of Furness and cons. by abp. of York in terms of arrangements of 1134 which were conf. during or just before his episcopate (v.inf.).

Note: electoral rights of Furness were conf. by Reginald king of the Isles prob. 1188 x 1190 (*Furness Coucher Bk.*,ii,711); and they were

given their first known specific papal conf. 23 May 1194 or 1195 (ibid., i,642-3; cf. ii,806 and i,661-5, 666-8). Metropolitan rights of Trondheim prob. reasserted after papal conf. of the subordination of this among other sees as its suffragans 13 Feb. 1206 (*Diplom.Norv.*,vii,no.7).

Nicholas/Koli 1203 x 1210 - 1217.
      An Argyll man, 'Nicholas' succ. Michael (*Chron.Man*,80,116); styled bp. of Sodor (*Mon.Ins.Man.*, ii,38-39); cons. as 'Koli' (a short form of Nicholas) 1210 (*ES*,ii,381), and obedience to Trondheim may be assumed since he is mentioned here in Icelandic annals; prob. there had been no bishop since 1203 until after the papal conf. of rights of Trondheim in 1206 (v.sup.); d. 1217 and buried at Bangor in Ulster (*Chron.Man,* 82,116).

Reginald   c. 1217 x 1226.
Nicholas   O.Cist. 1217 x 1219 - 1224 x 1225.
      Reginald was a member of the royal family of the Isles and succ. Nicholas/Koli (*Chron.Man*,82,116); not el. by monks of Furness (v.inf.) but prob. cons. at York since he is not mentioned in Icelandic annals (cf. *Diplom.Norv.*,xvii B,323) and since his rival had to seek cons. elsewhere (v.inf.); presumably appointed to see by King Reginald, and known to have been friendly also with that king's half-brother Olaf 1217 x 1223 (*Chron.Man*,84-88); buried at Rushen Abbey on Man (ibid 116), presumably some time before 1226 (v.inf.).
      Nicholas el. on death of Nicholas/Koli when abbot of Furness (*Chron.Melsa* (Rolls Series), i,380); it was prob. he who took the troubl at the time of his election to confirm the right of his fellow-monks to elect him as bp. of the Isles, and who got the monks of Rushen on Man and the archd. of Man to consent to his election (*Furness Coucher Bk.*, ii,711-12; cf. *Mon.Ins.Man.*, ii, 19-20); sent by his electing body to abp. of Dublin as metropolitan (by no known right) - a procedure prob. followed because York had already given cons. to Reginald (v.sup.;cf. *Diplom.Norv.*,xvii B,323), and because the Dublin abp. was also papal legate - and got conf. and cons. from him; but failed to obtain recognition from King Reginald as 'prince' (cf.*ES*,ii,427), went to the curia and got papal mand. to make the prince show him favour 9 Nov. 1219 (*Vet.Mon.*,no.31); got another papal mand. to abp. of York 15 May 1224 to receive his res. as bp. of Man and the Isles because of continuing exile from the see (*Historians of York*,iii,122-3; *CPL*,i,97); this was effective by 24 Jan. 1225 (*Reg.Gray*,153; see also Dowden, *Bishops*,275 and *Diplom.Norv.*,xvii B,323-4).

John 'filius Hefare' 1217 x 1226.
      Succ. Reginald, but d. soon after in an accident, and buried at Jervaulx Abbey, Yorkshire (*Chron.Man,* 116).

Simon 1226 - 1248.
      An Argyll Man, cons. bp. of Sodor as successor to John 1226, prob. Aug./Sept. by abp. of Trondheim at Bergen (*Chron.Man,* 116; cf.190 and 243-4; *ES*,ii,460; *Diplom.Norv.*,xvii B,324); prob. had not been el. by monks of Furness, who by 16 Mar. 1227 were needing help

of King Henry III against threats of King Olaf II of Man (*Rot.Litt.Claus.*, ii,175b); d. on Man 29 Feb. 1248 and buried in new cathedral of St German at Peel which he had begun to build (*Chron.Man*, 100,116;*ES*, ii,546-7).

Laurence 1248.
   El. 'by chapter (capitulum) of Man' when *I.archd.* on Simon's death; went to Norway for conf. and cons., but was refused these, the king of Man and the Isles insisting there on a new election back in Man in his presence by all the clergy and people; the king and bp. elect were drowned near Shetland on the way back Oct./Nov. 1248 (*Chron.Man*, 100; cf.200-1,248; *ES*,ii,547-50).

Richard (de Nafferton ?) O.S.A. 1253 - 1275.
   An Englishman but canon of St Andrews priory in Scotland and active at the curia when appointed to this see and cons. there at Perugia in Italy by abp. of Trondheim as metropolitan on or before 14 Mar. 1253 when papal notification was sent to chapter of Sodor (*Chron. Man*,315;cf.116; *CPL*,i,284); this followed soon after conf. of rights of Trondheim over this see 25 Feb. 1253 (*Diplom.Norv.*,iii,no.3); see G.W.S.Barrow in *Journ.Eccles.Hist.*,iii,29 for suggested surname; buried at Furness 25 Mar. 1275 (*ES*,ii,673).

Gilbert   O.Cist.   1275.
Mark   1275 - 1303.
   Gilbert, when abbot of Rushen in Man, el. by clergy and people on death of Richard, but this el. annulled by King Alexander III (*SAEC*,381-2).
   Mark was a Galloway man (*Chron.Man*, 116) whom King Alexander nom. to abp. of Trondheim for cons. (*SAEC*,382); cons. at Tunsberg, Norway 1275 or 1276 (*ES*,ii,674) or 3 Jan. 1277 x 2 Jan. 1278 (*Mon.Ins.Man.*,ii,133-4); d. 1303 (*Diplom.Norv.*,xvii B,327) and buried at cathedral of Peel (*Chron.Man*,118).

Alan x 1305 - 1321.
   A Galloway man (*Chron.Man*,118); cons. by 26 Mar. 1305 (*CDS*, ii,no.1717); presumably the man whom Anthony Bek bp. of Durham and lord of Man (x 1298 - 1311) imposed against wishes of monks of Furness (*Furness Coucher Bk.*,ii,694); d. 15 Feb. 1321 and buried at Rothesay on Bute (*Chron.Man*,118).

Gilbert MacLelan 1324 - 1326 x 1328.
   A Galloway man who succ. Alan and held see for two and a half years (*Chron.Man*, 118); occ. 16 Dec. 1324 (*Arb.Lib.*,i,220); occ. 20 July 1326 (*RMS*,i,no.487; cf. app.1,no.32 of 20 Dec. 1324, where name of this bp. is given as 'David'); d. before 14 Jan. 1328 (v.inf.), and buried at Rothesay on Bute (*Chron.Man.*,118).

Bernard (de Linton ?)   O.Tiron. 1327 x 1328 - 1328 x 1331.
Cormac Cormacii   1325 x 1331.
   Bernard was a Scot (*Chron.Man*,118); occ. still just abbot of Arbroath 9 Nov. 1327 (*Arb.Lib.*,i,no.357); el. before 14 Jan. 1328

(*ER*,i,59) being then chancellor of Robert I, who as recently as 20 Dec. 1324 had reserved to himself the patronage of this see (*RMS*,i,app.1, no.32); cons. 26 June x 12 Nov. 1328 (*ER*,i,114; Dowden, *Bishops*, 282), perhaps in Norway (cf. *Diplom.Norv.*,xvii B,330) but prob. not (v.inf.); said to have been bp. four years and to have been buried at Kilwinning Abbey, Ayrshire (*Chron.Man*,118); but d. before 10 June 1331 (v.inf.) - and so perhaps the 'four years' applies to Bp. MacLelan and his 'two and a half years' to Bernard (cf. *Diplom.Norv.*,loc.cit.).

Cormac el. by 'canons of Snizort and the clergy of Skye' on death of MacLelan, who sent proctors to get conf. from abp. of Trondheim; they reached him at Bergen 6 July 1331, and abp. ordered examination of the election there 12 July 1331 (*Diplom.Norv.*, xviii,no.10); presumably the abp. was not committed to Bernard in that he was at least willing to receive these proctors; but Cormac is not known to have been successful; cf. *I.archd.*

Thomas 1331 - 1348.

A Scot (*Chron.Man*,118) and Dk.canon when prov. to this see on death of Bernard 10 June 1331 (*CPL*,ii,341); had been cons. at curia prob. 7 x 10 June 1331 (*Diplom.Norv.*,xvii B,331); d. 20 Sept. 1348 and was buried at Scone in Scotland (*Chron.Man*,118).

William Russell O.Cist. 1349 - 1374.

A Manxman and abbot of Rushen on Man when el. by clergy of the Isle of Man following death of Thomas; went to the curia for conf. and got prov. 27 Apr. 1349 (*Chron.Man*, 118,336-43; *CPL*, iii,279; cf. Eubel, *Hierarchia*,i,456); cons. by 6 May 1349, prob. on 4 May (*Chron.Man*,349-50; *CPL*,iii,285); d. 21 Apr. 1374 at Ramshead (i.e. at Bolton-le-Sands, Lancashire), and buried at Furness Abbey (*Chron.Man*, 118-20).

John Donkan/Doncan/Donnegan 1374 - 1387.

A Manxman and Down archd. in Ireland when el. by clergy of Man 31 May/1 June 1374; went to curia for conf. and got prov. 6 Nov. 1374 and cons. at Avignon 25/26 Nov. 1374 (*Chron.Man*, 120, 394-400; *Diplom.Norv.*,vii,no.291; cf. Dowden,*Bishops*,285n; see also *CPL*,iv,28 and *Diplom.Norv.*,vii,nos.272,275 for variations of surname); installed at Peel 25 Jan. 1377 (*Chron.Man*,120); supported England and Pope Urban VI in Great Schism, and depriv. by Pope Clement VII 15 July 1387 (v.inf.); but retained recognition in Man and in England until trans. to another see prob. in Ireland 27 Sept. 1392 (*Diplom.Norv.*, xvii B,333-5).

Note: from this date only those bishops of the now divided see who obtained recognition in Scotland are noted here (cf. Dowden, *Bishops*,287).

Michael O.F.M. 1387 - 1409.

Trans. from Cashel abp. by Clement VII on depriv. of Donkan 15 July 1387 (Eubel, *Hierarchia*,i,456; *Diplom.Norv.*,xvii B,341); occ. as witness to act of Donald lord of the Isles at Ardtornish, Argyll 1

Nov. 1409 (*RMS*,ii,no.2264); d. before 20 Apr. 1422 (v.inf.).

Richard (Pawlie/Payl ?) (O.P. ?) 1421 x 1422.

Occ. as the bp. of Sodor called Richard recognised by an abbot of Iona who received conf. from him before 5 Nov. 1421 (*CSSR*,i,264; *CPL*, vii, 194); this Bp. Richard was known in Rome to have a vicar-general in spirituals who was rector of Kilchoman on Islay 6 Dec.1421 (*ACSB*, 3) - the same man who as early as 23 June 1427 is going to be found in company of Bp. Angus de Insulis (*RMS*,ii,no.2287); this bp. may possibly have been an otherwise unknown successor in the Scottish see of Sodor to Bp. Michael, and so d. before 20 Apr. 1422 (v.inf.); but more probably was same as the Richard Pawlie/Payl O.P. who was trans. from see of Dromore in Ireland to the undifferentiated see of Sodor by Pope John XXIII 30 May 1410 (*Diplom.Norv.*,xvii, nos.354-5, 967-8; *CPL*,vi,197; cp.301; cf. *Diplom.Norv.*,xvii B,336 Brady, *Episcopal Succession*,i,106, 296-7, and *HBC*,254, 294,317 for surname; name 'Richard Messing' appears to be erroneous), and who remained the bp. recognised in Man until 1429 x 1433 (*Diplom. Norv.*,xvii B,336); if this latter identification is correct, then he may have been recognised only locally and temporarily in the Western Isles of Scotland; it is noteworthy that Bp. Angus in 1426 was to be said to succ. a Bp.Michael, which may imply that this Bp. Richard was not by then regarded as having any rightful place in the list of bps. of the northern see of Sodor.

Michael de Ochiltree (Anchus, Anchir) 1422,

Prov. to see of Sodor in Scotland, which was vacant by death of unnamed previous bp., 20 Apr. 1422 (ibid.,xvii,no.418; Brady, *Episcopal Succession*,i,162); he was then *Db.dean (CSSR*,i,297-9), which ben. he continued to hold until prov. *Db.bp.* 22 June 1428; thus this prov. to Sodor was abortive.

Angus de Insulis/'Prole' 1426 - 1438 x 1441.

Prov. to see of Sodor or the Isles (said to be immediately subject to the holy see), which was vacant by death of Bp. Michael, 19 June 1426 (*CPL*,vii,478; *Diplom.Norv.*,xvii,no.447; Brady, *Episcopal Succession*,i,162), with faculty for cons. 29 July 1426 (*CPL*,vii, 465-6); occ. 23 June 1427 (*RMS*,ii,no.2287); letters of appointment delayed in the papal chamber because of a lawsuit (object unknown) until 2 Feb. 1428, and he offered his common services in person as late as 11 Feb, 1428 (*ACSB*, 8); occ. 10 Mar. 1430 (*APS*,ii,28); in poss. 19 Oct. 1433 (Reg.Supp.,289,fo.253), and prob. still in poss. 4 Feb. 1438 (*CPL*,vii,664); d. by 2 Oct. 1441 (v.inf.).

John Hectoris Macgilleon 1441 - 1456 x 1472.

Prov. when *I.archd.* on death of Angus 2 Oct. 1441 (*CPL*,ix, 225; cf. 152; *Diplom.Norv.*, xvii,no.562; cf. Eubel, *Hierarchia*,ii, 239); prob. son of Hector Maclean of Duart on Mull (cf. *RMS*,ii, no.2264); promised common services in person 6 Nov. 1441 (*ACSB*, 30); in poss. 11 Mar. 1456 (*CPL*,xi,261-2); d. before 3 Aug. 1472 (v.inf.).

Angus 1472 - 1479 x 1480.
    Prov. on death of unnamed predecessor 3 Aug. 1472 (*CPL*, xiii,871; cf. *ACSB*,68); cons. at Rome 27 Sept. 1472 (Brady, *Episcopal Succession*,i,p.xxii); occ. 3 Sept. 1479 (*CPL*,xiii,711); d. by c. Jan. 1480 (v.inf.).

John Campbell 1487 - 1510.
    Prov. when *Ar.archd.* on death of Angus after a seven year vacancy (PRO 31/9 - 52C/387-8). 18/19 Jan. 1487 (*CPL*,xiv,54; *Diplom.Norv.*, xvii B,344; Eubel, *Hierarchia*,ii,240n; *ACSB*,84; *SP*,ii,177; cf. Dowden, *Bishops*,290); ɔons. 21 Jan. x 13 Oct. 1487 (*Diplom.Norv.*,xvii B,344; *APS*,ii,175); granted abbey of Iona in commend for life 15 June 1499 (*Highland Papers*, iv,185-7); d. at Iona 14 June 1510 (*Taymouth Bk.*,115).

George Hepburn O.Tiron. 1510 - 1513.
    Crown nom. when abbot of Arbroath 21 June 1510 (*LP Henry VIII*,i,no.1112; *James IV Letters*, 173); prov. 10 Feb. 1511 *(Diplom. Norv.*,xvii B,345); temps. granted 11 May 1511 (*RSS*,i,no. 2250); cons. prob. by then, and certainly by 4 July 1511 (*Arb. Lib.*,ii,407); d. at Flodden 9 Sept. 1513 (*Adbn.Fasti*,116-17).

John Campbell   1514 - 1532.
Robert (?)   1529.
James Stewart   1529.
    Campbell had crown nom. before 18 Sept. 1514 (SRO,ADC,xxvi, fo.162; cf. *SP*,ii,180); prov. before 18 June 1515 (ibid.,xxvii,fo.15); but this was only a papal signature, which he never followed up with the necessary payments for a proper title to this see (*James V Letters*,162); therefore never cons.; occ. still as bp.- elect 3 Sept. 1528 (*APS*,ii,321); about this date he agreed to res. in favour of Farquhardsoun, but the relevant letters were said 1 Nov. 1529 not yet to have reached the pope, and he was then said by James V to regret his intention to res. (*James V Letters*, 163); res. his right in return for assignation of some of the revenues 17 May 1532, as conf. by pope 3/5 Nov. 1534 (Dowden, *Bishops*, 291;*Diplom.Norv.*,xvii B,346); d. after 7 Feb. 1554 (*ADCP*, 129).
    Robert occ. as bp.-elect 17 Nov. 1529 (SRO, ADC,xl,fo.141), but this is prob. an error for Campbell.
    Stewart, when abbot of Dryburgh, gets crown nom. to pope 1 Nov. 1529 (*James V Letters*, 162) unfruitfully.

Farquhard Farquhardsoun/Farquhardi Hectoris O.S.B. 1528-1544 x 15
    Expected to succ. to Campbell's right c.Sept.1528 (v.sup.); not y• effective 1 Nov. 1529 (*James V Letters*,163), when he was not the crown nominee; prov. on vacancy caused by death of Hepburn 17/21 Feb. 1530 (Eubel, *Hierarchia*,iii 302; Dowden, *Bishops*,291-2; *Diplom. Norv.*,xvii B,346; see *RSS*,iii,no.755 and *James V Letters*, 209 for best forms of his name); prob. cons. by time he was granted temps. 24 May 1530 (*RSS*,ii,no.685); agreed to allow Campbell to keep some of the revenues 17 May 1532 (v.sup.); crown lic. to res. to pope in favour of

Maclean, while retaining fruits and right of regress 18/19 Nov. 1544 (*RSS*, iii,no.977; *LP Henry VIII*, XIX,ii,no.640); perhaps d. before 28 July 1545 (v.inf.); see vacant 9 July 1546 (*RSS*,iii,no.1749); certainly d. before 7 Aug. 1547 (ibid.,no.2367).

Roderick/Rore MacLean (McClane, Machillienius) 1544 - 1552 x 1553.
Roderick/Rore Macallister 1545 - 1546.
Patrick MacLean (McClane) 1547 - 1552.

    Roderick MacLean, when *I.archd.*, gets crown nom. to pope as successor to Farquhardsoun 19 Nov. 1544 (v.sup.); occ. as bp.-elect 22 Feb. 1547 (*RSS*,iii,no.2164); but temps. granted to Patrick MacLean during vacancy 7 Aug. 1547 (v.inf.), and see was still vacant when he was expected to res. *I.archd.* 2 Mar. 1548; prov. bp. of Clonmacnois 30 Aug. 1549, though this was based on a false report of the death of the incumbent there (Brady, *Episcopal Succession*,i,246; *Diplom.Norv.*,xvii B, 347; Eubel, *Hierarchia*,iii,170), no mention being made of his right in this see; this prov. was not expedited, and he res. his right as elect of Clonmacnois when prov. Isles bp. (vacant on death of Farquhardsoun) 5 Mar. 1550 (*Diplom.Norv.*,xvii B,347-8; Brady, *Episcopal Succession*, i,163); d. 6 Dec. 1552 x 26 Nov. 1553 (*RSS*,iv,nos.1791,2253).

    Macallister regarded by upstart 'lord of the Isles' as bp.-elect 28 July 1545 (*Cal.State Papers* (Thorpe),i,53); claimed to have been el., when *Morvern dean*,Ar.dioc., by greater part of the country(though governor of Scotland had nom. another), and was seeking conf. from Henry VIII of England 13 Aug. 1545 (*State Papers Henry VIII*,iii,532; *LP Henry VIII*,XX,ii,no.120); still regarded in English eyes as bp.-elect 14 July 1546 (*Acts of Privy Council 1542-7,* 483) or even as bp. 25 Sept. 1546 (*State Papers Henry VIII*,iii,584).

    Patrick MacLean had been associated with the 'lord of the Isles' and Roderick Macallister 1545-6 (as above), but gets grant from governor of Scotland of temps. of see on death of Farquhard until such time as the pope makes prov. to it 7 Aug. 1547 (*RSS*,iii,no. 2367); still retained temps. of at least the attached abbacy of Iona (though temps. of bishopric are not further mentioned) when Roderick MacLean lit. against him before the Scottish council 31 July 1551 (*ADCP*,610); lost this lit. on the grounds that he had failed to prove prov. to this abbey 16 Jan. 1552 (ibid.,no.614); see also below.

Alexander Gordon 1553 - 1559, 1562 (?).
John Campbell 1557 (?), 1559 - 1560 x 1564.

    Gordon, when already abp. of Athens, granted temps. on Roderick MacLean's death 26 Nov. 1553 (*RSS*,iv,no.2253; see also no. 2536); occ. as elect of the Isles 12 Apr. 1554 (*APS*,ii,603); remained elect or postulate until as late as 10 Feb. 1559 and even (prob. wrongly) 8 Mar. 1562 (*Inchaff.Lib.*, 120,126); but did pay part of his financial obligations to the pope (*Mary of Lorraine Corresp.*, 385-6); trans.*Ga.bp.* 24 Mar. x 10 Apr. 1559.

    Campbell, when commendator of Ardchattan, occ. also as elect of the Isles 26 Dec. 1557 (*RMS*,iv,no.1240, where he has prob. been given a title which he obtained only later); see said to be vacant

8 Aug. 1559 (*RSS*,v,no.640); occ. as bp. of the Isles (prob. wrongly)
10 Nov. 1559 (*CSP Scot.*,i,262); occ. just as bp.-elect 10 May 1560
(ibid.,i,403) and 16 Aug. 1560 (*APS*,ii,605-6; cf. *CSP Scot.*,i,465);
but reverted to just commendator of Ardchattan by 10 June 1564
(*RMS*,v,no.691).

Patrick Maclean (McClane)	1565.
John Carswell	1565 - 1572.
Lauchlane MacLean (Makclane)	1567.

Patrick MacLean had had crown nom. to pope (perhaps since
1560, and not apparently in connection with his earlier tenure of
the temps.), but as elect of the Isles transferred his right to Carswell
in return for pension on or before 12 Jan. 1565 (*RSS*,v,no.1885).

Carswell gets crown grant of revenues of the see on res. of
Patrick MacLean 12 Jan. 1565 (ibid.); crown prov. 24 Mar. 1567
(ibid.,no.3373); d. 21 June x 20 Sept. 1572 (ibid.,vi,nos.1756,
1733); see prob. vacant by 11 Sept. 1572 (ibid.,no.1722).

Lauchlane MacLean suspected by 17 Apr. 1567 of getting
licence from queen to go to Rome to purchase this see; but swore
before council that this was not true, and renounced in favour of
Carswell any claim on this see which he might then have 21 May
1567 (*RPC*,i,511).

John Campbell 1572 - 1596 x 1605.
Lic. issued for an election on Carswell's death 20 Sept.1572
(*RSS*,vi,no.1733); crown conf. with mand. for cons. 22 Jan. 1573,
when also commendator of Ardchattan (*RMS*,iv,no.2116); prob.
cons. before temps. were restored 13 Oct. 1573 (*RSS*,vi,no.2817);
occ. 2 Sept. 1592 (*RPC*,v,10), and prob. still in poss. 15 Oct. 1596
(ibid.,322); d. before 12 Feb. 1605 (v.inf.).

Andrew Knox 1605 - 1618.
Crown prov. on Campbell's death 12 Feb. 1605 (Reg.Pres.,
iii,102v); crown nom. following el. for trans. to Raphoe 6/7 May
1610 (*CSP Ireland 1608-10,*nos.743,748); prob. cons. in Scotland
23 Jan./24 Feb. 1611 (Calderwood, *History,*vii,154); letters patent
for trans. 26 June 1611 (Cotton,*Fasti Ecclesiae Hiberniae,*iii,351);
retained see of the Isles until after 25 Aug. 1618 (Calderwood,
*History,*vii,304; *RPC,*xi,431); granted Irish letters of denization 22
Sept. 1619 (Cotton,*Fasti,*iii,351).

Thomas Knox 1619 - 1627 x 1628.
Crown prov. when *I.dean* 24 Feb. 1619 (Reg.Pres.,v,19); occ.
1 Nov.1627 (*HMC* 3,*4th R.*, 480); d. by 3 Apr. 1628 (v.inf.).

John Leslie 1628 - 1633.
Crown nom. for el. 3 Apr. 1628 (*Stirling's Register,*i,269);
crown prov. after el. 17 Aug. 1628 (*RMS,*viii,no.1305; RSS,ci.fo.30);
crown nom. for appointment to see of Raphoe in addition to this
see before 11 July 1631 (*CSP Ireland 1625-32,*nos.1991,2035);
but letters patent for trans. to Raphoe by itself followed with letters
of denization 1 June 1633 (Cotton,*Fasti Ecclesiae Hiberniae,*iii,351).

Neil Campbell 1633 - 1638.

Crown nom. for el. 17 Oct. 1633 (*Coll. de Rebus Alban.*,i,184-5); el. 17 Dec. 1633 (SRO, Misc.Ecclesiastical Docs.,no.79); crown prov. 21 Jan. 1634 (*RMS*,ix,no.17); depriv. 13 Dec. 1638 (Peterkin,*Records*, i,27-28); d. 17 Nov. 1643 x 29 Apr. 1647 (*Clan Campbell*, vii,305; Glas.Tests.).

CHAPTER OF THE ISLES

The right to elect the bp. was held by monks of Furness abbey, Lancashire from grant of Olaf I king of Man 1134 (v.sup.), as ultimately conf. by Pope Innocent IV 1244 (*Chron.Man*,ii,309,no.19; *Diplom.Norv.*,i,no. 28); right was only sometimes effectively exercised, and was finally rejected by King Alexander III of Scotland in 1275 (*SAEC*,381-2).

Bp.Simon (1226-48) began to build the cathedral of St German at Peel, Isle of Man, which existed by 1231 (*SHR*,viii,259); but the chapter of secular clergy who are found acting in episcopal elections from about the same time onwards was apparently of a synodal rather than a collegiate nature. (The archd. is the only dignitary known then.) In the elections of 1348-9 and 1374 it appears to have been the clergy of Man alone who formed this chapter.

A separatist trend in the Hebrides is already observable rather earlier 1326 x 1331, when a group of canons of Snizort could elect a bp. along with the clergy of Skye; perhaps this Snizort community had had a continuous existence from the days of a bp. of Skye in the late 11th century; the remains of a substantial 'early medieval structure' are still to be seen on the island in the river Snizort at Skeabost Bridge which is the site of the older churches of Snizort (*RCAHM* [Outer Hebrides, Skye and Small Isles] 192-3); certainly the clergy there provided a cathedral chapter of some sort for the bishops of Sodor in Scotland after the split of 1387, though by 1433 Bp. Angus de Insulis was getting papal approval for a plan to move his cathedral from Snizort ('Suusperdy'; cf. forms of name given in *OPS*,ii,354) to some other unnamed place, with the intention of creating a community of twelve prebendaries (*RSCHS*,xiv, 23-24, quoting Reg.Supp.,289,fo. 253); two ordinary prebends have been traced thereafter - Strath on Skye 1450 and Kingarth on Bute 1463 (cf. Cowan, *Parishes,* 112,190); but still the archd. is the only dignity known.

Request was made by crown to pope that Iona/Icolmkill abbey should be erected as the see of this bp. until the principal kirk on the Isle of Man should be recovered from the English 1 Apr. 1498 (*RSS,* i,no.184); but this was not successful, and the successive bishops from 1499 merely held this abbey in commend (*Highland Papers*,iv,168-75); there is no evidence that the Benedictine monks of Iona ever formed a cathedral chapter (*MRHS,*172; cf. 52); indeed a Sodor chanc. appears as a secular dignity by 1541 in addition to the archd. During vacancy in see 1547-8 a 'chapter of Icolmkill' and a 'cathedral church of Sodor' were said to exist (*RSS*,iii,nos.2370, 2744; cf. 2743); no unusual features in the chapter of this dioc. were noted at convention

of Leith 16 Jan. 1572 -it was certainly not then treated as a chapter of regular clergy - when arrangements were made for the participation of the old cathedral chapters in elections of reformed bishops (*BUK*,i, 221); a formal lic. to elect a bp. was sent to 'dean and chapter of cathedral of Sodor' 20 Sept. 1572 (*RSS*,vi,no.1733; cf. 1756), and they performed their task before 22 Jan. 1573 (*RMS*,iv,no.2116); it seems likely that a Sodor dean. must have existed before the Reformation, but there is no clear proof of this.

    Chapter was reconstituted June 1617 with a dean and subdean as the only dignitaries among its members (*APS*,iv,554-5); and by 1635 the old abbey of Icolmkill was in use as the cathedral of the see (*Coll. de Rebus Alban.*,187-8).

DEANS OF THE ISLES

First known date: 1572.
    Prebend: ch. of Soroby on Tiree and vic. of Iona in 1617 (*APS*, iv,554-5).

Note: dean acted with chapter in electing a bp. 20 Sept. 1572 x 22 Jan. 1573 (v.sup.), and then this bp. acted along with 'dean and chapter of Iona' 5 June 1576 (*HMC* 3, *4th R.*,476); no names known.

Thomas Knox 1617 - 1619.
    Crown pres. 4 Aug. 1617 (Reg.Pres.,v,fo.4); crown prov. as *I.bp.* 24 Feb. 1619.

Note: Bp. Thomas Knox acted with consent of unnamed dean and Chapter 1 Nov. 1627 (*HMC* 3,*4th R.*,480).

Farquhar Fraser 1633 - 1666.
    Occ. 17 Dec. 1633 (SRO, Misc. Ecclesiastical Docs.,no.79); occ.1 Aug. 1635 (SRO, Lord Macdonald,158/1,s.d.) and again after Restoration 21 Aug. 1662 (*Laing Chrs.*,no.2561) and 4 July 1666 (Part.Reg.Sasines Inverness, series 2,iii,fo.212).

CHANCELLORS OF THE ISLES

First known date: 1541.
    Prebend: unknown.

James Carmure/Carmuyr 1541, 1542 (?)
    Occ. as chanc. of Sodor of the Isles 3 Feb. 1541 (*SHR*,vii,362); occ. as canon of Sodor 29 July 1541 (Vatican Archives, Brev.Lat., 32, fo.483v); perhaps same as unnamed chanc. of Sodor or the Isles found 5 May 1542 (ibid.,33,fo.107).

SUBDEANS OF THE ISLES

First known date: erected June 1617 (v.sup.).
    Prebend: ch. of Rothesay on Bute in 1617 (*APS*,iv,554-5).

Patrick Stewart 1620 - 1635.
    Occ. 24 June 1620 (Part. Reg.Sasines Argyll,i,fo.205) and 1 Aug.
1635 (SRO, Lord Macdonald,158/1,s.d.).

ARCHDEACONS OF MAN : SODOR : THE ISLES

First known dates: Man   :   1188 x 1190 (?).
                      Sodor   :   1320.
                      The Isles :   1372.
    Prebend: ch. of Kirk Andreas in Man: 'from some unknown date'
(A.Ashley, *Church in the Isle of Man*, 16, no source quoted); not known
what happened after division of diocese.

Deremod/Dermicius (Man) 1188 x 1190 (?), 1217 x 1219.
    Occ. as Deremod the archd. 1188 x 1190 (?) and as Deremod
archd. of Man 1217 x 1219 (*Furness Coucher Bk.*,ii,711-12); occ. as
Deremicius the archd. 1187 x 1226 (*St Bees Reg.*,74).

Laurence (Man) 1246 - 1248 x 1249.
    In poss. 1 June 1246 (*CPL*,i,226); el. *I.bp.* 1248, but d. uncons.
Oct./Nov. 1248.

Dompnald 1253 x 1265.
    Occ. 3 May, 1253 x 1265 (*Mon.Ins.Man.*,ii,89-92).

Makaboy 1270.
    Occ. 1270 (Manx Soc.,vol.xxix,92,no source given).

A. (Man) 1302.
    Occ. 7 Feb. 1302 (*St Bees Reg.*, 77); cf. Alan who became *I.bp.*
by 26 Mar. 1305.

Cormac (Sodor) 1320.
    Occ. 17 July 1320 (*Diplom.Norv.*,ix,no.86); perhaps father of
(or same as) Cormac Cormacii el. *I.bp.* 1326 x 1331.

John Demester (Man) 1349.
    In poss. 14 June 1349 (*CPP*,i,169).

Nigel Mauricii (Isles) x 1372.
    Held it at death before 8 Nov. 1372 (v.inf.).

Note: from this date only those archdeacons who belonged to the
Scottish see of the Isles are noted here.

Bean Johannis (Sodor)   1372 - 1396.

Nigel Suari/Yvari   (Sodor) x 1396 - 1408.
Bean Macuilquen   (Sodor)   1407.
Cristine Macdonaillelygh/Donaldiyleich/Donaldi Elich (Sodor) 1408.
Gilbert Macdowell (Macduyl)   (Sodor) x 1416.
John de Carrick   (Sodor)   1416.
      Johannis gets prov. on death of Mauricii 8 Nov. 1372 (Reg.Av.,
183,fo.343v); new prov., when not in poss., 11 Dec. 1396, expedited
10/13 April 1397 (ibid.,301,fos.199-199v); cf. *Ar.dean.*
      Suari had some papal right to this ben. when in poss. 11 Dec.
1396 (ibid.); still in poss. 3 May 1408 (v.inf.).
      Macuilquen had coll. from ord. before 6 Apr. 1407 (Reg.Av.,
327,fos.178-178v).
      Macdonaillelygh gets *com.priv.* against Suari 3 May 1408 (ibid.,
329,fos.418-419); retained it until death before 2 Aug. 1441 (v.inf.);
cf. Macdowell below.
      Macdowell held it at death before 20 Aug. 1416 (v.inf.); cf.
Macdonaillelygh above.
      Carrick gets prov. on Macdowell's death 20 Aug. 1416 (*CPP*,
i,605-6); cf. Hectoris below.

John Hectoris Macgilleon (Sodor) 1441.
      In poss. when gets new prov. on death of Macdonaillelygh 2 Aug.
1441 (Reg.Supp.,375,fo.85v); cf. Carrick above; prov. *I.bp.* 2 Oct.
1441; granted rehabilitation regarding this ben 18 Nov. 1441 (*ACSB*,
130).

Andrew de Dunoon (Dunovin) (Sodor) 1441 - 1456 x 1457.
Nigel Cormacii (Sodor)   1455.
Angus de Insulis/Johannis (Sodor)   1456;
      Dunoon prov. in exp. of elevation of Hectoris 26 Aug. 1441
(Reg.Supp.,376, fo.176v); prov. on el. of Hectoris 22 Nov. 1441 (*CPL*,
ix,152); occ. 9 Aug. 1442 (SRO, Transcripts Misc.Chrs.,s.d. 15 Aug.
1458); still in poss. 28 June 1456 (*CPL*,xi,110); d. before 28 Apr.
1457 (v.inf.).
      Cormacii prov. on report of Dunoon's death 12 June 1455
(Reg.Supp.,482,fo.11).
      Insulis gets *com.priv.* against Dunoon 6 Apr. 1456 (*CPL*,xi,39-
40); res. his right without poss 28 June 1456 (ibid.,109-10).

Gilbert Smerles (Smeriles, Sineres) (Sodor) 1457 - 1460.
James Borthwick   (Sodor) 1457.
Duncan   (Isles) 1461 - 1462.
Christopher Bricii/Batii   (Sodor) 1463.
      Smerles prov. on Duncan's death 28 Apr. 1457 (Reg.Supp.,499,
fo.104v); is to res. in Borthwick's favour 21 May 1457 (v.inf.); seeks
expedition of letters delayed because of illness 15 June 1460, but
never had poss. (Reg.Supp.,532,fo.171v; 552,fo.158).
      Borthwick prov. on res. of Smerles 21 May 1457 (ibid.,499,
fo.270v).
      Duncan occ. 9 Oct. 1461 and 13 Feb. 1462 (*Rot.Scot.*,ii,407),
having prob. had ord. coll. and local poss.

Bricii prov. on Duncan's death 7/25 June 1463 (Reg.Supp.,563,fo. 105v; *CPL*,xi,482); promised annates 2 July 1463 (*ACSB*,146).

Gilbert Wright (Sodor) 1472.
In poss. 22 Dec. 1472 (*CPL*,xiii,324).

Nigel MacIlvride (McYlwryd, Makkilbreid) (Sodor) 1476 - 1479.
Occ. 20 Aug. 1476 and 6 Mar. 1479 (*RMS*,ii,nos. 1277, 1449).

Thomas Clerk (Sodor) 1501.
As archd. prov. Killala bp. 3 June 1501 (PRO 31/10 - 14/73-74; cf. *HBC*,350); perhaps in the English succession.

Thomas Fleming (Sodor) x 1516.
Held it at death before 5 Oct. 1516 (v.inf.).

Richard Lawson (Sodor) 1516 - 1541.
Crown pres. on Fleming's death 5 Oct. 1516 (*RSS*,i,no.2810); occ. 25 June 1541 (*Clan Campbell*,viii,13).

Roderick/Rore MacLean (McClane) (Sodor/Isles) 1544 - 1546 x 1548.
Occ. as Sodor archd. 18 Nov. 1544 (*RSS*,iii,no.977); occ. as Isles archd. 1546 (*OPS*,ii,133,377); regarded as *I.bp.elect* by 22 Feb. 1547; still in poss. 2 Mar. 1548 (v.inf.).

Archibald Munro (Sodor) 1548.
Crown pres. in exp. of dem. of MacLean 2 Mar. 1548 (*RSS*,iii, no.2660); perhaps error for Donald Munro (cf. Monro,*Western Isles*, 16).

Donald Munro (Isles/Sodor) 1553 - 1563 x 1584.
Occ. as Isles archd. 11 Sept. 1553 (SRO, Richmond & Gordon, 13/7/21; cf. *Spalding Misc.*,iv,222-3 and *SHR*,xxiv,173, where name is misread); occ. as Sodor archd. 25 Jan. 1563 (*RMS*,iv,nos.1455-6); d. before 11 Nov. 1584 (SRO, Comm.Edin.Decreets,xiv, s.d.).

Donald Carswell(Isles) x 1592.
Held it at death before 4 Jan. 1592 (v.inf.).

Alexander Campbell (Isles) 1592.
Crown pres. on Carswell's death 4 Jan. 1492 (RSS,1xiii,fo.108).

Patrick Stewart (Isles) 1620.
Occ. 24 Jan. 1620 (Part.Reg.Sasines Argyll,i,fo.205).

DEANS OF CHRISTIANITY

DEANS OF BUTE

First known date: 1514.

Finlay Lennox (Lenax) 1514.
Occ. 11 July 1514 (*HMC* 2, *3rd R.,* 403).

DEANS OF MULL

First known date: 1532.

Brinus 1532.
    Occ. as vic. of Iona 8 Aug. 1532 (*Cawdor Bk.*,158).

Fingonius Makmullen 1573.
    Occ. 1573 (*OPS*,ii,297).

OFFICIALS

OFFICIALS WITH GENERAL AUTHORITY

OFFICIALS OF MAN : SODOR : THE ISLES

First known date: Man   :   1219.
                     Sodor   :   1235 x 1241.
                     The Isles   :   1510.

M. (Man) 1219.
    In office 22 Sept. 1219 (*CPL*,i,69).

J. (Sodor) 1235 x 1241.
    In office 1235 x 1241 (*Reg.Gregoire IX*,iii,534).

Alexander MacLeod (Makloid) (Isles) 1510.
    Occ. 18 May and 21 Oct. 1510 (*RSS*,i,nos.2069,2142).

OFFICIALS WITH LIMITED AUTHORITY

OFFICIALS OF BUTE AND ARRAN

First known date: 1502.

Robert Abernethy 1502.
    Occ. as rector of Rothesay 18 Nov. 1502 (*Glas.Friars*,206).

OFFICIALS OF MULL

First known date: 1422.

Adam 1442.
    Occ. 9 Aug. 1442 (SRO, Transcripts Misc.Chrs.,s.d.15 Aug.1458).

COMMISSARIES

COMMISSARIES OF IONA

First known date: 16 Apr. 1573 (*Coll. de Rebus Alban.*, 7).

No names known.

COMMISSARIES OF BUTE AND ARRAN

First known date: 18 Dec. 1541 (SRO, ADC & S,xiv, fo.64v).

No names known.

COMMISSARIES OF SKYE

First known date: 16 Apr. 1573 (*Coll. de Rebus Alban.*, 7).

No names known.

MORAY DIOCESE

BISHOPS OF MORAY

First known date: c. 1114 or c. 1120.
    This see was directly subject to the pope until placed under metropolitan authority of St Andrews 17 Aug. 1472 (*Vet.Mon.*,no.852).

Gregory c. 1114 or c. 1120 - 1127 x 1131 (?).
    Occ. just as 'bishop' c.1114 if charter evidence is genuine (*Scone Liber*, no. 1; cf. *ESC*, 280-3; cf. also *Trans.Royal Hist.Soc.*, 5th series, iii,83, where date c. 1120 is suggested); occ. with style 'bishop of Moray' 25 Dec. 1123 x 25 Apr. 1124 (*Scone Liber,* no.4) and 1127 x 1131? (*Dunf.Reg.,* 4; cf. *ES*,ii,149); cf. Gregory *Dk.bp.*

William 1152 x 1153 - 1162.
    Occ. 1152 x 24 May 1153 (*St A.Lib.,* 184); d. 24 Jan. 1162 (*Chron. Holyrood,* 139; cf. 135-6).

Felix 1166 x 1171.
    See vacant 1164 (*Chron.Bower*,i,461); occ. 1166 x 1171 (Dowden, *Bishops,* 145,n.2).

Simon de Tosny (Tonei, Toeni) O.Cist. 1171 - 1184.
    El. 1171 (*Chron.Melrose,* 39); cons. at St Andrews 23 Jan. 1172 (ibid.,40); d. 17 Sept. 1184 (ibid.,44).

Richard de Lincoln 1187 - 1203.
    El. just as 'Richard' when a royal clerk 1 Mar. 1187 (ibid.,45); prob. same as the Richard de Lincoln found earlier as a royal clerk (suggestion of G.W.S. Barrow: e.g. *Arb.Lib.*,i, nos. 7, 18, 30, 54); cons. at St Andrews 15 Mar. 1187 (*Chron.Melrose,* 45); d. 1203 (ibid., 51).

Brice de Douglas O.Tiron. 1203 - 1222.
    Succ. Bp. Richard when prior of Lesmahagow 1203 (ibid.); his brothers Archibald and Henry at any rate certainly used the surname 'de Douglas' (e.g. *Moray Reg.,* nos. 74, 120; cf. *SP*,iii,134-5) and so prob. did he; d. 1222 (*Chron. Melrose,* 75).

Andrew de Moray (Moravia) 1222 - 1242.
    Succ. Bp. Brice 1222 (ibid.); prob. same as earlier *M.chanc.*; cons. 12 May 1223 x 10 Apr. 1224 (*Moray Reg.,* 63-64); d. 18 Sept. x 17 Dec. 1242 (*Abdn.Reg.*,i,16; *Chron.Melrose,* 90).

Simon (de Gunby ?) 1244 - 1251.
    El. when *M.dean* (q.v. for surname) and got papal mand. for conf. and cons. 3 Mar. 1244 (*CPL*,i,207); occ. 4 Feb. 1249 (*Moray Reg.,*no. 214; *Arb.Lib.*,i,no.237); d. 1251 (*Moray Reg.,* 359).

Radulf   c. 1252.
Archibald   1253 - 1298.
    Radulf el. when canon of Lincoln c. 1252 (*SAEC*, 369); not known to have had conf. or cons.; perhaps same as the Radulf canon of Moray who took leading place among witnesses of act of Bp. Simon (also prob. from Lincoln dioc.) 4 Feb. 1249 quoted above.
    Archibald cons. 1253 (*Moray Reg.,*359); occ. 22 Nov. 1253 (ibid., 116-17); prob. same as *M.dean* found earlier in 1249; d. 9 Dec. 1298 (ibid.,359).

David de Moray (Moravia) 1299 - 1326.
    Cons. at Anagni in Italy 28 June 1299 (ibid.); had been el. when
M.canon on death of Bp. Archibald, and got papal prov. following
cons. at curia 30 June 1299 (*Vet.Mon.*, no.364); d. 9 Jan. 1326
(*Moray Reg.*, 359; but note that his name appears as witness to a royal
chr. dated 10 Jan. 1326 - see *Melr.Lib.*, ii,328).

John de Pilmuir 1326 - 1362.
    Cons. at Avignon 30 Mar. 1326 (*Moray Reg.*, 359-60); said in
same source to have been *R.bp.-elect*; but this is prob. an error for
R.canon (cf. Eubel, *Hierarchia*,i,424n), which was his status mentioned
in papal mand. of prov. on Moray's death 31 Mar. 1326 (*Vet.Mon.*,
no.460); d. at Spynie near Elgin 28 Sept. 1362 (*Moray Reg.*, 360).

Alexander Bur 1362 - 1397.
    Said to have been el. on death of Pilmuir (*Chron.Bower*,ii,366);
but this is not clear from his mand. of prov., when *M.archd.*, 23 Dec.
1362 (*Vet.Mon.*,no.653); not yet cons. at that time (cf. *Moray Reg.*,
360, which mentions cons. at Avignon 17 Dec. 1362; cf. Dowden,
Bishops,153,n.2); cons. by pope 4/9 Jan x 7 Feb. 1363 (*CPP*,i,394,
397,401); d. at Spynie near Elgin 15 May 1397 (*Moray Reg.*,360).

William de Spynie 1397 - 1406.
    El when *Ab.dean* and *M.prec.*, and went to curia at Avignon for
prov. 1 Sept. 1397 and cons. 16 Sept., as announced by Pope
Benedict XIII to King Robert III 28 Sept. 1397 (*Moray Reg.*, 207,327,
360; Eubel, *Hierarchia*,i,350); granted temps. 16 Jan. and 3 May 1398
(*Moray Reg.*,207-8); d. at Elgin 2 Aug. 1406 (ibid.,360).

John de Innes 1407 - 1414.
    Prov. perhaps after el., when *R.dean*, 12 Jan. 1407 (Eubel,
Hierarchia,i,350); said to have been cons. at Avignon 23 Jan. 1407
(*Moray Reg.*,360), but prob. the itinerant curia of Benedict XIII in
Italy is meant; d. at Elgin 25 Apr. 1414 (ibid.).

Henry de Lichton 1414 - 1422.
    Present as M.canon when chapter met to elect successor to
Innes 18 May 1414 (ibid.,216-17); presumably el. then; prov. before
4 Mar. 1415 (*CPP*,i,602) and cons. at curia of Benedict XIII at
Valencia in Aragon 8 Mar. 1415 (*Moray Reg.*,360); trans. to *Ab.bp.*
1/3 Apr. 1422.

Columba de Dunbar 1422 - 1435.
    Prov., when *St A.archd. Lothian* and *Dunbar dean*, 3 Apr. 1422
(Eubel, *Hierarchia*,i,350; cf. *CSSR*,i,294). papal faculty for cons.
15 Dec. 1422 (*CPL*,vii,254); cons. 12 Feb. x 10 Oct. 1423 (*ACSB*,5;
HMC 44, *Drumlanrig*,i,33); d. at Spynie near Elgin 1435 (*Moray Reg.*,
360), before 7 Nov. (v.inf.).

John Wincester 1435 - 1460.
    El., when *Lincluden prov.* and M.canon, by 7 Nov. 1435
(*ACSB*,22); prov. on death of Dunbar 23 Mar. 1436 (*CPL*,viii,612-13);
cons. at Cambuskenneth Abbey 9 May 1437 (*Moray Reg.*, 360); d.

22 Apr. 1460 (*The Cathedral Kirk of Moray* (Ministry of Works, 1950 edn.),15, quoting tomb).

James Stewart 1460 - 1462.
    Prov. when *M.dean* 19 May 1460 (Eubel, *Hierarchia*,ii,196; *ACSB,* 50); cons. after 25 Oct. 1460 (*CPL*,xii,120); did not yet have temps. 11 Nov. 1460 (*ER*,vii,16); occ. as consecrated bp. 12 Dec. 1460 (*Moray Reg.*, 255); res. in curia in favour of his brother David 21 June 1462 (v.inf.); d. 5 Aug. 1466 (*Kinloss Recs.*, 7).

David Stewart 1462 - 1476.
    Prov. when M.canon on res. of James Stewart 21 June 1462 (*CPL*,xi,452); the two were prob. brothers (*Kinloss Recs.*, 7); had taken oath of fealty to pope at curia by 27 July 1462 when granted faculty for cons. (*Vet.Mon.*, no.823; cf. no. 820); cons. after 25 June 1463 (Dowden,*Bishops*,162) and prob. before 10 Dec. 1463 (*ACSB,* 54); occ. 18 July 1475 (Stevenson & Wood, *Seals*,i,154); d. 1476 (*Kinloss Recs.*, 7).

William Tulloch 1477 - 1482.
    Trans. from *O.bp.* on Bp. David's death 12 Feb. 1477 (*Diplom. Norv.*, xvii, nos. 705-6; *CPL*,xiii,556); occ. 23 Mar. 1482 (*ADA*,96); apparently occ. 18 Apr. 1482 (*RMS*,ii,no.1510), but said to have d. 14 Apr. 1482 (*HBC*, 296, no source cited).

Andrew Stewart 1482 - 1501.
    El. on Tulloch's death, when *M.dean*, *G.subd.* and *Lincluden prov.*, and then got papal prov. 12 Aug. 1482 (*CPL*,xiii,797-8; *ACSB*,77); while 'elect confirmed' had hopes of succeeding to *St A.abp.* 8 Nov. 1482 x 16 Mar. 1483; cons. after 22 Dec. 1485, when spiritualities of see were still vacant (*Arb.Lib.*,ii,238-9) and before 24 Oct. 1487 (*Moray Reg.*,257; cf. Dowden, *Bishops*, 164,n.2, citing *RMS*,ii,no.1581); d. 29 Sept. 1501 (*Moray Reg.*, p.xv, quoting Kalendar of Fearn).

Andrew Forman 1501 - 1514 x 1516.
    Postulated before 8 Oct. 1501 (*RMS*,ii,no.2602); prov. when commendator of May/Pittenweem 26 Nov. 1501 (Brady, *Episcopal Succession*,i,135; Eubel, *Hierarchia*,ii,196); occ. 24 Jan. 1502 (*CDS,* iv,nos. 1680-1); prov. additionally to Bourges abp. in France 15 July 1513 (ibid.,iii,135); granted pallium 3 Aug. 1513 (ibid.); promised services to retain M.bp. 22 Dec. 1513 (Brady, op.cit., 136); pope proposed his trans. to *St A.abp.* 11 Apr. 1514 and issued mand. of trans. 13 Nov. 1514, which became effective c. 4 Feb. 1516.

James Hepburn 1516 - 1524.
    El. before 12 Feb. 1516 (SRO, ADC,xxvii, fo.170v) on nom. of Governor Albany (Lesley, *History,* 106); prov. 14 May 1516 (Eubel, *Hierarchia*,iii,250; Dowden, *Bishops,* 168; cf. *St A.Form.*, i,168-9); granted temps. 28 Aug. 1516 (*RSS*,i,no.2803); occ. 19 Apr. 1524 (*Moray Reg.*, 401); d. a few days before 11 Nov. 1524 (SRO, ADC & S, vi, fo.207).

Robert Shaw O. Clun. 1525 - 1527.

Crown nom. to pope on Hepburn's death, when abbot of Paisley, 11 Jan. 1525 (*Vet.Mon.*, no.947; *James V Letters*,113; cf. 116); styled M.bp. 5 Feb. 1525 (*Arb.Lib.*,ii,444); prov. 17 May 1525 (Eubel, *Hierarchia*,iii,250; cf. Dowden, *Bishops*, 169); prob. cons. before granted temps. c. Sept. 1525 (*RSS*,i,no.3352); certainly cons. by 29 Oct. 1525 (*Moray Reg.*, 371); occ. 15 Jan. 1527 (ibid.,254); d. before Nov. 1527, when see is said to be vacant (SRO, ADC,xxxviii,fo.30).

Alexander Douglas   1528.
Alexander Stewart   1529 - 1537.

Douglas had crown nom. to pope (when earl of Angus was in control) on death of Shaw some time before 26 Apr. 1528 when James V wrote to Wolsey about him and the duke of Albany was opposing his appointment at the curia (Fraser, *Douglas*,iv,16; *LP Henry VIII*, IV,ii,no.4205); Henry VIII wrote pope in his support 31 May 1528 (*Vet.Mon.*,no.995; *James V Letters*, 145); project was presumably given up with fall of Angus in latter part of 1528 (cf. Dowden, *Bishops*, 170,n.1).

Stewart had crown nom. when *B.dean* and then got papal prov. 13 Sept. 1529 (Brady, *Episcopal Succession*,i,136-7); see still vacant 9 Dec. 1529 (Dowden, *Bishops*,170); and perhaps he was not cons. until soon before 16 Apr. 1532 when he received oaths of obedience from his chapter at Elgin (*Moray Reg.*, 373-4); d. 19 Dec. 1537 (*RSS*,ii,no.2493; cf. *Taymouth Bk.*, 121, which says 21 Dec.).

Patrick Hepburn O.S.A. 1538 - 1573.

Crown nom. to pope on Stewart's death when prior of St Andrews 1 Mar. 1538 (*James V Letters*, 342-3; cf. 345); got prov. 14 June 1538 (Brady, *Episcopal Succession*,i,137; Eubel, *Hierarchia*,iii,250); granted temps 24 Nov. 1538 (*RSS*,ii,no.2772); occ. 8 Oct. 1570 (*Scone Liber*,212); d. before 10 July 1573 (SRO, Acts and Decreets, 1,fo.274); said to have d. 20 June 1573 (Keith, *Bishops*, 150, source now lost).

George Douglas 1573 - 1589.

Lic. to elect issued on Hepburn's death with no name mentioned 12 Aug. 1573 (*RSS*,vi,no.2070); el. by chapter 20-22 Dec. 1573 (Calderwood, *History*,iii,330-1); crown conf. with mand. for cons. 5 Feb. 1574 (*RSS*,vi,no.2309); granted temps. 23 Mar. 1574 (ibid.,no. 2407); d. 28 Dec. 1589 (RSS, 1x, fo.103).

Note: after crown annexation of temps. of benefices 29 July 1587 (*APS*,iii,431 ff.), temps. of this see were largely granted to Alexander Lindsay (first Lord Spynie) 6 May 1590 and 17 Apr. 1593 (*RMS*,v,nos.1727, 2280); but he surrendered them to crown by arrangement with Bp. Alexander Douglas c. 17 Dec. 1605 (*Abbotsford Misc.*,i,214; cf. *Original Letters*,ii,277-8; *SP*,viii, 95-100).

Alexander Douglas 1602 - 1623.

Crown prov. 30 Nov. 1602 (RSS, lxxiii, fo.133); cons. at Edinburgh 15 Mar. 1611 (*Original Letters*,i, 265); d. 9/11 May 1623 (Forbes, *Kalendars*, p.xxix; cf. J.B. Craven, *History of Episcopal Church in Diocese of Moray*, 46, quoting tombstone).

John Guthrie 1623 - 1638.

Lic. to elect issued 28 June 1623 (RSS, xciii,fo.371); crown nom. 31 July 1623 (SRO,Guthrie, 19/3); crown prov. 16 Aug. 1623 (RSS,xcv,fo.45); cons. by 13 Oct. 1623 (Calderwood, *History*,vii, 580); depriv. 13 Dec. 1638 (Peterkin, *Records*,i,27-28); said to have d. 23 Aug. 1649 (Craven, *Church in Moray*, 56, no source cited).

CHAPTER OF MORAY

Before appointment of Bp. Brice de Douglas in 1203 the earlier bishops of Moray are said to have had no fixed see, but to have used as best suited them one of the three churches of Birnie, Spynie and Kineddar, all of which are in the vicinity of Elgin (*Moray Reg.*, 40, no. 46).

In terms of papal mand. of 7 Apr. 1206 (ibid.,no.45) Bp. Douglas established his see with a community of eight canons at Spynie Mar. 1207 x June 1208 (ibid.,no.46; cf.47).

In terms of papal mand. of 10 Apr. 1224 (ibid.,no.57; *Vet. Mon.*, no.52) Bp. Andrew de Moray transferred the see to Elgin 19 July 1224 (*Moray Reg.*, nos. 26, 58), and enlarged the chapter of canons to eighteen 5 May 1226 (ibid.,no.69) and to twenty-three before the end of his episcopate in 1242 (ibid.,no.81).

EARLY DEANS IN MORAY

Brice 1194 x c. 1197, 1197 x 1203.

Occ. c. 1197 (*Moray Reg.*,38-39, 131), having prob. become dean since 1194 x (ibid.,12); occ. 1197 x 1203 (ibid.,456, where names of archd. and dean are transposed).

DEANS OF MORAY

First known date: 1207 x 1208 (*Moray Reg.*,41).

Prebend: ch. of Auldearn with chapel of Invernairn in 1207 x 1208 (*Moray Reg.*, 41; Cowan, *Parishes*,11).

Freskin (de Douglas ?) 1207 x 1211 - 1226.

Occ. 1207 x 1211 (*Arb.Lib.*,i,141); occ. 19 June 1226 (*Moray Reg.*,78).

Hugh (de Douglas ?) 1226 x 1230.

Occ. 19 June 1225 x 4 Sept. 1230 (ibid.,110); prob. obtained it before 30 June 1228 (see *M.archd.*).

Simon (de Gunby ?) 1230 - 1244.

Occ. 4 Sept. 1230 (*Moray Reg.*,107, misdated 1240; cf. *Beauly Chrs.*, 33 where 'Simon' is miscopied as 'Duncan'); occ. 26 July 1232 (*Moray Reg.*,88); mand. for conf. as *M.bp.* 3 Mar. 1244.

Note: surnames suggested above belong to chapter personnel who appear to be identical with the men of the same christian names promoted to the deanery.

Archibald 1249 - 1253.
Occ. 4 Feb. and 20 Mar. 1249 (ibid.,277,114); prob. same as Archibald who became *M. bp.*, being cons. 1253, by 22 Nov.

Andrew de Dunn   1252 x 1253.
Nicholas de Hedon   1253 x 1254.
Dunn el., presumably on elevation of Archibald, but lost lit. with Hedon by 19 Dec. 1253 (v.inf.).
Hedon had earlier exp. grace (*CPL*,i,295, 325) and won sentence in his favour after lit. with Dunn 19 Dec. 1253 (*Reg. Innocent IV*, iii,362); occ. 22 June 1254 (*Arb.Lib.*,i,323).

William de Dunn 1260 or 1263 - 1275.
Occ. 11 Apr. 1260 or 13 Apr. 1263 (*Moray Reg.*,138) and 10 Jan. 1275 (*Beauly Chrs.*,57).

Walter Herok 1296 - 1329.
Occ. 28 Aug. 1296 (*CDS*,ii,211); occ. 23 Mar. 1310 (*Moray Reg.*, 148-9); still in poss. 15 Mar. 1329 (*CPL*,ii,288); el. *Ab.bp.* but d. uncons. before 21 Aug. 1329 (*Vet.Mon.*,245-6).

Andrew de Hirdmaniston 1329.
Prov. 19 Sept. 1329 (*CPL*,ii,298).

John Painter x 1349.
Held it at death before 8 Nov. 1349 (v.inf.).

William de Pilmuir 1349 - 1358 x 1368.
Had coll. by ord. on Painter's death and gets conf. 8 Nov. 1349 (*CPL*,iii,335); occ. 2 May 1358 (*Dunf.Reg.*,266-7). d. before 11 Dec. 1368 (v.inf.).

Thomas de Harcars 1368.
Prov. on Pilmuir's death 11 Dec. 1368 (Collect.,14,fo.175).

Alexander de Kylwos (Frulquhous) 1368 x 1370 - 1371.
Had prov. and poss. 1368 x 19 Dec. 1370 (Reg.Av., 176, fo.55v; cf. *R.dean);* prov. *R.bp.* 9 May 1371.

Robert de Sinclair   1371 - 1391.
Walter Trail   1383.
Sinclair prov. 28 May 1371 (Reg.Av.,176, fo.248v); occ. 18 July 1378 (*Moray Reg.*,182-3); prov. *O.bp.* 27 Jan. 1384; disp. to retain this ben. with this see 11 Feb. 1384 (*Diplom.Norv.*,xvii, no.163); trans. *Dk.bp.* 1 Feb. 1391.
Trail prov. 28 Nov. 1383 (Reg.Av.,238,fos. 13,61) unfruitfully.

John de Douglas   1391 - 1424 x 1428.
John Derling   1424.
Douglas prov. 21 Mar. 1391 (*CPP*,i,575); occ. 19 Dec. 1392

(*Morton Reg.*,ii,179-86); occ. 24/26 Mar. 1423 (*Univ.Evidence*,iii, 234); still in poss. 13 Apr. 1424 (v.inf.); d. before 10 Mar. 1428 (v.inf.).

Derling prov. 13 Apr. 1424 (*CSSR*,ii,61-62); retained right until death before 21 May 1424 (ibid.,202-3, 68).

Walter Stewart	1428 - 1433 x 1434.
Thomas Archer	1428 - 1428 x 1429.
Nicholas de Atholl (?)	1433.

Stewart el. on death of Douglas and had poss. when prov. 11 Aug. 1428 (*CSSR*,ii,235); still in poss. 26 Feb. 1433 (*ACSB*,231); d. before 9 Jan. 1434 (v.inf.).

Archer prov. on death of Douglas 10/22 Mar. 1428 (*CSSR*, ii,196, 202-3); res. in favour of Stewart in return for *Dk.treas.* before May 1429 (*CPL*,viii,153,411-12).

Atholl said to have some right 28 Feb. 1433 (Reg.Supp.,282, fo.29), but this is prob. an error for *M.archd.*

William Turnbull	1434 - 1435.
James Stewart	1435 - 1460.

Turnbull prov. on Stewart's death 9 Jan./29 May 1434 (Reg. Supp., 292,fo.258v; *CPL*,viii,510); lit. with Stewart and won sentence 11 Nov. 1435, but without poss. (*CPL*,viii,544-5).

Stewart had prov. and poss. before 11 Nov. 1435 (ibid.,544); cf. *ACSB*,21); prov. *M.bp.* 19 May 1460.

Andrew Stewart 1460 - 1482.

Prov. on James Stewart's elevation 19 May 1460 (*CPL*,xi, 414); prov. *M.bp.* 12 Aug. 1482.

Gavin Vaiche/Waich	1486.
James Chisholm	1486 - 1487.

Vaiche occ. 3 Sept. 1486 (St A.Univ.Mun.,SM110,B12,P 2.3); held it at death 26 Dec. 1486 (v.inf.; cf. *Ab.dean.*); prob. was seeking some exch. with Chisholm for *Ab.dean* at time of death.

Chisholm challenged by Vaiche as *Ab.dean* 5 Jan. 1485; had some right in this ben. when prov. *Db.bp.* 31 Jan. 1487 (v.inf.).

James Lindsay	1486 - 1487.
Gavin Dunbar senior	1487 - 1518.
John Spens	1488.

Lindsay prov. on Vaiche's death 26 Dec. 1486 (*ACSB*,217); promised annates 16 Jan. 1487 (ibid.); res. right in favour of Dunbar 28 Mar. 1488 (v.inf.).

Dunbar prov. on Vaiche's death and Chisholm's elevation 31 Jan. 1487 (*ACSB*, 217); surrog. to Lindsay's right 28 Mar. 1488 (ibid.,222); res. in favour of Dunbar junior, but promised annates to retain fruits 11 Sept. 1517 (PRO 31/9 - 31/322-3); prov. *Ab.bp.* 5 Nov. 1518, when instructed to res. this ben. (Dowden, *Bishops,* 137).

Spens had prov. and lit. with Dunbar before 29 June 1488 when he res. his right in return for pension on fruits (*CPL*,xiv, 231-2);

res. right again 14 Oct. 1488 (PRO 31/9 - 30/179).

Gavin Dunbar junior 1517 - 1525.

Prov. without fruits 11 Sept. 1517 (PRO 31/9 - 31/323-4); occ. 12 Dec. 1518 (*LP Henry VIII*,II,ii,nos.4645-6); cons. *G.abp.* 5 Feb. 1525.

Alexander Dunbar senior 1525 - 1549.

Occ. 26 Mar. 1525 (Fraser, *Sutherland*,iii,77); res. in favour of David Dunbar, but retained fruits and promised annates for right of return 12 Jan. 1548 (PRO 31/9 - 33/235-6, where names of parties are reversed; see also *St A.Form.*,ii,194-7); d. by 18 Dec. 1549 when testament was confirmed (Glas.Tests.).

David Dunbar 1548 - 1555 x 1557.

Promised annates and got prov. without fruits 12 Jan. 1548 (v.sup.); occ. 2 May 1555 (Pitcairn, *Trials*,i,376^X); d. by 28 Feb. 1557 (v.inf.).

Alexander Campbell 1557 - 1563.

Crown pres. on David Dunbar's death 28 Feb. 1557 (*RSS*, v,no.75; cf. no.1733; see *SP*,i,338); occ. 17 Mar. 1563 (SRO, Reg. Deeds, vi,fo.142); res. in favour of John Campbell on or before 29 Apr. 1563 (v.inf.).

John Campbell 1563 - 1566.

Crown pres. as *Kilmun prov.* on res. of Alexander Campbell 29 Apr. 1563 (*RSS*,v.no.1302); new crown pres. because of doubts on validity of Alexander Campbell's title 6 July 1564 (ibid.,no.1733); occ. 14 May 1566 (SRO, Reg.Deeds,vii,fo.273).

Alexander Dunbar junior 1566 - 1593.

Obtained poss. 9 x 25 July 1566 (ibid.,fo.385; cf. *M.succ.*); had had papal prov. and gets crown conf. 27 Jan. 1571 (*RSS*,vi,no. 1110); may have res. on or before 23 June 1590 (v.inf.); d. in poss. 13 July 1593 (Edin.Tests.).

Thomas Dunbar 1590 - 1619.

Crown pres. on res. of Alexander Dunbar 23 June 1590 (RSS, lx,fo.149); occ. 9 Oct. 1619(SRO, Part.Reg.Sasines Inverness,i, fo.210).

John Brodie 1624 - 1638.

Occ. 1624 (NLS, MS Chr.5774); occ. 24 Sept. 1638 (SRO, Part. Reg. Sasines Elgin,iv,fo,181).

PRECENTORS/CHANTERS OF MORAY

First known date: 1207 x 1208 (*Moray Reg.*,41).

Prebend: chs. of Lhanbryde, Alves and Rafford in 1207 x 1208 (*Moray Reg.*,41); then Rafford removed 1226 (ibid.,74); see Cowan, *Parishes*,6,132,167.

Richard (de Moray?) 1226 - 1230.

Occ. 5 May 1226 (*Moray Reg.*,74) and 4 Sept. 1230 (ibid.,107, misdated 1240; see also *Beauly Chrs.*,38-39); surname is suggested from an analysis of the chapter before and after the appearance of this Richard as prec.

William de Duffus 1232 - 1242.

Occ. 26 July 1232 (*Moray Reg.*, 88; cf. Macphail, *Pluscardyn*, 203 for surname); occ. July 1242 (*Moray Reg.*,110).

John de Hedon 1249.

Occ. 4 Feb. and 20 Mar. 1249 (ibid.,277,114).

Henry 1260 or 1263 - 1268, 1274-5 (?)

Occ. 11 Apr. 1260 or 13 Apr. 1263 (ibid.,138) and 9 Dec. 1268 (*Kel.Lib.*,no. 291); perhaps it was he who died in poss., 1274-5 (*SHS Misc.*,vi,46).

William de Cresswell 1296 - 1310.

Prob. in poss. by 28 Aug. 1296 (see *M.chanc.*); occ. 31 Oct. 1308 (*APS*,i,477) and 23 Mar. 1310 (*Moray Reg.*,148-50).

Roger de Inverness 1328.

Occ. 8/11 May 1328 (ibid.,150-4), having prob. got poss. since 22 Mar. 1313 (see *M.chanc.*).

Richard de Pilmuir x 1338 - 1344.

Moved from *M.treas.*, presumably before el. *M.bp.* June 1337 x Jan. 1338; prob. still in poss. 9 Jan. 1344 (*CPP*,i,33); prov. *Dk.bp.* 5 July 1344.

Duncan de Strathearn 1344 - 1347.

Prov. 8 July 1344 (*CPL*,iii,182); prov. *Dk.bp.* 15 Oct. 1347.

Gilbert Fleming 1347.

Prov. 10 Nov. 1347 (*CPL*,iii,256); d. by 18 July 1348 (v.inf.).

John de Flisco 1348 - 1349.

Prov. on Fleming's death 18 July 1348 (Collect.,14,fo.161); prov. Vercelli bp. 12 Jan. 1349 (Eubel, *Hierarchia*,i,521).

John de Rate 1349 - 1350.

Prov. 3 Mar. 1349 (*CPL*,iii,291); prov. *Ab.bp.* 19 Nov. 1350.

William Boyl 1351 - 1372 x 1373.

Prov. 8 July 1351 (*CPL*,iii,420-1; cf.483); in poss. 9 Dec. 1354 (*CPP*,i,265); res. on exch. with Spynie for *Ab.prec.* after 1 May 1372 (Reg.Av.,184,fo.369v) and before 14 Sept. 1373 (v.inf.).

William de Spynie 1372 x 1373 - 1397.

Got it on exch. with Boyl by ord. authority and gets papal conf. 14 Sept. 1373 (*CPL*,iv,188); cons. *M.bp.* 16 Sept. 1397.

James de Dunbar 1397 - 1397 x 1404.

Crown pres. on Spynie's cons. c.16 Sept. 1397 (*CPP*,i,625-6); held it along with *M.archd.* without disp. (ibid.,637); res. while still

a minor before 24 Mar. 1404 (v.inf.).

William de Felton 1404.
> Had ord. coll. on Dunbar's res. and gets prov. 24 Mar. 1404 (*CPP*, i,625-6).

John de Haliburton x 1413.
> Held it at death before 6 Jan. 1413 (ibid.,599).

Richard de Creich	1413 - 1420.
John de Spynie	1413 - 1415 x 1417.
Robert Stewart	1417 - 1419 x 1431.
William Croyser	1418.
Thomas de Sinclair	1418.

> **Creich** prov. on Haliburton's death 6 Jan. 1413 (*CPP*,i,599); no poss. when lit. and prepared conditionally to res. in Spynie's favour 20 June 1415 (ibid.,i,603); prov. on Spynie's death 11 Aug. 1417 (ibid., 607); still claiming a right without poss. 25 Nov. 1420 (*CSSR*,i,234);
> **Spynie** occ. 15 Feb. 1413 (*Kinloss Recs.*,125-8); lit. in curia when surrog. to Creich's right 20 June 1415 (*CPP*,i,603); d. before July 1417 (v.inf.).
> **Stewart** had coll. by ord. on Spynie's death c.July 1417 i.e. six months before 3 Jan. 1418 (PRO 31/9 - 51/102); had poss. when conf. 5 Sept. 1419 (*CSSR*,i,117); d. prob. in poss. before 20 Mar. 1431 (v.inf.).
> **Croyser** prov. on Spynie's death 3/20 Jan. 1418 (PRO 31/9-51/ 102; *CPL*,vii,92-93) unfruitfully.
> **Sinclair** prov. to Croyser's right on latter's getting *G.archd. Teviotdale* 25 June 1418 (*CSSR*,i,12).

Ingram de Lindsay	1431 - 1441.
George de Dunbar	1433.

> **Lindsay** in poss. when prov. on Stewart's death 20 Mar. 1431 (Reg.Supp.,267,fo.94; *ACSB*,104); lit. in curia and 'does not know if he possesses it' 12 Feb. 1433 (Reg.Supp. 283,fo.232v); in poss. 6 Aug. 1435 (*CPL*,viii,535); prov. *Ab.bp.* 28 Apr. 1441.
> **Dunbar** claims poss. 12 Feb. 1433 (Reg.Supp.283,fo.84v).

Thomas de Tulloch 1441 - 1441 x 1444.
> Granted it in commend as *O.bp.* 1/18 May 1441 (ibid.,373,fo.68; 377,fo.206v; *ACSB*,129); res. to ord. on exch. for can. and preb. of Caithness with Andrew de Tulloch before 9 May 1444 (v.inf.).

Andrew de Tulloch x 1444 - 1445 x 1448.
> Got it on exch. with Thomas de Tulloch and was conf. with poss. 9 May 1444 (Reg.Supp.,396,fo.174v; 401,fo.149), 21 Jan. 1445 (ibid., 401,fo.155) and 3 Apr. 1445 (*CPL*,ix,499); res. in favour of Piot (v.inf.) some time before his death, which is datable 5 June 1447 x 23 Sept. 1448 (see *C.bp.*;v.inf.).

Laurence Piot	1445 x 1448 - 1456.
Adam de Hamilton	1448 - 1441 x 1449.
Andrew de Durisdeer	1448 - 1449.

William Hog   1448.
Richard Clepham (Clapham) 1449 - 1449 x 1451.
Patrick Hog   1451.
Richard Holland   1453 - 1456.

Piot coll. by ord. on exch. with Andrew de Tulloch 3 Apr. 1445 x 23 Sept. 1448 (v.sup.), getting conf. 5 May 1450 (*CPL*,x,255); prob. still in poss. 2 Oct. 1451 (see Patrick Hog below); lost poss. during lit. with Holland after 12 May 1453; won lit., then res. in curia in favour of Lindsay 8 Jan. 1456 (*CPL*,xi,256-7), getting security in *Ab.archd.* 12 June 1456 in recompense.

Hamilton prov. on Andrew de Tulloch's death 23 Sept. 1448 (*CPL*,x,45-46); d. without poss. before 19 May 1449 (v.inf.).

Durisdeer prov. on Andrew de Tulloch's death 26 Sept. 1448 (Reg.Supp.,434,fo.321v); but alternative prov. to *Ab.dean.* was being arranged by 19 May 1449 (v.inf.).

William Hog prov. on Andrew de Tulloch's death 2 Oct. 1448 (Reg.Supp.,433,fo.256).

Clepham prov. 19 May 1449 (*CPL*,x,195,198). but res. right to Piot before 27 Feb. 1451 (ibid.,213).

Patrick Hog gets *com.priv.* against Piot 2 Oct. 1451 (Reg. Supp.,45 fo.159) unfruitfully.

Holland prov. 12 May 1453 (*CPL*,x,244); got poss. and lit. with Piot, and still in poss. 8 Jan. 1456 despite losing lit. (ibid.,xi,256-7).

James Lindsay 1456 - 1468.

Prov. on res. of Piot 8 Jan. 1456 (*CPL*,xi,256-7); perhaps in poss. by 12 June 1456 (Reg.Supp.,491,fo.242); occ. 11 Apr. 1468 (St A. Univ.Mun.,SCB, fo.48v); res. to ord. on exch. with Vaus for *G.dean.* before 7 Oct. 1468 (v.inf.).

Thomas Vaus   1468 - 1478 x 1480.
James Inglis   1468 - 1471 x 1474.

Vaus got it on exch. with Lindsay before 7 Oct. 1468 (*CPL*, xii,298-9); new prov. 12 Oct. 1468 (Reg.Supp.,633,fo.287); lit. with Inglis and got new prov. again 24 May and 25 Sept. 1471 (ibid., 667,fo.267v; 674,fo.232v); absolved with new prov. again 11 Feb. 1478 (ibid.,765,fo.42); occ. 4 Aug. 1478 (*Arb.Lib.*,ii,178); res. on exch. with Alexander Vaus before 8 June1480 (v.inf.).

Inglis gets *com.priv.* against Vaus and prov. on Lindsay's res. 7 Oct. 1468 (*CPL*,xii,298-9; Reg.Supp. 632,fo.83v); still lit. against Vaus 25 Sept. 1471 (ibid.,674,fo.232v); d. by 7 Jan. 1474 (see *Ab.archd.*).

Alexander Vaus   1478 x 1480 - 1485.
William Oliphant 1480 - 1482.
James Kinnaird   1480.
Giles Boyce   1480 - 1482.
John Fraser (Fresel) 1480.

Vaus got it on exch. with Thomas Vaus after 4 Aug. 1478 (v.sup.) and before 8 June 1480 (*CPL*,xiii,257-8; cf.106); had papal conf. but involved in lit. and dispossessed by 17 Aug. 1480 (*CPL*,xiii,257-8); paid

annates 19 Apr. 1485 (*ACSB*,255).

Oliphant prov. on death of Thomas Vaus 8 June 1480 (*CPL*,xiii, 106); lit. followed, and prov. *Si neutri* when not in poss. 30 Sept. 1482 (ibid.,763; *ACSB*,205).

Kinnaird in poss. 17 Aug. 1480 (*CPL*,xiii,257); lit. by 30 Sept. 1480 (ibid.,763).

Boyce prov. on death of Thomas Vaus 16 June 1480 (*ACSB*,199); in poss. 1 Mar. 1482 (ibid.,205); d. by 30 May 1482 (*CPL*,xiii,816).

Fraser lit. 30 Sept. 1480 (ibid.,763).

Adam Gordon 1485 - 1499.

Occ. 24 Nov. 1485 (*HMC* 4, *5th R.*,630); occ. 10 Sept. 1499 (*RMS*,ii,no.2503); prob. d. 3/4 Apr. 1508 (*Abdn.Reg.*,ii,212-13; cf.i, 343,350), but appears to have dem. before then (v.inf.).

Alexander Gordon 1504 - 1516.

Occ. 3 Nov. 1504 (*RSS*,i,no. 1045); prov. *Ab.bp.* 6 June 1516, but perhaps still uncons. when died 30 June 1518.

Alexander Lyon 1527 - 1540.

Occ. 15 Mar. 1527 (Boece, *Historiae* (1527),preface); occ. 23 Oct. 1539 (*RSS*,ii,no.3187) and 19 Feb. 1540 (SRO,ADC & S,xii, fo.18v).

John Thornton 1540 - 1562 x 1565.

Occ. 1539, presumably 1539/40 after 19 Feb. (*Moray Reg.*, xxiii;cf.sup.); occ. 1562 (*Moray Reg.*, xxiii); d. 24 Feb. 1565 (*PSAS*, ii,257), cf.inf.

James Thornton 1563, 1565 - 1577.

Occ. as early as 23 Feb. 1563 (St A.Univ.Mun., SS150/2,fo. 142); crown pres. on death of John Thornton 25 Apr. 1565 (*RSS*, v,no.2036); escheated 8 Oct. 1577 (*RSS*,vii,no.1208); d. before 24 Nov. 1577 (see *B.dean.*).

Patrick Auchinleck 1578 - 1581.

Crown pres. on death of James Thornton 8 Jan. 1578 (*RSS*, vii,no.1387); d. 5 Apr. 1581 (Edin.Tests.).

James Dundas 1582 - 1612.

Crown pres. on Auchinleck's death 30 May 1582 (Reg.Pres., ii,76); occ. 28/29 Sept. 1582 (SRO,Abbrev. FeuChrs.,ii,fo.181); crown nom. as Down and Connor bp., Ireland, 23 Feb. 1612 (*CSP Ireland 1611-14*,no. 437); but d. still retaining this ben. before 29 Oct. 1612 (v.inf.).

Gavin Dunbar 1612 - 1638.

Crown pres. on death of Dundas 29 Oct. 1612 (RSS,lxxxii, fo.65); occ. 24 Sept. 1638 (SRO,Part.Reg.Sasines Elgin,iv,fo.181).

CHANCELLORS OF MORAY

First known date: 1207 x 1208. (*Moray Reg.*,41).

    Prebend: lands of Fothervais, etc. in 1207 x 1208 (*Moray Reg.*, 41); then chs. of Inveravon (Strathavon) and Urquhart beyond Inverness in 1226 (ibid.,73; cf. 41,96); see Cowan, *Parishes*, 87,205.

Andrew (de Moray ?) 1207 x 1222, 1221 - 1223 x 1224.

    Occ. 1207 x 1222 (*Moray Reg.*,44); occ. 15 Oct. 1221 (ibid.,60; cf.61; see also 16); prob. same as cons. *M.bp.* 12 May 1223 x 10 Apr. 1224; ben. prob. vacant 5 May 1226 (*Moray Reg.*,73-76); identification of this Andrew is suggested from an analysis of the chapter before and after he appears as chanc.

Henry 1227 x 1230.

    Occ. early 1230 (*Beauly Chrs.*,38-39), having prob. got poss. since Mar. 1227 (see *M.treas.*).

William 1230 - 1239 x 1240.

    Occ. 4 Sept. 1230 (*Moray Reg.*,107, misdated 1240); mand. for conf. as *Ar.bp.* 16 Feb. 1239; cons. by 20 May 1240.

William 1242.

    Occ. July 1242 (*Moray Reg.*,110).

Andrew 1249 - 1250.

    Occ. 4 Feb. 1249 (ibid.,277) and 3 Aug. 1250 (*A.B.Coll.*,294).

Gamelin 1255 - 1257.

    In poss. when conf. *St A.bp.* 1 July 1255; lic. to retain benefices for two years 31 July 1255 (*Reg.Alexandre IV*,i,196,213).

Archibald 1255.

    Had local coll. and gets papal conf. despite lic. to Gamelin (v.inf.) 21 Dec. 1255 (ibid.,i,398).

Henry 1281.

    Occ. 2 Feb. 1281 (Fraser, *Grant*, iii,7).

William de Cresswell 1285 x 1294 - 1294 x 1296.

    Occ. 26/30 Oct. 1294 (*Moray Reg.*,144-5), having prob. moved from *B.archd.* since 10 Jan. 1285; moved to *M.prec.* by 28 Aug. 1296.

Henry de Banff 1296 - 1299 x 1310.

    Occ. 28 Aug. 1296 (*CDS*,ii,212); in poss. 30 June 1299 (*CPL*,i, 582); moved to *M.treas.* by 23 Mar. 1310.

Roger de Inverness 1312 - 1313 x 1328.

    Occ. 29 Oct. 1312 (*APS*,i,463-4) and 22 Mar. 1313 (*Diplom. Norv.*,ii,no.111); moved to *M.prec.* by 8 May 1328.

John de Inverness 1345 - 1358.

    Occ. 20 Oct. 1345 (*Moray Reg.*,157) and 2 May 1358 (*Dunf. Reg.*,266-7).

Henry de Pluscarden 1391 - 1394

Occ. 3 Nov. 1391 (*Moray Reg.*, 128); still in poss. 29 Oct. 1394 (*CPP*,i,582).

Duncan Petit 1400 - 1414 x 1418.

Occ. 6 Nov. 1400 (*Abdn.Reg.*,i,203-5) and 18 May 1414 (*Moray Reg.*, 216-17); prob. res. on getting *Ab.chanc.* by 10 Oct. 1418.

Ingram de Lindsay 1430 - 1431.

Prob. in poss. 11 Dec. 1430 (PRO 31/9 - 27/219, where date is wrongly given as 1431 and where he is called just 'canon of Moray'); in poss. 12 Jan. 1431 (*ACSB*,13); prov. *M.prec.* 20 Mar. 1431.

John 'Moderoch' x 1448.

Held it and res. to ord. on exch. with Green before 15 May 1448 (v.inf.).

John Green (Greyne) 1448 - 1464.

Coll. by ord. on exch. with 'Moderoch' and gets conf. 15 May 1448 (*CPL*,x,401-2); occ. 24 Sept. 1464 (Fraser, *Grant*,iii,26); cf. John 'Grahame' 20 July 1474 (*Invernessiana*,150, where name is wrong and date should be 1464).

Alexander Stewart 1472 x 1473 - 1492.

Occ. 28 July 1473 (Fraser, *Grant*,iii,31) having moved from *M.succ.* 5 Mar. 1472 prob. since Dec. 1472; new prov. having poss. 1 Apr. 1478 (Reg.Supp.,767,fo.35); occ. 10 May 1492 (*Cawdor Bk.*, 76-77).

Robert Forman 1506 - 1511.

Occ. 2 May 1505 (SRO, Seafield, 75/5); occ. 27 Aug. 1511 (SRO, ADC, xxiii,fo. 143).

Robert Maxwell 1519 - 1526.

Occ. 25 Oct. 1519 (*Glas.Mun.*,ii,136); prov. *O.bp.* 9 Apr. 1526 with disp. to retain benefices (Dowden, *Bishops*,264); promised annates to retain this ben. 26 Apr. 1526 (PRO 31/9 - 32/102-3); still in poss. 25 May 1526 (ibid.,32/88).

James Shaw 1527.

Occ. 29 July 1527 (SRO,ADC,xxxvii, fo.179).

Walter Maxwell   1532 - 1537.
Robert Crichton   1532.

Maxwell in poss. 11 June 1532 when he is to res. on exch. with Crichton (*RSS*,ii,no.1296); but retained it until res. in curia on or before 20 Aug. 1535 (PRO 31/9 - 33/10-11); occ. locally still 31 Aug. 1535 (Fraser, *Pollok*,i,268) and 6 Mar. 1537 (SRO,Sent.Offic.Laud., fo.261).

Crichton was to get it on exch. with Maxwell 11 June 1532 (v.sup.), but this was ineffective.

John Erskine 1535 - 1537.

Promises annates and gets prov. 20 Aug. 1535 (PRO 31/9 - 33/10-11); in poss. 13 Nov. 1537 when king proposed to pope that he res. in favour of Robert Erskine (*James V Letters*,338).

Robert Erskine 1537 - 1539.

Expects prov. 13 Nov. 1537 (v.sup.); occ. 18 Aug. 1539 (SRO, Seafield, 79/2).

William Gordon 1540 - 1546 x 1547.

Occ. 30 Dec. 1540 (*Prot.Bk.Cristisone*,no.318); cons. *Ab.bp.* 23 Dec. 1546 x 26 Jan. 1547.

James Gordon 1547 - 1564 x 1566.

Occ. 14 Apr. 1547 (*Moray Reg.*,428,no.468); occ. 9 Jan. 1564 (SRO, Seafield, 79/2); d. by 27 Feb. 1566 (*RSS*,v,no2662).

Robert Gordon 1566 - 1568 x 1573.

Crown pres. on death of James Gordon 2 Mar. 1566 (*RSS*,v, no.2669); occ. 10 Apr. 1568 (SRO, Gordon Castle, 12.5.1); d. before 13 Aug. 1573 (v.inf.); said erroneously to occur 1580 (Stevenson & Wood, *Seals*,ii,377).

Alexander Gordon 1573 - 1589.

Crown pres. on death of Robert Gordon 13 Aug. 1573 (*RSS*, vi,no. 2074); depriv. 15 Oct. 1589 (v.inf.).

Peter Udny 1589.

Crown pres. on depriv. of Alexander Gordon 15 Oct. 1589 (SRO, Reg. Signatures, xv, fo.10).

William Clogie 1606 - 1625.

Occ. 10 June 1606 (SRO, Gordon Castle, 15.2.4); agreed to demit 13 Oct. 1624 (SRO, Moray Synod Minutes,i,3), but found still in poss. 30 June 1625 (SRO, Part.Reg.Sasines Banff,ii,fo.273).

Alexander Innes 1625 - 1628.

Occ. 25 Oct. 1625 (SRO, Moray Synod Minutes,i,10) and 1 May 1628 (SRO, Part.Reg.Sasines Inverness,iv,fo,89).

John Chalmer 1631 - 1638.

Occ. 27 Apr. 1631 (SRO, Part.Reg.Sasines Banff,iii,fo.137) and 24 May 1638 (SRO, Part Reg. Sasines Elgin,iv,fo.183.

TREASURERS OF MORAY

First known date: 1207 x 1208 (*Moray Reg.*, 4l).

Prebend: chs. of Kineddar and Essle in 1207 x 1208 (*Moray Reg.*, 41); see Cowan, *Parishes*,62-63, 114.

Henry c. 1221 - 1226 x 1230.

Occ. c. 1221 and 19 June 1226 x 1230 (*Moray Reg.*,16,120); prob. still in poss. Mar. 1227 (*Arb.Lib.*,i,144; cf. *Moray Reg.*,22-23); res. by early 1230 (see *M.chanc.*).

Robert 1230 - 1260 or 1263.

Occ. as 'Robert' 4 Sept. 1230 (*Moray Reg.*,107, musdated 1240; see also *Beauly Chrs.*, 38-39) and 4 Feb. 1239 (*Moray Reg.*,277); occ.

as 'R.' 3 Aug. 1250 (*Kel.Lib.*,i,185) and 11 Apr. 1260 or 13 Apr. 1263 (*Moray Reg.*,138).

Henry de Banff 1310.

Occ. 23 Mar. 1310 (*Moray Reg.*,148-9), having moved from *M. chanc.* since 30 June 1299.

Adam Herok (Herert) 1326 - 1330.

Occ. as 'Herert' 28 Feb. 1326 (Felibien, *Histoire de la ville de Paris*,v, 631 ff.); occ. as 'Herok' 4/5 Dec. 1330 (*Familie of Innes*,57-59; Macphail, *Pluscardyn*,212-13); prob. res. on getting *C.chanc.*

Richard de Pilmuir x 1338.

Held it before moving to *M.prec.*before 9 Jan. 1344 (*CPP*,i,33), presumably before el.*M.bp.*June 1337 x Jan. 1338.

Martin   1343 - 1344 x 1351.
Richard de Moray   1344.
Donald de Mar   1344.
David de Mar   1344 - 1367.

Martin occ. 3 Dec. 1343 (*Family of Rose*,117); had had ord. coll. and has poss 9 Jan. 1344 (*CPP*,i,33-34); prob. still in poss. 28 Oct. 1344 and lost poss. by 8 July 1351 (v.inf.).

Moray prov. 9 Jan. 1344 (*CPP*,i,33) unfruitfully.

Donald de Mar prov. 9 Mar. 1344 (*CPP*,iii,126); res. at curia in exch. for *B.archd.*with David de Mar without poss. 28 Oct. 1344 (Collect.,14,fo.158v).

David de Mar prov. 28 Oct. 1344 (v.sup.); in poss. 8 July 1351 (*CPP*,i,215); prov. to another M.preb. 22 Apr. 1367 (Reg.Av., 264, fo.132v).

Thomas de Harcars 1367 - 1368.

Prov. 2 July 1367 (Collect.,14,fo.174v); prov. *M.dean.* 11 Dec. 1368.

William de Chisholm 1368 - 1401.

Prov. 11 Dec. 1368 (Collect.,14,fo.175v); occ. 12 Aug. 1371 (*Moray Reg.*,174); occ. 30 May 1399 (ibid.,213,328); res. in curia on exch. with Goldsmith on or before 22 Jan. 1401 (v.inf.).

William Goldsmith 1401 - 1437 x 1442.

Prov. on exch. 22 Jan. 1401 (Reg.Av.,305,fos.468-9); res. to ord. on exch. for another M.preb. with Innes 9 May 1437 x 27 Oct. 1442 (v.inf.; ord. was Bp. Wincester, q.v.).

James de Innes   1437 x 1442 - 1447.
David Stewart   1445 - 1446 x 1447.

Innes had coll. by ord. on exch. after 9 May 1437 and had poss. when conf. 27 Oct. 1442 (*CPL*,viii,314); new prov. 27 Oct. 1446 (*ACSB*,136) and 22 Apr. 1447 (Reg.Supp.,416,fo.213v); still in poss. 25 May 1447 (ibid.,418,fo.21); d. by 14 Oct. 1447 (see *R.dean.*).

Stewart gets *com.priv.* against Innes 20 Nov. 1445/19 Jan. 1446 (Reg.Supp.,408,fo.225v; *CPL*,ix,530); had given up suit by 27

Oct. 1447 (v.inf.).

William Wincester	1447 - 1492.
Donald de Harde	1447 - 1449.
James Lindsay	1447 - 1447 x 1449.

Wincester had coll. by ord. on Innes's death and gets conf. 21/27 Oct. 1447 (Reg.Supp.,420,fo.55v; *CPL*,x,346-7); new prov. after res. of Harde and lit. had gone against Lindsay 7 Jan. 1449 (Reg.Supp.,432, fo.245v); occ. 13 Aug. 1492 (*Family of Rose*, 156).

Harde prov. on Innes's death 17 Oct. 1447 (Reg.Supp.,420,fo. 139v); res. right in favour of Wincester 7 Jan. 1449 (ibid.,432,fo.245v).

Lindsay prov. on Innes's death 19 Oct. 1447 (*CPL*,x,364); lost lit. with Wincester by 7 Jan. 1449 (v.sup.).

George Hepburn 1497 - 1527.

Occ. 10 Oct. 1497 (SRO, Crawford Priory Inventory,no.24); res. in favour of James Hepburn, but promised annates to retain fruits 8 Feb. 1526 (PRO 31/9 - 32/94-5); still alive 28 Feb. 1527 (see *Dk.dean.*).

James Hepburn 1526 - 1554 x 1560.

Promises annates and gets prov. without fruits 8 Feb. 1526 (v.sup.); occ. 18 Jan. 1532 (*Moray Reg.*,422, no.461); occ. 10 Oct. 1554 (ibid., 411,no. 408); res. in curia before 21 May 1565 (v.inf.) and therefore prob. x 1560.

George Hepburn x 1560 - 1570 x 1574.

Had papal prov. on res. of James Hepburn prob. x 1560, and gets crown conf. 21 May 1565 (*RSS*,v,no.2068); occ. 8 Oct.1570 (*Scone Liber,*212); d. before 27 July 1574 (v.inf.).

Patrick Douglas 1574 - 1576 x 1583.

Crown pres. on death of George Hepburn 27 July 1574 (*RSS,* vi,no.2614); occ. 15 Oct. 1575 and prob. 27 Mar. 1576 (ibid.,vii, no. 540); res. on or before 26 Apr. 1583 (v.inf.).

William Douglas 1583 - 1617.

Crown pres. on res. of Patrick Douglas 26 Apr. 1583 (Reg.Pres., ii,88); occ. 2 Dec. 1617 (*RMS*,vii,no.1712).

Alexander Innes 1619 - 1625.

Occ. 9 Oct. 1619 (SRO, Part.Reg. Sasines Inverness,i,fo.210); had royal lic. to reside at Cambridge 22 Jan. 1624 and 5 Feb. 1625 (SRO, Guthrie,20/9), frustrating attempts by bp. to remove him on account of absence over a period of 4-5 years (Scott,*Fasti*,vi,382, quoting SRO, Moray Synod Minutes,i,50 of 12 Oct. 1624); but dem. before 30 June 1625 (v.inf.) and moved to *M.chanc.*

John Gordon 1625 - 1631.

Occ. 30 June 1625 and 27 Apr. 1631 (SRO, Part.Reg.Sasines Banff, ii,fo.273 and iii,fo.137).

David Collace 1635 - 1638.

Occ. 29 May 1635 and 24 Sept. 1638 (SRO, Part.Reg.Sasines Elgin,iv.fos.90, 181); occ. after Restoration 8 Apr. 1663 (ibid., 2nd series,i,fo.61).

SUBDEANS OF MORAY

First known date: 1225 (*Moray Reg.*, 21).
    Prebend: ch. of Dallas and altarage of Auldearn in 1226 (*Moray Reg.*,74; see Cowan, *Parishes*, 11, 44).

Adam 1225 - 1226.
    Occ. 1225 and 5 May 1226 (*Moray Reg.*,21, 75).

William 1227 x 1230.
    Occ. Mar. 1227 x 1230 (ibid.,120).

John 1232.
    Occ. 26 July 1232 (ibid.,88).

Walter 1232 - 1238.
    Occ. 11 Oct. 1232 and May 1238 (ibid.,96, 275).

William 1249.
    Occ. 4 Feb. 1249 (ibid.,277)

Ralph Reny 1275 - 1281.
    Occ. 10 Jan. 1275 (*Beauly Chrs.*,56-57) and 2 Feb. 1281 (Fraser, *Grant*,iii,7).

William 1310.
    Occ. 23 Mar. 1310 (*Moray Reg.*,148-9).

John de Dychtoun 1343 - 1346.
    Occ. 3 Dec. 1343 (*Family of Rose*,117) and 1 Apr. 1346 (Fraser, *Grant*,iii,9).

Simon de Crail 1351.
    Got papal conf. 13 May 1351, but did not get poss. (Collect.,14, fo.163).

Henry 1362 x 1364.
    Occ. 14 Aug. 1362 x 10 Dec. 1364 (*ER*,ii,166).

William Wys 1370 - 1378.
    Occ. 6 Mar. 1370 and 18 July 1378 (*Moray Reg.*,167-8, 182-3).

William Gerland 1383 - 1396.
    Occ. 9 Mar. 1383 (*Abdn.Reg.*, i,163-6); still in poss. 1 Aug.1396 (Reg.Supp.,91,fo.234v).

Alexander de Brothy 1405.
    In poss. 6 July 1405 (Reg.Av.,319,fos.391-391v).

John de Birnie (Birneth) 1414.
    Occ. 18 May 1414 (*Moray Reg.*,217).

Bean Mauritii (Moricii)/Bean Johannis Maelmolmar x 1433.
    Held it as Moricii and res. before 5 Aug. 1433, by which time he was dead (Reg.Supp.,287,fo.275v; cf.ibid.,289,fo.51v for alternative form of name); perhaps also called John Campbell (see *Ar.dean.*).

William de Birnie (Brynneth, Burnach, Birneth) 1433 - 1449.

In poss. when conf. following res. of Mauritii 5 Aug. 1433 (Reg. Supp.,287,fo.275v); occ 9 Jan. 1438 (SRO, Ross of Cromarty titles, box 7); occ. 30 Aug. 1449 (NRA, Transcript of Pluscarden Chrs.).

John Wincester 1464 - 1488.

Occ. 20 July 1464 (*Invernessiana,*150, where printed text has wrong date 1474) and 24 Sept. 1464 (Fraser, *Grant,*iii,26-); occ. 5 Dec. 1488 (*Moray Reg.,*259).

William Lyell 1500 - 1504.

Occ. 18 Jan. 1500 (Macphail, *Pluscardyn,*236); d.1504 (*The Cathedral Kirk of Moray,* 1950 edn. of guidebook, 16, quoting tombstone).

Adam Hunter 1506.

Occ. 2 May 1506 (SRO, Seafield, 75/5).

John Weddell/Vedall 1508 - 1509, 1516 x 1517 (?)

Occ. 13 Oct. 1508 (*Invernessiana,*189); occ. 31 July and 18 Aug. 1509 (*RMS,*ii,nos.3369,3373); perhaps res. on moving to *St A.Offic.* 14 Oct. 1516 x 28 Feb. 1517.

William Wincester 1518 - 1521.

Occ. 16 Oct. 1518 and 10 Nov. 1521 (SRO, St Andrews Chrs. nos.213,223).

Robert Reid 1524 - 1529.

Occ. 19 Nov. 1524 (St A.Univ.Mun,UY305/1,p.39); professed as a monk 11 July 1529 (*Kinloss Recs.,*11; cf. 49-50).

William Paterson   1529 - 1560 x 1562, 1577.
Nicholas Tulloch   1562 - 1574.

Paterson in poss. 1 Oct. 1529 (PRO 31/9 - 32/226); occ. 26 Apr. 1532 (*Beauly Chrs.,*209); occ. 13 May 1544 (*Invernessiana,* 217); res. to pope after Reformation (*RSS,*vii,no.648) apparently on or before 22 Apr. 1562 (v.inf.); but prob. retained some right until escheated on or before 5 Mar. 1577 (*RSS,*vii,no.938).

Tulloch prov. by pope on res. of Paterson 22 Apr. 1562 and got crown conf. 25 Sept. 1566 (*RSS,*v,no.3075); escheated on or before 20 Mar. 1574 (ibid.,vi,no.2401); said to be just factor and chamberlain of Subdean Paterson 5 Mar. 1577 (ibid.,vii,no.938).

Patrick Cumming   1576 - 1587 x 1588.
Alexander Bad   1581.

Cumming gets crown pres. on res. of Paterson by throwing doubt on Tulloch's title 6 July 1576 (*RSS,*vii,no.648); occ. 9 Sept. 1587 (SRO, Gordon Castle, 8.15.1); depriv. by 16 Aug. 1588 (v.inf.).

Bad gets crown pres. on res. of Cumming 1 Feb. 1581 (Reg. Pres.,ii,163) unfruitfully.

George Douglas 1588.

Crown pres. on depriv. of Cumming for non-residence 16 Aug. 1588 (RSS,1viii,fo.3).

Alexander Richardson 1606-1622

Occ. 10 June 1606 (SRO,Gordon Castle, 15.2.4) and 9 Oct. 1622 (SRO, Part.Reg.Sasines Inverness,i,fo. 210); d. 1622 (SRO, Reg. Retours,xx,fo.60).

George Cumming 1625 - 1638.

Occ. 18 May 1625 (SRO, Part.Reg.Sasines Elgin,iii,fo.53) and 24 Sept. 1638 (ibid.,iv,fo.181).

SUCCENTORS/SUBCHANTERS OF MORAY

First known date: 1225.

Prebend: chs. of Rafford and Ardclach (Fothervais) in 1226 (*Moray Reg.*,74-75; see also Cowan, *Parishes,* 8,167).

Lambert 1225 - 1235.

Occ. 1225 and 5 May 1226 (*Moray Reg.*,21,75); occ. 1235 (*St A. Lib.*, 327, cf. *Moray Reg.*, 107 which is misdated 4 Sept. 1240, prob. for 1230.

H. 1237.

Occ. 10 Oct. 1237 (*Moray Reg.,*133).

John 1239 - 1249.

Occ. 5 Mar. 1239 and 4 Feb. 1249 (ibid.,105,277).

Roger 1260 or 1263 - 1264.

Occ. 11 Apr. 1260 or 13 Apr. 1263, 16 Mar.1263, and Feb.1264 (ibid.,138, 277-8,278); perhaps same as Roger de Inverness (v.inf.).

Roger de Inverness 1299 x 1312.

Occ. 28 June 1299 x (*Moray Reg.,*147-8); prob. res. on moving to *M.chanc.* x 29 Oct. 1312.

Martin 1328.

Occ. 8/11 May 1328 (*Moray Reg.,*150-4).

Simon de Crail 1343.

Occ. 3 Dec. 1343 (*Family of Rose,*117); cf. *M.subd.*

John de Duffus 1350 - 1363.

In poss. 13 June 1350 (*CPP,*i,200); occ. 12 Nov. 1363 (*Moray Reg.,* 313).

John de Ard 1375 - 1394 x 1398.

Occ. 21 July 1375 (*Arb.Lib.,*ii,31-33); still in poss. 29 Oct. 1394 (*CPP,*i,582); prob. d. before 1 Aug. 1398 (*Moray Reg.,*327);

William de Felton 1397 x 1404.

Held it sometime after 16 Sept. 1397 (when Bp.Spynie was cons.) and before 24 Mar. 1404, by which time he held *M.prec.* (*CPP,* i,625-6).

John Brothy 1404 - 1406.

Had ord.coll. when Felton got prov. to *M.prec.* (v.sup.), and gets

papal conf. 21 Dec. 1406 (Reg.Av.,326,fos.375-375v); retained it until
death (Reg.Supp.,273,fo.263v. of 14 Jan. 1432) prob. before Nairn
got poss. (v.inf.).

William Davidson (Davison) x 1413.

Held it and res. on marriage more than six months before Nairn
had coll. i.e. x Nov. 1413 (*CPL*,viii,414; v.inf.).

Adam de Nairn (Narn)	1414 - 1435.
Thomas de Fordyce (Fordise)	1431.
John de Innes	1432 - 1435.

Nairn occ. 18 May 1414 (*Moray Reg.*,217); he had had coll. by
ord. more than six months after res. of Davidson (v.sup.); said 14 Jan.
1432 to have held it about seven years i.e. from c.1424-5 (Reg.Supp.,
273,fo.236v), but perhaps this is an error for seventeen years; res.
on exch. for *R.subd.* with Innes 5 Feb. 1432 (Reg.Supp.,275,fo.17);
tried to regain poss., but had no success by 23 June 1433 (v.inf.);
res. claim to Innes in return for pension 21 June 1435 (ibid.,307,
fo.187).

Fordyce got *com.priv.* against Nairn 17 Dec. 1431 (*CPL*,
viii,414).

Innes got prov. on irregular poss. of Nairn and death of
Brothy 14 Jan 1432 (ibid.; *ACSB*,107); prov. on exch. with Nairn
5 Feb. 1432 (Reg.Supp.,275,fo.17), but appears not to have in fact
res. *R.subd.* in exch.; in poss. 23 June 1433 (ibid.,288,fo. 107) and
21 June 1435 (ibid.,307,fo.187), when he agreed to a pension for
Nairn; res. before 14 Aug. 1435 (ibid.,407,fo.128v); cf. *C.prec.*

Robert de Tulloch 1437.

Prov. on res. of Tulloch 3 Nov. 1437 (ibid.,344,fo.30v).

Patrick Fraser	1441 - 1445.
John Monypenny	1441.
Malise de Tulloch	1445.

Fraser prob. in poss. 19 Apr. 1441 when wrongly said to have
res. or died (Reg. Supp.,377,fo.279v); res. on exch. for *M.archd.*
with Spens c. Jan./Feb. 1445 (*CPL*,x,355-6; Reg.Supp.,414,fo.154;
v.inf.); but still thought to be in poss. 14 Aug. 1445 (Reg.Supp.,
407,fo.190v).

Monypenny prov. on res. or death of Fraser 19 Apr. 1441
(ibid.,377,fo.179v) unfruitfully.

Tulloch gets *com.priv.* against Fraser 14 Aug. 1445 (*Diplom.
Norv.*,xvii, no.1028) unfruitfully,

Thomas Spens	1445 - 1449.
Thomas Penven	x 1447.
Robert Lauder	1447.
Gilbert Herring	1447.
Malcolm Rae	1447 - 1448.
Patrick de Birnie (Brynneth)	1448.
Hector de Tulloch	1448.
Nicholas Blair	1448 - 1449.

Spens got it on exch. through ord. with Fraser about two years before 7 Jan./13 Feb. 1447, when he got rehabilitation (Reg.Supp., 414,fo.183v,;*CPL*,x,355-6), in poss. 4 Apr. 1448 (Reg.Supp.,429,fo. 88); res. to ord. in favour of Forrester c.June 1449 (*CPL*,x,221; v.inf.).

Penven had prov. and then res. without poss. sometime before 2 Jan. 1447 (v.inf.).

Lauder prov. on Fraser's res. and Penven's res. 2 Jan. 1447 (Reg.Supp.,414,fo.154); res. before 3 Apr. 1447 without having had letters of prov. made out (v.inf.).

Herring prov. 28 Jan. 1447 (ibid.,414,fo.216); res. claim before 3 Apr. 1447 (v.inf.).

Rae prov. on res. of Lauder and Herring and supposed res. of Spens 3 Apr. 1447 (ibid.,417, fo.45v); new prov. on expected prov. of Spens to *M.archd.* again 11 Apr. 1448 (ibid.,426,fo.67v).

Birnie got *com.priv.* against Spens 4 Apr. 1448 (ibid.,429,fo. 88), but died before letters were made out (v.inf.).

Tulloch prov. on Birnie's death 5 Sept. 1448 (ibid.,430,fo.181v).

Blair prov. on Birnie's death 10 Dec. 1448 (ibid.,434,fo.327v); new prov. 24 Apr. 1449 (ibid.,436,fo.31v).

Gilbert Forrester	1449 - 1459 x 1462.
William Hog	1449 - 1450.
David Ogilvie	1451.
David Balfour	1458.
Richard Wylie	x 1462 - 1467.

Forrester had coll. by ord. on res. of Spens about two years before 22 June 1451 (*CPL*,x,221); new prov. 2 Nov. 1449, when it was Fraser who is said to have res. (Reg.Supp.,437,fo.228); still in poss. 28 June 1459 (*CPL*,xi,384); d. before 31 July 1462 (Reg.Supp.,553, fo.27).

Hog prov. on res. of Spens 30 Dec. 1449/3 Jan. 1450 (ibid.,438, fos,216,283) unfruitfully.

Ogilvie gets *com.priv.* against Forrester 22 June 1451 (*CPL*,x, 221) unfruitfully.

Balfour gets *com.priv.* against Forrester 16 May 1458 (Reg. Supp.,509,fo.227v) unfruitfully.

Wylie had prov. before 5 Jan. 1462 (ibid.,548,fo.48) and lit. with Forrester before his death i.e. before 31 July 1462 (ibid.,553,fo. 27); his prov. was based on res. of Spens, but he never had poss.(*CPL*, xiii,77); appointed abbot of Kelso 13 Nov. 1467 (*CPL*,xii,640).

William Fractoris	1462 - 1462 x 1477.
Patrick Lockhart	1462 - 1479.
Alexander Stewart	1464 - 1472 x 1473.
Archibald Whitelaw	1467 - c. 1476-7.

Fractoris prov. on Forrester's death 31 July 1462 (*CPL*,xi,456); res. right before 17 Dec. 1477, prob. without having had poss. (*CPL*, xiii,77).

Lockhart prov. on Forrester's death 10 Aug. 1462 (*CPL*,xi, 457-8); no poss. 7 Oct. 1462 (Reg.Supp.,562,fo.65); said to have res.

right before 17 Dec. 1477 (*CPL*,xiii,77), but then res. right in favour
of Chalmer 7 Feb. 1479 (v.inf.).

Stewart presumably had ord. coll. on Forrester's death; occ.
20 July 1464 (*Invernessiana*,150, where printed text has 1474 wrongly)
and 24 Sept. 1464 (Fraser, *Grant*,iii,26); occ. 10 June 1471 (*Cawdor Bk.*,53); got disp. to hold it with *R.archd.* 5 Mar. 1472 (Reg.Supp.,
677,fo.23); moved to *M.chanc.* by 28 July 1473, Galbraith getting ord.
coll. after Dec. 1472 (v.inf.).

Whitelaw prov. on Wylie's elevation to Kelso 19 Nov. 1467 (*CPL*,
xii,281-2); res.c. 1476-7 without having had poss (*CPL*,xiii,77).

William Galbraith	1472 x 1473 - 1477 x 1478.
Andrew Lyell	c. 1476-7 - 1479.
John Chalmer/de Camera	1478 - 1482.
Giles Boyce	1479.

Galbraith coll. by ord. Dec. 1472 x Dec. 1473 (*CPL*,xiii,77);
occ. 2 Aug. 1473 (*Moray Reg.*,256); still in poss. 17 Dec. 1477 (*CPL*,
xiii,77); res. to ord. (presumably in favour of Chalmer before 6 Mar.
1478,v.inf.), and entered a religious order before 7/8 Feb. 1479
(Reg.Supp.,777,fos.140,286).

Lyell got crown pres. to Whitelaw's right c. 1476-7 (*CPL*,
xiii,77); no poss. when conf. by pope 17 Dec. 1477 (ibid.); lit. with
Chalmer 8 Jan./7 Feb. 1479 (Reg.Supp.,776,fos.252v-3); promised
annates 10 Nov. 1479 (*ACSB*,196).

Chalmer occ. 6 Mar. 1478 (*RMS*,ii,no.1373); prov. *Si neutri*
8 Jan. 1479 (Reg.Supp.,776,fos.252v-3); surrog. to Lockhart's
right 7 Feb. 1479 (ibid.,fo.286); occ. 22 Mar. 1482 (*St Nich.Cart.*,
i,148).

Boyce prov. on reported death of Chalmer 4 Mar. 1479 (Reg.
Supp.,778,fo.119v); cf. *M.prec.*

John Ireland 1487 - 1495.

Occ. 24 Oct. 1487 (*Moray Reg.*,257); occ. 22 Feb. 1492 (SRO,
ADC,i,fo.209); still alive 11 Apr. 1495 (*Prot.Bk.Young*,no.790); d.
before 23 Aug. 1495 (v.inf.).

John Scherar	1495 - 1498.
Andrew Stewart	1497.
John Spens	1497 - 1513.

Scherar prov. on Ireland's death 23 Aug. 1495, but did not have
poss. when promised annates 1 Feb. 1498 (PRO 31/9 - 30/397-8).

Stewart lit. with Spens 31 Jan. 1497 (*ADC*,ii,63).

Spens lit. with Stewart 31 Jan. 1497 (ibid.); had become
M.offic. by 20 July 1499; occ. 3 Sept. 1501 (*Univ.Evidence*,iii,356);
occ. 10 Jan. 1513 (Fraser, *Grant*,iii,365).

Andrew Forman 1515.

Res. on or before 10 Feb. 1515 (v.inf.).

Thomas Chalmer 1515.

Mand. for prov. on res. of Forman 10 Feb. 1515 (*Leonis X Regesta*,
ii,26).

William Nory 1515.

Occ. 21 May 1515 (Fraser, *Sutherland*,iii,60).

John Dingwall (Druguual) 1523 - 1525.

Occ. 23 Apr. 1523 (SRO, Mey,no.19); in poss. and is to pay a pension from fruits 23 Aug. 1525 (PRO 31/9 - 32/80); prob. made exch. with Dunbar for *Ab.chanc.*

Patrick Dunbar 1525 (?), 1532 - 1535.

Prob. got poss. on exch. with Dingwall in 1525; occ. 16 Apr. 1532 (*Moray Reg.*,373-4); res. in favour of David Dunbar, but promised annates to retain fruits 10 Sept. 1535 (PRO 31/9 - 33/11-12).

David Dunbar 1535 - 1548.

Promises annates and gets prov. without fruits 10 Sept. 1535 (PRO 31/9 - 33/12-13); occ. 1539 (*Moray Reg.*, xxiii); res. in curia in favour of Alexander Dunbar, but promised annates to retain fruits 24 June 1548 (PRO 31/9 - 33/237-8, where names are transposed).

Alexander Dunbar junior 1548 - 1589.

Promised annates and gets prov. without fruits 24 June 1548 (ibid.); occ. 26 Jan. 1550 (*Prot.Bk.Rollok*,no.189); became *M.dean* also July 1566; when given crown conf. 27 Jan. 1571 he was thought to have had papal prov. 24 years earlier (*RSS*,vi,no.1110); res. on or before 28 May 1589 in favour of Robert Dunbar (v.inf.); d. 13 July 1593 as *M.dean.*

Robert Dunbar 1589 - 1619.

Crown pres. on res. of Alexander Dunbar 28 May 1589 (RSS,lix, fo.142); occ. 24 May 1615 (Edin.Univ.Lib., Laing Chr.no.2441; cf. *Laing Chrs.*,no. 1726); dem. on or before 16 Jan. 1618 (v.inf.).

Thomas Dunbar 1618 - 1619.

Crown pres. on dem. of Robert Dunbar 16 Jan. 1618 (Reg.Pres., v,fo.1); occ. 9 Oct. 1619 (SRO,Part.Reg.Sasines Inverness,i,fo.210).

John Hay 1625 - 1638.

Occ. 18 May 1625 (SRO, Part.Reg.Sasines Elgin,iii,fo.53) and 24 Sept. 1638 (ibid.,iv,fo.181).

ARCHDEACONS OF MORAY

First known date: 1179 x 1188.

Prebend: chs. of Forres and Edinkillie (Logie Fythenach) in 1207 x 1208 (*Moray Reg.*,41; Cowan, *Parishes,* 59,69).

Thomas 1179 x 1188.

Occ. 1179 x 1188 (*St A.Lib.*,290).

Robert c. 1197, 1197 x 1203, 1200 x 1206.

Occ. c. 1197 (*Moray Reg.*, 38-39,131), 1197 x 1203 (ibid.,456, where names of dean and archd. are transposed), and 1200 x 1206 (*Kel.Lib.*, ii,315).

Gilbert de Moray (Moravia) 1207 x 1208 - 1222 x 1224.
Occ. Mar. 1207 x June 1208 (*Moray Reg.*,43;cf.ibid.,274 for surname); occ. 7 Dec. 1221 (ibid.,456-7); cons. *C.bp.* 11 Sept. 1222 x 10 Apr. 1224.

Hugh (de Douglas ?) 1225 - 1227.
Occ. 1225 and 19 June 1226 (*Moray Reg.*, 21, 78); occ. Mar. 1226/7 (*Arb.Lib.*,i,144; cf. *Moray Reg.*, 22-23); surname is suggested from an analysis of the chapter before and after this Henry appears as archd.

Ranulf 1228 - 1232.
Occ. 20 June 1228 and 11 Oct. 1232 (*Moray Reg.*,122,96; cf. ibid.,107 which is misdated 4 Sept. 1240, prob. for 1230).

William 1235 - 1249.
Occ. 1235 (*A.B.Ill.*,ii,285; *St A.Lib.*, 326-7); occ. 4 Feb. 1249 (*Moray Reg.*, 277).

Archibald Herok c. 1258 - 1275.
Occ. c. 1258 (ibid.,135; cf. ibid.,138, 279 for surname); cons. *C.bp.* 10 Jan. x 22 Sept. 1275.

John 1281 x 1299.
Occ. 2 Feb. 1281 (Fraser, *Grant*,iii,7); still in poss. 30 June 1299 (*CPL*,i,582).

Stephen de Dunnideer (Donydeir) 1316 - 1317.
Occ. 18 Oct. 1316 (Fraser, *Grant*,iii,257); d. as *G.bp.*- elect 13 July x 18 Aug. 1317.

Adam Penny 1327.
Occ. 14 June 1327 (*Family of Rose*,115); retained poss. until death (v.inf.).

Alexander Bur 1350 - 1362.
Had earlier prov. on Penny's death and got conf. 5 June 1350 (*CPP*,i,199); prov. *M.bp.* 23 Dec. 1362.

William de Fores 1363 - 1370.
Prob. had poss. by 12 Nov. 1363 (see *C.dean*); occ. 6 Mar.1370 (*Moray Reg.*, 167-8).

Stephen 1371.
Occ. 30 Mar. 1371 (BM, MS Harley 4694, no. 8; Sibbald, *Fife*, 232-4).

Duncan Petit 1385 - 1385 x 1393.
Occ. 15 May 1385 (Fraser, *Menteith*,ii,260-2); res. on exch. with Dickson before 21 June 1393 (v.inf.).

Hugh Dickson/de Dalmahoy 1393 - 1394.
In poss. after exch. with Petit through ord. (Collect.,457,fo. 189v; Reg.Vat.,307,fo.565v); still in poss. 24 July 1394 (ibid.).

James de Dunbar c. 1397 - 1408.

In poss. by time he obtained *M.prec.* as well c. 16 Sept. 1397 (*CPP*, i,625-6, 637); occ. 5 Apr. 1408 (SRO, J.M. Thomson Transcripts,s.d.); d. before 2 Oct. 1408 (v.inf.).

Adam de Nairn   1408 - 1409 x 1414.
William de Camera   1408.

Nairn got ord. coll. on death of Dunbar, and gets papal conf. 3 May 1409 (Reg.Av.,332,fos.415-16); res. his right some time before 12 Apr. 1431 (v.inf.), presumably before 18 May 1414 (see *M.succ.*).

Camera gets prov. on death of Dunbar 2 Oct. 1408 (*CPP*,i,637); res. his right some time before 10 June 1430 (v.inf.).

John de Forbes x 1430.

Held it at death sometime before 18 May 1430 (v.inf.).

William de Dunbar   1430 - 1435.
Nicholas de Atholl   1430 - 1435.
Robert de Crannach   1430 - 1433.
Robert Scrymgeour   1435.

Dunbar was coll. by ord. on death of Forbes and got conf. 13 June 1430 (*CPL*,viii,372); new prov. 11 Mar. 1431 (*ACSB*,104); lit. with Atholl and Crannach by 12 Apr. 1431 (v.inf.); after nearly two years of lit. had succ. to Crannach's right in return for a pension before 23 Sept. 1433 (Reg.Supp., 288,fo.297), prob. had poss. then; lit. still with Atholl when he got ratification of his claim 18 Jan. 1435 (ibid.,301,fo. 297v); res. right before 13 Aug. 1435 (v.inf.).

Atholl had new prov. 18 May 1430 (Reg.Supp.,255,fo.37; *ACSB*,103); claimed poss. 21 Mar. 1431 (Reg.Supp.,267,fo.117v); lit. with Dunbar and Crannach by 12 Apr. 1431 (v.inf.); won a stage of lit. against Dunbar sometime before 18 Jan. 1435 (ibid.,301,fo.297v), when still claimed poss.; res. before 13 Aug. 1435 (v.inf.).

Crannach prov. in virtue of an exp. grace 10 June 1430 (Reg. Supp.,258,fo.87; cf. 301, fo.297v); lit. with Atholl and Dunbar by 12 Apr. 1431 (ibid.,266,fo.104v); res. right to Dunbar in return for pension sometime before 23 Sept. 1433 (when pension was conf.) after almost two years of lit. (ibid.,288,fo.297); still claimed some right 27 Oct. 1433 (ibid.,290,fo.105).

Scrymgeour prov. on reported death of Atholl 17 June 1435 (Reg.Supp.,320,fo.192); d. 23 May x 5 Nov. 1436 (see *C.dean.*).

Henry Hervy   1435 - 1438 x 1440.
John de Atholl   1435 - 1437.
Duncan de Lichton   1437.

Hervy got poss. on res. of Nicholas de Atholl (i.e. prob. by 13 Aug. 1435,v.inf.) and was conf. 7 Jan. 1436 (Reg.Supp.,318,fo.11); conf. again against any claim of John de Atholl 18 Mar. 1436 (ibid., 321,fo.113v); paid part of annates 30 Mar. 1436 (*ACSB*,263); occ. 8 May 1438 (*A.B.Ill.*,iii,265); prob. res. on exch. with Ogilvie for *Ab.prec.* after 5 Dec. 1438.

Atholl prov. following res. of Nicholas de Atholl, Crannach or Dunbar 13 Aug. 1435 (Reg.Supp.,310,fo.95v); claimed poss. when

incorporated at Basel 1 Oct. 1435 (Haller, *Conc.Bas.*,iii,529; cf.
Mon.Conc.Bas.,ii,824); but still had not yet expedited his letters of
prov. 18 Mar. 1436 (Reg.Supp.,321,fo.113v); lit. with Hervy in curia
by 2 Jan. 1437 (v.inf.).
    Lichton prov. on report of Hervy's death 2 Jan. 1437 (Reg.
Supp.,332,fo.236).

David Ogilvie   1438 x 1440 - 1443 x 1444.
Robert de Tulloch 1443.
    Ogilvie prob. got it on exch. with Hervy after 8 May 1438
(v.sup.); in poss. 8 June 1440 (*CPL*,ix,90); in poss. 30 Jan. 1443 when
res. on exch. with Tulloch for *Dk.dean.* (Reg.Supp.,388,fo.89v); but
this was ineffective because of Tulloch's death (v.inf.); res. effectively
on exch. with Spens for a parish ben. before 10 June 1444 (v.inf.).
    Tulloch prov. on exch. with Ogilvie 30 Jan. 1443 (v.sup.); d. still
Dk.dean before 10 July 1443.

Thomas Spens   1444 - 1447 x 1448.
Patrick Fraser   1445 - 1448 x 1462.
    Spens got poss. on exch. with Ogilvie before 10 June 1444 (St A.
Univ. Mun., St A.SCB, fo. 61-62v; cf. Reg.Supp.,417,fo.277); res. on
exch. through ord. with Fraser for *M.succ.* c. Jan./Feb. 1445 (*CPL*,x,
355-6); but occ. 23 June 1446 (*CDS*,iv,no.1187) and still lit. with
Fraser 19 Sept. 1447 (Reg.Supp., 410,fo.208v); lost case before 8 Feb.
1448 (v.inf.).
    Fraser got it on exch. c. Jan./Feb. 1445 (v.sup.); in poss. 13 Feb.
1447 and new prov. 19 Mar. 1447 (*CPL*,x,355-6,367-8); lit. with
Spens by 19 Sept. 1447 (v.sup.), but won and got conf. and new prov.
8 Feb. 1448 (Reg.Supp.,423,fo.42); d. shortly before 27 Aug. 1462
(ibid.,553,fo.229v; cf. *C.dean.*).

Archibald Whitelaw   1462 x 1463 - 1466 x 1467.
Thomas Cockburn (Kokarion)   1462.
    Whitelaw had ord. coll. on death of Fraser 1462 x 1464 (*CPL*,
xii,434); occ. 5 Dec. 1463 (Fraser, *Buccleuch*,ii,61); papal conf.
of ord. coll. 7 Feb. 1465 (*CPL*,xii,434); occ. 25 Dec. 1466 (*RMS*,
ii,no.898); res. on getting another ben. from ord. before 3 Sept.1467
(*CPL*,xii,579).
    Cockburn prov. on Fraser's death 27 Aug. 1462 (Reg.Supp.,553,
fo.229).

Archibald Knollis/Knowis   1467 - 1473 x 1475.
Robert de Forrest   1467 - 1467 x 1468.
Alexander de Meldrum (Ateldrany) 1467 - 1467 x 1468.
Andrew Forfar   1468.
John Edwardson (Edwardi)   1468.
    Knollis had had poss. for over a month by 3 Nov. 1467 (Reg.
Supp.,617,fo.191); had got it on res. of Whitelaw, and got new prov.
6 Nov. 1467 (Ibid.,616,fo.234v); occ. 2 Aug. 1473 (*Moray Reg.*,256);
d. before 4 Sept. 1475 (v.inf.).
    Forrest claimed poss. 25 Oct. 1467 when assigned pension on ch.

of Dalry by Knollis, who was rector there (Reg.Supp.,620,fo.174); d. before 8 June 1468 (v.inf.).

Meldrum (as 'Ateldrany') gets *com.priv.* against Knollis 3 Nov. 1467 (Reg.Supp.,617,fo.191); d. in curia before 20 Sept. 1468 (v.inf.).

Forfar prov. on Forrest's death 8 June 1468 (ibid. 626,fo.289).

Edwardson prov. on report of death of Knollis or on deaths of Forrest or Meldrum 20 Sept. 1468 (ibid.,634,fo.88 bis).

John Garden	1475 - 1479.
John Calder	1476.
John 'Ruch'	1476.
James Allardice	1476 - 1506 x 1507.

Garden got prov. on death of Knollis 4 Sept. 1475 (*CPL*,xiii,459); lit. with Calder and then Allardice prob. without poss., and res. his right 31 Oct. 1479 (ibid. 702).

Calder in poss. when lit. 11 June 1476 (Reg.Supp.,739,fo.11v); had had coll. by ord. on Forrest's death, and had had poss. for less then a year when conf. 16 July 1476 (*CPL*,xiii,518-9); d. before 29 Aug. 1476 (v.inf.).

'Ruch' prov. on Calder's death 29 Aug. 1476 (Reg.Supp.,742,fo.18).

Allardice had ord. coll. on Calder's death July x Dec. 1476, and then lit. with Garden (*CPL*,xiii,702); occ. 18 Aug. 1478 (Fraser, *Lennox*,ii,119); new prov. 31 Oct. 1479 (*CPL*,xiii,702); occ. 2 May 1506 (SRO, Seafield, 75/5); d. before 10 Nov. 1507 (see *St Mary, St A.prov.*).

Alexander Crichton x 1508.

Held it at death before 27 Nov. 1508 (v.inf.).

John Estoun 1508.

Crown pres. on Crichton's death 27 Nov. 1508 (*RSS*,i,no.1767).

Patrick Painter 1509 - 1513.

Thomas Nudry 1510 - 1526 x 1527.

Painter in poss. 18 Oct. 1509 (PRO 31/9 - 1/145-6); res. in Nudry's favour 19 July 1510, promising annates to retain fruits 9 Aug. 1510 (ibid.,31/228-9); occ. 7 Nov. 1510 and 27 Mar. 1511 (*RMS*,ii, nos. 3518, 3557); promises annates again 1 July 1513 (PRO 31/9 - 31/281 - 2).

Nudry prov. without fruits on res. of Painter 19 July 1510 (v.sup.); occ. Feb. 1512 and 3 Aug. 1513 (*James IV Letters*,229, 506n); still in poss. 26 May 1526 (PRO 31/9 - 32/87); still alive 7 July 1526 (*Laing Chrs.*,no.356); d. before 3 Dec. 1527 (v.inf.).

James Douglas	1527 - 1533.
Alexander Hervy	1529.
Sixtus Zuchellus	1529 - 1530.

Douglas had crown pres. on Nudry's death some two years before Dec. 1529 (*ADCP*,319); in poss. and lit. with Zuchellus 1 Feb. 1530 (*James V Letters*, 167-8); res. in favour of Bellenden, but promises annates to retain fruits 27 Aug. 1533 (PRO 31/9-32/267).

Hervy had prov. on Nudry's death, and res. his right in Douglas's favour 3 Dec. 1529 (*ADCP*,319).

Zuchellus prov. on Nudry's death 3 Sept. 1529 (PRO 31/9-32/135-6); lit. with Douglas when king seeks cancellation of his prov. 1 Feb. 1530 (*James V Letters*,167-8).

John Bellenden 1533   1538.
Promises annates and gets prov. without fruits 27 Aug. 1533 (PRO 31/9 - 32/267-8); occ. 16 Jan. 1537 (SRO, Prot.Bk.Thomas Kene, fo.79); occ. 20 Dec. 1538 (*RMS*,iii,no.1877); prob. res. on exch. with Dunbar for *G.prec.*

Archibald Dunbar 1539 - 1551 x 1565.
Prob. got it on exch. with Bellenden (v.sup.); occ. 9 Mar.1539 (SRO, ADC & S, xi,fo.244v); occ. 26 June 1551 (*RSS*,iv,no.1264); d. before 26 Jan. 1565 (v.inf.).

John Leslie 1565 - 1566-7.
Crown pres. on Dunbar's death 26 Jan. 1565 (*RSS*,v,no.1917); occ. 19 Oct. 1565 (SRO, Reg.Deeds, vii,fo.214); granted *R.bp.* 20 Apr. 1566/21 Jan. 1567.

Gavin Dunbar 1574 - 1613.
Occ. 12/18 Nov. 1574 (SRO, Abbrev.Feu Chrs.,ii,fo.52); occ. 22 July 1608 (SRO, Reg.Ho.Chr. s.d.); dem. on or before 1 July 1613 (v.inf.).

Patrick Tulloch 1613 - 1638.
Crown pres. on dem. of Dunbar 1 July 1613 (Reg.Pres.,iv,99); occ. 24 Sept. 1638 (SRO, Part.Reg. Sasines Elgin,iv,fo.181).

DEANS OF CHRISTIANITY

DEANS OF ELGIN

First known date: c. 1350 (*Moray Reg.,* 362).

John Hugonis 1375 - 1398.
Occ. 21 July 1375 (*Arb.Lib.*,ii,33), and 1 Aug. 1398 (*Moray Reg.* 327).

DEANS OF STRATHBOGIE

First known date: 1223 x 1226.

William 1223 x 1226 - 1227.
Occ. 1223 x 1226, 5 May 1226 and 18 Mar. 1227 (*Moray Reg.*, 69, 75, 23).

M. 1232.
Occ. 10 Oct. 1232 (ibid.,30).

Note: deanery still existed c. 1350 and c. 1400 (ibid.,363,366) and is mentioned 19 June 1566 (*Prot.Bk. Grote*,no.275); but no other names are known.

DEANS OF STRATHSPEY

First known date: 1226.

Gregory 1226 - 1227.
Occ. 5 May 1226 and 18 Mar. 1227 (*Moray Reg.*,76,23).

Note: deanery still existed c. 1350 and c. 1400 (ibid.,362,366).

Thomas de Fordyce (?) 1432.
Occ. as dean of an unidentified deanery and as vic. of Abernethy and Inverallan 9 Jan. 1432 (Reg.Supp.,273,fo.225); these vics. lay in Strathspey deanery.

DEANS OF INVERNESS

First known date: 1223 x 1226.

Robert 1223 x 1226 - 1227.
Occ. 1223 x 1226, 5 May 1226 and 18 Mar. 1227 (*Moray Reg.*, 69, 76,23).

Matthew Reny 1340.
Occ. 30 July 1340 (*Beauly Chrs.*, 87).

Adam Gobinol 1343.
Occ. as the 'rural dean' in a matter concerning chapel of Kilravock in Dalcross parish (which lay in this deanery) 3 Dec. 1343 (*Family of Rose*,118; cf. Cowan, *Parishes*, 43 and *Moray Reg.*, 362).

Donald 1398.
Occ. 20 Nov. 1398 (*Moray Reg.*, 211).

Patrick Fletcher (Flegear) 1462.
Occ. 25 Feb. 1462 (*Invernessiana*,140).

Martin Diverti/Dominici 1490 - 1499.
Occ. as Martin 20 Aug. 1490 (*Cawdor Bk.*, 75); occ. with surname read alternatively as Diverti or Dominici and as vic. of Brachlie and Petty 20 Dec. 1499 (*PSAS*,xli,319; NLS, Hutton MSS [Shires] xi, 52).

Note: Dr. John Durkan reports mentions of unnamed deans of Inverness in 1451/2, 1509, 1529 and 1542 in NLS, Hutton MSS (Shires).

OFFICIALS

OFFICIALS OF MORAY

First known date: 1233.

William 1233.
   Occ. as *M.chanc.* 1233 (Macphail, *Pluscardyn,*203).

William Agnus 1237 - 1238 x 1239.
   Prob. in office 10 Oct. 1237 (*Moray Reg.,*133, from place in witness list); occ. 6 Dec. 1238 (ibid.,121); prob. no longer in office 5 Mar. 1239 (ibid.,105, when he appears just as canon of Kingussie; cf. ibid., 97).

Walter Surays/Sureys 1275, 1254 x 1294.
   Occ. 10 Jan. 1275 (*Beauly Chrs.,* 57) and 1254 x 1294 (*Moray Reg..* 280).

Roger de Inverness 1294.
   Occ. 30 Oct. 1294 (ibid.,145).

John de Inverness 1345.
   Occ. as *M.chanc.* 20 Oct. 1345 (ibid.,157).

Walter de Birnie (Brennath) 1370.
   Occ. 6 Mar. 1370 (ibid.,168).

Thomas Young 1430.
   Occ. 17 Jan. 1430 (*Dunf.Reg.,*282-4);

John Basolis/Basok 1446 - 1455.
   Occ. 30 Aug. 1449 (NRA, Transcript of Pluscarden Chrs.); by 22/30 Dec. 1455 had been nine years in office, as he still was (*CPL,* xi,85, 286).

Thomas Grant 1464 - 1493.
   Occ. 24 Sept. 1464 (Fraser, *Grant,*iii,24), having perhaps taken office since 17 May 1464 (see *M.comm.*); occ. 8 Jan. 1493 (*Moray Reg.,* 249).

John Spens 1499 - 1513.
   Occ. 20 June 1499 (*Invernessiana,*179); occ. 10 Jan. 1513 (Fraser, *Grant,*iii,365).

Walter Maxwell 1519.
   Occ. 23 Nov. 1519 (*Glas Mun.,*ii,137);

Robert Reid 1527 - 1530.
   Occ. as *M.subd.* 9 Nov. 1527 (Fraser, *Sutherland,*iii,80); occ. as abbot of Kinloss 5 Nov. 1530 (*Arb.Lib.,*ii,502).

Gavin Leslie 1530s (?)
   Said to have held office apparently before 25 May 1529 when he would seem to have been dead (*Gen.Coll.,*ii,3-4); but in fact still

active 14 Aug. 1538 and 3 Jan. 1540 (*Moray Reg.*,402,420); his period in this office was prob. therefore before or after Sinclair; cf. *M.comm.*

Henry Sinclair 1537 - 1538.

In office when bp. died 19 Dec. 1537 and his commission lapsed (SRO, Prot.Bk.Edward Diksoun, p.17); still out of office 14 Jan. 1538 (ibid.); in office again 16 Mar. 1538 (ibid.,p.29).

Alexander Sutherland 1538 - 1549.

Occ. as *C.dean* and M.canon (under wrong name 'Sandilands') 9 July 1538 (Keith, *Bishops*,198); occ. as *C.dean* 28 Aug. 1542 (Fraser, *Grant,* iii,89) and 9 May 1549 (ibid.,374); occ. 15 Jan. 1552 (SRO, Sent.Offic. St A.,fo.255).

COMMISSARIES

COMMISSARIES WITH GENERAL AUTHORITY

COMMISSARIES OF MORAY

First known date: 1464.

Thomas Grant 1464.

Occ. (CG) 17 May 1464 (SRO, Mackintosh Muniments, no. 7); prob. moved to *M.offic.* by 24 Sept. 1464.

William de Birnie (Byrnetht) 1476.

Occ. (CG) as vic. of Essle and Dipple 15 June 1476 (Fraser, *Grant,* iii,2).

Anselm Robertson/Roberti 1521 - 1523.

Occ. (C) 5 Dec. 1521 (*Inverness Recs.*,i,184); occ. (GC) as *R.succ.* 23 July 1522 (*Moray Reg.,* 407) and 23 Apr. 1523 (SRO,Mey, no. 5).

Barald/Beroald Leslie 1525.

Occ. (CG) as M.canon 4 Mar. 1525 (Fraser, *Sutherland*,iii,72); buried 25 May 1529 (*Gen.Coll.*,ii,3).

John Hay 1530 - 1532.

Occ. (CG) 25 Aug./25 Sept. 1530 (BM, Add.MS 33245,fos. 107-8; see also *Arb.Lib.*,ii,502); occ. (CG) as M.canon 18 Jan. 1532 (*Moray Reg.,* 422).

Thomas Gaderar 1535 - 1536.

Occ. (C of Elgin) 16 Apr. 1535 (*RMS*,iii,no.1469); occ. (CG) as vic. of Nairn 27 Mar. 1536 (Fraser, *Grant,* iii,100); occ (C) 10 Oct. 1536 (SRO, Reg.Ho.Chr.no.1142A).

Gavin Leslie 1538 - 1545.

Occ. (CG) as M.canon 14 Aug. 1538 (*Moray Reg.*,402); occ. (CG) 13 Mar. 1545 (SRO, Sent.Offic. St A.,fo.106).

John Leslie 1549.
     Occ. (C) as M.canon 26 Dec. 1549 (*OPS*,II,ii,631; cf. Fraser, *Sutherland*,iii,20,n.l, where date is 16 Dec.).

Hugh Craigie   1551 - 1586.
John Gibson   1563.
Alexander Douglas   1570 - 1571.
     Craigie occ. (C) 4 July 1551 (SRO, GD 1/137), occ.(C) 13 Dec. 1558 (*St A. Offic.*,168); said to have held office 1559-1586 (*Intro. to Scottish Legal History* [Stair Soc.] , no sources cited).
     Gibson occ. (C) with Craigie 18 Mar. 1563 (SRO, Acts and Decreets,xxvi,fo.119).
     Douglas occ. (C) 4 July 1570 (*RMS*,iv,no.1964) and 24 Dec. 1571 (ibid.,vi,no.1410).

COMMISSARIES WITH LIMITED AUTHORITY

COMMISSARIES OF INVERNESS

First known date: 1522.

Magnus Vaus 1522 - 1540 x 1542.
     Occ. (C) as vic. of Dalcross 9 Apr. 1522 (NLS, Hutton MSS [Shires] ,xi,64); occ. (C) as vic. of Abertarff 25 Sept./20 Nov. 1536 (*Invernessiana*,209); occ. 16 Nov. 1540 (ibid.,213), d. before 17 Aug. 1542 (see *Tain prov*;cf. *RSS*,iii,no471).

James Duff 1556 - 1578.
     Occ. (C) as rector of Boleskine 2 Sept. 1556 (Fraser, *Grant*,iii, 122); in office until Reformation; then there was no judge in Inverness deanery until he was re-appointed by lords of council and session (being parson of Boleskine still) 12 July 1577/11 July 1578 (SRO, Bks. of Sederunt 1575-83, fo.50; *RSS*,vii,no.1578).

ORKNEY DIOCESE

BISHOPS OF ORKNEY

First known date: before 1035 (?).

These bishops prob. recognised York metropolitan authority in early 11th century; then Hamburg-Bremen supplied three bishops in the period 1043 x 1072; then York appointed three 1073 - c.1112, but failed to get poss. for the last of these; an alternative bp. appointed 1112 (?) prob. accepted metropolitan authority of Lund; there was a plan in 1151 to place this diocese under St Andrews as metropolitan (John of Salisbury, *Historia Pontificalis,* ed. M.Chibnall, 72), but this was rejected in favour of putting Orkney under Nidaros/Trondheim in 1153 (see A.O. Johnsen, *Studier vedrorende Nicolaus Brekespears Legasjon til Norden* (Oslo, 1945) 96-97 for date); it remained under Trondheim until after the political transfer of Orkney and Shetland to Scotland 1468-9, and was then put under the new metropolitan see of St Andrews 17 Aug. 1472 (*Vet.Mon.,*no.852; cf. *Diplom. Norv.,*xvii,no. 784).

Henry x 1035 (?)

Acted as bp. in the Orkneys, perhaps after being keeper of King Cnut's treasure in England, or perhaps by appointment of that king while holding this office i.e. perhaps before 1035 (Adam of Bremen, *Gesta Hammaburgensis Ecclesiae Pontificum,* ed. B.Schmeidler (1917), bk.iv, c.8; translation (1959), ed. F.J. Tschan, p.192); presumably an Englishman (see Thurolf below) and prob. under metropolitan authority of York (cf. *Diplom.Norv.,*xvii B, 294; cf. ibid.,197-8 for possible identification with a Bp. Henry active for two undatable years in Iceland), appointed later by king of Denmark to see of Lund c.1060-1 (Adam of Bremen, *Gesta,* loc.cit.).

Thurolf 1043 x 1072, perhaps c.1050.

Appointed by abp. of Bremen as bp. to the Orkneys (ibid.,iii, cc. 24, 77; ed. Tschan, 134,183), more specifically he was cons. to see of Birsay (presumably when this church was founded by Earl Thorfinn c.1048 x 1065) by this same abp. at the pope's order, the previous bishops having been selected from among the English or the 'Scots' (ibid.,iv,c.35; ed. Tschan, 216, cf. *ES,* ii,8; and see *Diplom.Norv.,xvii* B,295 for suggested date).

John 1043 x 1072.

Appointed to Orkneys by abp. of Bremen, apparently in succ. to Thurolf, following cons. in 'Scotland' (Adam of Bremen, *Gesta,*iii,c.77; ed. Tschan, 183; *ES,*ii,8); but perhaps in fact one of the 'Scots' who preceded Thurolf (cf. *Diplom.Norv.,* xvii B,295); perhaps same as the John 'Irski' (i.e. Irishman) who spent four years as a bp. in Iceland at some unknown date about this time (cf.ibid.,197; and see John *G.bp.* 1055 x 1060).

Adalbert/Albert 1043 x 1072.

Appointed to Orkneys by abp. of Bremen in succ. to John (Adam of Bremen, *Gesta*,iii,c.77; ed. Tschan,183; *ES*,ii,8); apparently cons. earlier elsewhere (Adam of Bremen, *Gesta,* schol. 148; ed. Tschan, 214).

Radulf 1073.

Nom. by Paul earl of Orkney, and sent to Thomas abp. of York, who arranged for his cons. at York 3 Mar.,prob. 1073 (Haddan & Stubbs *Councils*,II,i,162-3; cf. note in a version of the Anglo-Saxon Chronicle kept at Canterbury which gives date as 1077 - see *SAEC*,99); perhaps York was approached because the new abp. of Bremen did not yet have his pallium of metropolitical authority (*Diplom.Norv.*, xvii B,182); he is named as Radulf in a source dated x 1127 (Hugh the Chantor, *History,* 32), and a copy of his supposed profession of obedience to York was kept at York in the late 12th century (*Historians of York*,ii,363; cf. 372); just possibly the same man as Roolwer *I.bp.* (cf. *ES*,ii,96).

Roger O.S.B. 1100 x 1108.

As a monk of Whitby, Yorkshire, received cons. from Gerard abp. of York, after profession of obedience, as successor to Radulf Dec.1100 x May 1108 (Hugh the Chantor, *History,* 32; *Historians of York*,ii, 367); note that again there was no abp. of Bremen with metropolitical authority in the form of the pallium between 1101 and 1123 (*Diplom. Norv.*,xvii B, 183); prob. the unnamed bp. whom Anselm abp. of Canterbury commended to Hakon earl of Orkney, the implication being that this bp. had been to Orkney but was now in need of support to get the earl to submit to his authority (Haddan & Stubbs, *Councils*,II,i, 167-8; *Orkney-Shetland Recs.*,i,10-12); this letter cannot be dated before the period of Anselm's exile which began in April. 1103, as Hakon was not then yet earl (*Complete Peerage*,x, app.A); Canterbury was most likely concerned because York was vacant, so that the letter is datable between the deaths of Abps. Gerard and Anselm i.e. 21 May 1108 x 21 Apr. 1109; about this time an unnamed bp. of Orkney (presumably Roger) is known to have been available in England 25 May x 6 Sept. 1108 as a possible helper for a proposed cons. at York of a bp of St Andrews (Haddan & Stubbs, *Councils*,II,i,171; *SAEC*,130; *Sancti Anselmi .... Opera Omnia*, ed. F.S. Schmitt, v.p.389,no.442).

Radulf Novell 1109 x 1114 (perhaps 1112) - c.1147.
William 'Senex' 1112 (?) - 1168.

Radulf when a priest of York was el. by some Orcadians at York and then cons. by Thomas abp. of York with profession of obedience to that see June 1109 x Feb. 1114 (Hugh the Chantor, *History,* 32; *SAEC,* 134; *Historians of York*, ii,372); date was perhaps 1112 i.e. at same probable time as the rival appointment of William (cf. *Diplom. Norv.*,xvii B,297); accompanied Thurstan elect of York to his cons. by Pope Calixtus II at Rheims 19 Oct. 1119 (Hugh the Chantor, *Histor* 71, 72, 74, 76, 81); this pope had been led to believe that Radulf had been canonically el. and cons. when he commended him to Kings Eystein and Sigurd I of Norway 20 Nov. 1119 (*Historians of York*,iii, 39; see W. Holtzmann, *Papsturkunden in England*,ii,105 for dating); he had presumably not yet been able to get poss. of his see, though there

was no mention of any rival bp. on this occasion; but by time when Pope Honorius II wrote again to King Sigurd 9 Dec. 1128, another bp. was said to have been intruded, and this king was ordered to 'restore' Radulf (*Historians of York*,iii,50-51; see Holtzmann, *Papsturkunden*, loc.cit. for dating; cf. *ES*,ii,229); but his el. and cons. were not in fact acceptable to the clergy and people of Orkney nor to the 'princeps terrae' there (whether king or earl is not clear), so that he was never received in Orkney as bp., but served as vicar to bp. of Durham and abp. of York (*SAEC*, 164-5; see G.V. Scammell, *Hugh du Puiset*, 10, 264-5 for a grant to his sons c. 1133 x 1140); occ. on English side at battle of the Standard (when his surname is mentioned) Aug. 1138 (*Chronicles of Stephen*, etc. [Rolls Series] ,iii,162) and at cons. of William abp. of York at Winchester 26 Sept. 1143 (*Historians of York*, ii,222; cf.391); occ. in Lincon dioc. c. 1147 (*HBC*, 267, no source cited).

   William d. 1168 (*ES*,ii,266); said to have been bp. for 66 years, which would mean that he had succ. c. 1102; if this is true, it would have been at the time when the young Sigurd (later 'the Crusader' and king of Norway 1103 - 1130) was ruler in Orkney as king under his father King Magnus Barelegs (ibid.,ii,105,118); but there is no mention of him as a rival to Bp. Roger - unless the two unnamed bps. of Orkney mentioned above under Roger c. 1108-1109 are not the same person (in which case Roger could have been a resident in England as Radulf Novell was to be, and William had perhaps obtained cons. from Canterbury c. 1102 and was turning again to Anselm for support between time of that abp.'s return to England Sept. 1106 and his death Apr. 1109); it is more probable that '66 years' is an error for '56 years', and that William became bp. in 1112 after Bp. Roger had made himself inacceptable in Orkney and when King Sigurd returned from crusade (cf. *Diplom Norv.*, xvii B,297; cf. *ES*,ii,136); if so, his appointment was quite clearly a rejection of York metropolitical authority, presumably in favour of that of Lund, which had from 1103-4 replaced Bremen as the metropolitan see for the Norse kingdom (*Diplom:Norv.*,xvii B, 185); the language of the papal letters of 1119 and 1128 in favour of Radulf Novell need not be taken too exactly (for they are clearly *ex parte*) to imply that William can have been 'intruded' only at some date between the two letters, though it is just possible that for '66 years' we should read '46 years' i.e. 1122; it seems that he was already bp. at time of death of St Magnus 16 Apr., 1117 (?) (*Orkneyinga Saga*,ed. A.B. Taylor, 213; *ES*,ii,266; cf.160); by implication he must have been in poss. in 1119 as in 1128 (v.sup.), and he was certainly active in time of Earl Paul Hakonsson by Dec. 1135 at latest (Pinkerton, *Saints*, ii,246, 255-7; *Orkneyinga Saga*, 219-21, 144-6; *ES*,ii,192); was presumably active in the moving of his cathedral from Birsay to Kirkwall c. 1137 and later; in 1153 his see was firmly put under the authority of the new metropolitan see of Trondheim; in some sense he was remembered as the 'first bishop' in Orkney (*ES*,ii,266), a phrase which prob. means that he was the first of the Norse line of bishops under Trondheim (cf. *bishops of the Isles*); his nickname 'Senex' may mean that he was old, or more likely that the was the senior of two successive bishops called William (cf. Dowden, *Bishops*, 253).

William - 1188.

    D. 1188 as successor to Bp. William 'Senex' (*ES*,ii,324).

Biarne/Biarni Kolbeinsson 'Skald'   1188 x 1192 - 1223.

    Succ. the second Bp. William (*ES*,ii,324, 'Biarne' being the modernised form of 'Biarni'; cf. ii,6, for nickname, which means 'Poet'); occ. 1192 (*Orkneyinga Saga*,338) and presumably in poss. 27 May 1198 (*Die Register Innocenz III*,i,no. 218); occ. at a council at Bergen 28 July 1223 (*ES*,ii,455-6), and so death was prob. 15 Sept. 1223 (*ES*,ii,452, where date 1222 is given; cf. Dowden, *Bishops*, 256; *Diplom Norv.*,xvii B,297).

Jofreyr/Godfrey   1223 x 1224 - 1246.

    Prob. same as Jofrey provost of Tonsberg, Norway found 25 Dec. 1223 (*Icelandic Sagas* (Rolls Series),ii,85); cons. 1223 (*ES*,ii, 455, where argument for the name-form 'Godfrey' is given), prob. in Jan. 1223/4 before death of the Trondheim abp. 6 Feb. 1224 (*Diplom. Norv.*, xvii B,201; cf. 297); papal mand. to Trondheim abp. to induce this bp. to res. or accept coadj. following many years of paralysis which had confined him to bed 11 May 1237 (*CPL*,i,62); d. still in poss. 1246 (*ES*ii,544).

Note: an unnamed elect of Orkney was captured in a ship of war by some English pirates and killed sometime before 15 Sept. 1227 (*CDS*, i,nos. 981, 1007, 1009); called just 'a certain elect of Norway' in the first of these sources, and so perhaps the Orkney identification in the other two is erroneous.

Henry/Hervi   1247 - 1269.

    El. by chapter when canon of Orkney himself before 9 Dec. 1247, when granted papal disp. to receive this see despite illegitimacy (*CPL*,i, 241; *Diplom.Norv.*, i,no.42): cons. in Norway in winter of 1248-9 (*Icelandic Sagas*,ii,258; cf. *ES*,ii,551; see also *Diplom.Norv.*,xvii B, 298 for discussion of his name and argument that Hervi and Henry are the same person); d. 1269 (*ES*,ii,665).

Peter   1270 - 1284.

    Cons. 1270 (*ES*,ii,665), on or before 3 Sept. (*Diplom.Norv.*,iii,no. 14); prob. same as Peter *O.archd.Shetland* found 1269; a Bp. William erroneously found 1275 (*ES*,ii,672; cf. *Diplom.Norv.*, xvii B,298; Dowden, *Bishops*,258n); d. 1284 (*ES*,ii,685).

Dolgfinn/Dolphinn   1286 - 1309.

    Chosen by Andrew bp. of Oslo before 10 July 1286 and cons. by him 1286, perhaps 14 July (*Diplom.Norv.*,xvii B,299); d. 25 Mar. x 12 Sept. 1309 (ibid.; v.inf.).

William   1309 - 1339-40 x .

    El by chapter when *O.archd.* on death of Dolgfinn before 12 Sept. 1309 when Trondheim abp. ordered the usual enquiry into the el. prior to conf. (*Diplom.Norv.*,ix, no.83); cons. 1310 (Icelandic Annals quoted ibid.,xvii B,299); occ. 9 Sept. 1327 (ibid.,vii, nos.119-20); prob. the unnamed bp. in poss. at mid-winter 1339-40 (ibid., no.

169), but not known when died and was succ. by another bp. with the same name.

William x 1369 - 1382 or 1383.

Occ. 25 May 1369 (*Diplom.Norv.*,i,no.404). and was successor to previous Bp. William (Dowden, *Bishops,* 255,259); killed in the Orkneys 1382 or 1383 (Icelandic Annals quoted *Diplom.Norv.*,xvii B, 299); his usual agent still received the allowance for this see from the crown revenues of Aberdeen for term beginning Nov. 1382 (*ER*,iii,101-2; cf. 25, 76).

John 1384 - 1394.
Robert de Sinclair (Sancto Claro) 1383 - 1391.

John, when rector of Fetlar in Shetland, el. by chapter on death of William and then prov. by Pope Urban VI 10 Feb. 1384 (*CPL*,iv,336); cons. at curia soon afterwards, but had not had formal letters of prov. made out when that pope died 15 Oct. 1389 (ibid.; note that evidence that he promised common services to the rival Pope Clement VII 7 June 1387 (*Diplom.Norv.*,xvii,no.166) relates to *Ar.bp.* and not to this see); mand. from Pope Boniface IX to undertake admin. of his see 9 Nov. 1389 (*Diplom.Norv.*,xvii,no.169; *CPL*,iv,336); known at Rome to be absent from his see 27 Jan. 1391, though (Henry) bp. of Greenland was then in Orkney (*Diplom.Norv.*,xvii, no.175; *CPL*,iv,385); this latter bp. promised John's Orkney services for him at Rome 17 June 1391 (*Diplom.Norv.*,xvii,no.177), and was at curia again 9 Mar. 1394 when John was trans. to Greenland in exch. with him.

Sinclair described (formally, it seems, rather than in fact) as elect of Orkney 28 Nov. 1383 when Pope Clement VII made prov. to his *M.dean.* (*CPP*,i,566); but this prov. was never effective; prov. himself by same pope on death of Bp. William 27 Jan. 1384 (*Diplom.Norv.*, xvii, no. 161, wrongly numbered 160) with mand. for cons. by any catholic bp. 30 Jan. 1384 (ibid. no.162) and disp. to retain *M.dean.* 10 Feb. 1384 (ibid.,no. 163); cons. by 31 May 1390 (*CPP*,i,574; cf. 575); trans. by Clement VII to *Dk.bp.* 1 Feb. 1391; retained *M.dean.* until date of trans., and never had poss. of O.bp. (*Diplom.Norv.*,xvii, no.371); but did receive the traditional allowance from the Scottish crown revenues of Aberdeen from at least the term beginning May 1384 to term beginning Nov. 1391 inclusive (*ER*,iii,126,261).

Henry 1394 - .
John Pak/Colchester O.S.B. 1396 - 1397 x 1418.
Alexander Vaus 1398 x 1407 - 1414.
William Stephenson (Stephani) 1415 - 1419.

Henry trans. from Greenland bp. by Pope Boniface IX on exch. with John 9 Mar. 1394 (*Diplom.Norv.*,xvii,no. 180; *CPL*,iv,481); occ. 10 Aug. 1394 (*Diplom.Norv.*,xvii B, 300); d. before 21 Aug. 1396 (v.inf.).

Pak prov. when monk of Colchester, England on Henry's death by Pope Boniface IX 21 Aug. 1396 (*Diplom.Norv.*,xvii,no.183; *CPL*, iv,538); cons. by 13 Sept. 1396 (*Diplom.Norv.*,xvii,nos.184,944); occ. in Sweden 23 June 1397 (ibid.,xvii B,301); still in poss. 19 Dec.

1397 (ibid.,xvii,nos.191-2); d. before 19 Aug. 1418 (see Thomas de Tulloch below); had had poss;, but apparently experienced considerable opposition in Orkney (cf. *Spalding Misc.*,v,257-8; *Orkney-Shetland Recs.*, i,no.26, cf. Dowden, *Bishops*, 270).

Vaus, when *C.archd.*,prov. by Pope Benedict XIII 25 July 1398 x 7 Nov. 1407, prob. just before latter date (Reg. Supp.,102, fo.257v); mand.from this pope for cons. by any catholic bp. without prejudice to rights of Trondheim abp. 12 Feb. 1408 (*Orkney-Shetland Recs.*, i,no.85), but was not in fact cons. within the canonical period (*CPL*, vii,185); apparently dem. *C.archd.*, but still not cons. when trans. *C.bp.* 4 May 1414; on same date granted administration of O.bp. in commend for two years (*Diplom.Norv.*,xvii,no.371, where year is wrongly given as 1415; note that this mand. is addressed to the king of Scotland, not to the king of Norway); at this time the see had in the eyes of Benedict XIII been vacant since trans. of Bp. Sinclair 1 Feb. 1391 i.e. there was no one else between Sinclair and Vaus in the line of bps. obedient to Avignon during the Great Schism; not known how far he had poss. in Orkney (cf. difficulties of John Pak above), but at least he began to receive the traditional allowance from the crown revenues of Aberdeen (which had been diverted into other hands because of the Great Schism from Whitsun term 1392 to Martinmas term 1412 inclusive) from Whitsun term i.e. June 1413 (*ER*,iv,259; cf. iii,307, 579,iv,184; note that his putative relative John de Vaus remained as agent for collecting such allowances from Aberdeen under his successors in sees of Orkney and Caithness as late as Nov. 1425 - see ibid.,iv,331,397,422).

Stephenson had been chosen by Pope Benedict XIII for this see by Apr. 1415, though it was then uncertain whether Vaus's commend should be cancelled or he should be asked to consent to its termination (*St A.Cop.*,253-4); prov. as elect and canon of Moray on trans. of Vaus 13 Nov. 1415 (*Diplom.Norv.*,xvii,no.372, where date is wrongly given as 1416; mand. is addressed to king of Norway); promised services 19 Dec. 1415 (Reg.Av.,346,fo.308v), and cons. at curia of Benedict XIII prob. about same time (*CPL*,vii,103); got disp. to retain all his benefices in commend until a year after he should have full poss. of his see 12 Nov. 1415 (*Diplom.Norv.*,xvii,no.974; cf. *CPP*,i,604), and this was renewed by Pope Martin V 15 July 1419, when he claimed poss. of O.bp. but no fruits from it (*Diplom.Norv.*, xvii,no.392; *CSSR*,i,85; see also ibid.,120-1); trans. *Db.bp.* 30 Oct. 1419.

Thomas de Tulloch (Tulach, Turo) 1418 - 1461.

Prov. by Pope Martin V, his dioc. of origin being Brechin, 19 Aug. 1418 (*Diplom.Norv.*,xvii,nos.378,976; *ASCB*,17; misdated in Eubel, *Hierarchia*,i,378); see said to be vacant by death - presumably that of John Pak; promised services in person when residing in the curia at Geneva 26 Aug. 1418 (*Diplom.Norv.*,xvii,no.379)cf. *ACSB*, 1; *CSSR*,i,16); still elect 20 Dec. 1418 (*ACSB*,2); prob. no poss. (though possibly had some of the fruits) and not yet recognised in Scotland 15 July 1419 (see Stephenson above); had no rival after 30

Oct. 1419 (v.sup.); cons. by 10 June 1420 when active with other Scandinavian bps. in Denmark (*Diplom.Norv.*,xvi,no.75); occ. 12 July 1455 (*Spalding Misc.*,v, 392-3); presumably the unnamed bp. who occ. 28 June 1461 (*Diplom.Norv.*,v,no.836, where editor names this bp. as William; cf. Dowden, *Bishops*,261); res. on or before 11 Dec. 1461 (v.inf.).

William Tulloch 1461 - 1477.

Prov., when canon of Orkney and at curia, on res. of Bp. Thomas 11 Dec. 1461 (*Diplom.Norv.*,xvii,no.652); at this time he was called just 'elect' (cf. ibid.,no.653), but perhaps cons. by 23 Dec. 1461 when he paid some services (*ACSB*,52-53; but see 277); certainly cons. by 21 July 1462 when he swore fealty to king of Denmark and Norway at Copenhagen (*Diplom.Norv.*,v,no.842); trans. *M.bp.* 12 Feb.1477.

Andrew Painter (Pictoris) 1477 - 1503 x 1506.

Prov. when canon of Orkney on trans. of William Tulloch 12 Feb. 1477 (*Diplom.Norv.*,xvii,no.707; *ACSB*,73); prob. cons. by 31 Mar. 1477 when paid some services (ibid.,250), and certainly by 20 Feb. 1478 (*APS*,ii,193); given Stewart as coadj. from 4 Dec. 1498 (v.inf.); occ. 24 Nov. 1503 (*RSS*,i,no.1000); presumably d. before 18 June 1506 (v.inf.).

Edward Stewart 1498 - 1524 x 1525.

Crown nom. to assist Bp. Painter 8 Dec. 1498 (*RSS*,i,no.300), with crown nom. to pope as coadj. and successor to Bp. Painter prob. about same date (ibid.,no.299); prov., when canon of Orkney, as coadj. and successor 10 July 1500 (*Diplom.Norv.*,xvii B,304-5; cf. Dowden, *Bishops,* 263); promised services as elect of Orkney 19 Sept. 1500 (*Diplom.Norv.*,xvii,no.1154); occ. as coadj. still Nov. 1503 (Dowden, *Bishops,*263); first found as bp. in his own right 18 June 1506 (*RSS*,i,no,1286); given Benston as coadj. and successor from 27 Apr. 1524 (v.inf.); prob. d. before July 1525, and certainly before 13 Feb. 1526 (v.inf.).

John Benston (Beinston,Beynstoun) 1523 - 1525 x 1526.

Crown nom., when canon of Orkney, to pope as coadj. to Bp. Stewart 13 Dec. 1523 (*Vet.Mon.*, no.943); prov. as coadj. and successor 27 Apr. 1524 (*Diplom.Norv.*,xvii B,305; cf. Brady, *Episcopal Succession*,i,150-1); it was prob. he rather than the aged Stewart who occ. as unnamed O.bp. 10/17 July 1525 (*APS*,ii,291,294); d. before 13 Feb. 1526 (v.inf.; see also Dowden, *Bishops,* 264).

Robert Maxwell 1526 - 1540 x 1541.

Crown nom. before 13 Feb. 1526 (SRO, ADC,xxxv,fo.203), by which time both of his two predecessors were presumably dead; prov. when *M.chanc.* and *Dumbarton prov.* 9 Apr. 1526 on death of Benston (*Diplom.Norv.*,xvii B,305; Brady, *Episcopal Succession*,i,151); prob. cons. 25 June x 8 Aug. 1526 (*APS*,ii,307; *ER*,xv,282; but see *APS*,ii, 304 where an apparently consecrated O.bp. occ. 21 June 1526); occ. 10 May 1539 (*RMS*,iii,no.2882) and 20 Feb. 1540 (*Laing Chrs.*,no. 342, where wrong surname is supplied); d. before 5 Apr. 1541 (v.inf.).

Robert Reid O.Cist. 1541 - 1558.

 Crown nom. when abbot of Kinloss 5 Apr. 1541 (*James V Letters,* 423); granted temps. during vacancy 14 Apr. 1541 (*RSS*,iii,no.3974); prov. with retention of abbacy and other beneficies on Maxwell's death 20 July 1541 (*Diplom.Norv.*,xvii B,306; Brady *Episcopal Succession,* i,151-2); cons. at Edinburgh 27 Nov. 1541 (*Kinloss Recs.*,11); d. at Dieppe, France 6 Sept. 1558 (Lesley, *De Origine,*538-9; cf. *Diplom. Norv.*,xvii B,306-7).

Adam Bothwell 1559 - 1593.

 Crown nom. before 24 July 1559 (Brady, *Episcopal Succession,* i,152-3); prov. when canon of Glasgow on death of Reid 2 Aug. 1559 (*Diplom.Norv.*,xvii B,307-8; Brady, loc.cit); apparently cons. before granted temps. 14 Oct. 1559 (*RSS*,v,no.708); his connection with his diocese largely ceased after 27/30 Sept. 1568 when he became commendator of Holyrood (*SP*,iv,429; *RSCHS*,xiii,99-100); but retained title until d. 23 Aug. 1593 (monument at Holyrood, see *RCAHM* [Edin.] , 136-7).

James Law 1605 - 1615.

 Crown prov. 28 Feb. 1605 (Reg.Pres.,iii,98v); cons. 21 Oct. 1610 x 3 May 1611 (Spottiswood, *History*, iii,209; *Original Letters,* i,270), prob. 23 Jan./24 Feb. 1611 (Calderwood, *History*,vii,164); trans. *G.bp.* 20 July 1615.

George Graham 1615 - 1638.

 Trans. from *Db.bp.* 26 Aug. 1615 (Reg.Pres.,iv,122v); depriv. 13 Dec. 1638 (Peterkin, *Records*, i,27-28); d. 11 Nov. x 19 Dec. 1643 (MS Orkney Sasines, cited Craven, *Church in Orkney*, 193-4).

CHAPTER OF ORKNEY

First known cathedral was erected at Birsay by Earl Thorfinn 1048 x 1065 (*Orkneyinga Saga,* 189,213; *ES*,ii,2,266); after translation of remains of St Magnus from Birsay to Kirkwall, Earl Ronald-Kali built a new cathedral there from c. 1137 onwards, some of it apparently existing by 1155 (*Orkneying Saga,* 321,328; see also 338); the design of this building included two doors in the south aisle which have been thought to have been 'intended to communicate with the cloisters of a projected monastery' (L. Dietrichson and J. Meyer, *Monumenta Orcadica* (Kristiania, 1906), 61); Mr. R.G.Cant has pointed to this archaeological evidence and has suggested that a Benedictine community on the Durham model (which was being followed for the building) may have been intended; but then the plan of the building was altered when in fact it was a community of secular canons that was built up.

 First evidence of a chapter is at election of Bp. Henry in 1247; there is no evidence whether this chapter was of a synodal or collegiate character; but this Henry was a canon of Orkney when elected, and a group of such canons can be traced from then on; the

canons of the church of St Magnus had a sufficiently corporate character by 1266 to be appointed in the treaty of Perth to receive annual payments for the king of Norway from the king of Scotland (*APS*,i,420); prebends came to be attached to the canonries in the usual way by the early 14th century at any rate (e.g. *Diplom.Norv.*,ix,no.87 of 1320, and *CPL*,ii,313 of 1329); as many as twelve prebends have been identified in the 15th century, but the number had fallen to six by 1544 (*RSCHS*,xiv,39-40; cf.22).

The only known dignitaries in this period were the archdeacons of Shetland from 1215 and of Orkney from 1309; both offices may well have been considerably older than is now known, but it is at least possible that the archd. of Shetland was established before that of Orkney, and that the holder of the senior office (being the only one in existence when the community of canons at Kirkwall was being developed) was the customary president of the chapter; certainly no separate dignitary has been identified as head of the college of canons before the erection of the provostry in 1544 (v.inf.); and Mr Cant has pointed to the facts that not only did the current archdeacon of Shetland become the first provost in 1544 (while retaining his archdeaconry, which was given no place in the new chapter), but also that this new presiding dignitary was assigned the prebend of Holy Trinity which Henry Phankouth a previous archdeacon of Shetland is known to have held in 1508 (*Orkney Recs.*, 83-84); these facts point to the strong possibility that the new provostry in 1544 was conceived as a splitting off from the archdeaconry of Shetland of that part of this archdeacon's functions (and appropriate revenues) which had embraced the duty of presiding in chapter.

Bp. Reid gave his cathedral a new constitution 28 Oct. 1544, when in place of a community of six canons and six chaplains (with no mention of either archdeacon as such) he established one of seven dignitaries, another seven prebendaries, thirteen chaplains and six boys (Peterkin, *Rentals of Orkney*, app.v,pp.18-25; *RMS*,iii,no. 3102); but this new constitution was apparently not fully in effect until c. 1588/9 (*RSCHS*,xiv,24-25); the provost is described as 'dean of the chapter' 1614 (Craven, *Church in Orkney*, 108).

PROVOSTS OF ORKNEY

First known date: 1544.
Prebend: Holy Trinity i.e. parsonages and vicarages of Burray and South Ronaldsay in 1544 (*RMS*,iii,no.3102; Cowan, *Parishes*, 24,185-6).

Malcolm Halcro 1544 - 1554.
Pres. by bp. on new erection of ben. 28 Oct. 1544 (*RMS*,iii, no.3102); occ. 22 Feb. 1554 (ibid.,iv,no.898); d. by 15 July 1554 (see *O.archd. Shetland*).

Alexander Dick 1553 - 1576 x 1584.
Said to be in poss. 3 Feb. 1553 (*Orkney Recs.*,341, misdated by editor); occ. 20 Dec. 1575 and prob. 21 Dec. 1576 (*RSS*,vii,no.790);

d. before 1 Dec. 1584 and perhaps before 11 June 1570 (v.inf.).

Henry Colville 1579.
 Crown pres. on Dick's death 11 June 1579, but pres. never sealed (*RSS*,vii, no. 1928); perhaps Dick was not yet in fact dead; cf. *O.prec.*

Alexander Callander 1584.
 Crown pres. on Dick's death 1 Dec. 1584 (Reg.Pres.,ii,117).

Daniel Callander 1590.
 Crown pres. on death of his father Alexander 13 July 1590 (RSS, lxi, fo.5); apparently not effective (v.inf.).

Ninian Halcro 1592 - 1597.
 Occ. 9/30 Sept. 1592 (Craven, *Church in Orkney*, 29); occ. 6 Dec. 1597 (Wodrow, *Collections*,i,514).

Note: this ben. appears to have been vacant 6 Aug. 1611 when the other dignitaries res. to bp. (Craven, *Church in Orkney*, 109).

Daniel Callander 1614 - 1635 x 1636.
 Adm. shortly before 18 Jan. 1614 (*Original Letters* i,322); occ. 4/7 Nov. 1635, being then under censure by synod (Peterkin, *Rentals of Orkney*, app. 54-55); depriv. by High Commission before 22 June 1636 (v.inf.).

Walter Stewart 1636 - 1638.
 Crown pres. on 'silencing' of Callander by High Commission 22 June 1636 (Reg.Pres.,vii,68); occ. 24 May 1638 (SRO, Fea of Clestrain, no. 52).

PRECENTORS/CHANTERS OF ORKNEY

First known date: 1544.
 Prebend: ch. of Orphir with vic. of Stenness in 1544; vic. of Firth added c. 1551 (*RMS*,iii,no.3102; Cowan, *Parishes*, 66-67, 160, 187).

Nicholas Halcro 1544 - 1545.
 Pres. by bp. on new erection of ben. 28 Oct. 1544 (*RMS*,iii no. 3102); occ. 20 Apr. 1545 (*Orkney Recs.*, 338).

Magnus Halcro 1556 - 1574 x 1580.
 Occ. 2 Feb. 1556 (ibid.,256); occ. 17 Mar. 1574 (ibid.,348); d. by 6 June 1580 (v.inf.).

Henry Colville 1580 - 1596.
 Crown pres. on Magnus Halcro's death 6 June/24 July 1580 (*RSS*, vii,no.2376); occ. 1 Aug. 1595 (SRO, Orkney and Shetland docs., no. 193); murdered 9/12 July 1596 (Pitcairn, *Trials*,I,ii,386-8, 394, where described as parson of 'Urquhart'; cf. Scott, *Fasti*,vii, 246).

Robert Stewart 1611.
 Res. to bp. 6 Aug. 1611 (Craven, *Church in Orkney*,109).

Patrick Waterstoun 1617 - 1638.

Occ. 3 Nov. 1617 (*Orkney-Shetland Recs.*,III,i,14); occ. 24 May 1638 (SRO, Fea of Clestrain, no.52).

CHANCELLORS OF ORKNEY

First known date: 1544.

Prebend: ch. of Lady Kirk, Sanday, with vic. of all three Sanday churches in 1544 (*RMS*,iii,no.3102; Cowan, *Parishes*, 179-80.

Alexander Scott 1544 - 1554.

Pres. by bp. on new erection of ben. 28 Oct. 1544 (*RMS*,iii,no. 3102); occ. 23 June 1554 (St A. Univ. Mun.,Univ. Ch^r. M.16, no.1).

James Annand 1559 x 1561 - 1583 x 1585.

Occ. 12 Apr. 1561 (*Orkney Recs.*, 342); had been coll. by Bp. Hepburn i.e. 1559 x , and this was conf. by crown 5 Dec. 1566 (*RSS*,, v,no.3120; cf. SRO, Acts and Decreets, lv,fo.226, where this conf. is apparently misread and he is said to have been coll. by Bp. Reid i.e. x 1558); occ. 13 Mar. 1583 (SRO, Acts and Decreets, lv,fo.226); d. by 21 Apr. 1585 (v.inf.).

James Cok	1585 - 1631.
Alexander Cheyne	1585 x 1586.
James Stewart	1586 - 1587.

Cok had pres. from patron on Annand's death 21 Apr. 1585 and adm. 24 Apr. 1585, which were conf. by crown 20 Sept. 1592 (*RSS*, lxiii,fo.102); occ. 27 Jan. 1631 (SRO, Prot.Bk.David Heart, fo.266).

Cheyne gets crown pres. on Annand's death 23 Apr. 1585 (Reg. Pres.,ii,133); d. before 11 Nov. 1586 (v.inf.).

Stewart gets crown pres. on deaths of Annand and Cheyne 11 Nov. 1586 and 22 May 1587 (Reg.Pres.,ii,160,172).

Thomas Cok 1638.

Occ. 24 May 1638 (SRO, Fea of Clestrain,no.52).

TREASURERS OF ORKNEY

First known date: 1544.

Prebend: ch. of St Nicholas, Stronsay, with vics. of the three Stronsay chs. and Eday in 1544, though this appropriation of vics. was not effective (*RMS*,iii,no.3102; Cowan, *Parishes*,58-59, 192-3).

Stephen Culross 1544 - 1557.

Pres. by bp. on new erection of ben. 28 Oct. 1544 (*RMS*,iii, no.3102); occ. 20 June 1557 (*Orkney Recs.*, 261).

Francis Bothwell 1561 - 1574.

Occ. 12 Apr. 1561 and 10 Feb. 1574 (ibid.,342,348); d. 6 Oct. x 4 Dec. 1574 (Edin.Tests.,s.d.).

William Henderson 1578 - 1582.
Crown pres. on Bothwell's death 24 Sept. 1578 and again 30 Apr. 1579 (*RSS*,vii,nos.1662,1887); d. 19 Dec. 1582 (*RCAHMS [Orkney & Shetland]*,ii,132).

Walter Hay 1583.
Crown pres. on Henderson's death 26 Jan. 1583 (Reg.Pres.,ii, 84).

Cuthbert Henderson 1586 - 1595.
Earlier pres. by patron gets crown conf. 20 Sept. 1586 (RSS,liv, fo.91); occ. 1 Aug. 1595 (SRO, Orkney & Shetland docs.,no.193).

James Brand 1614 - 1615.
Occ. 1614 (Craven, *Church in Orkney*,108); occ. 22 June 1615 (SRO, Reg. Ho. Chr.,s.d.).

John Gardyne 1617 - 1631.
Occ. 3 Nov. 1617 (*Orkney-Shetland Recs.*,III,i,14) and 23 June 1631 (SRO, Prot. Bk. David Heart,fo.286).

Alexander Somervell 1638.
Occ. 24 May 1638 (SRO, Fea of Clestrain,no.52).

SUBDEANS OF ORKNEY

First known date: 1544.
Prebend: ch. of Hoy and vic. of Walls in 1544 (*RMS*,iii,no. 3102; Cowan, *Parishes*,83,206).

Peter Houston 1544 - 1564.
Pres. by bp. on new erection of ben. 28 Oct. 1544 (*RMS*,iii, no.3102); occ. 12 Apr. 1564 (*Orkney Recs.*,273).

Archibald Douglas   1564 - 1568, 1581 (?)
William Houston   1566.
Douglas occ. 20 July 1564 (Floors Castle, Roxburghe Mun., Bellenden Chrs.,s.d.); occ. 2 Aug. 1568 (*Orkney Recs.*,287); perhaps retained some right until 18 Nov. 1581 (v.inf.; and see *Thirds of Benefices*,203).

Houston gets crown pres. on forfeiture of Douglas for complicity in murder of Rizzio 11 Apr. 1566 (*RSS*,v,no.2757).

Magnus Murray x 1569.
Held it at death before 26 Apr. 1569 (v.inf.).

Thomas Stevenson 1569.
Had ord. coll. on Murray's death and now gets crown conf. 26 Apr. 1569 (*RSS*,vi,no.597).

John Stewart 1581.

 Crown pres. on Stevenson's death 14 Feb. 1581 (Reg.Pres.,ii,50); crown pres. again on sentence of barratry against Douglas 18 Nov.1581 (ibid.,62).

Henry Smyth 1621 - 1631.

 Occ. 27 Sept. 1621 (SRO, Craven Bequest, no.7) and 23 June 1631 (SRO, Prot.Bk.David Heart,fo.286).

SUCCENTORS/SUBCHANTERS OF ORKNEY

First known date: 1544.

 Prebend: Ch. of St Columba, Sanday in 1544 (*RMS*,iii,3102; Cowan *Parishes,* 180).

Magnus Strang 1544 - 1562.

 Pres. by bp. on new erection of this ben. 28 Oct. 1544 (*RMS*,iii, no. 3102); occ. 24 Jan. 1562 (*Orkney Recs.,* 269).

Jerome Tulloch 1562 - 1592.

 Occ. 1562 (*Thirds of Benefices,*151; cf. 204); occ. 9 Sept. 1570 (*Orkney-Shetland Recs.*,i,201); occ. 9/30 Sept. 1592 (Craven, *Church in Orkney,* 29).

John Gardyne 1620 - 1631.

 Occ. 5 Oct. 1620 (SRO, Fea of Clestrain,no.22) and 2 Jan. 1628 (SRO, Craven Bequest, no.17); d. 17 Apr. 1631 (Orkney Tests.,17 Apr. 1637).

ARCHDEACONS OF ORKNEY

First known date: 1309.

 Prebend: ch. of Orphir and vics. of Burray and South Ronaldsay in 1440 (*Diplom.Norv.*,xvii,441-2); vics. of Birsay and Harray in 1544 (*RMS,* iii,no.3102; see also Cowan, *Parishes,* 18,80-81; cf. 24,160, 185-6).

William 1309 - 1310.

 In poss. when el. *O.bp.* 1309, before 12 Sept. (*Diplom.Norv.,* ix,103-4); cons. 1310.

William de Buchan 1369 - 1372.

 Occ. 25 May 1369 (*Orkney Recs.,*16; *Diplom.Norv.*,i,308; SRO, Leven and Melville, 7/392/8); prob. moved to *O.archd.Shetland* by 12 Mar. 1372; d. before 28 Nov. 1383 (*CPP*,i,566).

John Thomson (Thome) x 1419.

 Res. sometime before 8 May 1419 (v.inf.).

John Patrickson   1419.
William Brown   1420.

Patrickson had ord. coll. on res. of Thomson and gets prov. 8 May/ 28 June 1419 (*CSSR*,i,45,81).

Brown prov. on res. of Thomson 10 May 1420 (ibid.,195-6).

Thomas de Grenlaw   1422 - 1424.
Simon de Grenlaw   1422.

Thomas said to have res. before 26 Oct. 1422 (*CSSR*,i,311); but occ. 4 Feb. 1424 (*Rot.Scot.*,ii,246).

Simon prov. on res. of Thomas 26 Oct. 1422 (v.sup.).

Andrew de Tulloch   1435 - 1447 x 1448.
Thomas Etal   1438.

Tulloch prov. 28 Sept. x 28 Dec. 1435 (*Diplom.Norv.*,xvii, 423-4); occ. 15 Jan. 1437 (SRO, St Andrews Chrs.,no.28); is to res. when prov. *C.dean.* 10 July 1445, but this prov. was unfruitful; in poss. 28 July 1445 (Reg.Supp.,407,fo.128v); d. 5 June 1447 x 23 Sept. 1448 as *C.bp.-elect.*

Etal prov. 13 Oct. 1438 (Reg. Supp.,352,fo.125) unfruitfully.

Christopher Gynnis 1448 - 1449.

Prov. on Tulloch's death 23 Sept. 1448 (*CPL*,x,194-5); is to res. without poss. 16 May 1449 (ibid.,195); perhaps in poss. when res. 24 May 1449 (Reg.Supp.,436,fo.200;437,fo.90); d. before 18 June 1449 (see G.subd.).

Nicholas Blair 1449.

Prov. on res. of Gynnis or death of Tulloch 24 May/18-22 June 1449 (Reg. Supp.,436,fo.200; 437,fo.90; *CPL*,x,199).

Andrew Wishart 1451 - 1456 x 1461.

In poss. 19 Oct. 1451 (Reg.Supp.,454,fo.115v); prob. res. when coll. to *C.treas.* 8 Jan. 1456 x 11 Dec. 1461.

James Kinnaird (Kynnardi) 1465 - 1481.

In poss. 7 Nov. 1465 (Reg. Supp.,587,fo.171); occ. 31 Jan. 1481 (*Orkney Recs.*,193).

Humphrey (Umfrid) Clerk 1513.

Occ. 10 May 1513 (*Orkney Recs.*,335; *Orkney-Shetland Recs.*, i,102).

John Tyrie 1527 - 1559 x.

Occ. 20 May 1527 (*Orkney Recs.*,208); re-presented by bp. on re-erection of chapter 28 Oct. 1544 (*RMS*,iii,no.3102); still in poss. under Bp. Hepburn i.e. 1559 x (*RSS*,v,no.3186).

Gilbert Foulsie/Fousy 1561 - 1580.

Occ. 1561 (*Thirds of Benefices*,1-2); occ. 18 Sept. 1566 (*Orkney Recs.*, 377); had had pres. from bp., and gets crown conf. 2 Mar. 1567 (*RSS*,v,no.3308); occ. 1 June 1580 (Comm. Edin. Decreets,ix,s.d.).

Thomas Swentoun 1586 - 1626 x 1627.

Occ. 6 Nov. 1586 (SRO, Fea of Clestrain, no. 2) and 14 Nov. 1626 (SRO, Prot.Bk.David Heart,fo.150); res. by 11 apr.1627 (v.inf.).

Francis Liddell 1627 - 1635.

Crown pres. on res. of Swentoun 11 Apr. 1627 (RSS,c,fo.89); occ. 28 May 1635 (SRO, Scarth of Breckness, no.84); d. 31 May 1635 (Orkney Tests.,31 Dec. 1636).

ARCHDEACONS OF SHETLAND

First known date: 1215.

Prebend: unnamed preb. attached in 1421 and 1429 (CSSR,i, 242; Reg.Supp.,249,fo.31); Holy Trinity parsonage i.e. Burray and South Ronaldsay attached 1508 (Orkney Recs.,83-84); this preb. came to be allocated to the provost in 1544 (cf. Cowan, Parishes,24,185-6); chs. of Tingwall, Weisdale and Whiteness attached at Reformation (PSAS,xliv, 304; see Cowan, Parishes,197,207,209).

Andrew 1215.

D. in poss. 1215 (ES,ii,406).

Nicholas 1226.

Occ. 3 Nov. 1226 (Orkney-Shetland Recs., i,28).

Gilbert 1260 - 1263.

Held it before 29 July 1260 (ES,ii,599,n.2); prob. still in poss. then and until cons. as Hamar bp. 4 Mar. 1263 (ibid.).

Peter 1269 - 1270.

Occ. 21 Aug. 1269 (Diplomatic Documents,i,291; see also Orkney-Shetland Recs.,i,35); prob. same as the Peter cons. O.bp. 1270, on or before 3 Sept.

Sigurd 1295.

Occ. 26 July 1295 (Orkney-Shetland Recs.,i,36); held an archd. which was prob. this ben. x 1299 (Orkney Recs.,67).

William Johnson (Jonson) 1360.

Occ. 4 Mar. 1360 (Diplom.Norv.,iii,251; Orkney Recs.,15).

William Wood (Wode) x 1372.

Held it and was depriv. by ord. before 12 Mar. 1372 (Diplom. Norv., vii,292-3); retained some right until death (v.inf.).

William de Buchan   1369 x 1372 - 1372 x 1383.
John Fule   1372.

Buchan prob. moved from O.archd. after 25 May 1369; prob. in poss. when found lit. with Fule 12 Mar. 1372 (Diplom.Norv., vii,292-3); held it for many years and at death before 28 Nov. 1383 (CPP,i,566).

Fule lit. with Buchan 12 Mar. 1372 (v.sup.).

Walter de Buchan   1383 - 1391.
Adam Easton   1381 x 1385 - 1391 x 1396.
William de Lancea   1383.

Buchan got poss. on William de Buchan's death and was still

in poss. 28 Nov. 1383 (*CPP*,i,566); occ. 23 Apr. 1391 (*Diplom.Norv.*, ii,402; *Orkney Recs.*,27); prob. dead by Jan. 1398 when Kirkness had poss. (v.inf.).

Easton prov. as cardinal by Urban VI on Wood's death 1381 x 1385 (*Diplom.Norv.*,xvii,142; cf. Eubel, *Hierarchia*,i,23,39); Boniface IX orders prov. to be put into effect, though Walter de Buchan is in poss. 27 Jan. 1391 (*Diplom.Norv.*,xvii,142; *CPL*,iv,385); res. on or before 5 Aug. 1396 (v.inf.).

Lancea prov. on Wood's death by Clement VII 28 Nov. 1383 (*Diplom.Norv.*,xvii,860; cf; *CPP*,i,566) prob. unfruitfully

Angus de Kirkness (Kerlues,Birknes) 1396 - 1429 x 1430.
David de Craigie (Cragy) 1420.

Kirkness prov. by Boniface IX on res. of Easton 5 Aug. 1396 and got poss. by Jan. 1398 i.e. 23 years before 7 Jan. 1421 when he got new prov. (*CSSR*,i,241-2); still in poss. 27 Nov. 1429 (Reg.Supp., 249,fo.31); d. before 17 July 1430 (v.inf.).

Craigie prov. on Walter de Buchan's death by Martin V 30 Dec. 1420 (*CSSR*,i,239) unfruitfully.

Malise de Tulloch 1430 - 1445.

Had ord. coll. on death of Kirkness and gets prov. 17 July 1430 (*Diplom.Norv.*,xvii,378-9); still in poss. 14 Aug. 1445 (ibid.,xvii,no. 1028; Reg.Supp.,407,fo.190v).

David Tulloch 1457.

Res. 9 July 1457 (Reg.Supp.,502,fo.94v).

Thomas Tulloch 1457.

Prov. on res. of David Tulloch 9 July 1457 (ibid.).

John Sinclair 1484 - 1484 x 1501.
James Sinclair 1484.
William Turnbull 1485 - 1487.

John Sinclair in poss. when prov. *C.bp.* 26 May 1484; but not cons., and so may have retained poss. or right until d. before 21 Jan. 1501 (v.inf.).

James Sinclair prov. on John's expected elevation 7 June 1484 (*CPL*,xiii,855) prob. unfruitfully.

Turnbull prov. on John Sinclair's expected elevation 27 Jan. 1485 (*ACSB*,215); paid annates 9 Feb. 1487 (ibid.,257) and so may have had poss. then.

Henry Phankouth/Phankouthin/Phantoutht/Phanteich 1501-1529.
Mawnys Herwood 1502.

Phankouth gets crown pres. on John Sinclair's death 21 Jan. 1501 (*RSS*,i,no.617); res., but promised annates on retaining fruits 23 Nov. 1529 (PRO 31/9 - 32/158-9).

Herwood got poss. on pres. of king of Denmark before 8 June 1502 when king of Scots ordered his removal in Phankouth's favour (*RSS*,i,no.755).

Malcolm Halcro/Hawcro 1529 - 1554.

Promises annates and gets prov. without fruits 23 Nov. 1529 (PRO 31/9 - 32/159-60); occ. 27 Apr. 1531 (*Orkney Recs.*,215); occ. 29 Aug. 1546 (ibid.,233); remained in poss. until death 22 Feb. x 15 July 1554 (see *O.prov.*, and see below).

Jerome/Jeremiah Cheyne 1554 - 1584.

Crown pres. as 'Jeremiah' on Halcro's death 15 July 1554 (*RSS*, iv,no.2785); occ. otherwise as 'Jerome' (e.g. Cardross Writs, no. 849; RSS,l,fo.94); res. to Regent Mar in favour of his son Thomas 31 Mar. 1572 (SRO,Erroll Chrs.,no.799); but apparently retained some right and occ. as archd. 5 Sept. 1580 (*RSS*,vii,no.2488) and 13 Feb. 1584 (SRO, Bks. of Sederunt,iii,fo.218v); d. by 9 Sept. 1584 (v.inf.).

Thomas Cheyne   1572, 1584 - 1586.
William Hay   1584 - 1628.
Alexander Cheyne   1592.

Thomas Cheyne gets crown pres. on his father's res. 31 Mar. 1572 (Reg.Pres.,i,76); not known how far he got poss. during his father's liftime; his crown pres. was conf. 24 Aug. 1584 (ibid.,ii,106); lit. with Hay 2 Nov. 1586, when process was stopped by royal warrant on his complaint that Hay was taking advantage of his absence from the realm (RSS,liv,fo.102).

Hay got crown pres. on death of Jerome Cheyne 9 Sept.1584 (Reg.Pres.,ii,109); then pres. by patron 20 Oct. 1584, and got crown conf. of this 16 Mar. 1586 (RSS,liii,fo.138); lit. with Thomas Cheyne stopped 2 Nov. 1586 (v.sup.); got ratification of his crown conf. 29 July 1587 (RSS,lv,fo.130); was being challenged by Alexander Cheyne when both were depriv. by synod for non-residence 17 Aug. 1592 (Craven, *Church in Orkney*,77); but retained right until dem. in favour of Mitchell 17 June 1628 (SRO,GD 1/314/1).

Alexander Cheyne had grant of a pension out of this ben. by Jerome Cheyne 4 Oct. 1578, which was conf. by crown 11 Mar 1584 (RSS,l,fo.94); became claimant to the ben. itself by 17 Aug. 1592 in competition with Hay, when both were depriv. by synod for non-residence (v.sup.).

John Mitchell 1629.

Crown pres. on dem. of Hay 21 Nov. 1629 (Reg.Pres.,vi,93).

DEANS OF CHRISTIANITY

DEANS OF ORKNEY

First known date: 1527.

Henry Pearson 1527.

Occ. 20 May 1527 (*Orkney Recs.*,208).

OFFICIALS

OFFICIALS WITH GENERAL AUTHORITY

OFFICIALS OF ORKNEY

First known date: 1461 (*Diplom.Norv.*,xvii,555,no name given).

Humphrey (Unfre) Clerk 1514.
    Occ. June 1514 (*Orkney-Shetland Recs.*,i,256).

John Tyrie 1527.
    Occ. 20 May 1527 (*Orkney Recs.*,208).

Alexander Craik 1532 - 1534.
    Occ. 27 June 1532 and 26 June 1534 (ibid.,336,216).

Peter Houston 1540.
    Occ. 24 Dec. 1540 (Fraser, *Pollok*,i,282).

Henry Barton 1543 - 1548.
    Occ. 29 Dec. 1543 (Fraser, *Pollok Cartulary*,65); occ. 7 Mar.
1548 (SRO, Sent.Offic. St A.,fo.158).

Malcolm Halcro 1550.
    Occ. 16 Apr. 1550 (*Orkney Recs.*,105); d. 22 Feb. x 15 July
1554 (see *O.prov.*).

Magnus Strang 1562.
    Occ. 1 Feb. 1562 (*Orkney Recs.*, 270).

OFFICIALS WITH LIMITED AUTHORITY

OFFICIALS OF SHETLAND

First known date: 1545.

Andrew Hiel (?) 1545.
    Occ. when vic. of Unst 26 Apr. 1545, his title (translated from
Norse) being 'official over Shetland in temporals' (G. Goudie, *Celtic
and Scandinavian Antiquities of Shetland*, 81-83).

George Strang 1558.
    Occ. 18 Oct. 1558 (*Orkney-Shetland Recs.*,i,80).

COMMISSARIES

COMMISSARIES OF ORKNEY

First known date: 1504.

John Stewart 1504.
    Occ. (C) at Kirkwall 30 Sept. 1504 (*Orkney Recs.*, 203).

ROSS DIOCESE

BISHOPS OF ROSS

First known date: 1127 x 1131 (?).

For possible foundation of see at Rosemarkie c. 700 see *ES*,i,205, 211; *Chron. Wyntoun*,iv,122-5. St Duthac (d. 1065) may have served as bp. in this area, though connected with Tain and Dornoch rather than with Rosemarkie (*HBC*,298,n.2; cf. *ES*,ii,10; *St A.Cop.*,4-6).

Bp. is usually designated 'of Rosemarkie' in 12th century, but thereafter usually 'of Ross'.

This see was directly subject to the pope until placed under metropolitan authority of St Andrews 17 Aug. 1472 (*Vet.Mon.*,no.852).

Macbeth 1127 x 1131 (?).

Occ. as bp. of Rosemarkie 1127 x 1131 ? (*Dunf.Reg.*,4; cf; *ES*, ii,149).

Simon (Simeon) 1147 x 1151 - 1155.

Occ. as bp. of Ross 1147 x 1151 (*Dunf.Reg.*, 8; cf. *Chron. Holyrood*, 121-2); occ. 27 Feb. 1155 as bp. of St Peter in Ross (Haddan & Stubbs, *Councils*,II,i,232; *AMW*,18).

Gregory 1161 - 1195.

Cons. to see of Rosemarkie by bp. of St Andrews as legate 1161 (*Chron.Melrose*,36); d. Jan. x Feb. 1195 (ibid.,49; cf. inf.).

Reginald (Reinald Ronald) O.Cist. 1195 - 1213.

El. when monk of Melrose at Dunfermline 27 Feb. 1195 and cons. to see of Rosemarkie by bp. of Dunkeld at St. Andrews 10 Sept. 1195 (*Chron.Melrose*,49); given nickname 'Macer' in *Chronica Rogeri de Hovedene* (Rolls Series), iii,284; d. 13 Dec. 1213 (*Chron.Melrose*, 57).

Andrew de Moray (Murevia) 1213 x 1214.
Robert 1214 - 1249.

Andrew el. to see of Ross on Reginald's death, but res. his right (without cons.) by papal licence 1213 x 1214 (ibid.; cf. inf.).

Robert appointed in Andrew's place when chaplain of King William (ibid.), and so prob. before that king's death on 4 Dec. 1214; occ. as bp-elect 17 Feb. 1215 (*Arb.Lib.*,i,74); cons. later in 1215, prob. before 7 July (*Camb.Reg.*,no.46; cf. no. 48; date must be before Bp. Malveisin left for England and the Lateran Council - see *CDS*,i,no.629); granted papal faculty to increase size of his cathedral chapter 29 May 1235 and took action accordingly (*Vet.Mon.*,nos. 80,182); prob. same as the Bp. Robert later remembered as having 'built' Rosemarkie, who was succ. by another Bp. Robert who was previously *R.archd.* (*Chron.Bower*,ii,114, where this succession is wrongly dated 1271); prob. d. 1249 (*Chron.Melrose*,108, where a 'Gilbert B.bp.' is said then to have been succ. by a 'Robert his archd.'; these facts do not fit Brechin dioc. at this date, but do reasonably fit

Ross dioc. if 'Robert' is read for 'Gilbert'; just possibly a Gilbert was R.bp. between the two Roberts, but this is not likely; cf. the language of *Vet.Mon.*,no. 182, which implies the direct succ. of Robert by Robert).

Robert 1249 - 1271.
Prob. succ. when *R.archd.* 1249 (v.sup.); certainly cons. 21 June 1249 x 20 June 1250 (*Rites of Durham*, 152); occ. 20 Sept. 1258 (*Moray Reg.,* no.122; cf. no.220); prob. d. 1271 (*Chron.Bower,*ii,114, on reasoning that this is the year chosen by Bower for his erroneous entry about two successive Bps.Robert).

Matthew 1272 - 1274.
El. when *R.succ.,* and received conf. and cons. from pope on or just before 28 Dec. 1272 (*Vet.Mon.,*no.254); d. at council of Lyons May x July 1274 (*Chron.Bower,*ii,121); see certainly vacant by Christmas 1274 (*SHS Misc.,*vi,49).

Robert de Fyvie (Fyvin, Fifyne, Syvin) 1275 - 1292 x 1295.
El. when *R.archd.* on Matthews's death and granted papal mand. for local conf. and cons. 8 Apr. 1275 (*Vet.Mon.,*no.261, where form 'Syvin' is used; cf. *Chron.Bower,*ii,121 for form 'Thomas de Fifyne'); see still in crown hands June 1275 (*SHS Misc.,*vi,49); occ. 16 Sept. 1278 (*Beauly Chrs.,* 64); occ. 17 Nov. 1292 (*Foedera,*i,780); d. before 18 Nov. 1295 (v.inf.).

Adam de Darlington	1292 x 1295.
Thomas de Dundee (Dono Dei)	1293 x 1295 - 1325.

Darlington, when *R.prec.,* was el. at one of two elections held on death of Bp. Robert; went to curia for conf., but res. his right on or before 18 Nov. 1295 (*Vet.Mon.,*no.348).

Dundee, when *B.dean,* R. canon and prob. *G.subd.,* was el. (after 24 Apr.1293 - see *Glas.Reg.,*i,207) at once of the two elections held on death of Bp. Robert;was then at curia, and after resigning his right to cardinal who then employed him got papal prov. 18 Nov.1295 (*Vet.Mon.,*no.348);cons. at curia by 2 Jan. 1296 (*Reg. Boniface VIII,*i,199);swore fealty of King Edward I before 31 July 1297 when granted temps. by that king (*CDS,*ii,no.928); occ. 1 Nov. 1321 (*C.A.Chrs.,*i,220-1); prob. still in poss. 5 Jan. 1325 (*Kinloss Recs.,*120-1); d. by 17 Apr. 1325 (v.inf.).

Roger O.S.A. (?) 1325 - 1350.
Prov., when canon of (apparently) Abernethy, Db.dioc., on Dundee's death 17 Apr. 1325 (*CPL,*ii,243); cons. at curia before 19 May 1325 (ibid.); occ. 30 Apr. 1350 (SRO, Transcripts of Misc. Chrs.,s.d.); res. in curia on or before 3 Nov. 1350 (v.inf.).

Alexander Stewart 1350 - 1371.
Prov. when *R.archd.* on res. of Bp. Roger 3 Nov. 1350 (*Vet. Mon.,*no.589); cons. by 9 Mar. 1351 (*CPL,*iii,388); occ. 4 Feb. 1371 (*Munro Writs,*3-4); perhaps still alive 27 Mar. 1371 (*APS,*i, 545-7); d. by 9 May 1371 (v.inf.).

Alexander de Kylwos (Frulquhous) 1371 - 1398.

El. when *M.dean* and R.canon on death of Stewart and then got
papal prov. 9 May 1371 (*Vet.Mon.*,no.689); cons. by 6 Mar. 1372 (*APS*,
xii,17-18); d. 6 July 1398 (Forbes, *Kalendars*,p.xxix).

Alexander de Waghorn (Kilbuines ?) 1398 - 1416 x 1418.

El. when *R.archd.* on death of Kylwos and got prov. from Pope
Benedict XIII 17 Aug. 1398 (Eubel, *Hierarchia*,i,424); authority for
surname 'Waghorn' is his seal used 1404 (Stevenson & Wood, *Seals*,
i,161; for the form 'Kilbuines' see *Beauly Chrs.*,202, no source cited);
occ. 17 Mar. 1416 (*Glas.Reg.*, ii,310); d. by 9 Mar. 1418 (*CPP*,i,608).

Thomas Lyell   1416 x 1418.
Griffin Yonge   1418 - 1422.
John Bullock   O.S.A. 1418 - 1439 x 1440.

Lyell, when R.canon (cf. *R.subd.*), el. by chapter on Waghorn's
death and went to curia of Pope Benedict XIII to seek conf.; but was
not successful (Reg.Vat.,329,fo.82-82v, dated 16 May 1419; cf.
CPP,i,608-9); presumably res. right on or before 9 Mar. 1418 (v.inf.).

Yonge was unnamed bp. trans. by Martin V from Bangor bp.
(where he did not in fact have poss. - see Le Neve, *Fasti Ecclesiae
Anglicanae*,xi,4) on Waghorn's death 14 Feb. 1418 (PRO 31/10 -
14/11, quoting 'Arch.Concist.Acta Misc.'; cf. Eubel, *Hierarchia*,i,424,
where date and source are wrong); occ. as Griffin R.bp. going from
Constance to Scotland as nuncio of Martin V 1 Mar. 1418 (*Vet.
Mon.*,no.739); failed to obtain poss. (*ACSB*,1; *CPL*,vii,119; cf.inf.);
but retained title until trans. to Hippo bp. by Martin V 1 Feb. 1423
(*CPL*,vii,288; see A.B. Emden, *Biog.Reg.Univ.Oxford*,iii,2134-5).

Bullock, when canon of St Andrews, prov. by Benedict XIII
on Waghorn's death 9 Mar. 1418 (Dowden, *Bishops*,216; cf. *CSSR*,
i,96), with faculty for cons. 11 Mar. 1418 (*Reg.Vat.*,329,fos.78v
79); in poss. of fruits by 1 Aug. 1419 (*St A.Cop.*,269; *ACSB*,310);
cons. 16 July x 16 Aug. 1420 (*Brech Reg.*,i,39; *Moray Reg.*,475);
prov. by Martin V on trans. of Yonge, with retrospective conf. of
his earlier acts as bp. 1 Feb. 1423 (*CPL*,vii,287); occ. 4 Sept. 1439
(*APS*,ii,55); d. by 26 Sept. 1440 (v.inf.).

Andrew de Munro   1440 - 1441.
Thomas de Tulloch   1440 - 1460 x 1461.

Munro, when *R.archd.*, postulated by chapter on Bullock's
death and sought conf. from Eugenius IV; but was not successful
and Tulloch got prov. 26 Sept. 1440 (v.inf.); in compensation this
pope granted him a pension on fruits of the see 4 Mar. 1441 (*Vet.
Mon.*,no.748; *CPL*,viii,239); he then sought conf. of postulation
from Pope Felix V at Basel, and got conf. there 30 May 1441 (*St
A.Cop.*,311-13; cf. 315,317); not effective (see *R.archd.*).

Tulloch prov. by Eugenius IV, when *R.dean* and *Dk.subd.*,
on Bullock's death 26 Sept. 1440 (*ACSB*,26); prob. cons. at curia
by 14 Oct.1440 (ibid.,26,27,127) and certainly by 10 Feb. 1441
(*CDS*,iv,no.1146); occ. 17 June 1455 (*APS*,ii,77); said to occ. 1460
(Keith *Bishops*,569, quoting inscription on cathedral bell);

presumably d. before 23 Mar. 1461 (v.inf.).

Henry Cockburn 1461 - 1476.

Prov. 23 Mar. 1461 (*ACSB*,51, where no reason for the vacancy is given); cons. 19 Oct. 1463 x 16 Aug. 1464 (*Dunf. Reg.*,366; *RMS*,ii,no.804); occ. 15 and 22 July 1476 (*APS*,ii,190; *RMS*,ii,no. 1249); dem. or d. before 20 Aug. 1476 (v.inf.).

John Wodman O.S.A. 1476 - 1480 x 1481.

Apparently prov. before 20 Aug. 1476 (*ACSB*,290); certainly prov. when prior of Pittenweem before 27 June 1477 (ibid.,189); occ. as bp.-elect 16 Aug. 1477 (*Cawdor Bk.*, 62, where surname is given); occ. still as unnamed bp.-elect 4 May 1478 (*ACSB*,291;cf.251) said to occ. as suffragan in York dioc. c. 1480 (*HBC*,271, no source cited); d. by 3 Aug. 1481 (v.inf.).

William Elphinstone junior 1481 - 1483.

Prov., when *St A.offic.Lothian* and perhaps *Db.treas.* and *Ar.archd.*, on death of Wodman 3 Aug. 1481 (*CPL*,xiii,105); occ. as bp.- elect 26 Nov. 1481 (*Laing Chrs.*,no.184); trans. to *Ab.bp.* still not cons. 19 Mar. 1483; still styled R.bp.-elect as late as 17 May 1484 (*APS*,ii,166).

Thomas Hay 1483 - 1488 x 1492.

Prov. when Ab. canon on trans. of Elphinstone 16 May 1483 (*ACSB*,80; cf. 81); occ. 12 Sept. 1487 (*RMS*,ii,no.1694) and 11 Jan. 1488 (*APS*,ii,180); dem. or d. before 26 Feb. 1492 (v.inf.).

John Guthrie 1492 - 1492 x 1494 (?).

Adm. to temps. (presumably for duration of vacancy) as bp.- elect 12 May 1490 x 26 Feb. 1492, prob. at very end of period (*TA*,i,197); prov. 26 Mar./11 Apr. 1492 (Brady, *Episcopal Succession*,i,144; Eubel, *Hierarchia*,ii,225); promised services 14 June 1492 (Brady, loc.cit.); said to have d. before July 1494 (*Beauly Chrs.*, 203, no source cited).

John Fraser/Frissell 1497 - 1507.

El. prob. before 10 Sept. 1497 (*RSS*,i,no.131) and certainly before 18 Sept. 1497 (*Prot.Bk. Young*,no. 947), when *Restalrig dean* and perhaps *Abernethy prov.*; adm. to temps. (presumably for duration of vacancy) as bp.-elect 30 Oct. 1497 (*TA*,i,314); prov. as G. canon on death of Guthrie 14 Mar. 1498 (Eubel, *Hierarchia*, ii,225; Brady, *Episcopal Succession*,i,144); still bp.-elect 3 Dec. 1498 (Fraser, *Carlaverock*,ii,452); prob. cons. by time he was granted temps. 3 Jan. 1499 (*RSS*,i,no.311); occ. 15 Sept. 1506 (*RMS*,ii,no.2991); d. 5 Feb. 1507 (*Chron.Frasers*,120).

Robert Cockburn 1507 - 1524.

Crown nom. to pope when *Dk.chanc.* 10 Mar./10 May 1507 (*James IV Letters*,62, 73); prov. on death of Fraser 9 July 1507 (Eubel, *Hierarchia*,iii,287); still bp.-elect 28 July 1507 (*James IV Letters*, 82-83); prob. cons. by 17 Aug. 1507 when granted temps. (*RSS*,i,no.1520); trans. to *Dk.bp.* 27 Apr. 1524.

James Hay O.Cist. 1523 - 1538.

Crown nom., when abbot of Dundrennan, prob. accepted by Pope
Adrian VI before his death 14 Sept. 1523 (*James V Letters*, 94; cf. *Vet.M*
no. 944), but actual prov. not granted until 27 Apr. 1524 on trans. of Co
burn (Eubel, *Hierarchia*, iii, 287); granted temps. 16 Sept. 1524 (*RSS*, i,
no. 3293); still bp.-elect 25 Feb. 1525 (*APS*, ii, 289); occ. Apr. 1538 (SRO,
Acts and Decreets, xliv, 56); d. by 3 Oct. 1538 (*RSS*, ii, no. 2736).

Robert Cairncross O.S.A. 1538 - 1545.

Crown nom. when abbot of Holyrood arranged on Hay's death 12
Nov. 1538 (Dowden, *Bishops*, 225, n.2) and carried through 15 Dec. 1538
(*James V Letters*, 356), prov. 14 Apr. 1539 (Eubel, *Hierarchia*, iii, 287);
granted temps. as bp. 23 June 1539 (*RSS*, ii, no. 3058); occ. 15 Apr.
1545 (*Laing Chrs.*, no. 495); d. 30 Nov. 1545 (*Kinloss Recs.*, 10).

David Painter 1545 - 1558.

Crown nom. on death of Cairncross when royal secretary before 2:
Dec. 1545 when granted temps. (*RSS*, iii, no. 1446); prov. 28 Nov. 1547
(Brady, *Episcopal Succession*, i, 145-6); still bp.-elect 13 May 1549 (SRO,
Acts and Decreets, iii, fo. 39); cons. at Jedburgh c. 1552 (Lesley, *History*,
244); d. at Stirling 1 Oct. 1558 (R. Holinshed, *Chronicles* (1577), 487).

Henry Sinclair 1558 - 1565.

Crown nom. on death of Cairncross when royal secretary before 2:
(*RSS*, v, no. 507); papal prov. as *G.dean* on death of Painter 2 June 1561
(Brady, *Episcopal Succession*, i, 146); granted crown lic. to go overseas
2 May 1563 (*RSS*, v, no. 1304); d. in Paris 2 Jan. 1565 (*Diurnal of
Occurrents*, 77, 79).

Note: temps. of this see granted for life to Henry Stewart (Lord Darnley
then earl of Ross 21 May 1565 (*RSS*, v, no. 2066); he d. as king 9 Feb.
1567.

John Leslie   1566 - 1592.
Alexander Hepburn   1574 - 1578.

Leslie had crown nom. 26 Mar. x 1 Apr. 1566 (Dowden, *Bishops*,
231, n.2); granted temps. when commendator of Lindores and *M.archd*.
20 Apr. 1566 (Keith, *Bishops*, 199-200); inducted as bp. apparently
following papal prov. and crown approval 21 Jan. 1567 (ibid., 200);
found as bp.-elect as late as 12 Mar. 1567 (SRO, Reg.Deeds, vii, 398);
occ. at queen's marriage 15 May 1567 (*Diurnal of Occurrents*, 111);
forfeited 19 Aug. 1568 (*APS*, iii, 49-55); said to have acted as bp. 9 June
1573 (*Lind.Cart.*, 331); renewed papal prov. on Sinclair's death on
nom. of imprisoned Queen Mary 22 Apr. 1575 (Brady, *Episcopal
Succession*, i, 147); rehabilitated in Scotland 13 Mar. 1587 (RSS, lv, fo
35), but this was annulled 29 May 1589 (*RPC*, iv, 388-9); trans. by pope
to Coutances bp. 16 Dec. 1592 (Brady, loc.cit.); d. near Brussels 31
May 1596 (Dowden, *Bishops*, 230, quoting tomb inscription).

Hepburn el. following lic. to elect with no name mentioned
issued on forfeiture of Leslie 14 May 1574 (*RSS*, vi, no. 2492); crown
conf. with mand. for cons. 20 Mar. 1575 (ibid., vii, no. 101); granted
temps. 3 Nov. 1575 (ibid., no. 324); d. 17 Sept. x 31 Oct. 1578 (ibid.,

nos. 1646, 1693); d. 22 Sept. 1578 (ibid.,no.2090).

David Lindsay 1600 - 1613.
     Crown prov. 5 Nov. 1600 (Reg.Pres.,iii,39) and again 22 Dec. 1604
(*RMS*,vi,no.1549); prob. cons. 23 Jan./24 Feb. 1611 (Calderwood,
History, vii,154); d. 14 Aug. 1613 (Edin. Tests.,17 Dec. 1613).

Patrick Lindsay 1613 - 1633.
     Crown prov. 23 Oct. 1613 (Reg.Pres.,iv,102v); cons. 1 Dec. 1613
(Calderwood, *History*, vii,178); renewed crown prov. 6 Nov. 1616 (Reg.
Pres.,iv,141); trans to *G.abp.* 16 Apr. 1633.

John Maxwell 1633 - 1638.
     Crown prov. 23 Apr. 1633 (Reg.Pres.,vii,2); prob. cons. by 18
June 1633 when he assisted at king's coronation (Spalding,*Memorialls*,
i,36);depriv. 13 Dec. 1638 (Peterkin, *Records*,i,26-27); crown nom. for
trans. to see of Killala and Achonry 29 June 1640 (*CSP Ireland 1633-
47*,242); letters patent 12 Oct. 1640 and 26 Feb. 1641 (Cotton,
Fasti Ecclesiae Hibernicae, iv,68); d. as Tuam abp. 16 Feb. 1647 (ibid.,
14).

CHAPTER OF ROSS

There were only four prebends for canons in ch. of Ross when bp. got
papal mand. 29 May 1235 to increase the revenues of these existing
prebends and add an unspecified number of new ones (*Vet.Mon.*,
no. 80); seven dignities and offices had been established in ch. of
Rosemarkie (situated in the modern Fortrose) along with other simple
prebends, and statutes had been drawn up governing the conduct of
the cathedral community, before 9 Feb. 1256 when these arrangements
received papal conf. (ibid.,no.182);

DEANS OF ROSS

First known date: 1212 x 1223.
     Prebend: chs. of Ardersier and Kilmuir Wester, with ¼ of chs. of
Rosemarkie and Cromarty in 1256 (*Vet.Mon.*, 69; Cowan, *Parishes*,
8,39,108,172) and still at Reformation (*RMS*,v,no.1625).

Henry 1212 x 1223 - 1227.
     Occ. 1212 x 1223 (*Moray Reg.*,app. to preface, no.III), and
18 Mar. 1227 (ibid.,23); occ. July 1224 x June 1228, perhaps Mar.
1226/7 (*Arb.Lib.*,i,144).

John 1278.
     Occ. 16 Sept. 1278 (*Beauly Chrs.*, 64).

John de Kinkell 1333 x 1350.
     Occ. 1333 x 1350 (*Munro Writs*, 1).

Alexander de Kylwos 1350 - 1368 x 1370.
Occ. 30 Apr. 1350 (SRO, Transcripts of Misc.Chrs.,s.d.); conf.
of el. 9 Sept. 1350 (*CPP*,i,204); occ. 1368 (*OPS*,ii,573); moved to
M.dean. by 19 Dec. 1370.

John Reid (Reed) 1371.
Prov. on res. of Kylwos 18 Jan. 1371 (Reg.Av.,176,fo.55v);
d. sometime before 10 Jan. 1372 (v.inf.).

William de Dingwall 1372 - 1389.
Conf. of el. after Reid's death 10 Jan. 1372 (Reg.Av.,185,fo.
260v); occ. 2 Nov. 1389 (*Moray Reg.*,353-4).

John de Innes 1396 x 1398 - 1407.
Prob. moved from *C.archd.* 1396 x 25 July 1398; occ. 1 Dec.
1404 (*A.B.Ill.*,iv,732); prov. *M.bp.* 12 Jan. 1407.

William Fayrhar 1407 - 1420 x 1436.
Prov. on elevation of Innes 18 June 1407 (*CPP*,i,635); occ.
16 Aug. 1420 (*Moray Reg.*,475-6); d. before 16 Oct. 1436 (v.inf.).

John de Innes (Innelli, James)   1436 - 1437.
Thomas de Tulloch   1436 - 1440.
Laurence Piot   1436 - 1440.
Innes prob. had local coll. on Fayrhar's death, being already.
R.subd.; claimed poss. when incorporated at council of Basel 3 Nov.
1436 (Haller, *Conc.Bas.*,iv,320, and *Mon.Conc.Bas.,* ii,910, where
name is given as 'Innelli' and 'James'); in poss. 13 Jan. 1437 (Reg.
Supp.,329,fo.139v) and 11 Sept. 1437 when he lost lit. with
Tulloch (*CPL*,viii,665); presumably lost poss. since he retained
R.subd.
Tulloch prov. on Fayhar's death 16 Oct. 1436 (*CPL*,viii,
583); lit. with Innes and won sentence in his favour 11 Sept.1437
(ibid.,665-6); got poss. but lit. with Piot (ibid.,ix,107); res. in
favour of James de Innes 23 Sept. 1440 (Reg. Supp., 367, fo.290v)
and prov. *R.bp.* 26 Sept. 1440.
Piot prov. on Fayrhar's death 16 Nov. 1436 (*CPL*,viii,610-11);
lit. without poss. 7 May 1437 (ibid.,667); gave up right on or before
26 Oct. 1440 (v.inf.).

James de Innes   1440 - 1447.
David Stewart   1445.
Innes prov. on res. of Tulloch 23 Sept. 1440 (Reg.Supp.,367,
fp.290v); surrog. to rights of Tulloch and Piot 3/26 Oct. 1440
(*ACSB*,127; *CPL*,ix,107-8); in poss. 27 Oct. 1442 (*CPL*,viii,314);
in poss. 26 Apr. 1447 (Reg.Supp.,415,fo.12); d. after 25 May
1447 (see *M.treas.*) and before 14 Oct.1447 (v.inf.).
Stewart gets *com.priv.* against Innes 20 Nov. 1445 (Reg.
Supp.,408,fo.225v) unfruitfully.

Alan Cant 1447.
Prov. on death of James de Innes 14 Oct. 1447 (*CPL*,x,363);
in poss. 16 Nov. 1447 (ibid.,360).

John Calder/Cawdor 1451.

     Occ. 1451 (*OPS*,ii,573); d. before 11 Apr. 1457 (v.inf.; cf. Reg. Supp.,499,fo.69 for name 'Cawdor').

David Stewart	1457.
William Ogilvie	1457.
Thomas Ross (?)	1457.
David Ogilvie	1457 x 1458.

     Stewart postulated by bp. and chapter (presumably on death of Calder) and prob. had poss. when prov. 21 May 1457 (Reg.Supp.,501, fo.55v).

     William Ogilvie prov. on Calder's death 11 Apr. 1457 (*CPL*,xi, 339); granted lic. to res. when he should get poss. 31 May 1457 (Reg. Supp.,501,fo.181); prob. did res. right in exch. for *B.chanc.* with David Ogilvie.

     Ross prov. 18 May 1457 (Reg. Supp.,500,fo.24, where this name is prob. an error for 'Vaus', v.inf.).

     David Ogilvie held it at death before 21 Oct. 1458 (*CPL*, xi,375-6), having prob. got it on exch. with William Ogilvie since 31 May 1457 (v.sup.).

Thomas de Vaus	1458 - 1466 x 1468.
David Balfour	1458 - 1463.
Alexander de Lumsden (Lomesden)	1466.

     Vaus prob. prov. under name 'Ross' 18 May 1457 (v.sup.); prov. on David Ogilvie's death 21 Oct. 1458(*CPL*,xi,375-6); lit. with Balfour by 28 Feb./5 Mar. 1461 (v.inf.); still in poss. and being molested when given new prov. 27 Dec. 1465 (Reg.Supp.,589,fo.234); in poss. 27 Sept. 1466 (*CPL*,xii,552-3); res. to bp. of Aberdeen in favour of Martin Vaus (v.inf.) before 14 May 1468 (Reg.Supp.,625,fo. 163v).

     Balfour prov. on David Ogilvie's death 4 Nov. 1458 (*ACSB*, 138); lit. in curia without poss. 28 Feb. 1461 (Reg.Supp.,536, fo.171); lit. with Vaus when given new prov. 5 Mar. 1461 (ibid.,537, fo.51v); said to be in poss. 25 June 1463 (*CPL*,xi,658); prov. *Si neutri* Sept. 1462 x Sept. 1463 (*CPL*,xii,p.xxviii); prob. still lit. against Vaus 27 Dec. 1465 (v.sup.) and then gave up.

     Lumsden got *com.priv.* against Vaus 4 Nov. 1466 (Reg.Supp., 603,fo.83v) unfruitfully.

Martin Vaus	1466 x 1468 - 1481.
William Hog (Hoge)/de Monteablo	1468.

     Vaus coll. by bp. of Aberdeen on res. of Thomas de Vaus to that bp., presumably before prov. of Hog 14 May 1468 (v.inf.) and certainly before 17 Nov. 1470 when given prov. (Reg.Supp.,661,fo. 66v); in poss. 7 Oct. 1475 (*ACSB*,329); occ. 7 Feb. 1481 (*RMS*,ii, no.1460).

     Hog prov. on res. of Thomas de Vaus 14 May 1468 (Reg. Supp.,625,fo.163v).

Martin Wane 1487 - 1504 x 1505.

Occ. 12 Sept. 1487 (*RMS*,ii,no.1694); prob. retained it until d. 15 Jan. 1504 x 12 June 1505 (see. *G.chanc.*).

Robert Fraser 1506 - 1523.

Occ. 10 Aug. 1506 (SRO,ADC,xix,fo.338); res. in favour of Paul Fraser, but promised annates to retain fruits 24 Apr. 1520 (PRO 31/9 - 31/350-1); d. 10 July 1523 (Dunrobin Castle, Kalendar of Fearn, fo.July).

Paul Fraser/Fresail 1520 - 1545.

Promised annates and got prov. without fruits on res. of Robert Fraser 24 Apr. 1520 (PRO 31/9 - 31/349); occ. 16 Sept.1523 (*HMC* 44, *Drumlanrig*,i,73); retired on pension, prob. after 10 Feb. 1545 (v.inf.) and certainly before 23 Apr. 1545 (Innes, *Sketches,*85n); d. 13 Sept. 1545 (Dunrobin Castle, Kalendar of Fearn,fo.Sept.).

Kentigern/Mungo Monypenny 1545 - 1575 x 1576.

Prob. moved from *R.archd.* after 10 Feb. and before 23 Apr. 1545 (v.sup.); occ. 8 Mar. 1546 (*RMS*,iv. no.508); occ. 3 Aug. 1575 (SRO, Abbrev. Feu Chrs.,ii,fo.30); dem. by 26 July 1576 (v.inf.).

David Monypenny   1566 - 1581.
Alexander Urquhart   1576 - 1582 x 1583.

Monypenny given crown pres. to exp. of this ben. 15 Dec.1566 (*RSS*,v,no.3122); occ. 20 Jan. 1581 (SRO, Mackintosh Muniments, no.121).

Urquhart got crown pres. on dem. of Kentigern Monypenny 26 July 1576 (*RSS*,vii,no.679); occ. 29 Dec. 1576 (*RMS*,iv,no.2624) and 2 Aug. 1582 (SRO, Reg. of Inhibitions, Perth, s.d. 6 Nov. 1590); depriv. before 8 May 1583 (v.inf.).

Hector Munro 1583 - 1588.

Crown pres. on depriv. of Urquhart 8 May 1583 (Reg.Pres.,ii, 89); occ. 12 July 1588 (*Munro Writs,*no. 118);

Andrew Crombie (Crambie) 1589 - 1630 x 1633.

Crown pres. on depriv. of Urquhart 15 Aug. 1589 (RSS,1x,fo. 48); occ. 15 Oct. 1590 (*Munro Writs,*no.127); occ. 8 Feb. 1630 (*PSAS,*xli,364); still described as dean 11 Mar. 1633 (SRO, Part. Reg. Sasines Inverness,v,fo.68), but by then had been succ. by Durham (v.inf.).

Patrick Durham 1633 - 1661.

Occ. 1 Mar. 1633 (SRO, Part.Reg.Sasines Inverness,v,fo.70) and 13 Apr. 1633 (Macgill, *Old Ross-shire,*no.65); claimed revenues of this ben. after Restoration 3 Apr. 1661 (*APS,*vii,106).

PRECENTORS/CHANTERS OF ROSS

First known date: 1255.

Prebend: chs. of Kinnettes and Suddy with ¼ of chs. of Rosema

and Cromarty in 1256 (*Vet.Mon.*,69); but perhaps something has been omitted from this text and these chs. were in fact then attached to R. chanc. as they certainly were by time of Reformation; no preb. mentioned 1274-5 (*SHS Misc.*,vi,49); chs. of Kilchrist/Tarradale and Kilmorack, with ¼ of chs. of Rosemarkie and Cromarty attached at Reformation (*RMS*,v,no.1625; cf. Cowan, *Parishes,* 39,98,106,115,172, 193).

R. de Eginton 1255.
> Occ. 16 Sept. 1255 (*Beauly Chrs.*,49).

Adam de Darlington (Derlington) 1255 x 1271 - 1296.
> Occ. 1255 x 1271 (*Moray Reg.*,282); cons. *C.bp.* 29 April.1296, but d. before 17 Dec. 1296.

Isaac Oliver 1350 x 1372.
> Occ. 1350 x 1372 (*OPS*,ii,574).

Thomas Wys x 1394.
> Held it at death before 26 Aug. 1394 (v.inf.).

John de Sinclair (Sancto Claro) 1394 - 1395 x 1400.
> Had prov. from Pope Clement VII on death of Wys with effect from 26 Aug. 1394; got new prov. from next pope 12 Oct. 1394, expedited 31 Dec. 1394/5 Jan.1395,still with effect from 26 Aug.1394 (Reg.Av.,282,fos.496v-498); d. before May 1400 (see *R.treas.*).

William Fayrhar 1407.
> In poss. when prov. *R.dean* 18 June 1407 (*CPP*,i,635).

John Barber 1407 - 1408 x 1417.
Richard Hunter   1408.
> **Barber** gets prov. 6/20 Nov. 1407 (Reg.Supp.,102,fo.258; Reg. Av.,329,fos.267v-268v); no poss. yet 16 Jan. 1408 (*CPP*,i,594); res. to ord. on exch. with Falconer before 16 Aug. 1417 (v.inf.).
> **Hunter** gets prov. on Fayrhar's move to *R.dean.* 21 May 1408 (*CPP*,i,636); d. before 5 Oct. 1408 (see *Dk.archd.*).

Thomas Falconer (Fauconer) 1417 - 1451 x 1454.
> Had coll. from ord. on exch. with Barber, and gets papal prov. 16 Aug. 1417 (Reg.Av.,349,fos.73-73v); occ. 1451 (*OPS*,II,ii,574); d. before 16 Mar. 1454 (v.inf.).

John de Duffus   1454.
Laurence Scot   1451 x 1455 - 1485.
> **Duffus** prov. on Falconer's death 16 Mar. 1454 (Reg.Supp., 471,fo.115v).
> **Scot** occ. 25 Feb. 1455 (*St A.Acta*,108); had had ord. coll. on Falconer's death and got conf. 8 Oct. 1455 (*CPL*,xi,257); in poss. 29 Mar. 1485 (*CPL*,xiv,322).

John (Thomas ?) Calder 1496 - 1519.
Adam Gordon   1514.

Calder occ. 15 June 1496 (*ADC*,ii,3); occ. 30 Oct. 1507 (*RMS*, ii,no.3298); res. in some way on or before 22 Sept. 1514 (v.inf.), but occ. 3 Aug. 1515 (*ER*,xiv,67); a *Thomas* Calder is said to have d. in poss. 8 Sept. 1519 (*The Cathedral Kirk of Moray*, guidebook [1950 edn.] ,16, quoting tombstone).

Gordon prov. by papal nuncio on res. of Calder 22 Sept. 1514 (*Laing Chrs.*,77).

Thomas Nudry	x 1521 - 1526 x 1527.
Patrick Hepburn	1522 - 1523.
Alexander Turing	1523 - 1527 x 1532 (?).
Thomas Hay (?)	x 1526.

Nudry in poss. before 1 Dec. 1521 and still in poss. 28 May 1522 (PRO 31/9 - 31/373-4); is to res. on pension in favour of Turing 30 Jan. 1523 (PRO 31/9 - 32/1; cf. *St A.Form.*,i,170-1); but retained some right until death (v.inf.) i.e. 7 July 1526 x 3 Dec. 1527 (see M. archd.).

Hepburn occ. 28 Feb. 1522 (St A.Univ.Mun.,UY305/1,p.76) and 23 Feb. 1523 (*St A.Acta,* 340).

Turing expects prov. on res. of Nudry 30 Jan. 1523 (v.sup.); promises annates and gets prov. 2 July 1526 (PRO 31/9 - 32/114); occ. 19 Mar. 1527 (SRO,ADC,xxxvii,fo.31v); perhaps retained poss. until he got *Methven prov.* 11 July 1527 x 6 Jan. 1532 (cf.inf.).

Hay said to have held it and res. before 2 July 1526 (PRO 31/9 - 32/114); prob. an error for Nudry.

Sixtus Zucchellus 1529.

Prov. on Nudry's death by a cardinal with powers 3 Sept. 1529 (PRO 31/9 - 32/135-6).

Walter Stewart 1532 - 1541.

Occ. 6 Jan. 1532 (*RSS*,ii,no.1104) and 5 Feb. 1541 (*RMS*,iii, no.2278).

John Cairncross	1548 - 1566.
John Elphinstone	1548 - 1551.

Cairncross occ. 27 Feb. 1548 (*RSS*,iii,no.2656); occ. 23 Dec. 1566 (SRO, Fraser, no. 210).

Elphinstone had a papal grace for this ben. 20 June 1548, then lit. with Cairncross, and res. in favour of Cairncross in return for a pension 1 Mar. 1551 (PRO 31/9 - 33/285).

Alexander Hume (Home) 1573 - 1587.

Occ. 24 Dec. 1573 (SRO, Reg.Deeds,xiii,fo.384) and 8 Aug. 1587 (SRO, Munro of Foulis, no. 110).

James Lauder 1606 - 1628.

Occ. 15 Sept. 1606 (SRO, Secretary's Reg. Sasines Inverness, fo.317) and 6 Mar. 1628 (SRO, Part.Reg.Sasines Inverness,iv.fo. 114).

CHANCELLORS OF ROSS

First known date: 1212 x 1223.
Prebend: only ¼ of chs. of Rosemarkie and Cromarty mentioned in 1256 (*Vet.Mon.*,69); but perhaps text here is corrupt and chs. of Kinnettes and Suddy were also in fact attached then to this dignity rather than to R.prec.; unnamed preb. existed 1274-5 (*SHS Misc.*,vi,49); chs. of Kinnettes and Suddy with ¼ of chs. of Rosemarkie and Cromarty were attached at Reformation (*OPS*,ii,501-2, 538; *RMS*,v, no.1625; cf. Cowan, *Parishes,* 39,172; cf. 106, 115, 193).

Maurice (Cecus ?) 1212 x 1223, 1225 (?).
Occ. 1212 x 1223 (*Moray Reg.*,app. to preface, no III); perhaps same as 'Maurice Cecus' who obtained papal mand. for investigation of his loss of chs. of Nigg (with chapel of Shandwick), Kilmorack (Altyre) and Kilchrist (Tarradale) 29 July 1225 (*CPL*,i,103).

R. 1255.
Occ. 16 Sept. 1255 (*Beauly Chrs.,* 49).

Duncan 1278.
Occ. 16 Sept. 1278 (ibid.,64).

William de Lindores 1327 x 1328 - 1333.
Occ. 24 Apr. 1327 x 8 May 1328 (*Yester Writs*,16); occ. 1333 (*OPS*,ii,575).

Alexander de Kylwos x 1350.
Held it when el. to *R.dean.* before 30 Apr. 1350 (cf. *CPP*,i,204).

John de Arbroath (Aberbrotht) 1350 - 1358 x 1370.
Had ord. coll. on el. of Kylwos and gets conf. 9 Sept. 1350 (ibid.); conf. again 11/12 Feb. 1358 (ibid.,324, 326); d. before 25 Feb. 1370 (v.inf.).

Thomas Lang 1370.
Had ord. coll. on Arbroath's death and gets conf. 25 Feb. 1370 (*CPL*,iv,84); d. soon after (Reg.Av.,172,fo.25v; cf. *CPP*,i,564).

Martin de Calder (Caldor) 1380 - 1381.
Occ. 11 Oct. 1381 (*Moray Reg.,* 183); in poss. 12 Dec. 1381 (*CPP*,i,561).

Thomas Hale x 1393.
Held it and res. to ord. on exch. with Munro before 21 Apr. 1393 (v.inf.).

Isaac de Munro (Monroy) 1393 - 1400 x 1404.
Had ord. coll. on exch. with Hale and gets conf. 21 Apr. 1393 (Reg.Vat.,306,fo.326); described just as R. canon 6 Nov. 1400 (*Abdn.Reg.*,i,205); d. in poss. before 3 May 1404 (v.inf.).

William de Tain (Tayn) 1400 x 1404 – 1404 x 1428.
Had ord. coll. on death of Munro and gets papal conf. 3 May.

1404 (Reg.Av.,309,fo.622v); retained it until death before 11 Aug.
1428 (v.inf.).

Thomas de Lochmalony 1428 - 1456.
        Had ord. coll. on Tain's death and gets conf. 11 Aug. 1428
(*CSSR*,ii,236); occ. 15 Nov. 1456 (*Bannatyne Misc.*, iii,100; cf. *OPS*,
ii,575).

John Stewart   1489 - 1497 x 1510.
William Dowy   1497.
        Stewart had held it for eight years before 14 Nov. 1497 when
his right was being challenged by Dowy (*ADC*,ii,88); retained right
until d. before 16 Oct. 1510 (see John Sanquhar below); obit dated
10 May (*PSAS*,ii,258).
        Dowy accused before king's council by Stewart of barratry
in connection with this ben. 14 Nov. 1497 (*ADC*,ii,88).

William Wawane/Wanay   1510 - 1515.
John Sanquhar/Schancar/Sanquhy/Sauchy   1510 - 1526.
P.B.   1514 x 1521.
A.K.   1514 x 1521.
        Wawane claimed poss. 16 Oct. 1510 when lit. with Sanquhar,
but had not had coll. (SRO,ADC, xxi,fo.203); not in poss. when
promised annates and got prov. as 'Wanay' 27 May 1513 (PRO
31/9 - 31/274); occ. 26 July 1515 (*RMS*,iii,no.111); d. c. May 1516
(see *St A. offic. Lothian*), prob. after res. (v.inf.).
        Sanquhar had ord. coll. before 16 Oct. 1510 when lit. with
Wawane (SRO,ADC,xxi,fo.203); promised annates and got prov. on
Stewart's death 13/23 Jan. 1511 (PRO 31/9 - 31/245) and
promised annates again in person 21 Mar. 1512 (ibid.); occ. 21 Mar.
1513 (SRO,ADC,xxv,fo.18); when an incumbent res. to Abp.
Forman of St Andrews as legate (called P.B., but perhaps Wawane
late in 1515), Forman conferred it on 'J.S.' and followed this act
by the annulment of local coll. of A.K. 1514 x 1521 (*St A.Form.*,
i,24-27; cf. Herkless & Hannay, *Archbishops*,ii,197-8; these
sources identify 'J.S.' as 'John Sauchy'); Sanquhar occ. 15 May
1520 (Fraser, *Eglinton*,ii,93) and 4 Mar. 1525 (Fraser,*Sutherland*,
iii,73); res. in favour of Chalmer, but promised annates to retain
fruits 27 Jan. 1526 (PRO 31/9 - 32/91-92).
        P.B. res. to Abp. Forman as legate 1514 x 1521 (*St A.Form.*,
i,24).
        A.K. coll. by dean, vicar-general and official of Ross on res.
of P.B. and got poss., but this was annulled by Abp.Forman as
legate in favour of Sanquhar 1514 x 1521 (v.sup.).

Note: lit. between *Gilbert Strathauchin* and *John B.* over this ben.
was ended by res. of Strathauchin on exch. with B. for vic. in
Moray dioc. (*St A.Form.*,i,41); but source is undated and perhaps
relates rather to lit. of Strathauchin and John Chisholm over
Db.dean.; see also *Dk.chanc.*

Duncan Chalmer 1526 - 1571.
David Chalmer of Ormont 1560 - 1593.
George Munro (two persons) 1571 - 1637.

Duncan Chalmer promised annates and got prov. without fruits 27 Jan. 1526 (PRO 31/9 - 32/92); occ. 23 Oct. 1526 (*Arb.Lib.*,ii,458); occ. 24 Nov. 1556 (*RSS*,iv,no.3349); res. retaining liferent to Pope Paul IV i.e. May 1555 x Aug. 1559, though date given is Mar. 1553; then renounced liferent on or before 13 Aug. 1560 (RSS,lv,fo.217); but occ. 11 Mar. 1566 (*Munro Writs*,no.79) and 6 Apr./21 May 1567 (SRO, Abbrev. Feu Chrs.,ii,fo.252); d. 13 Jan. 1571 (Dunrobin Castle, Kalendar of Fearn, fo.Jan.).

David Chalmer prov. by pope on res. of Duncan Chalmer 13 Aug. 1560 (RSS,lv,fo.217); occ. 28 Jan. 1564 (*Laing Chrs.*,194); still called 'successor' merely 6 Apr./21 May 1567 (SRO, Abbrev. Feu Chrs., ii,fo.252); escheated on or before 19 June 1568 (*RSS*,vi,no.311); d. retaining some right 22 June 1593 (Edin.Tests.).

Munro got crown pres. on death of Duncan Chalmer and forfeiture of David Chalmer 5 July 1571/23 Jan. 1572 (*RSS*,vi,nos. 1201, 1447); occ. 27 Feb. 1589 (SRO, Monro of Allan, no.5), Apr. 1607 (*Munro Writs*,no.146) and 18 May 1637 (SRO, Part.Reg. Sasines Inverness, vi,fo.44); there were two men of the same name involved here, grandfather and grandson, but family tree (SRO,Monro of Allan, no.291) gives no dates; the younger man was certainly in poss. by 6 Apr. 1630 (SRO, Part.Reg. Sasines Inverness,iv,fo.218).

TREASURERS OF ROSS

First known date: 1227.
    Prebend: chs. of Urquhart and Logie Wester, with ¼ of chs. of Rosemarkie and Cromarty, in 1256 (*Vet.Mon.*,69; Cowan, *Parishes,* 39, 138, 172, 205); still at Reformation (*RMS*,v,no.1625).

William 1227.
    Occ. 1 Feb. 1227 (*Moray Reg.*,82).

Walter Sybandy 1293 x 1314.
    Occ. 1293 x 1314 (*Panm.Reg.*,ii,159-60).

Adam Torrech/Tureech 1355 x 1362.
    In poss. 1355 x 1362 (Collect.,14,fo.180v; cf. 190v).

John de Sinclair x 1400.
    Held it at death which was six years or more before 18 May 1406 (*CPP*,i,634).

William de Ross c. 1400 - c. 1403.
    Held it for three years and at death which was three years or more before 18 May 1406 (ibid.).

Duncan de Forbes 1403 - 1406.

Alexander de Brothy   1406.

    Forbes in poss. 18 May 1406 and had by then held it for three years (ibid.).

    Brothy prov. 18 May 1406 (ibid.).

Simon de Ross   1406 x 1417.

    Held it and res. to ord. on exch. with Kylwos before 16 Aug. 1417 (v.inf.); in fact this exch. was prob. some time before c. July 1417 (see *R.subd.*).

John de Kylwos (Kylwhaus, Kylquhous)   1406 x 1417 − .

    Had coll. from ord. on exch. with Ross, and gets papal prov. 16 Aug. 1417 (Reg.Av.,349,fos.72-73); res. outwith curia some time thereafter before 13 Nov. 1430 (*ACSB*,102).

Henry Buge   1430 - 1444.
Henry de Rynd/Reid   1432 - 1433.
Launcelot de Ross (Ros)   1444.

    Buge prov. 13 Nov. 1430 (*ACSB*,102); lit. with Rynd by 14 Jan. 1432 (v.inf.); had had poss. for 14 years by 11 Jan. 1444 (Reg. Supp.,394,fo.79v); d. before 18 Oct. 1444 (v.inf.).

    Rynd lit. with Buge 14 Jan. 1432 (Reg.Supp.,273,fo.275); prob. same as the 'Henry Reid' who claimed some right in this ben. 12 Feb. 1433 (ibid.,282,fo.272v).

    Ross got *com.priv.* against Buge 11 Jan. 1444 (ibid.,394,fo.79v).

Thomas Tulloch   1444 - 1454 x 1455.
Launcelot de Ross (Ros) 1445 - 1448.
John Kennochson   1454.

    Tulloch had coll. by ord. on Buge's death more than three months before 18 Jan. 1445 (ibid.,402,fo.271v) and gets conf. 2 Jan. 1445 (*CPL*,ix,439); new prov. after lit. with Ross 1 May 1448 (Reg.Supp.,427,fo.185v); still in poss., having held it 10 - 11 years 26 Oct. 1454 (*CPL*,x,684-5); perhaps moved to *C.treas.* in which he had some right Apr. 1454 x Sept. 1455.

    Ross got *com.priv.* against Tulloch 18 Jan. 1445 (Reg.Supp., 402,fo.271v); lit. still 1 May 1448 (ibid.,427,fo.185v).

    Kennochson gets *com.priv.* against Tulloch 26 Oct. 1454 (*CPL*,x,684-5).

James Herring   1510 - 1512.

    Occ. 28 Oct. 1510 (*Arb.Lib.*, ii,399) and 12 Mar. 1512 (*RMS*,ii, no. 3716).

Thomas Heriot   1518.

    Held it at death 2 May 1518 (Dunrobin Castle, Kalendar of Fearn, fo.May).

Gavin Dunbar   1529 - 1546.

    Occ. 10 Sept. 1529 (*Moray Reg.,*418); occ. 12 Mar. 1544 (*Invernessiana*,216); d. 1 Sept. 1546 (Dunrobin Castle, Kalendar of Fearn, fo. Sept.).

Thomas Stewart (?) 1546.
    See *C. treas.*

John Hamilton 1546 - 1547 x 1548.
    Crown pres. on Dunbar's death 13 Sept. 1546 (*RSS*,iii,no.1892); occ. 26 Aug. 1547 (ibid.,no.2396); d. before 22 Apr. 1548 (v.inf.).

John Robertson/Robeson 1548 - 1596.
    Crown pres. on Hamilton's death 22 Apr. 1548 (*RSS*,iii,no.2732); d. 29 May 1596 (Edin.Tests.).

Robert Munro 1597 - 1615.
    Coll. after crown pres. on Robertson's death 16 June 1597 (Macgill, *Old Ross-shire*, no. 46); occ. 2 Nov. 1615 (*Munro Writs.*,no.158).

David Munro 1618 - 1634.
    Occ. June 1618 (SRO, Part. Reg. Sasines Inverness,i,fo.110) and 1 Mar. 1634 (*RMS*,ix,no.70).

SUBDEANS OF ROSS

First known date: 1256 (*Vet.Mon.*,69).
    Prebend: chs. of Tain and Edderton in 1256 (*Vet.Mon.*, 69; Cowan, *Parishes*, 59, 194) and at Reformation (*OPS*,ii,588); chs. of Alness, Cullicudden, Kincardine and Roskeen added by 1589 (*RMS*,v,no.1625; cf. Cowan, *Parishes*, 3, 41, 110, 172).

William de Balvin 1365.
    In poss. 16 June 1365 (*CPP*,i,505).

William de Dingwall 1371 x 1372.
    Res. on el. as *R.dean.* 18 Jan. 1371 x 10 Jan. 1372.

Thomas de Barry 1372, 1378.
    Prov. on el. of Dingwall 18 Jan. 1372 (Reg.Av.,186,fo.244v); still no poss. 27 Nov. 1378 (*CPP*,i,547).

William de Tarbart x 1395.
    Held it at death before Mar. 1395 (v.inf.).

John de Kylwos (Kylwhaus) x 1395 - 1406 x 1417.
Thomas Lyell   1395.
    Kylwos had coll. by ord. on death of Tarbart more than a year before 31 Mar. 1396 when he got prov. (Reg.Av.,298,fos. 523-524v); res. on exch. with Ross for *R.treas.* sometime after 18 May 1406 and before 16 Aug. 1417 (v.inf.).
    Lyell got prov. on el. of Dingwall to *R.dean.* 1 May 1395 (*CPP*,i,584); prob. unfruitful, as still held an unnamed can. and preb. of Ross when *R.bp.-elect* Mar. 1416 x Mar. 1418.

Simon de Ross 1406 x 1417.
    Coll. by ord. on exch. with Kylwos some time after 18 May

1406 (see *R.treas.*) and before 16 Aug. 1417 (Reg.Av.,349,fos. 72-73); prob. dem. or d. before c. July 1417 (v.inf.).

John de Innes	1417 - 1447 x 1448.
Adam de Nairn (Narn)	1432.
John de Leuchars (Luchris)	1433.
Patrick Fraser	1435 - 1436.
John Hacket	1436 - 1437.

Innes obtained poss. c. July 1417, for by 13 July 1433 he had been in poss. for c. 16 years (Reg.Supp.,290,fo.104); arranged exch. with Nairn for *M.succ.* 5 Feb. 1432 (Reg.Supp.,275,fo.17), but did not in fact res. this ben.; moved for a time to *R.dean.* by 3 Nov. 1436, but lost lit. 11 Sept. 1437 and returned to this ben.; prov. *C.bp.* 7/8 Apr. 1446, but d. uncons. 5 June 1447 x 6 Jan. 1448.

Nairn obtained some right by exch. with Innes 5 Feb. 1432 (v.sup.), but failed to get poss.

Leuchars prov. 13 July 1433 when Innes was in poss. (Reg. Supp.,290,fo.104); not fruitful.

Fraser had unfruitful prov. before 2 June 1435 on false report on res. of Innes (ibid.,306,fo.160); claimed poss. 30 June and 1 Dec. 1436 (ibid.,324,fo.73, 329,fo.202), but claimed only prov., not poss., 8 Nov. 1436 (*CPL*,viii,606).

Hacket got poss. on dem. of Innes i.e. prob. by 3 Nov. 1436 (v.sup.), and got conf. 13 Jan. 1437 (Reg.Supp.,329,fo.139v); presumably lost poss. when Innes reverted to this ben. after 11 Sept. 1437.

Walter Blair	1446 - 1448.
Patrick Fraser	1447.

Blair prov. on elevation of Innes 8 Apr. 1446 (Reg.Supp.,410, fo.235v; cf. *CPL*,viii, 307-8); had had poss. for more than a year before new prov. 12 Sept. 1447 (Reg.Supp.,419,fo.208v); had had ord. coll. more than a year before prov. 4 Jan. 1448 (*CPL*,x,290-1).

Fraser had prov. on elevation of Innes sometime before 26 May 1447 when not in poss., lit. 18 July 1447, and claimed poss. when given new prov. 24 July 1447 (Reg.Supp.,417,fo.274,418, fos. 148,159).

Thomas de Dingwall 1454 x 1455 - 1475 x 1477.

Prob. moved from *C.treas.* 21 Apr. 1454 x 18 Sept. 1455; occ. 3 Oct. 1456 (Fraser, *Cromartie*,ii,328-9); appears wrongly as 'John Dignail' 12 Nov. 1470 (Reg.Supp.,662,fo.191); occ. 6 Feb. 1475 (*ADC*,i, 347); d. before 21 Feb. 1477 (v.inf.).

Thomas Ross	1477 - 1489.
Richard Cockburn	1478.
John 'Strematau'	1489.

Ross. had coll. by legate on Dingwall's death and gets conf. 21 Feb. 1477 (*CPL*,xiii,84); occ. 12 Sept. 1487 (*RMS*,ii,no.1694) and 6 July 1489 (Fraser, *Cromartie*,ii,340).

Cockburn had ord. coll. on Dingwall's death and poss; gets

prov. on supposed death or res. of Ross 10 June 1478 (Reg.Supp.,770, fo.134).

'Strematau' had some right which he res. in favour of Maitland on or before 29 May 1489 (v.inf.).

John Maitland   1489 - 1525.
James Forrester/Forster   1489 x 1494 - 1498.
John Hepburn   1516 - 1539.

    Maitland promises annates and gets prov. on res. of 'Strematau' 29 May 1489 (PRO 31/9 - 30/163-4); lit. with Forrester 3 July 1494 (*ADC*,i,351); agrees to accept arbitration 17 July 1498 (ibid.,ii,281) and is successful; occ. 4 Nov. 1504 (*St A.Acta*,276); said to have d. 25 May 1518 (Bryce, *Grey Friars*,ii,306; *Spalding Misc.*,i,68), but occ. 18 May 1521 (*Laing Chrs.*, 84), 19 Nov. 1524 (St A. Univ.Mun.REP,fo. 21v) and 19 Nov. 1525 (*Univ.Evidence*,iii,181).

    Forrester had crown pres. on Ross's death and lit. with Maitland by 3 July 1494 (*ADC*,i,351); agrees to arbitration 17 July 1498 and presumably lost (v.sup.).

    Hepburn promises annates to retain a right which he held when recently elected *B.bp.* (PRO 31/9 - 31/299); not cons. until June 1522 x Feb. 1524; retained this right while *B.bp.* until 27 Apr. 1539, when (after lit. with Thornton) he res. in Thornton's favour (PRO 31/9 - 33/77-78; cf.62; *St A. Form.*, ii,84).

John Thornton   1525 x 1536 - 1565.
Thomas Rutherford   x 1536.
Patrick Liddell   1536 - 1539.

    Thornton prob. obtained poss. after death of Maitland and before Liddell's prov. *Si neutri* 17 June 1536 (v.inf.); occ. 4 Apr. 1438 (*Wigt. Chrs.*,217); prov. on res. of rights by Hepburn and Liddell 27 Apr. 1539 (PRO 31/9 - 33/77-78; cf. 62); d. 24 Feb. 1565 (*PSAS*,ii,257).

    Rutherford had some right at death before 17 June 1536 (v.inf.).

    Liddell promises annates and gets prov. *Si neutri* on Rutherford's death 17 June 1536 (PRO 31/9 - 33/42); lit. in association with Bp. Hepburn, and res. in Thornton's favour 27 Apr. 1539 (PRO 31/9 - 33/77-78; cf. 62).

James Thornton 1565 - 1577.

    Crown pres. on John Thornton's death 25 Apr. 1565 (*RSS*,v,no. 2036); escheated 8 Nov. 1577 (ibid.,vii,no.1208); d. before 24 Nov. 1577 (R.S.Mylne, *King's Master Masons*,55; cf. *B.dean.*).

William McQueen 1578 - 1586 x 1588.

    Crown pres. on John Thronton's death 25 Apr. 1565 (*RSS*,v,no. occ. 22 May 1586 (SRO, Mackintosh,no.142); at horn by 14 Aug. 1588 (v.inf.).

James Robertson 1588.

    Crown pres. on forfeiture of McQueen 14 Aug. 1588 (RSS,lvii, fo.172).

John Munro 1599 - 1616.
     Occ. 21 July 1599 (*RPC*,vi,614); occ. 14 Aug. 1607 (SRO,
Secretary's Reg. Sasines Inverness,fo.279); dem. on or before 5 Jan. 1616
(v.inf.).

Gilbert Murray 1616 - 1635.
     Pres. by bp. on dem. of Munro 5 Jan. 1616 (SRO, Misc.
Ecclesiastical Docs.,no.65); occ. 6 Feb. 1635 (SRO, Monro of Allan,
no.296/2).

SUCCENTORS/SUBCHANTERS OF ROSS

First known date: 1256 (*Vet.Mon.*,69).
     Prebend: chs. of Bron/Urray and Inverferan in 1256 (*Vet.Mon.*,
69; Cowan, *Parishes*, 88,206); these chs. known just as Urray by
Reformation (*RMS*,v,no.1625).

Matthew 1255 x 1271 - 1272.
     Occ. 1255 x 1271 (*Moray Reg.*, 282); conf. *R.bp.* 28 Dec.1272.

William 1278.
     Occ. 16 Sept. 1278 (*Beauly Chrs.*,64).

John de Hedlam 1296.
     Occ. 28 Aug. 1296 (*CDS*,ii,204).

Simon de 'Drumkudyn'/'Drumennadyn'/'Duncogvy'   1439.
     Occ. 12 May 1439 as 'Drumkudyn' (SRO, Ross of Pitcalnie,no.
15); had dem. before 17 July 1444 (Reg.Supp.,398,fo.94v,399,fo.4,
400,fo.92).

William Bayn/'Holme' x 1444.
     Bayn held it and res. to ord. sometime before 17 July 1444 (ibid.,
398,fo.94v; cf. *CPL*,ix, 426); 'Holme' held it sometime before 17
Oct. 1444 (Reg.Supp.,400,fo.92).

Alexander Ferguson (Fergucii) 1444.
Andrew Ross   1444.
     Ferguson in poss. 17 July 1444 (ibid.,398,fo.94v). perhaps same
as Gray below.
     Ross gets *com.priv.* against Ferguson 17 July 1444 (v.sup.).

Alexander Gray   1444 - 1445.
John Kennochson   1444 - 1445.
     Gray had had prov. and poss. before 17 Oct. 1444 when he got
new prov. (Reg.Supp.,400,fo.92); perhaps same as Ferguson above;
had got it on exch. (presumably with 'Holme'), then won lit. with
Kennochson and gets new prov. 23 June 1445 (ibid.,406,fo.235).
     Kennochson prov. on res. of Bayn 22 Aug. 1444 (*CPL*,ix,426);
lost lit. with Gray 23 June 1445 (v.sup.).

Anselm Robertson/Robesone (Roberti) 1508 - 1523.
Occ. 4 Nov. 1508 (*Munro Writs,*no.37); occ. 23 Apr. 1523 (SRO, Mey, no.19).

David 'Arlintoune' 1532.
Occ. 16 July 1532 (*Cawdor Bk.,* 155); prob. same as Haliburton.

David Haliburton 1539 - 1570 x 1573.
Occ. 27 Nov. 1539 (*Glas.Reg.,*ii 554); occ. 20 Oct. 1570 (*RMS,*iv, no.2170); depriv. on or before 18 Sept. 1573 (v.inf.).

Donald Adamson 1573 - 1580.
Crown pres. on depriv. of Haliburton 18 Sept. 1573 (*RSS,*vi,no. 2130); occ. 1580 (Macgill, *Old Ross-shire,*no.39).

John Malcolmson 1606 - 1635.
Occ. 15 Sept. 1606 (SRO, Secretary's Reg. Sasines Inverness,fo. 317) and 6 Feb. 1635 (SRO, Monro of Allan, no.296/2).

John McKenzie 1636.
Occ. 7 Mar. 1636 (SRO, Reg.Ho.Chr.s.d.).

ARCHDEACONS OF ROSS

First known date: 1223.
Prebend: chs. of Fodderty, Killearnan/Eddyrdor, Lemlair and Logie Wester in 1238 (*Vet.Mon.,* 38; cf. 32); but chs. of Fodderty and Killearnan only in 1256 (ibid.,69; see Cowan, *Parishes,* 67,101,129,138) and at Reformation (*RMS,*v,no.1625).

Robert 1223 - 1249 x 1250.
Occ. 6 July 1223 (Durham, Dean & Chapter MSS, Misc. Chr.no. 1151); cons. *R.bp.* 21 June 1249 x 20 June 1250.

Robert de Fyvie 1269 - 1275.
Occ. 5 Dec. 1269 (*Chartularium Studii Bononiensis,*xi,62); in poss. 28 Dec. 1272 (*Vet.Mon.,*102); cons. after el. as *R.bp.* 8 Apr. 1275 x.

John de Musselburgh 1279.
Occ. 6 Dec. 1279 (*Glas.Reg.,* i,194).

Alexander Stewart 1343 - 1350.
In poss. 22 July 1343 (*CPP,*i,66); prov. *R.bp.* 3 Nov. 1350.

Thomas de Urquhart 1358 - 1365 x 1376.
Occ. 12 Nov. 1358 (Fraser, *Grant,*iii,10); occ. 1 July 1365 (*A.B. Ill.,*iii,532); d. before 19 Aug. 1376 (v.inf.).

Alexander Man 1376 - 1381.
Had prov. on Urquhart's death shortly before 19 Aug. 1376 when he got new prov. (Reg.Av.,288,fo.287); prov. *C.bp.* 21 Oct. 1381.

Alexander de Waghorn (Kilbuines ?) 1398.

In poss. when prov. *R.bp.* 17 Aug. 1398; see *R.bp.* for notes on surname.

David Seton   1399 - 1418 x 1422.
John de Inchmartin   1409 - 1421 x 1422.
    Seton occ. 19 Oct. 1399 (PRO,E/404/15/39); in poss. 19 Aug./ 3 Oct. 1413 (v.inf.); occ. June 1418 x July 1420 (*ER*,iv,323); depriv. or res. before 6 Oct. 1422 (*CSSR*,i,311).
    Inchmartin occ. 24 Dec. 1409 (*RMS*,ii,no.56); gets prov. and *com.priv.* against Seton 19 Aug./3 Oct. 1413 (*CPP*,i,600; Reg.Av., 340,fos.625-625v,633-633v); occ. 2 Jan. 1421 (*Spalding Misc.*,iv,117); res. to ord. on exch. with Munro before 6 Oct. 1422 (v.inf.).

Andrew de Munro   1422 - 1451 x 1455.
Alexander Seton (?) 1424 x 1430.
    Munro got poss. on exch. with Inchmartin and got new prov. 6 Oct. 1422 (*CSSR*,i,310-11); new prov. again 11 Mar. 1431 (*CPL*, viii,333); occ. 1451 (*OPS*,ii,462,578); d. by 24 Oct. 1454 (v.inf.).
    Seton perhaps occ. 1424 x 1430 (*St A.Lib.*,407 - but text is doubtful; cf. *Bothwell prov.*).

William Ross 1451 x 1454 - 1455.
    Obtained poss., on Munro's death on strength of earlier exp. grace and got new prov. 24 Oct. 1454/7 Jan. 1455 (Reg.Supp.,475, fo.200; *CPL*,x,686; cf. *ACSB*,273).

Richard Forbes 1455 - 1460.
    Occ. 7 July 1455 (*ER*,vi,1); occ. 16 Oct. 1455 (*Gen.Coll.*,ii, 213); is to res. in favour of Vaus 19 July 1460 (v.inf.).

Patrick Vaus 1460 - 1466.
    Prov. on proposed res. of Forbes 19 July 1460 (Reg.Supp., 532,fo.256); had had ord. coll. and in poss. when given new prov. 21 Apr. 1461 (ibid.,527,fo.206); in poss. 26 Mar. 1466 (ibid.,592, fo.209).

Alexander Stewart 1472.
    Gets disp. to hold this ben with *M.succ.* 5 Mar. 1472 (Reg. Supp.,677,fo.23).

Gilbert Macdowell x 1480.
    Held it and res. to ord. on exch. with Maccullach before 10 Oct. 1480 (v.inf.).

Donald Maccullach 1480.
    In poss. after exch. with Macdowell 10 Oct. 1480 (*CPL*,xiii,85).

David Lichton 1483 - 1484.
    Occ. 3 June 1483 (*St Giles Reg.*, 143-4); res. to become a monk 15 Sept. 1484 (*CPL*,xiv,318).

Richard Muirhead 1484 - 1488.
    Prov. on Lichton's res. 15 Sept. 1484 (*CPL*,xiv,63-64); in poss.

22 Apr. 1488 (*ACSB*,222).

John Scherar 1492 - 1506.
    In poss. 19 June 1492 (PRO 31/9 - 30/242); occ. 23 Feb. 1506 (*Prot.Bk.Simon*,ii,115).

Robert Elphinstone 1510.
    Occ. 15 July 1510 (*RSS*,i,no.2099), having perhaps obtained it since 9 Aug. 1508 (cf. *Ab.archd.* and *Ab.treas.*); perhaps held it until death 23 Jan. x 30 July 1535 (see *Ab.treas.*).

Kentigern/Mungo Monypenny 1537 - 1545.
    Occ. 28 Feb. 1537 (St A.Univ.Mun.,UY305/2,p.4); occ. 10 Feb. 1545 (*RMS*,iii,no.3065); moved to *R.dean.* by 23 Apr.1545.

Donald Fraser   1545 x 1546 - 1572 x 1573.
Donald Munro   1568.
    Fraser occ. 28 Feb. 1545 x 26 Feb. 1546 (*St A.Recs.*,251); said to have d. 13 Feb. 1572 (Forbes, *Kalendars,* p.xxviii,); but occ. when at the horn 6 Mar. 1572 (*RSS*,vi,no.1512); d. before 2 Aug.1573 (v.inf.).
    Munro given this title, though an outlaw, 4 Oct. 1568 (*CSP Scot.*,ii,516); prob. error for Fraser; or error for *I.archd.*

Robert Graham 1573 - 1598 x 1602.
    Crown pres. on death of Fraser 2 Aug. 1573 (*RSS*,vi,no.2051); occ. 31 May 1598 (*RMS*,vi,no.802); d. before 10 Sept. 1602 (v.inf.).

George Graham 1602.
    Crown pres. on death of Robert Graham 10 Sept. 1602 (Reg. Pres.,iii,61) apparently without effect.

John Mackenzie 1602 - 1636 x 1642.
    Crown pres. on death of Robert Graham 26 Nov. 1602 (Reg. Pres.,iii,fo.65); occ. 7 Mar. 1636 (SRO,Reg.Ho.Chr.s.d.); described as 'formerly designated archd.' 18 July 1642 (*RMS*,ix,no.1181).

DEANS OF CHRISTIANITY

DEANS OF DINGWALL

First known date: 1530.

Donald Reid 1530.
    Occ. 12 June 1530 (*Munro Writs*,no.48).

OFFICIALS

OFFICIALS OF ROSS

First known date: 1451.

Henry Kennedy (Kynnidy) 1451.
Occ. 1451 (*OPS*,ii,579).

Robert Fraser/Fresell 1514 - 1514 x 1521.
Occ. 18 Jan. 1514 (*Beauly Chrs.*,177); occ. 1514 x 1521 (*St.A. Form.*,i,24); d. 10 July 1523 (see *R.dean.*).

Paul Fraser/Fresail 1524 - 1543.
Occ. 10 Sept. 1524 (Fraser, *Cromartie*,ii,342) and 31 Aug.1543 (SRO, Sent.Offic.St A.,fo.52); d. 13 Sept. 1545 (see *R.dean.*).

Duncan Chalmer 1553.
Occ. 1 Oct. 1553 (*RMS*,iv,no.856).

COMMISSARIES

COMMISSARIES OF ROSS

First known date: 1451.

Andrew de Munro 1451.
Occ. (CB) 1451 (*OPS*,II,ii,462); d. by 24 Oct. 1454 (see *R.archd.*).

Thomas Stevenson 1543.
Occ. (CO) 31 Aug. 1543 (SRO, Sent.Offic.St A.,fo.52).

Duncan Chalmer 1566 - 1571.
Occ. (C) 11 Mar. 1566 (*Munro Writs*,no.79); d. 13 Jan. 1571 (see *R.chanc.*), and retained office until then (*RSS*,vi,no.2493).

ST ANDREWS DIOCESE

BISHOPS/ARCHBISHOPS OF ST ANDREWS

First known date: before 1055.

This list begins with the first bishop for whom a firm date is known; for names of earlier bishops in the 10th and early 11th centuries, at least some of whom were probably associated with the church of St Andrews, see Haddan & Stubbs, *Councils,*II,i,173-4; *Chron.Bower,*i,339; cf. *PSAS,*1xxxvii,110.

Bp. Fothad may possibly have acknowledged metropolitan authority of York x 1093; but prob. none of his successors did so (v.inf.); King David I, however, was unsuccessful in his efforts to have this see made a metropolitan one in 1125-6 (Hugh the Chantor, *History,*126) and 1151 (*ES,*ii,212); and Malcolm IV may have been similarly unsuccessful 1159 (*RSS,*i,11,14); but the renewed efforts of York to exercise metropolitan authority over the Scottish church were frustrated in 1176, and its independence as a *filia specialis* of the apostolic see was conf. in 1192 (*AMW,*206-17,275-6; *Chron.Holyrood,* 159-61); this see therefore remained directly subject to Rome.

Bp. Graham became an archbishop and this see a metropolitan one with the sees of Glasgow, Dunkeld, Aberdeen, Moray, Brechin, Dunblane, Ross, Caithness, Galloway, Argyll, the Isles, and Orkney as its suffragans 14 Aug. 1472 (*Vet.Mon.,*no.852); when see of Glasgow was in its turn erected to metropolitan status 9 Jan. 1492, the sees of Glasgow, Dunkeld, Dunblane, Galloway and Argyll were removed from the province of St Andrews to form the new province of Glasgow (ibid.,no.889); Dunblane was transferred back to the province of St Andrews 28 Jan. 1500, and Dunkeld was similarly restored on or before 25 May 1515 (Dowden, *Bishops,*333-4); by 1617 the see of the Isles had come to be transferred from St Andrews to Glasgow (*APS,*iv,530).

Maelduin/Maldun 1028 (?) - 1055.

D. as bp. of Scotland 1055 (*ES,*i,599), being described as son of Gilla-Odrain or Gilla-Andriais; said in St Andrews tradition to have been bp. for 27 years (*Chron.Wyntoun,*iv,318-19, where surname is Makgillandris.; cf. *Chron.Bower,*i,339); known to have acted as bp. of St A. (*St A.Lib.,*116; *ESC,*no.6).

Tuthald/Tuadal/Waldef 1055 x .

Held see for four years following Maelduin (*Chron.Bower,*i,399), perhaps contemporaneously with Emperor Henry III (d.1056) and Pope Nicholas II (1059 - 61) as Wyntoun suggests (*Chron.Wyntoun,* iv,318); known to have acted as bp. of St A. (*St A.Lib.,*116;*ESC,* no. 7).

Fothad/Foderoc/Fodan/Modach x 1070 (?) - 1093.

D. as chief bp. of Scotland 1093 (*ES*,ii,49); known to be dead by 1093 x 1094 (*ESC*,no.12; cf. *SHR*,xxxvii,118-25); known to have acted as bp. of St A. under name Modach son of Malmykel (*St A.Lib.*,117; *ESC*,no.11); said in 15th century tradition to have performed marriage of King Malcolm III and Queen Margaret 1070 (*Chron. Wyntoun*,iv, 345, cf. *ES*,ii,25); remembered in York tradition (recorded x 1127) as having been cons. by the Scots, but having come later to abp. of York at wish of king and queen to make profession of obedience 1070 x (Hugh the Chantor, *History*,31; see also *Historians of York*,ii,363).

Gregory/Cathre/Godric 1093 x 1107.

St Andrews tradition of the 15th century listed a Gregory, Cathre, Edmar and Godric as having held this see 1093 x 1107, but having all apparently died as bishop-elect (*Chron.Bower*,i,339-40); Edmar is presumably Eadmer (v.inf.); but the other three names may well be various forms of the same name (suggestion of Mr. A.A.M.Duncan).

Turgot O.S.B. 1107 - 1115.

Cons. as bp. of St A. when prior of Durham by abp. of York at York 1 Aug. 1109 (*Chron.Melrose*,31; cf. Dowden, *Bishops*,2); but prob. never recognised York metropolitan authority (*SAEC*,130-2; cf. Hugh the Chantor, *History*,31, 35: *Historians of York*,ii,371); had been appointed by King Alexander I with agreement of King Henry I of England (*SAEC*,129-30), prob. 1107, either before 5 June or c. 20 June (ibid.,129,135); d. at Durham 31 Aug. 1115 (ibid.,135-6; cf. *Chron.Melrose*,31).

Eadmer O.S.B. 1120 - 1121.

As a monk of Canterbury was requested by King Alexander I for see of St Andrews and released for this appointment by abp. of Canterbury and King Henry 4 Jan. 1120 x (*SAEC*,138-40; cf.136; *ESC*, nos. 37-38); formally el. in Scotland 29 June 1120 (*SAEC*, 141); dispute followed over his investiture and cons.; took up office for a time, but res. without cons. and was back at Canterbury by early 1121 (ibid.,141-7; *Chron.Melrose*,32; see *Symeonis Dunelmensis Opera et Collectanea*, ed. J. H. Hindle (Surtees Soc.),114 for date), leaving validity of his res. uncertain (*SAEC*,151-4; *ESC*,no.39-42); d. 1128 or later, perhaps c. 1130 (R.W. Southern, *St Anselm and his Biographer*, 239-40; cf.380).

Robert O.S.A. 1123 x 1124 - 1159.

El. when prior of Scone at instance of King Alexander 25 Dec. 1123 x 31 Jan. 1124 (*Symeonis Monachi Opera Omnia* (Rolls Series), ii,275); cons. by abp. of York, but specifically without profession of obedience, prob. at Roxburgh on or just before 17 July 1127 (*Chron.Holyrood*,133; ESC,nos.73,75,76; cf. *SAEC*,164 where cons. is said to have been at York in 1128); d. 1159, presumably early in year (*Chron.Melrose*,35; *Chron.Bower*,i,340; cf.inf.).

Waltheof O.Cist. 1159.

Said to have been el. with the consent of his nephew King Malcolm IV (and so x May 1159 - see *RRS*,i,11) on Robert's death when abbot of Melrose; but declined office and d. 3 Aug. 1159 (*Acta Sanctorum*, August,i,267,paras.79-80; *Chron.Melrose*,35).

Note: William *M.bp.* and legate was suggested by Pope Alexander III to King Malcolm for trans. to St A.bp. 27 Nov. 1159 (*AMW*,52-54); but the king was then given an option to reject this suggestion and did so (v.inf.).

Arnold O. Tiron 1160 - 1162.

El. when abbot of Kelso 13 Nov. 1160 and cons. at St Andrews by William *M.bp.* as papal legate 20 Nov. 1160 (*Chron.Melrose*,36); d. 13 Sept. 1162 (*Chron.Holyrood*,140-1).

Richard 1163 - 1178.

El. when king's chaplain 1163, prob. at beginning of year (*Chron. Melrose*,36; *Chron.Holyrood*,141; cf. *Chron.Wyntoun*,iv,430-1); cons. by bishops of Scotland at St Andrews 28 Mar. 1165 (*Chron.Melrose*, 37; *Chron.Holyrood*,148), perhaps under special papal mand. (*Chron. Wyntoun*,iv,431; cf.430); d. 1178, prob. 13 May (*Chron.Holyrood*,164; *Chron.Melrose*,42; *Liber Vitae Ecclesiae Dunelmensis* (Surtees Soc., 1841), 143).

John Scot   1178 - 1188.
Hugh   1178 - 1188.

John el. by canons of St Andrews without consulting the king on death of Richard 1178 (*Chron.Melrose*,42; cf. *Chron.Holyrood*,165); appealed to pope against subsequent intrusion of Hugh by the king later in the same year before his own cons. and obtained an annulment of Hugh's appointment and conf. of his own el. (*SAEC*,273,275; *AMW*,228-9,231-2); John then returned to Scotland and was cons. by authority of a papal legate at Holyrood Abbey 15 June 1180 (*Chron.Melrose*,43; *Chron.Holyrood*,168), though he had to leave the country at once again for fear of the king; compromise with Hugh in Scotland and at the curia led to John's trans. to *Dk.bp.*1183, before July; but did not finally cease lit. with Hugh and renounce his claim to St A.bp. until mid-1188 (*SAEC*,298; *AMW*,276); as late as 16 Jan. 1188 Pope Clement III had been recommending his el. to St A. again by chapter of that see (*SAEC*,296-8; *AMW*,273-4).

Hugh nom. by King William when a royal chaplain following el. of John, and cons. by some Scottish bps. at St Andrews later in 1178 (*Chron.Melrose*,42; *SAEC*,271,n.2; *AMW*,224-5); his appointment was quashed by Pope Alexander III on John's appeal x 15 June 1180 (v.sup.); compromises arranged at a council in Scotland held by the king with two papal legates 1182 (*Chron.Holyrood*,168-9), and then between the two litigants at the curia led to Hugh's papal appointment to St A.bp. 1183, before July (*SAEC*,285-6;*AMW*,249-50); renewed lit. at curia raised by John against Hugh by 31 July 1186, led later in 1186 to Hugh's suspension (*SAEC*,290-3; *AMW*, 260-2); Hugh acted as bp. at a cons. at St Andrews 15 Mar.1187

(*Chron.Melrose*,45), but was deposed by pope on or before 16 Jan. 1188 (*SAEC*,296-8; *AMW*,273-4); went to curia and obtained absolution but d. at Rome 4 Aug. 1188 (*SAEC*,298; *AMW*,277; *Chron.Melrose*,46; *Chron.Bower*,i,358,496; for whole dispute 1178-88 see *Chron.Holyrood*, 164-8; details given in *Chron.Bower*,i,350-8 are confused and untrustworthy.

Roger   1189 - 1202.

El. at Perth when royal chanc. 13 Apr. 1189 (*Chron.Melrose*, 47; cf. *Danelaw Chrs.*, ed.F.M.Stenton,259-60,no.347 for proof that year was 1189); Roger was son of Robert third earl of Leicester (*Complete Peerage*,vii,533n), and has usually been given the name 'de Beaumont' (e.g. Dowden, *Bishops*,10), but there is no contemporary authority for this name (*Complete Peerage*,vii,527n); not cons. until 15 Feb. 1198 at St Andrews (*Chron.Melrose*,50; Dowden, *Bishops*,11); d. at Cambuskenneth Abbey 7 July 1202 (*Chron.Melrose*, 51 for year; *Chron.Bower*,i,359 for other details).

William Malveisin/Malvoisin (Malevicinus)   1202 - 1238.

Postulated for trans. from *G.bp.* at Scone 18/20 Sept. 1202 (*Chron.Melrose*,51; *Chron.Bower*,i,359,516); prob. conf. at once by a papal legate then in Scotland (*Chron.Wyntoun*,v,60-61), for he acted as bp. in St Andrews as early as 21 Sept. 1202 (*Vet.Mon.*,3); d. at Inchmurdo near St Andrews 9 July 1238 (*Chron.Melrose*, 86 for year; *Chron.Bower*,i,359 for other details).

Geoffrey de Liberatione   1238 - 1239.
David de Bernham   1239 - 1253.

Liberatione postulated by chapter for trans. from *Dk.bp.* on death of Malveisin, but pope refused conf. and ordered another election 12 Feb. 1239 (*Vet.Mon.*,no.98; *Chron.Wyntoun*,v,94-95; *Chron.Bower*, i,359).

Bernham el. when *G. prec.* and royal chamberlain 3 June 1239 (ibid.); papal mand. for conf. and cons. 1 Oct. 1239 (*Vet.Mon.*,no. 100); cons. 22 Jan. 1240 (*Chron.Melrose*,87; *Chron.Wyntoun*,v,94-95; *Chron.Bower*,i,359); d. at Nenthorn, Berwickshire 26 Apr. 1253 (*Chron.Melrose*, 110 for year; *Chron.Lanercost*,58; *Chron.Bower*,i,359; cf.ii,89).

Robert de Stuteville   1253 - 1254.
Abel de Gullane (Golin,Golyn)   1254.

Stuteville el. when *Dk.dean* (by a chapter which excluded Gullane among others) 28 June 1253 (*Chron.Bower*,i,360); lit. at curia ended 20 Feb. 1254 with quashing of this el. (*Vet.Mon.*, no.162).

Gullane when *St A.archd.* went as one of the crown envoys (King Alexander III being a minor) to curia to contest el. of Stuteville, and got prov. for himself on same day as el. was quashed 20 Feb.1254 (ibid.; *Chron.Melrose*,110-11; *Chron.Lanercost*,58); cons. by pope 1 Mar. 1254 (ibid.) and commended by him to government in Scotland for temps. 18 Mar. 1254 (*Vet.Mon.*,no.164); occ. at St Andrews 29

June 1254 (*Chron.Bower*,ii,89); d. 1254 (*Chron.Melrose*,111), perhaps 31 Aug. (*Chron.Lanercost*,60) rather than 1 Dec. (*Chron.Bower*,i,360; cf. ii,89; evidence that he was witness to an act of Oct. 1254 (*Dunf.Reg.*, 114-15,198) is suspect).

Gamelin 1255 - 1271.
El. when *M.chanc.* and royal chanc. 14 Feb. 1255 and obtained crown conf. (*Chron.Melrose*,111; *Chron.Bower*,i,360); papal conf. 1 July 1255 (*Vet.Mon.*,no 176); occ. as bp.-elect 22 Dec. 1255 (*Dunf.Reg.*,120; cf. 117); cons. at St Andrews 26 Dec. 1255 against wishes of new royal administration of which he was no longer a member (*Chron.Melrose*, 113); not reconciled with the government until it changed again and he could return from exile at curia to his diocese in spring 1258 (ibid.,115; cf. *Vet.Mon.*,nos.201-2); occ. 14 Apr. 1271 (*N.B.Chrs.*,22-23); d. at Inchmurdo near St Andrews 29 Apr. 1271 (*Chron.Bower*,i,360).

William Wishart 1271 - 1279.
El. when *St A.archd.*, *G.bp.-elect* and royal chanc. 3 June 1271 (*Moray Reg.*, 338-9; *Chron.Bower*,i,360); papal mand. for conf. and cons. 15 Mar. 1273 (*Vet.Mon.*,no.256); cons. at Scone 15 Oct. 1273 (*Chron.Bower*,i,360; ii,120); d. at Morebattle, Roxburghshire 28 May 1279 (*Chron.Lanercost*,103; *Chron.Bower*,i,361;ii,124).

William Fraser 1279 - 1297.
El. when *G.dean* and royal chanc. 4 Aug. 1279 (ibid.,i,361); cons. at curia 19 May 1280 (ibid.); papal mand. of conf. 21 May 1280 (*Vet.Mon.*,no.276); d. in France 20 Aug. 1297 and buried at Paris (*Chron.Bower*,i,361).

William Lamberton 1297 - 1328.
El. when *G.chanc.* 3 Nov. 1297 (*Chron.Fordun*,i,330); cons at curia 1 June 1298 (*Chron.Bower*,i,361-2); papal mand. of conf. 17 June 1298 (*Vet.Mon.*,no.362); d. at St Andrews 20 May and buried there 7 June 1328 (*ER*,i,109; *Chron.Bower*,i,362).

James Ben/Benne/de Edinburgh 1328 - 1332.
Alexander de Kininmund 1328.
Ben el. when *St A.archd.* and absent at the curia 19 June 1328 (*Chron.Bower*,i,362); conf. and cons. at curia on or just before 1 Aug. 1328 (*Vet.Mon.*,no.472); commended by pope to King Robert I 15 Oct. 1328 (ibid. no.473); left Scotland after battle of Dupplin 11 Aug. 1332 (*Chron.Bower*,i,363; cf.*Chron.Fordun*,i,354 for date), having apparently res. before 19 Aug. 1332 (v.inf.); d. at Bruges in Flanders 22 Sept. 1332 (*Chron.Bower*,i,363).
Kininmund when *St A.archd.Lothian* obtained some right at election of 19 June 1328, and prob. went to curia to challenge Ben's right (ibid.,i,362-3); but his right must have been quashed by Ben's prov. 1 Aug. 1328.

William Bell 1332 - 1342.
Said to have been el. when *Dk.dean* as early as 19 Aug. 1332 and

to have gone to curia to seek conf. (ibid,i,363; but in papal records this election is said to have followed Ben's death — see *Vet.Mon.*, no.550); hindered there by suggestions for English candidates for this see from Edward III 2/26 Oct. 1332 and 24 July 1333 (*CDS*,iii,nos. 1059,1061,1064,1080); remained unconfirmed, becoming old and blind, until res. his right at time of prov. of Landallis i.e. on or before 18 Feb. 1342 (*Chron.Bower* and *Vet.Mon.* ut cit.; *Chron.Wyntoun*, vi,156-7; cf.v,422-3).

William de Landallis/Laundels 1342 - 1385.

Prov. 18 Feb. 1342 following nom. to pope by King David II in France (and King Philip VI of France) and recommendation of the St Andrews chaper, who could not legally make a second election before Bell had res. (*Vet.Mon.*,no.550; *Chron.Wyntoun*,vi,156-9; *Chron. Bower*,i,363); cons. at the curia 17 Mar. 1342 (ibid.) with mand. to go to his see 18 Mar. 1342 (*CPL*,ii,557); d. at St Andrews 23 Sept. 1385 (*Chron.Bower*,i,364).

Stephen Pay   O.S.A.   1385 - 1386.
Walter Trail/Treyle   1385 - 1401.

Pay el. when St A.prior on death of Landallis, but d. at Alnwick, Northumberland on way to curia for conf. 2 Mar. 1386 (*Chron.Bower*, i,364,371; *Chron.Wyntoun*,vi,306-9).

Trail prov. by Pope Clement VII when *Dk.dean* and *G.treas.* and employed at curia, apparently without regard to election of Pay, 29 Nov. 1385 (Eubel, *Hierarchia*,i,89); cons. prob. at curia before 15 Feb. 1386 (*CPL*,iv,252); occ. 5 Mar. 1401 (*St Giles Reg.*, 37-38); d. before 1 July 1401 (v.inf.).

Note: two English archbishops were trans. by Roman popes of the Great Schism to this see (as if to *partes infidelium*) during reign of King Richard II; (1) **Alexander Nevill** from York 30 Apr. 1388; d. at Louvain, Brabant May 1392 (Emden,*Biog.Reg.Univ.Oxford*,ii,1346). (2) **Thomas Arundel** from Canterbury Oct. 1397; returned to Canterbury 1399, getting temps. 21 Oct. (ibid.,i,51-52; Le Neve, *Fasti Ecclesiae Anglicanae*,iv,4).

Thomas Stewart   1401 - 1402.
Walter Danielston   1402.
Gilbert de Greenlaw   1403.
Henry de Wardlaw   1403 - 1440.

Stewart el. with royal support as illegitimate brother of King Robert III when *St A.archd.* 1 July 1401; but there was delay in getting access to Pope Benedict XIII for conf., and he res. his right in favour of Danielston c.June 1402 (*Chron.Wyntoun*,vi,395-6, 398-9).

Danielston el. on res. of Stewart at instance of duke of Albany c. June 1402 and, though never conf., enjoyed temps. and exercised spiritual jurisdiction for just over six months until death at Christmas 1402 (ibid.,vi,398-9; cf. *CSSR*,i,141-2).

Greenlaw when royal chanc. was postulated by chapter for

trans. from *Ab.bp.* early in 1403, but did not manage to obtain papal conf. (*Chron. Wyntoun*,vi,399-400).

Wardlaw prov. when *G,prec.* and at curia of Pope Benedict XIII 10 Sept. 1403 (*SHR*,viii,246-8); cons. at curia 21 Sept. x 4 Oct.1403 (PRO 31/9 - 40/33; Reg.Vat.,323,fo.426); occ. in Scotland 28 Apr. 1404 (*SHR*,xxxv,134); d. at St Andrews 6 Apr. 1440 (*Chron.Bower*,i, 366).

Note: **John Trefor** St Asaph bp. was trans. to St A.bp by Pope Gregory XII during the Great Schism c.1408, but was apparently restored to his Welsh see before his death 1410 (Le Neve, *Fasti Ecclesiae Anglicanae*, xi, 38); this had no effect in Scotland.

James Kennedy   1440 - 1465.
James Ogilvie   1440 - 1447 x 1455.

Kennedy postulated for trans. from *Dk.bp.* 22 Apr. 1440 (*Chron. Bower*,i,336); he was then at curia of Pope Eugenius IV and got prov. 1 June 1440 (*ACSB*,25); occ. in Scotland 26 May 1441 (*RMS*,ii,nos. 266-7); d. 24 May 1465 (*SHR*,xxxi,196).

Ogilvie prov. by Pope Felix V at Basle with mand. for cons. 26 July 1440 (*St A.Cop.*,302-5); may have been in Scotland and able to draw revenues of the see for a time (A.I. Dunlop, *James Kennedy*,40); at Council of Basle as bp.-elect 23 June - 17 Nov. 1441 (J.H. Burns, *Scottish Churchmen and the Council of Basle*, 73-74; *St A.Cop.*, 204-9); never cons.; Felix supported him for a pension from the see 20 Mar. 1447 (ibid.,343-4), and he was reconciled with Kennedy by 25 Feb. 1455 when found back at St Andrews university (*St A.Acta*,107).

Patrick Graham 1465 - 1478.

Trans. by pope from *B.bp.* 4 Nov. 1465 (*ACSB*,56); appointed abp. on raising of this see to metropolitan status 17 Aug. 1472 (*Vet. Mon.*,no.852); given coadj. 13 Sept. 1476 (v.inf.) and a papal enquiry into his conduct was ordered 5 Dec. 1476 (*Vet.Mon.*,no.862; *SHS Misc.*, iii,176-8); depriv. 9 Jan. 1478 (*Vet.Mon.*,no.863); d. in prison later in 1478 (Dowden, *Bishops*,33).

William Scheves 1476 - 1497.

Prov. when *St A.archd.,Dk.dean* and *Crichton* prov. as coadj. to Graham 13 Sept. 1476 (*ACSB*,72-73), and then prov. as abp. on Graham's depriv. 11 Feb. 1478 (ibid.,73); prob. cons. at Holyrood Abbey 28 Mar. 1479 (Dowden, *Bishops*,33-34) and certainly by 15 May 1479 (Herkless & Hannay, *Archbishops*,i,88); forced by the Albany faction to appoint proctors to res. his rights in this see in favour of Andrew Stewart *M.bp.-elect*, prob. with a view to exch., in latter part of 1482; Stewart was raising money with expectancy of becoming St A.abp. 8 Nov. 1482 (*Edin.Chrs.*, 154-6; cf. Boece, *Historiae*,fo.396v); but Albany agreed with King James III to abandon his support for this plan 16 Mar. 1483 (*APS*,xii,33; cf. Dowden, *Bishops*,164,n.3); Scheves remained in poss. until d. 28 Jan. 1497 (*SHR*,xxxi,196).

James Stewart   1497 - 1504.

Postulated as brother of King James IV and when duke of Ross, and had royal conf. as commendator before 28 May 1497 (*Abdn.Fasti*, 15; cf. *RMS*,ii,no.2358 and *ER*,xi,66-69 for mention of him as abp. 22 May 1497); papal appointment as administrator until he should be of age to become abp. 20 Sept. 1497 (Brady, *Episcopal Succession*, i,124; cf. Dowden, *Bishops*,35-36); d. still without cons. 13 Jan. 1504 (*SHR*,xxxi,196).

Alexander Stewart   1504 - 1513.

Appointed by pope, being an illegitimate son of King James IV, as administrator until he should be 27 years old 10 May 1504 (Eubel, *Hierarchia*,iii,108; Dowden, *Bishops*,37); it was intended to provide him with a suffragen bp. to serve the see (*James IV Letters*,16-17, 19); d. at Battle of Flodden 9 Sept. 1513 when still too young to have become abp. (*Sc.Antiq.*,xiii,104; cf.xii,121; *Vet.Mon.*,no.899; Herkless & Hannay, *Archbishops*,i,270-1,app.7).

Innocenzo Cibo	1513 - 1514.
William Elphinstone junior	1513 - 1514.
Andrew Forman	1514 - 1521.
John Hepburn	1514 - 1516.
Gavin Douglas	1514 - 1515.
James Betoun (?)	1515.

Cibo prov. as administrator when a cardinal and nephew of Pope Leo X 13 Oct. 1513 (Eubel, *Hierarchia*,iii,108; cf.14); pope asked duke of Albany as regent to consent to plan that Cibo should res. his right to this see on exch. with Forman for Bourges abp. 11 Apr. 1514 (*James V Letters*, 8; Eubel, *Hierarchia*,iii,135); res. on this exch. without poss. 13 Nov. 1514 (v.inf.).

Elphinstone was postulated by chapter for trans. from *Ab.bp.* and got crown nom. from Queen Margaret and the council of magnates at end of Oct. 1513 (Edin.Univ.Lib.,Law MS,fo.17; Boece, *Vitae*, 105-6; *LP Henry VIII*,i,2nd edn., no.2443; cf.no.2406 for date; cf. *James V Letters*,4 and n.); Boece says that he refused this el. and nom. (loc.cit.); but in fact he had decided to send a proctor to Rome to presecute his claim for trans. by 25 Feb. 1514 , when he publicly announced his nom. and obtained the general support of an assembly of magnates, only Gavin Douglas dissenting (*ADCP*,11); crown letters of nom. sent to pope by Queen Margaret perhaps 22 June and certainly 5 Aug. 1514 (*LP Henry VIII*,i,2nd edn.,no.3532; *James V Letters*,12-13); d. without poss. 25 Oct. 1514 (see *Ab.bp.*;cf. *ADCP*,25); was thought at curia after his death to have effectively intruded himself into rule and administration of this see (*Leonis X Regesta*,i,792,no.13126 of 8 Dec. 1514), but this is doubtful.

Forman when both *M.bp.* and *Bourges abp.* was proposed by Pope Leo X to Regent Albany for trans. to this see on exch. with Cibo 11 Apr. 1514 (v.sup.); trans. by this pope from Moray and Bourges on res. of Cibo 13 Nov. 1514 (*Leonis X Regesta*,i,772-3);

pope commended him to Queen Margaret 8 Dec. 1514 (*James V Letters,* 15-17); bulls of provision published in Scotland in his continuing absence 15/17 Jan. 1515 (Fraser, *Douglas,*iv,69; *LP Henry VIII,*ii,no.40; *ADCP,*30); but government in Scotland is found still resisting the pope's appointment of Forman 14 Mar. 1515 (*James V Letters,*18-19); though he returned to Scotland soon after Albany did in May 1515 (Herkless & Hannay, *Archbishops,*ii,128,130), there was a long delay before he could get poss., Hepburn being now his opponent; see still vacant with Hepburn the vicar-general in the vacancy 8 Jan. 1516 (*Glas.Reg.,*ii,525); but Forman was granted temps. at last by Albany c.4 Feb. 1516 (*St A.Form.,*i,133; cf. Herkless & Hannay, *Archbishops,*ii, 143-4 and n.2; see also *James V Letters,*28,30); occ. as abp. 5 Feb. 1516 (*Pais.Reg.,* 357-8); d; 11/12 Mar. 1521 (Edin.Univ.Lib., Law MS,fos.12,17v).

Hepburn el. when St A.prior after death of Elphinstone i.e. Oct./Nov.1514 (ibid.,fo.17, where the fact that this election was in 1514 and not the year before is somewhat tortuously explained; *LP Henry VIII,*ii,no.40); he owed his nom. to the 'lords regents' or the 'whole nobility' (Lesley, *History,*101; cf: Dalrymple, *Historie,*ii,154) i.e. the magnates who were now at loggerheads with Queen Margaret since her marriage to the Douglas earl of Angus in Aug.1514; Hepburn laid siege to St Andrews Castle, which had been occupied by servants of his rival Gavin Douglas, before 23 Nov. 1514 (*LP Henry VIII,*i,2nd edn.,no.3468) and captured it shortly afterwards (Lesley, *History,*101); once the bulls in Forman's favour had been published in Scotland 15/17 Jan. 1515 (v.sup.), Hepburn retained support from various magnates (including now even Gavin Douglas) 2/3 Mar. 1515 (Herkless & Hannay, *Archbishops,*ii,119; *ADCP,* 30; cf. *James V Letters,*18-19), but he seems to have been worsted at a confrontation of factions in Edinburgh about this time, and is said to have left Scotland for the curia to further his claim in May 1515, prob. before the arrival of Albany on 15 May (Lesley, *History,*101; Dalrymple, *Historie,*ii,155-6; *James V Letters,*100-1; cf. ibid.,26 for dating); if he did in fact go abroad, he returned soon to be an active witness of crown charters under Albany 24 June to 4 Nov. 1515 (Herkless & Hannay, *Archbishops,*ii,137-8); put under papal interdict for his opposition to Forman 7 Oct. 1515 (*Leonis X Regesta,*ii,210); and eventually renounced his right (Edin.Univ.Lib.,Law MS,fo.17); but he retained poss. of fruits of the see until bought off with a pension and exemption from the archibishop's ordinary jurisdiction as his price for accepting Forman, as arranged by Albany c.4 Feb. 1516 (*James V Letters,*100-1; cf.ibid.,30; Lesley, *History,*106; *St A.Form.,*i,133; see Herkless & Hannay, *Archbishops,*ii,119; *ADCP,* 30; cf. *James V*

Douglas when *Edin.St Giles prov.* got crown nom. to pope with support of his new Aunt (Queen) Margaret before 23 Nov. 1514 (*LP Henry VIII,*i,2nd edn.,no.3468); had put his servants into poss. of St Andrews Castle apparently before death of Elphinstone, for on 8 Dec. 1514 he was ordered by papal mand. to give the castle up, presumably in favour of Forman (*Leonis X Regesta,*i,792, no.13126;

cf. Herkless & Hannay, *Archbishops*,ii,91,105); but by about the same date he had in fact to yield the castle to Hepburn (v.sup.); following this local setback to his claim and on the publication in Scotland of Forman's bulls 15/17 Jan. 1515 (v.sup.), Douglas got crown nom. to *Dk.bp.* instead 17 Jan. 1515, with papal prov. following 25 May 1515; Henry VIII was therefore out of touch with developments in Scotland when he supported nom. of Douglas to St A.abp. 28 Jan. 1515 (*Vet. Mon.*,no.901).

    Betoun when *G.abp.* may have had ambitions for trans to this see before 21 Jan. 1515, by which time Henry VIII was said to have twice written to Rome against him for some unspecified reason (*LP Henry VIII*,ii,no.44; Fraser, *Douglas*,iv,70); possibly still intent on reserving his own claim 3 Mar. 1515 when he did not support Hepburn's appeal against Forman (*ADCP*,30); but the nature of his claim (if any) is not known, and his motive of his claim (if any) is not known, and his motive on this latter occasion may simply have been support for Forman, whom he did in the end succeed in 1521-3 (v.inf.).

James Betoun 1521 - 1539.

    Crown nom. when royal chanc. for trans. from *G.abp.* 1 Dec. 1521 (*James V Letters*,85-86); papal trans. on Forman's death followed on 10 Oct. 1552, with grant of pallium 10 Dec. 1522 (Brady, *Episcopal Succession*,i,124-5); but this trans. was not effective until 5 June 1523 (*Prot.Bk.Simon*,337; cf. *St A.Acta*,340 for see being vacant still 22 Feb. 1523); given his nephew as coadj. 1537 (v.inf.); d. 14 Feb. 1539 (Dowden, *Bishops*,41).

David Betoun 1537 - 1546.

    Appointed coadj. to his uncle with right of succession 1537, before 5 Dec. (Eubel, *Hierarchia*,iii,108; cf. Dowden, *Bishops*,41,n.1); prov. to see of Mirepoix in France on nom. of King Francis I 5 Dec. 1537 (Eubel, *Hierarchia*,iii,246; Brady, *Episcopal Succession*,i,125); cons. 26 July x 13 Aug. 1538 (Dowden, *Bishops*,42); created cardinal by Pope Paul III, retaining administration of both his sees 20 Dec. 1538 (Eubel, *Hierarchia*,iii,25-26), with title of St Stephen on the Caelian Hill from 9 Sept. 1539 (ibid.,71); occ. as St A.abp. 25 Feb. 1539 (*RMS*,iii,no.1916); murdered at St Andrews 29 May 1546 (Knox,*History*,i,76; Lesley, *De Origine*,458).

John Hamilton   1546 - 1571.
Gavin Hamilton   1551 - 1571.

    John Hamilton granted temps. in vacancy on David Betoun's death when *Dk.bp.-elect* (though not so called) 31 May 1546 (*RSS*,iii,no.1696); trans by pope from *Dk.bp.* 28 Nov. 1547 (Brady, *Episcopal Succession*,i,126-7); but appointment not effective until June 1549 (*RSS*,iv,nos.283,310); given coadj. because of his ill-health

4 Sept. 1551 (v.inf.); executed at Stirling 7 Apr. 1571 (Dowden, *Bishops*,43-44,430).

Gavin Hamilton prov. when commendator of Kilwinning as coadj. to John Hamilton with right of succession 4 Sept. 1551 (Brady, *Episcopal Succession*,i,127-8; *Laing Chrs.*, no.584; cf. *Balclarres Papers*, ii,69-70); occ. as coadj. 11 Dec. 1553 (*SHR*,xxii,28; cf. 30,35,40); occ. as abp. 13 June 1571 (*CSP Scot.*,iii,604); d. 16 June 1571 (*Diurnal of Occurrents*, 225; cf; *RSS*, vi,no.1228).

John Douglas 1571 - 1574.
Crown prov. when *St A. St Mary's coll. princ.* on forfeitures and deaths of John and Gavin Hamilton 6 Aug. 1571 (*RSS*,vi,no.1228); commission appointed to examine his fitness as abp. 8 Sept. 1571 (ibid., no.2811); el by an *ad hoc* electoral chapter (following general arrangements of convention of Leith 16 Jan. 1572) 6 Feb. 1572 (Richard Bannatyne, *Memorials*, 223); cons. 10 Feb. 1572 (ibid.; cf. *RSS*,vi,nos. 1473-4); d. 31 July 1574 (*Diurnal of Occurrents*, 341).

Patrick Adamson/Constaine 1575 - 1592.
Lic. to elect issued with no name mentioned 10 Mar. 1575 (*RSS*, vii,no.87); crown conf. following el. on death of Douglas, with mand. for cons. 21 Dec. 1576 (ibid.,no.789); temps. granted 31 Dec. 1576 (ibid.,no.819); d. 19 Feb. 1592 (Calderwood, *History*, v,147).

George Gledstanes 1604 - 1615.
Trans. from *C.bp.* 12 Oct. 1604 (Reg.Pres.,iii,93); cons. Dec.1610 (Melville, *Diary* (Woodrow Soc.), 804; Calderwood, *History*,vii,152); d. 2 May 1615 (*Original Letters*,ii,437).

John Spottiswood 1615 - 1638.
Trans. from *G.abp.* 30/31 May 1615 (Reg.Pres. iv,117v; Calderwood, *History*,vii,198-9; cf. *RMS*, vii,no.1237); depriv. 13 Dec. 1638 (Peterkin, *Records*,i,26-27); d. 26 Nov. 1639 (*Spottiswoode Misc.*, i,6-7, quoting memorial in Westminster Abbey).

CHAPTER OF ST ANDREWS

The developing relationships of the various communities of clergy at St Andrews in the 12th and 13th centuries have been studied by Mr G.W.S. Barrow in *Journ.Eccles.Hist.*,iii,23-39; his salient points are noted here, together with some additional suggestions.

When Bp. Robert was appointed early in 1124, there was no group of clergy who regularly served the high altar of his cathedral ch. i.e. the modern 'St Rule's ch,(*Chron.Picts-Scots*,190), though its revenues were divided into seven portions, five of which supported

'parsonages' held by married clergy of some kind who did not lead a communal life (ibid.,189); quite separate from these *personae* was a community of culdees numbering thirteen c.1144 (ibid.,188); by this time the members of this community held their prebends hereditarily; they had no rights connected with the high altar of the ch. of St Andrew, but celebrated their offices at a side altar of that ch. (ibid., 190); there is no evidence to suggest that they had any exclusive right to elect the bp., though they may well have shared this duty in 1120 and 1123 x 1124 with the other clergy of the city and dioc. (cf. Barrow,op. cit.,33; see also *B. chapter* above).

Plans for the rearrangement of endowments to support the found-ation of a cathedral community of Augustinian canons were almost certainly under way at time of Bp. Robert's appointment by King Alexander I early in 1124; but there were delays until 1144, when the new community was finally established; by this time the model of the Augustinian chapter at Carlisle cathedral (founded 1133-6) was available (*ESC*,nos.162-5; see Barrow in *Trans. Royal Hist.Soc.*, 5th series,iii,83-84); this new community of regular canons succeeded to most of the property rights of the old personae of the ch. of St Andrew (*Chron. Picts-Scots*,189,193; *St A.Lib.*, 123,125,129), and it was King David I's intention c. 1150 that they should absorb also the property of the culdees — either at once if individual culdees wished to become regular canons, or piecemeal as each culdee incumbent died (*ESC*,no.233); Pope Eugenius III had already given permission for this gradual absorption of the culdees in his bull of 30 Aug. 1147, when he also granted to the Augustinian prior and convent the exclusive privilege henceforward of electing the bp. of St Andrews (*St A.Lib.*,48-50; see *Journ.Eccles.Hist.*, iii,33,n.1).

In fact the culdee community was never successfully absorbed by the Augustinian priory; their abbot occ. still in 1170s and 1180s (*Gen.Coll.*,ii,532; *St A.Lib.*,353); then Mr. Barrow dates a fresh departure to an agreement of Feb. 1198 x Aug. 1199 (ibid.,318-19; cf. *RRS*,i,217-18), whereby the canons made a settlement with the culdees which consolidated the latter's rights on a permanent basis; in the course of the next fifty years the culdee community came to be removed from the cathedral and transformed with royal and episcopal support into the chapter of the collegiate ch. of St Mary on the Rock at St Andrews; the prior and canons were hostile at various stages, and as late as 1248-53 were trying to enforce their old right of succession to culdee prebends (*St A.Lib.*,101; *Vet.Mon.*,no. 145; Reeves, *Culdees*, 113-15, *Inchaff.Chrs.*, 154-5); the issue became involved with national politics, the prior and canons looking to the supporters of Durward for help and the provost and chapter of St Mary to supporters of Comyn; prob. this is why no more is found under the Comynite Bps. Gamelin and Wishart or later of the priory's resistance to the permanent existence of the privileged chapel royal of

St Mary on the Rock.

There was a separate issue over the claim of the priory to exclusive rights in episcopal elections; two elements challenged this privilege — the two archdeacons and the culdees/chapter of St Mary; at least one archdeacon and prob. both were coeval with the Augustinian community, and successive archdeacons were prob. members of the chapter along with the canons from the first (cf. *Vet.Mon.*, no.162, pp.59-60); but it is not in fact known whether or not the archdeacons were excluded from elections between 1159 and 1202; after Bp. Malveisin's death in 1238 it was a matter of open doubt whether they were entitled to share with the canons in the election as voices of the 'community' of clergy throughout the dioc., and (perhaps in response to current troubles over *Ga.bp.*) it was agreed that they should do so for this occasion without prejudice to the rights of both sides (*Journ. Eccles.Hist.*,iii,39, appendix; note that the interpretation of this source suggested here differs from that offered by Mr. Barrow); and in fact at least the St A.archd. (and prob. that of Lothian too) was present when Bp. Liberatione was postulated later in 1238 (*Vet.Mon.*,no.162); it was the custom under the subsequent Bp. Bernham at any rate to install an archd. both in choir and chapter of the cathedral community, and it is clear from the way in which the canons tried to get Archd. Gullane's consent to their election of Stuteville in 1253 that they recognised that they would have to face litigation if they excluded him (ibid.); it may be assumed that the right of the two archdeacons to places in the chapter along with the canons was undisturbed thenceforward, and they certainly participated in the elections of 1271, 1279 and 1297 (*Moray Reg.*,338-9; *Vet.Mon.*,nos. 276, 362).

The case of the culdees was rather different; as a discredited group they are not likely to have had any share in the elections of 1158-1202; and they did not take part in 1238, even though their character had by then changed; two culdees did, however, take part in the elections of 1239 and 1255, in both cases apparently as a result of pressure from their probable patron the king, and in both cases at times when the chapter had recently conducted elections in 1238 and 1253 that were prob. unsatisfactory from the crown point of view (*Vet.Mon.*,no.177); the pope on 20 July 1255 granted the canons an indulgence that their having bowed to pressure in this way should not be prejudicial to their rights (ibid.); the chapter of St Mary on the Rock was apparently excluded from the elections of 1271 and 1279 (*Chron.Bower*,i,360-1); but the issue was revived in 1297 by William Comyn *St Mary, St A.prov.*, who objected to the election of Bp. Lamberton ostensibly because of the exclusion of the 'culdees' from the ceremony; but Pope Boniface VIII is said to have rejected the appeal which he made at the curia (ibid.,361-2); Comyn was still around at the next election in 1328 and renewed his objection as a matter of form, but no 'culdee' claim was raised in 1332 (ibid.,363); a place was eventually found for the *St Mary, St A.prov.*, however, by

papal privilege of 24 Jan. 1386 (in response to a petition from King
Robert II) that the holder of this ben. should henceforth have a place
in choir and chapter as a third secular dignitary along with the two
archdeacons (SRO, Transcripts from Vatican, i,250 ff.).

A fourth secular dignity in the chapter of St Andrews was the
chancellorship erected 1447 x 1449; but this ben, was dissolved 1461
x 1462.

By the convention of Leith 16 Jan. 1572 the surviving members
of the cathedral convent were left in control of the temporalities of
the monastery for life (*BUK*,i,222-3); Robert Stewart *C.bp.* was
commendator of the priory then and until his death in 1586; thereafter
the priory became a purely temporal lordship for his grand-nephew
Ludovick duke of Lennox by various stages 1586 - 1611 (*SP*,v,357;
MRHS,82); by 1606 the prior and convent had res. their spiritualities
and the priory had been suppressed and extinguished (*APS*,iv,353-5).

In 1572 also a separate chapter for episcopal elections and
spiritual affairs was erected under the commendator as dean; at first
this was done on an *ad hoc* basis, comprising 12 members of the old
chapter who had conformed to the Reformation; but a plan for the
future was also approved for a chapter of 21 reformed clergy including
four dignitaries i.e. *St A.prior/dean, St A.archd., St A.archd. Lothian.*
and *Edin.Trin.prov.* as *St A.chanc.* (*BUK*,i,222-3; Calderwood,
History, iii,186-8); it was such a chapter that conducted elections of
1572 and 1575 x 1576; then in 1606 and 1607 abp. Gledstanes was
empowered to choose seven parish ministers to form his chapter
(*APS*,iv,324-5,372).

In 1617 two distinct chapters were created; firstly there was to
be an ordinary or administrative chapter for the dioc., to replace the
suppressed chapter of prior/dean and canons, and comprising 24
beneficed ministers including *St A. St Leonard's coll.princ.* as *St A.dean,
St.A.archd., St Mary, St A.prov., Restalrig dean* and *Dunbar dean*;
and secondly there was to be an electoral chapter for approving the
crown nom. of the abp. of the province (as at Glasgow also), comprising
the eight suffragan bps. of the province (with *Dk.bp.* as convening
authority), *St A.St Leonard's coll. princ., St A.archd.,* and the vicars
of St Andrews, Leuchars and Cupar (*APS*,iv,530).

PRIORS OF ST ANDREWS

For lists of known holders of this office see *ES*,ii,205-6 (to 1313),
Chron.Bower,i,367-76 (to 1443), Edin.Univ.Lib., Law MS,fos.12v,
18-21 (to 1482), and *The Bibliotheck*,ii,24-26 (to 1304).

DEANS OF ST ANDREWS

First known date: 1572.

This dignity erected by convention of Leith 16 Jan. 1572 to be held by the prior/commendator of St Andrews (*BUK*,i,222-3); it was re-erected 28 June 1617 to be held by the principal of St Leonard's College, St Andrews (*APS*,iv, 530).

Robert Stewart 1572 - 1586.

Presumably took office on erection of dignity 16 Jan. 1572 (v.sup.); occ. as dean 6 Feb. 1572 (Richard Bannatyne, *Memorials*, 222-3) and 10 Mar. 1575 (*RSS*,vii,no.87); d. 29 Aug. 1586 (see *C.bp.*).

Peter Bruce 1617 - 1630.

Presumably took office on re-erection of dignity 28 June 1617 (v.sup.); d. 8 May x 17 July 1630 (see *St A. St Leonard's coll. princ.*).

Andrew Bruce 1630.

Crown pres. to deanery on death of Peter Bruce 18 Oct. 1630 (Reg.Pres.vi.97), being already in office as *St A. St Leonard's coll. princ.*

CHANCELLORS OF ST ANDREWS

First known date: x 1449.

Erected as a secular dignity 10 years or more before 3 Nov. 1459 (Reg.Supp.,525,fo.192).

Prebend: Soutra Hospital in 1454 (*CPL*,x,164); this property was detached and united to Trinity College, Edinburgh 23 Oct. 1460 (*MRHS*, 157).

Thomas Lauder 1447 x 1449 - 1452.

Prov. on erection of this dignity by Nicholas V i.e. 1447 x 1449 (*CPL*,xi,447-8); in poss. when prov. *Dk.bp*. 28 Apr. 1452 (*CPL*,x,559).

John 'Bonier' x 1457.

Held it at death before 29 Aug. 1457 (Reg.Supp.,503,fo.241).

Alan Cant 1456.

Occ. as *Chapel Royal dean* 13 Aug. 1456 (*St A.Acta*,114); perhaps d. before 3 Oct. 1457 (ibid.,121), and certainly before 3 Nov. 1459 (Reg.Supp.,525,fo.192).

John Tyrie (Tyri)   1456 x 1460 - 1461 x 1462.
James Gray   1460.

Tyrie had crown pres. from James II (i.e. x 3 Aug. 1460) on Cant's death and ord. coll. (*CPL*,xi,447-8, 450); in poss. when conf. 1 Dec. 1461 (Reg. Supp.,548,fo.172); res. to ord. before 18 June 1462 (*CPL*,xi,447).

Gray prov. on claim of long vacancy after Cant's death 14 Feb. 1460 (Reg.Supp.,527,fo.161); claims poss. 23 May 1460 (*ACSB*,139; f. 238,276).

Note: erection of this dignity cancelled by pope after 1 Dec. 1461
(v.sup.) and before 18 June 1462 (*CPL*,xi,447); it was re-erected by
convention of Leith 16 Jan. 1572, to be held in association with *Edin.
Trin.prov.* (*BUK*,i,222-3), but this may never have been effective.

ARCHDEACONS OF ST ANDREWS

First known date: 1147 x 1152.
        Prebend: ch. of Tarvit by 1209 x 1222, prob. 1209 x 1212 (NLS,
Adv. MS 15.1.18,no.14; Lyon, *St Andrews*,ii,306; cf. Cowan, *Parishes,*
195-6); then this ch. was exchanged for that of Kinneff 1363 (*CPP*,i,
409); and ch. of Rescobie was added by time of Reformation (Cowan,
Parishes, 170).

Matthew 1147 x 1152 - 1172.
        Occ. 24 Aug. 1147 x 12 June 1152 (*St A.Lib.*,187); occ. 1152
x 1159 (*Dunf.Reg.*,no.92, where this archd. is clearly distinguished from
that of Lothian, with Thorald *St A.archd.Lothian* in the senior place);
cons. *Ab.bp.* 2 Apr. 1172.

Walter de Roxburgh 1173 - 1179 x 1188.
        Occ. prob. 1173 (*Melr.Lib.*,i,no.51; cf. nos.50,52; cf. ii,no.443);
appears once as 'Gal.' 1178 x 1183 (*St A.Lib.*,334); occ. 1179 x 1188
(ibid.,290); for surname see ibid.,179; *Dunf.Reg.*,58; NLS, Adv.MS
15.1.18,no.47.

Note: John Scot is said (*Chron.Bower*,i,351) to have been archd. for
some time before his abortive el. as *St A.bp.* in 1178; but this is prob.
an error.

Hugh (de Roxburgh ?) 1189 x 1194 - 1199.
        Occ. as archd. and also as king's chancellor 13 Apr. 1189 x 1194
(*Lind.Cart.,* 284) and 2 Feb. 1194 (*ND*,no.462); as chancellor became
G.bp.-elect after 17 Mar. 1199, but d. uncons. 10 July 1199; had dem.
this ben. by 6 June 1199 (v.inf.); commonly given surname 'de
Roxburgh' (e.g. Dowden, *Bishops*,299; *HBC*,173), but authority for
this is not known.

Ranulf de Wat 1199 - 1209.
        Occ. 6 June 1199 (*ND*,no.467), having presumably obtained it
since 17 Mar. 1199 (v.sup.); d. 1209 (*Chron.Melrose*,54); surname
'de Wat' appears on his seal (Stevenson & Wood, *Seals*,i,98).

Laurence de Thornton (Thorenton) 1209 - 1238 x 1240.
        Succ. 1209 (*Chron.Melrose*,54); present at postulation of
Geoffrey de Liberatione as *St A.bp.* in 1238 soon after 9 July (*Vet.
Mon.,* 60; cf. *Journ.Eccles. Hist.*,iii,39, where document is misdated);
d. or dem. before 29 Mar. 1240 (v.inf.); surname is found only once
in a document of 1203 x 1204 (*Arb.Lib.*,i,117).

Adam 1240 - 1248.

Occ. 29 Mar. 1240 (*Dunf.Reg.*,137-8), having prob. been coll. since cons. of Bp. Bernham 22 Jan. 1240; occ. 2 June 1248 (*Lind. Cart.*,69-70).

Abel de Gullane (Golin, Golyn) 1250 - 1254.

Occ. 12 May 1250 (*C.Lib. R.*,iii,287); occ. 27 June 1252 (*Lind. Cart.*,62); prov. *St A.bp.* 20 Feb. 1254.

William Wishart 1254 - 1273.

In poss. 22 Feb. 1254 (*CPL*,i,296); el. *St A.bp.* 3 June 1271 and cons. 15 Oct. 1273.

Note: this ben. was perhaps still vacant in June 1275, for no tenth was collected from it for six-month term beginning then; but it had an unnamed incumbent by Christmas 1275, for tenth was collected for six-month term ending June 1276 (*SHS Misc.*,vi,62).

Alpin (Albiinus) de Strathearn 1278.

Occ. 1278 (Sarti & Fattorini, *De Claris....Bononiensis Professoribus*,ii,316); prob. same as the later *St A.offic.* and *Db.bp.*, his surname being found in 1292 and 1295 (*Chron.Rishanger*,263; *Reg. Halton*,i,34).

Gregory 1279 - 1295.

Occ. 4 Aug. 1279 (*Chron.Bower*,i,361; cf. *CPL*,i,462); occ. 13 Feb. 1295 (NLS, Adv.MS 15.1.18, no.8).

John Fraser (Fresel) 1296 - 1297.

Occ. 2 Sept. 1296 (*Rot.Scot.*,i,25); in poss. 3 Nov. 1297 (*CPL*, i,576; cf. *Chron.Fordun*,i,330).

Roger de Kingston 1299.

Pres. by Edward I 24 Mar. 1299 (*CPR 1292 - 1301*, 399), prob. unfruitfully.

Adam de Mauchan/Machane 1301 - 1304.

Occ. 31 Jan. 1301 (*St A.Lib.*,120); el St A. prior 27 July 1304 (*Chron.Bower*,i,369).

Robert de Lamberton 1308 (?) 1319 - 1323.

Seal of an unnamed *St A.archd.* was used 29 Sept. 1308 (SRO, Transcripts of Misc.Chrs.,s.d.); occ. 17 Feb. 1319 (*Dryb.Lib.*,245); occ. 30 Aug. 1323 (NLS,Adv.MS 15.1.18,no.36).

James Ben/Benne/de Edinburgh (Castro Puellarum) 1325 - 1328.

Occ. 20 Apr. 1325 (*APS*,xii,5); see *SHR*,xxvii,129 for his 'Edinburgh' surname on his seal in Apr. 1326; see *Dunf.Reg.*, 242 for surname 'Benne' 1322 x 1328; el. *St A.bp.* 19 June 1328 and cons. before 1 Aug. 1328.

William de Lindsay 1330.

Occ. 4 June 1330 (Fraser, *Lennox*,ii,23) and also 1328 x 1332 (*Balm.Lib.*,40) and 1328 x 1335 (*Pais.Reg.*,239).

William de Pilmuir (Pellemor) 1340 - 1345 x 1353.

Moved from *Dk.archd.* by 28 Feb. 1340; in poss. 18 Apr. 1341 (*Vatikanische Quellen*,iv,89; *Diplom.Norv.*,xvii,no.52); in poss. 25 Jan. 1345 (*CPL*,iii,162); d. before 15 Oct. 1353 (v.inf.).

Henry Stupy	x 1353.
William Wys	1353 - 1354.
William de Greenlaw	1353 - 1373.
William de Chisholm	1367.

Stupy said to have had ord. coll. on Pilmuir's death before 15 Oct. 1353 (*CPP*,i,253).

Wys had ord. coll. on Pilmuir's death and got conf. 20 Nov. 1353 (*CPL*,iii,490; *CPP*,i,254); in poss. 28 Nov. 1354 (Ob. et Sol..30,fo. 72v).

Greenlaw prov. on strength of papal reservation during Pilmuir's lifetime 15 Oct. 1353 (*CPL*,iii,476); occ. 11 May 1358 (*CPL*,iv,71-72); in poss. 23 Aug. 1373 (ibid.,108).

Chisholm prov. 28 Feb. 1367 (Collect.,14,fo.174) unfruitfully.

John de Peebles (Peblis)	1374 - 1378 x 1379.
Andrew de Trebrun	1378.

Peebles in poss 8 Oct. 1374 (*CPL*,iv,152); cons. *Dk.bp.* by authority of Urban VI c. June 1378; cons. again by order of Clement VII Feb. x July 1379.

Trebrun claims some right but no poss. 17 Nov. 1378 (*CPP*, i,546).

Thomas Stewart 1380 - 1430.

Prov. on elevation of Peebles 10 Feb. 1380 (*CPP*,i,551); in poss. 21 Dec. 1381 (ibid.,563); occ. 20 July 1430 (*SHR*,viii,234); d. before 23 Sept. 1430 (v.inf.).

George Newton	1430 x 1431 - 1433.
Richard de Creich	1430 - 1432.
Thomas de Myrton (Merton)	1431 - 1433.
William de Foulis	1432 - 1441.

Newton had ord. coll. and poss. on Stewart's death, and lit. with Creich and Myrton by 6/7 Apr. 1431 (Reg.Supp.,267,fo.198v); still in poss. 17 Sept. 1432 (ibid.,280,fo.101); res. to ord. on exch. with Foulis for *Bothwell* prov. 30 Jan. x 12 Sept. 1433 (ibid.,289,fos.200v, 246).

Creich prov. on Stewart's death 23 Sept. 1430 (*CPL*,viii,411); lit. with Newton 6/7 Apr. 1431 (v.sup.); new prov. 12/19 May 1432 (Reg.Supp.,277,fos.201v,243v; *ACSB*,109); still without poss. when prov. to another ben. 11 Sept. 1432 (Reg.Supp.,279,fo.299v).

Myrton had some right before 6/7 Apr. 1431 when lit. in curia with Newton (v.sup.); had had prov. but no poss. when given *com. priv.* against Newton 17 Sept. 1432 (Reg.Supp.,280,fo.101); new prov. 17 May 1433 (ibid.,286,fo.220v); still claiming a right 14 Aug. 1433 (ibid.,288,fo.204v).

Foulis prov. to Creich's right 11 Sept. 1432 (ibid.,279,fo.300); got Newton's right by exch. for *Bothwell* prov. 30 Jan. x 12 Sept. 1433, having poss. by latter date (ibid.,289,fos.200v,246); prov. in conf. of exch. 28 Apr. 1434 (ibid.,296,fo.86v); occ. 1 June 1441 (Fraser,*Pollok*, i,164).

John Legat 1443 - 1451.

Occ. 27 June 1443 (*HMC* 26,*12th R.*,viii,176); in poss. 3 Mar. 1451 (*ACSB*,272).

Hugh Kennedy x 1452 (?), 1454.

Perhaps moved from *G.treas.* x 21 Jan. 1452; occ. 4 Mar. 1454 (St A.Univ. Mun., SCB,fo.51v); occ. 24 Sept. 1454 (SRO,Bargany,no.1); d. before 26 Oct. 1454 (v.inf.).

John Kennedy 1454.
Hugh Douglas c.1454 - 1456 x 1457, 1458 (?).

Kennedy prov. on death of Hugh Kennedy 26 Oct. 1454 (Reg. Supp.,475,fo.214) prob. fruitlessly; cf. *St Mary*, *St A. prov.*

Douglas held it as a minor (ibid.,597,fo.116) for about two years, and res. under pressure from ord. (his uncle) on exch. with Stewart for *G.treas.* after 7 June 1455 and prob. 3 Nov. 1456 x 8 Oct. 1457 (v.inf.); still styled archd. 30 Nov. 1458 (*RMS*,ii,no.653).

Walter Stewart 1456 x 1457 - 1472 x 1474.
Hugh Douglas 1466.

Stewart obtained it on exch. with Douglas some time after 7 June 1455 (see *G.treas.*) and prob. after 3 Nov. 1456, when still described as *Dk.archd.* in a St Andrews context (*St A.Acta*,116); occ. 8 Oct. 1457 (ibid.,123); occ. 26 Apr. 1470 (Fraser, *Wemyss*,ii,95); res. to ord. in favour of Scheves prob. after 17 Aug. 1472, when bp. of St A. became abp. (v.inf.).

Douglas got new prov. on grounds that he had been improperly induced to res. while still a minor 4 July 1466 (Reg.Supp.579,fo.116) prob. unfruitfully.

William Scheves 1472 x 1474 - 1478.

Occ. 15 Apr. 1474 (SRO, Airlie, 29/1); had had local coll. on res. of Stewart from Abp. Graham, and gets new prov. 3/14 May 1474 (Reg.Supp.,704,fo.lllv; *CPL*,xiii,33-34); retained poss. after becoming coadj. to abp. 13 Sept. 1476, at least until 11 Mar. 1478 (v.inf.).

Robert Blackadder 1477 - 1480.
Andrew Stewart 1479.

Blackadder prov. on promotion of Scheves 25/26 Nov. 1477 (Reg. Supp.,761,fo.23; *CPL*,xiii,65); still no poss. 11 Mar. 1478 (Reg.Supp., 766,fo.59v-60); occ. 18 Aug. 1478 (Fraser, *Lennox*, ii,117); prov. *Ab.bp.* 14 July 1480, but not cons. until Apr. 1483.

Stewart as uncle of James III gets prov. on promotion of Scheves 19 Feb. 1479 (Reg.Supp.,727,fo.96) prob. unfruitfully.

Alexander Inglis 1480 - 1496.

John de Ireland (Irlandia)   1483 - 1485.

Inglis prov. on Blackadder's promotion 14 July 1480 (*CPL*,xiii, 93); el. *Dk.bp.* prob. on royal nom. 28 Aug. x 17 Sept. 1483, but never cons., and lost royal recognition as bp.-elect 26 May x 16 Aug. 1485; occ. 29 Apr. 1495 still in this ben. (*St A.Acta*,248); d. 25 Feb. 1496 (ibid.,263; tombstone in Queen Mary's House, St Andrews - identification depends on coat of arms).

Ireland occ. 29 Nov. 1483 (*Rot.Scot.*,ii,461); got crown nom. to pope for prov. (despite opposition of abp.) on promotion of Inglis to Dunkeld 4 Mar. 1484 (Reg.Supp.,833,fo.92); king and estates still hoped to make this nom. effective 9 May 1485 (*APS*,ii,171); see also *Crichton prov.*

Robert Wells/de Fontibus 1497 - 1501.

Occ. 22 May 1497 (*RMS*,ii,no.2358) and 26 Aug. 1501 (SRO, St Andrews Chrs.,no.171).

Alexander Stewart 1502 - 1504.

Occ. 20 Sept. 1502 (*TA*,ii,300); res. in favour of Dunbar on or before 10 Feb. 1504 (v.inf.).

Gavin Dunbar 1504 - 1519.

Crown pres. on res. of Stewart 10 Feb. 1504 (*RSS*,i,no.1019); occ. 27 Aug. 1518 (*ER*,xiv,344); nom. *Ab.bp.* by 31 Oct. 1518 and cons. 20 Feb. 1519; found still as archd. when witness 26 Nov. 1519 and 23 Jan. 1521 (*RMS*,iii,nos.187,196 - but these charters were recorded long after date of granting and error is probable).

Thomas Halkerston 1519 - 1521 x 1524.

Occ. 13 Mar. 1519 (*Cupar Chrs.*,no.7); occ. 18 Nov. 1521 (*Camb. Reg.*,249); d. after 20 May 1522 (see *Crichton prov.*) and before 24 Feb. 1524 (SRO, Sent. Offic. Laud.,fo.121).

John Cantuly   1524 - 1537.
George Dury   1526 - 1559.
Robert Pitcairn   1539 - 1584.

Cantuly occ. 26 May 1524 (*ADCP*,200); lit. with Dury and res. on pension in his favour with royal approval 30 May 1535 (PRO 31/9 - 33/17-18; *ADCP*,445); occ. 21 Feb. 1536 (*ADCP*,450); still has pension on fruits 18 Feb. 1537 (PRO 31/9 - 33/50).

Dury promises annates and gets prov. *Si neutri* 22 Jan. 1534 (PRO 31/9 - 33/272); claims poss. 1 Sept. 1534 (ibid.,287); occ. 28 Aug. 1536, by which time he had lit. for ten years (*James V Letters*, 323); res. in favour of Pitcairn 16 Sept. 1539 (PRO 31/9 - 33/96); but Pitcairn was his nephew and retroceded this ben. to Dury prob. at same date (*St A.Form.*,ii,94-97); the king asked his agent at the curia to stop this transaction 11 Dec. 1539 (*LP Henry VIII*,XIV,ii,no. 673), but it does seem to have been effective in the long run (v.inf.); occ. 20 Aug. 1558 (*RMS*,iv,no.2827) and 10 Oct. 1559 (SRO, E. 50/4,fo.35v, at back); prob. dem. by 12 May 1560 (v.inf.).

Pitcairn got prov. on res. of Dury 16 Sept. 1539 in terms of petition granted 18 July 1539 (PRO 31/9 - 33/96); retroceded ben. to Dury, but promised annates to retain right of regress prob. at same date (*St A.Form.*,ii,94-97); not known to occ. until 12 May 1560 (SRO, E. 50/4,fo.83, at back); occ. 1 July 1583 (SRO, Douglas, 3/74); d. 18 Oct. 1584 (*RCAHM* [Fife],113).

George Young 1584 - 1603.
Crown pres. on death of Pitcairn 12/19 Oct. 1584 (Reg.Pres.,ii, 113,117); occ. 11 Mar. 1603 (ibid.,iii,74).

Note: ben. of archd. was granted to *St A.abp.*, in part exchange for castle of St Andrews 1606 (*APS*,iv,283); it was re-erected by king to be held by the serving minister of parish ch. of St Andrews, the patronage being granted to the abp., 4 Apr. 1612 (ibid.,493-4).

Alexander Gledstanes 1612 - 1638.
Crown pres. as minister of St Andrews 4 Apr. 1612 (Reg.Pres., iv,68); occ. as archd. 18 Aug. 1614 (SRO, St Andrews Chrs.,no.402); depriv. 4 Dec. 1638 (Peterkin, *Records*,160).

ARCHDEACONS OF LOTHIAN

First known date: 1144.
Prebend: ch. of Kinleith/Currie in 1296 (*Foedera*,I,ii,724; Cowan, *Parishes*,42); as this ch. was still apparently an independent parsonage 1274-6 (*SHS Misc.*,vi, 33, 55-56), appropriation may be dated 1276 x 1296.

Thorald/Thor 1144 - 1165.
Occ. 1144 (*St A.Lib.*,123); said to have d. 1163 (*Chron.Holyrood*, 142); but occ. 28 Mar. 1165 x (*Dunf.Reg.*,no.96).

Andrew 1164 (?), x 1165 - 1179 x 1184.
Said to have been appointed 1164 (*Chron.Holyrood*,143); but see Thorald above; first occ. x 9 Dec. 1165 i.e. before death of Malcolm IV (*ND*,no.113); occ. 28 Mar. 1165 x 8 Dec. 1166 (*St A.Lib.*, 144); occ. 14 Oct. 1178 x 17 Sept. 1184 (ibid.,147).

William Malveisin/Malvoisin 1189 x 1194 - 1199.
Occ. 2 Feb. 1194 (*ND*,no.462), having got this ben. since 1189 x (*Arb.Lib.*,i,19; *ND*,no.116); occ. 6 June 1199 (*ND*,no.467); el. *G.bp.* Oct. 1199.

John de Leicester 1200 - 1212.
Occ. 17 June 1200 (*St A.Lib.*,153-4); el. *Dk.bp.* 22 July 1211; cons. after 13 June 1212.

William de Bosco 1214 - 1231.
In poss. 27 Oct. 1214 (*Glas.Reg.*,i,no.106); occ. 26 May 1227 (*Lind.Cart.*,no.97); d. 1231 (*Chron.Bower*,ii,59).

William de Bondington (?) x 1233.

Said to have held this ben before el. *G.bp.* and cons. 11 Sept. 1233 (Keith, *Bishops,*238 - no source quoted).

William de Maule (Maulia) 1235 - 1251.

Occ. 1235 (*Cold.Corr.,*242); occ. 29 Mar. 1251 (*Holy.Lib.,* no.75); obit at Chartres cathedral dated 10 June, no year given (*Obituaires de la province de Sens,*ii,175).

Thomas Charteris/de Carnoto 1260 x 1262 - 1267.

In poss. 13 Aug. 1262 (*CPL,*i,382), having got it since 30 May 1260 (cf. SRO, Transcripts of Misc.Chrs.,c. 1290); occ. 18 May 1267 (*ND,*no.652); but no longer described as archd. 19 Nov. 1267 (*CPR 1266-72,*167), and prob. res. in favour of Wishart.

Robert Wishart 1267 x 1271 - 1273.

Occ. 1267 x 1271 (*St A.Lib.,*376-7); prob. the unnamed incumbend who occ. 3 June 1271 (*Moray Reg.,*338); el. *G.bp.* later in 1271, but not cons. until 29 Jan. 1273.

Note: an unnamed archd. occ. 18 Dec. 1273 (*Kel.Lib.,*i,140-1); but ben. is not mentioned in tenth accounts of 1274-6 (*SHS Misc.,*vi).

Adam de Gullane (Golin) 1282.

Occ. Nov. 1282 (*Chartularium Universitatis Parisiensis,*i,no.510; cf. no.511; cf. *Midl.Chrs.,* 29; *ND,*no.418).

William Frere/Frater 1285 - 1306.

Occ. 10 June 1285 (*Newb.Reg.,*no.59); occ. 28 Oct. 1305 (*Foedera,*I,ii,975; *CDS,*ii,462); occ. 1306 (*Midl.Chrs.,* 43); for variants of surname see also *Melr.Lib.,*i,316 of 1291; *CDS,*ii,176 of 1296.

William de Eaglesham (Eglisham) 1317 - 1323.

Occ. 2 Mar. 1317 (*Kel.Lib.,*i,252); occ. 12 Oct. 1323 (SRO, Dalmeny Kirk Session Recs.,no.19).

Alexander de Kininmund 1327 - 1329.

Occ. 11 Aug. 1327 (*Holy Lib.,*77); prov. and cons. *Ab.bp.* 21 Aug. 1329.

William Comyn 1329 - 1336 x 1337.

Prov. 11 Nov. 1329 (*CPL,*ii,301); occ. 1336 x 1339 (*Cold.Corr.,* 20-21), but prob. d. before Feb. 1337 (v.inf.; cf. *G.chanc.*).

John de Douglas 1336 x 1337.

Occ. 19 July 1333 x 16 Feb. 1337 (*Mort.Reg.,*ii,90), presumably following Comyn in this ben.

Walter de Moffat 1340 x 1341 - 1357 x 1359.

Occ. Apr. 1340 x Aug. 1341 (ibid.,ii,42-43, nos.55-56); occ. 16 Oct. 1357 (SRO, Newbattle Chr. no.56); d. before 12 May 1359 (v.inf.).

Walter de Wardlaw 1357 x   1359 - 1367.

Had ord. coll. on Moffat's death and gets conf. 12 May 1359 (*CPP*, i,339); prov. *G.bp.* 14 Apr. 1367.

David de Mar	1367 - 1382.
Duncan Petit	1380.
Thomas de Barry	1382.

Mar prov. 22 Apr. 1367 (Reg.Av.,164,fo.132v); in poss. 13 June 1382 (*CPP*,i,565).

Petit prov. on supposed death of Mar 10 Feb. 1380 (ibid.,551) unfruitfully.

Barry gets *com.priv.* against Mar 13 June 1382 (ibid.,565).

Walter Forrester 1386.

Occ. 27 Mar. 1386 (*ER*,iii,132,679) and in poss. June 1386 (SRO, Transcripts from Vatican, i,no.58).

James Borthwick	1390 - 1408.
John Stewart	x 1405.
William de Lauder	1405 - 1408.
Alexander de Lilliesleaf	x 1408.

Borthwick in poss. 23 Nov. 1390 (Reg.Av.,268,fo.184v) and occ. 1395 x 1399 (*Yester Writs*,no.39); said to be dying July 1408, by which date he appears to have made an incomplete res. on exch. with Lilliesleaf for ch. of Calder-Comitis (*CPP*,i,638; cf. Reg.Av.,330,fos. 547-547v, which implies that he was dead by 9 July 1408).

Stewart had some right in this ben. before his prov. to *G.subd.*, i.e. before 9 Mar. 1405 at latest (ibid.).

Lauder had dispossessed Borthwick and occ. 27 Aug. 1405 (*Rot. Scot.*,ii,175); prov. *G.bp.* 9 July 1408.

Lilliesleaf had some inconclusive right based on an exch. with Borthwick, which he appears to have dem. before 14 July 1408, prob. in part-exch. with Cornell for *Dk.archd.* (*CPP*,i,638).

Richard de Cornell	1408 - 1419.
John Derling (Devlyn)	1409.

Cornell got prov. in conjunction with Lilliesleaf's prov. to *Dk. archd.* 14 July 1408 on occasion of prov. of Lauder to his see (*CPP*, ,638); in poss. 5 Oct. 1408 (Reg.Av.,330, fos.547-547v); occ. 22 Jan. 1419 (*Univ.Evidence*,iii,350); d. by 22 Mar. 1419 (v.inf.).

Derling got *com. priv.* against Cornell 18 Apr. 1409 (Reg.Av., 332,fos.442-443v) unfruitfully.

Columba de Dunbar	1419 - 1422.
William Croyser	1419.
Edward de Lauder	1419 - 1429 x 1430.

Dunbar had coll. by ord. on Cornell's death, and is in poss. 11 May 1419 (*CSSR*,i,47) and when given new prov. 23 June 1419 (ibid., 30); lit. with Lauder went in Dunbar's favour before 19 Mar. 1422 ibid.,291); prov. *M.bp.* 3 Apr. 1422.

Croyser prov. on Cornell's death 22 Mar. 1419 (*CSSR*,i,26-27); es. without poss. in Lauder's favour before 2 Apr. 1419 (v.inf.; see

also *G.arch. Teviotdale*).

Lauder prov. on Cornell's death and res. of Croyser 2 Apr.1419 (*CSSR*,i,28); after lit. with Dunbar got prov. *Si neutri* 19 Mar.1422 (ibid.,291) and then surrog. to Dunbar's right 5 Apr. 1422 (ibid.,293); in poss. still 26 Nov. 1429 (*CPL*,viii,155); d. before 25 Aug. 1430 (v.inf.).

David de Crannach	x 1429, 1430.
William Croyser	1429 - 1440 x 1441; 1452 x 1453 - 1460 x 1461
Thomas de Greenlaw	1430 - 1431.
Gilbert Forrester	1431.
Alexander de Newton	1431 - 1433.
Robert de Lythow	1440.
Thomas de Tulloch	1441 - 1444.
John de Lauder	x 1443 - 1452 x 1453.

Crannach wrongly reported 20 Nov. 1429 to have died with a right to this ben (v.inf.); prov. on Lauder's death 25 Aug. 1430 (*ACSB*, 102); res. in favour of Croyser on or before 18 Nov. 1430 (v.inf.) as part of a deal involving *Dk.subd.*

Croyser prov. unfruitfully on false report of Crannach's supposed death 20 Nov. 1429 (Reg.Supp.,257,fo.178); prov. in surrog. to Crannach's new right 18 Nov. 1430 (*ACSB*,102); surrog. to Greenlaw and Forrester 24 Jan. 1431 (Reg.Supp.,264,fo.297v); proposed to res. in favour of Lythow 4 Aug. 1440 (ibid.,366,fo.92v); instead was depriv. by Eugenius IV for adherence to council of Basel on or before 12 Aug. 1441 (see Tulloch below); restored 4 Dec. 1452 x 6 Dec. 1453 (*Rot.Scot.* ii.372: cf. Lauder below); prob. went abroad soon afterwards and died 19 July 1460 x 3 Sept. 1461 (*see G.archd.Teviotdale*); but though he continues to be styled archd. Teviotdale until his death, he is not found as archd. Lothian after 6 Dec. 1453.

Greenlaw prov. on Lauder's death 27 Aug. 1430 (Reg.Supp., 256,fo.86v); lit. in curia by 16 Oct. 1430 (ibid.,257,fo.62v); res. in Croyser's favour on or before 24 Jan. 1431 (v.sup.).

Forrester had some right and lit. in curia, but res. in Croyser's favour on or before 24 Jan. 1431 (v.sup.); still lit. 12 May 1431 (Reg. Supp.,266,fo.207).

Newton lit. 11 Mar. 1431 (*CPL*,viii,341); still claims some right 16 Oct. 1433 (Reg. Supp.,289,fo.140v).

Lythow prov. 4 Aug. 1440 (ibid.,366,fo.92v) unfruitfully.

Tulloch prov. in commend as *O.bp.* on Croyser's depriv. 12/30 Aug. 1441 (ibid.,375,fo.163; *ACSB*,129); commend cancelled 17 Oct. 1444 (Reg.Supp.,400,fo.198).

Lauder had coll. by ord. on Croyser's depriv. (presumably after c. Aug. 1441) and gets prov. 6 July 1443 (*ACSB*,131;Reg.Supp., 391, fo.149v); in poss. and lit. against Tulloch 14 Oct. 1444 (ibid.,400,fo. 198); new prov. 3 Nov. 1444 (ibid.,401,fo.24v); occ. 2 Dec. 1446 (*St A.Acta*,68); occ. 4 Dec. 1452 (ibid.,92) but dem. before 4 Feb. 1455 (ibid.,105); prob. dem. before 6 Dec. 1453 (see Croyser above).

James Lindsay (de Covington ?) 1461 - 1468 x 1469 (?).
    In poss. 23 Dec. 1461 (*Reg. Supp.*,547,fo.256); prob. same as *Lincluden prov.* and so d. 19 Nov. 1468 x 13 Feb. 1469 (v.inf.).

Nicholas Graham 1469 - 1469 x 1470.
    Prov. after ord. coll. on Lindsay's death 13 Feb. 1469 (*CPL*,xii, 311); d. before 3 May 1470 (v.inf.).

William Ferguson (Fergusii)   1470.
Robert Blackadder   1470 - 1472.
Archibald Whitelaw   1470 - 1498.
    Ferguson prov. on Graham's death 3 May 1470 (*CPL*,xii,347); in poss. at curia 29 Nov. 1476 (ibid.,392).
    Blackadder got poss. on strength of an exp. grace on Graham's death and has had prov.; gets extension of time for publishing letters of appointment at St Andrews 22 June 1470 (*Reg.Supp.*,659,fo.162v); res. in favour of Whitelaw 22 Apr. 1472 (ibid.,679,fo.180).
    Whitelaw occ. 20 June 1470 (*Wigtown Charter Chest*,no.417), having got poss. since 21 May 1470 (*RMS*,ii,no.991); new prov. 22 Apr. 1472 (*Reg. Supp.*,679,fo.180); in 60th year of age 5 July 1475 (ibid., 723,fo.166); gets Gifford as coadj. 26 Nov. 1494 (v.inf.); d. 23 Oct. 1498 (*Glas.Reg.*,ii,616).

Alexander Gifford (Gisford) 1494 - 1507.
David Arnot   1498 - 1503.
John Brady   1505 - 1525.
    Gifford promised annates and got prov. as coadj. and successor to Whitelaw 26 Nov. 1494 (PRO 31/9 - 30/380-1); pays some of these annates 9 June 1497 (ibid.,381); gets pension on fruits by 23 Mar. 1507 (PRO 31/9 - 31/168), but prob. never had poss. as at first intended.
    Arnot gets crown pres. on Whitelaw's death 26 Oct. 1498 (*RSS*, i,no.278); occ. 3 Dec. 1498 (Fraser, *Carlaverock*,ii,452); prov. Cambuskenneth abbot 29 Mar. 1503 (Dowden, *Bishops*,371).
    Brady occ. 27 Nov. 1505 (*RMS*,ii,no.2896); occ. 1511 (*TA*, iv,173); appointed proctors to res. this ben in favour of 'N.' but retaining fruits 'c.1512' (*St A.Form.*,i,38 - authority for dating is not known); retained it until his death (v.inf.), which was in Nov. 1525 (see *Edin.,Trin. prov.*).

Henry Forsyth (Frosith) 1525 x 1530 - 1531.
    Had prov. on Brady's death, but did not pay annates, and so a pension on the fruits is granted to a Roman clerk 3 Mar. 1530 (PRO 31/9 - 32/187-8); res. right in favour of Hay 4 Jan. 1531 (ibid.,201).

John Hay 1531.
    Prov. on res. of Forsyth 4 Jan. 1531 (ibid.).

Patrick Stewart 1532 - 1539 x 1542.
    Occ. 8 Feb. 1532 (*James V Letters*,206-7); occ. 23 Dec.1539 (SRO, GD 1/208/4); still alive 20 Nov. 1542, but prob. no longer holding this ben (see *B.dean*).

Walter Betoun 1546 - 1554.

Occ. 25 Oct. 1546 (*Glas.Mun.*,ii,168); occ. 12 Dec. 1548 (*ADCP,* 577); res. in favour of Alexander Betoun, but promises annates for right of return 30 Dec. 1548 (PRO 31/9 - 33/247, where it is Alexander who is said to res.); occ. 4 May 1554 (*HMC* 55, *Var.Coll.*,v,200).

Alexander Betoun 1548 - 1584.

Promises annates for prov. on res. and return of Walter Betoun 30 Dec. 1548 (PRO 31/9 - 33/247 - where it is Walter who is said to get prov.); occ. 31 July 1560 (*Prot.Bk.Glasgow*,v,no.1384); occ. 30 Jan. 1576 (Fraser, *Elphinstone*,ii,260-2); res. annexed ch. of Currie 28 Mar. 1584 (SRO, Reg.Ho.Chr.no.2709).
Note: This dignity was included in the reformed chapter of St Andrews (as from date at which incumbent would accept the Reformation) at convention of Leith 16 Jan. 1572 (*BUK*,i,222-3); but there was no mention of it when this chapter was re-erected June 1617 (*APS*,iv,530).

DEANS OF CHRISTIANITY

ARCHDEACONRY OF ST ANDREWS

DEANS OF FIFE : ST ANDREWS : CRAIL

First known dates: Fife: 1165 x 1172.
                        St Andrews: 1189 x 1198.
                        Crail: 1203 x 1209.

Cuthbert (Gillequdberit) (Fife) 1165 x 1172.

Occ. 1165 x 1172 (*N.B.Chrs.*,no.4; *St A.Lib.*,137,180); prob.dead before 1183 (ibid.,59).

Robert 1172 x 1178.

Occ. 1172 x 1178 (*St A.Lib.*,138; see also 259); but perhaps name is each time a misreading for Cuthbert (who appears also ibid., 260, which seems to be contemporaneous with or later than ibid.,259).

Patrick (Fife) 1178 x 1188.

Occ. 1178 x 1188 (*Dunf.Reg.*, 92).

William de Hales (St Andrews) 1189 x 1198.

Occ. 1189 x 1198 (SRO, Black Book of St Andrews, fo.xxxv).

John (Fife) 1200.

Occ. 17 June 1200 (*St A.Lib.*,154).

William de Crail (Karel) (Crail) 1203 x 1209, 1206 x 1209.

Occ. as 'William dean of Crail' and as 'William de Crail dean' 1203 x 1209 (*Lind.Cart.*,no.108; NLS, Adv.MS 15.1.18,no.33); occ. as 'William dean of Crail' 1206 x 1209 (*St A.Lib.*,397).

Radulf (Fife/Crail) 1212 - 1231.
Occ. as dean of Fife 1209 x 1222 and 1212 (ibid.,389,316); occ. as dean of Crail 1224 x 1231 (*Holy Lib.*, no.47) and as 'R.' dean of Fife 1231 (*St A.Lib.*,393).

Gerard (Fife) 1234.
Occ. 23 Apr. 1234 (NLS, Adv.MS 15.1.18,no.31).

Michael (Fife) 1240.
Occ. 29 Mar. 1240 (*Dunf.Reg.*,137).

William (Fife) 1239 x 1244.
Occ. 1239 x 31 Aug. 1244 (*Balm.Lib.*, 30).

Bartholomew (Fife) 1262.
Occ. 5 June 1262 (*Lind.Cart.*,no.142).

Roger (Fife) 1288.
Occ. as vic. of Cupar 8 Sept. 1288 (*St A.Lib.*,340).

John Abbot/Abbas (Fife) 1293 - 1306.
Occ. x Sept. 1293 (*Highland Papers*,ii,128); occ. 11 Nov. 1293 (*SHR*,xvii,158); occ. 16 Apr. 1306 (Palgrave, *Docs.Hist.Scot.*,i,327); see also *St A.dean.christ.Fothrif.*

Brice (Fife) 1350.
Occ. 22 Aug. 1350 (*Camb.Reg.*,77); see also *St A.dean.christ. Fothrif.*

Andrew Ramsay (Fife) 1459.
Occ. 22 Aug. 1459 (St A.Univ.Mun.,SS110.W 3).

David Ramsay (Fife) 1474.
Occ. 18 July 1474 (*C.A.Chrs.*,ii,68); see also *St A.dean.christ. Fothrif.*

James Gudesvane (Fife) 1502.
Occ. 17 Oct. 1502 (*Dunf.Recs.*,no.125).

Walter Small (Fife) 1507.
Occ. 2 Mar. 1507 (St A.Univ.Mun.,SS150/2, fo.56).

Alexander Arbuthnot (Fife) 1523.
Occ. as vic. of Anstruther 7 Jan. 1523 (*St A.Form.*,i,51).

David Guthynd/Guynd (Fife) 1537 - 1540.
Occ. 1537-8 (*MW*,i,229); occ. 1540 (*St A.Rent.*,223).

Henry Guthynd (Fife) 1541 - 1543.
Occ. 1541 and 1543 (ibid.,118,153).

Thomas Wemyss (Fife) 1544.
Occ. 1544 (ibid.,173); occ. 30 Oct. 1544 (St A.Univ.Mun., UY 412,fo.34v); d. 18 Jan. 1546 x 20 May 1549 (*St A.Rent.*,223).

Andrew Oliphant (Fife) 1549.
Occ. 1 Aug. 1549 with Robert Marschell as his substitute (SRO,

St Andrews Tests.,i,fo.2).

Robert Marschell (Fife) 1551.
Occ. 16 Apr. 1551 (SRO, St Andrews Tests.,i,s.d.).

DEANS OF KINGHORN : FOTHRIF

First known dates: Kinghorn   :   1195 x 1198.
                          Fothrif   :   1293.

John (Kinghorn) 1195 x 1198 - 1200 x 1202.
Occ. 1195 x 15 Feb. 1198 (*C.A.Chrs.*,i,7); occ. 1200 x 1202 (*ND*, no. 464).

John Abbot/Abbas (Fothrif) 1293 - 1306.
Occ. x Sept. 1293 (*Highland Papers*,ii,128); occ. 11 Nov. 1293 (*SHR*,xvii,158); occ. 16 Apr. 1306 (Palgrave, *Docs.Hist.Scot.*,i,327); see also *St A.dean.christ. Fife.*

Brice (Fothrif) 1350.
Occ. 22 Aug. 1350 (*Camb.Reg.*,77); see also *St A.dean.christ. Fife.*

David Ramsay (Fothrif) 1474.
Occ. 18 July 1474 (*C.A.Chrs.*,ii,68); see also *St A.dean.christ.Fife.*

Andrew Oliphant (Fothrif) 1539 - 1544.
Occ. 1539 and 1544 (*St A.Rent.*,43,173); see also *St A.dean. christ. Linlithgow.*

DEANS OF GOWRIE : PERTH : PERTH AND GOWRIE

First known dates: Gowrie   :   1165 x 1178.
                   Perth   :   1210 x 1225.
                   Perth and Gowrie :   c. 1283.

Simon (Gowrie)   1165 x 1178 - 1200.
Occ. 1165 x 1178 (*Scone Liber*,no.40) and 17 June 1200 (*St A. Lib.*, 153-4).

William (Perth) 1210 x 1225.
Occ. 1210 x 1225 probably early in period (*Lind.Cart.*,76;cf.78).

Elias (Perth) 1240 *or* 1245.
Occ. 5 May 1240 or May 1245 (*Scone Liber*,no.95; cf. *Lind.Cart.*, 80); occ. as dean and vic. of Perth prob. c.1240 (*Scone Liber*,nos.88-89; cf. *Inchaff.Chrs.*,no.69 for dating).

John (Perth) 1219 x 1257 *or* 1273 x 1274 *or* 1282 x 1296.
    Occ. 1219 x 1257 or 1273 x 1274 or 1282 x 1296 (SRO, Drum-
mond Writs,no.7).

Richard de Fedyn (Perth and Gowrie) c. 1283.
    Occ. c. 1283 (SRO, Maitland Thomson Notebook no.52,rev.1);
see also *St A.dean.christ.Angus* and *St A. dean.christ.Mearns.*
Robert (Gowrie) 1328 x 1329.
    Occ. Aug. 1328 x Feb. 1329 (*ER*,i,139).

Andrew (Gowrie) 1358 (?), 1362.
    Occ. as vic. of Perth 19 Feb. 1362 (*Camb.Reg.*,229); perhaps
same as unnamed vic. of Perth who occ. 14 Mar. 1358 (NLS, Adv.MS
15.1.18,no.79).

William de Donerdy (Gowrie) 1372.
    Occ. 26 Jan. 1372 (NLS, MS Chr.no.713).

Robert Logy (Gowrie) 1465 - 1471.
    Occ. 6 Nov. 1465 and 31 May 1471 (St A.Univ.Mun.,SCB,fos.
16,19v).

James Rattray/Retray (Gowrie) 1508 - 1514.
    Occ. 1 Mar. 1508 (SRO,ADC,xix,fo.228); occ. 14 Aug. 1514
(SRO, Reg.Ho.Chr.no.823).

Simon Young (Gowrie) 1517 - 1543.
    Occ. 15 Oct. 1517 (*RMS*,iii,no.229); occ. 1543 (*St A.Rent.*,153).

John Marschell (Gowrie) 1544 - c.1548.
    Occ. 1544 (ibid.,173); occ. 18 May 1545 (SRO, Erroll,no.442); occ.
c. 1548 (*Prot.Bk.Rollok*,43).

DEANS OF FORFAR : ANGUS

First known dates: Forfar   :   1195 x 1198.
                      Angus   :   1202.

John (Forfar/Angus) 1195 x 1198 - 1207 x 1209.
    Occ. as dean of Forfar 1195 x 15 Feb. 1198 (*C.A.Chrs.*,i,7),1203
x 1209 prob. early in period, and May 1203 x Aug. 1204 (*Arb.Lib.*
,115,118); occ. as dean of Angus Jan. x July 1202 (*C.A.Chrs.*,i,19;
see also *St A.Lib.*, 314); prob. same as 'John the dean' found in a Coupar
Angus context 1207 x 1209 (*C.A.Chrs.*,i,45).

Denis (Dionisius) (Angus/Forfar) 1212 - 1225 x 1239.
    Occ. as dean of Angus Dec. 1211 x Mar. 1213 prob. early 1212
Arb.Lib.,i,106); occ. as dean of Forfar 1211 x 1214 *or* Nov. 1220 x

Feb. 1222 (ibid.,93) and 1225 x 1239 (ibid.,263, 335).

Richard (Angus) 1245 - 1246.
　　　Occ. 1245 and 14 Nov. 1246 (ibid.,200,321).

Thomas de Trevequer (Angus) 1265.
　　　Occ. 11 Nov. 1265 (ibid.,187).

Richard de Fedyn (Angus) c. 1283.
　　　Occ. c. 1283 (SRO, Maitland Thomson Notebook no.52,rev.1);
see also *St A.dean.christ. Perth and Gowrie* and *St A.dean.christ.*
Mearns.

David (Angus) 1310.
　　　Occ. 25 July 1310 (*Arb.Lib.*,i,279); see also *St A.dean.christ.*
Mearns.

Adam (Angus) 1326.
　　　Occ. 18 Oct. 1326 (*C.A.Chrs.*,i,231); see also *St A.dean.christ.*
Mearns.

John Clerk (Angus) 1467.
　　　Occ. 27 Apr. 1467 (*Arb.Lib.*,ii,157).

Henry Barry (Angus) 1488 - 1490.
　　　Occ. 5 July 1488 and 31 May 1490 (SRO, Airlie,47/1).

Patrick Rossy (Angus) 1494.
　　　Occ. 12 Dec. 1494 (Glamis Castle, Strathmore Writs,box 2).

Gilbert Strattoun (Angus) 1497 - 1508.
　　　Occ. 18 Apr. 1497 (SRO, Airlie, 47/1); occ. 15 Sept. 1508
(SRO, Reg.Ho.Chr.no.726).

Andrew Byrkmyr (Angus) 1517 - 1522.
　　　Occ. 21 Dec. 1517 (*Arb.Lib.*,ii,423-4) and 20 May 1522 (SRO,
Airlie, 47/1).

Hugh Lindsay (Angus) 1533 - 1555, 1557 (?)
　　　Occ. 6/7 May 1533 (*Acta Sessionis* (Stair), 29-30; *ADCP*,403);
occ. as vic. of Inchbrayock 1544 (*St A.Rent.,*173); occ. 22 Mar.1555
(SRO, Airlie, 47/1); perhaps still in office 27 Apr.1557 (ibid.).

DEANS OF MEARNS

First known date: c. 1283.

Richard de Fedyn c. 1283.
　　　Occ. c. 1283 (SRO, Maitland Thomson Notebook no.52, rev.1);
see also *St A.dean.christ Perth and Gowrie* and *St A.dean.christ.Angus*

David 1310.
　　　Occ. 25 July 1310 (*Arb.Lib.*,i,279); see also *St A.dean.christ.*
Angus.

Adam 1326.
      Occ. 18 Oct. 1326 (*C.A.Chrs.*,i,231); see also *St A.dean.christ. Angus.*

Hugh Lindsay 1525 - 1544.
      Occ. 23 Sept. 1525 (*RMS*,iii,no.336); occ. as vic. of Inchbrayock 1544 (*St A.Rent.*,173); Inchbrayock lay in Angus deanery; see also *St A.dean.christ.Angus.*

ARCHDEACONRY OF LOTHIAN

DEANS OF LOTHIAN : TYNINGHAME : LISTON

First known dates:	Lothian	:	1150 *or* 1151.
	Tyninghame	:	**x** 1204.
	Liston	:	c. 1235 x 1238.

Aiulf (Lothian) 1150 *or* 1151 - 1186.
      Occ. just as 'the dean' 1150 or 1151 (*Kel.Lib.*,ii,no.445); occ. as dean of Lothian 31 July 1186 (*SAEC*,292).

Andrew (Lothian/Tyninghame) 1194 - 1209 x 1212, 1214 x (?).
      Occ. as dean of Lothian 2 Feb. 1194 (*ND*,no.462), 1209 x 1212 (NLS,Adv.MS 15.1.18,no.14) and 1 July, prob. 1212 (*Dunf.Reg.*,no. 166); prob. same as Andrew who was already parson of Tyninghame 1178 x 1188 (*St A.Lib.*,44-45) and occ. as dean of Tyninghame 1202 x 1214 (*N.B.Chrs.*,9), x 1204 and 1207 x 1209 (*Melr.Lib.*,i,53-54; see also *CPL*,i,28), and 1214 x (?) (ibid.,265).

Radulf Niger (Lothian/Liston) 1225 x 1227 - c. 1235 x 1238.
      Occ. 1211 x 1227, prob. 1225 x 1227 (*Glas.Reg.*,i,86),1227 x 1228 (*Dunf.Reg.*,136; *Holy Lib.*,47), 15 Jan. 1229 (*Glas.Reg.*,i, 125-6) and 1214 x 1240, prob. 1231 x 1240 (*Dryb.Lib.*,77); occ. in a series of documents relating to taxing of vicarages belonging to Holyrood abbey and of churches of Haddington and Linlithgow c. 1235 x 1238, being called once 'R.dean of Liston', but otherwise 'Ranulf dean of Lothian' or 'R.dean of Lothian' (*Holy Lib.*,65; *St A.Lib.*,402-3; cf. 158-9; Stevenson, *Illustrations*, 24-26; cf. *Dunf. Reg.*,64-65 for dating); presumably held ch. of Kirkliston in western part of deanery, but possibly the 'R. dean of Liston' was a successor to Radulf and the same as a Robert de Liston found also at this time among the chaplains of Bp. Malveisin of St Andrews (ibid.).

Baldred (Lothian) 1242 - 1246.
      Occ. 1242 and July 1246 (*St A.Lib.*,390,169).

Note: already by 1245 this deanery was beginning to split into two, for there is mention of a 'chapter of eastern Lothian' which met earlier than a meeting of the whole 'chapter of Lothian' on 5 Aug.1245

(*St A.Lib.*,329-31; cf. *Dryb.Lib.*, 77-78 for a meeting of same 'chapter of Lothian' 1214 x 1240, prob. 1231 x 1240 when Radulf Niger was dean); no dean of the whole area of Lothian is found after July 1246.

DEANS OF LINLITHGOW

First known date: 1246 x 1255 (see note above).

Robert 1255 - 1267.
　　　Occ. 22 Dec. 1255 (*Dunf.Reg.*,120) and 6 Apr. 1267 (*Camb. Reg.*,112).

R. 1307.
　　　Occ. 23 Jan. 1307 (*CDS*,iv,398; cf. *The Stewarts*,ix,325 for dating).

William Forman 1450 - 1464.
　　　Occ. 11 Feb. 1450 (SRO, Clerk of Penicuik,no.422); occ. as Dk. canon 11 May 1456 (*Holy Lib.*, 172); prob. still in office 5 June 1464 (*HMC* 44, *Drumlanrig*,i,38).

John Williamson 1523 - 1539.
　　　Occ. 29/30 1523 (*Prot.Bk.Foular 1514-1528*,419; *RMS*,iii,no. 238); occ. 1539 (*St A.Rent.*, 43,90).

George Cok 1541 - 1543.
　　　Occ.1541 and 1543 (ibid.,118,153); see also *St A.dean.christ. Haddington.*

Andrew Oliphant 1544 - 1545.
　　　Occ. 1544 (ibid.,173) and 28 Aug. 1545 (*Prot.Bk. Johnsoun*,no. 343); see also *St A.dean. christ. Fothrif.*

Hugh Curry 1550 - 1555.
　　　Occ. 7 June 1550 (SRO, Stirling Comm. Act Bk.,fo.11); occ. 4 June 1555 (*Prot.Bk. Johnsoun*,no.375).

DEANS OF HADDINGTON

First known date: 1246 x 1291 (see note above).

Robert x 1291.
　　　Occ. as vic. of Musselburgh x 1291 (SRO, Crown Office Writs, no. 7).

Henry late 13c.
　　　Occ. as vic. of Musselburgh in late 13c. (ibid.,no.8).

Michael 1307.
　　　Occ. 26 Jan. 1307 (*The Stewarts*,ix,326).

William de Knollis 1443.

    Occ. 20/28 Feb. 1443 (*Yester Writs*, 52; NLS, MS Chr.no.4775) and 27 June 1443 (*HMC 26, 12th R.*,viii,176).

John Balcasky 1456.

    Occ. 10/14 Sept. 1456 (SRO, Morton, nos.,114-16).

William Foular 1465 - 1471.

    Occ. 12 Nov. 1465 and 18 Mar. 1471 (*Yester Writs,* 63,71).

James Douglas 1479.

    Occ. as *Corstorphine prov.* 1 Sept. 1479 (*Mort.Reg.*,ii,239).

John Williamson (Valzamson) 1493.

    Occ. 4 Aug. 1493 (SRO, Prot. Bk. Peter Marche, fo.19v).

Andrew Brownhill 1517.

    Occ. Apr. 1517 (SRO, Reg.Ho.Chr.no.847).

Henry Lawson 1520 - 1521.

    Occ. 4 Aug. 1520 (SRO, GD 1/39/1/19) and 8 Oct. 1521 (*RMS.* ii,no.1962).

Thomas Boswell 1539 - 1540.

    Occ. 1539 and 1540 (*St A.Rent.*,43-44, 90).

George Cok 1541 - 1543.

    Occ. 1541 and 1543 (ibid.,118,153); see also *St A.dean.christ. Linlithgow.*

Andrew Myll 1544.

    Occ. 1544 (ibid.,173).

Robert Simson (Symson) 1549 - 1561.

    Occ. 21 Oct. 1549 (SRO, Justiciary Court Recs.,1548-9/1551, o.13v); occ. 14 Mar. 1561 (*Yester Writs,*198).

DEANS OF FOGO : STICHILL : MERSE : NENTHORN

First known dates: Fogo   : c. 1150 x 1162.
                           Stichill : c. 1170.
                           Merse : 1220.
                           Nenthorn : 1248 x 1258.

Samel (Fogo) c. 1150 x 1162.

    Occ. c. 1150 x 1162 (*Kel.Lib.*,i,no.138; cf. no.176); occ. 6 Jan. 161 x 13 Sept. 1162 (*ND,*no. 451).

Ocius 1165 x 1167.

    Occ. as 'the dean' 1165 x 1167 (*ND,*no.459).

Geoffrey (Stichill) c. 1170, 1165 x 1173.

    Occ. as 'the dean' c. 1170 (*Dryb.Lib.*,167-8) and as dean of Stichill 165 x 1178, prob. 1165 x 1173 (*Cold.Cart.*,46; v.inf.).

Patrick 1173.
Occ. as 'the dean' 1173 (*Melr.Lib.*,ii,409), 1173 x 1174 (ibid., i,42) and 1172 x 1177 (*ND*,no.454).

John (Fogo) 1194 - c. 1220 (?).
Occ. 2 Feb. 1194 (*ND*,no.462), 1203 x 1209 (*Cold.Cart.*,11,47), 21 May 1203 (*Kel.Lib.*,i,112) and c. 1220 (?) (ibid.,ii,292).

William (Merse) 1220.
Occ. 8 June 1220 (*Dryb.Lib.*,168).

D. (Merse) 1240 x 1245.
Occ. 1233 x 1245, prob. 1240 x 1245 (*ND*,no. 255).

Hugh (Nenthorn) 1248 x 1258.
Occ. 1248 x 1258, perhaps c. 1250 (*Kel.Lib.*,i,237).

William (Merse) 1268 - 1289.
Occ. as 'W.vic. of Swinton' 9 Dec. 1268 (ibid.,i,236) and as 'W.' 25 Feb. 1283 (Durham, Dean and Chapter MSS, Misc.Chr.no.1206; cf. Stevenson & Wood, *Seals*,i,99); occ. as 'William' 29 Nov. 1289 (Durham, Dean and Chapter MSS, Misc.Chr.no. 1049).

Note: a named dean of Merse occ. 5 Apr. 1379 (ibid.,no.663 - but writing has not been deciphered).

Richard de Spot (Merse) 1419 - 1423.
Occ. 9 June 1419 and 1 Apr. 1423 (*ND*,nos.499,500).

Richard Knoll (Merse) 1442.
Occ. 18/22 Jan. 1442 (*ND*,no. 501; see original i.e. Durham, Dean and Chapter MSS, Misc.Chr.no.1313 for date).

William Bertreme (Merse) 1456.
Occ. as vic. of Swinton 12/17 Sept. 1456 (ibid.,no.1315;cf.*ND*, no.505).

Edward Ramsay (Merse) 1516.
Occ. 3 Apr. 1516 (SRO, Swinton,no.80; see also *St A.Form.*,i,84 89).

James Schoriswood (Merse) 1539 - 1541.
Occ. 1539 and 1540 (*St A.Rent.*,54,118).

John Somervell (Merse) 1543.
D. in office Lent 1543 (ibid.,153-4,173).

William Cranston (Merse) 1543 - 1559.
Occ. 1543 and 1544 (ibid.,153,173); occ. 16 Jan. 1559 (SRO, Misc.Ecclesiastical Docs.,no.19).

OFFICIALS

OFFICIALS WITH GENERAL AUTHORITY

First known date: 1194.

Ranulf de Wat 1194 - 1198 x 1199.
    Occ. 2 Feb. 1194 (*ND*,no.462) and 24 Aug. 1198 x 17 Mar. 1199 (*Arb.Lib.*,i,103); succ. to *St A.archd.* by 6 June 1199.

Laurence de Thornton (Thorenton) 1203 x 1204 - 1224.
    Occ. 18 Aug. 1204 (*ND*,no.473), having taken office since 21 May 1203 (*Kel.Lib.*,i,112); occ. 1224 (*St A.Lib.*,327) and may have remained in office until death of Bp. Malveisin in 1238, but found after 1224 only as *St A.archd.*

Walter de Mortimer 1240 - 1242.
    Occ. 29 Mar. 1240 (*Dunf.Reg.*,no.221) and 1242 (*St A.Lib.*,390).

Andrew de Aberdeen 1245 - 1248.
    Occ. 5 Aug. 1245 (ibid.,330) and 2 June 1248 (*Lind.Cart.*,70).

Adam de Makerstoun (Malcaruiston) 1259 - 1260.
    Occ. 20 Dec. 1259 (ibid.,132) and 30 May 1260 (SRO,Transcripts of Misc.Chrs.,s.d. c. 1290).

Gilbert de Heris 1262.
    Occ. 5 June 1262 (*Lind.Cart.*,189).

Simon Walens 1267.
    Occ. 29 Jan. 1267 (*St A.Lib.*,311).

John de Musselburgh 1273 x 1274 - 1274 x 1278.
    Occ. 18 July 1274 (*Dunf.Reg.*,no. 207), having prob. taken office since cons. of Bp. Wishart 15 Oct. 1273; prob. res. before 21 May 1278 when occ. as a king's clerk (ibid.,no.87).

Baldred Bisset 1282 - 1289.
    Occ. 12 Oct. 1282 (*Camb.Reg.*,no.3); occ. 5 Jan. 1289 (Durham, Dean and Chapter MSS, Misc.Chr.no.3543).

Alpin de Strathearn 1289 x 1293, 1292.
    Occ. 1285 x 1293, prob. 1289 x 1293 (*Moncreiffs*,ii,641); occ. 1 Aug. 1292 (NLS,MS Accession 3958); see *St A.archd.* for surname.

Robert de Montfort 1293 - 1295.
    Occ. 30 Nov. 1293 (*Newb.Reg.*,no.172); occ. 13 Feb. 1295 (NLS, Adv.MS 15.1.18,no.8).

Nicholas de Balmyle 1297 x 1298.
    Occ. during vacancy in see Aug. 1297 x June 1298 (*Chron. Bower*,i,361-2).

William de Eaglesham (Eglisham) 1310 - 1324.
    Occ. 21 Feb. 1310 (*Lind.Lib.*, 12-13; *Abbotsford Misc.*,i,56); occ. 13 Mar. 1324 (*Arb.Lib.*,i,309); see also *St A.archd. Lothian.*

Adam de Moray 1327 - 1327 x 1328.
 Occ. 11/16 Aug. 1327 (*Holy Lib.*,77-79); cons. *B.bp.* 31 Oct. 1328.

Robert Oliveri 1330.
 Occ. 30 Nov. 1330 (*ND*,no.646).

Henry Stupy 1357 - 1360 *or* 1361.
 Occ. 18 Sept. 1357 (*CDS*,iii,300); occ. 20 Jan. 1360 or 1361 (Vatican Archives, Instr.Misc.no.2201).

Robert de Montrose 1386.
 In office when el. St A.prior 1386, after 2 Mar. (*Chron.Bower*, i,371).

John de Lichton 1387.
 Occ. 19 July 1387 (*Yester Writs*,32-33).

Thomas de Carnis 1407 - 1411.
 Occ. 19 Feb. 1407 and 11 Feb. 1411 (*St A.Lib.*,6-11,11-14).

John de Scheves 1413 - 1456.
 Occ. 22 Dec. 1413 (ibid.,15-19); occ. 2 May 1456 (SRO, St Andrews Chrs.,no.38).

Thomas Luthirdale (Luderdale) 1458 - 1467.
 Occ. 4 Apr. 1458 (R.G. Cant, *College of St Salvator*,80); occ. 29 Oct. 1467 (SRO, St Andrews Chrs.,no.48).

David Kay (Ray) 1469 - 1471.
 As 'Ray' had succ. Luthirdale before 4 Feb. 1469 (*CPL*,xii,652); occ. 25 Feb. 1469 (*Laing Chrs.*,no.40, where name is defaced in MS and 'Rede' is suggested by editor); occ. 8 June 1470 (Fraser, *Wemyss*,ii,96) and 12 Aug. 1471 (*HMC* 7, *8th R.*,i,307).

John Lock (Loch,Lok) 1475 - 1478.
 Occ. 18 Nov. 1475 (*Midl.Chrs.*,71); occ. 18 Nov. 1478 (*PSAS.* xli,316); d. before 10 May 1479 (see *St A. St Salvator's coll.prov.*).

David Meldrum 1479 - 1503.
 Occ. 4 Nov. 1479 (*St A.Acta*, 207); occ. 16 May 1503 (SRO, St Andrews Chrs.,no.172).

Hugh Spens 1505 - 1516.
 Occ. 3 Nov. 1505 and 14 Oct. 1516 (*St A.Acta*,279,318-19).

John Weddell 1517 - 1523.
 Occ. 28 Feb./2 Mar. 1517 (St A.Univ.Mun., UY305/1,p.65; *St A.Acta*,321; see *St A.Form.*.i.31-32 for letter of appointment); occ. 3 Nov. 1523 (*St A.Acta*,343).

James Simson 1524 - 1529 x 1530.
 Occ. 19 Nov. 1524 (St A.Univ.Mun.,REP,fo.21v); occ. 23 Sept. 1529 (SRO, Crail Chrs.,no.114); moved to *St A.Offic.Lothian* 26 Nov. 1529 x 24 Feb. 1530).

John Weddell 1530 - 1533.
    Occ. 18 June 1530 (St A.Univ.Mun.,UY305/1,p.87); occ. 7 May 1533 (*ADCP*,403); moved to *St A.offic.Lothian* Aug. x Nov. 1533.

John Spens 1533 (?), 1535 - 1539.
    Prob. occ. 5 Dec. 1533 (see *St A.comm.*); occ. 17 Feb. 1535 (*ADCP*,434); occ. 30 Apr 1539 (St A. Univ. Mun., UY 305/2,p.9).

Martin Balfour 1540 - 1545.
    Occ. 2 Mar. 1540 (ibid.,p.13); occ. 23 Dec. 1545 (SRO, Sent.Offic. St A.,fo.131).

Note: office is vacant 19 Jan. – 1 Sept. 1546 (ibid.,fos.132,149).

John Spittal 1546 - 1553.
    Occ. 27 Nov. 1546 (ibid.,fo.150) and 26 Jan. 1553 (St A.Univ. Mun.,UY 305/2,p.46).

William Cranston 1553 - 1558.
    Occ. 10 Mar. 1553 (SRO, Sent.Offic.St A.,fo.272) and 21 Aug. 1558 (St A.Univ.Mun.,SS150/2,fo.131v).

OFFICIALS WITH LIMITED AUTHORITY

OFFICIALS OF LOTHIAN

First known date: 1392.

Thomas de Strathmiglo (Stramiglot) 1392 - 1409.
    Occ. 20 Oct. 1392 (SRO, Morton Chrs.,no.68); occ. 5 Aug.1409 (*Holy Lib.*,133-4).

John Cameron 1420 - 1422 x 1427.
    Occ. 25 Aug. 1420 (*CSSR*,i,227); occ. 10 Dec. 1422 (Fraser, *Douglas*,ii,53); became king's chancellor 14 Dec. 1425 x 1 Sept.1426 (*HBC*,175) and cons. *G.bp.* 12 Jan. 1427.

John Laverok 1427.
    Occ. 27 Sept. and 6 Oct. 1427 (*CSSR*,ii,173; *HMC* 26, *12th R.*, viii,122-3).

John de Methven 1435 - 1436 x 1437 (?).
    Occ. 5 Sept. 1435 (*Holy Lib.*,129); occ. 23 Mar. 1436 (*ACSB*, 340); perhaps res. on becoming *Lincluden prov.* before 30 Nov. 1437; a William de Carnis occ. as commissary in the official's absence 17 Oct. 1437 (*Frasers of Philorth*,ii,213).

Nicholas de Otterburn 1440 - 1448.
    Occ. 26 May 1440 (*RMS*,ii,no.266) and 31 Dec. 1448 (Teulet, *Inventaire*,45); found in royal service from 7 May 1448 x 10 Dec. 1449 onwards as king's secretary and then clerk register until 8 Mar. 1460 x 28 Mar. 1461 (*HBC*,186,189), and so may not have retained this office.

John Otterburn 1464 - 1477.
      Occ. 5 June 1464 (*HMC* 44, *Drumlanrig*,i,38); occ. 17 May 1477 (*Mort.Reg.*,ii,234-5); see also *St A.comm.Lothian;* cf. *G.offic.*

William Elphinstone junior 1478 - 1483.
      Occ. 1 June 1478 (*ADA*,58); occ. as *R.bp.elect* 5 Mar. 1483 (Fraser, *Melville*,iii,49); see also *St A.comm.*; perhaps dem. on trans. to *Ab.bp.* 19 Mar. 1483.

William Wawane   1492 - 1515.
John Whitelaw   1495.
      Wawane occ. 6 Feb. 1492 (*ADA*, 161), 25 Aug. 1495 (*ADC*, i,385), 12 Dec. 1496 (*Arb.Lib.*,ii,299) and 26 July 1515 (*RMS*,iii,no. 111); d. c. May 1516 (SRO, Sent.Offic. Laud.,fos.3-4).
      Whitelaw occ. 13 Nov. 1495 (*ADC*,i,429); see also *St A.comm.*

Note: office is vacant c. May - Aug. 1516 (SRO, Sent. Offic.Laud., fos.4-13).

James Heriot 1516 - 1521 x 1522.
      Occ. 8 x 26 Aug. 1516 (ibid.,fos.13-14) and 16 Apr. 1521 (SRO, Calendar of Chrs.,no.909); d. before 18 Feb. 1522 (SRO, Sent.Offic. Laud.,fo.96).

William Preston 1522 - 1524.
      Occ. before 18 Feb. 1522 (ibid.,fos.95-96) and 9 Aug. 1524 (ibid.,fo.125).

Thomas Coutts 1524 - 1529 x 1530.
      Occ. 9 Aug. x 14 Dec. 1524 (ibid.,fos.125-6); d. after 16 Nov. 1529 and before 24 Feb. 1530 (ibid.,fos.167-9).

James Simson 1530 - 1533.
      Occ. 24 Feb. 1530 (ibid.,fo.169); d. 18 Jan. x 11 Mar.1533 (ibid.,fos.108-9).

Note: office is vacant c.Mar. - Aug. 1533 (ibid.,fos.109-14).

John Weddell 1533 - 1540.
      Occ. 29 Aug. x 26 Nov. 1533 (ibid.,fos.214-15; *St A.Offic.*,44) and 9 Aug. 1540 (SRO, Sent.Offic.Laud.,fo.297).

Abraham Crichton 1540 - 1553.
      Occ. 9 Aug. x 13 Oct. 1540 (ibid.,fos.298-9) and 10 Mar. 1553 (SRO, Sent.Offic.St A.,fo.272).

James Balfour 1553 - 1557.
      Occ. 15 July 1553 (SRO, Act.Offic.Laud.,fo.306) and 18 Dec. 1557 (SRO, Acts and Decreets,xxix,fo.57).

OFFICIALS OF ARCHDEACON OF ST ANDREWS

First known date: 1245 - 6.

Adam/Andrew Simplex 1245 - 1246.

'Adam Simplex' occ. as 'socius' of this archd. 26 Apr. 1245 (*St A.Lib.*,308); prob. same as the 'Andrew' who occ. as official of archd. specifically 14 Nov. 1246 (*Arb.Lib.*,i,321-2 - this name is prob. an error for 'Adam'; in same source Andrew de Aberdeen official of bp. of St A. is also mentioned).

Note: evidence for continuance of this office (though without names of the officials) is found in mid-13th century (*Oxford Formularies* (Oxford Historical Society),ii,482), on a seal used 28 Mar. 1284 (BM, Add M S 33245,fo.154). and on seal used 8 Dec. 1320 (*Arb.Lib.*,i,305).

Stephen de St Andrews (Sancto Andrea) 1336.

Occ. 24/25 Apr. 1336 (*Camb.Reg.*,131).

OFFICIALS OF ARCHDEACON OF LOTHIAN

First known date: 1219 x 1234.

Alexander de St Martin 1219 x 1234.

Occ. 1219 x 1234, perhaps near 1234 as official of Lothian (*Newb. Reg.*,55).

Adam de Tyninghame (Tynigham) 1268, 1267 x 1271.

Occ. as Adam vic. of Stirling 9 Dec. 1268 (*Kel.Lib.*,i,236); prob. same as 'A. de Tynigham official of Lothian' 1267 x 1271 (*St A.Lib.*, 377).

Nicholas de Lochmaben 1283.

Occ. 25 Feb. 1283 (Durham, Dean and Chapter MSS, Misc.Chr.no. 1206; prob. same source as mentioned under date '1282' in Dalrymple, *Collections*,292); cf. St Andrews below.

Nicholas de St Andrews (Sancto Andrea) 1273 x 1285 - 1293.

Occ. 1273 x 1285 (*ND*,no.418) and 30 Nov. 1293 (*Newb.Reg.*, 138); perhaps same as Lochmaben, or his successor.

Note: unnamed official found 12 June 1310 (Durham, Dean and Chapter MSS, Misc.Chr.no.135).

Thomas Extoun 1316 x 1327.

Occ. 16 July 1316 x 11 Aug. 1327 (*Midl.Chrs.*,42).

Note: unnamed official issued a document under his seal 8 Aug. 1372 (Durham, Dean and Chapter MSS, Misc.Chr.no.1164).

OFFICIALS OF PECULIAR JURISDICTIONS

OFFICIALS OF THE CHAPEL ROYAL AT STIRLING

First known date: 1511.

See under that heading.

COMMISSARIES

COMMISSARIES WITH GENERAL AUTHORITY

COMMISSARIES OF ST ANDREWS

First known date: 1447.

Henry Dryden 1447.
    Occ. (CB in absence of official) 9 Aug. 1447 (SRO, Soc.Antiquarie 'Cartae Variae', p.222).

David Kay 1471.
    Occ. (CB) 4 Mar. 1471 (*Yester Writs*,no.161); see also *St A.offic.*

William Elphinstone junior 1483.
    Occ. (CGB) 5 Mar. 1483, when also *St A.offic. Lothian* and *R.bp.-elect* (Fraser, *Melville*,iii,49).

John Whitelaw 1489.
    Occ. (CB) 21 Aug. 1489 (*HMC 4, 5th R.*,633); see also *St A.offic. Lothian.*

John Young 1495 - 1510.
    Occ. (CO) 29 July and 13 Aug. 1495 (SRO, Makgill,no.38; SRO, St Andrews Chrs.,no.139); occ. (C) 4 Nov. 1510 (*St A.Acta*,298).

Robert Davidson 1513 - 1516.
    Occ. (CO) 3 Nov. 1513 and 16 May 1516 (*St A.Acta*,306,317).

John Weddell   1516 x 1517.
Robert Schanwell   1517 - 1520.
    Weddell appointed (CB) by Abp. Forman while also *St A.offic.* 1516 x 1521 (*St A.Form.*,i,32-33), presumably before Schanwell, but perhaps along with him.
    Schanwell occ. (CO) 3 Nov. 1517 (*St A.Acta*,323) and (GCO) 8 Aug. 1520 (*Camb.Reg.*,281).

Martin Balfour 1528.
    Occ. (CO) 8 May 1528 (*St A.Acta.*,357-8).

Martin Balfour   1530.
John Spens   1530.
    Balfour occ. (CGO) with Spens 22 Feb. 1530 (SRO, Erroll Chrs., no.354).
    Spens occ. (CGO) with Balfour 22 Feb. 1530 (ibid.).

Martin Balfour 1533.
    Occ. (C) 29 Oct. 1533 (St A.Univ.Mun.,SS 150/2,fo.95v).

*Note:*John Spens occ. as 'principal commissary of St Andrews' 5 Dec. 1533 (St A.Univ.Mun.,UY 305/1,p.94); possibly he did hold office then with this unusual title; but it is more likely that he had already become *St A.offic.* and that the source is in error in describing a man who had been commissary and had now become principal official.

Walter Fethy 1542.
>   Occ. (CGO) 5 Jan. 1542 (*St A.Offic.*, 81).

John Brown 1545.
>   Occ. (CO) 26 Jan. 1545 (ibid.,91).

Andrew Trail 1545.
>   Occ. (CO) 11 Dec. 1545 (ibid.,93).

Robert McNair (Maknair)	1546.
James Rolland	1546.
Walter Fethy	1546.
Andrew Trail	1546.
Patrick Scott	1546.

>   McNair occ. (CG) 19 Jan. 1546 (*St A.Offic.*,150), 1 Sept. 1546 (SRO, Sent.Offic. St A.,fo.149) and 25 Oct. 1546 (SRO, Lord Forbes Papers, no.1696).
>   Rolland occ. (CG with McNair) 19 Jan. 1546 (*St A.Offic.*,150) and 11 May 1546 (SRO, Sent.Offic. St A.,fo.145).
>   Fethy occ. (C depute under McNair and Rolland) 11 Aug. 1546 (ibid.,fo.146)
>   Trail occ. (C depute under McNair and Rolland) 10 Feb. 1546 (*St A.Offic.*, 95) and 11 Aug. 1546 (SRO, Sent. Offic. St A.,fo.146).
>   Scott occ. (C depute under McNair) 21 July 1546 (ibid.,f.145).

Walter Fethy 1546.
>   Occ. (CGO) 27 Nov. 1546 (ibid.,fo.150).

David Guthrie O.S.A. 1548 - 1549.
>   Occ. (CGO) 28 Sept. 1548 (*St A.Offic.*,152) and 26 Jan. 1549 (SRO, Sent.Offic. St A.,fo.180).

Andrew Trail 1550.
>   Occ. (CGO) 21 June 1550 (*St A.Offic.*,104).

Walter Fethy 1550.
>   Occ. (CGO) 30 Aug. 1550 (ibid.,106).

Patrick Scott 1551.
>   Occ. (CGO) 21 Apr. 1551 (SRO, Sent.Offic. St A.,fo.236) and 4 June 1551 (*St A.Offic.*,111).

Andrew Trail 1552.
>   Occ. (CGO) 15 July 1552 (SRO,Sent.Offic.St A.,fo.261).

James Rolland	1553.
James Balfour	1553.

>   Rolland occ. (GGO) 12 Jan. 1553 (ibid.,fo.272).
>   Balfour occ. (CGO) 12 Jan. 1553 (ibid.); see *St A.offic.Lothian.*

James Rolland 1554, 1559.
    Occ. (CO) 13 Jan. 1554 (SRO, Fife Sheriff Ct.Bk.1575-6,fo.154);
occ. (CGO) 27 Apr. 1559 (St A.Univ.Mun.,SS 500.2).

William Skene 1565 - 1582.
    Occ. (C) under new organisation 3 Nov. 1565 (*St A.Acta,*424);
occ. 28 Mar. 1572 when conf. in privileges of predecessors (*RSS,*vi,no.
1532); d. 18 Sept. 1582 (D. Hay Fleming, *St Andrews Cathedral
Museum,*144).

COMMISSARIES WITH LIMITED AUTHORITY

COMMISSARIES OF LOTHIAN

First known date: 1456.

John de Otterburn 1456 - 1457.
    Occ. (CB) 11 May 1456 (*Holy Lib.,*165) and 10 Oct. 1457 (SRO,
Cardross, no.341); see also *St A.offic. Lothian.*

Robert Halkerston 1482.
    Occ. (CO) 22 Mar. 1482 (*St Nich.Cart.,*ii,131).

Richard Robertson (Roberti) 1482.
    Occ. (CO) 28 Sept. 1482 (Fraser, *Eglinton,*ii,5).

William Foular 1487.
    Occ. (CO) 24 Mar. 1487 (*Yester Writs,* 84); occ. (C) 9 Oct. 1487
(*HMC* 8, *9th R.,*ii,188; Fraser, *Elphinstone,*ii,257).

George Newton   1508 - 1516.
Patrick Craufurd   1513.
    Newton occ. (CO) 11 Apr. 1508 (SRO, Elibank,20/3); occ.(CO)
9 May 1516 (SRO, Sent.Offic. Laud.,fo.4).
    Crauford occ. (CO) 23 May 1513 (*Yester Writs,*115).

Robert Forman   1516.
Matthew Ker   1516.
    Forman occ. (CG) when *G.dean* 9 May x 19 July 1516 and 8 x 25
Aug. 1516 (SRO, Sent.Offic. Laud.,fos.4-13) i.e. during vacancy in office
of official of Lothian.
    Ker occ. (C depute under Forman) 19 July 1516 (ibid.,fo.5).

James Heriot c.1516.
    Occ. (CB) c.1516 (*St A.Form.,*i,61); see also *St A.offic.Lothian.*

Matthew Ker 1516.
    Occ. (CO) 26 Aug. 1516 (SRO, Sent.Offic. Laud.,fos.13-14).

Richard Cok   c. 1521.
John Wood   c. 1521.
John Letham (Lethane)   c. 1521.
James Hunter   c. 1521.

Cok occ. (CO) c. 1521 (ibid.,fo.87; cf.fo.94 of x 18 Feb. 1522).
Wood occ. (CO) c. 1521 (ibid.,fo.90).
Letham occ. (CO) c. 1521 (ibid.,fo.92).
Hunter occ. (CO) c. 1521 (*St A.Offic.*,18).

James Hunter 1522.
    Occ. (CO) 27 Mar. x 29 Apr. 1522 (SRO, Sent.Offic. Laud.,fo.99).

John Letham (Lethane) 1529.
    Occ. (CO) 26 Nov. 1529 (*St A.Offic.*, 39).

Thomas Melville 1531.
William Johnston 1531.
    Melville occ. (C) with Johnston 1531 (*Prot.Bk.Johnsoun*,no.36); occ. (CO) 7 Dec. 1531 (Fraser, *Keir*,337).
    Johnston occ. (C) with Melville 1531 (v.sup.).

Thomas Melville 1533.
    Occ. (CG) 11 Mar. 1533 (*St A.Offic.*,130); occ. (CG) 17 Mar.1533 (SRO, Morton,box 27); occ. (CG) 29 Aug. 1533 (SRO, Sent.Offic.Laud., fo.214) i.e. during vacancy in office of official of Lothian.

Thomas Melville 1534 - 1538.
John Williamson 1534 - 1540.
James Murray 1540.
    Melville occ. (CO) 22 Aug. 1534 (ibid.,fo.222), 20 May 1536 and 29 Nov. 1538 (*St A.Offic.*,63,133).
    Williamson occ. (CO) 20 Feb. 1534 (SRO, Sent.Offic.Laud.,fo.217), 11 Sept. 1537 (*St A.Offic.*,62) and 9 Aug. 1540 (SRO, Sent.Offic. Laud., fo.298).
    Murray occ. (CO) 9 Aug. 1540 (ibid.,fo.298).

COMMISSARIES OF STIRLING.

First known date: 1545 x 1548.

John Craig 1545 - 1552.
    Occ. (C depute) 2 Feb. 1545 (SRO, Comm.Edin.Decreets,i,fo. 101); occ. (C) 6 Mar. and 21 May 1548 (SRO, MS Act Bk.); prob. still in office (C) 9 Nov. 1552 (ibid.,end).

Alexander Chalmer 1569.
    Occ. (C) 16 Feb. 1569 (*RMS*,iv,no.1840); escheated by 11 Nov. 1569 for holding on to his commissary's register (v.inf.).

Humphrey Cunningham 1569.
    Occ. (C) 11 Nov. 1569 (*RSS*,vi,no.722).

COMMISSARIES OF PECULIAR JURISDICTIONS

COMMISSARIES OF THE CHAPEL ROYAL AT STIRLING

First known date: 1530.

See under that heading.

COMMISSARIES OF CURRIE (Archdeacon of Lothian)

First known date: 1543.

John Williamson 1543.
Occ. (C of jurisdiction of Currie) 16 Nov. 1543 (SRO, Sent.Offic. St A.,fo.57).

THE CHAPEL ROYAL

CHAPTER OF THE CHAPEL ROYAL

EARLY DEANS OF THE CHAPEL ROYAL

There were king's chapels/royal chapels/chapels royal (the terminology varies, but these phrases appear to be equivalents) of a collegiate character at *St Mary on the Rock, St Andrews* certainly from 1386 (and perhaps from before 1286 x 1296), at *Coldingham* 1473 - 1484 x 1485, and at *Restalrig* perhaps from its foundation in 1487 and certainly in the 1490s for a few years. These communities were headed by a provost, a dean, and a dean respectively (see under Heads of Collegiate Churches). The character of the office or benefice found with the title 'dean of the chapel royal' in the later fifteenth century cannot at present be exactly determined; but the evidence reviewed below suggests that it formed a prebend within the oldest-established of these chapels royal i.e. St Mary, St A. certainly from 1472 and prob. from as early as 1456 until the erection of the new collegiate church as the Chapel Royal at Stirling in 1501. This dean was subordinate to the provost of St Mary, St A. The list of provosts forms a separate succession in the same period, and in 1501 it seemed suitable to link this provostry (and *not* the old subordinate deanery) with the new and elaborately endowed benefice of the *deanery of the Chapel Royal at Stirling* for a few years (v.inf.).

Alan Cant 1456.
     Occ. as dean of the chapel royal 13 Aug. 1456 (*St A.Acta*,114); it is in a St A. context and he held *St A.chanc.* at same time; d. perhaps by 3 Oct. 1457 (ibid.,121) and certainly by 3 Nov. 1459 (Reg.Supp.,525,fo.192); as dean he prob. held a preb. in (or at least revenues derived from) St Mary, St A. as a successor certainly did in 1470s (v.inf.).

Note: an unnamed 'dean of the chapel royal of St Mary, St Andrews' found in poss. 10 Mar. 1472 (*CPL*,xiii,212); this title is clear evidence that by this date this deanery was in the old-established chapel royal at St Andrews; the duties then attached to it, however, laid on the dean responsibility for hearing royal confessions himself or deputing the task to one or two priests from St Mary's (ibid.); this is the earliest known evidence for a link between this office and duties at the royal court; in contemporary England the office of 'dean of the royal chapel' (which had no regular ben. attached to it) implied supervision of the clergy who served the king's chapel at court (*Liber Regie Capelle*, ed. W. Ullmann (Henry Bradshaw Society, 1961), 3-4, 7-9); in Scotland a similar body of clergy can prob. be traced back at least to 19 Nov. 1467, when there is mention of **John Spalding** (*B.dean* c.1456 - 1487) as 'master of the king's

chapel royal', being at the same time king's counsellor and confessor (*CPL*,xii,278-9); this title of 'master' was then a new one for Spalding, who as late as 10 Mar. 1466 had been described just as member of the household and chaplain of the young King James III (ibid.,xii,455; cf. xi, 686 for a predecessor as royal confessor in 1463); prob. the title implies duties similar to those of the 'dean of the royal chapel' in England; and certainly from 1473 onwards traces can be found in Scottish records which are not available earlier of an itinerant group of clergy serving the king's private chapel wherever he went (*TA*,i and ii *ad indices*); no connection is known between these clergy and any of the endowed chapels royal of the last thirty years of the fifteenth century; but at some stage the cleric in charge of them comes to be styled a 'dean' rather than the 'master', a change which had certainly come about by the 1490s in the last years before the drafting of the collegiate constitution of 1501 at Stirling (*Hist.Chapel Royal*,2); perhaps it had come about earlier when and because John Hume or James Oliphant assumed responsibilities for these clergy serving the chapel royal at court (v.inf.).

John Hume 1472 (?), 1473 - 1484 x 1485.

Occ. as dean of the chapel royal 11 Mar. 1473 (Fraser, *Lennox*, ii,93); had held a right in priory of Coldingham since 10 Dec. 1464 (*CPL*,xii,232-4; *ACSB*,148), and presumably had supported the king's request that this priory should be suppressed on his death or dem. and its revenues all allocated to the chapel royal of St Mary, St A., which the pope approved 6 Apr. 1472 (*CPL*,xiii,14; cf. *SHR*,xlvi,20); this suggests that he was prob. already dean and a prebend-holder in St Mary's as early as 6 Apr. 1472 and therefore prob. as early as 10 Mar. 1472 - with the implication of duties at the royal court attached to his ben. (v.sup.); but James III then changed his policy and appears to have supported Patrick Hume his rival as prior of Coldingham in a revised scheme for allocating only part of the suppressed priory's revenues to St Mary, St A., while the other part was to support another chapel royal at Coldingham, which pope approved 3 Apr. 1473 (see *Coldingham dean.*); occ. still as dean of the chapel royal 7 Mar. 1477, 6 Mar. 1478 (*RMS*,ii,nos.1413,1373) and 27 Oct. 1483 (*HMC* 26, *12th R.*,viii,163); said on 28 Apr. 1487 to have shared in the benefits of the papal mand. of 3 Apr. 1473 in that as dean of the chapel royal he had for many years (*pluribus annis*) taken his part with the other prebendaries of St Mary's in choir and chapter (*CPL*,xiv,47); prob. still in royal favour until after 12 Sept. 1484, since he obtained royal letters of recommendation to Pope Innocent VIII after that date to go to the curia; but presumably he forfeited his position as dean of the chapel royal before or soon after 26 May 1485 on misusing these letters in the matter of *Coldingham dean.* (q.v.) before then.

James Oliphant 1489 (?), 1495 - 1501.

Occ. in royal circle 17 Apr. 1489 and 5 Dec. 1491 with ecclesiastical duties (*TA*,i,108, 183); may possibly have already become dean of the chapel royal, but is not certainly found as such until 11

Apr. 1495 (*Prot.Bk.Young*,no.790); this may still refer to the preb. in St
Mary, St A. (v.sup.); occ. again as dean of the chapel royal 1 Dec. 1500
(*ADC*,ii,452); prob. now identifiable with the dean in charge of the clergy
at Stirling Castle mentioned in the act of 1501 creating subsequent
collegiate body (*Hist.Chapel Royal*, 2); from some date Aug. 1495 x
28 Jan. 1499 held also *Edin.Trin.prov.*, a ben. in royal patronage; still
alive 24 Mar. 1501 (*TA*,ii,70); presumably dem. when new collegiate
constitution for Chapel Royal was put into effect 6 Sept. 1501 and the
St Mary, St A.prov. became dean (v.inf.); his successor in *Edin.Trin.prov.*
was pres. 1 Sept. 1502.

PROVOST/DEANS/BISHOPS OF THE CHAPEL ROYAL
AT STIRLING

First known dates: provost: 1499 x 1501.
                     dean   : 1501.
                     bishop : 1505.
                     dean   : 1612.
                     bishop : 1615

David Trail 1499 x 1501.
      Occ. as 'provost of the new college in the castle of Stirling' 10
July 1499 x 14 July 1501 (*ER*,xi,314; cf. 318); prob. a caretaker
dignitary in office alongside or in succession to Dean James Oliphant
(v.sup.) while constitution for the new collegiate body was being
worked out.

Note: collegiate constitution authorised by pope 2 May 1501 was put
into effect 6 Sept. 1501 (*Hist.Chapel Royal*,1-18); deanery was to
be held by same person as held also (but separately) *St Mary, St. A.
prov.*

Deans of the Chapel Royal

James Allardice 1501 - 1504.
      Already in poss. of *St Mary, St A.prov.* before 6 Sept. 1501, and
so presumably obtained this ben. on that date (v.sup.); occ. 9 Aug.
and 28 Oct. 1502 (*RSS*,i,nos. 863,878); presumably lost this ben.
following papal mand. of 3 July 1504 (v.inf.); but remained in poss. of
St Mary, St A.prov.

Note: pope ordered separation of this ben. from that of *St Mary, St A.
prov.* 3 July 1504; deanery was henceforth to be held by successive
bishops of Galloway (*Hist.Chapel Royal*, 82-83).

George Vaus 1504 - 1508.
      Presumably held this ben as *Ga.bp.* as from 3 July 1504 (v.sup.)
until death in Jan. 1508; is found with joint title of bp. and dean e.g.
15 Apr. and 6 Aug. 1506, 25 Oct. 1507 (*RMS*,ii,no.2956; *RSS*,i,
nos. 1318, 1564); but is also found in same period as 'bishop of

Galloway and of the Chapel Royal' e.g. 30 Aug. 1505, 23 Mar. and
12 Oct. 1506, 15 Feb. 1507 (*RMS*,ii,no.2877; *RSS*,i,nos.1240,1341,
1431); king asked for papal approval for this change of title 3 Oct. 1506
and 6 Apr. 1507 (*James IV Letters,* 39-40, 68-69), and appears to
assume agreement to the change in a discussion of the vacancy after
the death of Vaus 1 Mar. 1508 (ibid.,98-99); formal grant of the new
title is dated 8 Sept. 1508 (*Hist.Chapel Royal*, 84-89).

Note: James IV in 1511 asked pope to declare that the authority of
the bp. of the Chapel Royal covered not only the collegiate ch.
in Stirling Castle, but also all the royal palaces throughout Scotland
(ibid.,209), and this was apparently put into effect (ibid.,241-2).

Bishops of the Chapel Royal

For details see *Ga.bp.*:

James Betoun	1508 - 1509.
David Arnot	1508 - 1526.
Henry Wemyss	1526 - 1541.
Andrew Dury	1541 - 1558.
Alexander Gordon	1559 - 1575.
Archibald Crauford	1564.
John Gordon	1568.
John Gordon	1575 - 1586
Roger Gordon	1578 - 1579 x 1587.
George Gordon	1586 - 1588.
Gavin Hamilton (?)	1605 - 1612.
John Gordon (?)	1610.

Note: it is doubtful whether either Hamilton or Gordon had any access
to the Chapel Royal revenues (*Hist.Chapel Royal*, cii - cxii).

Dean of the Chapel Royal

William Birnie 1612 - 1614 (?)
      Crown pres. to revived independent deanery of the Chapel Royal
20 Sept. 1612 (*Hist.Chapel Royal*,cxiii-iv); said to have res. before
16 June 1614 (ibid.,cxv, no source quoted).

Bishops of the Chapel Royal

William Couper 1615 - 1619.
      Succ. to deanery when it was re-annexed to *Ga.bp.* 2 June 1615
(ibid.,cxvi-vii); though apparently meant to hold this ben. just as 'dean'
he had by 2 Apr. 1617 revived title of 'bp of Galloway and of the
Chapel Royal of Stirling' (ibid.,cxxxvi-cxl); d. 15 Feb. 1619 (see *Ga.bp.*)

Deans of the Chapel Royal

Andrew Lamb 1619 - 1621.

Trs. to *Ga.bp.* 4 Aug. 1619; res. deanery on or before 16 July 1621 (v.inf.).

Adam Bellenden 1621 - 1635.

As *Db.bp.* succ. to this deanery when it was detached from *Ga.bp.* and annexed to *Db.bp.* 16 July 1621 (*APS*,iv,649; *Hist.Chapel Royal*, cxl - cxlii); trs. to *Ab.bp.* 19 May 1635.

James Wedderburn 1635 - 1638.

Appointment as *Db.bp.* and as this dean expected 10 Sept. 1635 (ibid.,cxci); occ. as dean 22 Sept. 1635 (*RPC*, 2nd series, vi,110); crown appointment as dean 14 Oct. 1635 (*RMS*,ix,no.412); in poss. when given crown pres. to *Db.bp.* 11 Feb 1636 (ibid.,no.480); depriv. 13 Dec. 1638 and d. 23 Sept. 1639 (see *Db.bp.*).

PRECENTORS/CHANTERS OF THE CHAPEL ROYAL AT STIRLING

First known date: erected 16 Apr. 1502 (*Hist.Chapel Royal*,27-29).

John Elwald 1502.

Crown pres. 9 Aug. 1502 (*RSS*,i,no.863).

Alexander Shaw 1508 - 1514.

Occ. 5 Jan. 1508 (SRO, Household Papers, no.1); occ. 17 Nov.1514 (SRO, Stair, box 79,s.d.); perhaps d. before 9 Dec. 1522 (see *Ga. archd.*).

John Cantuly   1529 - 1538.
John Scrymgeour   1529.

Cantuly occ. 18 Oct. 1529 (*RSS*,ii,no.371) and 14 Dec. 1538 (SRO, Prot.Bk. Edward Diksoun (NP 1/5B), p.57).

Scrymgeour gets crown pres. in exp. 18 Oct. 1529 (*RSS*,ii,no.371).

John Fethy 1545 - 1566.

Occ. 12 Jan. 1545 (*RSS*,iii,no.1026); occ. 20 Mar. 1566 (*RSS*,v,no. 2691); occ. as just usufructuary 12 Aug. 1566 (SRO, Reg.Deeds,vii,fo. 318).

George Gray 1565 - 1566.

Crown pres. in exp. 6 May 1565 (*RSS*,v,no.2042); occ. as titular 12 Aug. 1566 (SRO, Reg.Deeds,vii,fo.318).

Thomas Hudson (?) 1586.

Appointed as 'musitian master' of the Chapel Royal 5 June 1586, conf. in parliament of 1587 (*APS*,iii,489; cf. 563-4).

William Scott 1603 - 1619 x 1624.

Occ. as chanter 14 Sept. 1603 (*Hist.Chapel Royal*,cxxxv); still in poss. though absent 15 Feb. 1619 x (ibid.,cxxxi); depriv. on or before 7 July 1624 (v.inf.).

Robert Wynram   1624 - 1624 x 1628.

Crown pres. as 'musitianer' with revenues of chanter on depriv. of

Scott 7 July 1624 (*Hist.Chapel Royal*,clii); depriv. on or before 17 Mar. 1628 (v.inf.).

Edward Kellie   1628 - 1634.
　　Crown pres. as 'musitian' with revenues of chanter on depriv. of Wynram 17 Mar. 1628 (ibid.,clx - clxi); prob. still in poss. 12 Jan. 1634 (ibid.,clxxxvi, where date is wrongly given as 1634/5).

Edward Miller 1634.
　　Appointed 'musician' in place of Kellie 15 Feb. 1634 (Reg.Pres., vii,fo.24).

CHANCELLORS OF THE CHAPEL ROYAL AT STIRLING

First known date: 1512.

James Merchiston 1512 - 1514 x 1515.
　　Occ. 17 Aug. 1512 (*James IV Letters*,no.476); still alive 2 Oct. 1514 (see *Corstorphine prov.*); d. before 5 June 1515 (v.inf.).

James Inglis 1515 - 1529.
　　Crown pres. on death of Merchiston 5 June 1515 (*RSS*,i,no.2573); occ. 15 Dec. 1529 (ibid.,ii,no.455).

Alexander Wood   1529 - 1531.
　　Crown pres. in exp. 20 Mar. and 15 Dec. 1519 (*RSS*,i,no.4119; ii,no.455); occ. in between as if in poss. (*RMS*,iii,no.782); occ. 10 Aug. 1531 (*RMS*,iii,no.1093).

Michael Dysart 1551 - 1551 x 1552.
　　Occ. 16 Oct. 1551 (*RSS*,iv,no.1390); res. before 6 July 1552 (v.inf.).

Robert Lamont (Lawmond/Lawmont)   1552 - 1555 x 1558.
Michael Dysart   1554 - 1558.
　　Lamont gets crown pres. on res. of Dysart 6 July 1552 (*RSS*,iv, no. 1645); occ. 19 Apr. 1555 (ibid.,no.2961); perhaps res. on getting *Kilmun prov.* Mar. x Aug. 1557; d. before 9 Dec. 1558 (v.inf.).
　　Dysart gets crown nom. to pope for prov. 5 July 1554 (*RSS*, iv,no.2772); occ. 7 Dec. 1557 (*Prot.Bk.Grote*,no.124); gets crown pres. following Lamont's death 9 Dec. 1558 (*RSS*,v,no.527).

John Carswell 1572.
　　Held it at death 10 July x 20 Sept. 1572 (v.inf.; see *I.bp.* for date of death).

Thomas Buchanan   1572.
Archibald Sinclair   1573.
　　Buchanan gets crown pres. on death of Carswell 4 Sept. 1572 (*RSS*,vi,no.1716); res. right to annexed ch. before 14 Oct. 1573 (ibid., no.2153; cf. Cowan, *Parishes*,186).
　　Sinclair gets crown pres. on Carswell's death 18 Mar. 1573

(*RSS*,vi,no.1905).

TREASURERS OF THE CHAPEL ROYAL AT STIRLING

First known date: erected 4 June 1504 (*Hist.Chapel Royal*,53-57).

John Crauford 1506 - 1507 x 1509.
Crown pres. 6 Aug. 1506 (*RSS*,i,no.1318); occ. 14 Apr. 1507 (*Prot.Bk. Young*,no 1730); d. before 31 Dec. 1509 (v.inf.).

John Major/Mare 1509 - 1525.
Andrew Dury 1520.
Major gets crown pres. on death of Crauford 31 Dec. 1509 (*RSS*,i,no.1977); occ. 1 June 1520 (ibid.,no.3067) and 3 Nov.1525 (*St A.Acta*, 351).
Dury gets crown pres. in exp. 1 June 1520 (*RSS*,i,no.3067).

Robert Galbraith 1528 - 1532.
Occ. 19 May 1528 (*RMS*,iii,no.605); occ. 6 Jan. 1532 still (*RSS*, ii,no.1104).

Walter Stewart 1531 - 1541.
Crown pres. in exp. 16 June 1531 and again 6 Jan. 1532 (*RSS*, ii,nos. 940,1104); occ. 5 Feb. 1541 (*RMS*,iii,no.2278); perhaps d. before 27 Feb. 1548, by which time he had dem. *R.prec.*

William Myrton/Morton 1554 - 1558 x 1564.
Occ. as Myrton 31 Jan. 1554 (*Yester Writs*,no.645) and 16 Dec. 1558 (SRO, Reg.Deeds,iii,fo.129v); if same as Morton, had d. before 13 Mar. 1564 (v.inf.).

George Ross 1564 - 1565 x 1584.
Crown pres. on death of William Morton 13 Mar. 1564 (*RSS*, v,no.1635); occ. 24 Oct. 1565 (ibid.,no.2388); d. or res. before 11 Sept. 1584 (v.inf.).

Matthew Ross 1584 - 1584 x 1587.
Crown pres. on death or dem. of George Ross 11 Sept. 1584 (Reg.Pres.,ii,109); d. before 8 May 1587 (v.inf.).

Robert Hudson 1587 - 1587 x 1597.
Crown pres. on death of Matthew Ross 8 May 1587 (ibid.,170); d. before 16 Aug. 1597 (v.inf.).

William Hudson 1597.
Crown pres. on death of Hudson 16 Aug. 1597 (*RSS*,1xix,fo. 164).

Thomas Gray 1603 - 1619 x .
Occ. 14 Sept. 1603 (*Hist.Chapel Royal*,cxxxv) and 15 Feb. 1619 x (ibid.,cxxxi).

James Law (?) 1623.

Said to occ. 17 May and 14 Aug. 1623 (ibid.,cxlviii, 100-1, but is not in fact specifically called treasurer in the two sources quoted).

SUBDEANS OF THE CHAPEL ROYAL AT STIRLING

First known date: erected 2 May/6 Sept. 1501 (*Hist.Chapel Royal*, 1-18).

David Abercrombie 1503 - c. 1517 x 1531.
Occ. 10 July 1503 (*TA*,ii,379) and 5 Mar. 1512 (*Hist.Chapel Royal*, 90); still alive c. 1517 (see *Dk.subd.*); d. before 29 Nov. 1531 (v.inf.).

Robert Hamilton 1531 - 1534 x 1535.
Crown pres. on death of Abercrombie 29 Nov. 1531 (*RSS*,ii,no. 1066); occ. 24 Mar. 1534 (*Prot.Bk. Johnsoun*,no.71); res. before 23 June 1535 (v.inf.).

George Clapperton 1535 - 1574.
David Methven 1557.
Clapperton gets crown pres. on res. of Hamilton 23 June 1535 (*RSS*,ii,no.1703); new prov. on res. of Methven 22 Mar. 1557 (PRO 31/9 - 33/343); said to hold *Chapel Royal chanc.* 1558 (*OPS*,ii,211), but this is prob. an error; occ. 13 Mar. 1564 (*RSS*,v,no.1635); d. Apr. 1574 (Edin.Tests.).
Methven had prov., but now res. right to Clapperton without having had poss. and with no mention of pension 22 Mar. 1557 (PRO 31/9 - 33/343; cf. *RSS*,vi,no.2468).

John Duncanson 1574 - 1601.
Crown pres. on death of Clapperton and depriv. of Methven 8 May 1574 (*RSS*,vi,no.2468); d. 4 Oct. 1601 (*Hist.Chapel Royal.*, xcv, no source quoted).

Andrew Couper 1617 - 1623.
Prob. in poss 2 Apr. 1617 (*Hist.Chapel Royal*,cxxxix); occ. 15 Feb. 1619 x (ibid.,cxxxi); prob. in poss. 5 Aug. 1623 (ibid.,cl).

Bernard Lindsay x 1629.
Held it at death before 5 Mar. 1629 (v.inf.).

Andrew Ramsay 1629 - 1649.
Crown pres. on death of Lindsay 5 Mar. 1629 (RSS,ci,fo.199); occ. 16 Mar. 1649 (*APS*,vi,pt.2,720).

SUCCENTORS/SUBCHANTERS OF THE CHAPEL ROYAL AT STIRLING

First known date: 1506.

Robert Wemyss 1506.

Crown pres. 12 Oct. 1506 (*RSS*,i,no.1341).

John Fethy (?) 1563.
Occ. 28 Feb. 1563 (*RSS*,v,no.1268), but this is prob. an error for *Chapel Royal prec.*

ARCHDEACONS OF THE CHAPEL ROYAL AT STIRLING

First known date: 1507 x 1512.

James Silver (?) 1507.
Granted pension by king to reside in this collegiate ch. until he gets the archd. which is to be erected within it 8 Oct. 1507 (*RSS*,i,no. 1560).

Ninian Spottiswood 1512 - 1537 x 1543.
Occ. 5 Mar. 1512 (*Hist.Chapel Royal*, 90-93); occ. 1 Dec. 1537 (ibid.,89-90); d. before 7 Oct. 1543 (v.inf.).

William Hamilton 1543 - 1554.
Crown pres. on death of Spottiswood 7 Oct. 1543 (*RSS*,iii,no. 498); occ. 19 Feb. 1554 (SRO, Acts and Decreets,x,fo.106).

OFFICIALS

OFFICIALS OF THE CHAPEL ROYAL AT STIRLING

First known date: 25 Sept. 1511 (*Hist.Chapel Royal*,91).

David Abercrombie 1512.
Occ. as offic. of Galloway and of the Chapel Royal at Stirling 5 Mar. 1512 (*Hist.Chapel Royal*,90); see also *Chapel Royal subd.*

COMMISSARIES

COMMISSARIES OF THE CHAPEL ROYAL AT STIRLING

First known date: 1530.

John Letham 1530.
Occ. (C) 8 Jan. 1530 (PRO 31/9 - 32/215-22); cf. *Dk.comm. South of Forth.*

Thomas Erskine 1549 - 1550.
Occ. (C) 21 Jan. 1549 and 3 July 1550 (SRO, MS Act Bk. fragment).

HEADS OF COLLEGIATE CHURCHES

PRIORS/PROVOSTS OF ABERNETHY

First known date: 1276 x 1345, prob. 1328 x 1345 (*MRHS*, 74,174; see also Reg.Supp.,616,fo.132v for statement in 1467 that this collegiate church was founded by earls of Angus, which would have been after their marriage to the Abernethy heiress 1328 x - see *SP*, i,169-170).

Laurence Bell 1351 - c. 1380.
Occ. as provost 17 Mar. 1351 (*Lind.Lib.*,45); occ. as prior c. 1380 (Fraser, *Douglas,* iii,397).

Alexander Bell 1394.
In poss. as prior 23 Oct. 1394 (*CPP*,i,579).

John de Dalrymple (Dalrumpill, Dalywipil) 1395 - 1431.
Occ. as prior 2 Feb. 1395 (*RMS,* v,no.964) and in poss. as prior 29 Sept. 1431 (Reg.Supp.,269,fo.292v).

James de Dalrymple 1445.
Occ. as provost 13 Mar. 1445 (Fraser, *Wemyss,*ii,69).

John Fraser/Frissell 1476 - 1489 x 1499.
Occ. as provost 23 Feb. 1476 (*RMS*,ii,no.1538) and 3 Mar.1489 (*Prot.Bk. Young,* no. 175); succ. to *R.bp.* 1497-9; but perhaps res. 13 Nov. 1487 on prov. *Restalrig dean.*

George Clerk 1503 - 1510.
Occ. as provost 21 Feb. 1503 (*Prot.Bk.Foular 1500-3*,no.205) and 12 Oct. 1510 (Fraser, *Douglas*,iii,198n).

Thomas Boyd 1528 - 1550.
Occ. as provost 14 Jan. 1528 (*RMS*,vi,no.28); granted procurator for his res. 24 July 1550 (*Prot.Bk. Gaw*,no.72).

William Shaw 1550 - 1575.
Occ. as provost 13 Nov. 1550 (SRO, Dundas of Dundas,no.348) and 25 Jan. 1575 (*HMC 34, 14th R.,* iii,89).

John Provand 1575 - 1593.
Occ. as provost 6 June 1575 and 20 May 1593 (*RMS*,iv,no.2538; vi,no.29).

PROVOSTS OF BIGGAR

First known date: founded 16 Jan. 1546 (*MRHS*,174).

John Stevenson (Stevinstoune) 1546 x 1547 - 1563 x 1564.
Occ. 29 Mar. 1547 (*IR*,x,313), having prob. been pres. on foundation; occ. 14 May 1556 (*RSS*,iv,no.3240), and prob. retained it until death 11 Dec. 1563 x 1 Feb. 1564 (see *G.prec.*).

William Fleming 1574 - 1630 x 1631.
Pres. by patron 1 Jan. 1574 (*Wigtown Charter Chest,* 70-71); occ. 31 Jan. 1630 (SRO, Part.Reg.Sasines Lanark,iiiB,fo.111); d. by 31 Mar. 1631 (v.inf.).

Patrick Fleming 1631.
Pres. by patron on death of William Fleming 31 Mar. 1631 (SRO, Wigtown Chrs.,no.616).

PROVOSTS OF BOTHANS

First known date: erected 22 Apr. 1421 (*MRHS,*175).

John Richardson 1421 - 1432.
Prob. pres. at time of foundation, to which he consented as rector of the church (*Yester Writs,*no.54); occ. 13 Dec. 1432 (ibid., no.59).

Stephen Ker 1440 - 1449 x 1454.
In poss. 6 Aug. 1440 (Reg.Supp.,366,fo.77); occ. 23 Feb. 1449 (*RMS,*ii,no.332); d. before 28 May 1454 (v.inf.).

David Ramsay 1454 - 1454 x 1455.
Ord. coll. on death of Ker 28 May 1454 (*Yester Writs,*no.110); occ. 29 July 1454 (ibid.,no.114); d. before 7 Aug. 1455 (ibid.,no.116).

Fergus Macdowell   1457 - 1470.
Occ. 22 Apr. 1457 (*St A.Acta,* 119) and 20 Mar. 1470 (*ACSB,* 159); d. by 2 Nov. 1470 (v,inf.).

Gilbert Macdowell   1470.
Andrew Hay   1471 - 1494.
Macdowell prov. on death of Fergus Macdowell 2 Nov. 1470 (Reg.Supp.,664,fo.10v).
Hay coll. by ord. on death of Fergus Macdowell 18 Mar. 1471 (*Yester Writs,* no.162); after about a year of poss. on pres. of patron, gets new prov. 26 June 1472 (Reg.Supp.,681, fo.36); occ. 14 July 1494 (*Yester Writs,* no.235).

Thomas Young 1496 - 1505.
Occ. 6 Aug. 1496 (ibid.,no.239a) and 15 Mar. 1505 (*Prot.Bk. Simon,*ii, 82-83).

Robert Walterstoun   1513 - 1542.
Thomas Hay   1538 - 1543 x 1547.
Walterstoun occ. 22 May 1513 (*Yester Writs,* no.354); appoints proctors to res. in favour of Hay, reserving fruits 18 Jan. 1538 (SRO, Prot. Bk. Edward Diksoun, p.19); occ. as usufructuary 12 Dec. 1542 (*Yester Writs,* no. 602).
Hay expects poss. 18 Jan. 1538 (v.sup.); prov. on res. of Walterstoun who is to retain fruits 24 Dec. 1538 (*Yester Writs,*no. 541); occ. 19 Feb. 1539 (ibid.,no.542); described as future possessor 12 Dec. 1542 (ibid.,no.602); occ. 4 Aug. 1543 (ibid.,no.613); d. by

24 Sept. 1547 (v.inf.).

Thomas Hay 1547 - 1557 x 1558.
    As nephew of previous man of same name occ. following his uncle's death 24 Sept. 1547 (*RSS*,iii,no.2449); occ. 30 Jan. 1557 (*Yester Writs*, no.673); d. before 3 May 1558 (v.inf.).

Andrew Hay 1558.
    Pres. on death of the younger Thomas Hay 3 May 1558 (ibid., no.682; cf. nos. 684,685).

John Colquhoun 1558 - 1566.
    Occ. 26 Oct. 1558 (SRO, Peebles Burgh Prot. Bk.,1549-65,fo. 224); occ. 3 Aug. 1566 (*RSS*,v,no.3275).

William Dobsone x 1566.
    Held it at death before 21 Oct. 1566 (v.inf.).

Gilbert Brown 1566 - 1567.
    Ord. coll. on Dobsone's death 21 Oct. 1566 (*Yester Writs*,no. 741); occ. 13 May 1567 (ibid.,no.751).

Walter Hay 1580 - 1608 x 1609.
    Occ. 22 Aug. 1580 (ibid.,no.825); occ. 16 Jan. 1608 (Stevenson & Wood, *Seals*,ii,409); d. before 1 Feb. 1609 (v.inf.).

George Butler 1609 - 1628.
    Pres. on Hay's death 1 Feb. 1609 (*Yester Writs*,no.1065); **prob.** still in poss. 1628 (SRO, Yester Writs, no. 1459).

Alexander Hay 1630.
    Instituted 25 June 1630 following pres. by patron (ibid.,no.1370).

PROVOSTS OF BOTHWELL

First known date: erected 21 Feb. 1398 (*MRHS*,175).

Thomas de Barry 1398 x 1400.
    Said to have been first provost (*Chron.Bower*,ii,406); held it sometime before his death, which is datable July 1404 x Mar. 1405 (*Glas.Reg.*,i,293-4; *CPP*,i, 626,633), and presumably before 21 May 1400 (v.inf.).

John de Merton   1400 - 1423.
Thomas Trail   (?)   1409 - 1410.
Robert de Moffat (?)   1409.
John Elwald   1420.
    Merton occ. 21 May 1400 (Fraser, *Douglas*, iii, 401-2); occ. 30 Apr. 1405 (*St A.Cop.*,56); perhaps dispossessed for a time (v.inf.); in poss. 6 Nov. 1409 (Reg.Av.,334,fos. 494-494v) and when erection of provostry was conf. by Benedict XIII 18 May 1410 (SRO, Transcripts from Vatican,ii,no.46); in poss. 26 Jan. 1420 (*CSSR*,i,154-5) and prob.

until death Mar. x Dec. 1423 (*St A.Cop.*,451; *CPL*,vii,354).

Trail said to be holding rectory (not provostry) 6 Apr. 1409
(*CPP*,i,594-5); prob. did have poss. for a time (*TSES*,iii,115); appealed
to Alexander V against Moffat July 1409 x May 1410 (SRO, Transcripts
from Vatican,ii,no.45).

Moffat prov. to rectory (not provostry) by Benedict XIII at
request of the patron 6 Apr. 1409 (*CPP*,i,594-5) prob. unfruitfully.

Elwald gets *com.priv.* against Merton 26 Jan. 1420 (*CSSR*,i,154-5).

William de Foulis   1424 - 1433.
John de Ralston (Raulston)   (?)   1424 x 1430.

Foulis in poss. 28 Mar. 1424 (*CSSR*,ii,55); occ. 30 Jan. 1433
(*HMC* 21, *Hamilton*,i,18); res. on exch. with Newton for *St A.archd.*
before 12 Sept. 1433.

Ralston perhaps occ. 1424 x 1430 (*St A.Lib.*, 407 - but text is
doubtful; cf. *R.archd.*).

George de Newton 1433 - 1438 x 1441 (or 1443).

In poss. after getting poss. on exch. with Foulis through ord.
12 Sept. 1433 (Reg.Supp.,288,fo.231; 289,fo.246); occ. 8 May
1438 (*St A.Cop.*,162); said to have died before 6 May 1441 (*CPL*,
ix,413); but perhaps did not die until about four months before 27
Nov. 1443 (v.inf.).

Gavin Hamilton 1443 - 1462 x 1465, 1468 (?).

Got it on Newton's death and has held it some four months
when granted new prov. 27 Nov. 1443 (Reg.Supp.,393,fo.119); in
poss. 6 Apr. 1462 (*CPL*,xii,153); said to have d. before 9 June 1465
(ibid.,413); but occ. 23 Aug. 1468 (*RMS*,ii,no.985 - where source is
prob. not trustworthy).

Patrick Leche (Leich) 1468.

Occ. 26 Jan. 1468 (*Glas.Mun.*,ii,72); did not die until 8 Mar.
1493 x 16 May 1494 (see *G. offic.*); but not known whether he kept
this ben. so long.

David Arnot 1499 - 1500:

Occ. 20 Sept. 1499 (*RSS*,i,no.417) and 19 Mar. 1500 (*HMC*
44, *Drumlanrig*,i,54).

James Betoun 1502 - 1503.

Occ. 25 Nov. 1502 (Fraser, *Douglas*,iii,179) and 18 Nov.1503
(*Prot.Bk. Young*, no.135).

James Kincragy 1505 - 1507.

Occ. 12 Nov. 1505 (*RMS*,ii,no.2894); occ. 19 July 1506 (NLS,
Adv. MS 15.1.18,no.26); prob. res. on pres to *Ab.dean.* 24 May 1507.

William Elphinstone 1514 - 1514 x 1515.

Occ. 9 Nov. 1514 (SRO, Prot.Bk. Thomas Strathauchin,i,23v);
d. by 9 Sept. 1515 (*A.B.III.*,iii,465-6).

Alexander Hepburn 1525 - 1534.

Occ. 14 Apr. 1525 (*RMS*,iii,no.300); res. on pension on or

before 14 Aug. 1534 (PRO 31/9 - 32/279; cf. 283).

William Chirnside 1534 - 1552.

Promises annates and gets prov. 14 Aug. 1534 (PRO 31/9 - 32/279); res. on exch. with Hamilton 3 Sept. 1552 (v.inf.).

John Hamilton   1552 - 1594.
David Cunningham   1572.

Hamilton pres. on exch. with Chirnside 3 Sept. 1552 (*RSS*,iv,no. 1683); occ. 8 Mar. 1567 (ibid.,v,no.3319); decree of barratry given against him July 1568 (ibid.,vi,no.1988); and considered to have forfeited his ben. by 12 Mar. 1572 (v.inf:); but must have regained his right, for was said to have d. in poss. 19 Oct. 1594 (Edin.Tests.), or perhaps to have dem. just before then (cf.inf.).

Cunningham pres. on forfeiture of Hamilton 12 Mar. 1572 (*RSS*,, vi,no.1522).

Gavin Hamilton 1594 - 1604.

Crown pres. on dem. of Hamilton 2 Oct. 1594 (RSS,lxxvi,fo,224); occ. 3 May/8 Oct. 1604 (*RMS*,ix,no.420); perhaps same as prov. to *Ga. bp* Feb./Mar. 1605.

Robert Boyd 1621 - 1625.

Occ. 5 Dec. 1621 (*RMS*,ix,no.420); occ. 28 Sept./3 Nov. 1625 (*RMS*,viii,no.1532).

DEANS OF COLDINGHAM

First known date: erected 7 Apr. 1473 as a chapel royal with the king as patron (*Vet.Mon.*,472-3); suppressed 12 Sept. 1484 x 26 May 1485 (v.inf.); re-erected 28 Apr. 1487 ineffectively (v.inf.).

Patrick Hume 1473 - 1473 x 1478.

Had had claim to priory of Coldingham in commend since 6 Aug. 1461 (*CPL*,xi,425-6); prob. not recognised as such by James III when papal approval was given to suppression of this priory and allocation of all its revenues to *St Mary,St.A.* 6 Apr. 1472 (*CPL*,xiii, 14; but see *ACSB*,172); see *Chapel Royal early deans;* but had supplanted his rival for the priory (John Hume) in the king's favour by 3 Apr. 1473, when papal approval was given to a revised plan submitted by James III, whereby with approval of Patrick abp. of St Andrews Patrick was to res. his right to this priory, it was to be suppressed and its revenues applied only in part to *St Mary, St A.*, the other part now being applied to the erection of an additional chapel royal at Coldingham as a collegiate church with dean and prebendaries, and with prov. of Patrick Hume as first dean (*Vet.Mon.*,472-3; *CPL*,xiii,19); relevant letters released at curia 18 June 1473 (PRO 31/9 - 29/253); John Hume protected his position by securing Patrick's res. of his right to the priory and his own surrog. and new prov. as prior 2 Aug. 1473 (Reg.Supp., 694,fo.129v); but Patrick is found in poss. as 'dean of the chapel of the

king of Scots' (presumably Coldingham) 11 Oct. 1473 (ibid.,697,fo. 173), so taking the view that the erection of 3 Apr. 1473 had been effective; though John won lit. in the curia with Patrick over their respective rights to the priory and was in actual poss. of the fruits, James III supported Patrick's contention that the new collegiate ch. had been erected, and forced John to admit this (CPL,xiv,45-46); since Patrick at the same time accepted a pension on the Coldingham fruits from John as part of this settlement, he presumably res. his right as dean in John's favour sometime before his death 5 Oct. 1474 x 17 Oct. 1478 (see G.archd.Teviotdale).

John Hume 1473 x 1478 - 1484 x 1485.

Had prov. to this deanery in addition to the deanery of the chapel royal which he already held (see Chapel Royal early deans), presumably on res. of Patrick Hume 1473 x 1478 (CPL,xiv,47); he accepted the reallocation of the priory's revenues of 3 Apr. 1473 'for several years' as far as the share of St Mary,StA. was concerned; but as dean of Coldingham he did not press on with the erection of prebends there additional to the deanery in terms of the scheme of 3 Apr. 1473 (ibid.,46-47); occ. as 'dominus de Coldingham' 7 Mar. 1477 (RMS,ii, no.1413), a description which perhaps rightly describes his actual control there, but avoids the specific title of prior or dean; an act of presentation by him to one of Coldingham's churches was conf. by pope 21 Feb. 1484 (CPL,xiii,192-3), when his title of 'dean of the chapel of the king of Scots' appears to refer to this dignity (cf. Patrick Hume above, 11 Oct. 1473); went to Pope Innocent VIII (i.e. after 12 Sept. 1484) with royal letters of recommendation, on the understanding that he was to arrange for the erection of the additional prebends at Coldingham; but in fact misused his royal letters to obtain a revocation of the proceedings under mand. of 3 Apr. 1473; was later said to have maintained a minimum of one monk all along at Coldingham, and he obtained from Pope Innocent conf. of his rights as prior (and no longer dean) consequent to this suppression of the short-lived and only partially-erected collegiate church there (CPL,xiv,46-47); the letters restoring the priory must have been issued before 26 May 1485, when parliament decided that the pope should be requested to overturn this act of revocation and to order that the original scheme of 3 Apr. 1473 be carried right through by the erection of prebends at Coldingham (APS,ii,171); the Scottish embassy was delayed, but the pope eventually agreed to this 28 Apr. 1487 and ordered the full erection of a collegiate ch. at Coldingham (CPL,xiv, 47-48; cf. ND,no.445); in parliament of 13 Oct. 1487 it was declared treason to try to upset this erection at Coldingham (APS,ii, 179); but John Hume was presumably still active in working for restoration of the priory again, and in parliament of 11/29 Jan. 1488 some temporal persons (presumably his Hume relatives) were summoned to appear for trial on 1/5 May 1488 on charges of offences against the treason declaration of 13 Oct. 1487 (ibid.,182,184); but the Humes came into political power with the death of James III 11 June 1488, and John Hume appears soon after officially described as prior (not dean) of Coldingham (ibid.,215; ADA,143); nothing more is known of the scheme to restore and complete the collegiate ch. there,

and it was as a monastic not a secular foundation that this institution
survived into the sixteenth century (cf. *MRHS*,50; *SHR*,xlvi, 14,n.5;
24,n.3).

PROVOSTS OF CORSTORPHINE

First known date: 1429 x 1436 (*MRHS*,175; cf. inf.).

Nicholas Bannachtin 1429 x 1436 - 1473.
    Said to have become provost on erection of this church 1429
(*Midl.Chrs.*,1xx, quoting inscription on his monument); occ. 15 Sept.
1436 (ibid.,1xx); occ. 20 Sept. 1473 (*RMS*,ii,no.1320).

James Douglas 1479 - 1480.
    Occ. 1 Sept. 1479 (*Mort.Reg.*,ii,239) and 31 Oct. 1480 (*RMS*,
ii,no.1455).

Alexander Crag 1503.
    Occ. 16 Dec. 1503 (SRO, ADC,xv,fo.142).

Robert Forrester 1507.
    Occ. 12 Apr. 1507 (*RMS*,ii,no.3090).

James Merchiston 1511 - 1514 x 1515.
    Occ. 9 Aug. 1511 (*Prot.Bk. Simon*,ii,419); occ. 2 Oct. 1514
(*Prot.Bk. Foular 1514-28*,no.10); d. before 5 June 1515 (see *Chapel
Royal chanc.*).

Robert Cairncross 1527 - 1528.
    Invested with this ben. 5 Aug. 1527 (*PSAS*,ii,361); presumably
same as ordered to be admitted as canon regular 6 Nov. 1528 (Dowden,
Bishops,225).

Alexander Scott   1529 - 1544.
James Scott   1532 - 1564 x 1565.
    Alexander Scott occ. 6 Apr. 1529 (SRO,ADC,xl,fo.8); res. but
promised annates on retaining fruits 26 June 1532 (PRO 31/9-32/256-7);
occ. 4 Oct. 1540 (*RMS*,iii,no.2280); d. 14 May 1544 (SRO, ADC & S,
xxii,fo.45).
    James Scott promised annates and gets prov. but no fruits 26
June 1532 (PRO 31/9 - 32/257); occ. 30 Aug. 1535 (*RMS*,ii,no. 1887),
26 Oct. 1542 (SRO, Acts and Decreets, i,fo.120) and 10 June 1564
(SRO, Comm. Edin. Decreets, i.fo.52); d. before 24 Apr. 1565 (*RSS*,
v, no.2034).

William Scott 1564 x 1568.
    Said to have succ. his uncle James Scott (Scott, *Fasti*,viii,3).

Robert Douglas 1568 - 1585.
    Occ. 28 June 1568 (*RSS*,vi,no.327); d. 23 Jan. 1585 (Edin.Tests.).

Alexander McGill 1585 - 1628.
    Pres. by patron 23 Jan. 1585 and still in poss. 6 Mar. 1628

(*Midl.Chrs.*,pp.lxvii,lxxiv, citing SRO, Acts and Decreets, vol.412,fo. 145).

Florence Gairdner 1632 - 1659.
Occ. 25 Feb. 1632 and 21 June 1659 (SRO, Part.Reg.Sasines Edinburgh, xvii,fo.318, and 2nd series, viii,fo.169).

PROVOSTS OF CRAIL

First known date: 20 June 1517 (*MRHS*,176).

Alexander Dunbar 1517 - 1525.
In poss. of vic. of Crail on erection of provostry 20 June 1517 (*Crail Register*,55-60); res. on exch. with Myrton for vic. of Tarves 21 Jan. 1525 (*Arb.Lib.*,ii,442,no.584).

Thomas Myrton   1525 - 1533 x 1540.
Patrick Myrton/Morton senior   1525 - 1575.
Thomas Myrton succ. on exch. with Dunbar 21 Jan. 1525 (*Arb. Lib.*,ii,442,no.584); res. but promises annates on retaining fruits 21 Aug. 1525 (PRO 31/9 - 32/70 - 71); occ. 20 Sept. 1526 (*RMS*,iii,no. 389); occ. 25 Sept. 1533 (Stevenson & Wood, *Seals*,iii,516); d. 30 July 1540 (see *Ab.archd.*).
Patrick Myrton promised annates and gets prov. without fruits 21 Aug. 1525 (PRO 31/9 - 32/71); not known when or if he succ. Thomas Myrton (cf. *Ab.archd.*); but appears to be same as the Patrick Morton who was depriv. on or before 18 Dec. 1575 (v.inf.; cf. *Ab.treas.*).

Thomas Kinnear   1575.
Patrick Myrton junior   1576.
Kinnear gets crown pres. on depriv. of Patrick Morton 18 Dec. 1575 (*RSS*,vii,no.370).
Myrton gets crown pres. on depriv. of Morton 6 Apr. 1576 (*RSS*,vii,no.551); cf. *Ab.treas.*

Note: this ch. granted to burgh of Crail 10 May 1587 (*MRHS*, 176).

PROVOSTS OF CRICHTON

First known date: founded 26 Dec. 1449 (*MRHS*,176).

Peter de Crichton (Creychton) (?) 1449.
Rector of this ch. when provostry was erected 26 Dec. 1449 (*Midl.Chrs.*,306); perhaps became the first provost.

George Crichton x 1461.
Held it at death some time before 19 Oct. 1461, when his heir was served (*APS*,vii,144).

William Scheves 1474 - 1478.
> Occ. 26 Oct. 1474 (*Foedera* [O] ,xi,824); prov. *St A.abp.* 11 Feb. 1478.

Alexander Inglis   1480 - 1496 (?).
John de Ireland (Irlandia)   1483.
> Inglis occ. 23 Feb. 1480 (SRO, Prot. Bk. Darow, fo.252); dem. in favour of Ireland before 28 Dec. 1483 (v.inf.); but this was prob. part of consequences of his el. to *Dk.bp.*,and he prob. returned to this ben. c. 1485 as he did to *St A.archd.*
> Ireland in poss. 28 Dec. 1483 (Reg.Supp.,832,fo.113); prob. lost poss. by c. 1485 (v.sup.; cf. *St A.archd.*).

Thomas Halkerston 1501 - 1522.
> Occ. 6 Sept. 1501 (*Hist.Chapel Royal*,17); occ. 13 Mar. 1519 (*Cupar Chrs.*,no.7); res. on pension on or before 28 May 1522 (v.inf.); cf. Bryce, *Grey Friars*,ii,336, where obit is dated 1516.

George Lockhart 1522 - 1547.
> In poss. when agrees to pension on fruits to Halkerston 28 May 1522 (PRO 31/9 - 31/374-5); occ. 3 Nov. 1523 (*St A.Acta*,343); d. 22 June 1547 (*Glas.Reg.*,ii,614).

William Justice 1547 x 1549.
> Held it at death sometime before 3 Sept. 1549 (v.inf.).

John Johnston   1549.
George Ramsay   1553.
> Johnston gets crown pres. on Justice's death 3 Sept. 1549 (*RSS*, iv,414)
> Ramsay had pres. by patron on Justice's death, but was refused institution by ord.; res. in favour of Hepburn 8 Apr. 1553 (PRO 31/9 - 33/296-9).

James Hepburn 1553 - 1566 (?) x 1567.
> In poss. when prov. in terms of supp. granted 14 Aug. 1551 and following res. of Ramsay 8 Apr. 1553 (PRO 31/9 - 33/298-9); still alive 12 Oct. 1566 (see *Dk.dean.*) and perhaps still holding this ben. then; d. in poss. sometime before 8 Jan. 1567 (v.inf.).

David Chalmer of Ormont   1567 - 1593.
Adam Johnston   1570 - 1574.
> Chalmer prov. at Rome on Hepburn's death 8 Jan. 1567 (RSS, lv,fo.217); escheated on or before 19 June 1568 (*RSS*,vi,no.311), confirmed 19 Aug. 1568 (*APS*,iii,49); but prov. confirmed by crown 31 July 1587 (RSS,lv, fo.217); d. 22 June 1593 prob. still in poss. (see *R.chanc.*).
> Johnston occ. 1570 and 23 Jan. 1574 (*RMS*,iv,nos.2533, 2169).

Gideon Murray of Elibank 1597 - 1621.
> Pres. by patron 10 Feb. 1597 (v.inf.); occ. 1 July 1600 (*HMC* 57, *Home*, 62);original pres. conf. by parliament 28 June 1617 (*APS*,iv, 568-9); d. 29 June 1621 (*SP*,iii,506).

PROVOSTS OF CULLEN

First known date: founded 23 Apr. 1543 (*MRHS*, 176).

William Elphinstone 1543 - 1545.
　　In poss. at erection of provostry 23 Apr. 1543 (W. Cramond, *Church and Churchyard of Cullen*, 36); res. in favour of Duff 8 Dec. 1545 (v.inf.).

George Duff 1545 - 1575.
　　Crown pres. on res. of Elphinstone 8 Dec. 1545 (*RSS*,iii,no. 1420); occ. 7 Feb. 1567 (ibid.,v,no.3226); d. May 1575 (Edin.Tests).

PROVOSTS OF DALKEITH

First known date: erected 21 June 1406 (*MRHS*,177).

Patrick de Parkley 1438.
　　Occ. 15 Mar. 1438 (SRO, Duntreath, 2/10).

James Douglas 1453.
　　Occ. 2 May 1453 (*Foedera* [O],xi, 326).

Thomas Jaffray 1456.
　　Occ. 10 Sept. 1456 (SRO, Morton, no.114).

Alexander Gifford 1464 - 1469.
　　Occ. 4 Jan. 1464 and 4 Sept. 1469 (SRO, Morton, nos. 131,145); perhaps res. when he succ. to *Dunbar dean.* 25 June 1477 x .

Patrick Rule (Roul) 1478 - 1509.
　　Occ. 4 Nov. 1478 (*HMC* 57, *Home*,255); occ. 20 Dec. 1509 (SRO, Morton, box 56).

John Crichton (Crechton) 1510 - 1513.
　　Occ. 13/14 May 1510 and 11 Apr. 1513 (SRO, Morton, boxes 27 and 9).

Archibald Boyd 1520 - 1559.
　　Occ. 5 Nov. 1520 (Fraser, *Douglas,* iii,221); occ. 10 Feb. 1559 (Scott, *Fasti*,viii,72).

George Douglas 1619 - 1621.
　　Occ. 29 Jan. 1619 and 20 Oct. 1621 (SRO, Part.Reg.Sasines Edinburgh,iii,fo.67, and v,fo.110).

William Douglas 1625 - 1638.
　　Occ. 4 Aug. 1625 and 6 Mar. 1638 (ibid.,xi,fo.99,and xxvii, fo.155).

PROVOSTS OF DIRLETON

First known date: 1444.

John Burgon 1444 - 1447.
     Occ. 6 May 1444 and 30 May 1447 (SRO, Wallace-James Notes [GD 1/413], x, pt.1,p.201,quoting original charters 'penes me').

James Bracale 1464.
     Occ. 8 May 1464 (NLS, Adv. MS 29.4.2,v,fo.151v).

John Robeson/Robinson 1499 - 1509.
     Occ. 24 Jan. 1499 (*ADC*,ii,314 - called *Dumbarton prov.* in printed text, but 'Dirleton prov.' is a possible reading of MS); occ. 15 Apr.1505 (SRO,Biel,19); occ. 10 Nov. 1509 (SRO, ADC,xxi,fo.19).

Robert Hoppringill/Pringill x 1519.
     Occ. before 8 July 1519 (SRO, Sent.Offic.Laud.,fo.74); d. in poss. sometime before 9 Dec. 1561 (v.inf.).

Thomas Hay x 1553.
     Held it before 5 June 1553, by which date he is dead (SRO, Haddington Burgh Ct.Bk. [B.30/10],ii,fo.193v); cf. *Dunbar dean.*

Robert Hostlair 1561.
     Pres. by patron on Hoppringill's death 9 Dec. 1561 (SRO, Prot. Bk. Robert Lawder,fo.224v).

Henry Seton (Seytoun) 1565.
     Occ. 8 Dec. 1565 (SRO, Haddington Burgh Protocol Books (B. 30/1), no. 5,fo.442).

John Dalyell 1576.
     Occ. 7 July 1576 (SRO, Haddington Burgh Protocol Books (B.30/1), no.7, fo.48v).

Walter Ker 1580 - 1599.
     Instituted after pres. by patron 16 Mar. 1580 (ibid. fo.183); occ. 29 Jan./28 Feb. 1599 (*RMS*,vii,no.1667).

Mark Cas 1627 - 1632.
     Pres. by patron 25 Apr. 1627 (SRO, Biel Muniments [GD.6], no.1178); occ. 23 Mar. 1632 (ibid.,no.1179).

PROVOSTS OF DUMBARTON

First known date: founded 3 Jan. 1454 (*MRHS*,177).

George de Abernethy 1454 - 1475 x 1476.
     Assigned to provostry on erection of collegiate ch. 3 Jan. 1454 (Reg.Supp.,470,fo.193v); in poss. 22 July 1475 (ibid.,724,fo.57v); d. before Aug. 1476 (v.inf.).

Walter Abernethy   1476 - 1514 x 1519.
John Doles   1477.

    Abernethy had by 8 Aug. 1477 had poss. for more than one year but less than two, following death of George de Abernethy (*Reg.Supp.*, 755,fo.250); gets disp. to hold provostry and receive holy orders 17 Dec. 1477 (ibid.,762,fo.10v-11); occ. 10 Nov. 1488 (*Pais. Reg.*, 261); occ. 19 Mar. 1513 (*Prot.Bk.Simon*,ii, 475-7) and prob. again 3 Mar. 1514 (ibid., 451); d. before 4 Aug. 1519 (*RSS*,i,no.3044).
    Doles gets *com.priv.* against Walter Abernethy 8 Aug. 1477 (Reg. Supp.,755,fo.250) unfruitfully.

James Stewart   1520 - 1523.
    Occ. 19 Aug. 1520 (HMC 21, *Hamilton*,i,33); occ. erroneously under name John Stewart 4 July 1522 (*Glas.Mun.*,ii,146); occ. 19 Dec. 1522 (ibid., 141-2; cf. 148); nom. Dryburgh abbot 13 Dec. 1523 (*Dryb.Lib.*,xxii); promised annates for pension on this ben. which he had held before his promotion as abbot 29 Jan. 1526 (PRO 31/9-32/93-94).

Robert Maxwell 1523 - 1526 x .
    Occ. 4 Nov. 1523 (Fraser, *Pollok Cartulary*,95); prov. *O.bp.* with lic. to retain this ben. 9 Apr. 1526 (Dowden, *Bishops*,264); promised annates for retaining it 26 Apr. 1526 (PRO 31/9 - 32/102); perhaps dem. before 28 Mar. 1530 (v.inf.) and certainly before 24 Apr. 1539 (v.inf.), and so he did not retain this ben until his death 30 May 1539 x 5 Apr. 1541 (see *O.bp.*).

Robert Stewart   1530 (?) - 1564 x 1570.
David Hamilton   1544 - 1552.
    Stewart had perhaps moved from *Lincluden prov.* by 28 Mar. 1530; occ. 24 Apr. 1539 (*James V Letters*,370); retained it after nom. to *C.bp.* 8 Sept. 1541; res. 16 July 1546 (*RSS*,iii,no.2561) and was also depriv. before 15 Sept. 1546 when privy council refused reinstatement (*RPC*,i,41; cf. *St A.Form.*,ii,318-21); must have obtained reinstatement in due course, for he granted a chr. as provost 4 Nov. 1564 (SRO, Abbrev. Feu Chrs.,i,fo.7); res. on or before 21 Oct. 1570 (v.inf.).
    Hamilton gets crown pres. in exp. 8 July 1544 (*RSS*,iii,no.863;cf. nos. 1373, 1394); crown pres. again 16 Dec. 1547 (ibid.,no.2561); occ. 9 Feb. 1552 (ibid.,iv,no.1523).

Cuthbert Cunningham 1570 - 1613.
    Crown pres. on res. of Stewart 21 Oct. 1570 (*RSS*,vi,no.972); occ. 28 Jan. 1574 (SRO, Reg.Deeds,xiii,fo.63); occ. 2 June 1613 (*RMS*,vii,no.847).

Walter Stewart 1617.
    Occ. 1 Aug. 1617 (SRO, Fraser Chrs.,no.439).

DEANS OF DUNBAR

First known date: founded 21 Sept. 1342 (*MRHS*,177).

Laurence 1342 x 1363.
>Occ. before 1 July 1363 (Fraser, *Carlaverock*,ii,412).

David 1369.
>Occ. 23 Aug. 1369 (*HMC* 44, *Drumlanrig*,i,32).

Thomas de Merton x 1404.
>Said to have held it for more than five years before 12 May 1409, by which date he is called former dean (Reg.Av.,332,fos.399v-400).

William Stephenson (Stephani) 1409.
>Prov. 12 May 1409 (ibid.), prob. unfruitfully.

Columba de Dunbar   1412 - 1423.
Ingram de Lindsay   1422.
>Dunbar occ. 28 Feb. 1412 (*Univ.Evidence*,iii,173-4); prov. *M.bp.* 3 Apr. 1422; granted this ben. in commend for one year 5 Apr. 1422 (*CSSR*,i,294).
>
>Lindsay is said to have obtained it by 5 Apr. 1422 (ibid.,295).

Robert Young 1423 - 1433 x 1440.
>Occ. 28 Feb. 1424 (SRO, Swinton, no.20); but must have got it by May 1423, for by 27 May 1433 he had held it for ten yars as he still did (Reg.Supp.,286,fo.234); d. in poss. before Oct. 1440 (v.inf.).

Adam Hepburn 1440 - 1453.
>Had crown pres. on death of Young more than a year before 21 Oct. 1441, when he gets new prov. (Reg.Supp.,377,fo.58v); occ. 16 May 1453 (*Melr.Lib.*,ii,557,no.554).

Archibald Whitelaw 1467 - 1477.
>Occ. 31 Jan. 1467 (*RMS*,ii,no.900); in poss. and is said to have lately got it 3 Sept. 1467 (Reg.Supp.,614,fo.109v); occ. 25 June 1477 (*ER*,viii,401).

Alexander Gifford/Giffert 1477 x 1478 (?), 1493 - 1499.
>Perhaps moved from *Dalkeith prov.* x 4 Nov. 1478; occ. 1 June 1493 (*RMS*,ii,no.2154); occ. 11 Feb. 1499 (NLS,Adv.MS 9A.1.9 [vol.ii] , no.187); still alive 23 Mar. 1507 (see *St A.archd.Lothian*), but prob. had dem. before then (v.inf.).

Alexander Stewart 1504 - 1510.
>Occ. 13 Nov. 1504 (*TA*,ii,340; cf. 333); occ. 3 Nov. 1510 (*RSS*,i,no.2146); perhaps retained it until he obtained *B.dean.* 1512 x 1523.

Thomas Hay   1524 - 1552 x 1553.
George Hay   1529 - 1540.
>Thomas Hay occ. after coll. by abp. of St Andrews 29 Mar. 1524 (*Yester Writs*,no.408); patrons agree that he may res. in curia on exch. with his brother George Hay 10 July 1529, and king agrees also 6/8 Jan. 1530 (PRO 31/9 - 32/215-22); res. in cura in consequence in his brother's favour, but retaining poss. 21 Jan. 1531 (PRO 31/9 - 33/66-68; cf. 53-55); patrons notify curia that they have revoked their

earlier consent to this arrangement 19 Oct. 1534 (PRO 31/9 - 32/301);
occ. 25 Dec. 1552 (*RSS*,iv,no.1846); d. before 8 Dec. 1553 (v.inf.); cf.
Dirleton prov.

George Hay had expectancy to succeed his brother from 1529-30,
though patrons withdrew their agreement to this in 1534 (v.sup.); occ.
5 July 1540 (*James V Letters*,402).

John Row 1553.

Prov. on death of Thomas Hay 8 Dec. 1553 (*A.B.Ill.*,iv,487n).

Claud Hamilton 1556 - 1568.

Occ. 24 Jan. 1556 (SRO, Reg.Deeds,i,fo.360); occ. 24 Feb.1567
as 'Ludovicus' Hamilton 12 Jan. 1568 (*RMS*,iv,no.2516); forfeited 9
Aug. 1568 (*APS*,iii,54), but may have retained control of this ben. for
some time.

William Stewart 1571 - 1572.

Crown pres. on Hamilton's forfeiture 25 Jan. 1571 (*RSS*,vi,no.
1099); compensated by crown in Sept. 1572 for this ben. 'whereof he
was disappointed' (*TA*,xii,327).

John Reid 1579 - 1580.

Crown gift of fruits on forfeiture of Hamilton 10/21 June 1579
(*RSS*,vii,nos.1926,1950); crown pres. for same reason 5 Dec. 1579
(ibid.,no.2128); crown gift of fruits again for same reason 29 July
1580 (ibid.,no.2440).

Note: dean of Dunbar was named to the re-erected chapter of St
Andrews June 1617 (*APS*,iv,530); an unnamed dean occ. 17 Feb. 1637
SRO, Part.Reg.Sasines Edinburgh, xxvi,fo.151).

PROVOSTS OF DUNGLASS

First known date: erected 2 Jan. 1451 (bull in *HMC* 26, *12th R.*,viii,
127-8; cf. *MRHS*,178).

William Park 1459.

In poss. 12 Nov. 1459 (*Vet.Mon.*,422).

James Fleming 1475.

Res. in curia in favour of Edwardson, ord. having refused earlier
res. in favour of same 13 Apr. 1475 (Reg.Supp.,718,fo.46;741,
fo.217v-18).

John Edwardson 1475 - 1481.

Pres. made by patron to ord. earlier had been refused; now gets
prov. on res. of Fleming 13 Apr. 1475 (ibid.); in poss. 11 May 1476
(ibid.,739,fo.4); occ. 13 June 1481 (SRO, Reg.Ho.Chr.no.496).

Thomas Ker c. 1513-14.

Occ. c. 1513-14 (*James V Letters*, 6, 47), but became monk of
Kelso about the same time (*Vet.Mon.*,530-1).

James Haliburton 1515.
    Occ. 27 May 1515 (*HMC* 26, *12th R.*,128).

George Ker 1521 - 1535.
    Occ. 23 Jan. 1521 (*HMC* 34, *14th R.*,iii,68); occ. 24 July 1535 (*Camb.Reg.*,2).

John Chisholm   1536 - 1537.
Abraham Crichton   1537 - 1565.
    Chisholm was pres. by Lord Maxwell as patron and had poss. by 11 Feb. 1536 (*ADCP*, 450); occ. 15 July 1537 (*RMS*,iii,no.1695); after lit. with Crichton, res. in his favour on pension, with consent of other patrons 27 Aug. 1537 (PRO 31/9 - 33/70-73; cf. 57-60; see also *St A.Form.*,ii,50-55).
    Crichton prov. after lit. with Chisholm 27 Aug.1537 (v.sup.); occ. 31 July 1538 (*Spalding Misc.*,iv,203); occ. 15 Aug. 1565 (*RMS*, iv,no.1659); made will 17 Sept. 1565 (*RPC*,ii,497); d. by 8 Oct. 1565 (v.inf.).

John Hume 1565 - 1573 x 1577.
    Crown conf. of pres. earlier on death of Crichton 8 Oct. 1565 (*RSS*,v,no.2371); occ. 15 Aug. 1573 (*RSS*,vi,no.2078); forfeited before death, which was before 9 Aug. 1577 (*RSS*,vii,no.1133;cf.nos. 1104, 1108).

George Douglas   1577.
Richard Douglas   1577.
    George Douglas gets crown pres. on death of Hume 31 Aug.1577 (*RSS*,vii,no.1164).
    Richard Douglas gets crown pres. on death of Hume 10 Sept.1577 (ibid.,no.1175).

Thomas Ogilvie 1586 - 1608.
    Occ. 30 July 1586 (*HMC* 57, *Home*,55) and 10 Mar. 1608 (SRO, E. Lothian Sheriff Ct.Bk.,xiii,fo.247).

William Hume (Home) 1612 - 1619.
    Occ. 10 Apr. 1612 and 13 Dec. 1619 (SRO, Part.Reg.Sasines Berwick,i,fos.97,113).

John Hume (Home) 1621 - 1637.
    Occ. 26 May 1621 (*RMS*,viii,no.169) and 14 Feb. 1637 (SRO, Part.Reg. Sasines Edinburgh,xxv,fo.530).

Note: this collegiate church was suppressed and its property granted to Sir John Ruthven of Dunglass 29 July 1641, on res. of unnamed provost and prebendaries (*APS*,VI,i,267-9).

PROVOSTS OF ST GILES, EDINBURGH

First known date: supplication for erection granted 22 Feb. 1468 (Reg. Supp.,620,fo.229; cf. *MRHS*,178).

William Forbes 1468 - 1496.
  In poss. 3/12 Mar. 1468 (Reg.Supp.,621,fos.65v, 116); occ. 30 July 1496 (*St Giles Reg.*,no.111).

Gavin Douglas 1503 - 1515.
  Occ. 11 Mar. 1503 (*TA*,ii,360); still holding it when prov.*Dk.bp.* 25 May 1515 (*Dunk.Rent.*,332), and perhaps until cons. 21 Sept. 1516.

Robert Crichton 1517 - 1553 x 1554.
  Occ. 1 Sept. 1517 (Fraser, *Grandtully*,i,52; cf. *St A.Form.*,i,122-3); occ. 23 Aug. 1553 (SRO, Acts and Decreets, viii,fo.309); res. before 1 May 1554 (v.inf.), and having obtained *Dk.bp.* by then.

Alexander Campbell 1554 - 1556 x 1557.
  Crown pres. on Crichton's res. 1 May 1554 (*RSS*,iv,no.2741); occ. 17 May 1556 (SRO, Reg.Deeds, i,fo.319); res. on or before 19 Mar. 1557 (v.inf.).

William Chisholm 1557.
  Crown pres. on res. of Campbell 19 Mar. 1557 (*RSS*,v,no.92); d. before 5 Oct. 1557 (v.inf.).

James Chisholm 1557 - 1566.
  Crown pres. on death of William Chisholm 5 Oct. 1557 (*RSS*,v, no.214); occ. 2 July 1566 (*St Giles Reg.*, no.152); perhaps moved to *Db.archd.* in 1566.

PROVOSTS OF ST MARY OF THE FIELDS, EDINBURGH

First known date: x 20 Oct. 1512 (v.inf.; see *MRHS*,179).

Matthew Ker 1511, 1512 - 1515.
  Occ. as 'master' of the ch. *pro tempore* 19 Sept. 1511 (*Midl.Chrs.*, 261-2); occ. as provost 20 Oct. 1512 (ibid.,262-3); occ. 1515 (*St A Offic.*, 5).

Richard Bothwell   1523 - 1544.
David Vocat (?)   1527.
  Bothwell claims to have had reservation at Rome 18 Sept. 1523 (*ADCP*,178); occ. 30 May 1524 (*RMS*,iii,no.265); occ. 10 Apr. 1543 (*RMS*,iv,no.1801); res. in favour of Spittal with no mention of any pension 30 June 1543 (PRO 31/9 - 33/155; cf. 153; cf. *St A.Form.*,ii, 322-3); but occ. 26 Jan. 1544 (SRO, Sent.Offic.Laud.,fo.323); d. 1 Jan. 1549 (*Glas.Reg.*,ii,614).
  Vocat said to occ. 11 Dec. 1527 (*Midl.Chrs.*,p.cxi;cf.*MRHS*, 179); but source is ambiguous.

John Spittal 1543 - 1552.
  Bothwell res. in curia in his favour 30 June 1543 (v.sup.); occ. 19 Mar. 1549 (SRO, Reg.Ho. Chr.no.1455); occ. 18 Feb. 1552 (Fraser, *Douglas*,iii,245); presumably dem. before 20 Dec. 1552 (see Forrest below).

William Penicuik   c. 1550 - 1563 x 1566.
Alexander Forrest   1552 - 1561.
     Penicuik had pres. from patron and later claimed to have had poss. for two or three years before Forrest was intruded; gets crown conf. of his right 23 Jan. 1562 (*RSS*,v,no.965); occ. 25 July 1563 (SRO, Reg.Ho.Chr.,no.1919); res. on or before 9 Dec. 1566 (v.inf.).
     Forrest prob. moved from *Fowlis prov.* before 20 Dec. 1552; had been coll. by John Hamilton abp. of St Andrews (*RSS*,v,no.965); occ. 15 July 1553 (SRO, GD 1/39/5/3); occ. 20 Mar. 1561 (*RMS*,iv,no.2314)

Robert Balfour   1566 - 1579.
     Crown pres. on res. of Penicuik 9 Dec. 1566 (*RSS*,v,no.3123); forfeited 10 Nov. 1579 (*APS*,iii,137).

John Gibb   1579 - .
     Crown pres. on forfeiture of Balfour 7 Dec. 1579 (*RSS*,vii,no. 2136).

Note: this provostry was granted to provost, bailies, etc. of Edinburgh 18 Mar. 1581 (Reg.Pres,ii,73).

PROVOSTS OF TRINITY, EDINBURGH

First known date: founded 25 Mar. 1462 (*MRHS*,179).

Edward Bonkle (Boncle)   1463 x 1464 - 1495 x 1496.
     Occ. July 1463 x June 1464 (*ER*,vii, 241); d. Aug. 1495 x June 1496 (ibid.,x, 553).

James Oliphant   1499 - 1501.
     Occ. 28 Jan. 1499 (*ADC*,ii,317); occ. 1 Dec. 1500 (ibid.,452); still alive 24 Mar. 1501 (*TA*,ii,70); prob. d. before 2 May 1501 (see *Chapel Royal dean*.).

John Brady   1502 - 1525.
     Crown pres. 1 Sept. 1502 (*RSS*,i,no.865); res. while promising annates to retain fruits 26 Oct. 1525 (PRO 31/9 - 32/76-77); d. Nov. 1525 (SRO,ADC & S, i,fo,87).

John Dingwall   1525 - 1532 x 1533.
     Prov. and promises annates for future poss. 26 Oct. 1525 (PRO 31/9 - 32/77); occ. 19 Feb. 1526 (*Prot.Bk.Foular 1514-28*,no.664); occ. 6 Sept. 1532 (*SHR*,xxii, 30); d. before 7 Jan. 1533 (v.inf.).

William Cunningham   1533 - 1539.
     Crown pres. on death of Dingwall 7 Jan. 1533 (*RSS*,ii,no.1470); occ. 17 Feb. 1539 (ibid.,no.2892); prov. *Ar.bp.* 7 May 1539, following nom. 1 Feb. 1539.

Thomas Erskine   1539.
     Crown pres. on exp. of promotion of Cunningham 17 Feb.1539 (*RSS*,ii,no.2892); occ. 5 Sept. 1539 (ibid.,no.3138); res. before 13 Sept. 1539 (v.inf.).

Robert Erskine 1539 - 1540.

Crown pres. in exp. 5 Sept. 1539 (*RSS*,ii,no.3138); instituted 13 Sept. 1539 (*Spalding Misc.*, iv,32); occ. 28 July 1540 (*RSS*,ii,no.3594); res. before 1 Aug. 1540 (*James V Letters*, 406-7).

George Clapperton 1540 - 1566.

Crown pres. in exp. 28 July 1540 (*RSS*,ii,no.3594); presumably in poss. by 1 Aug. 1540 (v.sup.); occ. 25 May 1542 (*ADCP*,519); occ. 23 Dec. 1566 (*RSS*,v,no.3146).

Laurence Clapperton 1566 - 1571 x 1572.

Crown pres. in exp. 23 Dec. 1566 (*RSS*,v,no.3146); occ. 12 Mar. 1571 (*RMS*,iv,no.1990); held it at death before 27 Jan. 1572 (v.inf.).

Note: by convention of Leith 16 Jan. 1572 this ben. was associated with the new dignity of *St A.chanc.* within the reformed chapter of St Andrews then established, to take effect from such time as the incumbent should accept the Reformation - as was not apparently the case at that date, since a temporary substitute chanc. was named (*BUK*, i,222-3).

Robert Pont 1572 - 1585.

Crown pres. on death of Laurence Clapperton 27 Jan. 1572 (*RSS*,vi,no.1456); occ. 20 Jan. 1585 (*Midl.Chrs.*,242).

Note: provostry granted by crown to burgh of Edinburgh 25 June 1585/ 26 May 1587 (Reg.Pres.ii,134,172; cf. *MRHS*,179).

PROVOSTS OF FOWLIS EASTER

First known date: 1538 (*MRHS*, 180).

Malcolm Mortimer (Mortymor) 1538.

Occ. 1538 (Prot.Bk. Thomas Ireland,fo.3).

Alexander Mortimer (Mortymor) 1540.

Occ. 1540 (ibid.,fo.7).

Alexander Forrest/Forrous/Forret/Forres 1549 - 1550 x 1552.

Occ. 5 May 1549 (SRO, Acts and Decreets, iii,fo.428); occ. 7 Oct. 1550 (Prot.Bk.James Harlaw,fo.20v); moved to *St Mary, Edin.* prov. prob. after 18 Feb. 1552 and before 20 Dec. 1552 (cf.inf.).

Nicholas Spittal 1552 - 1559.

Instituted 20 Dec. 1552 (Prot.Bk.Thomas Ireland, fo.21); occ. 20 Dec. 1559 (SRO, Maitland Thomson Notebook no. 6,p.147, from Fowlis Easter Chrs.no.100).

Gilbert Gray 1568 - 1576.

Occ. 3 May 1568 (*HMC* 26, *12th R.*, viii,108); occ. 12 Jan. 1576 (*RMS*,iv, no.2505).

PROVOSTS OF ST MARY & ST ANNE/
OUR LADY COLLEGE, GLASGOW

First known date: erected 29 Apr. 1525 (*MRHS*, 180).

Christopher Boyd 1532.
    Nom. by founder while holding vic. of Dalry 15 July 1532 (*St Mary Lib.*, 10-12).

Archibald Crauford 1543 - 1566.
John Sinclair (?) 1552.
    Crauford occ. 25 June 1543 (*Glas.Mun.*, ii,293); occ. 18 May 1566 (*RSS*,v,no.2834).
    Sinclair occ. as 'provost of college of Glasgow' 3 Sept. 1552 (Fraser, *Maxwell Inventories*,163); perhaps error for *G.college princ. regent.*

PROVOSTS OF GUTHRIE

First known date: erected 19 May 1479 (*MRHS*, 180).

David Guthrie 1483 - 1505.
    Prob. in poss. when annates promised in name of unnamed provost 24 July 1483 (*ACSB*,207); occ. Nov. 1486 (*St A.Acta*,224); occ. 30 Sept. 1505 (*RMS*,ii,no.2910); said to occ. 4 Oct. (?) 1506 (*James IV Letters*, 40), but this is prob. an error for Thomas Dickson.

Thomas Dickson 1506 - 1510 x 1512.
    Occ. 24 Oct. 1506 (SRO, Reg.Ho.Chr. no.695) and 13 Nov.1509 (*RMS*,iii,no.834); moved to *Restalrig dean.* 1510 x 18 May 1512.

John Hay 1512 - 1529.
    Occ. 5 July 1512 (SRO, Erroll, 257) and 3 Aug. 1529 (*Yester Writs*, no.451).

John Garden 1532 - 1535.
    Occ. 12 July 1532 (SRO, ADC & S,i,fo.62v); in poss. 21 Jan.1535 (PRO 31/9 - 32/302).

Gabriel Guthrie 1577.
    Crown conf. of earlier pres. by patron 3 Feb. 1577 (*RSS*,vii, no.882).

John Lindsay 1594.
    Occ. 22 Sept. 1594 (SRO, Guthrie, box 1, bdle 1).

David Lindsay 1598.
    Pres. by patron 29 Jan. 1598 (Scott,*Fasti*,v,436, no source cited).

Thomas Glover 1604.
    Pres. by patron 18 Jan. 1604 (Scott, *Fasti*,v,436, no source cited).

PROVOSTS OF HAMILTON

First known date: erected 4 Jan. 1451 (*MRHS,* 181).

William Turnbull x 1462.
　　Held it before 10 Apr. 1462, by which time he is dead (Reg.Supp., 549,fo.218v).

Martin Vaus　　　　　1462.
George de Graham　　1462.
　　Vaus had a claim based on pres. by Thomas Vaus (as dean of Glasgow and rector of Cadzow/Hamilton i.e. 1456 x) which he res. in favour of Graham 10 Apr. 1462 (*CPL,*xi,438-9; *HMC* 21, *Hamilton,*i,48).
　　Graham said to have been installed as provost 4 Apr. 1462 (*OPS,* i,106, quoting MS sources); his claim was based on pres. by Lord Hamilton at first vacancy after erection of this ben; after dispute with Vaus, he gets conf. and mand. for induction 10 Apr. 1462 (*Vet.Mon.,* no.817; *CPL,*xi,438-9; *HMC* 21, *Hamilton,*i,48).

David Cunningham 1490 - 1509.
　　Occ. 10 July 1490 (*Glas.Mun.,*ii,255); occ. 22 Nov. 1506 (*Prot. Bk. Simon,*ii,150); prob. retained it until d. 18 Apr. 1509 (see *G.offic.*).

Arthur Hamilton 1514 - 1514 x 1515.
　　Occ. 19 Mar. 1514 (*Prot.Bk.Ros,*no.63) and 30 Mar. 1514 (*HMC* 21, *Hamilton,*i,49); d. before 8 June 1515 (*Prot.Bk.Ros,*no.111).

Arthur Hamilton 1516 - 1566.
　　Son of predecessor; occ. 11 Nov. 1516 (*HMC* 21, *Hamilton,*i,52); occ. 3 May 1561 (*RMS,*iv,no.2585); prob. still in poss. 15 Feb. 1566 (*RSS,*v,no.2630).

Gavin Hamilton 1605.
　　Occ. 28 Dec. 1605 (*RMS,*ix,no.890).

James Hamilton 1617 - 1632.
　　Occ. when *G.dean* 15 Nov. 1617 and 13 July 1632 (SRO, Part. Reg.Sasines Lanark,i,fo.16, and ivA,fo.346).

PROVOSTS OF INNERPEFFRAY

First known date: x 25 Oct. 1542 (*MRHS,*181).

John Drummond　　　1549.
John Sinclair　　　　1549 - 1567, 1574 (?)
　　Drummond lit. with Sinclair 11 Feb. 1549 (*ADCP,*581).
　　Sinclair lit. with Drummond 11 Feb. 1549 (ibid.); occ. 17 May 1567 (*RMS,*iv,no.2378); perhaps still in poss. 17 May 1574 (see *C.archd.*) and may have d. soon after.

William Lindsay 1575 - 1584.

Occ. 21 May 1575 (Stevenson & Wood, *Seals*,iii,467); d. in poss. 15 Mar. 1584 (Edin.Tests).

John Drummond 1592.

Crown pres. on Lindsay's death 28 Jan. 1592 (RSS,lxiii,fo.148).

PROVOSTS OF KILMAURS

First known date: x 8 Jan. 1462 (v.inf.; cf. *MRHS*, 181).

Patrick Cunningham 1462 - 1483.

Occ. 8 Jan. 1462 (SRO, Reg.Ho.Chr.no.364) and 1 Feb.1483 (SRO, Craigens, 27).

Walter Nory 1507 - 1508.

Occ. 1 Feb. 1507 (*Prot.Bk.Simon*,ii,154-5) and 13 May 1508 (*HMC* 57, *Home*,256).

Christopher Boyd 1511 - 1527 (?)

Occ. 28 Feb. 1511 (SRO, Reg.Ho.Chr.no.763A); see also *Methven prov.* where source for his res. 11 Feb. 1527 perhaps applies to this ben.

Note: an unnamed provost occ. 10 Nov. 1596 (*Laing Chrs.*,no.1320); but charters of 5 Nov. 1603 (SRO, Secretary's Reg.Sasines Ayr,ii,fo. 251), 5 Mar. 1626 and 17 Oct. 1638 (SRO, Part.Reg. Sasines Ayr,iii,fo. 498, and vii,fo.176) were granted by the prebendaries with no mention of a provost.

PROVOSTS OF KILMUN

First known date: erected 5 Aug. 1441 (*MRHS*, 181).

Note: an unnamed provost was prob. inducted at once, for whom annates were promised 5 Oct. 1441 (*ACSB*,129.

Peter Wilson (Vulsun/Yulsun/Wilstan) 1448 - 1452 x 1465.

Occ. 30 Oct. 1448 (*Highland Papers*,ii,182); occ. 6 July 1452 (*RMS*,iv, no.791); res. to ord. in favour of Ochiltree sometime before 17 Dec. 1465 (v.inf.).

David Ochiltree (Outhere/Outhert) x 1465 — 1476.

Prov. after coll. by ord. on res. of Wilson 17/27 Dec. 1465 (Reg. Supp.,589,fo.148·*ACSB*, 154); occ. 25 Oct. 1475 (*Glas.Mun.*,ii,84) and prob. still in poss. 12 Nov. 1476 (ibid.,ii,87).

John Dewar   1495 - 1511.

Occ. 18 July 1495 and 30 July 1511 (*RMS*,ii,nos.2353,3622).

Archibald Leche (Leych) 1520 - 1522.

Occ. 7 May 1520 (*Cawdor Bk.*, 135) and 1522 (*OPS*,ii,71); perhaps same as MacVicar (v.inf.).

Archibald MacVicar 1529 - 1548.

Occ. 26 Aug. 1529 (*RMS*,iii,no.932) and 27 Sept. 1548 (SRO, Reg. Ho.Chr.no.1445); perhaps same as Leche (v.sup.).

John Campbell 1555 - 1557.

Occ. as prior of Ardchattan 31 Jan. 1555 and 1557 (SRO, Reg. Ho. Chrs. nos. 1639, 1691); same as *elect of Isles* found 26 Dec. 1557.

Robert Lamont (Lawmond/Lawmont) 1557 - 1557 x 1558.

Occ. 28 Aug. 1557 (*Lamont Papers*, no. 1443); occ. 26 Dec. 1557 (*RMS*,iv, no. 1240); d. before 9 Dec. 1558 (see *Chapel Royal chanc.*).

John Campbell 1559 - 1573.

Occ. 2 Dec. 1559 (SRO, Prot.Bk. David Watson,fo.85v), being a natural son of 4th earl of Argyll (*SP*,ix,26, being corrigendum to i,340); d. in poss. 18 Sept. 1573 (Edin. Tests.).

Note: unnamed provost known c. May 1595 (*Cawdor Bk.*, 210).

Archibald Campbell 1597 - 1600.

Occ. 19 (Dec.?) 1597 (SRO, Reg.Ho.Chr.no.3488); d. in poss. Mar. 1600 (SRO, Reg. of Retours, viii,fo.59)

Duncan Campbell 1601 - 1602 x 1604.

Crown pres. on death of Archibald Campbell his brother 27 Mar. 1601 (Reg.Pres.,iii,36);pres. by bp. of Argyll 3 June 1602 (*Clan Campbell*, viii,291, citing SRO, Acts and Decreets,vol.492, fo.259); d. before 7 Feb. 1604 (see *Ar.archd.*).

Alexander Colville 1611 - 1614.

Crown pres. on death of Duncan Campbell 20 Nov. 1611 (Reg.Pres., iv, 60); occ. 16 Dec. 1614 (*HMC* 3, *4th R.*,480,no.129).

PROVOSTS OF LINCLUDEN

First known date: erected 7 May 1389 (*MRHS*, 182).

Elisaeus Adougan 1389 x 1390 - 1406.

Occ. 25 Nov.1390 (Dowden, *Bishops,*366; SRO, Maitland Thomson Transcripts, box 33, file 5); prob. had been the master of the hospital who became first provost on erection of the collegiate church (SRO, Transcripts from Vatican,i,no.62); prov. *Ga.bp.* 28 May 1406, with lic. to retain this ben. 24 June 1406 (Dowden, *Bishops,*367n).

Alexander de Carnis 1407 - 1424.

Occ. 16 July 1407 (NLS, Adv.Chr. no.B 49); in poss. 31 Mar.1424, but a leper (*CSSR*,ii,56); prob. d. 14 July 1424 (Fraser, *Douglas*,i,381, n.4 — this seems to be the date on his tomb).

John Cameron 1425 - 1427.

Had pres. from patron after death of Carnis and occ. 17 Jan. 1425 (*RMS*,ii,no.14; cf. *CSSR*,ii,93); occ. 28 May 1426 (*RMS*,ii,no.53), though had been el. *G.bp.* and prov. 22 Apr. 1426; cons. 12 Jan. 1427.

Gilbert de Park   1427.
John MacGilhauch   1427 - 1434.
        Park had some right which he res. in favour of MacGilhauch before
19 Sept. 1427 (*CSSR*,ii,170-1).
        MacGilhauch in poss. when given absolution for the way he had
come to terms with Park over this ben. (ibid.); occ. 10 Oct. 1432
(SRO, St Andrews Chrs.,27); in poss. when incorporated at Basel 8 Feb.
1434 (Haller, *Conc.Bas.*,iii,21; *Mon.Conc.Bas.*,ii,579); d. before 19 Nov.
1434 (v.inf.).

John Wincester   1434 - 1436.
Thomas MacGuffok/Malgusar   1434.
James Kennedy   1434.
        Wincester had pres. by patron and institution, and gets prov. 20
Dec. 1434 (Reg.Supp.,301,fo.75v); occ. 14 Apr. 1435 (*HMC* 5, *6th R.*,
i, 691); prov. *M.bp.* 23 Mar. 1436.
        MacGuffok gets papal mand. for this ben. to be assigned to him
on death of MacGilhauch 19 Nov. 1434 (*CPL*,viii,493) and pays some
annates 30 Nov. 1434 (*ACSB*,263).
        Kennedy prov. 18 Dec. 1434 (Reg.Supp.,300,fo.284) prob.
fruitlessly.

John de Methven   1437 - 1440.
        Occ. 30 Nov. 1437 (*Foedera* [O] ,x,679); occ. 11 Aug. 1440
(*RMS*,ii,no.245).

Thomas Spens (?) x 1450.
        Said to have held it on crown pres. at some date before promotion
as *Ga.bp.* 8 Jan. 1450 (Boece, *Vitae*,37).

James Lindsay de Covington 1448 x 1449 - 1468 x 1469.
        Occ. 18 June 1449 (*RMS*,ii,no.1705), having got poss. since 16
Jan. 1448 (*CPL*,x,342; cf.9); in poss. 19 Nov. 1468 (Reg.Supp.,633,fo.
22); d. before 15 Mar. 1469 (*CPL*,xii,706-7; cf.x,9); prob. same as
St A.archd. Lothian and so d. before 13 Feb. 1469.

James Crichton (?) 1469.
        Perhaps occ. 23 Nov. 1469 (*Pais.Reg.*,323, where text is corrupt).

Andrew Stewart   1470 - 1488.
David Livingstone   1483 - 1486.
William Turnbull (Tornabul)   1484 - 1486.
        Stewart in poss. 18 Jan. 1477 (Reg.Supp.,746,fo.74v-75); prov.
M.bp. 12 Aug. 1482; provostry annexed to his *mensa* on same date
(*CPL*,xiii,907); this 'pretended' annexation dissolved 16 Oct. 1488
(*APS*,ii,209).
        Livingstone occ. 29 Apr. 1483 and 31 Mar. 1486 (*RMS*,ii,nos.
1564, 1646).
        Turnbull promises annates 1 July 1484, and pays some of them
31 July 1486 (*ACSB*, 83, 257, 297).

George Hepburn 1499 - 1505.

Occ. 21 Jan. 1499 (*ADC*,ii,309); postulated as abbot of Arbroath 9 Feb. 1504 (*Arb.Lib.*,ii,349, no.438).

Andrew Makbrek 1504 - 1505.

Crown pres. in exp. 6 Feb. 1504 (*RSS*,i,no.1017); occ. 2 June 1505 (*Prot.Bk.Young*,no.1542).

Note: provostry united to Chapel Royal, Stirling 3 June 1508 (*RPC*, xii,445; *MRHS*, 182).

John Duncanson 1512 – 1536.

Lit. in curia for this ben. despite annexation to Chapel Royal 9 Apr. 1512 (*James IV Letters*,no.439, where name is given as 'Duncan'); res. some right in favour of Henry Wemyss, presumably after 1525 (v.inf.); but still drawing pension on fruits as late as 23 Dec.1536 (PRO 31/9 - 33/48-49).

Note: annexation to Chapel Royal came to be dissolved in time of Henry Wemyss bp. of Galloway 1525 - 1541; in fact this must have taken place before 14 July 1529 (v.inf.); Wemyss retained some right as bp., which (together with some right gained by him through res. of Duncanson in his favour) he res. in favour of William Stewart 1529 x 1533 (*St A.Form.*,i,310-11; cf. 321-3).

Robert Stewart 1529.

Occ. 14/26 July 1529 (*RSS*,ii,nos. 210,245); perhaps moved to *Dumbarton prov.* by 28 Mar. 1530 (v.inf.).

William Stewart   1529 - 1536.
John Stewart   1535.

William Stewart gets crown pres. in exp. 14/26 July 1529 (*RSS*, ii,nos. 210,245); occ. 28 Mar. 1530 (*ADCP*,325); prov. *Ab.bp.* 13 Nov. 1532, but continued to hold this ben. in commend (v.inf.) ; occ. 12 Aug. 1536 (*RSS*,ii,no.2118); res. but promised annates to retain fruits 23 Dec. 1536 (PRO 31/9 - 33/48); did not die until 10 Apr. 1545 (see *Ab.bp.*), and so possibly may have retained it until then.

John Stewart gets crown pres. in exp. of res. of William Stewart from his commend (*RSS*,ii,no.1742) prob. unfruitfully.

George Marschell 1536 - 1546 x 1547.

Crown pres. in exp. of res. of William Stewart from commend 12 Aug. 1536 (*RSS*,ii,no. 2118); promised annates and gets prov. without fruits 23 Dec. 1536 (PRO 31/9 - 33/48-49); occ. 16 Dec. 1546 (Prot.Bk. Herbert Anderson 1541-50, fo.49); d. before 16 Sept. 1547 (v.inf.) and testament conf. 4 Nov. 1547 (Glas. Tests).

Robert Douglas 1547 - 1609.

Crown pres. on Marschell's death 16 Sept. 1547 (*RSS*,iii,no.2433); occ. 3 May 1568 (Prot.Bk. Herbert Anderson 1566-69,fo.112); escheated on or before 26 Jan. 1572 (*RSS*,vi,no.1454); conf. in poss.for life when William Douglas given pres. in succ. to him 6 Dec. 1585 v.inf.); still in poss. when made testament 12 Sept. 1609 (*HMC* 44, *Drumlanrig*,i,31), and prob. d. soon afterwards.

William Douglas of Drumlanrig 1585, 1609 - 1640.

Crown pres. with reservation of fruits for life to Robert Douglas 6 Dec. 1585 (Reg.Pres.,ii,139; *APS*,iii,415); conf. as an exception when estates of benefices were annexed to the crown 1587 (ibid.,436); got poss. 12 Sept.1609 or later (v.sup.); occ. 23/27 Aug. 1615 soon after he had succ. to estate of Drumlanrig (*RMS*,vii, no.1526); his grant of this provostry was for life, and this was conf. June 1617 (*APS*,iv,574-5, no.53); d. 8 Mar. 1640 (*SP*,vii,134).

PROVOSTS OF MARKLE

First known date: 1515.

Status of this foundation is not clear (cf.*MRHS*,187); in title-deeds of the barony of Hailes it is customarily described just as a chapel, not a collegiate church (e.g. *RMS*,ii,no.3635,v,no.218, and vi,no.166 of 1511, 1581 and 1594); but clergy with title of Provost are found as below.

George Scougall 1515.

Occ. 28 July 1515 (*Lag Chrs.*,no.76).

John Donaldson 1539 - 1540.

Occ. 29 Sept. 1539 and 12 June 1540 (SRO, Prot. Bk.John Feyrn, fos.66v,84).

James Scott 1617 - 1629.

Occ. as just chaplain 27 Nov. 1617 (SRO, Part.Reg.Sasines Edinburgh,ii,fo.24), occ. as 'provost and chaplain of the chaplainry of St Mary of Markle' 20/22 Apr. 1629 (ibid.,xiv,fos.317,320).

PROVOSTS OF MAYBOLE

First known date: founded 1 Mar. 1384 (*MRHS*, 182).

Thomas de Buittle (Butil) 1384 (?). 1388 - 1401, 1415 (?);

May have been the incumbent senior priest who became provost at erection of provostry (*HMC* 4, *5th R.*,613); in poss. 1 Feb. 1388 and 15 July 1401 (*CPP*,i,570,617); may have held it until prov. *Ga.bp.* 14 June 1415.

Note: an Eliseus is found as provost of Maybole 10 May 1399 (*Melr. Lib.*,ii,508), but this is prob. an error for provost of Lincluden.

John Kennedy x 1439 - 1454 x 1456.

In poss. 31 July 1443 by which date he had held it for four years and more (Reg.Supp.,391,fo.236); granted papal rehabilitation 30 Nov. 1443 (*ACSB*,132); in poss. 23 Sept. 1451 (Reg.Supp.,454,fo. 43v); prob. res. on becoming *St Mary, St A. prov.* 24 Sept. 1454 x 28 June 1456.

Eustace de Maxwell 1454 x 1459.

Held this ben. for a time and then res. on exch. with Seres for vic. of Maybole i.e. 1451 x 1459, prob. 1454 x 1459 (Reg.Supp.,571, fo.82).

John Seres 1459 - 1462 x 1464.

In poss. after exch. with Maxwell 1 Mar. 1459 (Reg.Supp.,517, fo.187; cf. sup.); new prov. 26 Sept. 1461 (Reg.Supp.,544,fo.190v); pays annates 9 Jan. 1462 (*ACSB*,240,277); d. before 28 Jan. 1464 (v.inf.).

Eustace de Maxwell 1464 - 1469.

Returns to this ben. by prov. on death of Seres 28 Jan. 1464 (Reg.Supp.,571,fo.229); occ. 4 Jan. 1469 (SRO, Ailsa, 1/107).

David Robertson 1477 - 1480 x 1494.

Has had pres. by patron on or just before 3 Dec. 1477 (*Scot. Antiq.*,x,141); occ. 25 Jan. 1478 and 18 June 1480 (ibid.,x,141; xi,36); d. before 28 Nov. 1494 (*ADA*,185).

Gilbert Kennedy 1521.

Occ. 26 Mar. 1521 (*Prot.Bk.Ros*, no.459).

Walter Kennedy 1525 - 1540.

Occ. 25 Oct. 1525 (*Glas.Mun.*,ii,150) and 1 Mar. 1540 (SRO, Bargany, no. 1018).

John Kennedy 1588.

Occ. 20 May 1588 (SRO, Reg.Ho.Chr.no.2966).

Thomas Kennedy 1600.

Occ. 1/4 Nov. 1600 (SRO, Secretary's Reg. Sasines Ayr,i,fo.75).

Gilbert Ross of Millenderdale 1602 - 1624.

Occ. 27 May 1602 (SRO, Secretary's Reg. Sasines Ayr,i,fo.295) and 15 June 1624 (*RMS*,viii,no.772).

Ralph Weir 1624 - 1638.

Occ. 11 Aug. 1624 and 18 Jan. 1638 (SRO, Part.Reg.Sasines Ayr,iii,fo.153, and vii,fo.119).

PROVOSTS OF METHVEN

First known date: founded 1 May 1433 (*MRHS*, 182).

John Stewart 1433 x 1435 - 1443 x 1445.

Prob. pres. on erection of ben. in 1433; occ. 19 Mar. 1435 (*Brech.Reg.*, i,133); new prov. 27 May 1437 (*CPL*,viii,647); occ. 26 June 1439 (*A.B.Ill.,iv*,190-1); d. 21 Dec. 1443 x 14 July 1445 (see *Dk.dean.*).

David Weir (Werre) 1463.

In poss. 16 Sept. 1463 (Reg.Supp.,568,fo.95).

John Otterburn 1467 - 1471 x 1473.

Occ. 20 July 1467 (SRO, Reg.Ho.Chr.no.406); granted lic. to res. on exch. with Patrick Young for *Ga.archd.* 27 Nov. 1471 (Reg. Supp.,673,fo.245v); this exch. was effective certainly by 20 Sept. 1473 (see *Ga.archd.*).

Patrick Young 1471 x 1474.

Granted faculty to receive this ben. on exch. with Otterburn 27 Nov. 1471 (v.sup.); this exch. was effective before his death, which was before 20 May 1474 (see*Dk.dean.*).

John Young 1474 - 1489 x 1491.

Occ. 25 Oct. 1474 (*Glas.Mun.*,ii,82); occ. 3 Aug. 1489 (Fraser, *Wemyss*,ii,112); d. before 5 July 1491 (*RMS*,ii,no.2051).

John Tyrie 1498 - 1519.

Occ. 10 Mar. 1498 (*RMS*,ii,no.2470) and 26 Nov. 1519 (*Spalding Misc.*,iv,197).

William Douglas   1525 - 1527.
Christopher Boyd (?)   1527.

Douglas occ. 23 Apr. 1525 (*Prot.Bk.Foular 1514-28*,no.580); promises annates to retain it with abbacy of Holyrood 17 July 1526 (PRO 31/9 - 32/117); gets lic. to exch. with Blackadder for priory of Coldingham 11 July 1527 (*RSS*,i,no.3839).

Boyd said to have appointed proctors to res. this ben. 11 Feb. 1527 (SRO, Prot. Bk. Makneill,i [B 22/22/18], fo.49); but source is prob. in error for *Kilmaurs prov.*

Adam Blackadder 1527.

Granted crown lic. to receive it on exch. with Douglas 11 July 1527 (*RSS*,i,no.3839).

Alexander Turing 1532 (?), 1537 - 1538 x 1540.

Perhaps in poss. by 6 Jan. 1532, by which date he had dem. *R.prec.*; occ. 7 May 1537 and 28 Feb. 1538 (*RSS*,ii,nos. 2250, 2457); prob. res. on exch. with Colden for *B.chanc.* before 6 Mar. 1540.

John Colden (Culdene, Caldowme) 1538 - 1541 x 1547.

Crown pres. in exp. 28 Feb. 1538 (*RSS*,ii,no.2457); prob. got poss. on exch. with Turing by 6 Mar. 1540 (v.sup.); occ. 21 Mar. 1540 (*ADCP*,482); occ. 27 Dec. 1541 (*Prot.Bk.Johnsoun*,no.312); d. before 27 Sept. 1547 (v.inf.).

Henry Mowe/Moun 1547 - 1549.

Crown pres. on death of Colden 27 Sept. 1547 (*RSS*,iii,no. 2458); dem. on or before 19 Apr. 1549 when he promises annates for pension on fruits (PRO 31/9 - 33/248).

David Haliburton   1549 - 1573, 1588 (?)
James Herring   1572 - 1600 x 1602.

Haliburton in poss. 19 Apr. 1549 (PRO 31/9 - 33/248); occ.

2 Sept. 1550 (*RSS*,iv,no.869); depriv. 1573 (v.inf.;cf. *R.succ.*); perhaps still in poss. 22 Sept. 1588 (Stevenson & Wood, *Seals*,ii,389— date may be an error for 1558).

Herring pres. by patron on depriv. of Haliburton 10 July 1573 and instituted 2 Sept. 1573, getting crown conf. 10 Sept. 1573 (*RSS*,vi,no.2123); occ. 17 Aug. 1583 (*RMS*,vi,no.650) and 16 Sept. 1597 (*RPC*,v,687); prob. still in poss. 1600 (*Provosts of Methven*,85); d. before 7 Jan. 1602 (*RMS*,vi,no.1275).

William Buchanan 1607 - 1614.

Occ. 19 Sept. 1607 (*RMS*,vii,no.12); d. in poss. 15 Dec. 1614 (St A. Tests., 2 Mar. 1615).

Robert Murray 1631 - 1639.

Occ. 28 Oct. 1631 (SRO, Reg.Deeds.,vol.549,fo.87) and 23 Aug. 1639 (*RMS*,ix,no.2061).

PROVOSTS OF PEEBLES

First known date: founded 28 Mar. 1541 (PRO 31/9 - 33/Diversorum Paul III (1541-2),fo.160; cf. PRO 31/9 - 33/133-4 of 31 Aug. 1542; cf. *MRHS*,182).

Gilbert Wightman 1541 x 1545 - 1557.

Prob. pres. on erection of ben. in 1541; occ. 29 Oct. 1545 (Gunn, *Peebles Ch.*,128); appointed a proctor to res. annexed ben. in favour of David Gibson 28 Apr. 1557 (ibid.,150,155) prob. unfruitfully.

Andrew Betoun 1558 - 1573.

Installed as provost 4 July 1558 (Gunn, *Peebles Ch.*,153); depriv. of all his ecclesiastical livings (this ben. not specifically mentioned) because he is out of Scotland 8 June 1573 (*RSS*,vi,no.1981).

DEANS OF RESTALRIG

First known date: erected 13 Nov. 1487 (*MRHS*, 183).

This foundation is sometimes styled a chapel royal e.g. 15 June 1493 (Foedera [O] , xii,545), 1493 x 1494 and 1497 (*ER*,x,408;xi,2).

John Fraser/Frissell 1487 - 1498.

Prov. on erection of deanery 13 Nov. 1487 (*CPL*,xiv,211-13); prov. after el. to *R.bp.* 14 Mar. 1498.

Henry Wood 1497 - 1500.

Crown pres. in exp. of Fraser's election 10 Sept. 1497 (*RSS*,i, no.131); occ. 4 July 1498 (Fraser, *Eglington*,ii,57); res. on exch. with Boswell for *Dk.prec.* on or before 10 Jan. 1500 (v.inf.).

Robert Boswell 1500 - 1511, 1513 (?).

Z

Promises annates and gets prov. on exch. with Wood 10 Jan.
1500 (PRO 31/9 - 31/3); occ. 26 Aug. 1505 (*RMS*,ii,no.3151) and
1510 (*RSS*,i,no.2064); res. on exch. with Dickson on or before 26
Jan. 1511 (PRO 31/9 - 31/255); apparently still in poss. 11 Mar.1513
(*Prot.Bk.Simon*,ii,474), but source is incomplete and possibly
erroneous.

Thomas Dickson   1510 - 1513.
     Crown pres. in exp. 1510 (*RSS*,i,no.2064); prov. on exch.with
Boswell 26 Jan. 1511 (v. sup.); occ. 18 May 1512 (*RSS*,i,no.2394);
occ. 1 June 1513 (SRO, ADC, xxv,fo.56); apparently killed at Flodden
9 Sept. 1513 (*Scot.Antiq.*,xiii,106; cf.xii,121).

Patrick Coventre   1514 - 1517.
John Douglas   1515.
     Coventre occ. 18 Sept. 1514 after having had crown pres.
(*ADCP*,21; cf.35); occ. 14 Nov. 1517 (*HMC 5, 6th R.*,712).
     Douglas had prov. at Rome before 8 June 1515 (*ADCP*,35);
res. in favour of Coventre 27 June 1515 (ibid.,39).

William Gibson   1526 - 1542.
     Occ. 12 Apr. 1526 (*Midl.Chrs.*,207); prov. suffragan bp. of St A.
with title of Libaria 16 July 1540 (Dowden, *Bishops*, 42,n.2); cons.
28 Aug. 1541 (*St A.Rent.*, 122); d. 7 July 1542 (*James V Letters*,440).

John Sinclair   1542 - 1566.
James Lauder   1547 - 1573.
     Sinclair had crown pres. and gets papal prov. on death of Gibson
27 Aug./22 Sept. 1542 (*HMC 55, Var.Coll.*,v,67; PRO 31/9 - 33/141-2);
gets crown lic. to res. in favour of Lauder 5 Apr. 1547 (*RSS*,iii,no.2237);
res. in curia, but promises annates to retain fruits 3 Aug. 1548 (PRO
31/9 - 33/242-3); lit. with Lauder 6 Aug. 1548 (*HMC 55, Var.Coll.*,v,68);
occ. 2 July 1552 (ibid.); d. in poss 9 Apr. 1566 (*Diurnal of Occurrents*,
98).
     Lauder gets crown pres. in exp. 5 Apr. 1547, promises annates and
gets prov. without fruits 3 Aug. 1548, and lit. with Sinclair 6 Aug.1548
(v.sup.); occ. 12 Apr.1568 (*HMC 55, Var.Coll.*,v,69) and 14 Sept. 1573
(*RSS*,vi,no.2126); res. before 10 Nov. 1573 (v.inf.).

Thomas Douglas   1573 - 1575.
     Crown pres. on Lauder's death 10 Nov. 1573 (*RSS*,vi,no.2197);
d. June 1575 (Edin.Tests.).

George Ramsay   1575 - 1600.
     Crown pres. on death of Douglas 29 Oct. 1575 (*RSS*,vii,no.313);
occ. 15 Aug. 1600 (*Midl.Chrs.*, p.cxiii).

Note: fruits of deanery were divided into two parsonages for benefit
of ministers of Lasswade (then George Ramsay) and Dalkeith and
their successors 15 Mar. 1591, conf. 5 June 1592 (RSS,lxii,fo.19;
APS,iii,551); but the dean of Restalrig was named to the re-erected
chapter of St Andrews June 1617 (*APS*,iv,530).

PROVOSTS OF ROSLIN

First known date: ch. was collegiate x 1456 (*MRHS*,183); erection under a presiding prebendary conf. 12 Feb. 1477 (Reg.Supp.,747,fo. 75-76); provostry erected 1521 x 1524 (*St A. Form.*,i,348-50; cf. *Midl.Chrs.*,xcvii).

John Dickson 1524.
Occ. 5 Feb. 1524 (*Midl.Chrs.*,328).

David Huchesoun 1540.
Escheated after condemnation for heresy (*RSS*,ii,no.3612).

John Sinclair 1542 - 1555 x 1556.
Occ. 13 Feb. 1542 (SRO, ADC & S, xviii,174) and 7 July 1555 (*RSS*,iv,no.3030); d. before 20 Sept. 1556 (ibid.,no.3312).

John Robeson 1563 - 1583.
Occ. 22 Apr. 1563 (*HMC 5, 6th R.*,717) and 26 Feb. 1572 (*Midl.Chrs.*,xcviii); a 'John Dickson' said to occ 28 Apr. 1571 (ibid.), but this is prob. an error in the quoted source; d. 25 Apr.1583 (*Edin.Tests.*).

Henry Sinclair 1601 - 1606.
Occ. 6 Oct. 1601 (SRO, Secretary's Reg. Sasines Edinburgh,v,fo. 339) and 23 Oct. 1606 (*RPC*,vii,265).

PROVOSTS OF ST MARY ON THE ROCK, ST ANDREWS

First known date: 1250 (*MRHS*, 184).
See *Journ.Eccles. Hist.*, iii,36 for argument that it was erected 1248 x 1249.

Perhaps a chapel royal as early as 1286 x 1296 (see seal from that date described in *Laing Chrs.*,5); regularly so regarded by 1386 (Reg. Av.,245,fo.397v) and until at least as late as 1514 x 1521 (*St A.Form.*, i,nos.131-2).

Adam de Makerstoun (Malcarniston) 1250 - 1280.
Occ. 7 Nov. 1250 (NLS, Adv.MS 15.1.18,no.20); occ. 11 Sept. 1280 (Durham, Dean & Chapter MSS, Misc.Chr.no.1052).

William Comyn	1287 - 1329.
John Benstede	1298.
William de Rasen	1309.

Comyn gets conf. after local coll. 7 Mar. 1287 (*Reg.Honorius IV*, i,572-3); prob. dispossessed for a time during the Wars of Independence; in poss. when prov. to *St A.archd. Lothian* and is to res. this ben. 11 Nov. 1329 (*CPL*,ii,301).

Benstede pres. by Edward I 15 July 1298 (Stevenson,*Documents,*

ii,288).

Rasen pres. by Edward II on res. of Comyn 2 Aug. 1309 (*Rot. Scot.*,i,67).

John de Roxburgh 1342.
Occ. 1 June 1342 (*ER*,i,499).

Gilbert Armstrong 1363 - 1373 x 1376.
Occ. 14 May 1363 (*Chron.Bower*,ii,369-70); still alive 27 Aug. 1373 (*Rot.Scot.*,i,960); d. in poss. before 25 Jan. 1376 (v.inf.).

William de Dalgarnoch 1376 - 1376 x 1377.
Instituted by bp. on crown pres. on death of Armstrong 25 Jan. 1376 (NLS, Adv.MS 15.1.18,no.39); occ. 5 Mar. 1376 (*ER*,ii,469); d. before 1 Mar. 1377 (Reg.Av.,201,fo.509).

Duncan Petit 1378 x 1381 - 1397.
Occ. 11 June 1381 (*John of Gaunt's Register* (Camden Series),ii, 376), having got it since Oct. 1378 (*CPL*,iv,248); occ. Feb. 1390x Feb. 1391 (*ER*,iii,238); still alive 14 Jan. 1397 (see *G.archd.*); prob. d. before 5 June 1397 when his successor as royal chancellor is first found (*HBC*,175).

Robert de Lany 1408 - 1432 x 1437.
Occ. 21 Dec. 1408 (*CDS*,iv,158); occ. 31 Mar. 1432 (*RMS*,ii, no.200); d. before 9 June 1437 (v.inf.).

Hugh Kennedy 1437 - 1454.
Had crown pres. on death of Lany and gets papal conf. 9 June 1437 (*CPL*,viii,663); in poss. 7 Dec. 1452 (Reg.Supp.,464,fo.239); d. 24 Sept. x 26 Oct. 1454 (see *St A.archd.*).

John Kennedy 1456 - 1472.
Occ. 28 June 1456 (Stevenson, *Letters Illustrative of English Wars in France* (Rolls Series),i,325); occ. 15 Apr. 1472 (*St A.Acta*, 184); still alive 3 Nov. 1472 (ibid.,185).

William Scherar 1477.
In poss. 14 May 1477 (Reg.Supp.,751,fo.263-4).

James Allardice 1480 - 1506 x 1507.
Occ. 18 Jan. 1480 (*ADC*,i,47); occ. 1 Apr. 1506 (Stevenson & Wood, *Seals*,ii,227); still alive 2 May 1506 (see *M.archd.*); d. before 10 Nov. 1507 (*Prot.Bk.Foular*,i,no.362; cf. no.415); see. also *Chapel Royal dean*.

James Kincragy 1508 - 1539 x 1540.
Occ. 5 Dec. 1508 (*St A.Acta*,290 i.cf*SES*,i,p.cccvii-viii); occ. 31 Oct. 1532 (SRO, Prot. Bk. Thomas Kene [NP 1/2A] ,s.d); still alive 17 Sept. 1539 (see *Ab.dean,* where date of death 27 July 1539 is also suggested); d. before 30 July 1540 (v.inf.).

James Lermont/Leirmonth   1540 - 1578.
Patrick Bellenden   1554.
Lermont gets crown pres. on Kincragy's death 30 July 1540 (*RSS*,ii,no.3598); occ. Feb. 1576 (Martine, *Reliquiae*,216); d. 20 Mar.

1578 (Edin.Tests.).

Bellenden gets crown pres. on report of Lermont's death 12 Dec. 1554 (*RSS*,iv,no.2876).

Thomas Buchanan 1578 - 1599.
Crown pres. on death of Lermont 1 Apr. 1578 (*RSS*,vii,no.1531); d. in poss. 12 Apr. 1599 (Edin.Tests.).

Robert Buchanan 1599 - 1618.
Crown pres. on death of Thomas Buchanan 12/13 Apr. 1599 (Reg.Pres., iii,24); occ. 4 June 1616 (SRO, Crawford Priory,no. 377); d. Feb. 1618 as minister of Ceres (St A.Tests.,15 Apr.1618).

Note: this ben. was granted to *St A.abp.* in part-exchange for castle of St Andrews 1606 (*APS*,iv,283); but its incumbent was named to the re-erected chapter of St Andrews June 1617 (ibid.,530).

PROVOSTS OF SEMPLE

First known date: founded 21 Apr. 1504 (*MRHS*,184).

David Dunn (Done) 1514 - 1516.
Occ. 14 June 1514 (SRO, Reg.Ho.Chr.no.818) and 25 Oct.1516 (*Glas.Mun.*,ii,129).

Archibald Laing 1518 - 1525.
Occ. 6 Mar. 1518 (*Prot.Bk. Foular 1514-28*,no.101) and 14 Oct. 1522 (Fraser,*Keir*,320); d. 21 Mar. 1525 (*Glas.Reg.*,ii,614, citing obit).

John Reid 1532 - 1533, 1540 x 1541 (?).
Occ. June 1532 (*James V Letters*, 224) and 18 Aug. 1533 (SRO, Justiciary Ct. Recs.1531 - 39,fo.94); if same as *Ab.chanc.*, d. 18 Dec. 1540 x July 1541.

John Semple (?) 1557.
Occ. 22 Mar. 1557 (*Arch.& Hist.Coll.Renfrew*,ii,59, but source is suspect).

PROVOSTS OF SETON

First known date: erected effectively 22 Dec. 1492 (*IR*,xiii, 71-76).

John Williamson 1533 - 1548.
Occ. 18 Aug. 1533 (SRO, Justiciary Ct.Recs. 1531-39,fo.96); occ. 14 Mar. 1548 (*Laing Chrs.*,no.528; Stevenson & Wood, *Seals*,i,221).

William Cranston 1549 - 1562.
Occ. 27 Nov. 1549 (Patrick,*Statutes*,86) and 18 Mar. 1562 (*RSS*, v,no.1008); d. by 24 Sept. 1562 (*CSP Scot.*,i,653); cf. *St A.St Salvator's coll.prov.*

Thomas Raith 1567 - 1582.
Occ. 13 May 1567 (*RMS*,iv,no.1842); d. Jan. 1582 (Edin.Tests.).

William Seton 1595.
> Occ. 26 May 1595 (SRO, Reg.Ho.Chr.no.3327).

PROVOSTS OF TAIN

First known date: erected 12 Sept. 1487 (*RMS*,ii,no.1164; cf.*MRHS*, 186).

Thomas Monylaw/Monelaw 1487 - 1491.
> Prob. pres. on erection 12 Sept. 1487; occ. 8 Oct. 1487 (Fraser, *Cromartie*,ii,322); d. in poss. 25 Jan. 1491 (*HMC* 1, *2nd R.*,179).

William Spynie 1492 - 1514.
> Gets papal conf. of appointment 17 July 1492 (Macgill,*Old Ross-shire*,no.2; occ. 18 Jan. 1514 (*Beauly Chrs.*,180).

Donald Munro	1534 - 1546.
George Ogilvie	1541.
Magnus Vaus	1542.
Hugh Gray	1542.
John Thornton	1544.

> **Munro** occ. 28 Aug. 1534 (*Cawdor Bk.*,162), 22 Feb. 1541 (*RSS*, ii,no.3870), 31 May 1541 (*RMS*,iii,no.2380) and 14 Sept. 1546 *(Munro Writs,* no.57).
> **Ogilvie** gets crown pres. on possible res. or death of Munro 22 Feb. 1541 (*RSS*,ii,no.3870).
> **Vaus** occ. 1 May 1542 (Fraser, *Grant*,iii,88); d. before 17 Aug. 1542 (v.inf.).
> **Gray** gets crown pres. on death of Vaus 17 Aug. 1542 (*RSS*,ii,no. 4841).
> **Thornton** occ. 24 Mar. 1544 (SRO, Fraser Chr.no.131).

Alexander Gray 1549.
> Occ. 20 Mar. 1549 when expected to res. (v.inf.).

Nicholas Ross 1549 - 1566 x 1567. 1569 (?).
> Crown pres. in exp. of res. of Gray 20 Mar. 1549 (*RSS*,iv,no.166); occ. 5 Nov. 1553 (Macgill, *Old Ross-shire*,no.902); occ. 20 June 1566 (ibid.,no.14); dem. before 13 May 1567 (v.inf.); but said to have d. 17 Sept. 1569 as commendator of Fearn and Tain prov. (Forbes,*Kalendars*, p.xxix).

Thomas Ross 1566 x 1567 - 1584.
> Had pres. on res. of Nicholas Ross and gets crown conf. 13 May 1567 (ibid.,v,no.3533); occ. when also abbot of Fearn 10/28 Feb.1571 (ibid.,vi,no.1127); res. but retained liferent 26 Feb. 1584 (Reg.Pres.,ii, 104; *OPS*,ii,419).

Walter Ross 1584.
> Crown pres. on res. of Thomas Ross 26 Feb. 1584 (Reg.Pres.,ii, 104).

HEADS OF UNIVERSITY COLLEGES

KING'S COLLEGE, ABERDEEN

PRINCIPALS

First known date: erected 17 Sept. 1505 (*Abdn.Fasti*, 54).

Hector Boyce/Boece 1505 (?) - 1536.
   First holder of this office (*ESL*, 77-78); not yet fully qualified to hold it in 1506, being only bachelor of theology then (Abdn. Univ. Archives, Parchment Cartulary, 94-96), and did not in fact become the required doctor of theology until soon after 5 Sept. 1528 (*Abdn.Counc.*, i,121); but prob. held office from 1505, though first known appearance as principal is as late as 8 Feb. 1515 (Fraser, *Colquhoun Cartulary*, 418); occ. 18 Jan. 1536 (*RMS*,iii,no.3004); d. before 22 Nov. 1536 (*RSS*,ii, no.2192).

William Hay 1538 - 1542.
   Succ. prob. after 12 Feb. 1538 (*RMS*,iv,no.2496) and before 16 Dec. 1538 (*Abdn.Fasti*,lll, where his successor as sub-principal occ.); occ. 17 Apr. 1539 (ibid.,112); occ. 25 Mar. 1542 x (ibid.,576).

John Bisset   1542 - 1564 x 1565.
William Cranston   1547.
Alexander Anderson   1552, 1564 x 1565 - 1569.
   Bisset occ. 11 May 1542 (ibid.,115); res. before 26 Feb. 1547 (v.inf.), but ineffectively; occ. 6 Aug. 1549 (*Abdn.Fasti*,259); res. accepted at curia 7 Feb. 1552 (ibid.,123), but found still as principal thereafter e.g. 3 Nov. 1553 (Abdn.Town House, Sasines, x, fo.65) and 20 Oct. 1558 (SRO, Cal.Chrs.,viii,no.1767); presumably formally in office still as late as 10 Aug. 1564, when Anderson occ. as vice-principal (v.inf.); styled principal at death, which was before 29 May 1565, when his testament (now lost) was registered (*Edin.Tests.*,i,27).
   Cranston prov. on res. of Bisset 26 Feb. 1547 (*Abdn.Fasti*, 120-1) unfruitfully.
   Anderson prov. on res. of Bisset prob. 17 Feb. 1552 (ibid., 123-5. but dates are not consistent); but found still as sub-principal 22 June 1556 (*RSS*,iv,no.3280), 20 Oct. 1558 (SRO, Cal.Chrs.,vii, no.1767), 5 Jan. 1559 (*Abdn.Reg.*,i,p.1xv), 18 Mar. 1563 (Abdn. Town House, Sasines,v/2, fo.66), and as vice-principal 10 Aug. 1564 (ibid.,xi,fos.455v-457); presumably Bisset was still formally in office during this period, but exceptionally Anderson occ. as principal himself 9 Feb. 1559 (*RMS*,v,no.861) and 31 Mar. 1563 (*Abdn.Fasti*, 127); perhaps principal in his own right when occ. as such 21 Feb. 1565 (Abdn. Town House, Sasines,v/2,fo.90v), and certainly when occ. 29 Sept. 1565 (ibid.,fo.89v);depriv. 30 June 1569 (*BUK*,i,142-4); d. 23 Jan. 1578 (*Spalding Misc.*,ii,44).

Alexander Arbuthnot   1569 - 1583.
>   Crown pres. 3 July 1569 (*RSS*,vi,no.662); d. 17 Oct. 1583 (*Spalding Misc.*,ii,56).

Note: after annexation of *Ab.dean.* to this college 8 Apr. 1579, the office of dean of Aberdeen came by 1585 (v.inf.) at latest to be attached specifically to this principalship, an arrangement conf. 28 June 1617 (*Abdn.Fasti,* 142).

Walter Stewart   x 1585 - 1587 x .
>   Occ. as principal and dean of Aberdeen 1585 (Edin.Univ.Lib., Laing Chr.no.445; cf. *Laing Chrs.*,no.1100); occ. 11 Mar. 1587 (*Abdn. Fasti*,133-4).

David Rait   x 1592 - 1629 x 1632.
>   Said to occ. 25 Dec. 1592 (*Abdn.Grads.*,25); occ. 5 Apr. 1596 (SRO, Reg.Ho.Chr.no.3397); occ. 19 Nov. 1629 (SRO, Part.Reg. Sasines Abdn.,vii,fo.225); d. before 24 Aug. 1632 (*Abdn.Ct.Bk.*, ii,325).

William Leslie   1632 - 1639.
>   Occ. 31 Aug. 1632 (SRO, Part.Reg.Sasines Banff,iii,fo.232); pres. and adm. 5 Nov. 1632 (*Abdn.Fasti,* 289); threatened with depriv. 12 Apr. 1638 (ibid.,288); still in office 27 Dec. 1638 (ibid.,412); depriv. before 18 Aug. 1640 (ibid.,417); date of depriv. was prob. 11 Apr. 1639 (Spalding, *Memorialls,* i,166).

MARISCHAL COLLEGE, ABERDEEN

PRINCIPALS

First known date: erected 2 Apr. 1593 (*Fasti Mariscal.*i,42-43).

Robert Howie   1593 - 1598.
>   In position of responsibility from 1593 (*Fasti Mariscal.*,i,92); took up full office July x 25 Sept. 1594 (G.D. Henderson, *Founding of Marischal College,* 89); el. minister of Dundee Mar. 1598, and moved there by 26 Sept. 1598 (*BUK*,iii,948; *Abdn.Counc.1570-1625,* 164).

Gilbert Gray   1598 - 1614.
>   Took up office 29 Sept. 1598 (*Fasti Mariscal.*,i,60); buried 29 Dec. 1614 (ibid.,ii,27; cf. i,154-5).

Andrew Aidy/Adie   1615 x 1616 - 1619.
>   Recommended by King James to Earl Marischal and town council 5 May 1615 (*Aberdeen Council Letters*,i,no.134); but the earl approved two other candidates before 21 June 1615 (*Fasti Mariscal.*,i,167-8), and the council decided to approach one of these, Patrick Sandis, 1 Aug. 1615 (ibid.,168); council still hoped to appoint Sandis 10 Jan.1616 (ibid.); Aidy said to occ. 15 Mar. 1616 (ibid.,ii,28); certainly occ. 28 Aug. 1616 (*Abdn.Counc.1570-1625.*346); occ. 16/21 Sept. 1619

(*Abdn,Fasti,* 278-80); dem. some three months before 1 Mar. 1620 (v.inf.), i.e. late 1619

William Forbes 1620 - 1621.
    Appointed by town council 1 Mar. 1620 (*Fasti Mariscal.*,i,186-7); dem. on or before 11 July 1621 (v.inf.).

Patrick Dun 1621 - 1649.
    Appointed by town council on dem. of Forbes 11 July 1621 (ibid., i,187-9); dem. on or before 20 June 1649, by which time his successor had been pres. (*Abdn.Counc.1643-1747,*97); d. 1650 x 1653 (*Fasti Mariscal.*,ii,214; H.F.M. Simpson, *Bon Record,* 75).

THE COLLEGE, EDINBURGH

PRINCIPALS

First known date: 1586.

Robert Rollock 1586 - 1599.
    Appointed 9 Feb. 1586 (*Edin.Recs.1573-1589,* 449); d. 8 Feb. 1599 (*De vita et morte Roberti Rollok* [Bannatyne Club], 55).

Henry Charteris 1599 - 1620.
    Appointed on Rollock's death 14 Feb. 1599 (*Edin.Recs.1589-1603,* 242); res. 20 Mar. 1620 (*Edin.Recs. 1604-1626,*205-6).

Patrick Sandis 1620 - 1622.
    El. 20 Mar. 1620 (ibid.,206); res. 7 Aug. 1622 (ibid.,234).

Robert Boyd of Trochrague 1622 - 1623
    El. 9/18 Oct. 1622 (ibid.,238); res; 31 Jan. 1623 (ibid.,240).

John Adamson 1623 - 1651.
    El. on removal of Boyd 21 Nov. 1623 (ibid.,246); occ. 28 May 1651 (A.Dalzel, *History of the University of Edinburgh,* ii,161, quoting graduation book), and d. towards end of 1651 (ibid., quoting testament); certainly d. before 23 Apr. 1652 (*Edin.Recs.1642-1655,* 279).

THE COLLEGE, FRASERBURGH

PRINCIPAL

First known date: 1597 x 1600 (*Fasti Mariscal.*,i,78).

Charles Ferme/Fairholme 1600.
    Minister of Fraserburgh from 1598 (Wodrow, *Selections,* 270-3); ordered by general assembly to undertake this principalship 18 Mar. 1600 (*BUK,*iii,958); escheated 18 July 1605 and, after imprisonment soon after, banished to Bute at king's pleasure 23 Oct. 1606 (*RPC,*vii,

82-83, 260-2); returned to his parish perhaps after total of two years in prison, and said to have d. 24 Sept. 1617 (Wodrow, *Selections,* 179).

Note: no other officers of this college known.

THE COLLEGE, GLASGOW

PRINCIPAL REGENTS/PRINCIPAL MASTERS/PRINCIPALS

First known dates: principal regent in faculty of arts   : 1460.
principal regent of college of arts   : 1480.
principal regent of pedagogy   : 1485.
principal regent of university and pedagogy : 1557.
principal master of the college   : 1574.
principal of the college   : 1615.

Principal Regents

Duncan Bunch 1460 - 1473 x 1474.
Occ. 6 Jan. 1460 (*Glas.Mun.*,i,10; iii,404); d. 3 Nov. 1473 x 19 Dec. 1474 (ibid.,ii,217; iii,405,cf.xxvi-vii; *CPL*,xiii,42; *ACSB*,179).

Walter Bunch O.Cist. 1475 x 1478.
Incorporated into university 1475, prob. 1 July x 1 Oct., when prior of Gadvan (*Glas.Mun.*,ii,83); undertook rule of college sometime thereafter, and depriv. 25 June 1478 (ibid.,ii,226).

John Goldsmith and **John Doby** 1478 - 1480.
Appointed jointly to rule college for following year 25 June 1478 (ibid.); prob. still in office 20 Jan. 1480 (ibid.,i,27-28).

John Brown 1480 - 1483.
Adm. on pres. of bp. and faculty of arts 7 Oct. 1480 (ibid.,ii,232); d. 3 July x 3 Nov. 1483 (ibid.,ii,239; iii,405-6).

Walter Leslie 1483 x 1484 - 1485.
Occ. Nov. 1483 x Mar. 1484 (ibid.,ii,239-40); asks faculty to be allowed to res., is asked to stay on until Whitsunday, and agrees c. Mar. 1485 (ibid.,ii,242).

John Goldsmith 1485.
Acted as temporary principal again in spring of 1485 (ibid.,ii, 243).

George Crichton 1485 - 1488.
Adm. on pres. of bp. (ibid.,ii,243-4); letter of dismissal from bp. received by faculty 18 July 1488 (ibid.,ii,250).

John Goldsmith 1488.
El. by faculty of arts 18 July 1488 (ibid.).

John Doby 1490 - 1498.

Occ. 25 June 1490 and 3 July 1498 (ibid.,ii,253,271); d. before 24 Dec. 1498 (ibid.,ii,273), and presumably before 25 Oct. 1498 (v.inf.).

Patrick Coventre 1498 - 1509.

Occ. 25 Oct. 1498 and 4 Aug. 1509 (ibid.,ii,114,285); still in the university 27 Nov. 1509 (ibid.,i,46; *St Mary Lib.*,210).

Thomas Coutts 1510 - 1513.

Incorporated in the university after recent institution as principal regent 7 Oct. 1510 (*Glas.Mun.*,ii,124); occ. 25 Oct. 1512 (ibid.,ii,125); continued in office 25 Oct. 1513 (ibid.;ii,127).

David Melville (Melwyn) 1514 - 1515 x 1517.

Occ. 25 Oct. 1514 (ibid.,ii,128); prob. still in Glasgow 11 Dec. 1515 (ibid.,ii,129); moved to St Andrews university by 7 Mar. 1517 (*Univ.Evidence*,iii,65); see *St A.ped.princ.*

David Abercrombie 1517.

Incorporated in the university as principal regent 18 June 1517 (ibid.,ii,130); occ. 25 Oct. 1517 (ibid.,ii,131).

John Major 1518 - 1523.

Incorporated in the university as principal regent prob. soon after 25 Oct. 1518, when the current rector took up office (ibid.,ii,134); certainly at Glasgow by 22 Nov. 1518 (Major, *History*, 435-6; cf.*IR*, ,90); occ. 25 Oct. 1522 (*Glas.Mun.*,ii,147); incorporated in St Andrews university 9 June 1523 (see *St A.ped.princ.*).

James Lindsay 1526.

Occ. 25 Oct. and 30 Nov. 1526 (ibid.,ii,151;*IR*,v,100).

John Sinclair (?) 1552.

Occ. as 'provost of college of Glasgow' 3 Sept. 1552 (Fraser, *Maxwell Inventories*, 163); perhaps error for *G. St Mary & St Anne prov.*

John Houston (?) 1556.

Occ. just as bursar 25 Oct. 1554 (*Glas.Mun.*,ii,174); occ. as principal regent in a rubric dated 8 Feb. 1556, but only as regent in related text (ibid.,i,59); occ. again just as regent 15 June 1556 (ibid., i,60), and as dean of faculty of arts 14 Mar. 1557 (ibid.,i,61).

John Davidson 1557 - 1574.

Occ. as principal regent 14 Mar. 1557, following incorporation in university 24 Oct. 1556 (ibid.,i,61; ii,175); occ. 6 May 1570 (*RMS*,iv, no.2332; cf. *Glas.Mun.*, i,81-82); occ. just as regent, but acting in name of pedagogy 8 Oct. 1571 (*Prot.Bk. Glasgow*,vi,no.1794); prob. unnamed principal regent 29 Apr. 1574 (ibid.,vii,no.2044); presumably dem. before 1 Nov. 1574 (v.inf.); res. attached vicarage of Colmonell 5 Jan. 1575 (ibid.,vii,no.2112).

Principal Masters

Andrew Melville 1574 - 1580.

Commenced duties c. 1 Nov. 1574 (Melville, *Diary* [Bannatyne Club], 38); occ. 5 Jan. 1575 (*Prot.Bk.Glasgow*,vi,no.2113) and 1 Oct. 1580 (*Glas.Mun.*,i,132); left Glasgow Nov. 1580 (Melville, *Diary*,64-65) after crown pres. to *St A.St Mary's coll. princ.*

Thomas Smeaton 1580 - 1583.

Prob. in poss. Nov. 1580, following nom. by general assembly Oc: 1580 (Melville, *Diary*,64-65; *BUK*,ii,471); crown pres. 3 Jan. 1581 (*Gla. Mun.*,iv,1xxxi, quoting RSS,xlvii,fo.61); d. 6 Dec. 1583 (Spottiswoode, *History* (1847-51),ii,320).

Patrick Sharp 1586 - 1614.

Crown pres. on death of Smeaton 10 Jan. 1586 (*Glas.Mun.*,iv,lxxx quoting Reg.Pres.,ii,140); res. 10 Aug. 1614 (*Glas.Mun.*,iv,lxxxii).

Principals

Robert Boyd of Trochrague 1615 - 1621.

Expected to be successor at time of Sharp's res. Aug. 1614 (Wodrow, *Collections*,II,i,115-16); arrived in Glasgow from France 31 Dec. 1614 (ibid.,122); adm. 20 Jan. 1615 following crown pres. (*Glas.Mun.*,iii,367; iv,lxxxii; cf. Wodrow, *Collections*,II,i,125-6 which gives 30 Jan.); intends to res. 24 Mar. 1621 (ibid.,II,i,154-60); occ. still 6 Nov. 1621 (ibid.,162) and 20 Dec. 1621 (*Glas.Mun.*,i,215).

John Cameron 1622 - 1623.

Took up office after 12 July and before 7 Aug. 1622 (Wodrow, *Collections*,II,i,172-3), though did not yet have formal crown pres. (*Glas.Mun.*,iv,lxxxiii); occ. 6 Jan. 1623 (ibid.,ii,300); left Glasgow c. Ma 1623, as he certainly arrived in France by July 1623 (Wodrow, *Collectio* II,ii,182; cf. 168).

John Strang 1625 - 1649 x 1650.

Already offered this vacant post by Oct. 1624 (Wodrow, *Collections*,II,i,197; cf. 205-7); crown pres. on departure of Cameron 10 Oct. 1625 (Baillie, *Journals*,iii,417,n.7; *Glas.Mun.*,iv,lxxxv); adm. 22 Feb. 1626 (ibid.,iii,367-8); occ. 26 Dec. 1649 (ibid.,iii,540); arrangements made for his pension on res. 19 Apr. 1650 (H.M.B. Reid, *Divinity Principals of the University of Glasgow*,286-7); res. 1649 x 1650 (*Glas.Mun.*,iv,lxxxv).

ST JOHN'S COLLEGE, ST ANDREWS

MASTER

First known date: 1419.

The college buildings are mentioned as early as 19 June 1416 (*St A.Acta*,7).

aurence de Lindores 1419.
Named as master on formal erection of this college 22 Jan. 1419
*Univ.Evidence,*iii,350).

ote: no other masters known; but building prob. still in use 1456 and
461 (*St A.Acta,*115,117,147).

THE PEDAGOGY, ST ANDREWS

PRINCIPALS/PRINCIPAL REGENTS

irst known dates: principal   : 1430.
                     principal regent : 1505.
A less official second pedagogy sometimes existed e.g. 1432 (*St
.Acta,*33; cf. 28-29, 74).

aurence de Lindores 1430.
El. by faculty of arts 28 May 1430 (ibid.,29); d. 16 Sept. 1437
ibid.,45).

ohn de Atholl 1454.
Appointed by faculty of arts 29 Jan. 1454 (ibid.,101).

ohn Lock 1460.
Appointed by faculty of arts 5 June 1460 (ibid.,137); cf. *St A.
t Salvator's coll. prov.*

homas Ramsay 1498 - 1500 x 1505.
Prob. appointed by faculty of arts 16 Jan. 1498 (ibid.,266; cf.
.cclxii,n.7); moved to become prebendary of St Salvator's college
7 May 1501 x 3 Nov. 1505 (*Univ.Evidence,*iii,355; *St A.Acta,* 279).

ames Lyne/Lyn 1505 - 1509 (?).
Occ. 3 Nov. 1505 (ibid.,279); still at university (but not called
rincipal regent) when dem. office of bursar of faculty of arts 5 Oct.
509 (St A.Univ.Mun.,UY 412,fo.17v); moved to *Dk.dean.christ.
trathearn, Fife and Lothian* before 11 June 1511.

eter Chaplain (Capellanus) 1510 - 1512 x 1513.
Occ. prob. as principal regent 8 May 1510 (*St A.Acta,*295; cf.
.cclxii,n.9); occ. 12 June 1512 (ibid.,p.cclxii); moved to become
rebendary of St Salvator's college by 3 Nov. 1513 (ibid.,306 and
ote).

David Melville 1515 x 1517 - 1521.
Occ. 17 Mar. 1517 (St A.Univ.Mun.,UY305/1,p.66), having prob.
oved from *G.coll.princ.* 11 Dec. 1515 x 7 Mar. 1517; occ. 4 Nov.
521 (*St A.Acta,*338); found at Dunkeld Nov. 1521 x Nov. 1522 (St A.
Jniv.Mun.,UY412,fo.20) and so may have dem. by then.

ohn Major (?) 1523 - 1526.
Incorporated in university 9 June 1523 (*St A.Recs.,*218) on

moving from *G.coll. princ.*; perhaps took up similar position at St Andrews and became head of the pedagogy, though he is not found specifically as such, being usually described as *Chapel Royal treas.* (cf. ibid.,p.xxxix); certainly taught in arts faculty, for George Buchanan was his pupil in dialectic ('Georgii Buchanani Vita', in J.M.Aitken, *The Trial of George Buchanan,*p.xiv) and it was in the pedagogy that Buchan incorporated 28 Feb. 1525 x 28 Jan. 1526 and determined during Len 1526 (St A.Univ.Mun.,UY305/1,p.80; *St A.Acta,*350); Major last foun at St Andrews 22 Jan. 1526 (St A.Univ.Mun.,UY305/1,p.79); returned to Paris by 20 Nov. 1526 i.e. prob. in summer or autumn of 1526 after eight years in Scotland (cf. *IR,*v,92-95).

Robert Bannerman 1526 - 1539.
Occ. 3 Nov. 1526 (*St A.Acta,*353); remained in office until erect of St Mary's college 1539 (v.inf.).

ST MARY'S COLLEGE, ST ANDREWS

PRINCIPALS

First known date: 1539.

Robert Bannerman 1539 - 1546.
Inducted when principal of pedagogy as first principal of St Mary college 7 Feb. 1539 (*St A.Acta,*p.cclxiii); is found erroneously as sub-principal 10 Feb. 1539, with David Guthynd/Guynd (the true sub-prin as principal in same document (St A.Univ.Mun., SM 110. B1.P1.17); re 13 July 1546 (*St A.Acta,*p.cclxiii).

Archibald Hay 1546 - 1547.
Crown pres. on expected res. of Bannerman 29 June 1546 (*RSS,* iii,no.1738); coll. 13 July 1546 (*St A.Acta,*p.cclxiii); d. before 27 Sept. 1547 (v.inf.).

John Douglas 1547 - 1574.
Crown pres. on death of Hay 27 Sept. 1547 (*RSS,*iii,no.2457); coll. 1 Oct. 1547 (St A.Univ.Mun.,SM110.B15.7); retained poss. after cons. as *St A.abp.* 10 Feb. 1572; occ. 6 Mar. 1574 (Calderwood,*History* iii,303); prob. retained it until death 31 July 1574 (*St A.Acta,*p.cclxiii, n.6).

Robert Hamilton 1575 - 1579.
Occ. 17 Jan. 1575 (ibid.,p.cclxiii,n.7); gets crown conf. after el. on death of Douglas 27 Feb. 1575 (*RSS,*vii,no.60); prob. depriv. 13 Dec. 1579 (*Univ.Evidence,*iii,190), and certainly before 17 June 1580 (SRO, NP1/35,fo.83v).

Andrew Melville 1580 - 1607.
Took poss. on moving from *G.coll.princ.* Dec. 1580 (Melville, *Diary* [Bannatyne Club] , 84), after crown pres. and approval of general assembly in Oct. 1580 (*BUK,*ii,466); depriv. 9 Mar. 1607 (*Original Letters,*i,457[X]).

Robert Howie 1607 - 1641.

Adm. 16 June 1607, after being appointed 9 Mar. 1607 (*RPC*,vii, 396); res. July 1641 (*Acts of General Assembly 1638-1842*, 46); d. by 1647 (J.K. Cameron, *Letters of Robert Howie*,lxxix).

ST SALVATOR'S COLLEGE, ST ANDREWS

PROVOSTS

First known date: 1450.

John Athilmar 1450 - 1473.

Coll. at foundation of college 27 Aug. 1450 (R.G.Cant,*College of St Salvator*, 52); occ. 7 Dec. 1473 (*St A.Acta*,p.cclxiii,n.13).

James Ogilvie 1474 - 1475 x 1476.

Coll. before 26 July 1474 (*CPL*,xiii,366); occ. 3 Nov. 1474 and 9 Feb. 1475 (*St A.Acta*,192; p.cclxiii,n.15); res. before 8 Dec. 1476 (v.inf.), and then granted pension on fruits 29 Dec. 1476 (Reg.Supp., 745,fo.156; cf. *ACSB*, 195 where year is wrong; and cf. *St A.Acta*, xxxiv).

John Lock 1476 - 1479.

Occ. 8 Dec. 1476 (Fraser, *Haddington*,ii,238); had been el. and had got prov. by an apostolic commissary on res. of Ogilvie (Reg.Supp., 745,fo.156, as above); occ. 18 Nov. 1478 (*PSAS*,xli,316-17); d. before 10 May 1479, prob. soon before (*St A.Acta*,207,n.1).

John Liston 1479 - 1505.

Occ. 3 Nov. 1479 (ibid.,207) and 14 Apr. 1505 (*RMS*,ii,no.2850).

Hugh Spens 1505 - 1534.

Occ. 3 Nov. 1505 (*St A.Acta*, 279); d. 21 July 1534 (ibid.,p.cclxiii, no.21, quoting tombstone).

John Major 1534 - 1550.

Occ. 3 Nov. 1534, after serving previously as coadj. (ibid.,375 and p.cclxiii,n.22); d. 1 May 1550 (D.Camerarius, *De Statu Hominis* [Chalons-sur-Marne, 1627] , 188).

Peter Chaplain (Capellanus) 1550 x 1551.

Occ. 18 Sept. 1550 (*St A.Acta*,p.cclxiv,n.1), after serving as coadj. from as early as 29 Apr. 1544 (St A.Univ.Mun.,SS150/2,fo.112v); d. before 6 Feb. 1551 (v.inf.).

Martin Balfour 1551 - 1553.

Occ. 6 Feb. 1551 following death of Chaplain (*St A.Acta*,p.cclxiv, n.2); still in poss. when made his will 12 Dec. 1553 (St A,Univ.Mun., SS150/2,fo.128v); d. before 18 Dec. 1553 (ibid.,fo.128r).

William Cranston 1553 - 1559 x 1560.

Occ. 18 Dec. 1553 following death of Balfour (*St A.Acta*,p.cclxiv, n.4); occ. 23 Apr. 1559 (St A.Univ.Mun.,SS110,E4.5); left for France

24 Sept. 1560 with hopes that he would return (*CSP Foreign 1560-1*, no.619/9); but appears to have dem. at this time (v.inf.); d. after 18 Mar. 1562 (see *Seton prov.*) and before 24 Sept. 1562 (*CSP Scot.*,i,653).

John Rutherford 1560 - 1577.
     Occ. 22 Oct. 1560 (St A.Univ.Mun.,SS110.Y25); res. 29 Aug. 1577 because of old age (*St A.Acta*,p.cclxiv,n.6).

James Martine 1577 - 1620.
     Coll. by rector of university 29 Aug. 1577 (ibid.,n.7); d. Mar.1620 (*Gen.Coll.*,ii,190).

George Martine 1620 - 1645.
     Occ. 9 Aug. 1620 (St A.Univ.Mun.,SS110.G11.22); d. Oct. 1645 (*Gen.Coll.*,ii,194).

ST LEONARD'S COLLEGE, ST ANDREWS

PRINCIPALS

First known date: erected 30 Aug. 1512 (J. Herkless and R.K. Hannay, *College of St Leonard,* 128-30).

John Annand (?) O.S.A. 1512 (?).
     Said to have started this college i.e. *huic collegio in re literaria......* *exordium dedit* (Boece, *Vitae,* 87); had occ. already as regular canon of St Andrews by 3 Nov. 1511 (St A.Univ.Mun.,SL110.PW78), and so may well have been appointed the first principal, though he is not found at this time with this title,

Alexander Young   O.S.A.   1517 - 1531 x 1533.
Gavin Logy   1523 - 1534.
     Young occ. 20 Apr. 1517 and 14 Jan. 1531 (*St A.Acta*,p.cclxiv, nn.10,12); moved to office of sub-prior by 28 Feb. 1533 (St A.Univ. Mun.,UY305/1,p.91).
     Logy occ. concurrently as 'principal' or 'principal regent' 3 Nov. 1523 and 3 Nov. 1534 (*St A Acta*,p.cclxiv, n.11;cf. p.xlviii,n.3).

Thomas Cunningham O.S.A. 1534 - 1539.
     Occ. 29 Nov. 1534 (*College of St Leonard,* 54); occ. with unusual title of '**direc**tor principalis' 8 June 1536 (St A.Univ.Mun.,SL110.A25); occ. 30 Apr. 1539 (ibid.,UY305/2,p.9).

Alexander Young O.S.A. 1540 - 1543.
     Occ. in office again 2 Mar. 1540 and 20 Oct. 1543 (*St A.Acta,* p.cclxiv,nn.15,16).

John Annand O.S.A. 1544 - 1546.
     Occ. (perhaps during a second spell as principal) 8 June 1544 (St A.Univ.Mun.,SL155,p.253) and 15 May 1546 (ibid.,SL110,PW105).

John Law O.S.A. 1549 - 1552.
     In office by 11 Nov. 1549 when in receipt of the stipend (ibid., SL515,p.17); occ. 29 Feb. 1552 (ibid.,UY305/2,p.44); apparently still

alive and in office 1 Nov. 1552, when he was reported to have received the stipend for the term beginning Pentecost 1552 (ibid.,SL515,p.42).

John Duncanson O.S.A. 1552 - 1566.
    Paid stipend as principal from 11 Nov. 1552 (ibid.,p.55); occ. 20 Apr. 1553 and 8 Nov. 1566 (*St A.Acta*,p.cclxiv,nn.20,21); d. 20 Dec. 1566 (SRO, NP1/26, fo.2v).

George Buchanan   1567 - 1570.
Patrick Adamson/Constaine   1570.
    Buchanan succ. 8 Mar. 1567 (ibid.); occ. 10 Aug. 1569 (*CSP Scot.*, ii,667-8); res. in favour of Adamson at request of the lords of the secret council, with right of return if Adamson was not acceptable to John Winram superintendent of Fife and the masters; Adamson subsequently res. his right back to Buchanan 3 Apr. 1570 (SRO, NP1/26, fo.90); Buchanan dem. 5 Apr. 1570 (ibid.,fo.2v).
    Adamson had pres. from lords of secret council, but res. his right presumably because he had not satisfied the attached conditions 3 Apr. 1570 (v.sup.).

James Wilkie   1570 - 1590.
    Occ. as 'regens principalis' in absence of Buchanan the Magister principalis' 3 Sept. 1568 (SRO, NP1/26,fo.76v), and again 2 July 1569 (ibid.,fo.88); appointed as Buchanan's successor 15 or 28 Apr. 1570 (*St A.Acta*,p.cclxv,n.3; cf. SRO, NP1/26,fo.2v); occ. as 'magister principalis' 12 June 1570 (ibid.,fo.93v); d. 18 Aug. 1590 (*St A.Acta*, p.cclxv,n.4).

Robert Wilkie 1590 - 1611.
    Paid stipend as principal for term beginning 11 Nov. 1590 (St A. Univ.Mun.,SL515,p.439); occ. 1 Mar. 1611 (ibid.,UY305/2,p.113); dem. on or before 8 Apr. 1611 (v.inf.); d. 26 June 1611 (monument in St Leonard's church).

Peter Bruce 1611 - 1630.
    Adm. 20 June 1611, following appointment 8 Apr. 1611 on dem. of Robert Wilkie (St A.Univ.Mun.,SL110,MB18.4); occ. 8 May 1630 (ibid.,SL110.R5); dem. on or before 8 June 1630 (v.inf.); d. before 17 July 1630 (Edin.Univ.Lib.,MS DC.6.7 [St Andrews Statutes], p.43).

Andrew Bruce 1630 - 1647.
    Adm. 11 June 1630, following appointment 8 June 1630 (St A. Univ.Mun.,SL110.MB18.5 and 6); d. May 1647 (ibid.,SS110.AM1).

INDEX

This index is limited to personal names, and to just the main entries about each person. Casual mentions in the course of discussions of other persons are not included, nor are mentions in introductory or connecting material.

Where persons are known only by christian name, a help towards separating those with the same name is offered by an indication of the century or centuries in which they are known to have held office e.g. '(13c)' or '(13c - 14c)'. The same indication is provided for persons with the same full name.

References to the same person have been brought together wherever possible. But it often happens that the sources cited in the Fasti for the earliest and latest tenure of selected offices do not happen to be those which prove contemporaries of the same name to be the same person. No full research has been possible into sources not cited in this work, and some of the present identifications depend on probability rather than certainty. More identifications will emerge as the careers of individuals indexed separately here are further explored. The editor will welcome corrections and additions.

*